THE PEOPLE OF THE VALLEY

VOLUME II
THE JOURNEY

BY FRANCES ELLEN CRARY

ASHBROOK PUBLISHING
10089 BARTHOLOMEW RD.
CHAGRIN FALLS, OHIO 44022

ISBN: 0-09629950-2-9 Volume II
ISBN: 0-09629950-3-7 Two Volume Set

Library of Congress Catalog Number: 91-073346

A publication of Ashbrook Publishing
10089 Bartholomew Rd.
Chagrin Falls, Ohio 44022

Printed in the United States of America

Copyright (c) 1992 by Frances E. Crary--All rights reserved

This book is dedicated to the world of humanity which is very rapidly growing into a spiritual consciousness that brings its souls to an awaress of the eternality of the unity of all life. There is modest hope that the book may contribute to this great birthing of spiritual consciousness. It is a novel, a fantasy, but yet it deals with a reality that may well help to carry this human race out of their world of illusion.

I want to express my gratitude to Helen, Emily, Anne, Cheryl, Eunice and Elbert who actually read, advised, edited etc.; and to every other friend who has encouraged me, and to my daughter Jennifer, to Kit and Linda, Justin, Nathan and Linda K. who have taught me much about life.

> How can we lose our desparate clutch
> At ourselves as the central actors on Life's stage
> And welcome Life, Mother of all lives?
> How can we shake from our humanity
> Dark strains of fear,
> Where greed and lust are nourished
> And wake ourselves to Light?
> To breathing Love
> While Life transforms all Vision.
>
> Frances Ellen Crary

This is a story about possibility. It is a dream about what might be, of what is presently shaping itself, of the phoenix-like rising up of a new civilization out of the ashes of our old and sorry world. A new Earth and a new People whose eyes are opened and whose hearts have welcomed the inflow of Light and Love radiating through this universe. A new people accepting their own transcendent nature.

It is the story of humankind's waking from millinia of sleep and beginning finally to accept Vision, the nature of reality and the wonder of Life, and to do this through an Earth itself wakened to new dimensions of relationship. The recovery of humakind from the anguish and greed of historical civilization, from pain and hunger, from power misused by selfish leaders, could only happen through new vision. This new vision has filled the eyes and hearts of the People of the Valley. With struggle and steady realization, pain and joy, tearing old patterns from their minds and hearts, they lead us into possibility.

WEBS

Web of spiders!
Trap for the unwary fly, the burdened bee.
Carnal house of insects, wrestling with their shrouds.
And yet - webs hung in sunlight,
Glimmering wheels of light
Gleaming filiments of startling streanth
Tangled carelessly to dry whisps on the horn of a cow.

Webs of living!
Humankind caught in ancient patterns,
In rituals of assumption that the real is known.
What dark one sits upon the webbing of our life
And hears our desparate writhing and our pain,
Keeps us captive, blind in shrouds of fear

Web of Spirit!
A shimmering whorl of light, catching at mind,
Strung with beads of consciousness,
Bright in cosmic sun
That rises just behind our eyes,
Reflecting Being in those shimmering beads.

Seeing through, we know there cannot be
A path upon the web, but only through.
Seeing through, we long with Hearts of grief
For that which breaks one strand and let's us See.

Grown still in weary hopelessness we glimpse
Between our strands of darkness, beads of light
Unnamed, unknown, reflecting what is real!
On that reflection, catapulted through,
We see the real - are Joined - we know!
Mind soars, Heart Sings, Life IS.

Frances Ellen Crary

CHAPTER ONE

Children.

 Andrew stood up from his work bench, Stood a moment looking at the figures on the computer screen and listening to the combination of sounds that he had arranged. His young face was puzzled,intent. He felt vaguely troubled by the 'music' of this arrangement of sound sequences and harmonies interspersed with disharmony. The strong underlying beat drew at him, troubled him even more. He could accept the discomfort, that was his whole point, to find what sounds were related to specific emotional responses. But this time it was different. There was something here he didn't understand and he'd have to hunt up the Master Teacher and work it out with her. He nodded, his face smoothing with the decision and punching the off button he turned away.

 He watched the youngsters at the other end of the room, talking among themselves,writing up their reports and so involved in them they were unaware of him. He stretched his body, reaching as high as he could, caught the edge of a beam above him and swung to stretch and loosen cramped muscles.Then he turned,"Hey, kids, it's time to go home isn't it? It's way past my dinner time."

 One young girl looked up at him, her eyes still so full of the thoughts she was struggling with she did not focus on him for a moment. Then she recognized what he's said and nodded,."We'll be through soon, Andrew. You needn't wait. We can close up. I'm thinking of coming back this evening." She smiled that odd vague smile of absorption and bent again to her work. The others seemed not to notice. He knew they did,he knew also they didn't need him They were on their own, when they needed him again they would call.

 He turned, caught up his jacket, and went out. He grinned thoughtfully to himself as he remembered the day. They'd begun to understand what he was teaching and understanding, had become totally absorbed in going on with the concepts on their own. He thought it was their own bright minds, rather than his skill. But they'd been off on their own before two o'clock. He looked up at a call and saw Anna across the court. Those kids might be 'reinventing the wheel' but that's what most kids did at that age, rediscover the basic knowledges of science and of social life as well. He thought how exciting it was to him to watch their minds begin to grapple with the problems, to see a way to search out solutions, and he wondered whether he ought to consider being a teacher. He thought he didn't have the kind of Talent to be a Master Teacher and he didn't want normal teaching as a life work. There was enough of that in ordinary living.

 He caught up with Anna and she was primed to talk. She said,"Andy,I get so mad when someone borrows files and then doesn't record their names or bring them back on time. I wish I didn't feel so furious at them though."

 He nodded, " You admit it though. You claim the anger- you don't project it. Let yourself be, Sis. They were wrong, and it IS frustrating. To anyone, except maybe a Saint." She glanced up at him,,her mind swiftly acknowledging. She grinned quickly at him."How'd it go with the kids today?"

He grimaced, his hands reached out as they walked, spreading themselves wide like great brown wheels. "They do so well, they don't need me much. But when they do, it's crucial I be there. I like to teach, Anna. You know that. You know, no matter how interested they are, they need help just like I need help right now from my Master Teacher before I can go on. Master Rolf in the physiology lab,has helped me figure out the equipment I need to study the way sounds affects the body. He says lots of the work I'm doing's been done, but if I do it my way, I'll understand more and maybe find something the other researchers didn't notice. Maybe I'll have to include the affect of odors to get a full picture. And also the music that's developing out of this is different from anything I've ever done." He shrugged,"It might be something new or I may be off balance completely."

She laughed, "That's creation,Brother. Have you got data on specific sounds with specific people? Do people react pretty much the same or do we all have our own set of triggers?"

That's what we've got in the computer, the figures, the data for the tests we did last month. I asked Jimmie, to help me, he's going into psychology and literature, and he's fascinated with the problem." Andy grinned at the memory of the two of them talking excitedly as they fed their data in to the computer."You know, Sis. I've gotten so fascinated that I've not had a serious affair with a girl for six months. I'd not tell that to anyone else you know."

She snorted,"Andrew, how serious is a relationship between two sixteen year olds? You mean you haven't been playing with sex." She was amused and he was relieved that she was not playing that old role of prude that he thought she played sometimes. She knew his thought and frowned."Oh, that! Well, Andy, thanks to your nagging, I've been watching myself."

"Whatever you've done, the restraint becomes you, Sis." He laughed and dodged her fist at his shoulder. "But then, you have to admit that I'm a pretty good looking guy. At least other girls think I am." He preened obviously and she giggled. "How about you,Sis? I haven't seen any special boy keeping you company. After all,I do hear the talk. With your brown skin and blond hair you catch attention. You're a lovely young - woman." He stopped, realized he'd never thought of her as a woman before and she felt herself glow at the comment." You know that you are ?" He met her eyes, "We've got a lot going for us, you know Sis."

She nodded,her eyes sparkling, she always enjoyed Andrew even when they fought. "Well, I'm taking some time out from boy friends. I want to try out some other things. Mom says that she worried about you, though. She says you've been so withdrawn and moody lately she thinks something must be bothering you. She says you haven't seemed willing to talk." Her mouth went down in a frown- smile. "Maybe after last Gather she'll even Touch and see for herself." Their eyes met, and he shrugged,"But she's set to ask you! So look out!"

He was silent, the foolishness fading out, a serious frown furrowing the young smooth, face. "Sis, I've got a lot of things on my mind. I've just gotten over my resentment about Dad's being gone so long. After all, a boy needs his Dad as much as a girl does. But it wasn't just the usual. I've resented it when I couldn't ask him for help. I never understood why he had to go." He was quiet. "I think I do now though." Again he shrugged as if putting that in the past. "But now that he's back, other things've changed. We've changed, you and me, Sis. And our friends. And now, the family's finally talking about - what's happening. There's something wonderful going on, Anna, but I understand too why some of the family is scared. It's strange too. the changes. The energy! It's increasing all the time, isn't it?" His voice was soft, and he searched her eyes for recognition of his thought. "I'm conscious of more than I understand, and I think you are too."

    Anna nodded, her hands suddenly rolled into fists, then released themselves. She was nodding as he talked and tucked one arm into his elbow to walk more closely with him. "I know, Buddy, I resented Dad's going too, but mostly I resented having to keep still about it so as not to make it worse for Mom. But as for things changing, its about time folks woke up. Things've been changing for years. Jessie's like a catalyst. No one can pretend it isn't happening any more." She was quiet, then softly, she added, "Jessie will help you with all that you realize. She really will, Buddy."

    He nodded. and said nothing for several minutes. Then, matter-of-factly,

    "I was surprised at Dad. At the Gather I mean."

    "Well, there it is. He's begun to admit that he Sees, that he knows and experiences more than the surface of things. Have you tried Reaching to him, since the Gather?"

    He laughed, "Old habits die hard. I just haven't had the nerve to try just the two of us. How about you, Sis?" Andy turned to frown at her. She shook her head absently but said, "Only with Jessie".

    They walked silently for minutes, through the second Ring gardens toward the exit archway of the Outer Ring. Then he said, nearly stopping to speak the thought," I can't believe what's happened to them all. We can actually Reach to them. I've gotten such a habit of shielding when I'm around them that I forget and continue to do it. I think Mom is more aware than she'll admit. I've thought that a long time. She's so perceptive and sometimes I feel her there when I lift, when I'm focussed. It's as though at that point, we're not separate. And that's what Jessie showed us at Gather. No doubt of it. The communion was pretty intense. But I'm not adept enough to know if Mom is there with me or not."

    He was speaking softly as if the thoughts needed saying in this slow shaping of words. "It's not easy to talk of it. 'The place of Knowing'. That's what you and I have called it. My Master Teacher says it's a good name. He said just to watch and listen. Words are so clumsy, they don't hold the knowing .But when we Touch, especially JOIN, then the realization flows like a liquid of perception. But words cut it up and harden it so it's not accurate." He grinned and she nodded. Maybe it's just as well we've never felt right about talking to our family about these things. We'd've really got them confused."

"Well, Brother, it's obvious to me you teach well, you put that better than I've heard it."

He shrugged, but she could tell the compliment pleased him. He picked up a small branch fallen from a tree, to break it up then throw it from the path,the automatic action of any teenage child in a town where the young were the scavengers and gatherers."What d'ya think of Jessie?"

She nodded, as if all this needed talking about. I like her. After the Spring planting -- well, I knew she was something more than just an old lady. Jessie's brought a new energy to this family. You can feel it alive in our house. No one's able to deny the changes happening in themselves, or hide it anymore. She's an amazing old lady,isn't she?"

"Yeah, I thought I didn't like her at first. She bothered me. then I realized one day , -when she was looking at me - that I didn't like it to have someone know me so well." He laughed."Damn, I hadn't thought that was what it was." He shook his head. "Just seeing that unplugged me."

"Seeing that she knew you?"

"Yeah, she did. She really did and when I saw it, I saw what she knew." He frowned and shrugged, "No use foolin' myself. There it was. Like a mirror,she is.It's why she made me uneasy at first."

Anna nodded, They walked in silence. After minutes he said, "Anna, you seem to really go for Jessie. But you're not half as much involved with our other friends as I am. Why's that?" He watched her serious young girl's face,thinking how young she looked. She said,"Well, there's just something special. She just understands things." She hesitated, glanced at him." I think she was my mother in a past life. There's no reason for how I feel otherwise." He nodded,searching her eyes and then she grinned and but he knew she was serious. They kept their Touch bluntly withheld. Practicing without even the images of mind Touch. To shape ideas with words alone. It seemed to enhance the wonder of their open reaching minds later. And it gave them a sense of connection to their family.

He leaped to a low wall, balancing like a child and waving his long arms. She laughed to see him and then was beside him. She balanced,then, moving with cat-grace, raced along the narrow ledge - leaped over shrubs that wound in low hedges down the short bank. He watched her astonished, for a moment, then frowning sourly, he followed, a wind mill of arms and legs but moving fast enough to catch up with her by the time she was jumping down into the path way again. She laughed up at his frown, "Just because I haven't stretched out eight inches in the past two years doesn't mean I can't keep up with you." They were exhilarated by the run. He looked at her and then relented and laughed.

She said,"Mom says I can go mountain camping alone next week. I'll spend a week up beyond the north gap where the River drops into rapids." She knew she was bragging, teasing him.

He frowned again,"Mom won't let you do that. Or Dad won't. I know."

"She talked him into it, Andrew, actually, I was surprised.I didn't think they'd let me either after that wild Camping when I found Mayda, my cat friend. She scared them, you know. But, I've had plenty of self defense training, I've camped alone before, I've met and made friends with my wild animals when I was in the wild world program at Center, -- and I'm not afraid of anything." She made a face at him. They said they wanted me to take Rob, and I might. He'd be good company at any rate. And he's never been the least bit put off by Mayta when she comes here to see me." She frowned, "Although, I think it's better for me to go to see her in the west mountains. It's always exciting to meet her cubs. Anyway, two of my friends have already done the solitary survival test -- so I just have to." She laughed, touching his arm, "Now that everybody's finally admitted we can Mind Touch,they might believe that I can call for help if I have to.I only know one person who had to do that,and it was a broken leg. He called the Healers but the Monitors had already alerted them,they were there just as he'd made his contact. You know, those Monitors really do watch."

He studied her face, so animated with her plans but so innocent,"Well, you could call me, you know." Their eyes met and she nodded.

It's a relief that Mom's admitted the Sending. I don't know what else. But after the summer Gather,I think she's really ready to tell us about her cliff place." She grinned. "She thinks no one knows. Wonder what she'd do if I DID Reach to her while I was so far away. She'd probably panic." She laughed. "Maybe she'll really accept us, one day, Andy. But I don't know whether she would be able to receive that far. It'd be interesting to find out. Maybe I'll call just before I come home just to see. If any problem comes up I can't handle, I'll call you, Buddy". She stood on tiptoe to kiss his cheek and then gave a little leap and ran along the winding path.

He followed her for a moment then stopped,his attention acute,there was someone there among the trees. They were just a few yards from the Outer archway, to the side, a cluster of tall trees hid the side of the great curving building. He heard a low whistle. He knew the signal,and knew Anna wouldn't fit in. The excitement of secret meetings roused his love of adventure. He felt a little like a child again, the budding man in him denied his interest, but he was not yet far enough past his childhood to resist. The fantasy of danger, of mystery, still attracted him. He said to Anna, "Look we've nearly reached the Dining Hall. Will you go ahead and have a cup of chocolate and I'll meet you in a little while. I want to talk to someone here." With a sudden confidence, he Reached to her briefly and she knew a swift image of that clandistine game. She stared at him, then controlling her impulse to look where she too knew someone waited, she nodded quietly and turned to go on.

He turned then, to cross the short distance to the trees, and observed that he felt irritated with her and that it was unreasonable. She might tell? After all, why should she? They weren't children. But he was acting like one. The inner conflict irritated him more. He heard himself laugh, a strange sardonic sound. Why were they scuttling in the shrubs so? Why not? The whole matter was one of intrigue , of subtle excitement. He grinned and admitted that it was like children playing. But it WAS fun. Remembering how the boys had been at their last meeting, he thought they were so serious, so intense in their convictions. Maybe it wasn't play to them. And they did have convictions. He frowned, facing himself with those facts. He heard the faint whistle again and went to join them.

He moved through the grounds with the trained trackers silence , enjoying this part of the charade. But he back tracked, wound around a farther garden and came on them from the other side. Then silently he burst through into their midst and they whirled,one leaping to grab him with a flying tackle. Another boy sank out of sight among vines. A third stood with his mouth open unable to grasp that they had an intruder they had not heard. Andy laughed,,unwrapping himself from his assailant. His face was bruised,it hurt but he was so pleased with the success of his ruse, that he ignored it. The two sat up from their tussle and the other boy, Argrid, said, " Why'd you sneak up?"

Andy smiled, fingering his scrapped skin and feeling some obscure victory,"Isn't that what we're supposed to do?"

At his voice the boy who had slid back into the vines, a strong, tall boy named Roger, emerged frowning, angry, he said in a fierce whisper."Shut up both of you,. What do you think you're doing. You make that kind of noise and you won't last an hour in the deep woods." He was training as a Hunter and was proud of his skills. He envied Andrew's arrival. Even he himself had not known Andy was near. At the same time he saw the hopelessness of training Argrid. He said, "Argrid, what d'you think you accomplished?"

"Why, I was the one who got him., If he'd been an enemy he could've --", He was cut short by Roger, his voice steely."Shut up, don't you have any sense at all. You're making enough noise right now to attract everybody in the Center. If he had been an enemy everyone of us would be dead. Yes, had we been in the forests among wild creatures we'd be dead, or maimed!" Andrew felt Roger's anger and knew part of it was at himself. That anger, hot, sharp hurtled against him so sharply it literally stung in his mind. He couldn't repress the thought. He doesn't even know he's throwing that much anger around. He remembered the statement that 'had they been in the wild they'd all be dead'. Could it be these boys didn't respond to the wild creatures, that they feared them? He felt outward, reaching tentatively, but finding nothing, withdrew. He dodged the implications of the thought.

He met Roger's eyes, hard with the fierce intensity of one determined to remain hard in every circumstance. Andrew realized the fear, and discomfort behind the fear, the hardness. He ignored the knowledge, and focussed attention . Roger was taller than Andrew, a year older and heavier. He had the forceful personality of the born leader. Andrew felt an obscure attraction, admiration, and knew he wanted to be liked by this hard bodied hunter apprentice. He was distrustful of his strong attraction but had not stopped to think about it.

He wanted to be part of this gang and he didn't want to think about that. He heard the mind call from Anna and swiftly Sent to her to wait a moment longer. He said aloud,"I'm sorry Roger, I didn't think. I could have se -- " He stopped in time, with a jolting suddenness he realized that he could not speak of Sending here. He put aside that thought,"I should have given the signal."

THE JOURNEY

Roger studied Andy, He didn't trust him, Andy knew. He felt things in Andy that put him on edge. He suspected Andy was not the simple boy he seemed to be. But at the same time he needed him, his standing in the community of boys, everybody liked him,, most even looked up to him though Andy seemed not to be aware of that. Andy was important to Roger's plan.Andrew could lend some prestige to this conspiracy that it didn't have. He knew that Andy was also friend of Dave's.Roger envied that. Andrew's folks were Founders. Roger's were new comers and although they worked hard,they couldn't seem to keep abreast of what was happening. His parents seemed discontented, resentful of something, and he couldn't figure out what. It was a mystery. The town welcomed them, got them jobs, established all of them in the Learning Center and asked them to do service on the Council. They were going into business for themselves with Council help. But they couldn't seem to fit. He thought there was some old resentment from the last place they had lived. They never would talk to him about it.But they'd recently joined the Builders and that seemed to make them less irritable.

Now, this boy, native to the Valley,seemed another kind of mystery. His Dad warned him to watch out for children who went into those 'trances'.Roger himself had seen strange things. He didn't talk about it. But he felt angry. Sometimes he'd seen some look pass between a Master Teacher and students at the Center, a held look and then, sometimes a silence that puzzled him.He had begun to watch, and now, this. Andrew should not have been able to approach them without his - at least his - knowing.

Andrew felt the turbulence of thought, the emotional ebb and flow, and waited. He wanted suddenly to prove himself, to really be a part of this 'gang.' He didn't understand its attraction, but he felt it so strongly that he couldn't give it up. He pushed all doubts, all questions into the background. He would not debate decision. He would make the other boys accept him. After all, they were almost grown men and they wouldn't be able to play at the old games much longer.

Finally Roger made his decision,"All right, But don't let it happen again." He was pleased with himself,the command coming from his mouth as if it were natural. He had studied old movies, old history and he knew the way it was done. He said, "We've got to train the others, and you're the one who can do it now."

Andrew was puzzled, he could not Touch to know Roger's meaning. He asked, "What d'you mean? Train them to what?"

Roger allowed his lips to curl, to sneer in the manner he thought to be appropriate."Dumb Ass! Train them to do what you just did. To move through the town without a sound, to sneak up on people."

But anyone could - " Andy stopped himself. Yes, most of his friends would have mind heard another coming. Few he knew who could quiet their minds enough not to be mind-heard.He said,"Well, anyone could learn that. Yes, I'll teach them."

Roger turned to leave,then turned back, a contemptuous look on his face, a stage look,as though he played a role. Well, of course, it was a game to him too.

Andrew felt better, then doubted his own thought. Roger really believed the role. He thought such a look would keep underlings in their place.It wasn't a game to him after all. The insight startled Andrew but he shrugged it away. He suddenly wanted to laugh, but he also wanted to win back approval and his reaction was to suppress the laugh utterly, even the knowledge of it. He asked hesitantly,"Why d'we need to sneak?"

"You idiot, We're gonna have to find out things people are trying to keep hidden,.We're gonna have to get places we don't want anybody to know about. We have to protect ourselves from attack. We have to spy! Yes, spy on people who can't know we're there." He said the last as a sudden inspiration . Surely there were those who would be after them,when he fulfilled his plans.

Andy nodded silently, amazed and glad to be reinstated. He turned, knowing something was very wrong here, but not wanting to discover it now. He told himself that Roger really knew how to play a role. Make it seem real. There was also something intriguing,some 'happening' such as he had not known. These games were theatre of the best sort. It was exciting. His mind was attentive, listening, seeing more than he could have explained. Why were they playing this game? Why was he so intrigued? But he turned from any attemmpt to answer. A lifetime of watching his own behavior, knowing his own thought and attending to his motives and actions, seemed suddenly in this moment to fail him. This was only some strange and fascinating charade, a game. He told them he'd meet them tomorrow and made the date. For the first time in his life he closed his mind to his twin sister and the experience of excluding her was both exciting and difficult.

He met her in the Dining Hall and drank a hot cup of cocoa that she had ready. "She sensed his preoccupation and they talked little. Then they left to begin the trip home. When they were on the path again, Andy looked up at the sky."It's going to storm, Anna, we'd better be moving." She nodded and they set out rapidly.

He reached to take her hand, feeling a desire to make up for his distance., They had arrived at the forking of the path outside the Center Buildings,when they heard a shout. They stopped , looking back toward the wide covered walkway circling the vast Ring building. A child stood against the corner,just outside the Archway in the distance. Two other children were running off toward the other side. They saw it was Cassandra who called. She seemed to be laughing,then she stopped. Anna and Andrew glanced at one another, their minds open again, communicating as usual.

Cassandra was dressed in blue shorts and shirt. Her feet in light sandals. The wind blew a bright orange and yellow scarf across her face and her hair was tied back, red-brown and shoulder length.She was looking down at her feet as they approached and they were startled at the sharpness of her Mindshout. It wasn't like Cassandra. Now they could see her face was anxious, her sturdy little body shook with exertion and her arms,still held stiffly at her sides seemed strangely at odds with the whole situation.

THE JOURNEY

Anna caught her breath, muttered softly,"Not again!" Cassandra was tied up, tied to the drain spout on the side of the circling walls.They knelt beside her. She was their little sister, they felt a surge of anger. They worked silently to free her from the ropes that held her. Andrew stroked her arms , his dark fingers gentle on the child's pale skin. Anna finally loosed the last knot and let the ropes drop. Andrew slid an arm around the little girl's shoulders and drew her close to him.

She began to chatter then, freed and less anxious, "It's only a game. It's nothing. It's nothing to worry about. We were playing that we were capturing people and we tied them up and I was last and the other kids had to go. It's just a game."

Andrew was startled at the similarity to his own reminders just a short time ago. Could this be the same? He shook his head, angry, No, these were just little kids.

Anna looked at this little bright eyed girl that she had known so long."Sweetheart, surely they weren't going to just leave you there?" Then she saw the fear, (and guilt?) in Cassandra's face and knelt down to speak,"It's all right, Dear, we aren't going to worry. We've got you loose and we've got to hurry home or we'll all be soaked."

Cassandra had begun to repeat her protestations rapidly as if it were a chant, and Anna tipped her face up,"Don't worry now, we just have to get home.It's all over."

Andrew shook his head, "No, Sis, she needs to talk about this. We need to know what's going on. It's crazy, her tied up like this. This is the second time, you know. That's too much. " He felt his own anger, his desire to protect the child, "She knows we don't buy that story. She's too mind strong not to know."

Anna hesitated, looking sadly at Cassandra's face. She already knew what Cassandra felt, both the fear and guilt. But Cassandra was looking up at them eagerly, expectantly. Her eyes moving from one face to the other, relief and tiredness showing now in her own pale face. She nodded , no words were needed and they were silent, a distinct communion going on among them, intimate and tender. Then her tears began. Andrew lifted her up and carried her over his shoulder as she cried.

They walked slowly away from the Center. They did not see the worried eyes of children who had run away. Not the concerned glances of adults still moving here and there in the pathways. Anna radiated feelings of well being, for those who could receive. Had they seen themselves they might have realized how the solemnity of their faces caught attention. Just as they turned into the branch of the path that led to the farm, they nearly collided with two men . One tall and black, the other medium height and much older, but with skin so tanned he looked mulatto.

Ned swiftly looked from one child to another and went to them, lifting Cassandra from Andrew, he held her high, and when she realized who it was,,she threw both arms around his neck and sobbed twice as loud , then suddenliy she was still.

THE PEOPLE OF THE VALLEY

The old man, Emery, was familiar to the children. He stood silently watching, feeling the worry of the children, but unable to fathom what could cause it.

Ned looked at Andrew and Anna, then said gently," Her hands have been tied." Swiftly he Reached, and his touch was harsh against their minds. They felt surprise at his skill.It took something like this for him to Touch them so."Now, wait," he said aloud," You know that kids need to talk aloud about things like this." He sounded angry, then swiftly checked himself and smiled,

The twins nodded guardedly and he knew they would not talk more. He stood Cassandra on her feet, knelt so that his face was level with hers. She had lost the strained look,ceased to cry. She was smiling now and clung to his hands. He looked seriously into her eyes."Tell me, Cassandra, what happened?"

The little girl looked away a moment and then with resolution, she met his eyes. Seriously,she answered."The other kids,tied me to the wall,not too tight, you know, they didn't want to hurt me. They were careful, Uncle Ned, honest." She seemed anxious that he understand that. At his nod,, she went on,falling into the pleasure of telling her story. "You see, they wanted me to do it again. You remember I'd done it once before but couldn't seem to make it happen again. But then,I'd promised and I didn't really want to either, It was a little scary. Because the other time,I'd got caught in a corner and I was afraid to stay there, so I just WILLED it,Uncle, Ned.I just WILLED it hard and there I was, out of the corner. It surprised me too. But they wanted to see it and they didn't believe it happened, even when they saw it themselves the first time. I didn't want them to think I was a lier. So I said I would try."

"Try what?" He was patient, his voice gentle and very quiet. She glanced up at Andrew and Anna, their worried looks, and hesitated. Swiftly,the twins reminded her they would not betray her friends and she nodded quickly and said,"Why to fly away from the ropes, to lift myself out and escape, like I did before."

Andrew and Anna looked at each other smiling but Ned continued, his eyes holding hers,"Fly away? How do you do that, Casandra?"

Her forehead puckered in worry and she looked from one face to the other,"I just do it. It just happens when I want it to very much. But it's WILLING it, like the Teachers say. You know, Uncle Ned!"

"And it was to test you that they tied you?"

She nodded, fidgeting with his hand, not meeting his eyes,"And it was, well, I -". She took a deep breath and burst out,"Well, I was bragging, Uncle Ned. I did do that!" She looked up at him with such appeal for forgiveness that he had difficulty remaining serious.

He nodded then,"Bragging, Huh? So that's it! I think I see." He stood up, lifting the little girl to hold her high above his head. He looked up at her smiling face and laughed. Not every man could lift a nine year old girl so easily and so high. He seemed to do it as easily as when she was only three. She laughed too then, looking down at that black shining face, tender with his love for her. "Hey, little lady up there, How would you like to come down and hurry home before you

THE JOURNEY

get caught in this storm?"

Cassandra nodded, and he tossed her up a little, then set her down between the twins. He winked at her as he studied her face. Whatever was happening here he would have to talk to the rest of the Family. He was glad he had found it out. These kids kept things to themselves too much.he noticed the swift interchange between the twins, realized they excluded him as naturally as if he would not know. He smiled inwardly. Family talk was still not good, habits of exclusion were already formed. He Reached, Touched, and felt surprise and a trace of guilt in their minds. They both stared at him and Anna blushed.

"Uncle Ned, Of course. We promised too, didn't we? That we'd not pretend anymore." She shook her head,"I'm sorry."

Andrew nodded, but he said only,"Thank you, Uncle Ned,She needed a little pick up." He grinned at his poor pun, then added,"I don't think it's anything to worry about,do you? It's just kids play, you know."

Ned watched them,their faces so relaxed, even amused. Puzzled, he finally said with a sigh," We'll talk about it later, Son. I'll get belts for the three of you.You won't make it now walking. It's already sprinkling." He turned, assuming acceptance, and they followed. Ned set his credit card into the slot and got belts from the public rack at the entrance to the Learning Center and distributed them."Not many left. People have been scurrying out of here this last hour." He was frowning, his mind racing. He saw laughter in their eyes, " Kid play indeed, Andrew. It doesn't seem you'd find this funny. What if you hadn't come by."

Andrew met his look firmly," Someone would have heard. But I don't find it funny, Uncle. Just pleased with her." He glanced at Cassandra and nodded,"She's O.K."

Ned looked at them both, his face still unfamiliar with stern seriousness,"All right, Son, but you and Anna both know the fear in the Valley. You know we have to be careful. You know what people are afraid of!" He stopped, aware that he did not state that name himself. The fact disconcerted him. The two children stood silent and he thought they knew his chagrin. But then, a faint guilt touched thier eyes, and they nodded. Ned went on, aware that he was talking as much to distance himself from his own uneasy feelings. ."You both know that there is a growing polarity. This Valley is literally splitting apart, and yet you think it's all right for Cassie to demonstrate to every body walking by that she has power that frightens most people, frightens even herself, actually." And he added silently, 'frightens me'. He thought they sensed that last.There, he'd said it then, what needed to be said clearly, without mincing words. The first time he'd spoken his fear so bluntly. From their looks he knew they were not used to hearing adults speak so."The worst of it is that she thinks her greatest mistake was in bragging about her Talent. That IS bad, but to ignore public reaction is worse, right now. Can't you children remember that?" This time he included Cassandra in his glance and she frowned, and ducked her head.

He glanced sharply at Anna, saw her eyes meet Andrew's and suddenly clearly knew their mind's Touched. The knowledge left him cold, he felt his own refusal so strong it shuddered through his muscles. He forced himself to admit his fear. He knew, could not deny, the power he felt between them. Young people with old Minds. The thought flashed to him startling him. He shrank from acknowledging his own awareness .Then he knew the thought,"My God, am I still afraid of all this ?"

Anna turned to him then, as if unaware that he had closed himself away with his fear. He felt anger. Damn her, as if she didn't know. She was so calm about it. She said serenely,"Uncle Ned, we do know how it is.But some people just don't want to see! We think there shouldn't be a problem." Her own bigotry was instantly obvious to her. She blanched.

Ned shook his head, his eyes on hers, refusing to shift and she looked down,biting her lip. Why would she try to fool Uncle Ned. She needn't pretend with him.Why would she want to pretend with anyone. What was wrong with her? The old habits were strong. An arrogance lurked in their shaadow. She reached out one hand to him, wanting help, wanting forgiveness. Wanting to see the familiar brilliant smile. But she withdrew that hand, this was her own problem.

Andy was nodding,"It's true, Uncle Ned, everything we're realizing -- together!" He would not yield, held Ned's eyes."We know it. We've got a lot to learn ourselves.. We'll be more careful. Cassandra will to, won't you, Sister?" She nodded, solemly.

Ned nodded then."Well, just do it. You don't have to like it." He watched them lift away, stood thoughtful in the chill gust of the wind.

Rose saw them coming from her cottage at the far end of the pathway from the Hall. She had come to change clothes, the storm was making the air colder and summer clothes were not enough. She watched the storm approach, the thin grey curtain moving closer. The three dots that were the children grew larger but the clouds were swift above them. The River glinted through the trees,it's surface rough in the wind. Surely Ben won't try to come by belt. The storm would be too high for belts by the time he got back from Altos.

She watched the rain move slowly toward them, saw the children riding ahead of it, and sighed with relief when they landed safely on the deck, running to get inside the Hall. Rose let her eyes sweep far across the Valley beyond. No creatures roamed the meadows, except for small herds of deer or cattle, here and there,she could see them still grazing. This summer rain wouldn't drive them to shelter . Half a dozen head of cattle lay quietly under great spreading beech trees on the far hillside. They were so calm. She pulled on a glowing blue sweater over summer skirt and matching hose. Then pulling a feather light parka over it all, she went out to walk to the Hall. It would be dinner time soon. She'd better see to it.There was something bothering those three children too. She decided she'd find that out before Ben got home.

CHAPTER TWO

Meetings in Adwin

    Early on a June morning , a week after the children had brought Cassandra home from town, a morning when the light of coming dawn had barely replaced the darkness and the cool air drifted with pale mists across the Valley from the River,Rose stood at her door, open to this new dawn. She looked out beyond the slope of hills, along the River,at the sudden whir of hundreds of water fowl as they raced across the water away from the northern shore. They had been startled by some hunter, either man or beast. They summered here in the swamps of Matta and provided Adwin what small harvest she needed of geese and ducks which always preceeded the second harvest of Matta . Most northern towns depended on their swamps for these double crops.
    The birds settled, and the water finally stopped trembling in the sharp rays of sun. There was silence again. A cow bawled in the distance and then there were three short sharp staccato barks. The stillness seemed to cradle these sounds, to be stained with the grey of the landscape which was rapidly becoming blue of sky and green and gold of land as light grew. Lights still glowed softly along pathways everywhere, and in towns and forests where people lived. Rose walked slowly through the already warm air to the Temple, she savored this quiet, peace. What would this day bring? Entering the Temple, she selected sound, color and fragrance, then stilled them all. She would contemplate utter silence. She focussed,attention reached beyond thinking, into stillness. The void, the emptyness, open and receptive. Was that void Mind itself? A greater universal, unlimited Mind shared by all living things?
    She knew she was acutely aware of every nuance of sound and color and smell, of thought or feeling, even as those were given no attention. She entered deeper, beyond senses, silence. And that silence held where thought could not follow. The indefinable present.
    After some time,she stirred from her absorption, rolled back in the ebbing of her reach,descending out of that place of knowing, she felt the flood of personal life surround her. Now she noticed fragments of thought, a few sounds of life outside the Temple, they came and went. Now she turned to them, but they did not claim her. Realization of a knowledge out of stillness was printed into her mind in a language pure and indelible. Thought would come later.
    Then, the flow outward again, from herself, into stillness. Herself forgotten, her attention diffuse and extended through the Valley, through Earth. She could feel those lives, waking now to the imminent dawn, registered in her consciousness as an unfolding pattern of steadily growing energy and she felt it as fully with her body as her mind. Through everything was a stillness that led toward - what? She remained in communion, realizing through the immensity of

Earth Life, something larger than Life Itself that nourished all life? In that case it was herself being nourished also. The thought spun through her mind, weaving a web of new thought. It sparkled with the lingering reflections of Light. She sat, unmoving. She had dressed carefully in a soft green, knee length plasilk dress, belted and full for walking. She had put on Bondeel fibre walking boots, tougher and more flexible than leather had ever been. She planned to ride the belts to town She had tidied her room knowing she wouldn't return until night. She looked down at herself, as if her body had a life of its own.

In this self remembering attention shrank again. She felt content, to sit and to remember. But yawning realizations drew her attention. She was grateful for the solitude of the Temple when no one was there. She thought something of herself remained there, like a thread that nourished her through the day. She pressed two tiny gold discs set into the cubicle, and there was the sound of a drum, so deep it seemed to rise from Earth's depths. It began to surge, then in long slow measures to hold a steady pattern. At the same time a brass chime, round noted, silvery and full, rang out in syncopation to the drum, its voice creating a dialogue that caught up the attention of her absorbed mind. Rose settled into that steady framework of sound, and offered herself again to stillness.

She noticed the quiet of her limbs, the beat of her heart, a pain in her hip, the slow activity of her bowels. The click of a switch outside, the stillness, and her right foot itched. She watched, aware of being an animal alive in this quiet place. Attention held, moved outward toward the world around the Temple, beyond, extending, following consciousness in a widening circle. On and on, beyond the Valley itself, beyond the nation, her mind held images of seas and cities, passed them by and then the Earth Herself hung in a dark void. Bright, blue and white, the Earth hung and the gold light of the sun made brilliant her seas. Rose was still, the universe and the effort drew her closer - conscious of Being at that farthest point. Waiting, Listening. A single focus of awareness.

Then, like the extinguishing of a light, her mind emptied, images, form, dissolved in nothing. Held, supported by effortlessness, in a void of lightlessness. No time, nothing. And there she knew.

Suddenly, light pierced consciousness. She stood awake limits unknown. Soul Conscious, containing Rose? She Touched against others as though conscious minds were flickering lights she swept toward. She felt the power of endless Reaching. Possibility! Then that small self curdled, fell like a blind stone down into its limits, lost awareness of Self. A flickering thought intruded and was gone. "Soul Conscious?"

Without effort she accepted the fall. Sitting silently, her body functioning, her mind ranging, Reaching into its small distance. Stillness was a rising state, nothing occurred and she sat in the midst of it. Knowledge pulsed and woke in that held attention. She bore that knowledge willingly, it was not unfamiliar. But the memory of that vast Soul Reach held something that was other than familiar. What? The overwhelming power of that Touch, the wind that breathed against her mind, as if to quicken it, to impress upon it, hinted at its Self. And she quailed to faintly realize. Far reaches of Soul? The willing immersion of her self in that Self was a memory that could be thought about. But the sweep of fiery wind? There had been the impossible. She felt her heart ache with a longing her mind thrust aside.

Memory! Consciousness a centered calm. Perception thrust beyond the thinking part of mind, outdistancing thought, until vision was a lance of light, pressing beyond knowledge into knowing. And that Touch, there, contact with what? The awe-ful pressure of a living wind, that swept past all barriers, banging like a doorway blown through consciousness. Her mind shuddered before IT. And that Wind finding her, touched and left its imprint, an imprint that loosed its own breath into this human consciousness. Then, there was no time, but being - what was not?

The impact of that Touch tore the inner structure of her being into shreds. Hurt with an ache that would not heal. She cried out,and the cry was her heart's bleeding. Later, Rose sought to hold memory, to name, to define that impossible Touch but there were few hooks in her mind by which to reconnect. That brilliant wind could not be held, named, but it could be remembered. There was memory of wonder, of hollow immensity, of a wind that created itself even as it filled that hollow , a wind that was itself Light. She felt her body softened, tears running, her hands curled, strengthless. She sat in receptive stillness absorbing that reflection of Light, conscious before she slid down the inevitable narrowing tunnels from Mind to mind. She lifted her hand, looked in surprise at the fine wrought structure and marveled. She was quiet then, for some time. tears flowed across her face,and a tiny moan like a plea issued from her half opened mouth.

Gradually she steadied, drew herself back and cut off consciousness beyond herself. Words shaped, thought fed them.Familiar words that seemed so crucial to understanding. She said aloud,"Oh, my God, how broken is my heart, how torn from sanity my mind. I ache with dispair and with Joy." And she thought those words were strange, yet accurate.

After a while, she sighed. Began repeating familiar words, realizing their comfort.

> All people are One and I am one with them.
> I seek to Love, not hate,
> I seek to serve and not exact due service.
> I seek to heal, not hurt.
> Let pain bring due reward of Light and Love
> Let Soul control the outer form and all events,
> Let Light reveal the Love that underlies
> the happenings of our time.
> Let insight come and wisdom.
> Let the future stand revealed.
> Let inner unity demonstrate
> and outer cleavages be gone.
> Let Love prevail, Let all people Love.

As the words faded, she held to one line, "For me this day, 'let outer cleavages be gone, let inner unity demonstrate'. THAT I must practice during this day, steadily and without ceasing".She would start the day from here, this quiet and this committtment.From this point, personal needs seemed distant and small. Without doubt the shining wind had left its imprint in the substance of her mind and heart.

When she rose to leave, there were three others in their own cubicles and one person, Anna in the open central room.The main Hall was adrift now in shimmering gold, but only Anna had come to sit there. Rose left and stepped outside, seeing the dawn had come and the Valley below filled with the colors of the day. On the high peaks the sun already was glowing a soft gold and the snow glistened where it caught the light. She stood a moment, lost in the wonder and beauty that soared mile upon mile before her.

She reflected now,her heart blazing with all that had Touched her. It was all still available to her, all present, all right here now. She could not suppress the soft cry,"Oh dear, oh dear, how can I understand?" But thoughts coursed into view, swelled from a mind taut with realization.

There, just behind thought was that point where Light still beckoned. The place of Soul Consciousness and all that meant. It was not a dream. It was reality. She, aware so that what she knew here, in this little self, was a revelation. When she looked into a tree deeply enough, she saw beyond that life, into its source. Even though she carried all her learnings of Earth, of living things,like a barrier between herself and that Earth life, she could shed all that, free herself and stand naked of everything, except awareness. When she looked into Earth deeply enough, she entered into Her life, Her nature as into a vast dimension and what she knew folded around the small cluster of her learning and absorbed it. She could not -- would not -- forget. Yet, the memory throbbed through her heart, making her almost afraid. How could she , how could humankind be - what all that Vision implied? Her entire living self was stretched, renewed, aware,so that something of her longed to sleep and forget. Something of her felt Joy like a current running through her veins, blazing in her heart. She deliberately turned her attention to her familiar physical world.

She saw the lights go off in the towns, they still gleamed in forest and mountain side. The sunlight spread deeper, ran swiftly over low western hills,but the low Valley was like a dark pool. She felt again the power of that Valley world. Her eyes lifted to that point on the cliff where she so often fled for solitude. She sat on the wide railing that ran along this path before the Temple and reflected on the fact of these years of secrecy.That inner waking, the stretch of mind to Mind, of self to Self, had been a secret happening within individuals, unspoken. But this other, the Talents, the movement from physical to astral planes, had also been secret and it was simpler. That too they had denied. She had. And fear had held her from speaking of the times she visited, out of body, that secret point on the cliff?

THE JOURNEY

Why did she never explore other possibilities of travel in that state? What fears stopped her. Surely she needed to know, all that she could, if she were to understand the fears of the Builders? After all, wouldn't that astral world be another entrance way into that greater way of Soul consciousness. Or would it hamper realization? Somewhere she had heard that it might. But she thought it was only if one got so fascinated with it that she forgot to go on. And what did that mean? Surely she ought to know, now that she was delving in it! There was a whole lot to learn. She'd better be about it.

Now there was more! Couldn't they acknowledge that humanity -- not just a few, but all humankind, traveled finally into new realms? What would happen if they did? She slid one hand along the fine texture of the oiled wood seat, propped her elbow on one knee and fitted her chin into her hand. Her mind still full, reverberating with the impressions that flight beyond it had made on it. She said aloud,"We are awake. Everyone admits that. We see ourselves - we know what we've been. We know what human kind has been. We don't pretend we are more good than we are evil. We know both. We know we have to choose."

The words seemed to bring clarity, seemed to rise out of the impressions from Soul Light."Now we know what our pattern has been. We know how to break it. How to see further. But now, how do we step on, cross over the interface between animal human and Soul human? What would we be like, how would we live were we to stand permanently Soul conscious? Already we've begun-- where will we go?" She stopped, musing on those questions, unable to find answers. But hearing the questions as bells that rang to warn of an ending and a beginning.

"Look what we've been! We see ourselves now, see how we locked ourselves into old lusts, hates, fears, and selfish ambitions; how we acted out of neurotic needs to build a world full of greed and dispair, pain and suffering. We thought our goal was to find comfort and peace for our self. We didn't know. I believe that we did not know, that no peace, no comfort, nor joy can be ours until all humanity is lifted from suffering and dispair. We were self defeating all these centuries. And those who did lift, did become Soul Conscious, were killed because they hinted at what we suspected deep in our own hearts. Our very culture eternally lashed back on us, on the best of us. We were caught, locked into a never ending circle. We found ourselves betraying our own dreams, our highest visions. We, trapped in minds that could not perceive selflessness, could not dare harmlessness, we forever have fallen back down to our lowest natures in times of stress." Her heart hurt to say the words, yet she felt she must. She must speak of all she realized.

"Yet, in us has always been the longing, the hope for being all that we are -- for being Soul conscious. But to be so, meant rising out of the devouring ambitions of this little hungry self. That then was evil? The refusal to see, to transcend self, to stand firmly at our highest vision, and persist toward it." The words set a decision for her.

She stood, walked slowly toward the Hall, strange that no one seemed around, no one called or walked this path with her.

She stepped slowly up the low steps onto the deck,"Maybe we have been afraid to be fully human. Afraid of what that would mean. The loss of littleness, the loss of this poor fragment of awareness we call our lives, and our hungry needs." A sense of amusement that seemed to rise from depths beneath knowledge, startled her. Why? She looked around. Was she missing something?

The mountains brightened, light slid down lower and reached the Valley floor. House lights through the forests faded. Across the miles of wild grass land between the arms of dark forest, a shimmer of mist rose from the heavy evaporating dew. The Valley was awake. she felt the Earth beat, like a Heart, pulsing through her feet,into her body. And in response to it, the slow chime of the vast arching sky. Her mind heard,received the Sound of Earth Life. Could she simply live in this wideness of being? Must she shrink to the smallness of her own fear?

With surprise she saw Jane coming up the pathway from the River fields. She had a streak of mud across one brown leg below her shorts. She was whistling loud enough that Rose knew she assumed she was alone. She whistled a well as many people sang, her notes true and sweet.But when Rose stood and called out, Jane started a little, looked slightly embarrassed then shrugged. She came up on the deck and dropped tiredly into a chair. Rose sat too, smiling,glad to be drawn from her thoughts.

Jane said,"Ah, Rose, it isn't often I finish my work this early, before the day has well started, but this time of year, there's not much to do but keep tabs on things. It's too hot by the late morning for labor, unless it can't be helped."

Rose nodded, watching her silently, until Jane frowned and asked,"What's going on with you? You look as if I've interrupted something."

Rose shook her head,"I've just spent more than an hour realizing a lot of things. Things I don't fully understand at all." She brightened, meeting Jane's clear,direct gaze,"Maybe you could help me figure it out?"

Jane laughed shortly, lifting her hands lightly in self deprecation,then leaning to rub the drying mud off her leg. "If I could be of help, I'd like it. But I doubt if I'd be."

Rose ignored Jane's usual self denial,and said,"You'd be a real help, Janey. I'm like a water logged tree in the river, only I'm thought logged." She laughed. Jane was watching her, she nodded, inviting Rose to go on."This morning, in the temple, I realized - something --"she resolved to say it."Soul Consciousness, Jane. We're capable of it. We ARE sometimes. When we Reach - when we are as aware as we can be" She watched Jane, wondering whether these words would put her off.

Jane nodded seriously,"That -- Soul consciousness - I know, its what we seek." With a shake of her head, she quoted, "To lift the mind, the attention, beyond everything we know or have been, to reach to that which is the highest we are, and know ourselves ONE life." She shook her head again."That what you mean Rose?"

Rose had to laugh,"You've remembered the words. Now what do they mean?" At Jane's raised eyebrows, she went on,"Yes, that's it. I've got to understand what it all means, Jane. The Reach, the Joining, the searching out how to live? What does it mean to plan the Journey. Why would people be doing such a thing? Those are the questions I've been asking." She looked so dispairing that Jane reached to take her small hand in her slim long fingers.

Oh, Rose, no wonder you're tired. That's harder than the work I've been doing."

Rose shook her head, suddenly impatient,"I mean it, Jane. What is the point of everything? We've recognized Talents, we know we practice living, practice emotional balancing, and we stretch for that highest state of consciousness. And it has to be so we can live as human beings at some level beyond this one. Then what will we be?" Her voice broke, she leaned to Jane, both her hands clutching Jane's,"What will we BE?"

Why, Rose, we'll be more-- just more human, I think. We'll be AWARE, we'll know life, at least Earth life, as if it were ourselves." She said it so quietly that Rose stared at her unbelieving.

"It can't be. I can't believe you've understood already what I'm struggling with.And you always tell us you're ignorant of these things." She shook her head again.

"Rose, tell me what you've been thinking, that's made you feel over whelmed. Just tell me."

Rose nodded, she could find again the thought, could speak it now."I think the task is to learn to live through Earth. Just as you say. To live through each other, as one people, one Humanity. Just that! I think that's it, Jane. And I think then, we'd be standing at that state of Soul Consciousness, knowing from there. I think that's what it is, the total inclusion of life with Life."She breathed a long sigh. "There, that seems to say it." She looked with relief at Jane and Jane laughed.

"Then, there's how to live so. That's the real question. How can we live from that Soul level? "She frowned, let go of Jane's hands, sat back and added,"And still be human?"

Jane laughed,then sobered, knowing Rose was deeply serious, "Why don't we wait til we ARE Soul Consious and see?"

Rose's eyebrows went up, she frowned. "Obvious,isn't it?" But her heart beat hard, an eagerness, a Joy, broke through the resistances of body and mind. She stopped, holding out her hands, realizing anew, aware and willing at that moment,she said,"After all, what is the alternative? To live only in this small human condition with all its pain, its constant unceasing hurting of others, of life, of hunger so insatiable it ruthlessly destroys whatever frustrates it? Denies all Love!"

In that moment she forgot Jane, forgot everything except this committment. It seemed to ravage through her, tearing away old habits of thought, searing through her own needs and dissolving them as if they were a darkness before the flood of light. She almost shouted,"Yes, I want to know of Life and of Love and to live in that knowledge. But I will have to live this life too. I must learn to bring one into the other. I will begin by listening to Earth and listening to the simplest of people. Listening with all my heart! I MUST understand!" She felt released from some constriction, freed. It was exhilarating, she knew she had committed herself. Whatever it cost, whatever the inner pain of adjusting her self, her mind, her physical life to that committment, she would persist. She would be WILLING!

It was as though a greater Consciousness beyond her, invisible, drew her toward itself, and she realized she WAS that which drew her. The sense of subtle amusement, of smiling delight, swept through her. She caught her breath, surprised.

At any rate, she had decided. She would no longer fight her Self, but offer herself in service to that Self. The decision swept past years of grief and fear leaving them behind, reduced to powerlessness. Her mind seemed empty, fragile, fluid as a quiet pond, utterly responsive.

Her eyes moved to include the plants blooming all over the gardens, the hill side, the winding paths among them, the small octagonal ponds of clear, green water. The whole thing so alive. Birds rustled searching for insects, a clutter of wild turkeys chirped at her from outside the garden. Jane watched her, silent, so deeply with her. Rose marveled at that. Jane was more conscious than anyone seemed to realize. Than she herself realized. When the thin walls of her resistance fell, she would be a wonder to know. She looked at her in awe, and Jane frowned, puzzled at the expression. Then she smiled. She reached out her hands again, took Jane's and said,"Jane, perhaps there's just the decision to live at our absolutely highest point of awareness. All the time!" She grinned at Jane's skeptical look and said, "Have you had breakfast? I haven't, will you join me?"

Jane nodded,"To do that would be asking a lot. More than we've done. But -- maybe you're right. Maybe it's the task we have." Then, turning to meet Rose's eyes, she said,"No, I've not eaten and I'm hungry. Let's go.

They went in to breakfast, sharply aware of the breath of wind, the smells, the endless complexities of this Earth life. She closed the Hall door as though she shut herself off to rest. Food seemed a wonderful gift, a blessing and Rose ate reverently for the first time in her life. They talked a little of the day, of their plans. Rose said she was on her way to town. Jane shook her head and said she would stay and go to her cottage, Steve would meet her there later. She smiled so that Rose wanted to ask whether there would one day be a wedding. But she didn't.

Rose pulled on a light, wind proof coverall over her clothes. It would fold into a package small enough to put into her pocket when she reached town. Then she strapped on a belt. The sky was clear, she could see the high trails of a huge transworld air craft crossing far above. Here and there air cars, like gaudy birds, moved from town to town, a few freight cars rumbled slowly through the low altitude traffic level, but the skies were emptier than she had ever seen them. The building of Transmitters in the largest towns of the Valley, of the world, in fact, had made the constant drift of freight cars gradually decrease. The small northern towns took their products to Santiago and picked up their incoming freight there.

THE JOURNEY

She watched the silvery blink of the high air craft. She looked down then at the fields passing beneath. The belt lifted her only a few feet off the ground, but it was fast enough that the wind pressed her clothes against her body hard.. She was in Adwin in minutes.

She dropped down in the Central Civic Center. The Outer Ring held the big new World Market screens and viewing rooms. Wisteria traveled around one whole side of the building, reaching up to the second story, it would eventually climb to the third. Now, however, she could smell the fragrance of its blooms,hanging thick, lavender, delicate and lovely in a cascade from the strong young vines. She looked at it a moment and then at the ever moving screen. It drifted through its constantly changing images of products. Familiar, strange, new and old, world products, in three dimensions, and moving to show their function, followed one another without ceasing. She wanted to go inside this day and study some products carefully but that would be later. Right now,she must meet her friends.

Before her the walkway wound through little groves of trees, young, early apples and a stand of citrus. There were young boys and girls busy among the apples trees. They had ladders and baskets. These were the town gatherers, doing the spring thinning. She stooped to pick a handful of fragrant violets growing along the brick path. She felt with pleasure the sun on her back, the sounds of the town, the chatter of the children. the whole morning seemed to her to have a magic quality, a vividness. The sense that she could not hold all the beauty within herself,that she was too full with it, brought tears suddenly to her eyes.Then she laughed with sheer joy. But ached with the beauty, the recognition, as if her heart were not yet large enough to hold it all. Would the pain be as great as this joy when she must meet with one who suffered? She knew it would be so. Aware then, she realized shadows of that suffering, farther away, but sensable. She drew herself inward, Coward. But the grief lived beneath the joy.

Then she noticed the children had become utterly silent.She looked up. Saw several of Andrew's and Anna's friends among them. Carl, leaned from the tree to whisper down. " Hey, Rose, watch and you'll see something great." There was a mischief and a question in his eyes. Suddenly there was a soft thud against her head and a small, green apple bobbed about in the air in front of her eyes. She watched as it floated on down then to the basket. Another and another followed until there was a light rain of them, all descending and funnelling properly into the waiting baskets. The children were grinning at her surprise. She saw Andrew then, high up, his weight mostly on the ladder and one foot on a limb.

She shook her head,"Careful Andy, they are young trees, you know. They can't take much weight yet."

He nodded,"We know Mom. We are. But we've got a contest going and we have to work fast,so look out below.'

She thought some of the children were disappointed that she was not shocked, or better, frightened at their skill. She was, but she intended not to satisfy them. She smiled,"Well, you all know there aren't that many apple trees in town gardens. The groves along the river are a better test. Is it a fair trial?"

Someone laughed,"It might not be except they know it too and they insisted we divide the trees by number. Don't worry, Rose, we'll lose or win fair and square." She nodded and started on, then saw Anna's face among the leaves of another tree. She waved to her and then wondered at how unfamiliar her own children had become. Without warning, sensitive now to the nuances of emotions around her, she knew that playful delight of her son, the dominant feeling among these children, was not all. The sour,tightness of jealousy, the rasping,grip of resentments, others, also colored this group of children. She stifled herself. How could one endure sensing so sharply? But the question needed consideration -- later. She grimaced. These children were aware of that kaliedescope of emotions among themselves. Aware and accepting. The thought made her frown. How could they?

But she was cheered by that encounter as she went on. These were not children as she had been. They already used Talents without shame or fear. They already knew that working together, that mutual welfare was necessary to create a world they valued. Their study, their games, work, exploring of the wild lands, everything worked from mutual cooperation. They learned it by living it all the time. She had never done that. It was a given among them. So vastly different from her own childhood. They were beyond their own parents. She wonderd whether the Builders included children, or were most children talented? Even more,had most children, waked to that higher consciousness within themselves? She must find out.

She took a fork in the walk where it changed from tiles to brick again. Here there was a busy, noisy, color filled open market. She loved the variety. Goods were sold here from all over the world, but mostly they were local products.Bright and acreous odors, fragrances, exotic food smells, almost anything could be found even in this little town market or the wide malls inside the two outer Rings. Around her as she walked, were little stalls under huge curving umbrellas that curled down to within three feet of the ground and gave privacy as well as creating a bright colorful marketplace. In some shops were shopkeepers, talking and visiting with the shoppers. Some had no owner present but rather a computer watch that told the price of things and received the credits. She studied the interweaving of tile and brick where two more paths joined. She knew that teenages had done this whole great stretch of plaza, and marveled at their skill. She liked the fact that children had done it.

She thought again of the children working there to thin the fruit crops. A consciousness of the yawning gap between herself and these young ones troubled her. How did they feel? What did they think of those among them who could not do these things? What did those lacking such skills think, feel? She was reminded of Will. They should give thanks that he was their only mind blind member. She felt grief at that reminder.She said aloud,"My God, how many are

THE JOURNEY

there among us?"

As the question was spoken, she wished she could simply go to the library and program a computer to find out the number of people with and without talents in this city. If only they hadn't been so secret about them!

Could they do a Video News story? A series? The Master Teachers could put it together, build and present it as part of the Valley News? She ought to get that started surely. We've got to know, where we stand and so we'll start talking. Builders would have to talk too.

She passed through the center Arch into the inner Ring gardens. It was as if she saw the whole town anew, everywhere she traveled, it seemed fresh and vividly alive. Even the dead leaves, of last fall now nearly rotted beneath thick trees against the curving side of the Ring buildings seemed to her vivid, beautiful with the new life that rebuilt in them. Nothing seemed to her to be out of place. What small debris was left by people had been carefully removed from these gardens by the town Gardeners. Order shaped itself even in the chaotic looseness of the plots of 'wild garden'. And yet, even in this blooming world of beauty, of serenity, there was suffering.

Now she allowed herself to notice. Small deaths, small hungers, a diseased tree, only recently noticed by the gardeners. Then, refusing avoidance, she felt the human pain, the ache of struggle, confusion, emotions in turmoil among the many people walking through the early morning light. She turned to look around at them, some full of her own kind of joy, yes, there were those, but many who weren't. She withdrew her attention to shield herself for this moment. Beneath it, here and there, the swift hurt and death of creatures, finding food, or becoming it. To know it as part of a whole took more balancing than she had learned as yet. To distinguish between suffering imposed by thoughtlessness or cruelty and that which was simply the ordinary hurts of living, she would need to learn more. She said aloud,"Whatever depths or breadth of awareness we reach, there are simply more balances to discover and practice."

She walked beneath an arbor of clematis and grapes, past the Agricultural offices where the master Farmer would be. She turned to look around. Should she go directly to the cafe where they were to meet? Could she spend more time wondering this way. The day was still very early, she could take a little more time.

Three small children played along the path way around a cluster of great granite boulders. Their bright clothing flashed in the sun. One child had removed his clothes and climbed to the top of the highest boulder where he sat, seemingly oblivious of the others. Others were tediously and utterly absorbed in arranging twigs and leaves into designs on several yards of broad flat stone. She watched but could not devine their game. She thought there were resemblances to the rituals of Summer festival in them. They were transforming the rituals in these games just as they would one day transform the Valley rituals.

Suddenly the child at the top of the boulder raised his arms, sang a high keening tone. A minor melody,,sweet and penetrating and at that signal the others, moved away from their design, stood around it, and began to dance,

THE PEOPLE OF THE VALLEY

moving finally in and out of the design, serious, absorbed, as children are when they create their own games.. The singer sang on,the beat of his rhythm kept with his clapping hands. They did not notice Rose. The intensity of their play tugged at her mind,reminded and faded, and then she murmured to herself,"Is this a Teaching Game, have their Teachers sent them here?" Then, watching, "Are they closer to Earth than I? They are singing of Earth consciousness from whose strength we all drew to build this Valley?" She silently watched them, realizing more as she did so." Of course" The explanation, right or wrong, comforted her even though she was not sure of the reason. She extended her mind, felt the tight womb of their intermingled attention,joined in a play, a joy and an absolute necessity that held them and that she would not touch. She moved away.

    She thought of Benjamin and Tom gone to Altos to see William, to reassure themselves that he was still their brother regardless of their differences. She felt that old,astringent of resentment, like a shredded mist of memory, that Benjamin had left again. She smiled at her recognition. It did seem that he'd been gone a long time,two days. But she shook her head at her resentment. And smiled sadly at herself. She easily lifted herself out of the morass of emotion and it collapsed. She drew her thoughts together, accepted.

    Just as the speaking out of the Builders in the Valley, had changed the Valley itself, at least for her, so the denial by William of the realizations of his family had changed the Family itself. Must have changed him. Of course it had. She wanted to deny that, and would not.After all, Ben had resisted the Reach of their minds for so long, But he had learned to recognize that he was able, that he COULD. Even though he was still hesitant. So perhaps Will might.But she let the thought fade. No,it was waste of hope. For Will it was not choice. He was like one crippled. They must accept his handicap.

    She stepped out from the grove of pear trees through which she had walked, into a small lawn of lemon grass. The fragrance rose as she walked and she felt it lift her spirits. In sudden gratitude, she sent her own energy downward, outward, unblocking the flow of herself, and she felt calmed.

    She saw people moving through the gardens, intent on their own errands. She passed through a crowd coming from the business offices, wove her way through them,smiling and speaking: comforted .Walking through the town always had relieved tensions for her. She entered the inner Ring, and a small court where scuptures were standing. The central figures were professional and very fine work, one of Annette's, two of other artists. The others near them were the work of students, and she could see Anna's there beside a wild lilac blooming dark blue flowers . Andrew's piece was gone and she remembered it was being taken to the farm . They would set it into their own garden. It might be his last sculpture. She walked slowly but steadily until she had passed on through the Rings of the Center and out through the fields beyond it. Surrounded by a paved circle and then a wider circle of bright green ground covers, was the Temple. She could see it flaming brilliantly through the groups of select trees around that wide lawn. Adwin's pride it was. It was always open and she wanted to stop there a moment.

THE JOURNEY

She let her eyes follow the slim central spire rising a hundred feet into the blue air and the smaller spires surrounding it. The light played on the orange-red-gold of those spires. They looked like a fire , a grand flaming that burned always on this projection of the Center Ring. It was the heart of the three great Triple Rings of Adwin.

She walked up the low broad steps and entered. The stillness caught at her heart, so deep it seemed. The wide entrance held tables on which were the bibles of all religions. Each was left open where some one had been reading. The central circle was paved with tiles in rich colors and designs then it opened out into seven triangles that altogether shaped a star. From each of the seven points brilliant color poured through stained glass all the way to the top of the spires so that the central circle was splashed with that color throughout the day. Making glass for that Temple and Santiago's had established the glass industry that was Denlocks major income now. Rose stood for several moments, breathing in the loveliness and calm. Then she left.

How could a people who would build such a Temple for such a small town, not be able to meet these present dangers? Her heart filled with hope. How could she come to terms with the loss of William? She shrugged. The questions brought grief. Then like a stab of pain, she was ashamed. They had lost nothing. It was only at ego focus, not Soul focus that there seemed to be loss. William was as he had always been. He was not like the rest of the family,, but he was William, their brother. To know a brother less conscious was not to know loss. The pride that saw it as loss would be enough to destroy them. Ego needs permeated their attitudes, were endemic,ancient. How could they stand beyond them? The ego was essential to being human too. Then what? Could they stand at Soul level, where ego was no longer controlling life?

"We have been taught and we know better. We can't excuse ourselves, we see more and must act from that vision." She spoke with a sudden conviction that startled several people passing by. Two large dogs crossed the path, looked up at her with concern in their large brown eyes because they heard the tone of dispair. She touched their heads in reassurance and they went on. A woman and child walked toward her nodding but sensing her desire for solitude, said nothing.She walked back from the Temple toward the Civic Center's outer Ring again and found a bench to sit on. After a moment she lifted her head, listening. She felt a delicate Mind Touch. Who? She Reached in welcome.

It was Ted, walking with confident stride he came through the shrubbery where she could see him. She Touched more firmly and he turned to her, his face lighting up. Perhaps his own thought had been grey.

"Rosy,Ah, we're early, you and I. I wanted to take the long walk through town this morning. Just seeing and gloating about all we've done. We've done what we intended all those years ago. I feel like an old man now. Yet we were so young when we began. You and Ben just Mated, me and Aileen just meeting actually. And now we've got half grown children.I'll never live anywhere else. I love this town." He looked at her speculatively, his cheerfulness a balm to her heart.Then he frowned,"How sad you look this morning, dear friend. Tell me!" He sat next to her.

She smiled ruefully, then made a decision to take a risk,"Ted, it's too hard to tell. Would you Touch with me? Let's try and see whether I can send adequate imagery. It'd show you better than any words." He hesitated,surprise, relief and amusement crossed his face, then he nodded and she felt his Touch. She responded swiftly and the communication occurred smoothly. The closeness seemed a healing in itself. The images of her morning's worry, the concerns of the Family for William and such like him, formed swiftly and informed him well. He nodded as they separated, their attention back into the sunlight shining through the temple glass. She had not even tried to make an image of that recognition in the Temple. It wasn't until much later that she wondered at herself. Why was suffering, worry, easier to communicate than joy or wonder?

He said,"It's true, Rose. I'm having the same trouble. I found myself out though when I saw that I grieve for Will and for my own cousin and have not felt such grief for all the others.Pure self centered nature, still dominating my life. My selfishness is obvious and I'd prided myself on having a bigger Heart than that."

She nodded, took a long breath. "I've struggled wtih that too, Ted. It's a revelation you know, though I hadn't thought that word would fit for such a sad thing. To see myself that narrow isn't pleasant. I WANT to think of them as only different,not less.I'm ashamed of myself and that makes me angry." She laughed shortly, "Angry with the Builders."

"Well, Kiddo,, it's the way we've been. If we don't cop to it we'll stay that way. I know that I'd go tearing off to save my Maria faster than I'd go off to save another child. Although, I give myself credit, I'd surely go fast for either. I've had experience to prove my behavior, so at least I know that's not wishful thinking."He breathed a long sigh."All the teaching, the aim to selflessness. With my ego, it's a hard climb." He shook his head, but his self criticism was gentle.

"We're more selfish than we'd like to think we are, aren't we?"

"We've begun to see that though. Let's not be too hard on ourselves." He looked at her sadly, but with a brightening face. Together they recited the old Teaching,"To acknowledge the facts of our nature is the first step in growth." Rose was smiling then in remembrance of those unburdened days.She said,"I suppose I ought to be less dispairing, but we still have a lot to learn. I want to think better of myself." She grimaced. "All I can say for myself is that I know the difference between ego and Self.I know which powers my living most of the time."

"Well, we can think better now, because we've begun to question ourselves . I know that when I walk there, near the Temple, feel the wonder of all we've done, all we've learned about ourselves, I feel such a great joy. I can almost convince myself that we're really beginning to live the life we want to learn to live. Then I find myself thinking and acting the way I've been lately and --" He shook his head. "I want to put it all aside and indulge myself, comfort myself with remembering

THE JOURNEY

how great we are." He did not smile, and the lack of joking in Ted, sobered her more."Because you know, Rose, we HAVE done mighty good work here. But we do it because that Vision is there ahead, guiding and enlightening us."

"Well Ted, we know we've got to learn a lot. I think we have to do that together. I doubt it can be done by one alone." She was silent, her heart hammering, and she was surprised at how nervous she felt."Have you, your Family, have you been taught about 'Joining'?" At his hesitation, then determined nod, she said," What d'you think of it?".

He was gazing off into a shimmering fountain, he said,"I think maybe that might be a way for us. A way to find out what we need to know. But too many of us are afraid of it." He glanced down at her then,"Don't you see people being afraid of it?"

She went on,"Jessie drew us into Joining. Yes, we were afraid at first. But I don't think now, after we all - afterward, that we feel any fear. At least I don't. I think we live at Soul level then. Jessie says, the nature of Soul is Love. It makes a difference. To think that. Finally my ego can tolerate knowing that there's something greater than itself". She was amused at the thought.

He looked at her thoughtfully for a moment, then he laughed,"What a way to put it! But I think you're right. It's in knowing the difference. It's right in front of us, you know.I think when we experience what we call Seeing, that's when we've lifted a little out of our selves. Lifted into Soul level. We do realize something, then when we remember what we realized,we get excited and our ego swells itself out and imagines it did it all. Then we convince ourselves we're very special. And that blinds us all over again. But we've seen that place where the wonder is. The Wonder IS Soul Consciousness. To remember even a bit of that is enough to live on for -- " his voice softened,"a long time."

She nodded, staring at him in surprise,"Ted! It's as if you realize all we've been struggling with in our Family. Surely, it must be common to us all."

He was frowning, and nodded slowly,"I'm sure it must be. It's good to talk to you. We've had trouble talking to each other at home. But you see, Rose, we're waking up. It's as though I break the tendrils of a vine by which I've been held captive, and as each one snaps, I realize anew that the vine is part of me. There's pain and loss and fear and grief. Such strange griefs. Old identities die hard."

She stood, took hold of his hand,"I know, Ted. Yet we've come to terms with ourselves in certain ways. We've got a crucial problem here in this Valley and it's disrupted all our complacence. This division between us could destroy us -- or from what we've just realized, it may be, it could save us. Make us realize!". She was silent, they sat hidden in their corner for several moments, watching people go by. Children chattering, adults with faces full of intent. Then Rose said," We've got a lot to meet in ourselves, you know, my friend. If we fail in that, we will lose our Valley."

"I know, I've been angry. I wanted to fight someone. The builders especially. But I know if I do, then I've lost everything. I need to talk like this a lot more, Rose. We don't do that, you know."

THE PEOPLE OF THE VALLEY

She nodded, sober,"We've never trusted enough, even with all our talk of trust. It amounts to whether we've capable of -- of Love actually." She shrugged.

He listened, his eyes moving as if caressing the gardens, the people passing.I think that's the only power great enough to bring us out of this as a whole people. The question must be met. We talk of freedom, talk of human realization. Well, talk's cheap, the idea is empty. Look there," he pointed at a half opened daisy, "that's the miracle. It's literally so. Everyday, I see how common miracles are. And we have to understand the miracle. That's what we have to study, pay attention until we understand. After all, the Builders are part of the miracle." His eyes were shining, he was full of a power she hadn't seen in him.

She met his eyes, his words had stirred her, brought her own mind into his Vision. She slowly shook her head, " Just pray God it doesn't take so much time that the Builders have laid the Valley waste before we can learn." For moments they sat, their hands lightly clasped and staring into the bright pattern of the pathway. Then with a shrug, Rose turned, stood and pulled him after her. "We've got to get on. The others will be there. After all our efforts to be early, we'll be late."

They walked from their sheltered spot and went on into the Outer Ring toward the little cafe where they would meet their friends. They saw Maria and Ralph first, then Eric stood from a clump of grass where he'd been lying. They went together into the cafe, it's windows warm with the light of glow globes that drifted about the ceiling. Esther and Deborah were there waiting with Alrik. They held a table for them all. They were so absorbed in paintings that hung on the walls all round,they didn't see the newcomers. Rose began to study the paintings. She had seen none of them before. They were Eric's work. He had not shown any of his work for more than a year, and these were different. They all gathered silently, studying the paintings. Eric watched them at first with his usual attenpt to hide the tension and then gradually relaxed as he saw that they were at least absorbed. He went to order nuts and little cakes, and a big pitcher of icy beer.

After some time, Ralph heaved a sigh and turned to Eric and held up his hand with fingers closed into an O. He nodded and winked. Marial turned to find him and went to him immediately to kiss him saying, "I like what you've done,Buddy.". And then she sat down. The others turned one by one, giving various responses, Ted offered the only real critique,but it was positive enough to please Eric. Eric seemed to have waited to hear his response, for after that, he smiled. They asked about the use of color to achieve his intention and listened and ate as he explained, enjoying talking now. Until now, no one had seen these paintings, they were not yet detached from their creator. Suddenly he ceased to talk and said,"I don't want to talk about them. I want just to enjoy this morning eating good things with my friends. I haven't got long, I'm scheduled to help do some repair work on a processing furnace for the new mine. "

Marial looked up curiously, "Well, how's the little mine going. I've not heard since you folks first started taking ore out.Imagine Adwin having her own little mine." She laughed.

THE JOURNEY

Eric nodded,"It isn't ever going to be a mine like Altos' mines, but it'll give us another trade product and the quality of the ore is better than we thought. But I like the work there. It's a good change for me."

"Looks as though that's where you got material for this group. But there's something abnut these, Eric, something - different. Something's happened to you!" Ted frowned, studying Eric's face.

Eric laughed then, "It's pretty obvious isn't it?"

"Unless you take us for idiots,"Marial said testily, Her own work was waiting and Ted's reminder of Eric's talent and accomplishment gave her an urgency to get back to it. She was a musician and one of her own compositions would be performed by the Adwin orchestra this autumn. She worried and fretted more than even the average artist. Eric looked at her thoughtfully, seeing much of her feeling. Rose realized her unease and shifted the conversation. There would be no way to convince her that orchestra members who were practicing the music were playing it because they liked it. Not even when she heard the final performance would she be satisfied, but that was the way of the creator, perhaps. Rose said,"Well, this is a nice way to start a day. What are your plans? Anyone want to come with me to the World Market?"

They finished their eating, talking lightly of the day's events and finally began to prepare to leave. Rose found herself alone with Deborah and Esther. Ralph had dozed off in his chair, and they woke him persuading him to go with them. They walked slowly through the streets, greeting friends, acquaintances. When they arrived at the World Market , the great screen was running a series of traffic organizers used only in large cities.

They watched it a moment then it changed and a product manufactured in Dresden began showing itself in action. They went into the building to find a cubicle to look at the products they were interested in.

Rose moved into a cubicle and sank into the comfortable chair,then adjusted the selector to find the film that she must review for her students. As soon as this's done, I can look over those new transparent submarines." She grinned at Esther, "You've heard of them?"

Ralph, who had slid into a chair and closed his eyes, sat up alert."Oh, you mean the ones they call the 'water skate'? Yes, let's take a look. I'd be interested in one of them for River running. I've seen one and you can travel around underwater as if you're in a body shaped bubble. It fits easily around you and has extensions that are just like hands." He seemed ready to go on but Rose had nodded and turned to her review. She had the ear phones in and wouldn't hear him. He sighed and sank back.

Esther prodded him,"Tell me, Ralph, How long can you stay under?"

He opened his eyes, interested again,"Why indefinitely, I suppose. No, that wouldn't be possible, oxygen and all, but then, it's for hours at least. As long as I'd want, I'm sure." He returned to his nap and Esther and Deborah dialed into view the little water skate, looking at it with eager interest. Finally Rose drew off her ear phones and turned to them. Glancing at the sleeping Ralph, she dialed the submarines. Esther woke Ralph and insisted he study it with them. "What's wrong with you Ralph, what's happened to your energy?" He shrugged and grinned and she went on,"Well, whatever, look at this. We might be able to get one for ourselves if you join us, you know. Adwin Council won't buy them for the recreation system, for at least a year, but we might get one between us and if it proves worth it, then they'd be interested. After all, if they're what they say, we could use them for children to study underwater life ." He grinned,"Wouldn't they love that?"

They talked and compared and finally decided which model would seem most suitable. The craft skimmed along the surface like a leaf in the wind, the person inside appeared to be suspended and blown along without effort. Then when it submerged , it was flexible and literally seemed to'swim' so easily did it dart and probe into corners, under logs or boulders, and to light its own way brightly enough that visiblility was good.They were elated and convinced."Well," Ted conceded, "That demonstrator was really skilled. We couldn't get that kind of action right off."

When they came out again into the afternoon sunlight, Ralph took Deborah's shoulders and turned her to face him."Hey,Babe, how about it? Wouldn't you like to get one?" All his tiredness was gone, his energy restored in this enthusiasm. "We could send in an order now and it would be here the next shipment from Santiago. Tomorrow perhaps." Deborah loved the water and used every kind of boat in the Adwin dock. Ralph fairly danced around the two women.

Deborah smiled and looked at him thoughtfully,"Ralph, I don't think it's that important to me to have one but if it is to you, then you go ahead."

He said,disappointed,"But I don't have the credit to do it alone" He turned, still holding to Deborah's hand,"How about you, Rose and Esther? Are either of you interested?"

Rose nodded and Esther said,"Yes,I am, and I knew I couldn't do it alone either. Besides, none of us would use it enough for single ownership. We'll be better off if several of us buy it."

Rose said,"Well, then Ralph, you go on in and order it. Here's my card and we'll own it three ways. Unless someone else wants to join us." He grinned happily and gathered their two cards. The thought flashed into her mind,"What children we are after all." And she was content at that.

Ralph bent to kiss them both and ran back to the Market.The three women walked then slowly across the oval court before the Market entrance and paused at the crossing of the path ways. The hill fell sharply there and they could see two bald heads bobbing up toward them. Next appeared shoulders on which green hoods fell back on the grey robes that signified monks of the Asana discipline. Must be a traveling assignment, Rose thought, half envious. The secure,very quiet, highly ordered life, appealed to something in her.The two men smiled and murmured a whispered greeting to the women as they passed.

Rose watched them disappear, then turned to go on with her friends." What do you know of the Asanas?" She looked at the other two women and caught a swift wistful look in Deborah's face that surprised her. Deborah spoke then with that longing ill concealed.

"Their Mother House is still in Tibet. There is a daughter house here in this Valley. They are a teaching order, and I do know that they spend part of their initiate years studying with our Monitors. I spent a term studying with them."

"You were of them then?" Rose was surprised "My retreat time was with the Elders at North Station." She laughed,"Once I thought I hadn't learned much, but now I keep noticing that my attitudes are changed from the old days. What I learned is incorporated in my very living. It's a kind of basic foundation." She was silent a moment then said,"I suppose I wanted such Teachers to make miracles, give me insights into the very nature of being, etc. I wanted instant enlightenment, and I had my own idea of what that was. I think now that I imagined it would be a state of eternal bliss in which I would be worshipped and admired and would live a life of no worry." She laughed then, gently,shaking her head.

Deborah said,"And since then, you've gone back haven't you, Rose? For a weekend now and then?" At Rose's nod, she said,"It's a good teaching."

Esther sighed,"I still wish that someone would come here, to us, and give us a greater Teaching; one that would make everything clear. Someone who could lead us into a swift path, a way that would reveal to us all that is glorious and change our lives in a day" She smiled sheepishly, and Rose felt grateful at her confession, she had felt that same wish. She was pleased that they three could talk so easily of these matters. Not all her friends did. And that thought woke the yawning worry that her own family did not.

Esther spoke then out of a silence, "Do you know of those who get stuck there, at the Retreats? Ones who seem unable to come back and join daily life? What happens to them? One of my childhood friends did that. He wanted to stay but the Fathers sent him home."

Rose Reached timidly, felt sorrow in her friend, sorrow held in abeyance. She knew with certainty that that sorrow was old, ingrained, and it roused the same response in herself. Are we ever really separate? she wondered.

Rose took Esther's hand and drew near to her friend in steady support. Deborah looked at the two of them, measuring and said,"I think it was the rituals that I used to love,. They fascinated me and I thought I could reach enlightenment through them. Of course I never did know what I meant by enlightenment.I think it was similar to what you thought, Rose.Then, later, in my life, I realized those rituals were symbols and I'd not interpreted them at all.They were the pointing of the Way. I had to give them up, to let go of them,in order to walk on. But it was a long time before I admitted that I used them to avoid even looking on in the direction they pointed." She shook her head, and Rose felt her tears rather than saw them."I've never told anyone else these things.I don't know why I am now."

Rose's voice held anger,"It's time we did. It's time all of us did if we want to understand what we're about here in this Valley. If we don't talk, we just pretend." She turned to them, facing them, stopping their walk. "Listen, we've all got to talk.To speak about - these understandings, and also the Talents, the things we realize that puzzle us. We've begun to know something of the dimensions of Spirit, and yet we won't talk of it.We even avoid what we know, what we actually know and won't admit to. Why is it? Why do we do that?"

Esther nodded, watching Rose with bright,hopeful eyes."It's true. I know that, but I didn't know you did. I don't know why except because there's so much to understand and it's all so - different. After all,Rose, you're right, human consciousness, not just our own, but all human consciousness is expanding and becoming -- something more. If we don't respond,acknowledge that, we're going to be left behind. Like the Builders, in fact. I think that's why I keep longing for a new Teacher, one who can tell us everything." She shook her head, a frown tightening her face,"Rose, Rose, we've known each other for years and haven't talked like this. Not at all like this!"

Rose met her eyes, her own full of a new fire,"Well, now that we've begun, we'll keep it up. Don't you think that's exactly what you just said, that we're becoming -- conscious of our own changing? We will talk! But I don't think we need a new Teacher. We've had Teachers and we didn't listen. Anyway, I think a real Teacher would tell us what our Learning Center Master Teachers tell us, that we must, absolutely must, do this ourselves. We have to meet all the reasons why we don't. They've already told us,you know."

Deborah sighed,and looked absently at her as if she had not heard."I've heard it said that if a True Teacher came among us we wouldn't recognize such a one at all.I think that's true, that we wouldn't know. How do we know but that there's such a person here with us now?" They were silent, looking at one another. She went on,"I've heard some amazing things about Jessie, and yet, when we're with her she seems so ordinary. Like us!

She stopped their responses with a raised hand,"Wait! We all know we've learned things from her, yet those things strike us later, as if we didn't really hear at the time. Lately,I've been looking at those thoughts coming from her talks with us. And I see they also Point the Way. And there's another thing, You notice that we don't ask her questions much, we seem to resist asking and yet, by her very behavior, her way of living, she speaks. I think we must ask. How can she speak to our need if we don't even have the right question? Her life is a like a still pool among us, the quiet of her nature never inflames or fails, it simply seems to nourish." She stopped, astonished at her own words, looking at them. "Wow. I didn't know I knew that, but I do."

Esther was watching Deborah intently, finally she nodded, Then, that's it, I see things differently when she's around, and after she's been with people, they seem to think differently but don't notice it right away.She is like a -- like a Light."

They were all silent again, looking at her, caught in troubled thought of what she had said. After a few minutes Rose said,"I think you're right, Deb.I think my idea, my notion of what a True Teacher would be like has blinded me to knowing one who was right here with us.I never could have fitted a real human being into it and maybe that's why I didn't see this. I wanted some shining stereotype of an angel, I suppose."

THE JOURNEY

Esther nodded,"Maybe we don't want to see. Maybe a glamourous image - the familiar idea of success, for instance - dissolves before what is Real. " She watched the others,aware that she needed their acceptance in order to go on, "We denied that we were denying, that was the worst. We kept it like a secret, or at least I did, not to be taken out except when I was alone and secretly."

They were silent, standing under trees, heavy with young fruit, in the outer gardens of the Civic Center. They were aware of a stirring of their attention,aware of the silent presence of the hundreds of plants around them. Rose saw fear in the eyes of her friends, but pushing that fear out, lay a new hope."It's been more. We've refused to talk, to admit that we Touched one another." She stopped, glancing at them all, remembering with an acute new recognition."It was Jessie who taught us how to Join. That -- the Joining, is like another way of - of being."

Deborah nodded slowly,"Your Family too? Then,it's true," She was whispering,awe filling her voice,"She taught us that too, and we've not dared try it since."

"There are strong people, especially in the Valley Council, who Join without hesitation and obviously, drawing anyone able into that Joining.It's not as - as intense, it's only a start of what she showed us, but - it IS Joining. So we've known, as a people. We've known! Grace initiated it in the Council but we acted as if it were only to be done during a Council meeting. Now, I don't know why we don't practice everywhere, with anyone who will. Why don't we ask Jessie to teach us more. We're ashamed, I think. Stopped by old, old patterns of fear. What are we, that we refuse our own best realizations because someone might make fun of us? I want to talk about Joining. I want to know that we can do that together". Her eyes were bright with tears and the courage it had taken to speak.

Deborah,took Rose's hand and glanced at her, "We will do that, Rose. I promise at least that I will.I think that our worry about the Builder's has prodded us to be more aware, but it's also made us more fearful. Or maybe it's more accurate to say, we've become aware of our fears. We've assumed we're right to deny what they accuse us of. But what they accuse us of is exactly true. They're right, we do what they accuse us of." She turned fierce eyes on them, drawing Rose along with her hand, and they went into the shadows of the Archway through the Outer Ring.

Then Deborah visibly made a decision,"In my Family, we've done that. We've spoken to one another a little. And when we did that, some of us found that we could Join, could Reach and Touch and they had not, genuinely had not known, they could. So now you're saying we have to do this with everyone?"

Rose felt excitement an ascending Joy,"It's true, We did that too. Oh, Deborah, then, it's possible that lots of people have noticed that. Something's happening in this Valley,something we haven't known about, or wouldn't. And we've got to pay attention. What's happening has brought us to a point of crisis. Look at us! We're talking finally about what we've either denied or kept secret. We're TALKING! And Ted and I talked the same way this morning. It's happening! But whatever's happening in this Valley, it's disturbing a lot of people.

And that's frightening."

Esther turned to them then, they walked across the outer fields and sat on a bench at the fork in the path. One forked to the Farm and Rose knew it was time to go but they did not want to part. "Listen! You're right. There's restlessness, a heightening of our senses, children are aware of things that we don't even notice. I hate to admit it, but it's true. We've been so separate, so alone, in our little Family groups, and maybe our peer groups too, but essentially separate. We didn't really know what was wrong, and only now, when we admit to Joining, do we finally realise the loss." She searched their eyes, wanting them to understand, hoping they did. "And we've only just touched on what Joining is. All it might be. I think it scares everybody at first, its such a total immersion in mental - life! To choose to merge, to be together so deeply,takes courage, you know. I was afraid of getting lost so I couldn't find myself again. Until I saw how easily I can return to just being myself."

Rose was nodding eagerly, and murmured,"I see there's no real separation between us - ever! Slowly, I've begun to lose some deeply ingrained fear that has haunted me, maybe all of humankind, during all our existence. That fear of being outside, of being cut off, of being separate.But even more, the fear of the unknown". She laughed suddenly, "See, Esther, how fearful you were that we would either laugh at you or think you're mad? It's inborn. We've struggled for centuries to be individuals and to be reasonable, and we are! But we need so much to be perceptive and to risk knowing what we find."

She drew a long deep breath, an excitement rising, unfamiliar and strong."Now, to be together, to truly be Joined. And to See what isn't reasonable at all. To actually See! Oh, there it is, It's not a denial of what we are at all." They were silent, Then she cried out,"But you see, it's so habitual. So obvious. We're doing it again. We're afraid." They looked at each other, trembling, their hands reaching out to lock fingers. They sat in a stillness that was half reluctance, half hope.

"Why not?" Deborah, sighed,"Why not?"

"You know, Jessie doesn't preach to us, she doesn't even repeat the Teachings. Obviously pointless. If we didn't hear them before, we won't now. But she just lives, just lives her life and talks to us about ourselves." Esther spoke softly.

Rose nodded,"Yes, that's it, she just lives. But then, it's a real depth of living, you can feel it when you're around her. That energy of something so alive in her. She's not at all afraid of it." She hesitated,"She did tell us that she wanted to prepare us for the Journey."

"What Journey?" Deborah nearly held her breath.

"She said it was to the Silent City. She said that we would know when we were ready. It's something similar to the stories the People of the Way tell. Jessie says it's true." The others watched her, their minds racing."

Esther nodded, "My father said something of that last week. He said Jessie had reminded him of something he'd forgotten and that the Journey was what

THE JOURNEY

he'd forgotten. He said our Family must go together. He wanted to call a Gather. Right away, he called one for tomorrow."

Rose squeezed her friend's hand and leaned to kiss them both lightly before she turned to go home. "There's a lot to think about. Let's each go home and talk to our Families and insist on everyone talking this time." They nodded and drew from one another. Each turning to her separate way.

CHAPTER THREE

Under the Pine Tree

    Jessie walked among the people of Adwin, Jasper and Denlock. She rode the belts out into mountain towns, learned the ways of tiny villages, the many nooks and crannies of each town, She visited each place of learning, of crafts, laboratory,of machine works, industrial center, fabric and paper mills, mines, library, studio, theatre, music halls, in fact every aspect of Northern Valley life. She visited small shops and saw how they were places of pleasure and profit for those who ran them, how they created a natural social life for young and old. She talked to editors of Video News, and watched the make up of the news strips on the Computer screens of every household. And she visited and laughed at the foolishness going on in the amusement parks. She was familiar with all that went on at Learning Centers. She knew what the people of this Valley sought, played at, worked for. She knew the Valley within weeks as well as people who'd lived there for years. The changes that had occurred since she was last here were tremendous. She learned the needs and aspirations of the people.
    She also found whether there had been change in the nature of what the people now called sin. Or forbidden pleasures. For these made a statement as to the development of a people. In all north Valley she found three of the old-world entertainment houses operating, where gambling and sexual extravagance was fed or exploited, two where people might lose themselves in drugs of various kinds.In three of these were also the painful (for her) florid whole room Holograms William had seen in his visit to the Black Mountain. He would have been astonished to see her there.
    She talked to a man who lounged near the entrance to a place called the Holo-delight. A stupid name, she thought, and wondered whether it attracted many people. As many, for instance as the library or the Learning Center work rooms? She dressed for these visits in a grey dress and low soft shoes,with a light cloak thrown over her shoulders, as nondescript as she thought she could be. She stood several minutes reading the lurid billboards, knowing he watched her. Finally he said,"This's not a place for a woman like you lady. You'll be seeing things you don't want to see."
    She turned to him, "Oh, but I'm curious. What's it like in there?"
    He studied her face for a minute and frowned,"I can't figure you. You don't look like a lush, but you don't walk straight either.The boss's not gonna want you out here. Not good for business."
    "Is business good? With all the color, lights and everything, it must be drawing a crowd." She waved a hand, appearing to be an old lady out of her element.
    "He laughed, a harsh unamused laugh," Business! It hasn't hardly started up

good yet. But it'll get there. It just takes time, you know. People got to hear about us."

"You wanta know what I think?" She didn't wait for his answer,"I think it's gonna have to go some to beat the one over in Bennett. They've got no day business yet, but their night business is pretty good. Of course, you can get drugs there, make you forget the misery of your life a little."

"They got nothin' we haven't".He seemed actually defensive. Then with a frown he said as if it'd been on his mind,"It's the way this Valley's run that makes it hard to get a business on it's feet. The people've been reciting those convictions to themselves. They actually believe them. A whole fucking Valley of do gooders. It'll take some time to show them how to have fun again."

Jessie nodded sympathetically,"Maybe things'll change. It's the Healers to blame for a lot of it. Can't even lie without them knowing anymore." She shook her head, "How'd you get permission to set up here?"

This time his laugh was genuine,"Nobody to stop us. Don't you know them very convictions make it all right to do whatever you want." He frowned again, "But the people aren't comin' in much yet, like they still can't get used to it. Havin' time to have fun, I mean."

Jessie nodded again, and turned away,"We'll maybe I'll come in one night this week. See what's new." She smiled then, surprising her companion,he looked startled and then, when their eyes met, almost fearful. He reached out a hand and touched her arm as she turned, "Who are you lady? Just who are you?"

But she waved and walked off, the shimmering lights of the advertizements blinking behind her,garish in the sunny day. She felt better. The Learning Center was far ahead on numbers so far. It wasn't easy for crime to get a start in a Valley where every citizen served some time on the governing councils and knew what their officials did from personal experience. But he was right, people were just beginning to realize their free time. That didn't explain why there was the same pattern in south Valley. They had finished their cities, most of them, years ago. And Santiago, had only one of these three houses she had so far located.

She walked off, thinking about the Black Mountain Holorooms that had cropped up in recent months. People came, but attendance was scattered. The proprieters promised riches for those who invested in them or operated them and kept insisting to her that it was only a matter of time until they would gain universal popularity. But Jessie knew, and some of those operating them had begun to suspect, that the people of the Valley had found other fulfillment. The ones she talked to felt frustration, they couldn't explain the lack of interest.

That night Jessie did as she had promised and went in to try the entertainment. She watched the torn hearts of those who frequented these places and grieved, but sought to Reach to them, offering them a different hope. Some of these were receptive,though they did not know of their benefactor. Such people began to seek out the Master Teachers and ask for help. But there where some who had slipped too deeply into that spiderwed of hungers and twisted distractions. Twice she traveled there. She'd learned enough, and went home to rest for a few days and think of all she had found. A sorrow that was painful lodged itself in her heart and sobered her.

The next morning she left her cottage to sit near the great pine that grew bent from the boulders protruding out of the hillside. It was a fine June morning, and it would be hot soon. Her place under the pine would be cool and give her a grand view across the Valley on which to meditate. Here too, she must attract some of the Family because it was time for some intensive Teaching, if they were to be ready for that coming Journey.

She sat on a stone that had been chiseled enough to make a rough seat. Sandy boulders had dissolved through years so that there was pool of rough red-brown sand that flowed past the tree trunk and filled the narrow spaces between the boulders. Rank grass grew here and there, sometimes making a thick green carpet for several yards. As she sat, she could see a figure coming up from the barn. She called out, her voice ringing into the air. Gently she Reached and felt the answering Touch of that alert young mind. Anna would come to sit with her.

Anna leaped lighty down from the broad path that led eventually into Adwin and stood a moment on a sharp edge of a boulder before jumping down. She scuffed the coarse sand with one foot, then found a flat piece of sand stone to sit on.

"Hi, Jessie. I saw you there and wished you'd call." She seemed pleased to be here.

Jessie looked at her, considered thoughtfully this young girl. Her strong supple body folded gracefully on to the stone. Honed and trained by daily practice of Aikido-chan and gymnastic exercises, her favorite sport, that body would be prepared to meet what came to it. She sat straight backed, bare legs, dark brown in contrast to her pale yellow shorts and shirt. Her fair hair was tied back, falling across her shoulders and her round brown face shone with contentment. Jessie laughed, 'You look like the proverbial cat that caught the bird."

Anna nodded. They were silent then, their eyes met, then Anna looked around herself, locating the small creatures who lived in this spot. Jessie noticed with pleasure how naturally Anna did that. A squirrel moved curiously down a limb, peered over at them, chattered and backed a little into a hole in the trunk then ran busily behind the tree to disappear among the boulders. Lizards lay against the rock in the sun, and now and then an insect droned by. The Valley below was partly cut off by Jessie's cottage but to the west, Denlock was visible over the fields and forests that curved like a paint of every green shade with a weaving in of brown and yellow. Here and there brilliant patches of bright blue, rose and orange splashed where legumes bloomed wild. A wondering human could subsist comfortably in almost any part of that Valley. Legumes returned nourishment, fixed nitrogen and added the normal mulch of their fallen bodies to Earth. The land was rebuilding from the centuries of misuse more rapidly than anyone could have hoped. For Anna this was all a normal condition, but for Jessie, it was the miracle resulting from the new consciousness among humankind.

Jessie smiled. Yes, Valley people were advanced beyond their ancestors in more ways than they knew. They were however also advanced in ways they did not yet seem to understand. They must become more aware. Surely plants that were producing so many of the needs of humankind; oils,fuels, proteins, ,medicines, and refreshment for the soils, as well as raw materials for paper,fabrics, paints, roofing, building materials, in fact, much of what petroleum and forest products had once provided, marked this renewed life of Earth. And the forests were intact. Wood was a precious commodity, never wasted, always reused. Silica industries were expanding, pushing aside the small petroleum comeback. But it was the careful ending of waste that had changed industry the most.

People of the Valley were ready to go on. Jessie was finally satisfied that this was one of the twenty three truly advanced communities on Earth. Her thoughts were open to Anna,and though Anna did not read them as thoughts, she knew the trend of Jessie's attitudes and the feelings that accompanied them. Jessie let these reflections comfort her sorrow. The renewal of this Earth was for her a miracle. She remembered when it still suffered.

They conversed in this quiet, way and felt the comfort of it. Gradually Anna was aware that a powerful Earth current was flowing through her body. For the first time in her life she knew acutely of its presence. That recognition of being part of Earth power brought tears to Anna's eyes. This consciousness of Joining was new, was so great, so far extended, that she marveled. She had not even asked! Or had she?

She felt a great silence spread through her. The tree seemed to whisper, to sing and the comfort of its strength behind her was good. Feelings surged into her attention. She felt them, identified them and let them settle back into calm. Emotional silence - Ah, it seemed a new kind of peace. She tentatively played with the lift of emotion and then its absence. It was a whole dimension of perception and its presence or absence vastly changed things.Clutters of busy thoughts swept across her attention and she let them subside without drawing her attention. Her mind Reached, sensed, experienced and then was still. For some time she sat with Jessie thus.

Anna remembered her Journey time with the Vagabonds, the People of the Way. She remembered the depth of their relationship with Earth and Sky. She wondered at that reverence now with this new sharp closeness. Jessie nodded. A thought shaped,"Earth is like a Mother but she is the symbol of her own reality, just as my body is a vehicle for life to - to manifest through." She looked at Jessie and smiled. She continued," Yes, that's right. Earth, grand as She is, is a vehicle for a greater Life. The People of the Way don't worship the Earth, they reverence that Life that lives her. Their sense of reverence is deep. And they gave that to me when I was with them. They taught me." The two were silent again. After a while, Anna said, "Jessie, I'd like to talk."

Jessie nodded and Anna frowned. She gathered her thoughts together. "I've been unable to stop thinking about what we talked about the other day. About

Andy and his friends, about the way people aren't acknowledging what's happening. Not just our parents, but all of us kids too.I've been thinking about all of that. Jessie, what's going on?"

" A lot is going on. What do you see?"

"Well, there're people in town I never thought about, never knew were there,People who don't --don't know the way we do.I think that's it. They aren't -- aren't denying anything, they just don't know! Sometimes they seem so sad. I talked to Jacob the other day. He's Jeremy's uncle and I've known him a long time. But there it is. I didn't know him at all. He works in the news center, edits the Adwin news. He gets people's poetry published, their stories, etc.. Sometimes even their music. He's really dedicated to getting local artist's work out to be known. He did our work when we were kids, our poems and we had a little book of them.It was so wonderful for us." She smiled remembering. "He used to laugh and I could see he knew our poems weren't all that great but he liked them anyway. He's always been a person I liked. Now,he's full of sadness that he can't understand. He says he can't shake it and he doesn't know why.I think it's actually dispair."

"Dispair? How did you know that?"

"I could feel it, Jessie. He doesn't know that he sends, that we can feel it and it just floods out sometimes. It's painful, you know." She was silent, remembering."You know, he went away for a while,and when he came back he wouldn't continue writing the book he'd started. Said he wasn't good enough to do it right! In fact, one day, I heard him say that he didn't see much point to living and wished he'd die. He seemed more indifferent then, than sad. That was worse." Her face was full of woe, the memories drew her mouth into a downward curve. Jessie nodded. Anna glanced at her, her mind loosely receptive,,wanting to talk, not to Touch.

"You see Jessie, I suppose that if a man feels like dying, he might just do that. But then,I wonder whether a person has a right -- that's my question.I've thought of dying, of leaving this body, as I sometimes do, but choosing not to come back. But then, how could a person refuse to live their life out. It's true that beyond this life there's so much more than we can know here. But why would anyone refuse this life because she's dispairing, or miserable? It's what we're here for, isn't it? To meet all the dispair? That'd be dying to escape, and that would be terrible. Because you can't escape, you know. Not at all." She spoke so naturally, so matter of factly that Jessie had to restrain a smile. For many this would not be matter of fact.

She sat then frowning,meeting Jessie's eyes but her own were not seeing. After a bit she went on." What is it Jessie? Death? I've thought about it often. But now, there seems to be trouble coming. Death could be an accident, could be caused by violence. I saw some fights last week. These were old fashioned fist-clubbing. They just pounded each other until one was bleeding and then someone stopped them. Jessie what was awful was they weren't defending themselves, they WANTED to hurt! I know one of the boys well, I've practiced aikedo-chan with him. No one could have ever hit him if he hadn't left himself exposed. I didn't know the other boy well, he may not -- may not Reach and that might make the difference, you know. But that was between kids who've never hit anyone in their lives. It was like something got lost from inside them. I felt betrayed, Jessie, like somehow I'd been lied to." She shook her head slowly, her bright fair hair catching the sun in gleaming gold.

She took a long breath, "That's not all. The Builders've gathered at the Great Meadow south of town, you know, between the Jasper Forest and Adwin, and farmers came there and they couldn't seem to talk and then three of those folk were fighting .The same thing only this time ADULTS!" She seemed outraged. Her eyes full of pain and confusion.

"People were hurt, Jessie, one man fell,hit so hard he couldn't move. Some tried to stop them and got hurt too. Luckily no one had knives with them. Because I think some of those people were so angry they might have used them. The Healers came then, and things just lost energy. I think the Healers damped out their anger. They can you know." She looked up at Jessie to see if she agreed, and Jessie nodded."But then, death like that, Jessie! What if someone killed someone else. That would be a kind of death for both of them. And not even chosen! Not chosen!" Her voice was suddenly shrill with pain."Oh,Jessie,what's happened to people? They've lost their vision." She was suddenly crying and Jessie looked at her thoughtfully. How much of this must the children endure?

Jessie turned her eyes out to the Valley beyond them. They swept across the Valley, crossed the River, and up into the peaks, seeking there further strength and wisdom for herself. As she followed her own gaze with attention, she saw - knew, of two people who sat there among those high peaks. Rose and Ben, finally! Bodyless, aware. They were unaware of one another however, each on opposite sides of the curved cliff. More,it was even stranger that they were each aware of her Touch,but unaware of one another. Why? And how had Benjamin intuitively found to that site for his first time? She withdrew. It would wait.

She relaxed visibly and turned back to Anna,"Death? Anna, death is our friend. It is the final reward of life. After living as well as we can, Learning what we must, it's the reward to return home. How well do I know that!" She spoke the last few words so softly Anna barely heard. The words shocked her, She wondered how such simple words should have such impact. The idea of death as something bright, as a reward, arrested her thought. She found herself clinging to the words, holding the thought like a comfort. Jessie spoke again.

"Death is to have the right to step through into a fuller consciousness, to be able to throw off this narrow limited little self. There, out of this physical body, this Life breaths free, is alive in another greater way. To return into this life can be a painful thing sometimes especially when one has roamed far, has lost touch with this -- little self.In this form,I am so small,this brain has difficulty handling much consciousness. It is clear then - clear that I am not my body." and she smiled gently,"Though I live throughout it."She nodded pensively,"It is made up of so many little lives."

She was silent, and Anna waited, sensing that Jessie spoke as much to herself as to Anna. What must it be like, thought Anna, to be so near the time when 'Death' would be a right choice? When it would be 'time to die'? Jessie turned suddenly to Anna, her face alight, her eyes shining, she seemed eager to speak.

"Of course, if I've lived my life well, if I've succeeded in my task of living, as a human being, as a woman, there would be a Joy in the ending of this body time. Wouldn't there?" She sighed, her voice soft. Anna felt almost an eaves dropper. Jessie said, "Then there is also that extension of life. There are those who live in this physical world and are able to live at the same time through the extended universes. To live as persons here and live though, BEYOND - - consciously - at the same time. That is the amazing fact. Consciousness that penetrates two or three dimensions.

She sighed, "Does one ever know that her life is completed? Perhaps that is how one knows it is right to end it." Anna realized that she shared in an inner soliloquy concerning a dilemma of Jessie's inner life. Jessie's voice was very soft but clear. For moments there was silence, then -" It's obvious that death is an end and a beginning, but I've always longed to be able to live in both worlds at once. Yes, while I am still here in this body, to be conscious in at least one other dimension. Then there would not be what we call death, but merely an easy movement into another state of consciousness. It is perhaps that which we humans practice a little when we leave our bodies to know that astral world. It is so close to this one."

"Then you do not live in several worlds at once? I thought, I assumed you would have."

Jessie laughed, "You've read that in your books, my dear one. And it's true, I do live so." Now her voice again dropped, her eyes far seeing, "I do, but only intermittently, not fully as an adept would do. So I miss much and cannot see all I need to see."

Anna frowned, puzzled, "Jessie, what we call the 'out of body' world, that's only a short step on isn't it. The FULL consciousness you speak of is -- is larger?"

Jessie nodded, half attentive, "It is very much so. The out-of- body experience has to do with crossing an invisibile barrier but only like a window into the Astral dimension. A world only a step beyond this one. But beyond it, what I enter into only a little, is so vast, so incomprehensible actually to human minds. So much so that to be consciously even OPEN to That, when living as a human being, is very difficult - for me. Not for all." She shook her head slightly, refocussing on Anna's attentive face, her hands lifted as if letting go of something and she smiled. "You know how some people are able to know they are asleep and dreaming while they are asleep. Lucid dreaming? They are conscious in two states. After all that is one of the first human transitions. Your Teachers must be teaching you to do this." Anna nodded silently and Jessie went on.

"That transition is symbolic of all we will begin to learn to do. To wake from one stage and enter another. That one of conscious dreaming and waking within

THE JOURNEY

the dream is another. Then the movement out of body to astral experience, is another and so on, until finally, one is aware of -- of more. To know one moves from one to the other WHILE DOING IT is a primary practice which I know you are adept at, little one." She smiled and Anna nodded too. Jessie glanced at Anna, frowned and then said slowly,"To know, to be awake even in these beginning ways, can bring harm, if our heart is not full, if we are not aware of the Presence of Love. Harm to our self or to others." She watched Anna carefully.

Anna nodded slowly,"I think I can see how that would be so, Jessie. You call it transition. There must be several a person has to pass." Jessie let out her breath in relief, and nodded. Anna went on."But you say there're other states of consciousness? More beyond the ones we know?

Jessie laughed, "Oh, my dear child, there is limitless expanding of consciousness, beyond everything we know as Life. How can we realize so much? Well, there it is, memory is like a thread, to help keep some continuity. After so many goings and comings, we learn how to keep a thread of consciousness connected beyond birth and death. One does get to know the others, and yes, there are many. Each greater, each deeper, each more vast. The life of Spirit is never ending. Each state is less physical. For this Physical world is the hardest to infuse with Spirit, you know. It is most resistant. But then, even for me, death is only like waking up from having slept. It is without real change."

She hesitated, as if deciding whether to speak of something. Then nodded curtly to herself and said," You see, even at beginning levels one can live consciously in what we've always called dream, can also live in the astral state, and then one can live in both even while perfectly aware of living in this lovely physical world. Because these are not separate worlds, but separate states of consciousness, until we expand and live inclusively.

Anna nodded, fascinated, listening with her whole being,"Jessie, You do that. Live in several states at once?"

Jessie nodded, frowning,"It's to make it clear to you that I tell you, Dear. Yes, it is one dimension that is constant along with dream and the physical world. The world of Mind and of Spirit, is constantly present. Then further dimensions, I only glimpse." She laughed,"If you think it hard sometimes to Balance emotions and reason, think what it is to balance two or three further dimensions. But you must in order to keep clear sight in either."

Anna's eyes were shining, her face full of interest. "Jessie, I've not talked to anyone like this, not even the Master Teachers. Because they -- well, you know they are not so personal in their talks."

Jessie nodded,"I've thought that not always wise, but then it is the rule, I know."

Anna nodded,"But how does one know, how does one know when her life is well lived. When she is - is - finished?"

Jessie started, looked piercingly at the young girl and frowned,"That's a question I'm not sure I can answer. Because I ask it of myself also. Perhaps you could help me then. If one has spent one's life learning to be always aware of the

Presence of Love, to allow that Energy to flow without restriction through oneself, then one might say life is complete. But then, what if one is born unaware of Love at all. Then the completion might be different. I think that it depends, this condition for completion."

Anna nodded,her face so absorbed she seemed to drink more than Jessie's words,"It's true, people are at such different places. But how can I know where I am?"

Jessie nodded, absently as if just realizing that,"Of course, and then, the service of living, serving others, that might give some clue. Or if one's body were worn out, then that would be a time to leave it." She chuckled,"I think that's going to be my signal." She looked down at her round, strong old body.

Anna persisted,"How could one know whether one could have loved more, could have been more open to Love Itself?"

Jessie stopped her inward attention, this young girl was truly asking, and hadn't she reminded them they must ask? She settled herself and turned her attention,"It's true we might never know for sure. But, paying attention, practicing daily the centering of one's life within Love might be a way to know. Love Itself, the Heart will inform the mind if you pay attention. You do realize, Anna, you children are taught to know yourselves better than any generation in history. So perhaps it's necessary to carry that skill farther, to know oneself much more deeply within, to know one's very Soul nature,and to see how this personal self balances within that knowledge. That might be the way to watch and to discover? Mightn't it?"

Anna nodded, and they sat, letting these thoughts resound in their minds for a while. Then Anna was aware of a sadness,,a great welling of grief.It threatened to engulf her, to draw her from balance. She wanted to avoid thinking of this woman's death, because she didn't want to lose her. To lose such talks as these. With whom could she talk in this way if not Jessie? She knew clearly that this time next year, in that summer sun, Jessie would not be here.

And suddenly without warning, she sobbed. Startled herself by the intensity of grief. In an instant attention swept through her looking at that explosion of emotion.And accepted it. It was right to weep, to release this grief. And so she did,then, crying like a child, she went to Jessie's lap and comforted herself in that touch and warmth. Jessie let her cry. Stroking her hair lightly. And finally Anna stopped, sniffled, wiped her nose and face. She felt something lifting her heart, something strong and pure. It was a gladness rising from Jessie's touch, a bright touch of Joy. She saw how eager Jessie was to know that greater Life. She felt it's nearness herself and was comforted. And then, she knew clearly, that Jessie would not be beyond Reach. She was shaken by images that swept through her mind, wonderful images that promised what she had not known. She hugged Jessie's waist, her face still bent into Jessie's lap.

Jessie nodded, smiling, her own eyes bright with tears. The two nodded then, accepting something. Jessie said,"Anna there's more to be talked of here. We need to talk of your worry about the violence you've seen. But first,do you

THE JOURNEY

know where your parents are right now?"

Anna blinked, shifted her body, drew back to her old place on her round flat stone. Her mind immediately protective, watchful. Then she laughed. Of, course, Jessie would know. She Reached and found a picture. She smiled with a profound sense of relief, it was like a great stricture had been released from her heart. How wonderful not to have to always watch what one said, what one thought even. She squirmed with a sudden pleasure but her words still held some of the restraint."Why Jessie, do you?"

Jessie looked at her and nodded, smiling. "Yes, I do know, Anna. And I also know that you do."

Anna nodded slowly, she couldn't keep the grin from her face. "Oh, Yes, Jessie, I've known so long, and couldn't ever talk about it. Except with Andrew. We always talk. And lately, some of my friends talk of it too. Other people are doing that, only differently, you know."

Jessie nodded and sighed."It's all right. This Family's willing to talk more. Now you have learned to Reach and even soon to fully Join." Her smile was full of a mischief, "Dear One, they don't really know what that is yet, do they? As for those who have lost their balance, who resort to fury without restraint, well, Anna, we'll just have to present them with an atmosphere so filled with Love that the violence damps out completely."

"We will have to learn!" Anna's eyes were steady on Jessie's. The young girl felt Jessie's eagerness, her delight in that promised realization. And her face was at ease. They sat in companionable stillness, at peace with one another. After some time, Jessie lifted her head, studied Anna's face. Was she able to be aware of the approach of another person? That other person who came now toward them? Jessie Reached, Touched very gently. And withdrew. That one was sensitive, so very much so. She had learned to overprotect herself and she didn't know of her skills. Jessie knew that strange tender Touch, unacknowledged by its owner. Jane had much yet to learn. But mostly it was to acknowledge herself. Jane saw them and would come near. She glanced at Anna and told herself that educating was needed here ."Anna, who is it who comes."

Anna was startled, shrank, then in remembrance, she Reached freely, a powerful Reach that surprised even Jessie. She smiled,"I do know, Jessie. I've been aware of her for some minutes, since you were." She laughed at Jessie's look, "Well, there it is. You've given me permission. It's Jane. She's just coming from down at the home field. She still throbs with the Earth music in herself.She's absorbed by it. Just as always. I can feel her footsteps against Earth, Jessie, they seem to merge, they seem not to be separate, as though her feet grow from the soil and carry Earth green up through her body even as she walks. She is so true, Jessie. I am sometimes afraid of her, but my fear is an awe, not a terror."

Jessie nodded, she understood that. Jane was a rare one.But she only said,"Let's call her, see if she hears." She watched Anna closely.

Anna grinned, knowing she was being tested,"She'll hear but she won't know that she does." It was so matter of fact that Jessie caught her breath. This child's development was surely rapid. Perhaps there were more of these clear,conscious minds among the young that she did not rightly recognize. Their habit of concealment was better than she would have dreamed. They had intuitively learned to shield. She frowned.

Jane turned from her path, hesitated, then without thinking it out, came on to them. She approached the two under the pine and said,"Anna, Jessie, may I join you?"

Anna nodded, but Jessie turned and greeted Jane with warmth. Jane sat down in the sandy floor, picked up a pine needle and gently slid her fingers up and down its smooth length. "You'll never know what's been on my mind. Maybe because I've been walking up the path from the River fields so often through the years, seen that long wonderful stretch of land curving with the River, the power of Earth rising beneath my feet every day. But whatever, I've an idea that won't go away." She hesitated, then studying them a second, shrugged,"Well, it's not just an idea, it's more, it shapes within my whole body. Perhaps it rises out of that saturation of beauty that spring time always is for me, but there it is. I've got to tell somebody."

Jessie nodded,"It shows, my Dear.You are radiant with something creating itself within you. Just as a woman radiates the beauty of her unborn child. Tell us!"

Jane nodded, so ready that she needed no persuasion,"You see Jessie, it's just that I love the Earth. I would like to see the Earth taken up the way one's garden is. See the land of all the countries, the ocean, the great lakes and Rivers, and the mountains themselves, looked to as though they were our garden. To care for Her, to landscape, to plant, to nurture, and to heal Her where we have harmed her. Not just as we try to earn a living from Her, but with Love and appreciation for all she's done for us. All she constantly IS for us." she stopped a moment, her voice softened, as if she spoke from deep within her self,her eyes distant, seeing a truth she was just realizing. " A celebration of She whom we express most fully, our Mother Earth. Imagine humanity to be Her eldest child. We are part of the mind of Earth." She was silent for several minutes, lost in some far imagining and that very unity that she knew so well.Jessie wondered how she might help Jane become conscious of all she knew.

Then Jane said, her eyes moving cheerfully from one to the other. "I would like to see us as gardeners of the Earth. Making all her parts healthy and full of that wonder that she could be. That she once perhaps was, before humankind began to hurt her living surface."

Jessie watching, thought,'She does not acknowledge that Earth only needs humankind to cease its harming and She will heal Herself. She doesn't yet know all her power.

They were silent, listening, seeing that Jane wanted time to think out loud. "We've done a lot you know. It's been fifteen or more years since Altos began bringing the new legumes, the trees and vines, the meadow plants, that replenish Earth as they grow. And there,"She pointed at the far hills,"You can see the most

THE JOURNEY

recent legumes spreading like a bright, many colored paint, one or another blooming through every month of the year, and the trees, bearing fruits as well as fixing nitrogen in Earth. Every one of those plants nourishes Earth and us and all animals.And they offer another nourishment, our heart's delight from their color and fragrance. Earth can provide for us if we care for her as though she were a loved Mother rather than a pantry." She laughed, suddenly shy.

Anna was nodding enthusiastically,"Yes, the history films show us how we've changed, Jane. Where there were scars of bombs, open mines, gouges from old Highway building, cutting at the land to make flat endless entensions of old sprawling cities, we've helped the deep meadows to cover them. We planted new forests , new vines, and we've never allowed another sprawling city to be built. The cities are units. Aunt Annette says they are modern sculptures." She stopped, suddenly thinking that she'd taken attention from Jane. It was not her idea, but Jane's. She flushed,"Tell us more about your idea, Jane."

"Jane was content,"Oh, you do understand, Anna.You see what I mean! I was sure you would. We've covered the old scars and made beauty where uglyness was, but we've only just begun to see Earth as a whole Being"

"And you're reminding us that we're part of that Being. You think we're a growing out of Earth Herself?" Jessie was smiling, delighted with this turn of thought.

Jane looked puzzled,tipping her head to look at Jessie questioningly, "I do, Jessie, I do think that. But I didn't know I did until now." She laughed pleased to discover. We've got to remember, we're part of Earth, not just here 'on Her'. We LIVE out of Earth Consciousness." She stopped, the thought startling her, embarrassed by her own vehemence. Then she grinned apologetically. Jessie was smiling broadly, when this girl became fully conscious of her own powers, she would be something. She realized she must encourage her to talk out loud more, talk to explain herself. For in that she informed herself.

Jane went on, talking slowly now,"That does make a difference, doesn't it?" She absorbed that and then said,"Have you seen the forests that run up the slopes behind Banig, beyond where the grain fields end? Have you been there? The western foothills go for miles before they climb into those western mountains that separate us from the sea, you know." They were nodding, of course, everyone has seen those forests

But Jane went on." "Well, you see the forest does not nourish itself as well as it might. The hardwoods Clandor takes for their industry, their lumber and furniture making, comes from old replantings that run into the snow line. But there has only been hardwood and the very highest conifers. Now, when they take out a tree, they take root and all. And the plant wizards come in and plant a new kind. Here and there through the forest there are clumps of Golden Shower, Coral tree, hardy jacaranda, another with a deep blue blossom that hangs a foot long, and bears a seed pod that is edible for us as well as most animals. The Jacaranda has red bloom, and round nutlike fruit, the others each have fruits or long thick sweet pods, but the wonderful thing is that each of them are nitrogen fixers. The falling leaves and flowers provide other nourishments. They are forest feeders."

She took a quick breath, as if afraid to stop the flow of words. "There are shrubs in the middle of old meadows that do the same. All those bright colors you see yonder on the hills are legumes that were seeded into the meadows and foothills. So you can see, we've already begun. But we did it mostly for ourselves, to improve our crops, our forest product. And also to care for the wild creatures. But we could do it thinking of Earth Herself first. A gift for our Mother!" Her eyes were shining. The speaking out of her dream was stimulating and joyful.

"We'd be making some very great changes. We'd have to take care." Jessie cautioned.

"But we have the Wizards. They can communicate with the plants, can't they? They know what the plants can do. Perhaps they can find what the Earth wants and needs too."

Jessie's face smoothed, she nodded, "We'd have to trust that they would listen carefully." She stopped, creating a moment of silence, then said slowly,"But where would we find Earth Wizards?" When Jane simply looked puzzled, she added,"But then, the important thing is that they are able to listen."

Jane nodded enthusiastically,"Oh, yes, I don't think of this as something we know how to do. We must learn so much. We must listen. We must not re-shape Earth. We must discover the best way to help Her. For instance, there - "She pointed at an outcrop of boulders ,tangled in briars, dead weeds, old shrubs some of which had begun to die. "You see, just looking, one does not see the beauty of line, the lovelyness of those great stones, lying there in that mess. We hardly notice the blooms on that vine that curls along the edge, because it's crushed under that dying bush.Yet, the little ones of the meadow can live under healthy vines as well as these, can make burrows under stones exposed and clean as well. That could be a small garden in itself, that spot there. We could trim a tree to reveal it's beauty, we can cure disease of plants whether they are 'useful' to us or not. The great oaks, there, the group nearly against the Highway down there. They were planted at least ten years ago and they produce acorns as sweet as apples and as large as golf balls. They've fed hundreds of animals. And yet, the limbs the Vagabonds trimmed last winter because of the heavy snows, made them more beautiful as well as healthier."

Jessie was nodding, smiling wistfully,"So long, so many centuries a few people had such dreams, not so well envisioned, perhaps, but so impossible for them. Now, now that we've no wars to use our time and wealth, and no desparate need to use all our lives in doing each other out of empires, we might have time for such new vision." She nodded, "Go on, Jane what else have you imagined?"

But now Jane was silent, doubt beginning to disturb her face. Jessie was relieved . After a few minutes she went on, her eyes down, studying the patterns of the sand at her feet,"Well, we've got a lot to learn. We still don't know how to listen as well as we must." She frowned, trying to find words for something that disturbed her. Finally she burst out, " We'd destroy possibility if we limited Earth to our imaginations." Surprised at her own words, she looked at the two women,

THE JOURNEY

puzzled then added,"We need a larger vision, I suppose." Her doubt seemed to fill her now, and she seemed less excited. She looked up at the other two women, Jessie and Anna laughed gently and then Jane smiled.

Jessie nodded, her heart light now that Jane could doubt."It's a great dream,Jane. Surely it needs more thought, but it is a wonderful dream. Perhaps we can learn to respond to Life rather than to manipulate Life. Perhaps you yourself might be the one to meditate upon the living Earth and discover what you need to know."

Jane met Jessie's eyes, saw there something more, a request, a plea that surprised her."Why yes, Jessie. I must ask Earth herself, mustn't I. She'll tell me. I can feel her speak, hear her music. I listen to her movements far down inside her and I know that she can speak if I can learn to listen. " She was silent,"Ah, that's the hard thing, isn't it, to hear beyond one's own intentions." She shrugged, shaking off the introversion."But then, I really would like to do it the way I've thought of it. I'd like to make the Earth into a great glorious garden. How could it hurt at all?"

Jessie nodded,"Keep thinking on it, Dear. I remember how our ancestors harmed our Earth .I remember as a very young child that I grieved but I did not know how to stop anything, even when I heard clearly the cry of torn and bleeding trees. It was worse for my grandmother who used to tell me of vast fields ripped apart as though they were not alive by huge unconscious machines, and almost as unfeeling people. I always thought the people must have felt the terrible rape of Earth, but they hardened themselves. They denied, just as you still deny so much now."

Jane looked from one to the other. "But what do I deny?"

Jessie was patient,"Listen, pay attention. You sense so much more than you are willing to admit. You know so much more. You have power to communicate with Earth herself, perhaps, not just with her plants and animals. perhaps you will be our first "Earth Wizard."

Jane caught her breath. "Oh no, Jessie, I cannot. I could not presume. To do that, it would be - be - wrong, unnatural."

"Why, Dear? What is so wrong. You know and admire plant Wizards.How is this more wrong?"

Jane was shaking. "Oh, it's -it's such an assumption. I couldn't presume so."

Jessie was quiet, they sat in stillness for minutes, Then Jessie said, "We have learned a lot. communication that we have not talked of before. You were at our Spring Planting and the recent Gather and you do know, Jane. You do know that we were together there in a new way." At Jane's hesitant , half fearful nod, she went on,"We have much to teach. We of this Valley have no interest in personal wealth. We use our time to understand, not to 'pass' it away. We enjoy each other,our local pub is small and for talking, singing, and people are forever meeting each other at the Learning Center at all hours. Many new teas and coffees are sold equally with wines and beer. When, in fact have you seen anyone drunk in Adwin." They shook their heads, "Nor has anyone. The pleasure gardens lose patrons, the theatres are performing plays that would not have been imagined in my time. There is change, and people do not entertain themselves with distractions to avoid themselves. War has long been a thing of the past. What's happened? Surely a new dawn rises. Do you think humankind climbs out of its lowest and begins to seek its highest potential?"

She let them think, absorb those ideas. Because she knew that they opened vistas even these two had not seriously considered." What will we do now to enjoy our lives? Maybe we'll travel further into the inner dimensions, develop vast and world encompassing thoughts such as your own. But we must acknowledge ourselves."

She watched them, they listened raptly, knowing something important was happening. Jessie said, "Now! LOOK!" She used that Voice, the sound shaped into words that caught at them and drew them to a very acute attention. And then, there was silence. Jane closed her eyes and gradually she began to know an inner contact, a Touch, so gentle, so delicate that it seemed at first only a sharpening of her senses. Then it grew, broadened, and deepened. She could feel herself more, she knew her own nature extending and she began to feel a loosening of denials. Then like a delicate tingling,she felt Presence, a closeness that had never been there. An intrusion? Yes! She closed herself in reflex defense. But then, because it was so very delicate, she wanted to know, she wanted to allow, to open her self. She held herself attentive. Not even with Steve had she felt such intimate Touch. The thought wisked away. All thought faded, her mind stilled, empty. Aware of Presence! She was aware of more than she had ever been conscious of. And Earth beneath her, pressing against her flesh, an extension of her own consciousness, felt to her alive. As alive as she herself was.But most astonishing was this sense of an 'other' Touching her-- touching her very mind. That Earth consciousness vast and endless seemed to include her in Itself. And she was home. How could this be? But the experience could not be denied. It was! She was Earth Conscious! Time fled,thought ceased.

Then in one swift tightening, withdrawing,a fierce racing flood of thinking, broke the contact. Her eyes, stared into Jessie's and she cried out,"Earth is not only a physical object!"

Jessie nodded, her voice stern, filled Jane's mind like a rumbling of the sea,"You know! You are aware of Earth! If you weren't so busy shielding yourself from your own astonishing,deep nature you'd have seen that long ago." Then, her eyes smiling, her voice softened, "Will you please let yourself imagine that there is more to yourself than you've noticed ?" She was smiling tenderly, as if amused.

Jane nodded, numbly, her heart full. There was so much beauty in that Touch. This had been more than the Touch of another human mind, it was more powerful than what had happened at the Gather, and that had frightened her. This was not a Mind Touch, but 'other'. She had felt something underlying all awareness, something as vast and deep as Earth. The thought awed and silenced her. Now she could not avoid! The experience reverberated in her mind and would not be denied. Surely, she must listen, must learn. With a long surrendering sigh, she was slowly nodding, her eyes large, staring at Jessie as if the old woman were never seen before." I will learn, Jessie. That was - real. I can't deny! I - oh, my God, Jessie, it shook me to my bones." She was silent, remembering,"But it was wonderful, it was as if I had come home!" For long minutes she was still, the other two watched her, smiling hoping. Finally with a decisive nod, she said,"I'm a little afraid, but I must understand." Then with one hand rubbing her temples, she said softly,"My head hurts, as if, as if my very brain was affected. But I am willing to focus attention and to understand." She drew a long deep sigh, trembling with decision."That's what I must do."

Jessie smiled,"I know you can. You are learning."

Jane stood up. wrapped her long legs around one another in a gesture of unease, then straightened them, stood quietly, laughing at herself. "I've felt -- something. The other times. Something I didn't know how to describe. But I didn't think. I assumed it was just an aberration. Now there is - what you call Joining? Could Joining be -- with Earth Herself?" She trembled at the question. Both of the others laughed,glanced at one another.

" Jane. we've known you could Touch deeply into Earth. Andy knows that too. We've watched you and longed to talk about it.Tell us about it."

Jane nodded,"I may have done that, but it was -- so much less, so scattered in comparison to what I - I almost knew just now. I think with the -- the little ones, the animals and the plants too,there is a kind of Touching. As though I sense, their thought. The animals, such simple, direct thought, but very clear. The trees too, so utterly different, but then the Wizards would know of that. But this! This Earth Touch is different. It's not thought, like we think of it. It's something very much deeper. You know ,trees are one way Earth speaks out to us. One way only.People! We could be another way that Earth speaks. We ARE extensions of Earth after all. I suppose she does speak through us, but we've deafened ourselves with our own loudness. We won't learn how to be still enough to hear Her! But the trees are still. They carry Earth voice. And that, I hear. I do hear that." She was silent, and then, softly, she murmured,"Sometimes there's a kind of Earth 'knowing' a simple knowledge, that - that grows, fills my heart even at its slightest Touch. Could it be that is the way Earth would speak through us if we listened? If I could bear listening?"

"Believe it, Jane. You must learn how to focus and to attend." Jessie's voice was nearly a whisper. "Here is the beginning. You already stand far ahead of most. You are a special Talent. And it must not be lost. There is a slow opening of our minds, my Dear. It keeps on happening as we are willing. As we focus and pay attention. There is something happening within humankind, and we are the outward expressions of that happening. Life is waking us up. We begin to live the changes in humankind. We could not be aware of such things without living them."

"You don't remember the old world,the terrible things humankind did. Nor do you remember the brave courage of those of great heart among them. You live in the world they dreamed of, and often died to bring to life. Be alive to what you are, child, to what we all are!"

Anna moved to sit nearer Jessie. She looked up through the pine tree to the blue above them, feeling the serenity, the beauty like a great still wave that slowly surged over everything else. Within that stillness a part of herself continued to think, to speak, a paradox that amused her. She said, "It's sad, Jessie, that all the old times are gone. That world is dead."

Jessie shook her head, partaking of that stillness and speaking from it as well. She Touched and was received, offering to the young girl's mind imagery, teaching pictures that showed her what might be. Then she said, "You see? There is a sadness of loss, always, for what is gone, for the years of our youth, whether for individuals or for humanity."

Jessie said, "Now for your other question." Swiftly as mind can Touch mind, Jessie began to show her the way to live in two worlds at once, to let state penetrate state. Anna was receptive. She thought it was something like lucid dreaming but Jessie showed her the difference. The strength of a ranging mind that could sustain consciousness through subtle worlds and yet keep its centered point, where stillness offered a gateway, was for Anna miraculous. Jessie felt her own perception shaky, she saw Anna stabilize, aware of the contradictions yet finding harmony among them. Anna stood beyond Jessie's own edge of perception. Her mind seemed to loosen, to break free from restrictions, to taste something so alien at first, she felt burned, torn. Her head ached, her body quivered with energy rising through it, the beginnings of a new realignment. She ignored them. She could faintly See, but the strain was too much. She must go slowly.

Jessie knew the child's leap, suspected her realization but she could be only a sign post for her. And wait for her return. Anna sat so carefully still, awareness blossoming through the air, through each object, the sunlight, the dense grey stone beside which they sat. She was present to her world more wholly than she had imagined possible. Finally Anna's attention receded, fell back into single recognition, she had seen through things into the life that lived them. She sat, shaking her head, tears wetting her face. She looked at Jessie, remembering.

Jane nodded, biting gently on the bitter sap of a pine twig. She knew nothing of what had happened for Anna, but she was deeply aware of the wave of stillness, it inundated her mind, she could not think within it. She shook herself. Jessie was looking at her. She saw Jessie's eyes encouraging her to speak. She felt herself break through a delicate membrane that had surrounded her. She looked around, lost, feeling the whirl, the immediacy of objects, as though seen in a clearer light. The stillness lifted her so she floated upon it. All around her the Earth radiated a glowing light as of diamonds shimmering through air and she knew it was just the ordinary air and she was finally Seeing.. Now she looked literally through physical objects, through the trees to the Light within them, into the great boulder beside which Jessie sat. She accepted. She had always seen that light that filled things, enlivened them. But she had never admitted it. Now she nodded, holding to Jessie's presence as to a safety strap. Her body quivered with

THE JOURNEY

the penetration of her own perception. She knew that the world around her, sentient, vibrant, was everything that was. She said softly, "There isn't any separation between anything at all, is there?" She could never deny again.

Everything seemed clear, the whole Valley filled with that silvery gold glow. She turned to Jessie and she could see that shining white light around her shot through with color here and there. She could see Anna, her own sweep of color and a pearl white radiance penetrating them. She looked around, all the world seemed to glow. She murmured, looking every where with wonder in her eyes, "Oh, dear, and its been here all the time. Just this, the Earth world!" It was as if she saw THROUGH each form to its source. She sat in amazed silence, looking around. Conscious of all she saw, and also conscious that Jessie and Anna were there as normal people within all the Light. "Is this a world of light, Jessie? There seems so much light. Special kind of light too. Such glistening light. I think it shines even in the dark."

Jessie was grinning like a delighted school girl, "Yes, yes, Dear. It is that, a world of Light. And you see that you have seen us here and that you have spoken to us while you realize we are all part of that world of Light. Does that surprise you?"

Jane thought of that. Her mind seemed engaged so deeply in that great aura of stillness. But at the same time, there was this small thinking, going on. She smiled suddenly, "Yes, it does. But it's as though I finally am remembering something." She frowned.

But Jessie and Anna looked at one another and laughed. "Yes, that's it exactly." Jessie said softly.

Jane looked at her thoughtfully, "Jessie, why is all this happening? Why are we able to realize so much when we could not before?"

Jessie nodded, turned away, looking far over the distant hills, feeling the beauty of the land reach through herself. Finally she said softly, "Is it new? Or is it as you say, we are finally remembering? Surely you have always realized, but have not acknowledged what you knew." She was silent then and after a little while, she went on.

"It was so long for the people of my time. We kept expecting that such change must come. We dreamed, prayed, hoped for it and yet, we were so stubborn, because we wanted the change to be as we ourselves imagined it. We didn't notice that it was already happening within us. Within many people. Then certain ones began to withdraw from our society, we thought they were simply people drawn to a religious life. Others began to live differently, a life of service. Humankind gave them little notice. They began to found retreats in the high mountains. And they are now what you call the Monitors. They took up the task of watching, being there to help, but not to interfere. And they began the schools. It was from people trained in their schools that the ideas of the Valley itself began to form and develop". She was silent, then shook her head, but I think you must know something of that. You want to know WHY?"

Jane nodded, and Anna reached out a hand to touch Jessie's. "Perhaps it's because the human race is ready to go on now. To take that leap, that step beyond what we have been. To literally become more than we ever were."

They were silent. Anna said,"I remember now, the teachers told us when the desire to share became endemic, fixed in our hearts, that we began to change. Because we cannot know alone, but with and through one another? Isn't that what they meant?"

"Yes, that as much as anything, an attitude change. that survival wasn't worth it without everyone's survival. That wealth wasn't worth it, without everyone having wealth. And then, knowledge that that could be done." She turned to them smiling."You have no idea what a revolutionary idea that was at first. We saw that we must learn to share, that we must agree that sharing was a basic survival skill, not simply altruism.That it is absolutely necessary if the human race is to go on.Unless we learned that Life itself was absolutely important, all life, every kind of life, then we could not survive as a people. Because we ARE that Earth life. That knowledge the Earth Herself taught us,but only with great pain. It is one characteristic of Love and Love has entered our world view. We are beginning to be aware of Love as a reality. The return of the Christ some called it. Some called it the recognition of the Buddha Mind. What ever name it went by, it was that that began the changes."

Anna nodded," When I was studying in Santiago, Master Teacher Jem used to tell us that we finally saw that we must stop trying to change others and change,or grow up ourselves. He said when that knowledge spread into national consciousness, that the end of the old ways was in sight. It was a radical idea then, I suppose,that a whole nation could take itself in hand."She met Jessie's eyes questioningly, but Jessie nodded.

"My Mother used to say that when peace was in her own heart, then she felt peaceful toward others. Even when they were distressed. She would tell us then that we could meet anger or fear, without losing our own peace. She reminded us that we could not expect anything of another, but only of ourselves.So we must watch ourselves only. She would shake her fingers at us, and say,'You notice that when I am angry you get angry too, or else you get afraid.' " She smiled in memory and Anna watching, picked up a clear picture of Jessie's mother and Jessie as a child. The glimpse pleased her. But Jane, returned now to her old attention noticed nothing. She murmured,"And all that was supposed to be a mystery, is not at all. It's simply paying attention!"

A squirrel that had been running among the rocks came near to study them. Anna met the bright eyes, felt it listen. She turned to Jane, whose attention was acute. The squirrel turned to Jane, as though drawn and began to walk steadily nearer, watching her closely. Jane reached out one hand, and the little creature came and touched that hand with its nose, then reached out a paw to feel the skin. It sat a moment and then turned away, as if suddenly losing interest. A cool breeze had come to sweep across the hills, making the trees rustle but the great rocks they leaned against sheltered them from its force. They were relaxed in the sun's warmth. The pine above them sang in the strong wind.

Jane sighed, "Well, there's the whole Earth to know. To share with. I think my idea, the idea of the Earth as Garden is good."

Jessie laughed, "It's only because I know of your deep love for Earth that I am not terrified at that idea, my Dear. In my mother's time, that might mean that someone wanted to make the Earth over to their own image,. But you are sensitive to Earth. You have been trained to recognize your own desires, to evaluate them. Now you admit that you are conscious of the Light all around us, within the trees and I know you hear the music of Earth, the Earth Song. So I do not fear." She held Jane's eyes, but smiled, "You have known much of the dark within yourself as well as the light within you. And so, you will find struggle, for between these there is always struggle, but I have confidence in your basic life sense."

Jane said, nodding slowly," Ah, Jessie, I've known - I've known the languages of animals and plants. So many years and I've denied knowing. I concealed it in a kind of fantasy game that I played. But I'll not do that again. I do hear. All I have to do is pay attention and acknowledge. That Soul consciousness,that you spoke of, centers us. It's why our Valley has no army, no military defense system."

"To battle one another is to lose everything we hold dear. It is worse than death." Anna spoke frowning, "But then, how do we teach those who cannot see at all if we die?"

Jane nodded,"Jessie, you see the implications. It's pretty revolutionary! Yet, when I see the things that are happening now, I wonder whether we can keep our vision."She looked sad, "But at least, I will not deny myself."

"You are an honest person, Jane. One person who doesn't argue once she sees a thing. It's refreshing."

Jane nodded, " It's as though a living Spirit inhabits everything, me, the trees, - everything. It's like Earth, perhaps, flowing into everything, or like Sun, who penetrates everything. That's the way I can think of this.I have to listen to myself!"

Jane shrugged finally, sitting loosely sprawled on the sandy floor,"Well, I'm glad there's something useful in my nature. I watch the rest of you and wonder if I will ever catch up."

Anna and Jessie both laughed, at the same time poured their love toward Jane,"Oh, Jane Dear, you've already begun. You realize so much,Dear. Everyone doesn't sense what you live with daily. You must teach us as we teach you."

Jane stood up then, staring at them both surprised and pleased. Then looked away with a wry smile, chagrined;she had seen herself again as inadequate."Thank you, I'll have to think about this. It's new to me. But it's getting late and I've got chores".Then admitting the excuse, she shook her head and said softly, "No, I just need to be alone." She turned, then went back to kiss them both before she ran off up the hill to the path.

The old woman and the young sat unmoving for some time. Sometimes they held themselves alone, sometimes, one or the other, would Reach, then Touch briefly, sharing an image, a perception. They did not think about it, they were aware. Finally Anna stirred, looked at Jessie and said,"There is so much to learn,Jessie, so much to learn. The teachers tell us everything they know and they are good teachers, I think. But the Master Teachers always seem to be holding something back. They seem not to speak of --whatever it is that --" She shrugged,"Well, I can never discover what it is."

"Have you asked? Do you insist on knowing?"

Anna looked at her speculatively, this was a new thought."Oh, of course". She smiled apologetically, "Why haven't we? We know they will not push us, not intrude. They set tasks that leave us with questions. Why haven't they set tasks that will bring questions of what is hidden?"

"What kinds of tasks would lead you to what is hidden?"

Anna sat nodding slowly,understanding flooding her mind," You've said that living is the task. That's it isn't it? Out of our living come these questions and we keep denying what we inwardly know. So we don't form questions of them. It isn't easy to form questions of such matters, Jessie."

" Why not try?"

When we pay close attention, which they themselves have taught us, then we grow conscious of Light, of a dim perception of something there, beyond thought; just THERE far to the edge of our minds. It IS Light,at first anyway. So much Light we cannot see more. Then it becomes a radiance that fills everything around us, just as we spoke of earlier,a radiance that Jane sees within the trees themselves. It's as though we begin to see THROUGH the Light. But, I just don't see how one can ask what is needed."

"Anna, aren't you just avoiding. Isn't it the same old habit? Come, now, ask as a question what you need."

Anna laughed like a child embarrassed,"It would seem silly." She saw that was not true, and shrugged again, "Well, Jessie, first I don't understand why the Light is intermittent, why it doesn't hold, why when one focusses one's attention on it, it seems to shift away. It's almost as though one can See only by looking from the corners of the eye, from the 'not looking'. And yet, Jessie, often when I enter deeply into absolute silence in the temple, I am risen, moved into that Light, standing there, and it is unceasing." She shrugged, but then, I'm seeing things from inside, from -- in my mind? I always feel as though I'm 'coming back' after meditation. As if I've been somewhere beyond myself?" She wanted Jessie to recognize the question.

" And what do you see there?"

"I see things differently, as from such a larger view. It's as though I am inside the Light and Light is the air I breathe. It is the highest point I know."

"Have your Teachers taught you what that Light is?"

"They've told us that there will be a Light before us, that we will discover Light and that within that Light we will know." She gestured impatiently, then sober, she frowned,"Well, I do remember they did tell us that it's the Light of Soul Consciousness."

"What does that mean?"

Anna grinned, amused at Jessie's catachism, "It's being more conscious. Because, seen from that point of view, a quarrel changes completely and sometimes is completely meaningless. Sometimes, my friends and I enter that Light together when there is a quarrel, and there we - we - " She stopped floundering, uncomfortable, then she heaved a great sigh and said,"then we Touch, so we know together, even there together, and we both see all around the problem and it dissolves." She shook herself, frowning and looking with concern into Jessie's eyes added hastily,"We don't do that often Jessie."

Jessie sighed sadly then,"Anna, Anna. There is no cause to hesitate, or minimize your practice. You know I'm aware of such things. You must not hesitate to speak of whatever you experience. All of us MUST speak out, must talk with one another."

Anna looked down, then straightened her body as in decision,"You're right, Jessie, I'm doing what I've always done." She sighed again,"But with my friends I talk. We've seen how Joining occurs in Light!" She waited, as though unsure.

"Yes, you and your friends talk of these things then?"

"Oh, yes, Jessie. we always have. We wouldn't manage without being able to talk to each other."

"There, it's just that. The process is an entering into knowing, to give full attention to knowing is to realize what is known and though you may not consciously be aware in both states at once -- yet --, you can bring what you've realized down in memory. You are blessed, dear, that you have such friends. Your Mother has not had." She caught Anna's guilty look and waved her hand, "No, let's go on with your question. What is this place that you speak of as Soul consciousness?"

"I don't know. I have no words. But when I stand there, within that Light, that seems to me what is meant by Soul Consciousness. For it is so large, there is such vision. You see, Jessie," She struggled with words."There's such -- such stillness. Sometimes as though everything - life itself - has stopped. Yet there is another kind of Life that" -- she shook her head,"I can't describe it. We onliy glimpse it. It's scary at first, You know. If my friends hadn't talked about it so many times, I couldn't tell you even this much. But we all thought that what the Teachers call "Soul identity' must be what is meant here. Is that so?"

Jessie held Anna's eyes, Her gaze seemed to stir something in the child's mind, to waken some memories, to lift her now into that state of stillness."Tell me," she murmured,"What is that for you, that Soul identity?"

For a moment an expression of great impatience crossed the little girls face, then she frowned and lifted her head. After a moment, her gaze inward, she smiled slightly,"Why, of course, it's when I'm immersed, in that Light. I remember myself lost, then suddenly realizing, as though the word 'I' has no more meaning at all. Impersonal, yes, but so very -- inclusive. So then, whatever 'I' am, is more than this 'I' with which I am familiar." She nodded slowly, as if seeing and speaking from that greater Self. Then she drew her gaze back to the immediate moment,"But you know I think it's - where I discover Love. Maybe Love is the strongest quality of Soul. It's as though that word finally has meaning. Because Love is never absent. It's at that time that Love seems so very Present, Jessie. I've thought of it and that's the only way I could say it. You've told us something of that, and I agreed, remember? It's what it was like,there. In that Soul Light." She was silent. Then softly she added,"It changes the way you think, you know, the way you see! Abigail said she thinks it changes our attitudes toward things. Permanently, Jessie, It's permanent, you know. And then, people don't act the way they did before, before they were aware of Love present all the time? None of us have. We've ALL talked about that."

Jessie nodded,"You've known all along! You simply haven't believed yourself. You are Soul conscious!"

"I don't know very much about it, Jessie except it is real and that it's changed the way we think. We thought at first it was just getting older then we saw that - " she was embarrassed, then shrugged and went on,"adults didn't see the way we do.So we knew it couldn't be just getting older. It had to be that we were standing there,in that Light of Love. We talked about the - the Knowing, the realization that Humankind is more then anybody'd ever thought.But we couldn't be absolutely sure because we kept wondering whether we might have made some mistake and we couldn't talk to our folks." She stopped, was silent for several minutes then shook her head resignedly,"I don't know why we didn't ask our Master Teachers. I think it seemed so very strange we were embarrassed, but they ARE adults, you know." She had spoken so forcefully, so confidently that she suddenly looked at Jessie in alarm, had she overstepped her good manners ?

She shrugged, knowing she was committed to everything, now she had begun, she might as well tell it all, she said,"We helped each other, you know. We lift, we KNOW!"

Jessie chuckled, "You were JOINED and you didn't know. Enthusiasm belongs with young ones, without it they are incomplete. It was right that you did that, and that you discovered all you have." She spoke to comfort her. They were again silent, letting these thoughts settle.Then Jessie said, "And the other children know that they're different!"

Anna was nodding eagerly, glad to complete the telling, to relieve herself of these secrets."Oh, Yes, Jessie, they know!

Things we used to think were important just don't seem important at all. And that makes us feel different, but then, it seems all right too. We try to be interested in what everyone's interested in. But, now, more and more of our friends are -- are like us!" She shrugged, looking down at her feet, smoothing the sand with a bare toe. "I don't think the others notice." She frowned again, glanced up at her Teacher, then said," But sometimes I worry about Andrew - Andrew is pulled into the games of the boys who -- who can't See at all." She frowned again, hesitant, then. "I don't want him to be lost that way!"

"And that is something important.You fear for him."

Anna smiled ruefully, after a sharp glance upward, "I do Jessie. He seems sometimes to draw apart from us." Her face had grown stern and she was frowning."But you see, Jessie, none of us, us kids that is, thought we could talk to our folks."

"And you couldn't! But now you can! There is true Good Will among us. Good Will that comes of the heart and it's endemic in this Valley today. It's one reason the Monitors know that the Valley people are ready." Anna was shocked, Jessie had never spoken casually of the Monitors.

" There are many people who don't understand. That worries me. I can tell my own twin brother sometimes refuses his knowledge.Yet, sometimes, he does not refuse at all. That must make for a terrible conflict, as bad as Mama's maybe. He sees as I do. I know! We've talked of these things. But now, he seems caught somehow, caught into some kind of trap. He's with us, then all at once, he's gone. He rushes off with those young men,most of whom don't realize much at all. They seem caught in some fierce desire that he can't resist." She was silent, reflecting and then said, hopefully, "At least he doesn't react with fear or anger at the Builders, because he Sees too well their inner state. He does remember that."

" He rushes off with whom?"

" Kids we've always known, but who're mostly mind blind.It's as if he sinks to his littlest self, some fierce urge in him." Her lips quivered and tears filled her eyes, this worry she had kept to herself and Jessie knew a deep pity. After all, in so many ways, this remarkable young woman was still a very young girl.

Jessie said,"Be grateful that the fire of your own youth, your old personal feelings do not drown your vision. He has much to meet. The battle will not be easy. You have met it in other ways and you may have another meeting of it as you grow." her gaze softened, and Anna felt the tenderness of her caring. Then," Do you see at all what brought him and his friends to this place?"

Anna stared at her for a moment, her head began to nod slowly and finally she said,"Oh, I suppose it's because he wants adventure, the hideouts, the secret games they play. I see that, Jessie.But it seems to stupid, so wrong. " She swallowed, old angers rising and being balanced. Finally she shook her head again and said, "Maybe, without knowing, he's testing himself?" She was silent, then taking a long, deep, slow breath, she seemed to right herself, looked up with a wry smile,"The Teachers say, 'No one can find the Way for another.' I suppose that's what is meant. So you've got to leave other people alone sometimes. But, he's my own twin, it's hard.". Her smile was troubled.

Jessie waited. She could see that fine mind working at this knotty problem. Anna said,"Then maybe it's my task to learn why I think I've got to find his way." For some time they did not speak, Jessie gazing across the Valley, drinking in the bright day, the scudding clouds in a clear blue sky,the movement of people far away on the Highway. Such beauty, she thought was its own purpose.

They sat in quiet, watching the day pass across the Valley below. The bright sun rose higher, warmer, and the blue of the sky seemed to reach down to their very eyes. The breeze was still cool from yesterday's rain, but the sun warmed things rapidly. It would be warmer tomorrow, and humid, Jessie thought. She listened deeply, undisturbed, and heard the birds like brilliant notes, sweet bits and pieces of an unfinished song. Then the sounds of insects, needling through the bark of the old tree. The rustle of squirrels beneath the surface of Earth. She was surprised at all she could hear when she focussed. Jane had alerted her to an attention she had let become dimmed. She smiled her gratitude and chagrin at her self. She was so absorbed that she started when Anna spoke."Jessie,I also worry about the Builders."

Jessie nodded,"You realize that you see from a higher vantage point, you see the whole extent of the River, you see the entire forest and all its paths, and they cannot, for they are like wingless birds, confined to Earth.Unable to see through the distances."

"And the Builders are afraid of that greater vision in us?"

" When a child is deep in meditation alone or with friends, or teen agers are doing part of their gathering of the crop with mind power assisting their hands, it frightens those who do not see that this is natural to those young people."

"But Jessie, we can't hide forever!"

"No, of course,not. We must meet and we must admit to what is real among us. Then maybe you'll be able to talk to them." Just then they were interrupted by a shout from behind the boulder. Two children stopped their race down the slope so suddenly they tipped forward, then caught themselves. Then they came up to kiss each of the two women, who embraced them with amusement."What is this, we've been invaded by whirl winds." Jessie laughed.

"Oh, Jessie, we heard. You're talking of the doing of Talents. You're talking about what we're practicing. We want to know."

Jessie and Anna looked at one another, a swift Touch was enough to find their agreement. Anna said,"Sweetheart,you were eaves dropping. That's not polite."

Casssandra blinked, her smile fading a little, "Oh, well, we didn't mean - we only heard and didn't think to --- " She blushed at last, recognizing her fault.

Jessie turned to her,"Please,,it's of no matter, Dear. But it is important that you learn, automatically to turn from Touching unless invited." Anna marveled that in her voice was only sweet gentleness, no trace of condemnation.

The two little girls looked at one another,,a hint of mischief in their smiles. "We do see, Jessie, we'll remember. But let us join you now, will you?"

Jessie nodded, her own eyes laughing."What do you think, Anna, shall we include them?"

Anna nodded and the girls squatted on the sand. Cassandra jumped right in with her request,"I want to learn how to move things with mind. You know what that is? Look." With a soft movement of her hand, she lifted a small twig,still holding needles. It lay on the palm of her hand. Then a swift thought passed between the girls, they were attuned to one another,Jessie was amazed at their control.They hadn't at all shielded. Maybe they didn't know how, what they did was so obvious. The twig rolled, it's little brush of needles wobbled then it turned completely over and the needles swayed as if a wind blew. The whole twig lifted then fell." Cassandra turned to them, her eyes full of pride and mischief, She grinned.

Jessie nodded, That's quite good, Dear. Janice, you are her equal, I see." Both girls nodded, looked at each other and giggled."What have your Teachers told you of this?"

"Oh, we haven't told them. We thought- " they looked at each other,their minds racing with images,obvious to the other two, as though they were shouting. "We thought they'd think we were wasting time".

"You know better than that. It's almost a lie." Jessie's voice was more severe than Anna remembered hearing it. They shrank from the Sound, and Cassandra started to back away. Then she said,"You're right, Jessie, I apologise."

Janice did not lift her head, she grinned sheepishly and finally nodded,"You're right, we shouldn't pretend so."

Jessie nodded a curt dismissal of the matter. "Now then, you are concealing you're talents and you know that would not please your Master Teacher.?"

"Oh, sometimes we show our teachers. They don't mind. They think we're funny."

" Cassandra!" Jessie waited until Cassandra looked at her. "You know very well that I refer to your Master Teacher and he would not think it funny."

"Well, Jessie what's wrong with some fun? We're just having fun."

"Nothing at all, Dear.Nothing is wrong with fun. But what is the reason you hide that Talent from those who could really understand?"

Cassandra was silent again, her eyes shifted quickly to her friend, and Janice bent her head, refusing to meet them. Cassandra looked at Anna, then back to Jessie, seeing that no refuge was handy. "Well, Mother,I don't exactly know. I just felt that they'd tell us to --- not to do it." She screwed up her face in a frown."Actually, now you ask. I don't really know why."

Jessie nodded, "Then let's look at it. You can do these things, and that is a great Talent, surely. It is something you can feel pride in. In another year you will be part of a team of Gatherers, and that skill will come in right handy. It's these Talents that makes the work go faster." She looked at Cassandra and saw the surprise. She smiled, surely these girls must know that older young people used mind power to pick fruit and vegetables. She glanced at Anna, and saw the slight shake of her head. Good, obvious proof that they were truly careful not to flaunt their powers. Jessie asked,"Tell me now, what's the purpose of what you do, why move things?"

Cassie looked from one to the other, the question seemed to have an obvious answer."Why it means we're developing, advancing in consciousness, that we've begun to overcome physical limits. You know Jessie, just what the Teachers say. We're developing spiritually."

"Why then do you feel reluctance to demonstrate to your Master Teachers?"

Cassandra flushed, looked down, then frowned,"Well, its just that, just that -- I don't know, Jessie. I just feel as though they wouldn't like it."

"Ah, then they might not like to have a Valley of flyers and movers,of people who can send apples flying off into a basket. But then, they tell you to develop your Talents, don't they?"

Both girls nodded, Janice was troubled, there was something here she hadn't thought of.She said,"Yes, all the teachers have told us to "develop the powers of mind, body and heart." You know, that's the way they say it. They say that we must conquer our lower Nature." She looked hopeful."

Jessie was patient, her voice seemed very gentle, as though she sought informatioon only. But they felt a mild riprimand."Then do you children all think that this is of the higher nature? This using of your mind to control physical forms?"

Cassandra nodded, reassured,"Yes, yes, of course. We focus mind power to search ourselves for new Talents."

Jessie's voice softened, lost the stern tone it had had. She smiled, and they felt the force of her Love for them clearly enough to relax."Then, how do these skills make for the finer purer life? How does manipulating things make us better people?"

Both girls huddled a little, leaned against each other as if seeking comfort."But Mother, then -- then, have we done wrong? Somehow it felt a little wrong"? Janice spoke so softly Anna had to lean to hear, but Jessie nodded.

Cassandra said,"Then having control over our bodies isn't of the Spirit?"

Jessie shook her head."First, Janice, training your mind is not WRONG. It is in purpose that you've gone astray. And, no Cassandra, it wouldn't seem accurate to say something is NOT of Spirit. For isn't Spirit the nature of reality after all? But I would ask whether lifting things about, or even yourself from one plane to another, as when we leave our bodies and explore the second level, has value to teach us to be open to the forces of Love, or to know how to care for our Earth, or to realize the needs of our fellows. Those are the characterists of Spirit in us, not mental gymnastics." She sighed, letting her mind Touch in comfort,"Listen Sweethearts, you say that you seek what your Master Teachers call 'enlightenment' that is what you've been taught all your lives,, and yet, how do these Talents enlighten?"

Cassandra looked unsure, finally losing all arrogance."Why Jessie, I don't know . I don't know. I just thought it was part of it. That if we worked hard to learn, we'd know." She seemed surprised,"I guess you're right, there really isn't much value in moving things from one place to another, except it helps us get our chores done sometimes."

"There might be many values, Dear. After all, people have spent all history trying to find more efficient ways to move things. Perhaps this is the simplist way. And there is a certain mental discipline and training of focus in that skill. But as for being a Spiritual value, it is perhaps spiritually equal to the invention of the locomotive or the air car. They all increase mind power, and that strengthens the ability to search the Heart, to Reach toward Mind Itself. They each give us new perceptions, traveling in air cars gave us knowlege of the world in a new way. So there it is.Each of these has been important. Such minds can be turned then to higher tasks."

There was a united sigh of relief. Janice said,"Then it would be for focussing the mind. That would be the value? Learning to focus?"

Anna nodded as Cassandra glanced at her for help. Jessie seemed to recede, almost as if she withdrew herself a little, and Anna felt suddenly brought into her place as teacher."For what other reasons do we want to learn to focus?"

Cassie looked at her friend, and they both shook their heads? "Well,I don't know." she finally admitted.

Anna glanced at Jessie, felt her refusal of help.She'd have to do this on her own."Are you sure?"

Janice was turning a twig round and round in her fingers, her eyes intently on Anna's face,"I think, it's to find the Center. To Center at the point of Light." Cassandra looked at her in astonishment, then suddenly nodded, as if remembering.

"Yes, yes, that's true, isn't it."

Anna spoke softly, "There's something to discover . They tell us there is the spark of Spirit in each of us, that we have that spark and must bring it into flaming fire. And there is focussing, paying attention so sharply that we can experience something of that fire! That seems to me to be the way it begins." Then she was silent, and a look passed over her face that caused the little girls to hold their breath.

"Sometimes,there is something more. Sometimes a person can sustain attention, focus high enough to Touch that point where Soul consciousness is. Then a bright wind comes to pour through us, and the power of it seems so great it -- it may frighten you, but it blows that spark into life, and then it begin to burn. In us that flame will not go out, it will not cease. .So it is easy to know whether we stand in Spiritual life or personal life, or a combination, because what is thought and done in the Spiritual state is not for oneself alone at all, but for others, ALL others, not just those we love. And it is never for personal welfare even of others, but for welfare of Life ." She turned then again to Jessie."Is that right, Mother? I'm getting in over my head."

Jessie's face was serene and her delight in Anna's teaching was evident. Anna was gazing at the sandy scuff marks on the stone at her feet,"Jessie, how did I know that? I didn't know all that until you asked me.Until I said it, in fact."

"Sometimes it's like that, Dear. Sometimes that's the way we learn. By speaking out from within ourselves. What within you has spoken?"

Anna lifted her eyes shy, hesitant, frowning,intent,"Could that be Soul? That which spoke . The Teachers say that through the intuitive mind comes the voice of the Soul at times when we are personally quiet. Could that be? I never knew how that could be."

"It might well be, Anna. For it was not a selfish thought you had, but one of true search."

Jessie said nothing more, the girls were silent, listening astounded. Finally Anna drew a great breath and said, "I think that's right. I know of that knowledge in meditation but I have never shaped it into thought - or into words. I don't always hear that inner voice. I suppose it's possible to hear all the time." She was nodding her head, a discovery for her. She felt a deep sense of gratitude as though a gift had been given her.

Jessie nodded, said softly, "Spirit is the very breath that breathes through all life from the smallest atom to the planet itself. So to practice the Spiritual life,one wants to practice living as a loving, selfless, harmless human being who honors all life as he does his own. Such a person is aware - intensely aware of Life. Wouldn't that seem logical?"

The little girls let out their breaths finally in free breathing,looking at one another, they did not giggle,then looking at Anna and Jessie, they did. Janice said,"I never thought to see it that way. "

Cassandra shook her head," I've heard about that business of being selfless. But I can't see how a person could do that.It must be terribly hard." She seemed sad.

Jessie laughed, reaching out a hand to touch Janice's shoulder lightly, then she Touched them each with a tenderness that brought smiles to their faces."It is only hard when the mind is small. When the Heart is open, it's simply natural, Cassandra, it is indeed. We don't TRY to be selfless, we simply ARE and when we know that,we live that way.

She smiled and in her eyes was that twinkle of amusement that was so familiar. Cassandra went to her and Jessie took both her hands and kissed them. "You are growing well, Sweetheart. Don't worry." Then when Janice stood and came to her, she placed one hand on her head, and with the other held both the child's hands. "You too, my Dear, you have much to learn and there is a great life ahead for you." They kissed her and turned to leave the grotto. Turning to wave as they reached the last big boulder behind which they would disappear.

Jessie nodded to herself, and Anna stood up to go. She said,"That was a great lesson for me. I appreciate you very much,Mother." She looked around a moment, feeling the day, the warm summer afternoon and realizing a lot of time had gone by. "Oh, I've got several things I must do.I've got to go."

"Go with God, my child." Jessie whispered. And Anna went off leaving Jessie watching the day grow to evening. A flock of birds turned,banked and then swept across the sky,one mind of many parts. Far off a small lake among the foothills gleamed and then a flock of geese rose from its surface and formed a steady flight pattern. She could hear their far off honks. Another melding of small sharp minds. The Valley seemed to flame beneath the summer sun. Crops were ripening, trees where heavy with fruits. the fragrance of the Valley was like a Touch from Earth Herself. Jessie sat, acknowledging the Life power around her, feeling its rise and gentle subsidence. It was a good world she lived in.

CHAPTER FOUR

A Visit in Altos, a New Traveler and a lesson.

    Two days later , on a cloudy late morning, Jessie stood on the Highway between Adwin and Denlock. She stood looking back,setting into order all she had learned in Adwin and under the pine tree at the Farm. The garden city was nearly invisible even from this small distance. There was color, and here and there a roof extending through the trees. The Temple soared above everything, but the three rings protruded only slightly out of the foliage. She had walked through the industrial Ring talking to people going to work there. The young ones who learned the various businesses, the old who worked part time. She had stopped to visit the new chemical plant where Field Loaders were setting down for unloading. Huge bundles of plant fibers,leaves, flowers,roots,bark, etc., separately gathered into tight four foot baskets or bags, were brought into the drying sheds. Barrels of extracted oils, were stacked ready for pickup at oneside of the huge storage room. The plant was in production and she could smell the many odors rising from three warehouses. Tons of dried leaves would be shipped to Green City for making medicines. Stalks would be refined for fabric and others crushed for their oils. Adwin's first harvest of paper vine would go to the mill next to the labs.
    Jessie had climbed to the third story of the massive Ring buildings where the white coated laboratory technicians worked in an easy busy atmosphere. A number of young apprentices, learning the basic chemistry, busied themselves among the staff.Out of those young ones only a few would become chemists,but all would know something of the process and the knowledge. She watched and listened and learned.
    After she had left the town, she walked down the steep western path until she reached the Highway bridge crossing the River and had walked on that Highway, chatting with any passing Vagabonds. She wanted mostly to just walk, and to watch and to sense the manner of people she met. Sometimes people walked with her a while on these journeys and sometimes they talked. Often they simply accompanied her in silence and often they shared images of their lives in a flowing exchange that did not interfere with occasional thought. But now, she stood alone.
    These towns were already producing well. The pride they felt in that was endemic. She heard a shout, and turned to watch a team of Gatherers loading transparent boxes of vivid green Gombos onto floaters to be taken to market and to the processors. Near by the rumpled thick growth of Cassava vines ripened the first of several crops of large golden melons. Across the Highway, was a wide field where narrow strips of legumes,blazing with their dark purple blossoms,alternated with long strips of short, thick stalked corn already at its

maximum height of four feet. Twelve inch ears of corn stood low on the heavy stalks, and she knew though she could not see, that they held three to a stalk, average.

Just as she began the climb up the long curve of the ancient cloverleaf that joined several old road beds, a short, strongly built man waved and called. He came in off one of the grass covered side roads and hurried to walk with her. Long ago there had been a city here. Now it was open grassland spotted thickly by great trees. The forest was dark to the west. She stood looking down through vines that shielded the rising concrete roadway and made sun spangled caverns of the broad arches beneath it. It's maintainence crew lived, when they were here, in houses built into the heavy structure. The People of the Way considered it a lark to live in their cloverleaf centers now and then. Only at the time for Gathers was it filled to overflowing and surrounded for hundreds of yards by the gathered carts of their people. Underneath the great, valting halls formed by the curving cloverleaf crossings,were held these sacred meetings. The people of the Way Joined traditionally with towners during festivals, but they held their own separate Gathers. Several shaded spaces were enclosed to form travel inns, and places for special celebrations.It was the only building the Vagabonds did, and it seemed out of character. In all the Valley they maintained four cloverleaf 'towns' for a citizenry that passed constantly through them and never remained for more than a few days. Jessie stood now on the highest ramp and gazed down over the land below.

She turned to her companion and said,"Look,the Silent City is so clear from this point. I like to come here just to get such a good view."

He glanced at her, his face solemn,"It is so, Mother. And yet,it does not welcome us."

Jessie laughed,"It does not. Unless we decide to climb to her. And that is a task indeed, Alfred."

From below them they could hear the sound of music and the rhythmic pounding of feet on the Earth. A dance was underway among the Vagabonds who had stopped here .Above them a huge Air freight Car gained altitude out of Adwin rapidly to get out of the local travel lanes. Alfred's face had that look of amused amazement that often Jessie saw on older people of the Valley.

"There it goes and those big fellows are already nearly obsolete. Yet it was only yesterday that they were our pride. The big transworld air craft, that fly beyond sight, will be needed no doubt, but these freight cars have few years left."

Jessie nodded, but asked,"You think then that the Transmission Stations will be cheap enough for small towns?"

"Maybe not, but we don't need many freight cars to bring our supplies. One or two a day for the whole north Valley is enough, at least now.." He looked seriously at her,"But then, you've no concern with that, you're worry is with us, isn't it?" He searched her face as she turned to him but found there only a gentle amusement.

""Oh, isn't it all one matter, actually. The Valley and her works are not separate. But then, Alfred, what do you see happening?"

He sighed,"Trouble, Ma'am. Trouble but we'll handle it.I'm sure of that."

"And how will we do that?"

He frowned,then relaxed and smiled,"Ah, you imagine that I might think of violence, of putting those who are so different down with our anger." He shook his head,"We're not so foolish,Mother, even those of us who don't know the way to do that thing my sons call the Mind Reach. We have hearts as wise and strong as any who do." He gazed out over the fields and forests. Breathing deeply of the warm perfumed air and nodded slowly,"Yes, we'll manage, Jessie."

She smiled and felt a surge of confidence that she had needed. She turned to look at him and they both walked on."Then,Alfred, you don't feel envy, you don't feel resentful of those who do these things you cannot do?"

He was silent, then after several minutes, he said slowly,"Oh, to be truthful, I suppose I have felt some envy. I don't know what they do, however, I can't really feel much resentment if I can't know whether it's really worth while. They don't speak of it, my sons, nor do their Mates. I think it's like having any other skill, I don't envy the pipers there below us,nor that wonderfully talented harpist we can hear with them." He shrugged,"Why should the Builders envy so?"

"I don't think it's envy exactly that powers the Builders.But rather simply the lack in themselves that makes them unable to fill their lives full as people like your sons can do. Your sons don't need the excesses of the old way to entertain them anymore. The Builders feel they have nothing else.They feel life losing it's meaning now with our basic building done." She grinned at him easily,"As for you, is there no inner lack that you must try to fill?"

He shook his head, serious, leaning against the massive railing along the old roadway," I hear about that need, from more people than you would believe, I think. But I live with my heart full, of love and of pride in us as a people. I'm watching all these changes. wondering, it's true, whether I'll be included, but," he hesitated and she saw a faint sadness," it's no great matter. The life of Earth fascinates me, I'll never reach an end to all there is to learn of Her." He was silent,looking over the low land forest and interpenetrating fields."Look there, the miles of meadow and wild grains, and the clumps of oaks, apples, whatever, like islands here and there through those lakes of grass. Look at the blue of that string of ponds between here and Denlock,two of them white with wild fowl." We're balancing things here finally. the land is healthy, all the creatures are included and there is food for all. How can we ever grow weary of such lives as we live." Then they were silent again, and he sighed finally to add,"I can see how it might be with some though, Jessie. Those who feel a lack, something lost with the old days, but I think their hearts must be closed, otherwise they wouild see there is all we can desire here. Right here. When people don't understand, and their hearts are empty, then they envy and fear. You know of some who do, don't you?"

"Well, that's what I've got to find out. Surely there's talk of it. What kind of talk do you hear?"

THE PEOPLE OF THE VALLEY

He sighed, laying one gnarled hand on her shoulder,"It's said,that the Black Lodge sends teachers among the Builders. And I went one time to hear, and they preach, not teach, but preach that they have a mission to stop the Devil's work in the Valley. They feed what little fears people have, you know, and they become big fears. That's what seems to me so terrible, Jessie, so out of character for us, for Valley people. To even listen to such things." He turned again, to walk a little way,"We've only recently, in my life time, gotten such notions out of our heads. So when I heard that, I was sick, truly sick at heart."

She nodded,"Then it is a deliberate attempt to undo all that's been gained in the Valley?"

"It seems to be. But we know, and we can meet it. I am confident." His clear dark eyes, were shining with that confidence and he smiled. She was glad that he had not been afflicted with dispair, but had found delight instead. "You and I, Mother, we are not young, it won't be long before our departing, and that I look forward to, but in the meanwhile, we must speak our heart's Love out, must be sure that the young hear."

Jessie was comforted to hear his words, she felt deeply the love this old one had and the trust. She thought there must be many like him. And as they parted, and she turned back to return to Adwin, she cleared her mind easily of the worry and allowed that underlying Joy of her heart to surge forth, filling her with itself.

She met Anna , Andrew and Cassandra at the Adwin air grid above the Learning Center. They would go with her to Altos today.They came laughing and talking of the trip ,eager to visit their Family in Altos. Once they were air born, Jessie turned the little craft toward the Silent City. She wanted to visit again that point of all her hope. And as they flew over, felt again the emergy, breathed the fragrance, listened to the soft music,flowing on the mountain winds, she felt her own heart at peace.They all felt it's power. She watched the children, noticed Andrew and Anna smiling quietly at each other, in the old habitual secrecy of their young lives. She felt satisfied.

Cassandra had moved to the seat beside Jessie and took her hand, holding it tightly, she looked at Jessie once,then turned her gaze down toward that source of beauty. She was not chattering now,but was unusually silent. She seemed utterly absorbed. Jessie felt her need for reassurance and kept that physical contact, until gradually Cassandra felt the delicate Touch from Jessie's mind, felt and acknowledged that deeper contact. She glanced up at Jessie a moment, and her hand relaxed.But Cassandra was absorbed, Jessie had never seen her so intent and silent. She looked over at Anna and felt as much as knew the twin's delight at Cassandra's response. Jessie Reached out to them, refusing any denial and felt their surprise and pleasure. They too 'saw'the City. Their relief was a great outward sigh, as though they'd been holding their breath. Jessie couldn't resist smiling.

"So, you're still denying, still hiding a little,arent' you?"

They looked at one another,Andrew said, a look of embarrassment on his face,"It's true, Mother, we were. We keep forgetting, but then, it's so good when we know you're with us." They were both grinning now, too delighted to keep straight faces.

Cassandra was silently weeping, but without sadness, she looked at them all, turning her face slowly from one to the other."It's such a wonderful place. Why haven't we come before?"

The twins looked surprised,"But we do. We have. YOU could have, you know."

Cassandra studied their faces,, then looked at Jessie."I'm glad you brought me here, Jessie. I will come again."

The air car moved off toward the south east. Already they could see the brilliant gleam of sunlight reflecting off the Great Domes far above. They had long miles of travel ahead, and they were silent, each busy with her own thoughts. Finally they landed on the Grid at the pyramid of homes among which Paul and Annette lived. They descended in the Air lift and the children regained their exuberance, laughing and trying out this unusal wonder that lifted without any visible means.

When they reached the apartment Paul was waiting for them at the roof garden beside the door. Annette came immediately and their children came hurrying from their rooms to greet their 'cousins'. With lots of talking and questions, they met and embraced.Then cool drinks were offered and they separated, the adults settled in the living room the children went to Steve's room. Jessie spoke of the detour over the Silent City. Annette and William were late and this time she was glad.

Paul went to get refreshments. Dressed in a loose blue plasilk shirt and flaring slacks, he looked much like a Vagabond himself. He looked at Jessie,"You flew over the City? Few do it you know. It's another thing we avoid, even when we know we're avoiding. People joke that she has an aura that scares them, but I suspect it isn't a joke."He grimaced as he filled his cup at the autoserv turned and sat with them in the large brightly lit living room. The late morning sun had just begun to slant into one edge of the room, but glow globes bobbed gently around the ceiling.

Jessie met his eyes,"It's no joke!" He felt sudden relief.She sighed,smiled slightly,"But then,the People of the Way are not fools, you know.They're sensitive to Her everywhere in the Valley. Do you know what that name,'People of the Way,' means?"

Paul shook his head,Jennifer said ,"Well,I assumed it meant the Highway as a way of life."

Jessie shook her head, "It refers to the path of life they travel. Their Way, their growth in understanding about the nature of reality."She looked suddenly stern, a hint of anger entered her voice,"Paul! Jennifer! They acknowledge their inner Teachings everywhere, openly, and for that they are considered quaint at the best. Among so many Families, this infuriating avoidance is persistent. Why is that?" She leaned forward."Have you not all been taught?"

He was surprised at her vehemence, glanced at Jennifer, then nodded curtly,"That's something else that needs more talking,Jessie. Even after the two last Gathers, we're still hesitating. We do talk to one another more, but not about the City. Mostly of our own changes. It's unhealthy to avoid any of it. We've not said anything at all to William. And that's not going to help. We know he resents the City. He's unreasonable about Her and he's not just joking either. For Will to be unreasonable is something I never thought I'd see."

Jessie spoke softly,"Paul, Jennifer,have you spoken with your children about Joining? Do you know their capacity?"

Paul flinched, got up to refill his cup, took theirs and refilled them and waited, wanting Jennifer to speak.She said,"Jessie, we have done that. We've talked to them about the talents after the last Gather, and to our amazement,they already knew so much more than we guessed . They -" she groped for words, her eyes cast down,"they seemed to think we were making a fuss about nothing."

"They didn't resent not being able to discuss these things in the past?"

"Yes, they did,Jessie. Steve said it was about time we woke up." He smiled ruefully, "Now they do talk about their inner lives a little, but it takes getting used to. It's us who are uneasy now, not the kids." He shook his head,sadly. Jennifer took her fresh cup and cradled it with both her hands,sipping lightly. Jessie nodded, and they were silent.

Paul sat down again, after placing Jessie's fresh cup on the table at her side. He looked at her face, framed by soft grey-white hair and brightened by the delicate lavender of her dress. "It's Will I worry about, not the kids. I think he's afraid he'll find something he doesn't want to face if he really visits the City. He says the Family is insane to consider that Journey you've talked of.He's really resentful of you now. And he doesn't think he's unreasonable at all. Usually Will can spot flaw's in his own logic faster than anyone else.But then, he doesn't deal with strong emotions well and that's what this is."

Jennifer spoke softly, her usual diffidence gone. "He's become more and more involved with the Builders. I don't know much about their ideas,I haven't paid attention and that's probably a mistake.But I know they want the City put off limits,and they've started their 'investigation'. What ever that means."

" Jennifer, how do you feel about that City?"

"I'm afraid." Jennifer smiled wanly, then was serious,"But I recognize my fear as without cause. I also am drawn to Her, I want to go there again. And that, I can't explain. So I'm divided."Jessie nodded, satisfied at more than her words,"Well,there's one thing to comfort us. She's not defenseless. We can rest assured of that." Jennifer heard those words with a surge of unease, they seemed suddenly ominous to her. Their talk stopped at the sound of the chime and the auto butler announced the arrival of their friends.

They spent the rest of the day together, Jessie listening,drawing them to talk, seeing the shape of their lives here, Will was not reluctant to talk of the Builders, told them that they were a strong and growing group. Jessie asked him directly about the City and he answered evasively at first, until she insisted and then with characteristic sternness, he said,"It's a manace,or else it's simply a place we

THE JOURNEY

ought to take the mystery out of so people will come to their senses about it. The idea, calling that city 'Her'. And I hear you all doing it. That's an example of the problem." The talk shifted to other things, they did not argue, but simply talked of all that was happening in their lives.The children came to sit on the floor for a while,listening and joining in now and then. Rachel and Steve wanted to take their guests out to have a run on the high slopes where there was still snow for skiing.The five children left with much noise and excitement. They came home when the sun was setting.

It was not until evening had begun to darken the windows and dinner was over that they all gathered in the living room again. They sat quietly together. Paul felt grateful to Jessie for creating an atmosphere that seemed more harmonious than such gatherings had been for a while. There was nearly the old familiar closeness among them. Then when they sat, sipping a fine delicate liquor imported from Belgium,and Annette's favorite, Jessie, Reached, gently. Then, she focussed,found a response from Paul and shaped the Reach into a light Touch. Paul met that clearly, and then hesitantly, came Jennifer,her strength not great yet, her focus a little off. However they were surprised at the sudden entrance among them of Annette's force.Clear, focussed, and decisive.

Annette's smile told them much, and the Joining proceeded,firm,deep, entering into a rappour that melded mind and thought.Suddenly, the children were there, all except Steve, and their minds seemed to bring laughter, Joy,delight of surprise into the meld. Paul drew in, focussing fully,offering precision and shape. As usual 'idea' was shared,but specific thought did not tranfer. Rather they shared images and sensation. Paul felt the strength of their Joining grow. Wondered why they let this powerful gift become lax in their lives.

The linking was swift after that. Eighteen year old Steve stood,lost in wonder,watching them, his eyes moving from one face to the other, and then with a mental shout that startled the Joining, he entered in, giving a new strength, a powerful mind control.The faces of the children were lit with delight and shone with Joy. The Joining held several moments longer and it was deep and good

During this time, William sat feeling the sudden intensity,knowing nothing of what was happening, yet aware enough to know something was. He frowned, glanced at Annette and saw that Joy,then suddenly the strange familiar grief that maddened him so.They all felt that grief, met it with her and supported her in it. Will said, "What this? What's wrong here?"

Jessie broke the Joining after that swift plea from Annette,"Be careful! Do not hurt him." After the Joy, was this Grief. Jessie said aloud,"I think Will, that you sense there is something happening here. Can you tell me what you think of it?"

He frowned, scowled at her as if he thought it all her fault,which he did. "You were all looking so strange, so distant, and so silent. A different silence, I can recognise the difference. I've seen it before and it infuriates me. It's as if I'm being left out of something, some secret affair." His voice rose slightly, still fully under control. "But what really disturbs me is you, Annette! That look! My God, it's as if you're in pain, or a terrible grief's come over you. What is it?"

Annette nearly cried out, his perceptions were acute,"Oh,Will,I don't know.I don't know how - how -"

Jessie spoke with the Voice that instantly claimed their attention, though it was soft. "Will, you must listen. You must be willing to know that we are Joining our minds into a melding that is wholly complete and intimate., That is the truth. We would welcome your attention so that you might enter into this Mind Touch."

He pointed a finger,"I don't want to hear this mumbo Jumbo,this trying to avoid facts. My wife's got some trouble she refuses to speak to me about. That's all. Mind Touch! Telepathy! These things are your imagination. It's rot! Childish superstition. I can't believe that you're serious." He was so agitated that Jessie drew in and made a Sending of clear healing energy and surrounded him with it. He went to the window,restlessly turned from them, then finally quieting a little, he turned back. "Well, do we have any of that wonderful liquor left?" His face was relaxed, he almost smiled.

Jessie was astounded, he couldn't - couldn't simply refuse everything like that.She wanted to laugh,then cry. But she persisted, refusing to let him so totally avoid."Will, you have not acknowledged that we have just Joined together in a Mind Meld that we are consciously creating. Will you recognize that this is possible?"

He looked at her sternly then,his face no longer troubled,"Jessie, I cannot possibly believe that you are serious. I have to assume that you think you're doing something, but it sounds like the foolishness of centuries ago. People do not do such things. I cannot understand what you mean by that word 'Joining'. I'm not sure the children should be exposed to this talk either."

She was steadily holding his eyes, though they constantly tried to escape. "Will, the children are part of the Joining.Their minds are as strong as ours, in some cases stronger, they practice Joining with their friends. It is not something we can ignore any longer in this Valley."

He tore his gaze from her,looked again out the window, then with suddenness that was again denial, he turned to Annettte,"Then, what is it, that you conceal from me. Why do you so often look so grieved?"

She gulped, not ready, but drew her strength from the others,said,"Will,Dear, I love you, you are my Mate.But I won't pretend any more. I do Mind Join just as Jessie says. It IS true! I grieve because you won't acknowledge and for a time I didn't even try it, to avoid hurting you. And that is a great loss to me,Darling. " She heaved a great sigh, stopped his attempt to speak with one hand,"No! No! Let me say it now, it has been too long that I have not.I have denied my own self, refused to allow myself to grow into this new knowledge. This can't change my love for you. Please, my Love, let's think about it reasonably. It is only a gift and everyone does not have all gifts."

He looked at her in amazement, utterly unable, for the first time in his life, to speak. Finally in a tightly controlled voice, he said,"I can't believe this. You're serious. You really believe this happens!" He stared at her, and slowly his gaze softened. He nodded curtly, "You're right. We'll have to think about it. I don't know

now what to say at all." He looked at them, seeing a look of pleading in their eyes. It first angered him and then suddenly, so suddenly he was surprised, (because he could not imagine Jessie's flow of Healing energy) he relented and nodded quietly. " Then let it be for a time. We've got to talk between ourselves, Annette. We must understand."

They were able to reach almost the old degree of good comradery in their talk of local matters before the evening ended and they all said good bye. The children and Jessie went to catch the air car that made the evening trip to north Valley. They would be home late. It was a sober group that climbed into the car and headed toward Adwin. But the children could not repress their Joy either, and soon they were talking with great eagerness with Jessie about that wonderful new ability among the adults to do these things they had taken for granted among themselves. While they talked, Jessie focussed her attention farther. She knew much had happened that day, while they were gone from the Farm.

Early the next morning, Rose stirred uneasily in her sleep. Ben, lying beside her, one arm flung across her body, murmured, aware of her restlessnes. The bright moon outside allowed dim visibility in the room, then,covered by a cloud,left darkness. Rose's body relaxed, she easily slipped away, far into the bright night. Instantly she was there,on her cliff face, the place of safety during these flights. Why had she come to the cliff? Why had she not traveled into realms of that Astral world, strange and fascinating, creating as she went the desires and the dreams that she might enjoy?

Jessie had thought of that question early in her visit,when she knew of that flight, and realized that for Rose, this'travel' was not for personal entertainment, but rather for greater understanding. Therefore such travels as she did, testing herself to see whether she could stand unseen before a friend in London,or seek out her parents to talk to in that non- physical realm,were brief. She had once found her parents but they were busy with matters beyond her. However, she saw the futility of such personal 'play'. She could actually build a new reality for herself, astral matter was responsive to strong desire, but she knew it was seductive and harmful. After a few self indulgent 'creations', she turned away from that waste of living. This was another dimension. To use this precious time 'playing' with astral possibiities would teach her little of the world she was now living in. Teach her little of her self. She knew that she needed to learn to live in the physical world.And tonight, as usual, she stayed in this favorite place.

She sat on a boulder broken from the cliff face, it's sharp edges worn down by years of weather, and contemplated her situation. The Valley below appeared unchanged. She wanted to see more,she was willing to see more.

With focussed concentration she opened the eyes of her mind.She was 'willing'to SEE. There were other people here, of course, those permanently gone from their physical bodies, but not yet gone on to further states of being. She could see people moving below, people walking through gardens where snow lay in her own world. Below her, on a forested slope, a small town clung. The world was not the same.It was as though those people could shape their world as they willed. Though it seemed so solid, the Earth could be flexible beyond imagination. What then was reality? Was it a mental phenomonon? Or was it more than her mind could conceive? She decided on the latter.

But people lived here! It was a busy world. She thought of the way these Astral beings reshaped their world, with mental energy, and then, compared that with the way her own physical world was reshaped, She said,"We do it with our minds too, but it takes longer. Can't be done with thought only, but with muscle power, time, and great effort. But here, since it was astral matter, strong emotion could itself create change, when focussed by Mind.

She watched as two forms glided by, aware of her but giving no attention. Then she looked out over the Valley, intrigued by the clear rosy light that permeated everything. There, to the west of Jasper, was a tiny hut in the forest and in that hut was someone - someone who radiated another Light, golden and clear.She caught her breath. There must live a Traveler of the Monitors. She let her eyes sweep across the Valley, there,another such hut, across the River, beyond the fields and Skenna swamps, high on a rocky outcrop. This one glowed as if a fireburned within it. Rose saw then, in town or city, other such pools of Light,intensifying the general radiance. She was awed,caught up in wonderment at this revelation.

She looked around her, here on the cliff face,her vision seemed to shift, refine itself. She cried out,"Who are they? They're everywhere. There are so many smaller ones.They're like fireflys." She looked back to the home farm. She said," The cottages, our farm is like a cluster of bright, tiny lights and one deep pool of brilliance. Ah, yes, it's Jessie who lives where that pool lies. She is One who Travels. If I ever had doubt,there is an end to it." Searching through Adwin, she found lesser lights but many much brighter.Then there were myriads of tiny bright points. She thought, "Well, there it is. The Master Teachers must radiate so much more than the rest of us. And those firefly lights, who of us blazes with even that kind of brightness?" A wistfulness entered her mind, a strange longing,to be able to offer Light.

She persued the search, fascinated now. She found a village where not even a fire fly light appeared, except one house in which seemed a dim glow. Here, near the village, a spot of such intense darkness that she felt it pull at her,was like a pit, a well within the bright growth of the land. She shuddered and turned away. Surely she must be mistaken. Yet, perhaps if she could see deeply enough, even in that village there might be some with that spark alive in themselves Surely Jessie had told them that spark burned in every human being. And yet, she must learn how to see it. Must be knowledgeable of that in people, if she were to teach. If she learned to see more would she see other such dark pits? Her heart grieved at the idea. She resolved to ask Jessie about them.

"Surely I am mistaken,even those who cannot Reach out, who cannot mentally Touch,have in themselves that heart of Light." She stood watching and letting her attention return to the citizens of this realm, those who seemed busy with their own affairs. And she did not notice that pool of Light that had shaped itself on the other side of her cliff.She began to bring her attention back from that search,and was surprised at how suddenly her vision shifted. No one would miss the strong pools of brilliant light here and there,but she might never have noticed all the other lights had they not made her attend.

Then she noticed a difference around herself. Someone was near! She let her mind Reach into cliff caverns, and found only the small minds of little rodents and snakes. She mentally reached out across the cliff face. She must know. She felt a throb of fear,then gently releasing that, she knew! Someone, a person was nearby.

Immediately she knew who it was, and the wonder of it fought with a sudden and real jealousy. That surprised her. How could she be jealous? Hadn't it been her long wish that Benjamin would be able to know of these things? Well, there it was. She could not deny the emotion. She swallowed, felt a twinge of shame at herself, then let that subside. She smiled at herself, turning her attention from that same self.

There he was, there beside her and unaware of her presence.He who had refused even to Reach such a short time ago. Benjamin was here!

Then she realized that he Reached toward her, blindly Reaching out to her,not knowing where she was. She thought that it was the way an unborn child might make its presence known by kicking and crying out. Yet, this was different. Ben woke within himself more than he was willing to acknowledge, just as he did with those other Talents he finally had accepted.

She moved, stepped across the sharp projection between them,and stood watching him. He had not fully arrived. He was not clearly defined and she thought that could be dangerous.She started to Reach, wanting to help, then knew she must not interfere. Slowly he stabilized, slowly with an act of will, he released himself to this new world.

She could see him now, clearly, his face a glow of amazement. He looked all about,far off across the Valley, and she was startled to know that brilliance with which this man she loved shone. The brightness was like those she had seen among towns below. Not great like the pools of Light, but surely radiant. Her own Ben! Her own Family! Why had she not known before?

For a moment as she watched, she thought he might escape in terror and amazement back into his room, but he steadied, she could see the determination in his eyes. She Reached gently,Touched, and felt a sudden snap as though a restraint was broken.He was firm, clear and strong,, looking at her.

He was startled, but seemed to accept her presence."Oh, Rose,you're here! I might have guessed you'd be." He took her hands,drew her nearer seeking her reassurance."Look, Look, there is the Valley, just as in our everyday world. There it is and here we are." He seemed to have trouble absorbing it."This world is unbelievable! I came once before, but I didn't stay, I couldn't".

She watched him as he looked out, his eyes sweeping across the miles of Valley below. He muttered to himself,"Even though it's altogether different, I can't say what the difference is." She knew his need to adjust to this new experience.

THE PEOPLE OF THE VALLEY

Several times he shook his head, wiped his hands across his face as if to clear his vision. She remembered doing the same long ago when she had first come here. He turned to her finally in a tone of astonishment and awe,"Rose,there's more going on here than I could have imagined. Is it possible I may be hallucinating?"

She smiled then, "That you'll have to decide for yourself,since I can't know what you see. But I do agree there's much,much more going on than you realize. That's sure. It takes time to absorb, to learn how to See. And there's still much we can't ever see, I'm sure, because we are still tied to that physical world. I think there are things we should not see. You must know, Love,that we're only here at an edge of things,not fully here. And this is only the first of many such dimensions that are beyond this one."

Much of what he realized there he could not shape into thought. It eluded his thinking mind. He allowed himself simply to be aware. And then suddenly he turned to her, drew her to him,held her as though he must find some comfort from all that was so alien. For some moments they held each other. She knew he saw only what he could bear to see, realized only what he could bear to realize. And so he must learn. Slowly, he would allow himself to be conscious of more. Slowly he would extend into this world more fully. She waited a little and he lifted his head, met her eyes and said softly,"Come with me,my Love,let's go home"

Rose shook her head,"No, Benjamin. No. You must wait a while here. You must meet this because you've come to do that. Find your own way here, find your own limits. If you don't you might find resistance to return and then you'd lose it all." His head was bent, but he listened. She wanted to help, to stay with him but recognized the desire as her own flaw. She must let him be. She gathered herself and left.

Ben didn't take much note of her departure. He stood still for several minutes, and finally lifted his head, looked again at the grand vista below, trying to decide what was so different about it. His mind reeled, the old patterns seemed torn askew; old patterns of perception were suddenly clearly false. He realized that perception was many layered and in this moment, for the first time in his life, he SAW that nothing was truly as it seemed.

The old narrow vision seemed a darkness from this point of view. Here was energy, here was Light, here was depth and dimensions of Vision such that the old vision seemed blindness. He cringed with memory of assumptions he had insisted were all of reality for all his life. Why had he so long refused? There was a pulsing energy in the Earth, the universe, seen from this larger perception, he could not deny. There was vitality and possibiity and there was also a subtle and seductive trap here, just as there had been,as there still was, in that old familiar physical world.

How did he know? His mind seemed looser, more willing. Yet,he still wanted to limit himself to what was present,to look no further. This,itself, was too much! Every level of perception had its own barriers to what was beyond itself. That was probably necessary for human sanity. He grinned, amused at the idea. However,

THE JOURNEY

if there was this, just outside his ordinary sight, then, how much more might there be?.

He remembered that Rose had managed all this some time in her life, had survived the mind torturing dilemma. He was aware that a real pain throbbed in his head. Stretching the mind was painful. Strange, he could think perfectly well here. This was not like the stillness in which perception ranged beyond thought. This was - was almost ordinary! The idea amused him.

As he tried to think, to explain to himself, images grew sharper, the scene before him shifted, became more accurately a picture of his thought. As if when he intently imagined, he created? The whole experience seemed to him similar to dreaming. Yet he could and did walk about, touch his own body, clench his hands and hear himself talking clearly. Besides, everything was so recognizable, there were familiar hills, and below, the great River gleamed like a broad silvery snake down through green land, the heavy thickness of forest, and the lighter smoothness of meadow and crops. So much color, the hillsides painted with living flowers, blooming and brilliant with color and meadows a kaliedescope, the whole so sharp, so clear. And yet, it had been night when he woke from sleep to come here. The world he knew was subtly changed, or perhaps it was his eyes that had changed. He pressed against a curtain, a curtain of dim light.

The details of that changing became clearer, he was finally through that transparent curtain, on another side of it. Here the same land seemed to glow with a light that held the dust of diamonds powdered through it. It excited him to see, to breathe it. It filled him with energy. And through that light, he could see. The relief of happiness filled him, and he imagined a castle there, on that sharp high knoll, and as he imagined, a brilliant pink- gold, stone, turretted castle, took shape there in the midst of a medieval fairyland garden. Astounded, he saw it appear there before him. He could himself change what he saw, what the world was like. And he marvelled and was again afraid.

He turned away, cleared his mind of imaginings, saw the castle fade. He wanted to keep his mind clear, he wanted to know the real not the imagined or at least know the difference. As he cleared his vision, watched with open attention, he saw that there were flickers of light, here and there, many like a scattering of stars flung over the fields and hills. He did not ask what they were. The unknown lights flickered and he saw them mostly from the corners of his eye. When he focussed, they disappeared, or flickered.

He turned again, focussing, his mind centered, observing with no thinking. And he saw the visible energy of the land, the glow of living things and the matrix from which they existed. He knew the 'sea' of energies from which all life all Earth in fact, manifested Itself. He could see that the forms of things were only the shaping and gatherings of substance supported by that ceaseless flow of energy. Physical things were themselves not solidly stable at all! He stood caught in amazement at the recognition.

He realized these things, not knowing how, for all logic denied them. But he did not entertain logic just now. He let his senses receive and attend. There was an intensity of impression from that sea of energy that pressed itself against his mind,insisting on recognition. He absorbed what was experienced,absorbed it as one might absorb sunlight. He could not explain and it did not matter. But gradually, he began to feel the demand for explanation force aside all perception and cover his senses with their dim questions. His mind wavered, closed about itself and hid. This was all impossible. He knew, even as he thought he could not know.

What he finally thought, then rejected as foolish, was that the primary quality of the atmosphere in this universe was magnetic. Was it Love itself, or an aspect of Love, Certainly it was related. And his own will, drawn by the deep desires in him, created as he willed. Will! It was a direct force then. Ordinary human will. How dangerous, how wonderful, it could be. Some part of his mind smiled, confident in that truth. The other parts of his mind refused, stood balking. The impossiblity of Love as 'atmosphere' forced him finally to consider that he must be dreaming, for now his mind raced releasing floods of thoughts,of questions . He felt drowned in them. But pleasantly recognized that he did not have to answer them.

There was so much more, so much that he could not understand enough to think about but he was aware that it was there.

He just knew that this world held endlessly fascinating possibility. The struggle in awareness baffled him, boggled his thinking mind. But there was another part of his mind that seemed elated , that luxuriated in this, literally stretched itself in Joy. He distrusted that new part of himself.

He made a choice. He was here,by God,he would know! Fear rubbed against the edges of thoughts, theatened thinking but he resolutely refused it. He WOULD know!

Steadily balancing himself,,quieting the urge to go to sleep and deny, he remembered Rose. She had been so calm. He thought of the luminous extension of her shape that made the familiar human form within it take on a look of fragility. It was then as the Teachers said after all? Could that be what people of the past had seen and called an angel? He was amused then, and everything seemed to relax at that amusement. His tension released, he could see better.

But moments later, he felt the tightness return. He desparately tried to create order in his thought, grasping at old patterns to make sense for his thinking. Why could he not just allow experience to occur, allow his mind to absorb without understanding at all. MUST he understand everything? Yes, he had to bring this that he recognized, saw, felt, KNEW and yet could not explain,down into some explanation. It had to 'make sense',otherwise, where was he after all. He could imagine that he was deluded utterly. It would not be so difficult if it were not so very Real!

"Well", he said aloud, surprising himself that he could make sound.But how could one make sound without flesh? The question had to be left behind. He heard himself, so it must be sound."I've got to keep calm." At these words he knew the full range of his terror as emotions fought with reason. That awareness within him, who stood quiet and observed this battle between these two familiar adversaries, was patient. He felt both terrified and exalted, neither of which could he believe. What was real then? He focussed attention on a nearby rock, the very dense stuff of the cliff, and felt it, slid his hands over its surface in reassurance. But instantly he knew he could walk through it. Then what was he? A ghost? Was he perhaps dead down there in his room? The thought nearly precipitated his return but he managed to catch himself. No, he would know this thing.

He could not know how utterly different from Rose was his response to these experiences. She had never questioned, rather wanted to accept and keep the delight of strangeness. She had not probed, had questioned only a little. She accepted! In this place she felt relief from the need to explain. But Ben was trained as a scientist and he had to find explanation. Slowly he found this thought shaping again and thought he might not ever explain it all. Not now. His mind could only realize so much. He would ALLOW himself to realize only so much. He felt the barriers slide into place, firm, opaque and yet absolute. He did have choice. That seemed a very important realisation.

"Well, to sum it up, it looks as though I'm aware of two worlds at once when I'm here, in this state. There is that one I've always known, a very limited world, it seems. And there is this one, so much more vast, flexible, possibly unlimited even, though I doubt that. I suspect it's limits simply aren't so easily known. Am I creating this world?" He laughed, that seemed even more impossible. " But then, this world does seem to be much more responsive to the Mind's direction. Laws are different. The world does shift somewhat in response to strong thought. Therefore how can I know what is real? Is only thought real? Or is all substance fluid and responsive to thought?

I wish there were someone here to help me. It's so hard to hold firm thinking. As if thinking here denies or adjusts reality. That's pretty unsettling."

He felt himself drift, as if he were taking flight back to his body. He stopped himself, held firm. "That's the only term I can use, surely it's actually the same world, just a different state of being. But I also have got to understand!"

"Somehow, I know this is the way it should be. That this is the normal world on a higher level. The physical aspect is heavy, so slow, so - limited. I want to simply accept and to realize, to BE here." As he said that, thought ended, he felt immersed in a radiant Silence, so deep it throbbed. It was an entering into Light. It was so lovely he wanted to deepen it, to enter more fully. He wanted to drink in the beauty of it. But he felt a clear, firm barrier. He knew suddenly, as though some one had told him, that he could enter no further. He was still alive, and with a body waiting. He could not step further into this condition of being. He watched thoughts pour in to vision and then drift off. He need not attend them. He wondered if in meditation he had touched that same Light.

He tightened his resolve. How had Rose born this? Born so much all alone, not even knowing whether others knew of it? Not having that knowledge to deny insanity. He felt jealousy, anger at her knowing, and smiled at those feelings. He remembered his own inner Earth travel, when he had entered into the tree world.

Something of that related to this strange unknown world. What is the connection? How do these various states of being fit into human consciousness? There must be so much going on all the time all around us and we don't even know. He realized the last thought suddenly and a panic siezed him. It was too much. He turned away from himself. It made no sense at all to panic at that thought, but he knew that to persue the idea, would be to enter danger. A lot of things here didn't make 'sense'.

He looked out across the Valley and saw with new Vision the vitality of the life there. The Valley itself is ALIVE. Just as Earth is Alive. Of course.I've not thought of that. He laughed with the joy of it and said,"If I were to describe the Valley now, how would I do that?"

He felt the energy rising from the great vast mountains, the power in them, the Life that they radiated.This mountain that he stood on, carried meaning so vast his mind only realized its possibility of existence but could not begin to imagine their nature. He felt tossed against that meaning, but it was to great for him, he shrank to himself. Then, in that moment of closure, he saw the spots among those mountains where, in this reality, a chalk grey blight seemed to have struck. He could see with eyes grown unnaturally sharp, eyes penetrating the rich green that stood surrounding those spots. He'd never seen that with physical sight. Did that mean it only existed here? His heart lurched, and tendrils of fear thrust their way into his well being. Such places ought to be searched out? Some appeared to be in small villages, one in the center of Denlock. Surely they must be a fading of that Life that radiated through everywhere else.

With an acute and sudden desire for the familiar, he turned to the trees. The great gnarled trees that grew from the rock walls,in the narrow crevasses, and on narrow ledges. Seed fallen into cracks of the mountain had cracked their shells and probed upward into the light. Fighting their way through storms and winds through years of struggle,,they were veterans of suffering and of LIfe. He bowed mentally to them. He let his eyes move across the clean face of the stone behind him, and knew clearly what was meant by the 'living stone'.

Ben reached then, to those familiar trees, and felt their response. He was so fragile beside them, they accepted his Reach reluctantly but with humor. He felt himself a reed against their strength, then he withdrew, and was alone, standing against the cliff. He liked the way the short limbs of the bent trees leaned against the prevailing winds,held themselves curved and twisted to fit the need for balance.

With sudden recognition he was no longer separate from those trees, or from the life of the mountain. The inclusion was vast, he was swept into the expanding metaphor that is Earth. Aware! He knew humankind was an extension of Earth Herself and the realization made him laugh with Joy. "Is this what Jane knows? Does she realize that sense of being part of Earth the same way?" He wished he could ask her. Then was swept with a profound sorrow,beyond reason. He said,"And she too denies her own knowledge!"

The insignificance of himself against the depths of all he knew now as 'Being' made him conscious of how great was human ignorance. The realization shuddered against his joy. He could not bear more! With a jolt he shriveled down to the tiny personality that contained all the humanity he could personally know at the moment.

Our teachers have said that humanity is a flowering of Earth herself. An extension of Earth. That we are no less a part of Earth than the mountains. I thought they spoke symbolically, and now I see they meant it actually. We are exactly that, extensions of Earth. The strangeness of that knowledge reverberated through his mind, and he absorbed it. His mind had been impressed with knowledges that he could not think about. Consciousness was stretched and he ached. The aching of his body seemed chronic lately, an aching that rose from within, deep beyond muscle and nerve. Was his body having to adjust too?

He saw a thought, as if before his eyes,"Will I remember? Will I be able to think about all this when I leave this cliff, this dimension?" He felt afraid that he would lose too much, as if thought would sift through a dark screen and he would keep only part. "Must that always be?"

He was quiet, wanting to experience nothing more, weary. Then he felt a presence, some one near. Looking around, he saw that Rose had returned to him. With a great shivering sigh, he turned to her, his whole being seeking comfort, his mind holding the question like a sword that pierced him."Rose how can we remember? How can we remember?"

"Slowly and with time, we do, Love. We learn how to know ourselves and then we remember more." She sighed, taking his hand."That's what the Teachers have told us and we thought they told allegories. But we have to find words, language to hold all we realize. We have to allow our minds to stretch. Consciousness EXTENDS and we have to stretch with it. It is painful, sometimes, it is frightening, and it does not 'make sense' until later, but it is right."

Suddenly he cried out,"Rose, let's go home, Let's go home. This is too much to endure!"

Without answering she held his hand tightly, and suddenly the flight occurred, he was drawn as surely back as though he was on an elastic band. There they were, in their room, and he was moving, feeling the physical weight of his body a great burden for seconds before the familiarity returned. And his body, his physical brain, attempting to absorb all that he now was, knew, ached, was sore. He felt hot tears, the sobs of a broken heart, he was filled with crying that would not seem to end. For some time he lay, crying, letting himself adjust. He felt an unnameable grief. And peircing upward through it, like a sweetness of wonder, was that unnamable Joy.

Finally he drew himself up, pulled Rose into his arms, kissed her and held her as if he held his salvation. For sometime, he sat, holding her, stroking her hair absently, feeling the joy of her presence."You know, Rose," He finally began, softly, "For so long I envied you. I knew you 'went' someplace and I couldn't even ask you what it was. I just wanted to go too. I longed to be able to be there, where ever you were, but lately I've lost the longing. The ache to find you faded, and then, there I was. As though that desire itself blocked my path. I think it has something to do with learning how to Join. To focus my attention. The press of consciousness against the edges of our assumptions finally results in its rupture and the entering into greater consciousness. That is where the pain comes. That is where the Wonder is!

She laughed, Surely that's true, Love. You ceased to bind yourself up with either desire or denial for what you imagined to be and allowed yourself to enter into what IS." She stretched her body beside him. The setting moon slanted its last light across their bed, and to her it seemed a golden Touch. She said,"You know, Benjamin, my Love, there were so many times when I felt life had become empty, without meaning. Nothing life held was what I longed for. Such entertainment had palled utterly. And so I thought I must go to the Healers. But then, one day, I risked, because there seemed no longer any reason not to, and Reached as far as I could. Just Reached out to Life Itself. And passed through this membrane of perception." She laughed shortly, a bitter sound."I haven't ever talked about it. I don't think I've ever told that to anyone."

"And in all that time, I couldn't help you, my Darling., I knew, I could see that there was something missing. I grieved, and sometimes it was part of what drove me away. To try to find something for you." They were silent for some time, curled around each other, taking comfort for old pain. Then he said, smiling, "Well, it's good to know that I'm not losing my reason. That scared me for a while there."

She nodded absently, missing his smile, then said, "You know, Ben, the Builders aren't separate from us anymore than you and I can be separate from that mountain we stood on. If we can remember, then we may be able to act with Love. If not, then I'm afraid we won't. We must understand what they tell us."

He turned to her, his attention sharp, "Yes, if we have the courage, Rosy."

They looked out the window, at the morning sky taking the grey light of the unrisen sun. They could see a light in Jessie's cottage. Benjamin felt suddenly an overwhelming sense of being a part of that rising sun, as though he too rose there, hung far in cold space and poured out Light onto that rolling world below,as Earth turned to receive the light that spread down over the Valley. He felt it's touch faintly, and it was as though he was there in that Light that entered into this darkness of dawn. He did not notice the tears pouring over his face. The experience was so great it hurt in his body, but he tightened his grip on Rose's waist so that she cried out in sudden pain. He reeled back,unable to tell her. Contrite to have hurt her,but speechless.

She Reached and found his Touch. In an instant they had Joined so that she knew his image of that coming of the Sun. His mind acutely sensitive, perceiving beyond himself. There, he within himself, watching himself through these small human eyes, this narrow conscious mind. And he knew then irrevocably that he was more than that mind. Identity had shifted into that greater Soul state, and would not forget Itself.

After some time, Rose said, "Ben it's hard the first time. There's so much and you've been so ready except that you were blocked so bitterly. Now, it all seems to be opening up at once for you. " She wiped the tears from his face, gently and went on,"We've pushed aside something that's been choking us for years. Choking our whole family. You and I Ben, we must not forget.We must lead the way,when we can. And we must follow the others when they can show us how to go."

He sat up, rubbed both hands over his face, shook his head,and sighed."You saw?"

She nodded,"I saw. Ben. It's real.That recognition of your true Self.It's real."

Then he grinned,"As for taking the lead, Sweet,we may already be too late. I think our children may have done so ." A swift pain came and went in his eyes and she nodded. They held each other in silence for some minutes. Then he said,"The human body has so much to offer, you know.It has such great beauty too. I love the feel of your skin, the movement of muscles and the joy of being alive in this body. I don't want to leave it often. Maybe I can learn, out there, but there is so much to learn right here. That's why I was born,after all. Other dimensions must wait." He kissed her, "The smell of your breath is wonderful."

She melted into him and they began the slow delightful process of making love. His hands gentle and skilled found her body responsive and she thought there could be no better beginning to a day. He murmured softly as he kissed her ear,"My Darling,I am so much more conscious of you, we begin to Join so deeply already even as we touch one another this way." Their lips met and all talk was of sensuous languages, of silence and an arousal of flesh to its greatest Joining. Ben's face was full of the wonder of their love, this new deeper intimacy. Mind linked to mind,heart to heart, in such depth and intimacy that neither would have dreamed possible a year ago.

She responded eagerly, tides of desire roused and joyous. The tenderness of their bodies increasing as though it would not end. She cried out his name, and the image they shared through linked minds was one of an almost infinite tenderness. The wonder of it lifting them into its own heights. And as they found each other in these new ways, the day brightened,the tipping world rolled to let the sunlight pour across mountains and Valley, stretching long dark shadows behind every tree or hill.

Later, they lay, still locked into one another, and Rose let the wonderful quiet grow. After a while, she roused herself,smiled and kissed the tears wet on his face. "That was the most wonderful of Joinings ever, Love. The most wonderful!" He leaned on an elbow to look down at her face, stroking back the moist hair from her forehead. She laughed and went on, "But more than this, I cannot find words to say how lovely it is to be able to talk to you of all the things that fill my heart. For so long I have wanted to."

He nodded, not trusting himself to speak for a minute. "I know that. It is as though a dam has broken, a great holding within me has drained away. I am freed of desparate longing for what I searched all my life. Now I must understand what it is I have found." He laughed suddenly in a joyous great roar,"Oh, Rose Love, look at the day out there!"

THE PEOPLE OF THE VALLEY

She laughed "I want to go out and stand in that sun naked and run as far as yonder hills." She leaped from the bed, stood sliding her hands down her hips, and then turned to him inviting him. He nodded, laughed again and said,"Yes, let's do it."

They ran naked from the cottage, waved at Jerry , who turned from entering the hall to laugh at their high spirits. They ran down the slope to the River. Ben plunged in and swam with fierce swift strokes that took him half way across before she jumped in after him. The three dogs had followed them, leaping and barking a welcome to their Joy. Rob watched as they leaped in the River and then watched with a faint whine now and then as they disappeared underwater, playing and racing each other to see who could stay under longest. His mate and pup churned the water with the man and woman. Rob watched, studied the silent surface, then barked once, leaped in and began swimming rapidly to find them. With a start he jerked his head up, slowed his swimming. Rose Reached to him to comfort him with knowledge of their safety, and immediately, they both surfaced. Rob swam back to shore. He didn't like to swim. He sat there, soaked and dripping so much like a disapproving nanny,that Rose and Ben laughed.

When they climbed out of the water they went to him and stroked his great head, his mate whined, dug at his side, then licked his face, with eager concern. Rose sat and hugged his wet body to her,"We're a trial to you, aren't we Rob? We should have told you we were going to play underwater." Ben stroked the big friend, meeting his eyes, and nodded,"She's right, Friend, we should have told you.I'm sorry."

Rob was molified, and began to wag his tail again. They began to run again, taking hold of each others hands. The brown,round bodied woman and the white sturdy body of the man racing along pathways, laughing . They ran across the fields of grass beneath the willows along the River banks. Through the trees they glimpsed the fields they had planted months ago,already many vegetables were being harvested, and the fields looked full and ripe. Their bodies were full of their own delight of life and they enjoyed them. Then they turned and ran back, up the hill to their cottages where they put on shorts and shirts and retuned to the Hall. Ben felt the heat of the morning sun with pleasure. They were aware of the stillness, of the fragrant air, the boundless energy of growth around them. Jane and then,Silvia came slowly from the Temple, but no one else seemed around. The Earth everywhere seemed waiting for an event unknown.Rob stood with them, watching the cat slowly winding her way down the walnut tree to join them.

When the four of them entered the Hall they heard voices Immediately they knew that Jessie was telling a story of the old days. The children loved to hear them, for though they had seen all the history films of those old days, Jessie was a born storyteller.

The morning air was still cool but the sun was already hot.It promised a hot day, but far to the north west there were banks of clouds gathering. There might be a storm by evening if they were lucky. They needed rain.

Cassandra and Steve came in following them and they were all there, at the dining table, The newcomers dialed their breakfast and Jerry asked,"Couldn't wait to get dressed, today,you two?" He told the others of the flight of these oldest members of the family down the hillside. And the children laughed, eyeing them with renewed respect, but with doubt. But they had interrupted a story and Anna insisted that Jessie be allowed to finish.

Jessie, nodded,"Many folks owned stores, markets, and even huge shopping malls such as only great cities have today. But they had to spend their lives sitting in them, or hiring others to do so. It was a strange way of life, but some seemed to like it. In the small town 'stores', they called them, because it was where goods were stored, the town people came in all day, in and out and they could visit and enjoy a social life right in the midst of their work. But big places, were not like that at all. A monotonous job that many people did only because they could find nothing else to do. I could never have been a clerk and I'm glad that we don't have to watch over our goods, that we have Market screens and depos where people can see things but simply insert their card and the item will be sent right out. It's so much more efficient and does not waste human life."

Cassandra was intrigued, leaning against her father's side,nibbling a piece of toast, she said,"But the little shops, they sound like the open markets where you can buy all kinds of interesting things. That would be fun, I think."

Jessie nodded,"Yes, it would be for a little while, at least.But then, people were trapped in jobs in those days. They had no choice. The little store my uncle had was what they depended on for survival."She leaned back, and they knew the history was turning into a story which they had hoped for.

"I was just ten. My family was poor and I went to work for my uncle in his little corner store. You see when you were hired,you must stay there without leaving at all for long hours all day and every day. People couldn't go to a learning Center to search out something that interested them because we didn't have learning Centers. You just had to stand there. We had schools which were equally as confining. Children had to sit and stay in one room all day." A flash of old anger passed across her face,and then she smiled sadly,"I suppose it was a little better for my father and uncle who were able to leave to travel a little just to buy the supplies, but most came by mail order, and they seldom left either. They really couldn't deviate from the exacting days work. We were all hidden away from the sun and Earth for days at a time."

"My uncle couldn't pay much but he sold us food at cost. At first I enjoyed it, the feeling of responsibility, and learning something new .Neighbors came in and talked to me and I began to learn for the first time to like strangers and make them friends. That part was good for me. My parents were rather shy people. We never had visitors at our home, so this was a whole new world for me.I did find out I could make friends, but then,gradually when all the newness wore off, I didn't like being indoors so much. I would go out to rearrange the outside display,meet a neighbor who was looking things over, anything to get outside. On cold rainy days, it was cozy and sometimes I could read. But my uncle didn't really like that, he wanted me always attentive. And there wasn't anything to be attentive to."

Rose said," It was a good business then? They were able to make a living?"

"Only a small living, but it sufficed. My uncle loved people and loved to talk to the neighbors when he was there. But he had no business sense. If it hadn't been for my aunt he would have failed. I did learn something of business from my aunt. But then, after a while, my cousin was old enough to take over for me, and they didn't need me. My uncle was unable to tell me but I knew and told them they couldn't afford me. I went into a bigger town and got a job as a checker in a huge market. That was exciting at first, and I felt so proud because they paid better. But in no time at all, I felt that awful feeling of being trapped, there behind that counter, watching the days of my life go by outside. It was a kind of torture to me." She shook her head,"My parents were pleased, we needed the money, but they hated to see me spend my life that way too." She was silent for so long they thought she had ended the story.

Benjamin asked,"Was that at the end of the Times of Trouble, Jessie. The economy had to be still in bad shape, because that was less than a hundred years ago. Our Valley would have been nearly deserted by then. Abandoned."

Jessie let her eyes return from far memory and nodded,"Yes, it was only in small towns that the old life still flourished and then, in a slovenly fashion. The banks had failed and money was worthless, too many people died in those terrible years. People were afraid in the big cities, no one trusted anyone else. People seemed to have gone mad with frustration and so many had nothing to live for." She stopped, memory bringing frowns. Then said softly," But beneath everything, there were those seed groups who were the beginnings of our new age. They had begun to create a new way to live with one another." She sat silent, remembering and those who were attentive, saw the images.

"When I started working, the local farms were producing a fair amount of food again. But the poor were still poor. People still followed pretty much the old patterns there. We didn't have bright young people to wake us up. I didn't know what was happening out in the rest of our world until I was older. In our town there was the endless monotony of old ways, the rigid system of using people to produce, to make things, most of their lives used up in repetition, that broke out hearts, lost us our connection to our Souls. Too many even denied that Soul existed." She smiled with a shake of her head," For me that means they denied their true Self. We had never known what we were at all." The story was taking her back, reliving those scenes, those years of blind, unconscious living. And the flickering steady run of images through her mind were visible to most of the family as they listened and Reached to her.

Cassandra said,"But Jessie, what happened in the big store?"

Jessie nodded then, took a new breath and began again,"The manager wouldn't pay me full wages because I was so young, but as soon as I got out of high school he said he would pay better. I was in school all day, expected to stay at my desk, not allowed to walk around, or study what interested me, as you all do. Oh, how I envy you children sometimes, and how I rejoice that that old way is gone. After school, I felt chained to the counter at that store . I felt so frustrated. I think that was what broke my heart.I was so completely cut off from Earth". She was silent,remembering and the images of that time made it real to the listeners.

She went on in a subdued tone, speaking as if the memory needed to be exorcised,"On ten minutes breaks I would run outside, find a quiet place behind the building and sit in the sun, for there were no trees near these big buildings. I felt as though I cried inside. No one should spend youth so. Cut off from Earth strength." The Family listened in silence, "I finally saw the danger nearly too late. I realized one day that I was avoiding going out to the light and air. It hurt too much to return to the prison of the work place. And I had begun to 'adjust' they called it. I was beginning to deny that I wanted anything else,I tried to convince myself that this was right. That it was a good job. That I was childish to be so unhappy."

Tears were in her eyes, reliving this emptied old pain. "But I was hearing new ideas here and there, reading the news, watching the new programs on television, there were things happening in other places. Finally, I left our town, and went off to work and go to college. And in those years, I determined that I would not lose touch, that I would keep my trysts with Earth. I found small weed filled empty lots where old buildings had fallen or were in ruins, and I searched out the plant and animal life there. It was amazing to me how much there was. It was then I first knew I could enter into plant consciousness, could understand the small mental Touch of animals. Find comfort there, in fact! My own inner development was beginning to make itself felt." She looked around smiling blandly,"But I also began to meet young people who were living a different life, who thought and were already Reaching out, already practicing the Balancing among themselves. They taught me that there was another possibility for life. And then, I met John, my husband and my life changed forever." Her face lit and she smiled with such joy that everyone breathed a sigh of relief.

Cassandra broke the silence,"Jessie, people were very strange when you were growing up"

"Strange? Yes, I suppose we were. But everything was changing during those terrible years when so many people were poor, so many without homes even."

She drew herself out of these memories, and said,"God in Heaven, I'm glad that you see it as strange. It was the normal way for my people. But now it's over,that way of life. It was a terrible price we paid,but I think it was worth it. We had to see ourselves! We HAD to find a new way! And so we did."

Andrew reached out a hand, "But Jessie, couldn't you stop. Stop doing what you felt so trapped by?"

"Well, my parents saw how unhappy I was and told me to stop.But by then, I'd found that having a little money was pleasant.I almost got trapped again with that one, came close to sacrificing my life for comfort. Then there was a pride in the discipline required to keep going at both school and the job and proving I could do it.I felt strong,somehow.But it was a hard time. I saw the wrongness of that desire for comfort itself, because that's what money bought. Comfort is a high price to pay for the loss of one's Soul. The loss of Earth. I knew it was not what life was about, even before the market failed and I lost my job."

Cassandra nodded, wondering exactly what she meant, how could one 'lose Earth? After a moment she said, "Well, I would like to work in a small shop. I wish I could."

Ben nodded, "You don't have to worry about exploitation hidden behind economic necessity the way Jessie did, Love. You can try that out. Why not, Sweetheart? You know which are the student run shops, and you can apply for the next opening. You learn how to run a business and how to judge good merchandise, and you do some travel for buying. It could be a good education for you."

Cassandra grinned, "I did apply, Uncle Benjamin. My teacher said she'd know my date for working there by the end of this week." She laughed, "My teacher said I had a romantic picture of working in a shop. She says there's lots to learn there . All the merchandising and book keeping, and finding supplies, etc. She said that I'd have to work with older students until I learned enough." She seemed confident and the notion was still exciting to her.

Jessie laughed, "In my childhood, you would have been given a job as salesman. You love to talk to people and you have a way, a kind of charisma that goes with the role. You can persuade and convince others."

Cassandra grimaced, "My Master Teacher already told me that. She says it's the chief thing I must learn. How to take responsibility, because that talent can be so easily misused. I don't know exactly what she meant."

Jerry slid back his plate, "Oh, yes you do! You must remember that there are people who want to persuade others without regard to what is for their welfare. But worse, you know that you meet people now and then who take advantage of another persons laziness or weakness, or even ignorance." He sounded angry. "That's what we mean by responsibility."

Jessie's sigh was almost inaudible, "Jerry, she lives with a different kind of people. The caution is not amiss, but there are few today who would be so influenced. We are not the same people that my parents were even. You MUST know that. Yet you refuse to acknowledge it." He looked puzzled and she frowned, then went on, "Surely, all of you, you must see that. We aren't the same people. Our very attitudes are different. We think differently, our values are different." She looked around and then with a faint touch of amused exasperation noticeable, she asked, "Don't you all know these things?"

They looked sheepishly at one another, Rose frowned, nodded, then shook her head, "Well, if we are truly different, wouldn't it be hard for us to see that? To compare?"

Jessie stared at her a moment and then laughed, "Of course. It does depend on a comparison. And that's so easy for me. But look at people like our friend Henry. He would be seen as a normal man in my time."

"Tell us then! What is the difference?"

" Yes, that might help. For one thing, People today would laugh at an old time salesman. We wouldn't be responsive to him or her. That was already changing in my time. Sale people had to be so much more subtle. But today, people won't be persuaded against their better judgement and we have been taught, we practice from childhood to carefully evaluate ideas, goods, works of art, a good glass of wine, whatever we've valued. We know ourselves, we know the patterns that pull us to old desires and some know that if we succumb to a persuasion it's because we want to. We know ourselves! Perhaps that's the most crucial fact. But we also know one another more deeply. How can one who Mind Links, who senses anothers intentions and emotions, be seduced to what he does not want,or think? We pride ourselves on being able to make conscious choices.But more, the sense of responsbility for one another is great. We dispise one who takes advantage of another's weakness even in business.A person who did that would be filled with self disgust today."

But aren't there weak minds that can be convinced by stronger minds just as in the past?" Jerry persisted.

Jessie was silent for such a long time that they began to wonder whether she had heard. Then, sadly she nodded, "There is always difference. It is still possible that there are those irresponsible to others too .It was once the greatest fear of my life. Certainly one able to sustain a strong Joining could use that Talent to dissuade others, or to lead them to his own interests. He could do terrible harm. Because you're right, there are still a percentage of people who want to be dependant, who will allow persuasion against their better judgement."

Rose broke in,"But Jessie, any person who can mind touch would see such an intention. We haven't given that Talent enough credit for reducing crime in the Valley."

"I worry about those who do not Reach, or Touch. . Those unable to defend themselves. After all, you know the early expression of that Talent was called charissma, or called a 'silver tongue'. It did persuade and only the ideals and ethics of the leader saved us. In the old days ethics were based on getting what you wanted."

"We have some protection, we have all been taught. We know better. Valley Convictions are deep in our nature now, they're second nature." Silvia spoke with the force of one hoping to convince herself.

Jessie was nodding ,"You trust that honor, that the Convictions are stronger than human greed. I hope it is so and it may be in this new day. It is what we trust will bring us safely through this time. Transitions are always troubled times."

"My father said that new creative ideas were actually suppressed bcause they would disrupt the status quo in business. A useable air car was developed and suppressed many generations before we built ours. The automobile industry would have been devastated. Or so they thought. Hundreds of other ideas were squelched in fear of economic disruption to a major industry. Solar power went begging for decades. He thought it was that kind of subtle suppression that brought about the explosion when finally the world monetary crash occurred. He believed you cannot hold down creative thought forever. They had thought atomic bombs or worse would destroy society. But you know it was world wide protest of the inequalities in opportunity and refusal to be exploited anymore, that did it! An early awakening of humankind was to economic reality." She grimaced, flung out one hand," That and a clear recognition of how we had been treating one another. It was a painful recognition. Then there was REAL disruption..The changes came so swiftly then, My Dad said, that institutions - and people - had been built on rigidity and couldn't give enough to adjust. They hadn't left themselves room for change within themselves."

Rose got up to refill her cup and get an apple. "We simply don't think the way our grandparents did."

Steve was watching her, his eyes heavy lidded, his big work roughened hands clasped across his daughters waist, she dozed against his shoulder."You mean most of us don't".

There was silence again,sudden and abrupt. No one even shifted about, it was as though they froze in place. Jessie finally spoke out of the quiet."That's true. Exactly that."

Rose's face was full of a dawning understanding," You mean that even though we value every life, we can still be filled with contempt for anyone less conscious." She said the words with obvious pain.

"The measure of our growth, of our consiousness is given by that refusal of all contempt, or fear either.An innate compassion is one sign of an unfolding Mind." Jessie looked seriously at each of them. "When Builders imagine the empire they would build,they imagine one controlled by each one. Each imagines himself or herself in power and with the greatest wealth. Of course, each imagines that power to be used with some compassion, for we have taught compassion to all our children."

"Compassion of that kind can result in benevolent dictatorships. No modern mind-aware citizen would allow such thoughts to survive an hour. They are narrow and self indulgent at heart." Jerry spoke angrily, aware that his anger hid his own similar thoughts."I've watched how insidious such notions can be.That,I, myself, could run this world. And how I'd do it!" He shook his head and suddenly laughed."It's a seductive notion."

"Well, there's the other end of it, you know."Anna's voice seemed light and young in the room,grief filled her eyes, strange sudden grief that the others did not understand because her mind shield was clearly visible." When we want to set out a space, a country, a farm, and completely control it, keep others out, only allow our personal life to be lived there, then we act the way animals do. How do we know we have a greater capacity? Have human beings ever really transcended animal behavior except in style? In variety? How do we differ from the animals?" She sighed and shook her head. "Can we be more?"

Jerry looked at her in surprise. "Honey, you sometimes come up with surprising observations. It's true. And so obvious we don't think of it. We are animals. All of us. We have highly developed minds, but they have minds that are developing also." He saw her look of gratitude as he turned to Jessie. "You're teaching us that human's are capable of something truly more advanced in consciousness? Something even beyond thought?"

They sat contemplating the idea and its reverberations, and then Rose said thoughtfully, "It's caught the attention of more than one philosopher, that our differences are minor. We still live in caves, though ours are refined and polished, we still gather in hives or packs, and we were recently still fighting each other over food. We make nesting places, whether one family or a nation and we fight to keep others out. We haven't seen a greater pattern for living in our past." She frowned, and drew a long breath,"There is difference in us, Jessie, difference in our very hearts. We are becoming something OTHER than animal!"

"Then what is it? How are we different?" Jessie prodded.

Rose stared at her, frowning, trying to think, "What each one of us keeps realizing and entering into. What we've all experienced and been unable to 'think' about at least while we realized it. The spark of Spirit in us, awakened, is transforming us. We are whatever Spirit is!" She stopped and then her eyes falling to her hands, said so tly. "It has to be that!" There was silence, they absorbed that idea.

After a while Ben said,"I saw Rob bringing in the sheep this spring. Organized, working with his gang of dogs, all of them handling the sheep with care and gentleness and bringing them into the barns for shearing. They knew the ones for town and for us. They were remarkable. Change is happening in them too. I thought their intelligence is greater than ever in human history. But human beings have had something to do with that increase in intelligence." He turned to Jerry,"What happened Jerry, when you sent Rob out for your stallion?"

Jerry grinned, "That was the day of that bad storm. Rob went early and the storm got so bad he finally came in. He told me that Berne would be in later. I was skeptical, thought I'd misunderstood. I've never known him to carry such a message. But before night fell, and the storm was really bad, there he was, standing just in the barn door, sheltered,and looking smug. And behind him, eating quietly the hay he'd got for them by pushing the lever I taught him to use, were all his mares. I couldn't have been so surprised. They'd come for shelter and safety in that storm. And two were close to dropping colts and they stayed for that. Surely, you can't deny animals aren't developing too. It's true. But the change in humankind is another thing. You used that word 'transforming'. I think it's true." He was nodding, a far look in his eye.

Jessie nodded, frowned a moment then said gently,"When you say that we are Spirit you suggest Spirit is something separate. Isn't all life also Spirit? Perhaps the more conscious we are, the more Spirit can transform our nature toward what is greater, finer. We know we have minds and can use them. Animals are not that self aware. But now, we begin to know we are Spirit and can live as such. Which makes us Self aware. A much higher level. We've said this before. We must remember.!"

Our ancestors, a billion or so years ago had no idea what their waking self awareness would lead to. Certainly they could not have imagined our modern civilization. We cannot imagine what we are becoming. The nature of Spirit baffles us. Just as the nature of the intellect baffled primitive people. A person with an early good intellect could think of things and so understand things that seemed magical to the others. So they were leaders." They were silent, thinking of what she'd said.

Then Jerry said,"I think we've got to understand that difference. Use it. Practice that awareness, if we are to meet this crisis in our Valley." Jerry's voice came in a whisper, but clearly heard. They began slowly, one by one to Reach,extending flickering tendrils of mind to Touch, linger, include. There were none who resisted. Each one slowly focussed and Reached, and was drawn gently into the whole mental radiance. The power of that melding lifted them. It revealed to them depths of a Universal consciousness that swept through them,extended beyond their united awareness, but left a brilliant trail of light pointing the way to their own new path. There WERE other dimensions.

Out of those depths a new knowledge waked them to itself. Troubled them, with responsibility, and a necessity for steady committment. yet, it also filled them with a tender Joy that nourished them as they had not felt nourished before. For some time there was silence.The conversation seemed ended, redundant. This realization, this awakening as a group,seemed as holy to them as a prayer. They each felt reluctant to break the beauty of that moment. Rose murmured the idea over,"We can't imagine what we are becoming."

After some time, Ben looked over and met Jessie's eyes, his own full of love. Steve nudged Ben, and when he turned to follow Steves pointing finger, he saw Cassandra, now in a large chair where she could curl up easily,and sound asleep. Her body, relaxed, seemed poured into the soft chair. Steve was smiling, but Benjamin grinned. He saw that Cassandra was not there in that body.

Anna looked speculatively from Rose to Benjamin, then said,"Have you noticed that Cassandra does that rather often now?" She waited, but except for a look of surprise, no one interrupted,"At least four times this week I've found her slumped in some odd corner chair, sound asleep. Do you wonder at that?"

Rose was watching Anna closely, Jessie smiled, and nodded to Anna.This too needed talking about. Steve responded with a worried frown. "But Anna, I know she's been getting to bed early and she sleeps the night through. How can she be so tired.You think something's wrong?"

Anna went on, continuing to watch the response. "The other day she was asleep in the film room. I thought that strange because she'd gone with Doug and Gary to review early American cities for a history paper they're writing together. They plan to enter it in the children's essay contests at Fall Festival and they 've been excited about it, so I was surprised she'd go to sleep.I thought too that something must be wrong, so I - I Reached a little." She stopped, as if embarraassed. "Well, what do you think?"

Steve looked quickly at Anna, then at his daughter, a new concern in his eyes. Ben met Anna's eyes, knowing more, Rose swiftly met Anna's eyes too, then as swiftly studied Cassandra.And caught her breath in surprise. Anna grinned in relief and pleasure at having brought them astonishment. Rose said,

THE JOURNEY

"Cassandra, Cassandra, hey, come on back, Honey."

Andrew moved in his seat, watching, his eyes flickering from one to the other, Rose was suddenly smiling. She felt delight, wondering how Steve would handle it. Or Silvia, or even Jane? What would they feel? She was abruptly aware that her own children knew well this skill, that they had not been fooled by her own travels. The knowledge seemed to come with an apology and she gulped.

Cassandra lifted her head, focussed her eyes and looked around. A sheepish smile met them. She could see that her father was worried and she knew he did not understand what she had done. She wondered whether it had been smart to do this here while the family was together. But it had seemed the only way she knew to make them see. She wanted to have the others close so that her father would have their support and so would she. She looked at Anna and Anthony. They at least could help her. Then she looked around, met Rose's eyes, surprised to see an amused loving smile, and at Ben. He didn't seem so accepting but he KNEW. She saw approval in Jessie's face.

She said, "Daddy it's just that I got tired of trying to move my whole body and some of the kids were leaving their bodies behind. They said it was better, more interesting. Some of them play games with this, and I don't know whether that's good or not, but I don't, at least I haven't. I wanted to ask about it." Her words tumbled over one another.

Jessie was smiling like a proud mother might whose seen her child take a first step. "She's done exactly what she says, Steve. She's learned how to fly only in a more sensible way. Maybe if the others who do this will confess to the family, then it will not seem so strange. Will you just raise your hands to acknowledge?" There was a gasp from the others as four hands lifted, then another. Jerry seemed reluctant, but then he grinned and nodded. Silvia looked around quietly but simply nodded her head. She understood finally how this fit into some things that had puzzled her.

Steve was angry, "Why hasn't anyone said anything?"

Rose shrugged, "Oh, Steve, it's the same as with so much else we've not talked about. I've glad we've begun to talk. It's time. We've let the business of building this Valley absorb us far too much. I surely haven't told you of the struggles I've had. I'm sure all of us have suffered for our silence, our secrecy. I didn't even notice my own children, because to do so would've meant I had to admit to myself what I only half accepted. Surely I couldn't imagine children doing such things. I thought I was abnormal. I am so sorry. How could I have been so blind. I could've prevented a lot of the pain I felt and surely our children would have benefitted by having a mother they could talk to". She seemed so contrite that Anna wanted to go to comfort her.

Jessie smiled, "You and Ben are still thinking of these young people as children in that old sense. Shake yourselves loose. Realize what they are! What you are! The Valley's not the place for any more refusal. You speak of acceptance of Spirit, of normal Spiritual nature, Self Consciousness, well, look about you. This business of leaving the body to extend into the astral dimension is part of a developing mental power. It is something that happens because we are more sensitive, aware. It is a result of expanding consciousness, not its cause. Even so, each acceptance brings further vision. You've got to stop denial. We've got a lot of work to do. The Valley needs your clearest vision." She suddenly spoke a short phrase in that Voice of power, and her face was stern."Now attend to it."

The order fell like blow against their attention. Breaking old fibers of habit. Rose felt it rip loose reluctance. She bent toward Jessie, her eyes clear, her mind opening, freshened, as though a breeze blew through, dislodging dust of dissolving habits. She Reached and felt Benjamin's struggle, felt his pull to break away from himself, He resisted but the Will that Jessie had set among them would not budge. He railed against it, afraid,and suddenly the edge of that fear was lit by such an overwhelming flow of Love that it was liquid Light pouring into him. It flooded his mind, rose like a fountain out of his own exultant heart. He could recognize. He could accept himself. He felt his mind clear, as if a curtain had been dropped away. Awed, he was silent.

Anna and Andrew held their attention joined in that flow of penetrating Love, that influx of power that dissolved fear. For that Love rose from their own hearts, and Jessie had only unlocked it with the powerful flow to them through herself. They held steady,allowed and received. Tears filled their eyes. Tears of Joy and relief. Darkness seemed pushed away, out of this circle that was their family.

With great tenderness, they felt their circle growing, felt it flame into greater Light. It was a tide that swept into then through them.Jessie focussed it. Where did it come from? What source brought that unbelieveable tide of Love Itself into their midst? Slowly they acknowledged that the tide rose from their own awakened and Loving Hearts. The living Spirit that was their Heart nature, was the source of the flowing Love that was not 'theirs' but was Life Itself flowing through them.

Then it was that Silvia was drawn to them, the blindness of her mind ended. The power of this energy broke that barrier. She Reached out, tremulous, but clear, and Touched with pure awareness.

After some time, during which they realized and accepted, Cassandra stirred, stood up and said,"Well, I guess I thought I was pretty smart and I wasn't so smart after all." She looked disappointed but there was a gleam of amusement at herself that made Jessie laugh, and turn to Rose.

Rose met Jessie's eyes, and said,"Tell us about that Cassandra.About what it's like for you. You are mighty young to be doing such things,you know." Her familiar warm, loving smile gave the little girl courage. Her face cleared and was full of eager excitement. She could tell the whole story after all.

"I tried and tried to lift myself, my whole body. But it was such a struggle and it wasn't working. I just don't have enough Talent. I can move little things, but no more. And Anna and Andrew said I might get hurt anyway. So then one day, I was lying in my room just thinking about all that, and I could see the western hills, up into the coastal mountains, and I began to imagine myself there, It was so real,I could feel the trees, see the shade under them, I found a trail that ran among the deep leaves and ferns, and I found a little cave, clean and empty.It was really empty, and I went in. Then, suddenly I knew that this was not imagining, it was real. I was there and then I got scared, because I didn't know how I got there, and I looked at myself, and then I saw that I was not solid, like my body is,but different. I don't know how to say it. Then I felt more scared and suddenly I was back here, inside my body and home. And I knew that I had left it and gone on that trip." She grinned proudly at them.

"Didn't you wonder how you did it?"

"Oh, yes, once I relaxed and thought. It was so scary at first. Then I tried some things, and then I talked to Anna, and then I tried again, and pretty soon, I knew how to do that when I wanted to." She looked around, and then with hesitation,she added,"I don't like to travel in that strange world though.It's a different place, strange things happen and the people are odd. Some just smiled at me, some looked at me as if they thought I shouldn't be there. But they wouldn't talk."

"Or maybe you couldn't hear them?"

Her eyes narrowed, she frowned and then nodded,"Yeah, I think that's it. Like I couldn't quite hear.Like there was something between us, that I could see through easily but it wouldn't open up." She was nodding emphatically now, her eyes distant with the memory. "Anyway,I don't need to talk to them.I don't want to go too far. I just want to see this world through the astral light. I can't make my eyes shift well enough to see that way except when I really try to focus." She spoke as matter of factly as any child puzzling out a new problem.

Rose laughed,"I never thought of it that way, Sweety, but it's exactly right,isn't it. You have to shift your vision in a certain way to be aware of that Astral world while you're here.Being out of body in this world makes it much easier. Going to visit people who can't see you is risky though."

Jessie was laughing and shaking her head,"When I was her age,if I'd admitted to such talent and anyone thought I was still sane, I would have been used only for military secrets, to spy."She turned attention back to Cassie. "Do you do this often,child?"

Cassandra shrugged,"No, actually Mother, I don't. I tried doing it around here a few times because I wanted someone to notice.But I don't really do it often. I have too much to do." She did not notice the expression of relief on Jessie's face.

Rose nodded,"That's good, after all, it's this life we're here to manage, not that next one." After a second of thought,Cassandra's puzzled look shifted to understanding.Rose went on,"It's important that you realize that yourself."

Steve was still staring at his daughter with amazement and he finally said,"Honey, I don't know much of what you've done. It seems strange to me but I wish that you'd not do it."

She smiled at him, pleased to hear his concern,"I won't Daddy.I don't really have time, but I want to practice now and then just to explore things."

He was still worried,"Would you, at least talk to Rose maybe about it when you do? I'd feel better."

She was on the verge of arguing, how could it matter, when she caught Rose's eye and stopped,"Well, O.K. Dad. If it'll make you feel better, I suppose I can." Her high handed manner of agreement got a frown from Steve but smiles from both Anna and Andrew. Then, still beaming with satisfaction at the success of her surprise, she went to Steve and kissed him. He took her hand and drew her near.

Out the window the sky was changing, clouds gathered and swept swiftly across the open blue, promising a shower, but little more. Jessie said, "We still go by old assumptions even though we're thinking of new recognitions. The Spirit is sharply alive in us,is always alive, we know that. We still don't know how to describe that Presence. Yet we are also over whelmed by a little far vision, and a single extension into one other dimension. How will the people understand the depths of Spirit,the Sacred Universe alive with vivid color, stately dance, orderly movement of cosmic proportions, that includes everything that is! How begin to understand that when they are non-plussed by talents cropping up,especially in children? How can adults learn to acknowledge all that touches us, even though they are afraid?"

Silvia spoke frowning, realizing at this moment more than she had ever realized,"That is exactly what the artists in our Valley are speaking of, the paintings, the music, the sculpture. I've felt it, but never actually identified it. That's exactly it, Jessie!" She was excited at discovery,"Remember what the Video News art critic said at last Festival? Dodge Hunter said, 'Our artists depict a stable and numinous equilibrium, surrounding and infusing ever changing world patterns.'Look, yonder!" She pointed a finger at two paintings hung along the inner wall of the room.

They all turned to look, seeing as if anew those familiar paintings by a Santiago artist. Startled eyes were turned on Silvia, but eager for them to see what she saw, she went on, "The changing of appearances is exposed for what it is. We too, are exposed for what we are. And remember Annette's last symphony. It caught us all in surprise, fascinated, but left most of us lost, wondering what it was that burned in our hearts when we listened. There! Some felt disturbed, some felt wonder, but nobody was unmoved. And we didn't know then." She looked around at them, wanting to see their recognition to support her own.

Benjamin said, "Neither did she, I think. At least, not then." They were silent, taking all that in. Ben went on, "I'm going to take a new look at our art, and at our poetry too. It's there,Silvia. You're right. It's there! That recognition, and we do know it at the edges of our minds." After a moment he shook his head, "You asked how adults can begin to See, Jessie. Well, that's one way.But we'll need the help of all the Master Teachers of the Learning Centers all over the Valley. You've already got them teaching, Jessie, but they don't reach those who don't come to listen. Can't we ask them for other kinds of help?"

Jessie nodded,"I've done so. They're calling extra Gatherings in each of the towns they serve in these next two weeks. and there will be at least one Monitor contact. But they don't really need Monitor help with this."

"You've already asked? Already talked to them of it? Jane was startled,"But Jessie, have you always known that - that people could do these things, had these Talents?"

"It was obvious to anyone really noticing. It would have been obvious to you all had you admitted to it." She did not smile, but looked at them seriously.

"But that other? That recognition of that Presence - of Spirit. Have you known, seen, always?"

She shook her head, "No, although I was first perceptive of what is called mystic experience when I was a child. Then I thought it natural, I did not know it was different. But it made me watchful for that Presence in everything else. And so I began to See, to know that It is always present. Omnipresent, in fact!" Then she stood and went to the windows, watching the rapidly shifting sky,"Look our Mother the Earth and our Father the Sky, are combining forces to bring us storm. They too must balance forces in themselves. Clouds are gathering like anger, and roaring in as if they cannot wait to dump their rain on us. It's going to be a wildstorm but very little rain this time." Her eyes when she turned back to them were intent, wanting them to notice that violence of wind and water joined to bring new life into this Valley."We do need that rain, you know." She looked penetratingly at them each one,"The clouds darken the land, the powerful winds may rip leaves down, may even break weak branches from the trees, but in the end, the storm will renew our land." And Rose shivered.

CHAPTER FIVE

Discoveries for Benjamin

Where Great Highway branched toward the south Valley west of Bend into the foothills of the Coastal mountains, a vagabond family traveled. Winding through deep rolling forest and dense grasses of wild meadows, the tight low grass of the roadway showed no sign that another family had passed this way for weeks. It was, for Deborah, as she sat in the low bench of the Slow Cart a most beautiful land. Every curve of the road exposed a new vista, every shadowed section of woodland held in it small worlds of hidden glens, crystal streams, small unexpected pools, or even high meadows where little lakes had gathered before spilling down in swift cataracts over exposed rock. Another time, she might look through an opening between steep hills out over wide miles of open grassland, and then climb again where dark entrances to caves were half hidden behind thick stands of shrubs and trees. The cart moved with a gentle rumble, and she felt the frustration of the sprained knee that made it necessary for her to sit today. The Clan Healer had met them when they called, and had given her a True Healing. It was so much improved, there was almost no pain but she must give it another day to finish the Healing. Adam strode as always there beyond, walking the hills and vales with never dulled eagerness to see again what was beyond.

They had not traveled this Road often. But lately, Adam seemed to want to travel the little side roads more and more. She enjoyed it, the change, the new scenery. But she thought some deeper reason brought him here on the road that eventually would wind all the way through the Coastal mountains to the Coast. They were only a few miles from Afton. She would enjoy seeing the mills there where half the Valley Glasteel was manufactured. Barnes produced the rest and was a strong competitor but Afton had the advantage of being only a few miles east of fine coastal sands for the melting vats, and even less distance from Glemma's iron ore to the north. She pictured Afton from memory in her mind and smiled. For a manufacturing town, it was clean and built up and down small ridges of this wrinkled land. Streets edged with trees and shrubs wound around houses up the steep hillsides and leveled out on the highest ridges. At the base of the hills, by the wide creek that emptied far to the south into Green River, was one curving wall of multi- story apartment buildings, and another along the flat topped ridges. They were all painted with a rainbow of pastel colors, their balconies bright with flower boxes. It could have been a village of old Europe. She thought she had rarely seen a more picturesque town than Afton and wondered what changes it might have made since their last visit.

Adam, stopped, waited until the cart caught up then whistled to the tall young people ahead to come back for a lunch stop. He reached out a hand to draw Stacy and Kit, who had been pacing the cart, toward him. The couple, already

THE JOURNEY

entering their seventies, walked with the straight stride of young people, but they were slower. They laughed at him,"Ah, Adam, we've not held you up, have we?" Adam smiled, shaking his head. They needed no reassurance. He had noticed that when people reached the ending of their fifties,it took several years for the transition from middle age to old age to occur.Years when there must be an adjustment to new limits. But neither of these needed help with that adjustment. Their minds were so full of the deep thought, the Vision was radiant in their eyes, They entered these years with an accumulation of tolerance, of knowledge and purpose, of suffering, of joy and sorrow and of struggles to define the relationships that made their lives have meaning. Adam thought it all added up to wisdom and he valued these two more than they knew. He repeated the old apology,"There's never been a reason for the People of the Way to hurry, you know. We travel but we are not 'going some where'.

Kit laughed,"Well, there it is, Love, you've heard that before. We've got to let it be. If we cannot hold the pace, we can always ride a bit." He turned to his mate,Stacy. She was not tall, and beside him she seemed shorter, beside Adam she seemed slender,small. But her wiry frame was strong, a vigor of movement told of the fire that still burned in this small body. Kit seemed almost cadaverous in his slimness, he stood several inches taller than Adam and everyone knew the power of that lean,body. Age had eroded some of that vitality that had once allowed them to dance, leap down from the clover leaf gathering places doing flips, rolls and turns as they fell, then land in a tucked roll that carried them into another leap and spin. They had been acrobatic dancers seldom bested.Now they could not leap so, but they taught others how.

Stacy's hair, nearly white,had once been reddish gold, and so curly it clung like a cap. Kit's thick mop of grey seemed never to change now that it had got this far from black. Her eyes laughed up at Adam and he knew that she had long met the onset of old age, evaluated it and had decided the gifts out weighed the loss. She was content. But Kit still fought against that restraint that grew from his very flesh. He sometimes could dismiss the loss, knowing that the extensions of his mind more than compensated but he could not forget the joy of the leap, the beauty of a flexible body. The two of them trained acrobats at the Clover Leaf halls. Persistently they sought a young one who could equal their talent, and so far, had not found that one. Stacy thought that when he did, he would accept his own loss.

Now, she stood a moment, watching the receding figures of the young people ahead, children and grandchildren, talking to one another and not aware of the signal Adam had given. She threw back her head, and suddenly, there was the Call. Her voice, husky, full and able to carry further than that distance, was nothing to what it had once been, when she sang in Festival celebrations but it was still a great voice. The young ones stopped, turned and began slowly to come back. Adam felt the power of the Call. The use of Voice in such Calling was not common, and she did it so that it carried more than the message. She threw a power of Love that raced through her, and the air seemed literally to sparkle with it. He felt an impulse to bow to her and he did so. Deborah, clapped her hands twice, smiling and pleased.

You honor us lady. Such a Call is like a gift."

Stacy seemed a little embarrassed, but shrugged and said,"Well, we'd best be making lunch, or have you got it all done there,Deborah. The cart has some uses, after all."

Deborah held up a plate with a stack of sandwiches on it. "If I could not be useful at all, with this helplessness, I would suffer even more. It was a relief that I could do this."

They moved to the shelter along the road, where heavy carved wood benches made a half circle around a stone fire place. They need not use that fire, but the benches would be welcome. The two young men, three women and two children who came striding up clustered around the plates. Adam brought bowls of fruit to set on the stone, and cups of cold teas.They gathered to eat.

Jed, one of those who had been walking ahead, oldest of the men, and an adopted son who grew up in Brandhover, until he made his choice, took a few bites, then stopped, "There ahead, Adam, there's a deep vale beneath that hill where a little creek winds down and fills it, remember the swamp that was there? Just small enough to grow an acre or so of Matta and nourish a covy of ducks each winter. The land above was always fine deep pasture for the wild ones. But now, it's been drowned. Actually drowned, Adam. The fields above the swamp are drowned."

Adam stopped eating, his eyes dark,"Then you're talking of Builder work for nothing else would do it?"

"It looks so", piped up Tod, his young face full of indignation."Grandpapa, how can it be right?" He turned from Kit to Adam, "Adam, shouldn't we make it right?"

Adam could see that Tod wanted to leap into action. to move into that Vale and make things right again and he knew Tod might do just that. He felt a weary urgency to teach this lad what he must learn if he was to live. There seemed so many to teach these days."Tod, it's not for us to interfere until we know more. If the land's been meddled with, then surely we must look into that."

Kit, met his grandson's eyes, a look of pleading in them,"Son, let it be. You've been taught that your Talent must be used with care. Don't let it make a wrong into another wrong."

The boy stared at him a moment, abashed, and then angry,"But are we to do nothing?"

Deborah brought more tea, refilled glasses and said,"Is there anyone living near?"

"I couldn't see." Jed shook his head," We were just barely in sight of the Vale.But you'll see when we go on."

It was only half an hour they kept the lunch time this day, all eager to see what Jed had reported. It took only a few minutes to reach the top of the hill. They stood looking down. There, as Jed had said, were the swamps, and the sloping fields around them, but now a dam was built at the lower edge of the swamp and the land around scraped down to half fill the old swamp so that the water spread over twenty or so dry acres. Where once a deep, century old meadow had been, was the stiff tall stalks of Matta, blooming now, it filled the Vale with its deep purple blossoms and the sharp,sour sweet fragrance. Everybody looked down, the trees along the edges of the meadow were already showing signs of harm from the drowning, some had been felled and pulled back for further cutting and to allow room for more Matta here in these hills. How long had it taken to rebuild this land, these meadows, to get new grasses and legumes planted to begin the renewal of the over pastured hills. There to the left had been a small patch of Oca, a fine root that tasted much like a potato but finer, tender and delicious when the People of the Way stopped here in their travels. It too was gone. Five years ago, at their last visit, Deborah had slipped in to a corner of the field a few Arracacha, large apple sized, vegetables, that tasted like celery and carrots combined in one and yet different from either. Another of the thousands of plants Altos imported from foriegn lands and gave to the Valley. She had hoped that a few might grow but they had flourished and contributed to the dinner of many a traveler. She searched with her eyes and saw only a few forlorn plants clinging inside a rocky upthrust.

They stood looking at the scene, and finally saw the cabins built back in the hillside. Utilizing a large cave, the cabins were set close against the steep banks, butted up against cave entrances. They were neatly built, finely crafted from logs and glasteel,and sealed into the side of the cave wall so that the stone rooms in the hill would be an extension of their homes. They surely had finished and polished that natural stone and shaped the space into pleasant rooms. The idea seemed ingenious, and the small group of houses, so natural there, nestled into the hill, made Adam want suddenly to forget the whole thing. But he knew that they must not.These folk had built and dammed the land without making known their intention. The Valley Law held that all lands half a mile along the Highways and Roads, were to be left clear unless agreements with the People of the Ways had been made. These folk had ignored that Law. Besides, large swamp lands here were going to need constant maintainance since they were not part of the land's shape but had been imposed on it.

Adam turned to Deborah, wanting her response, and she shook her head, a sadness filling her throat too deep to speak, but she Reached and felt their minds respond."There is too much of that, there have been too many fields used without thought. The Valley needs no more Matta fields. Were there need, the River has yet unused wild Matta swamps that could be developed. Swamp's that are part of the normal shape of the land.. But our mills must already ship more than three quarters of the production out Valley. We have all we need, it's a rape of the land when it's for no true need."

"But look! That Matta isn't our river Matta. It's the weaker fiber plant, the disgard from Altos. They want their carpets and draperies to have short life. They say they can create new markets by hiring many artists to make many new designs but such that will last only a few years and must be replaced. They insist on variety and replacement to make great wealth." Jed, spoke softly, he had visited a Builder Gather in the past month, to find out the cause of these sudden new farms.

Stacy laughed,"They don't know their own people. No one will buy. No one wants a design not fine enough to live with for years, nor a fabric poor enough to need replacement in half a life time. They don't know their people."

Jed studied her confident face,"It's possible,that old desire for things can be reborn, can be wakened in us again. To change things in our homes for variety alone?"

"Would you change the walls of our clover leaf Gather place, the color, the tapestry hanging there? Do you ever grow weary of that? A thing done well enough constantly delights the eye."

Jed shook his head, but Elizabeth spoke quietly from behind him,"A thing made with great care is new each time it is seen. And look around you, just as the Earth is new each day. I need make no changes in our tapestries, nor even here in our own rugs or clothes. They were made for ourselves, and they took some time to make. The tapestries take many years. They delight every eye and will for many life times. But our clothes, our carpets, all that we have is made to last generations. How can we want less. The people of the towns, surely they are not less particular of their homes".

Deborah cried out,"But most important, we have no time to keep making things that won't last. We have too much else to busy us, too much of inner learning, of finding the Life, the Spirit. It's a waste of living to repeat simply for no purpose."

"I understand that the purpose is to distract. To entertain. But I ask to distract from what?"

Deborah nodded, "To distract from the press of that very inner Life we seek. It is a way to avoid that Life". She shook her head. " Some of us have entered to deeply into that inner life to be distracted from it." The sorrow in their faces as they saw the drowned fields was deep. They looked at one another, anger kindling in the young folks eyes. But they listened to their elders and were quiet. Then Deborah sighed and said sadly,"And we thought the Valley people were ready for their Journeying. The time of Journeys is near. Are they going to retreat, refuse? How can such a thing be? Many of us have already made that Journey, many are ready."

"You are", Adam, reminded her, "But that doesn't mean everyone is. I fear there might be reason for this hope of the Builders."

Stacy laughed, "Adam, think. Let your heart listen. You will know better. The Valley Life leaps within us all, too many of us, far too many. There is no worry."

He was impatient."Don't be so sure, Stacy. How can you be so sure?"

Adam felt a clutch of sorrow, a strange grip of anger combined with fear, and he attended that feeling, surprised at it. "What do these Builders mean? What is their need? They want what our People have long since lost interest in." He felt them listening, Touching enough to realize his intention. He said aloud,"We must go on, we'll be in Afton soon. There, new crops are coming into fruit. We'll sample the melons. And we'll find out what is happening and maybe we can find some reasons why.

" Elizebeth spoke again,"Father,Tod could, couldn't he?"

Adam sighed, nodding. "He could, I think, empty the water, tunnel beneath the dam and let the water run it's natural way. But they would only be angry and rebuild it. They would be more than ever sure that we are demons. No! It was not their right, but neither is it our right to bring harm to another's place without due work of the Law. Two wrongs don't make a right."

Tod grumbled to himself, for his Talent was just recently known to him, the ability to move and effect the land. He was planning to spend the next two years in Santiago studying Geology, and Archeology, and then another studying with the Earth Teachers among his own people. Those Master Teachers knew the depths of Earth energy and could teach the Way so that he would not harm life in his effects on land and cavern. He had no doubt as to the necessity of that training. He had once seen an untrained 'Mover' and had been appalled at the destruction.

They gathered themselves together, Deborah settled down again and the family continued on their way to Afton.They must wait until the council met to make these choices.

At the Farm, north of Adwin, the Family was gathered for the evening meal. Everyone home again. Everyone talking excitedly about the coming Summer Festival. There was time yet, but preparation was vigorous. The young ones already were planning for Autumn Festival. Anna had been in a rare mood of excitement and was talking more than anyone had heard her in a long time. Rose listened, relieved, she had thought Anna much to quiet these past months.

Anna was laughing and her face seemed so much like a child's that Rose, watching, felt a pang of loss for that little girl. Pleased delight animated her, and she said,"Mom, my friends are planning a play. A satire, it will be, perhaps, a joke, about all our Valley troubles. There're so many and we seem so preoccupied with them. We want to have some fun instead."

Rose felt her swift frown come and go because she wanted to present an accepting face to this child who was too often serious. She glanced at Jessie recognizing her own distrust, "That sounds good. A play is always fun to do. But a satire? Mightn't it be too sensitive a matter just now?"

Andy scowled, muttered,"People've got to get used to these ideas, got to face up to the problems."

Benjamin looked at him, his fork stopped before it reached his mouth, his eyes stern,"Just be careful. A lot of people are having trouble. Emotions are strained!"

Rose spoke thoughtfully, looking now off beyond the room,"I don't know. I remember not long ago, a joke might have tipped me out of my sanity, a joke having to do with --with all that we've had to realize."

Jessie smiled at her,"You mean about the Talents? Or about the Soul awakening that we know is happening. The Valley Wakes! No one can avoid that fact. Is it still frightening?"

Rose was silent, moving the food around on her plate, she suddenly wasn't hungry."It is both perhaps. But then, how can one joke about that Awakening? It is too overwhelming, too new."

Anna grinned,"We've got a term, Mom. You know it but you won't use it. We call it 'Soul Jump'.It means that we're CONSCIOUS! That's the point. People've always thought they were conscious, but they never knew the half of it."

"But you won't joke about that - about Soul Consciousness?"

Andrew laughed, "If we can, we will. We may not be able. Master Teacher Don says that it takes understanding and acceptance to joke. We might have to limit the satire to the Talents. After all, we do understand them pretty well."

Rose nodded warily," Yes,the talents're understandable enough. Joke about them. We need better names, but Soul Jump does sound a bit - extreme, doesn't it? For so long it was just an idea. We need what sounds real!"

Ben finished eating, drank a sip of hot coffee and nodded."Well, the first experiences of -- that 'far perception' rouses so many feelings. Most of us get lost in THAT. We can't help it. I think I confused the emotional storm with the experience itself,the Vision of Light."

Rose sighed and broke in,"Good God, yes! I've been drowned and then spewed up out of that emotional sink so many times I would appreciate knowing how to avoid it altogether. Now we've begun to talk of Spirit, there're students asking questions and how can I answer? I've never avoided the dispair of those times, nor the overwhelming wonder. If I don't know how to meet it all, I've no business teaching anything."

They had forgotten the children, who sat listening quietly, glancing at one another now and then, their minds already Joined, sending silent comments on this conversation and finally smothering their own laughter. They were determined to find a joke in this. But Ben, hearing Rose's plea, turned to her,"You didn't learn how to meet it during your time at the Retreat? I thought that was what that retreat was for."

Rose shook her head,"Oh, I remember the Monitors talking to me about emotional reactions that I must be prepared for, but then they were only ideas.It wasn't until later, at home, that the real experiences began."

Jessie stood up, setting her cup aside,"Then we must learn. I will teach you. We will begin tonight." Her abruptness and efficient recognition surprised all of them. Never before had she spoken of actively teaching them something. Jessie studied them then turned briskly to the Hall." You all know that the time of the Journey is coming near. You must prepare, must be ready! Come, we might as well begin now."

But Anna cried out."You didn't hear what we said at all." Her hurt and anger was clear.

"Oh, but we did, Dear. We just didn't know what to do with it. How can anyone joke about something that's torn their heart so?" Rose was apologetic, she sensed their disappointment. "But then, maybe you young ones can. I'd like to see it happen." She felt more than saw Anna's acceptance. But both the children finished their dinner and came to the Hall with them. It was still light outside, the long days made time stretch. But Anna slid to stretch herself on the floor and Andrew on a couch across the room. They would listen.

And so began that series of formal Teachings. Sometimes others came, sometimes it was only the Family, but the talking continued, the exchange of experience. Understanding grew through focussed attention. The idea of the Journey became real to them, though it was still only an idea. Informal, with questions welcomed and even attempts to make questions out of badly misunderstood experience, they shared their insights, their Touch with that Divine Spirit that illuminated their minds enough to wake them from racial sleep. The teachings became an important weekly activity. Rose listened in astonishment. How strange it sounded, the differences. She had so long thought she was alone, and though that was corrected at the Spring gather, she had assumed that everyone must suffer as she had. Now she knew she must help to ease that suffering where it occurred and encourage those who walked through the barriers without those old fears.

----------- -----------

A few days after this first of these 'Teachings', Ben walked alone into Adwin. The sun was barely risen, and broke fitfully through rolling clouds. He watched the sky, enjoying the beauty of this clearing weather and the cool sharp breeze. Rain had broken the hot spell, and now, cool winds promised another respite.

During the past week he had spent much time in Adwin helping prepare for the Summer Festival. The game fields were carefully mowed, the shopping Mall that took up most of the central Ring of the Business and Civic Center, was decorated as though a party was in progress. Adwin celebration would begin tomorrow. Festival in Santiago had already ended and small towns between were in the midst of their celebration. People who loved the Festivals had already gone to enjoy these neighboring ones.

Bright banners flew above the town Centers. He grinned, looking across the fields to the Town beyond. Flags and embroidered banners were rippling in this mornings wind from the tops of the Ring buildings of every Center in town. He could already hear the music, but he knew it was practice. Bands and orchestras and the Players practiced today in dress rehearsal. He could see the flashing color of boats on the water, some partly decorated already. Boat Racing was popular, dozens were entered and ready. There was one big double deck River Palace, carrying crowds who would have dinner and music and dancing into the night while they drifted along between tree lined banks. The Green River became so busy the fisherman had trouble getting their nets in, and gave up for three days. Runners ran along the Highway, he could see their bright shorts gleaming in the sun. Crowds of them this year, of all ages. He laughed, he had run himself yesterday with Jane and Steve in the rain at twilight time, and had gotten so soaked Rose had thought they would be sick. They had begun to feel chill by ten oclock when dark finally fell and admitted it so that Rose made them get into warm beds and brought hot drinks for the three of them.

Musicians, acrobats, singers, troupes of clowns, performers of all kinds were already roaming the streets and eating everything in sight. People constantly came and went through the small bar in the Market Building and the supply of mead, good wine, coffee, teas, carbonated juices, and a whole lot of other drinks would be well depleted if they didn't finish this Festival soon. He had never seen so many people so excited about a Festival. It was as though they caught at this distraction to take their minds from the troubles of the day.

Yesterday Ben had arranged for the Tents in the paved courts, the small stalls of the bazaars that were already setting up their goods. By tonight most would be ready. Tridimensional Video would record the events. Each town kept its own records. He could see freight cars coming in, bringing special foods, last minute supplies. And there were the lower flying passengers cars bringing in people who followed the Festivals for the fun of it. He wondered how anyone could take time from work or study to entertain themselves at some other town's Festival. Well, maybe they had reason.

He walked down the hill, watching in the distance as teams trooped out onto the acres of practice fields below town. Three or four games could be played at once, but he could see other teams standing watching while they waited their turn. Bright suits created a pattern on the green fields. Crossing the Highway, greeting the people from the gathering of Vagabonds camped along the edge of town, he began the climb up into town. He stopped a moment, turning to see better the rapid change and shifting design of players on the nearest field. It was a game of Tilloc. A game of high speed,, based on careful strategy, could only be won if its teamwork was exemplary. Ben knew, because he played often, that a loose mind-joining of team members was needed. Members cooperated with one another to harmonize the intentions of the opposing team. That harmonizing meant that their configuration could be identified and swept into a different one. Then his own team had to be able to plan a double design, to fool the opposition enough that they would be able to complete their plan before they were found out. It took skills that Ben had not been able to admit to before this summer. Mind blocking and Joining, release and closure, protection and disclosure, all being done so smoothly and in precision that the spectators saw an amazing movement of changing patterns, moving into and out of one another. He began to realize how skilled his team was, how disciplined, as he watched these others.

Ben walked on, odors of the morning rose about him, grasses, early ripening fruits, animals. He could see cattle and deer moving through the deep meadows on low hills. Predators would not be apt to be hunting this late in the day, but watchful deer lifted their heads constantly testing the breeze, alert. He felt himself move, a part of the Earth life, a conscious participant in that greatest of all games. He spoke softly. "The vitality of Life flowing through us all is so great that it is as if every living thing were on the edge of an expansion , a breaking out of old patterns. Not just humankind, but all of Life." He was silent, walking, his senses alert to every nuance of life around him. "We'd better get ourselves ready, because it's happening and we're not ready. Whatever that Journey is, it has to depend on whether we're ready!"

Yes,he had felt a new power this summer. Since Jessie had begun the Teaching Gathers, there was real difference. He blessed her that she had seen to do that.

He felt full of a new and fiery power flowing through his veins and Heart. An electric energy that woke in his mind,and stimulated consciousness. Yes, it was becoming a new world, a new and wonderful world. He stopped, dropping to sit on a blue-grey boulder at the edge of the path.

He drew attention into focus. Calmed body and mind. It took seconds to still himself. Attend! Thoughts came and went like gnats against a sky. If he paid attention to them, they would draw him into their narrow focus. He held steady, letting thought drift away like a scattering of snow. Constant thinking, intent focus in one direction only, to find a conclusion, was like having blinders on. Even though his thinking mind drew ideas from every perspective, it was only one dimension of vision. He knew that more surely now than ever in his life.

Now here, standing open, in this large awareness, thoughts seemed fragile, tiny, incomplete. He could see that there were sets of thought, each one with its own rational. Each defendable. But here, in this detached state, standing back from himself, he saw that thinking mind behind the barrier of its own patterns. A thought flickered through that wide perception. One - he must create language to contain all he knew. He smiled, felt sweat running down his neck and face. He allowed everything,attending everything, aware! Thought drifted unnoticed, he had extended beyond it.

The tide of attention fluxuated. Its ebb and flow brought rhythm. He observed the flow of thought,the sensations, rising and falling within dimensionless stillness. He was not caught by these, but could measure himself thus. The flow carried him away again, extended far beyond senses, and in that reach, Life whispered. With rhythmic retreat an easy humor, amusement, grew. He was a point of perception aware of the Valley world. As though looking through himself he saw the Valley was an extension of himself, of humanity, after all. He was here and it was good. He walked, alert within the skin of his body. The balance shifted. After a while, thoughts drew him,and shaped themselves insistently.

He shook his head,then, nearing the top of the hill. "Something is changing,,something in us. In our minds and hearts. and so we are changing as never before. I feel that and know it is true. Yet I cannot define it at all. It must be true for all people, not just for me. The Valley itself seems different. Is it? Or is it our perception of it? He remembered yesterday during a teaching with Jessie and Rose had said,"Change is like a rising current around us. What can we do?" And Jessie had said, "Go on living your lives the best you know how. And practice the highest point of attention."

Ben smiled when he remembered Rose's reply,"Living our lives at that point IS the steady change, isn't it?" She had turned then to meet his mind,that swift thrust of her responsive Touching was a pure joy to him. He remembered now the power of it,the sense that they were part of a current running Valley wide and deep. He acknowledged, with sober reflection, the slight shrinking away from that very Joy. Why? Surely it could not but be good. Yet there was resistance to growth, to that unknown measure to Life. A faint grief rose and tightened in his throat. There was so much yet to learn.

He stopped walking, stood, remembering the Practice. They did not need to be overwhelmed by the emotions that were so charged.He steadied himself,acknowledged the grief, the anger below it. He focussed thought, Reached higher again, stood at that point where he could watch himself, and saw in amazement how those thoughts had already taken that imprint,that stain of dispair. Surely she's right. One must make the choice. Otherwise, emotion could surge, thoughts cascade full of sorrow, fear, and rouse more of their kind. Surely it was a simple pattern and he could choose to end it. That was the amazing freedom. That he had choice!

He stood with his head bent, his eyes seeing the rich Earth life at his feet, aware, yet slightly separate. He said aloud,"I choose direction and Joy rather than descent into grief. I choose to KNOW, whatever the cost." And he laughed at the success of that fearful part of him in having to add that last phrase.

He Reached, listened and was so implacably there in this point,this place, that he Touched the Life in the grasses of the pathway. It fascinated him. He thought there was no less than a life time of wonder here in this one moment and place.The fact shook him. He heard with a sharpness that astounded him, felt the movement of living beings all around. He extended into them, they into him. And there was stillness so deep that the small sounds of the day flickered like fireflys in sunlight. He attended.

At times little strings of thought rose, sometimes following one another like a shower of dim sparks emitted from old patterns and the tight organization of their limits. That organization broke, loosened and was left in a disruption that hurt. It - reality must reorganize itself and include -- include ---all this?

Well, perhaps! But now, he felt a freedom, a great exultant breath that filled him, extended him beyond himself.His mind seemed to shiver with the immensity of it. He felt as though an envelop had surrounded him,and that envelop was splitting, was broken so that Light shone through. And what was that beyond? That Light? He could not see through that Light. It was as though another universe examined him more than that he examined IT.

Light filtered through his whole being, as though it permeated his flesh, surely permeated his mind. It was a living and breathing Light. He felt himself grow calm, still with this knowledge. It grew in him, overturning the knowledge of his littleness. It exposed him to Himself. He grieved to see himself and at the same time, he exulted to glimpse his Self!

He stood firm, bearing the intensity, the vastness of what he knew and comforted that he did not have to know more. He felt his body grow limp and slide down to lie against the grass.

It seemed strange to him that he must limit himself to that body. Yet, natural too. He was a wind playing free through time and space, penetrating density as if it were empty, then, in its natural course, he sucked swiftly downward and into this small personal self, into a brain-mind too taut with wonder to fully realize it's extension. Shrinking, he withdrew from that Wonder of Light and Life and was Ben lying on the grass overlooking the playing fields. He lay still, staring up at the blue patch of sky just above, the blue allowed his mind room, to let his stillness live in it's depths.

He sighed, letting his mind draw itself into focus, centering on the day, the sounds of people shouting, singing, the thrum of music coming from the Highway, the sound of town life. He sat up, looked around. It was all here. Yes, the world was overlaid with beauty, seemed to glow, as if from some inner Light that he had not seen before. He felt rising within his body something so -- great - so persistent he could not resist. It's surgance upward took his breath. He knew it, and finally with a great sob of relief, he allowed that in-pouring.

This was what Joy could be. It was Joy such as had no cause. He stood, smiling foolishly. He leaped up and laughed, his hands clapping, his body unable to express it's feeling, and all sorts of emotions raced through him, fear, anger, delight, hope, dispair, grief, disbelief, awe, and he drew them into one stillness of wonder. How could Life be so? How could he know all THAT? And THAT was not separate from this! He knew no passage of time, though it seemed afterward as though time had stood still.

Finally, he descended to familiar limits. He sat some time, quietly reviewing all that had happened, wanting to keep hold on it, seal it into his memory, and he knew that he only held the after glow, the remnants of what had really been. One could not hold onto such Wonder. But its effect on his life was permanent, its stretch of his mind was real. He was sure of those facts. Now with quiet steady focus I can See through all the stuff of living. All the littleness, the frustration and resentments of daily life. And I can do this at the point of Life.

"Even this beauty, the wonder of our Valley as I see it now, is like a candle in comparison. We are so small! So small!" His tears still fell unheeded. His body adjusting itself. "I know the difference now, between the old life and this. But I don't sustain awareness. I think it's because I cannot bear to. It's so much!" He shook his head, a grief rising like a knife shaft to part the unceasing flood of Joy, "What is this grief?" He caught his breath, tears overflowing his eyes. Then the answer came as if already there, waiting. "The sorrow is knowing but being unable to bear all I know. It's also letting go of myself as the center of my life drama. A kind of death!" He was silent, drawing deep breaths to bring himself calm. "But the Joy too! It's almost as hard to bear. And what is that?" The answer again was there. "Knowing that there is That!" He shook his head, "So little do I know, and yet, that little is a revolution in my Heart!"

But the knowledge that surged through him, demanded response and rasped at his whole self like a slow changing was - w hat? He attended, his eyes closed, looking in to that knowledge. "It is the necessity to LIVE what I now know, live it so that it is manifest through this life. And I have no idea how to do that! It's something we must do together! For nothing - nothing of Life is separate from anything else." His throat hurt with the pain of that demand, that clear understanding. "It is for us to live what we are becoming, together." After a while he sat up, looked around again.

He shook his head, "What is it that I've seen this day? My grandparents would have called it God,I think. Maybe hid from IT, and I wanted to do just that! Yet I think it's only a glimpse of what might be surroundings of the Eternal. For the Eternal, Life Itself, is more vast than I can know. We do have the glimpse of a promise for all humankind, if we can grow enough to bear it." He was silent. He remembered yesterday, when Jessie had talked to them of that strange pattern of dispair that they recognized, that Rose had asked her about. It came so often just as they were on the verge of perception, just as they resisted, held themselves in refusal, and did not know they were refusing.

At least had not until now. And that dispair was like a slough of despond, into which one fell and was so drowned that nothing else seemed real for as long as it took to struggle out. And that dispair was called depression and it was the refusal to look beyond oneself and to See. The refusal to accept that humankind COULD live so. Live as that knowledge required. That together they were able.

Yet Ben knew, had known for long, that this world, the life of physical living was not enough, not enough at all.So there seemed nothing else. The refusal to meet all that we are. All that Life is. The refusal to live so. "Yes," he said aloud now,"I think that's what has made me so hopeless lately. Yet, even now, when I see as I do, what can I do." He stood up, righted his vision, looked around slowly.

He laughed then, ran like a child back onto the path, and commenced climbing the trail."She said that too" he said aloud as if counciling himself." Just being more aware will be enough. Doing that, we'll live well with Earth, with life here. I didn't think that included me, because I had only begun to See. But now!" He shook his head, he couldn't avoid it. But he need only be calm and pay attention, listen and watch -- watch himself mostly to see what he was doing with his life. He sighed, that task would demand all of his time. He had only to Be Alive -- and be aware of being alive!

"But right now, I want to enjoy, I want to remember and be full of this Joy. I can find it even in the blackest time. Look, at everything -- everything shines out with it. Everything is full of light. The trees are full of a life I've never noticed. They shine, even in the daytime. This impossible magic of life itself is almost too much to bear. Right here in this little, narrow and dark world, even here, it is so full. He was brought about by a whisper of feathers rushing through air and saw a hawk,dive,swift as an arrow, impaling a smaller bird with its claws. He watched the fluttering victim, heard its faint scream and silence. Sobered, he nodded. "Everything fits. Everything, even sorrow. Even death.

He remembered that Paul,Rose,then Jennifer, had told Jessie that the Light

THE JOURNEY

had seemed too much. That sometimes it was painful at first. And she had said that even the wonder of life must be balanced. They had spent their lives learning to balance ordinary emotion, both negative and positive, and now they must learn to balance extraordinary perspective. These might bring utter serenity or pain, or a wonder so great with joy that it hurt in its greatness. The body had to learn to bear such experience.

He started to run, to relieve himself of excitement, to express the joy. He wanted to run away from this fullness, and yet he wanted to hold it in him forever. He ran uphill, feeling his body reach, use its energy fully, the proud strong movement, the different joy of that. He laughed as he topped the slope that brought him to the paved path into town. His face was glistening with sweat, his shirt dark with it.

But he could not deny the Joy, the underlying stream of Joy that seemed now to have taken up its place beneath all else. He must learn to live with this and never forget. He said aloud, "Well, there's a lot to do today. I understand now more than ever why we hear each other talking of 'changing' so often." He had stopped his run, stood at the crossing of paths, on to the Civic Center, the other to the winding way into the residence saddle and then on to the Learning Center. He dropped to a bench, his mind full, his heart aching. "I need to stop and think this through. To let myself tolerate what I realize." He watched himself, aware and gentle.

"My thinking mind shakes itself and demands order, demands explanation like a suspicious monkey who has come upon wonder lying like a jewel in the grass and cannot explain the unceasing light that emanates from it. It is true, when that curtain parts, when the recognition occurs, even without warning, then it is like that found jewel. I have not imagined it, because I could not imagine it. Even now, I couldn't imagine another step or describe that one. I can't even speak of it! It's hard to even think about it. No, I could never have imagined THAT. It makes no sense, it just IS."

"My monkey mind wants to USE that jewel for something. To break it like a nut, or to show it to others and get their admiration. If it won't work for me that way, then I want to deny it. To refuse its reality. Part of me is baffled that I cannot make it 'work' for me, while the rest of me stands utterly delighted in the wonder of real knowledge. I'd rather not speak of it. I feel content not to argue, but content to simply be with it."

Thought of the hawk's kill wove into his mind. "Yes, everything gives up its life that everything can live. There is no choice. Only humankind has choice to be kind or cruel, to create or to destroy. We can protect the helpless from human cruelty, even from massive natural disaster, if we care, or we can refuse and see people drowned, or starved, or worse. We are responsible because we have choice." The idea seemed to burn into his mind. The universe is Good, evil is our denial of Love.

He was filled with the idea, it reverberated through his mind, like something that shifted whole patterns of thought there. "Only humankind can know that it is only the loss of a body when death claims her or him. The tragedy, even the suffering,is so much greater for those unknowing.

He walked slowly into the Civic Center, past the Market screens, glancing idly at the display. He looked around, seeing the town through new eyes, the play of light through the brilliant colored glass in the roofs of the walkways around all the rings of the Civic Center. He heard the noisiness of the outer ring where the colors and smells of the main markets were. The shoppers came and went, people talking and laughing, stopping to eat and talk in the small bright cafes, each unique. He moved across the gardens surrounding the Middle Ring where quieter business was being done, in law offices, adminstrative offices. Through the archway looking outside the outer ring, he could see the new Healing Center nearly done, so rapidly had everyone pitched in to build that important center. It could be ready for dedication at Summer Festival. Well, they were all experienced buiders now, it was no surprise they could put up a building in a few months. People had learned how to work together.

He wanted to be with people just now. He wanted to listen to ordinary talk, settle himself back into this world, accept its limits and let this glory in himself subside a little. "I could say that I must hold this Jewel in my heart, knowing it is too precious to use for mundane things. Too wondrous to show, for perhaps others would not even see it. It is my own Jewel and others must find their own. But I can talk to -- to Jessie." Then the fact of their family committment hit him with renewed relief."But not just Jessie, I can talk to my Family and they will hear."

The realization was so reassuring that he felt as though a second inestimable gift had been given them. "She did that! Jessie did that. She showed us how to meet each other and this new knowledge". Only a year ago he would not have thought to talk of such things to anyone at all. How changed things were already.

He stood a moment, within the center of a small paved court, the fragrance of summer flowers filling the air, and thought,"If I can just live here, using this practical reasoning mind, and feeling 'normal', is that enough? Would I dare? Would I find a way to live this ordinary life and still be aware of all that I know? Could it be done? What would life be like then? How could I manage." He shook himself,people were glancing at him, a few, catching the reflection of his worries, smiled. He was aware but his attention was not on them.

"That,what I just realized, surely it is what is called Soul consciousness. That wider, greater, deeper state. The energies that came flooding in, that lifted me, and that were part of that consciousness, those were energies of Love. They were normal to that Soul conscious state. And the thoughts that grew from that awareness. They were gifts. Surely he must learn to endure that power, and direct himself within it, if he were to live so. To function consciously in this world. In full consciousness. Could that be done? How could he learn enough? BE enough. The sense of well being, of a deep rooted will toward Good, to bring Health, and beauty and Life to every living thing, reaffirmed his committment to the Convictions. "To allow, to nourish, to husband living things and live as though

THE JOURNEY

we're all one Life here! That's it! There's need for profound compassion and I - I don't think I have enough."

Then a strange thought interrupted,"And the Builders want us to drink more, eat more, redecorate our houses,,rebuild our farms, produce and produce. They want us to make money by indulging our neighbors lusts. They want us to -- " He sighed, nodding slowly,"to be what we've always been. How could such things matter anymore."

He stopped thinking, deliberately turned his attention to the gardens, to the people. He felt surrounded by the familiar and it was comforting. He walked on past the market then, into the wide tree filled slopes that were the residential part of Adwin, winding through the paths that led down and gradually flattened out past cluster-homes, through small vegetable gardens enclosed among the blooming hedges. He climbed finally upward again toward the Learning Center. There the practice for the Festival was in full swing. People of all ages crowded into the practice rooms, ran through the courts to playing fields, or down over the steep hill side at the other end to join runners on the Highway. The wordprocessors were all in use, people writing their poetry, essays,stories or reports of their year's studies. The busy hurry of things pleased him. He walked on into the Outer Ring. Bells pealed the morning chimes and he was astonished that so little time had passed.

He saw a small, short man pulling off a sweater. He stood behind some shrubs that were nearly as tall as he was. Dark purple blooms covered the bushes, but clustered among them, were large nuts,already ripening,the smell of them sharp in the clear air.Benjamin called out, "Hey there Henry, it's good to see you. I've wondered where you've been"

Henry turned to look at Benjamin, his face a dark scowl."It's them blazing bells. I never have liked them. Good thing they don't go on at it any longer. I'd never stand it." Then he grinned, tied his sweater by its sleeves around his waist, and walked to meet Ben. "I'm glad you came along, I want to talk a bit". He shifted his glance, watching to notice any change in Ben's expression, any refusal. But Ben smiled, nodded and so he went on."I was gonna go eat. Would you join me?"

Ben nodded, "I've eaten at home but I'll join you for a cup of tea. I eat in town so seldom now that it's a treat to join everyone in the Public Hall." He frowned, aware of his own powerful feelings, the longing to talk of his realization, the resistance to doing it. He noticed Henry was looking better, more relaxed, yet that strained look was still there in his eyes. Would he have even noticed before this morning?

Henry glanced at him as they began their fast walking into the Hall."So it gets lonely at the farm then?"

"Not lonely, I need a lot of solitude, Henry, and I have a large family, you know.But it's good to have a change. " He shrugged,"I've been stuck in the laboratory pretty steadily lately, or else at home, working at the computers there, so I've missed people. I'm glad you were here." Henry glanced at him, surprised, then a slow smile tugged at his mouth,pleased.

They crossed the plaza at the Dining Hall, greeting the swarm of people coming in to breakfast. They found a small alcove that gave them a little privacy and sat down. Henry nodded, satisfied, he didn't want others near. They began punching their order, and got cups of hot tea .Henry looked at his and shoved it back. He changed his order to coffee. Benjamin looked around. People were talking quietly, the tables filling outside the alcove, and the smell of food was good. Henry sat down, sipped from his steaming cup and said,"Do you know how much power you could have in this town. That you already have actually."

Ben looked at him in sheer surprise, and shook his head. Henry went on,"No, don't deny it. You must know it's true. You must know that I've been here long enough to have a fairly clear picture of the conditions. I just can't understand why you haven't done more with this Valley around here. Why Ben, I've sounded out people and they think of you with great respect, an amazing respect. They have the same attitude about Rose. You two could - could - do a lot more than you do." He fixed Ben with a baleful eye and waited.

Henry's breakfast' came through the wall slots and Ben got up to collect it and set the plates before his friend. He felt a strange distance, a mild,calm, attentiveness, as though he watched and listened from a very wide spectrum. He was aware of Henry's intensity, his press of persuasion, and was wary of it. But he was also aware of Henry's lonliness. Some people avoided him and since he would not join any peer group and work out the problem he had with others, it wasn't about to be relieved. He said,"What could we do that we're not doing, Henry?"

An impatience thinned Henry's voice, He thought he must be talking to a man less intelligent than himself,yet how could that be. Every body said Benjamin was a 'brain'. But people in this Valley seemed somewhat obtuse,, generally, he had long since decided."Why the governing and control of the town,would be a starter. This town is just sitting here doing as little as it can. It isn't rich, it isn't building big business with other cities, let alone with the world. Have you seen the fabric you produce? You could make a fortune on that alone. The designs are remarkable. And yet none of you do anything about it!" At Benjamin's start at protest, he raised a hand. "Oh, I know you trade your fabric, I know Adwin makes some money with it, but you could make so much more!" He sighed, waved his hands in a wide gesture then recommenced eating, "But from another angle, you, YOU, Ben, could win an election. You could run for Council and take a top position and run things. You could. I know it. People like you and you're a friendly man."

Ben said,"But we already have a system that works."

"You mean that rotating system in your government. Every town in the Valley insists on that system and it's a crazy system. Where does the power go? How can you build any influence? Why even where I came from we had elections and people stayed in their elected jobs for several years. They had time to get control of things, to build a machine that would go on working after they left office. Don't you see? People here don't seem to have any political sense." He searched

Ben's face, decided he was interested and went on, "We always had a jolly fight every time an election was run. Excitement! Stirs a man's blood."

Ben nodded, his eyes narrowing,"We know there're towns to the north where the old ways dominate still. I've never understood why. They didn't work for the old ones, so why would they work for us? If everybody takes a turn, everybody is involved and knows what's happening and has to be concerned. Corruption is not easy in our system. Everyone knows what's going on and can't be fooled, if someone were foolish enough to try." He looked sharply at Henry, wanting him to see that, but Henry shook his head and went on.

"Just doesn't make sense to me, Ben, never has. But regardless of how you run your town, do you realize that you could develop this whole Valley., It's sitting here waiting for someone to exploit all the possibilities. If you expand Adwin, it could grow into grand city, biggest in the Valley, you know. With all the hills, it'd be a beautiful city too. There're resources, look at the labor possible out of that Vagabond crowd. Offer them something. Offer them fun, life ! There could be road houses along the highway.It's wasted as it is.You've got that Industrial Center, but there's room for another one that could be bigger, a mile in diameter. It'd hold enough industry to make this town equal to Santiago or Bend. I say you could have a dozen more big industries if you got in a good sales force to sell for you." He was excited, thinking that Ben's attentiveness was a sign he was being persuaded.

Ben smiled, "What else d'you have in mind, Henry?"

Henry grinned, his eyes shining, "Why, Ben, this Valley's got room for an empire, and no body seems to notice. You could make Adwin into the richest city in this Valley, maybe in the west. The crazy thing is that when I try to find out who's the power behind things, the one who can pull the strings, I come up empty. And I'm not used to that. I can usually find the hidden power in any city machine. First two years I was here, I tried to pry things out, talked to a lot of people, sat in on the courts, the councils, pried around among the workers in the factorys and the winery,the brewery. You've got only one of each, not selling near as much as you ought to be." He regarded Ben thoughtfully, then went back to his point. "God in Heaven, Man, I couldn't believe it. There doesn't seem to BE any power. It's actually as you say. You ALL do it.And nobody using the power the way it ought to be. How the nobby hell d'you get things done? Who tells you what to do?" He was honestly puzzled, and his face reflected that, but under that, moving beneath that puzzlement was a bitter resentment,and Ben, seeing it, was himself puzzled. The realization was like a jolt to him.

"It's insane, you know. One of these days someone is going to come in here and take over and clean up. You know that. It's like you're a bunch of babies, just waiting for the hatchet." He frowned,"Oh, I don't mean that unkindly, I know you all mean well. In fact, I've never lived with a better bunch of people, anywhere. I like that. But it makes you mighty vulnerable.You don't have any protection at all. None!" He was intense now, leaning forward,, his eyes insistent.

Benjamin felt a flood of emotions and examined them all with a strangely

THE PEOPLE OF THE VALLEY

steady, observing eye. He wondered at his own calm. Yes, there was anger, resentment, piqued pride, and then amusement. Amusement won out, and he felt his body relax. Henry ate for several minutes, now and then shaking his head, glancing at Ben and then shaking it again. After a few minutes, he said in a stage whisper, that nearly set Ben into an explosion of laughter, it seemed so incongrous."I've heard of these Valley Builders. I can't find where they meet, but I plan to talk to them. They sound like sensible people. Do you know who to contact?"

Ben felt a surge of fear, wondered at it and caught it like a bubble that broke. "Yes, we know of them, but you simply have to ask around. They're pretty vocal. They've got into the news a lot lately. Call at the Civic Center and ask for their next meeting. I hear it's going to be telecast." He said it matter of factly.

Henry stopped eating, stared at him. "You mean they don't meet secretly? A group that different? I heard they want to change things around here. I'm for that but I never thought they'd be allowed to. Not openly," His voice dropped to conpiratorial tones.

Ben said, " Come on, Henry. Who's to stop them? You know the Law, every group has a right to be heard. To practice it's ideas. You must know that."

Henry nodded, grinning again,"I've heard that's the law, but I never thought anybody'd be held to it except maybe the poor slob on the street." At Ben's chagrined head shake, he went on."I did hear one name, read it in the news sheet. A William of Altos. Now he sounds like one I need to talk to. Sounded like he was big in that group."

Ben felt his heart lurch, he had never heard William referred to by anyone outside the family as a member of the Builders. This time the feelings rose and choked off the quiet, the amusement. William! Their William,his own family and yet even Henry had heard of him..Ben wanted to deny knowledge , not to tell Henry how to reach William. Wanted to deny to his own heart too. He knew denial was cowardly, and hated it,but did it. He simply said,"I've heard of him." Even as he said the words, he felt himself shrink, the light grow less golden. He struggled for balance.

He wanted to shift the conversation, get Henry on some new tack, wondered at himself. He looked down into the last of his tea, then up at Henry and said,"I think I'm going to have a glass of wine. Just a minute."

Henry held out his credit card, Get one for me to, will you Ben?"

Ben took the card and got their wine. He shook away the surging clamor of questions then, with sudden recognition, listened to himself.'You've got to fortify yourself to hear a simple truth that's unpleasant? Where's the vision gone now,Ben?' He sat in miserable silence, looking down into the glass of ruby wine, knowing his discomfort and refusing to deny it.

Henry was sipping appreciatively, "Wine's pretty good here in Adwin. Best I've found's in Brandhover, though. Their vineyards are on the western slopes of the Valley, get the afternoon sun. D'you buy Brandhover wine?"

Ben nodded curtly, glad the talk had shifted but not wanting to talk about wine either. He glanced again at Henry, whose face was flushed, his body alert, ready to move, like a spring wound. There was still that hovering sense of intrigue, secrecy, in Henry's attitude. That at least brought back Ben's sense of humor. Clearly he realized that the sense of intrigue, secrecy, and the pleasure of manipulating people and events, was a chief attraction of the Builders. And that was exactly what Henry missed. Abruptly, he asked,"Henry, where'd you come from." He sipped his own wine, enjoying the feel of it as it went down, the slow spread of relaxation his body felt. Smiling at himself, he spun the glass in his fingers, watching the wine swirl, waiting.

Henry shook his head, suddenly angry and impatient."What's that got to do with what I'm telling you.?" Ben didn't answer and Henry relaxed a little ,his eyes distant."I was born in Center City, Kansas. the people there aren't quite so ignorant as you folks,but they were beginning to change. I saw it. Leaving the old ways too. I got into too many arguments, but then it wasn't long until the people wouldn't argue. Just looked as if it didn't matter. Like maybe I was daft. I went north,into the far west, and ended up in the land just north of the Valley for a few years. The old ways are still respected there, but the people are too settled for me. I'd done a lot of traveling by then. People in the plains may not be as ignorant as you folks seem to be,but they wouldn't listen to my plans either. I tried to push things a little, I was young then. Some of them didn't like somebody young as I was trying to talk to them about running their town. I left." He shrugged, grinned ruefully, "Funny what makes people think they're always right. Some suggested I go to the rehabilitation center in Arizona. Made me mad. But then, when I began to get into trouble with so many, I thought I ought to look into it." His eyes were bleak, his voice softer,less sure.

"I lived there a couple of years. Rehab! My God! Their ideas were worse than yours. That community's going no where, nobody wants to take over, run things right. Kept teaching us how to work together, they said. Said we'd got to learn the 'Convictions'. Pretty much the same as yours, but I didn't see much sense in learning them. No one was going to pay any attention to them." He leaned his chin on his hand, his eyes distant, remembering.

" Actually, there were some that did! Those Healers did! They were a strange bunch, couldn't rile them even if you insulted them to their faces. I left. It wasn't for me. There were a lot of really crazy people there, you know, Ben. People who really needed help. But me? No, there wasn't much for me. I left!"

Ben nodded, but said nothing, then coming to a decision he asked,"Tell me, Henry, if you were asked to do it, how would you go about developing this Valley? What'd you do exactly?"

Henry's face lit up, his body straightened and he leaned toward Ben, sipping his wine, enjoying himself."It's simple. At first, I'd get some earth movers, and get into those unused lands. Rip down a lot of that forest. We'd sell the timber, to Clandor, or make our own mills. Right now all that timber's wasted. It's wasted! Then, when I had a good few thousand acres of open land, I'd start with grapes. But I'd leave the empty prairie south of Santiago clear. I'd round up the cattle out

THE PEOPLE OF THE VALLEY

of the hills and the sheep. We'd have beef for the world, wool and lamb for sale to supply half the western part of the nation. You folks don't know what you're wasting. All them wild critters huntin' each other out there. Make a game preserve and let hunters come in for a fee. For a FEE, Benjamin! You could make money there too." He sighed, shook his head, looking so sad Ben felt sorry for him.

"It's a shame the way you waste. But the grapes would grow in south Valley you know. Hot summers, dry enough and high hillside slopes. I heard the Builder's want that too, and I agree. We could raise the best and sell wine all over the world. What we got from the timber would pay the cost of getting started. We could make a small profit from the brush even, selling to the paper mills. Leave clean fields ready to be planted. Good land too. Then, there're a couple of other crops we could plant. Get heavy production going and then build a market."

"I can't believe you've not heard the Builders talk. That's nearly the way they think". Ben frowned, amazed.

"Well, that's what I've heard, that's why I want to get into it." He ate a fork full of steaming food, grinning, his eyes shining with pleasure. "But the clean up wouldn't take long. Then we could - "

Ben interrupted, he felt himself drawn out of balance, and frowned, but spoke angrily, "No! Henry, you know no one rips the land anymore. We don't even when we plant. Don't need to. Those big earth movers are museum pieces. Except for the three we keep for emergency in case of bad storms and fallen trees."

Henry shook his head,"Don't matter, it's what I'd do. Go through this Valley, clean it up. Get it into use. I thought of beer once, but I think wine would go better. There's plenty of beer out Valley. All kinds. But not really enough wine."

"Have you ever been unable to get some?"

"No! You don't understand. We've got to make a bigger market, get people to enjoying it more, drinking more. More desire, more sales, more money for us!" He grinned, " There's an old stone outcrop that opens into some fine caves near Denlock. With some finishing and enlarging, they'd make fine storage and aging caverns. Just the right temperature, a wine chemist told me. They already plan to use them, 'one of these days'." He laughed, "Can't you see? People don't know how to exploit the market, build it. People've forgotten! It's your ignorance."

He was staring off into the distance, seeing there his dream."It's the way our great grandfathers did it. Adwin makes wine, yes, and a very good one, but you don't produce more than a few thousand bottles to trade. Same with Denlock. Even Brandhover, hasn't got more than three winerys and they trade out Valley. It's their biggest product. So they could expand a lot." He drew a deep almost trembling breath, "Look, Ben, there in the hills, where you've got all those clovers, and fine grasses growing. We'd put cattle, wouldn't even have to fence, use those wonderful force lines you folks use for your fields." He was excited and Ben listened. Henry would build another market in meat and build a great slaughter house on the outskirts of Adwin. "There're only a few dozen chicken ranchs in the whole Valley, people've forgotten how to eat meat. The ones there are use up hundreds of acres,letting the birds run free over the fields . They could be raised like people used to in stacked cages in ten story buildings and come out faster and easier. Water fowl too. Look at the thousands that never get used. We could supply restaurants and City Processing plants all over the Valley, ship out Valley." He continued, his memories distorted by his own dreams. He would get people involved in advertizing, in making other people want that. And Ben listened silently, his heart heavy. Henry might have actually been an empire builder in the old world. He thought,'Oh,Henry, how can you be so blind.' The irony was that Henry thought that Ben was the blind one.

"Why Ben, there's a whole hunting trade to build out there. Best hunting country in the nation, I bet. People like to travel. You know, people with enough money and nothing to do. It's a natural. We could bring in tourists and the like to hunt. Make a big tourist industry, and that'd need hotels along the Highways, and on hill tops where the view was fine, and that would make a market for our wine and beef, etc. Don't you see? We could change the Valley, make money enough to travel, even to the planets on the new star ships when we wanted to. Build fine homes, all of it." He was smiling now, a big conspiratorial smile."Get enough markets going and you'd have people with a lot of money and nothing to do. Those people like to be entertained. There's the business for Vagabonds. Get those beggers into some real work."

Ben said shortly,"You think people'd want to hunt, just to kill?"

" Why not? They always used to in days gone. We'd need to bring the old days back. When men were men, Ben." Ben heard Henry's voice, his mind probing, like a tongue does a sore tooth, the tenderness of vision that this morning had revealed to him. This talk had brought a screen before that memory, distanced that deep Joy. He felt suddenly desparate to find it again, shook his head to help him rebalance. But it didn't help.

Henry said,"What d'you think?"

Ben nodded slowly,"But Henry, what'd we get from all this? "

Henry's look was a combination of astonishment and dispair. How could Ben not see? But he shifted, enjoying the telling, enjoying describing the wonders possible with enough money. "We'd get rich, Man! We could build mansions, Ben, real mansions, with servants, and with holographic fun rooms. We'd be the important people of the Valley, the ones who started it all. We'd ride in air cars like nobody's got yet,. We'd have people working for us enough to begin a little empire. We could give parties like you never dreamed of, invite people from all over the world. And there're the games, the war games, the Valley needs at least one place for them? Excitement, a new Dream Park and Fantasy Land. My grand folks used to tell about them. It's been so long, but now we could do it! You know, Ben! You HAVE to know! All kinds of excitement and action., This Valley is so dull, today."

Ben sighed,"But building all that, having all those people coming here, to just look at things,eat, drink, entertain themselves with too much of -- of all that, even just to hunt, and kill, wouldn't that ruin our Valley? What of the creatures we have responsibility for, our friends? We've already planted our share of the Valley, the human share. The rest belongs to them, you know. We've got new groves of food trees among the forests."

Henry was distracted,"Yeah, I've seen that new oak forest. Biggest acorns I ever saw. Good too. You can eat them like a nut. How'd you do that?"

"Altos, of course. Took them a while though, we've got several small groves of trees that produce big acorns but not as sweet. Animals eat them. But with these new ones our acorn flour industry is starting to grow. It was a good investment. But to get back, Henry, we've got a committment to all Life, not just ourselves."

Henry made a gesture of impatience, his hands flung up and then slapped down flat on the table, he leaned forward," That's the dangdest thing I've seen in this whole country. And you know that the people back east are getting to be the same way now. That notion that creatures are just like people. I say they're not! Not at all! So we clear them out. Send them back up into the mountains. Who cares? They ought to be in their place. This is our earth,man, not theirs. We can do what we want with it. There's MONEY, POWER, there for the taking,and you'd let a bunch of wild animals stop you? We could be men the whole world would reckon with?"

Ben nodded, he understood that pronoun 'we'. He felt sadness, and helpless to express himself with this man. Then, he drew himself back, rebalancing. The vision of the morning was there, behind everything again. And he felt amusement,an amusement stained with sadness. The whole idea was an anachronism, rising from a time he hoped was gone. He sat looking thoughtfully at Henry while he talked, realizing as he never had before that here was himself as he had been once. All the age old desires personified. The life, the great opening beauty of Heart was hidden away within Henry, just as it had once been in himself. His sorrow was as much for humanity as for Henry and himself. His joy as much for every part of life that would wake, would lift up its head and know, eventually. He said as gently as he could,"Henry, I don't know how to say it, but neither Rose nor I want any power in this Valley. We have every thing we need. What we long for now, is the life that is of the highest Vision that the Valley people begin to know. We don't need power over other people, or over living things anymore.We need to - to open our eyes and remember!"

Henry was too distressed to hear. He went on thoughtfully talking of his plans for several minutes, as if not wanting to believe he had failed again. Then he stopped, heaved a long deep sigh that seemed to come from his legs. "That word you used, Vision, Man there's no reason we can't build Churches. Or use the Temples, but put some chairs in and get a preacher. They seem so empty to me."

Ben shook his head,he thought he'd try one more,"Temples aren't for preaching, Henry, but for finding the Self." At Henry's stare he went on. " Making big markets would be very difficult. People think for themselves. We would have made more wine if we wanted it. We could have told the Hunters to bring in more meat, if we wanted it. To try to convince people they want what they don't want would be the height of idiocy.People have been thinking for themselves for several generations now. Have been taught to do that from childhood. When we

THE JOURNEY

have an election we get ninety percent voting. No nation ever did that before. You can't influence people easily today. To try would be to insult their intelligence."

Henry listened and his face fell, he was instantly full of that old dispair that had become habitual with him. "Oh, Man, Oh, Man, that's just about the same story the others gave me. It just doesn't make sense. I'm tired of hearing it. But nobody else has listened as well as you Benjamin. I'll give you that."

Ben spoke slowly, his eyes distant, "We've begun to know of something so much greater than our selves that when we touch upon it, we lose ourselves to it altogether." He realized that he himself had not thought this out, that he had experienced and accepted and had not yet set into words all that he knew. How could he tell another. And wouldn't that be just another kind of 'religion' if he did? He shook his head."No, Henry, we can't tell you. You have to exprience, you have to See for yourself."

"Henry simply shook his head,"I don't understand, I just don't understand. The whole world seems crazy to me." He jumped to something he did understand a little,"It's too much sentiment. What's wrong with clearing out a few squirrels and foxes?"

Benjamin laughed, choosing between that or anger,"I've said we're an ethical people. It isn't ethical to destroy the natural world for our personal desires. It's that simple, Henry. The Valley is important, its health. Notice how clear our air and water are. We can drink water anywhere it runs. The whole Valley is healthy.It's full of LIFE.There is a creative energy building a healthy world around us, a healthy people and a people who create, think, Love. Don't you see that?"

Henry was sadly shaking his head,"Words, words, just like always. People don't really think, not the average man. They don't want those things. People aren't like that. What you're talking about isn't what people want! You'll see. Ben. One of these days, we'll get it going and you'll see."

Ben sighed, "People don't want to build things that don't last because they don't want to spend their lives doing nothing but building things over again.We don't want more than just enough to keep our bodies healthy. We've got other things to do now, Henry, Don't you understand? OTHER THINGS TO DO!"

Henry was looking down at his empty glass.His eyes pained.He said,"You just don't seem to understand, Ben. You're living in a dream. People aren't like you say they are!"

Benjamin was nonplussed, Henry wasn't hearing at all. And worse, Henry thought Benjamin did not hear. Was that true? Could it be he wasn't hearing Henry either? He sighed wearily and said,"I do live the way I describe. I believe that others do. It's taken us too long to gain control over our lives and we have no desire to have control over other people's lives. I like going out every day knowing I can control my life a little and that other people will control theirs. I don't want to be responsible for hundreds of people working at humdrum jobs that drain away their very spirits, their minds and hearts. I like knowing that other people have the same chance and enjoyment of life that I have. It makes my life infinitely better to know that." He met Henry's eyes, his own intent and almost pleading,"Surely you see that?" Henry sighed again, his eyes suddenly moist. He stood up so abruptly it startled Ben, stood for a second, then sank tiredly into his chair,"Then I guess there's no use at all."

Ben was puzzled,"No use?"

"No use to keep hoping that we can make it like the old days."

Ben nodded, understanding his disappointment,"I don't know what to do, Henry. Surely there is work you'd like among us."

Henry was staring off into space,and he spoke as if from an old dream,"You see, my family were some of those who held onto the old ways and I know how they thought.My old man used to tell me how I could get things in control some day. He said people were ripe for a change. He said people were like sheep,you just had to get them turned the right way. But maybe he was wrong after all. People today already seem changed, they just don't have the old drives. They've lost them. Just look at you. You don't WANT to run the world. I'll bet you don't even run your own family? Well,I think this town was my last try. I've tried too long. And if it isn't going to work, then -then -" he dropped his head to hide tears of frustration. "then I don't know what to do".

Ben leaned to him,wishing he had Healers Talent,"Wait,Henry, there is something for you." He knew he must help Henry now, immediately, if he were to be helped. He could not let him rush out to deal with his dispair alone."Henry, there's something right here in Adwin that needs your special talents. Just as you've told me. Someone with a strong head for organization. If you think you'd like to try to I could arrange for you to see the town manager and I know he'd agree."

Henry's misery twisted his face, and for a moment Ben thought he had not heard, then with a visible pulling of himself back to the moment, he drew a long breath, frowned and asked, "What kind of job would that be?"

Ben searched his mind to find a proper title,"Well, it's the job of - of Administrator of Supplies. The name didn't seem right but it was the best he could do for the moment. "We need a man to organize and arrange all the incoming products, raw materials for the mills and farm equipment, office equipment market goods for the street markets, and supplies for cafe's restaurants, library, public kitchens and food procesers, -- there're a million things a town needs to function right and we've been getting along with business training students. They're pretty good but we need someone to coordinate the whole thing. The town's finished, we're starting full production. Someone has to see that it's smoothly run. Someone who knows how to take charge of things." He began to worry as to whether Henry had ability for the work after all. Another failure would finish him.

"You have computers already in use.?" Suddenly Henry was all business, Ben felt relief like a cool breeze. "You've got someone whose been doing this, to get me started?" An edge of unease in his voice. Ben's mind raced, He'd have to talk to several people fast.

" We have both and they'd be glad to get you started."

Henry's eyes lost that terrible bleak look,"Well, how do I go about getting into this work. It sounds like it might be something I could do for a while at least. After all,I've got to do something. I'll got crazy if I don't."

Ben started to say, "Why all you do is go down to the city Hall and talk to Mayor Tom and he'll take you over and get you started . "But he stopped himself, he realized that he had to play this game Henry's way. He said,"I'll go put in a word for you with the Mayor. I've got some business with him anyway, and I'll meet you here again at noon. You can do business with Tom, he's a good man. Very sensible." He squirmed, he never felt good in a drama of this kind. One part of his mind resented having to dissemble. But Henry's response was enough to reward him for the effort. His face lit up, he understood that kind of action.

"Good, you put the word in. I told you that you had influence around here. And I'll be here. I've nothing much else to do anyway." The last phrase in a forlorn, lost tone that both amused and disgusted Ben. This man had to be rehabilitated and a job was the first step,in his opinion. He'd talk to the Healers though, they needed to find a way to talk to him too.

So Ben left Henry to go and find Tom. He had not seen his friend for two weeks and was looking forward to good talk. He found him at home, reading and drinking from a big hot pot of coffee. Benjamin could see him across the gardens of the Outer Ring of the Civic Center. Tom lived in the first cluster of homes at the upper edge of the wide shallow residence saddle that sloped away between the center knoll and the hill the Learning Center was built on He was one minute from his office. Through the triangle of window Ben looked in and waved. Tom got up immediately to greet him at the door, shaking hands, then embracing him vigorously, his lean face and dark eyes shining. His grin was broad as he stood back, delighted to see Ben.

"Tom, it's no wonder you get elected every year. You actually make your friends feel good just seeing you. That Talent hasn't been named yet though."

"Ah yes, it's called charisma. Only people never thought it was a Talent. It's got its dangers like any Talent, my friend.But basically this part of it is just letting your happy feelings show. Most people love seeing their friends,they just don't always let them know". He chuckled as they went to the table. It's a good talent for a politician though." He got a clean cup and plate, "Come have a bite with me. I know I'm late,but last night was a long night. We've been having a few problems with young Hunters lately. A young man and woman who've chosen that work but who don't seem to respond to the training very well yet. If they can't correct it, they may not be chosen for Hunter and that would devastate them." He shook his head.

"Can you tell me?"

"No problem there,it'll be on the Video News sheets all day. We've found two young people shooting birds, and other small animals just for practice. As if we didn't have enough practice sites with moving targets. I've never seen a young person willing to kill, but these were doing it --" he stopped, frowned, shaking his head in perplexity,"They said it was in 'fun'.Didn't see the problem.That was what got to me, Ben, they didn't see the wrong of it."

THE PEOPLE OF THE VALLEY

Ben stared at him. "That's never happened before since the town was begun. Our young people all learn the use of firearms,and can shoot a straight true arrow, but they've been horrified at the idea of killing anything. It takes special training for the Hunters to learn that they can and must." He waited, Tom must enlighten him.

Tom grinned, feeling the mind Touch,"You're right, I ought to. But I can't. It's in the hands of the Healers now. They've got both of them. One came from Clandon and the other is one of our own. Only two things in common. They are both Builders. They are both angry at those who aren't." He waved the cup, "Well, will you have breakfast with me?" Ben shook his head,"How about a cup of coffee?"

Ben nodded and sat down while Tom got food for himself and coffee for them both."Where are Mary and the kids? I know Angela is in Sea Town, this month, but you're not alone again are you?"

Yep. Mary went to New London and took the kids because they haven't been there. She's going to spend next year studying with Clarence Appleton, Drama Master. He specializes in designing and building small town theatres. She wants to learn and come home and build and direct a theatre here in Adwin. She was so excited because theatre there has changed, we're very backward evidently. I'd like it if she did start working seriously here. At least she would be living home again. Angela is always going to be a visitor I think. She's really wedded to the Sea City. Mary'll send the kids back next week, they need to continue with their study here."

"Well, it's too bad, Tom that a man with two women in his life can't always have one at home." He laughed at Tom's grimace. Tom's ability to love two women always amazed Ben. None of the three had mated, not wanting that, and since each had a love of solitude, they'd done well with their loose arrangement.

Angela will be here for a month or so soon, Ben. The undersea City is nearly complete, just as our town is, but she'll be there a lot, she loves it. But she needs to be up here too,in the hills. She says it's not right for her to live there constantly. She thinks maybe children born there might find it completely satisfying. She's learning about building under stress and wants to use that knowledge for some of the high mountain villages here. There's as much stress in high peaks as in the sea."

Tom's eyes sparkled, he was a happy man, but Ben felt his wish for Angela to return. Racial mixtures were obvious in Tom; the slant of his eyes,and dark skin, hair that couldn't decide whether to be straight or to curl, told of both oriental and negro background, his blue eyes, of a nordic father. His hair hung to his shoulders and he wore often a fullbeard, carefully trimmed. Now, he wore a plain maroon cotton robe and slippers. They sat silently a moment, sipping coffee and just enjoying each other. Then Tom said,"You've got something on your mind."

Ben nodded,"I suppose it's obvious, especially to you. You know you've got another Talent, my friend, and it's a vital one for your work. You do what used to be called,'read people'.Were you ever tested for Healing?"

Tom nodded,"I was. And you're right, I've a lot of that Talent, but not enough for Healing. It's one Healers must have a whole lot more of than I do. But it does help me. I sense the state of emotions in people. Acutely, actually. It bothered me when I was a child until the Master Teachers taught me how to manage it. So I failed the Healers test, but they advised me to go into this work."

Ben said, "You could read the whole picture from my mind, couldn't you?"

Tom sobered, shook his head, "Wish I could. I get general information, but I couldn't do more than Touch. I didn't know that's what it was until our spring Gather. I'd not really consciously Touched, until then. Though I've done it intuitively since I was a child. I don't think I've practiced consciously choosing to Touch more than once or twice since the last Gather. It scares me a little. But then, maybe I ought to practice with you." He was silent, thoughtful, "One of my boys does that too, the other, doesn't. I don't know whether he ever will. I didn't know that either until after the Gather and then I asked them, and Angy and Mary did too." He grinned, shaking his head, "You know our family hasn't talked any more than yours."

"Well, then, I'll tell you the details, and you can go on from there. But, did you know that Jessie's going to teach a class in Joining at the Center. It's for adults who've hidden their Talent and so don't know how to manage it. So it's for us. That's the first public statement that's been made in this town and the Builder's are opposing her. They've mounted a strong protest."

"But the Master Teachers have taught the kids all these years."

" Yes, but only those who came to them and therefore there wasn't a public statement made, and of course those who didn't come had no idea such a thing was going on. Besides, people our age didn't know what it was about, not enough to ask." He turned to look directly at Tom, "I think Jessie sees that training as part of getting ready for the Journey, you know".

Tom nodded, "I need to ask her about that. I don't think I understand what it means at all." They were both silent, thinking of that. Then Tom shook his head and said, "Well, tell me what's on your mind."

Ben frowned, "It's Henry." At Tom's nod, he went on, told him the story of the morning's talk, and what he had advised. Tom listened silently, looking out the big triangle of window before him. He watched the sun slanting into the broad court before the house, through scattered paths and gardens that gave the residence areas privacy. A row of huge citrus trees, all full now of green fruit and fragrant new bloom, separated the cluster from the Civic Center. They were rare this far north and therefore prized by town people when they grew. People drifted by, walking toward the Ring Archway. He watched idly, listening and letting his eyes fall on the high unbroken curve of the wall. No windows here. But lilac bushes and camelias shaded its length, throwing shadows along the pale rose stone. He loved the scene before him. Had chosen this house for it as much as for the house itself - and for the friendliness of the four other families that would inhabit the other three houses of the cluster.

Ben finished the story and waited, feeling a sense of relaxation and relief. Tom was silent, absorbing all he'd heard. Ben thought Tom could handle this and he could go on to his own work with the team assigned to solve problems rising from the attempt to build the foundation for a city on one of the moons of Jupiter. The work had sent him traveling to Laboratories in Europe and in the eastern part of the United States during the past month. This day of respite would be well used. He always gained insights when his mind was off on some ordinary human problem. Ideas came unexpectedly through. But theory and practice were too often far apart. And until it was used there, on those barren Worlds, it would not be known how it would work. He hoped he would not have to go there with the team that would act as consultants. The gift of this morning to relax and wander about a little, seemed a very great joy.

Tom was speaking,"I appreciate that you took the time, Ben. We've been trying to get something going for him but he's been so resistant to anything we thought of. I think this might work. He wants to control things it's true, and we can allow that a little in the job you suggested. Let him run it however he likes as long as he gets it done and doesn't offend anyone too much." He turned to look at Ben, but Ben was now gazing out the window, lost in the movement of people and plants. "When anyone has tried to interest him before this, he's just argued. I suppose you got him when he was about to give up. Or maybe your talent is to explain things so they impress the listener." He laughed, "Whatever, it worked."

Ben nodded,"You don't think he'll offend people with that officious attitude he has?"

Tom shrugged,"Well, there might be something we'll have to watch, but we'll choose people to work with him who can manage or who are themselves working on learning to handle authority figures or people with poor self esteem.. Students you know, help out in that work a lot. He doesn't know his emotions splash all over every mind around him and wouldn't understand if you told him. So we'll have to adapt to that." He stroked the gleaming coarseness of his beard, and grinned," He sends like a baby, no control at all, and it's mostly emotion, stained with the color of his attitudes." He laughed again, "I should talk. I probably do the same. I've not practiced much. Kept away from it out of fear."

Ben nodded, "Well, that's true for most of us, friend. If Jessie hadn't started the Teaching she does for us at home, we'd all be lost." He was silent, thinking of that. But word will get around about Henry, and people will want to help."

Tom laughed,"He sure tried to convince us, didn't he?"

Ben smiled,:"You too? I suppose almost everyone around."

"He kept telling me that he could 'cut me in on the profits' whatever that meant. And still, it never dawned on him that I don't need any more than I have. I think he really believes people haven't changed in that."

"Hopes more than anything, I'd say. But then if he fits in, it'll be all right. After all, he isn't the first drifter we've had to deal with. But he's the only one who insisted on tearing up the Valley."

Tom got up to slide his dishes into the autowasher and wiped the table . They stood, Ben stretched and they turned to the doorway,"What I wanted to do, Ben, was catch up on our own lives. What's been happening at the Farm?"

THE JOURNEY

They began to talk. The sun rose higher, sweeping light into the corners of the town and warming the air so that the perfumes of the trees and gardens were caused to stir and pour forth into that air. Ben stayed with Tom until he dressed for work and then walked with him to the entrance to his office. Then he struck off across town to find Henry. He felt like a conspirator in one of Henry's fantasys. "I could get caught up in playing this game too." He laughed at himself, "There's a rascal in me somewhere who'd like the intrigue of it. Seeing if I could fool people. But then, most of my friends would be on to me before I started. Manipulating people won't work in a Self-conscious community.

He went to the Physics lab in the second story of the inner Ring of the Learning Center, where he worked with total concentration and attention with his associates and students. He relaxed at the shedding of all thought but this work. But he WAS supposed to take this day off so finally, with a sigh of relief, he left to go for a late lunch. He walked the short distance to the main plaza of the inner Ring. The two outer Rings seemed especially busy today, Everywhere, through more than forty rooms and in the libraries, film view cubicles,hologram stations ,labs and workshops, people came and went. He could faintly hear the noise in the south third of the outer Ring where children and adults worked in the vocational workrooms. The hum of machinery, of saws, drills, etc. and the soft sputter now and then of a welding tool, told him it was busy today. Many of these products of students would be displayed at the Festival and they must be finished. He watched the flow of people coming and going, went in to the Public Dining Hall and got his lunch and brought it out to sit in the sun. He wanted to watch the flow of people of every age through these busy rings.

From where he sat he could glimpse the high spires of the temple through trees that had already grown to tower over the two story outer Ring. Sitting silently, enjoying the quiet, eating and listening, he saw Tom approaching. His head bent,he seemed lost in thought. Ben hailed him, and he raised one hand and hurried over to join him.

"It looks as if it will work, Ben. You know the feeling Henry gives me is that he thinks the world has gone crazy and he is the only sane man here. He seems to have decided that he must just put up with us. But then, maybe he's right."

Ben nodded,"Had lunch? Why not get some and join me?"

Tom glanced at the Dining Hall, and nodded. He went in and came out again with a tray. He sat down,"He wants to own his own house. He says the council ought at least to allow that. To do as he pleases with it, he says. He's suspicious, he seems to think someone will deprive him some how. He doesn't believe me when I tell him that any citizen has a lifetime home and no one can oust him unless he himself decides to change. He's an anachronism, that's all, and we have to bend a little to let him fit in.

"We could make a contract stating those very rights in legal language."

"Yes, good idea. He'd be satisfied I think. A contract would content him that we're not going to throw him out. It'll make him feel as though he's got some power."

Ben shrugged. They were silent. Then Ben said,"I've wondered what it was like, since I talked to him. The old days he talks about. D'you suppose they ever really existed? I think he's got a fantasy rather than a reality. We ought to let him play them out in the holograph studios where such games can be played.

"Yeah, I can imagine living as a Lord, having servants, people , waiting on me, having a gold lined air car, and a palatial home set apart, inside a great wall, or on a high hill with a river diverted at its base to surround my lands. .It's easy to imagine, but then when you settle in and decide what you would do there, it falls flat. What DID people do".

Ben snorted, "If they were really rich, they indulged their appetites. They enjoyed -- no exploited all the senses as fully as they could, indulged their own worst lusts, tried out their fantasies by using their subjugated people. They controlled their financial world because that was fun for them, kept them busy and with a feeling of power. Set up all kinds of little spy networks, spies spying on spies, etc." Benjamin grinned, "I've read the old tales, most of them exaggerated perhaps. Then they had fights and insulted each other so they could go to war. That was the main diversion for men. But then, what else was there? It would not keep me interested. I've thought of it. Decided it wasn't for me."

"Well, just before the time of troubles, in the best of the world, business was sophistocated and morals were at least argued about, no one could use people so obviously. You had to at least be secretive. War was as subtly arranged. It was orchestrated as a noble cause.

" Maybe that was worse, after all. The darkest part of our nature has a chance to come out in secret. Who knows. But men and women spent days sitting around council tables arguing about the compelling world of finances and business, of networks that ran communications, about all the twisted complexities of government. It had become a paper world, built on the assumption that you couldn't trust anybody and had to triple check on every move.Paper snowed ordinary inventiveness under. People sat at their desks reading papers and making copies and exchanging them, then filing tons of them. They thought computers would change all that but they only made it worse until we developed modern information storage banks that weed themselves out constantly. I've read the histories. I think it was worse than the era of castles and knights."

Yeah, when Henry told me his dream, trying to find things that would entice me,he didn't include any of that dull life. He said there would be every kind of servant, even lovely young girls -- and boys." He watched Ben's expression, which changed only by a raised eyebrow. "He said he didn't tell you any of those ideas because he thought you'd be angry. He considers me a man of the world." Tom stopped a moment, looking away, then laughed. "Oh, he had more to offer. He said if we wanted we could try things people had forgotten about.He spoke of gambling halls that were like halls of indescribable luxury. Well, for me, life is all the gamble I need. I felt such a feeling of dispair - when I noticed that there is still in me an attraction, I actually felt a stir of desire - I felt sick, sick and sad." He was embarrassed, then amused,"Oh, Ben, we've not met all the old darkness in us yet."

Ben nodded,"But you're ready to recognize them when they do surface. That's a step on."

He looked across the gardens, letting his eyes rest on the sun and shadow playing against the soft red of the buildings through the green leaves. The tall wide windows in which could be seen people busily moving and working, seemed to reflect the lovelyness of the gardens and increase them.

They were silent for long minutes, then Benjamin shrugged. "We've got to get our priorities straight, they aren't to unmask the Builders."

Tom turned abruptly to stare at Benjamin, "You're right. We've got to let the Builders alone and be about our business of discovery."

Tom stood and began to pace back and forth,oblivious of those coming and going about them," Our Teachers are trying to show us. We've got to learn."

"Tom, it's not the same today. We KNOW our old methods don't work to study this - - other dimension. We call it Spirit, but what is that actually? I don't know, but I know that the whole material universe, is only one dimension of Reality. We've begun to know a little of the others, only a little and we don't know how to think about them yet." He frowned in frustration, "We can't test what we experience, can't prove it by old methods."

Tom's eyes were fast on his, he nodded slowly,"I think I see the problem you would have as a scientist. But that doesn't hinder me."

Benjamin nodded slowly, "It was the Mind Touch, the Joining! Tom, do you know what that did to my sense of balance? The absolute fact of it that I could no longer deny?" He looked almost frightened for a second and then broke into a wide grin."It nearly tore me apart trying to explain until I saw I couldn't explain. That something existed that I couldn't explain at all. I just had to accept it because it was my own experience!"

"So it's no wonder the people who do not experience anything of Joining are angry when we do.It's no wonder that we've not paid attention to them too. We were busy first just trying to deny and then to admit for ourselves?" He was slowly nodding, understanding something that seemed important for their town. "We've refused to notice that a lot of people were very discontented because we hadn't admitted what they could be discontented about?"

Ben laughed, stood and the two of them paced across the gaily colored tiles of the court, seeing little of the design except the shift of color as they walked. He said,"That about says it, Tom. I've not ever put it so clearly to myself."

For several minutes they contemplated those thoughts that seemed to sum up and to warn them of so much. Then Tom sighed, and stopped, taking the green leafy twig full of scarlet currents from a bush at the edge of the court into his hand to eat."Well, Ben, we've still got a problem, and Henry's stated it about as well as anyone could. We're none of us immune to the feelings he talked of. The old lusts, the old feelings and desires. To what extent are they there? Do we want to deny them? Or do we want to admit them and see how strong they are?

THE PEOPLE OF THE VALLEY

Because they don't fit into my perception of Life anymore. I feel sick to my stomach at the thought of some of the things already being shown -done, in the entertainment centers that the Builders are setting up in the Valley towns."

Ben looked at him quickly,"I hadn't heard! What's that?"

Tom sighed, and they stopped again at the bench to sit down. Tom rubbed the red stain from his fingers and said,"Surely you must know. They've been busy at it for several weeks. In Santiago first, then Clandor, then they began with the smaller towns. Bend," He laughed, "That little town in the lower lake country, Joseton, refused! The whole town! Such an uproar, you must have seen something of it. It's all been on the News." He stood, a wry smile tipping his mouth upward,"I suppose that tells us something. If I were truly detached, I'd not be so nauseated. Joseton wouldn't have been so angry. In Windhover, people all went in to see, tried out the place, then that was it. Only two people ever came back." He grinned,"Must've stumped them."

Ben glanced quickly at him, then ignored the last sentence,"I don't think I've heard. I've been busy, as I told you." He was sad,"Some scientists refuse to even discuss it still. But those of us who Join, who experience these things, who stand out of body seeing another dimension for ourselves so clearly we can no longer refuse to admit what is happening, those of us who See - cannot do anything else but research it. Not if we are Scientists!" He was full of a rightous anger so that it blew like an energy through him and he suddenly felt it, sobered, then laughed again, "Wow, I'm wound up! But it's good to talk of it."

"I can see that. I see why you haven't heard of the entertainment centers too." Tom smiled ruefully.

Ben nodded,"You say they've set one up here? In Adwin?"

Tom nodded,Yep! Right down town in the Civic Center outer ring. They said it belonged in the Market Ring, but we got them a little farther from that. However, Ben, How could we refuse and still profess that all people had a right to their interests? Unlike Bend, there were a few who were interested but most people were like you Ben, they didn't seem to notice."

Ben stood up, agitated, he slapped his hands against the side of a stone sculpture that he knew a child had done, and felt the smooth curve of it hurt his hand."Damn it, Man, surely, there must be limits?"

"Not if you actually mean that all people must be accomodated."

Ben was silent, walking toward the inner Ring, turning and walking back, he dodged a group of talking,laughing young men and women, their bright faces seeming so free of worry,to him. He resented them irrationally. Noticed that and frowned at himself. "Tom, let's go see that. I've got to see what's been done."

"I've already done that. You can go today if you like, I think Rose's seen it. The whole Council went down, and that includes our dear Jane. What SHE must have thought, I haven't heard. She wouldn't like that though. Not because she's a prude. Jane isn't that."

"What? What is there?"

"Oh, the old fashioned peep show type thing, only now it's the latest

THE JOURNEY

technology, holograms that put you into rooms full of living people engaged in every type of sexual or violent - - perversion." He hesitated, "Well, I wondered if I were being fair, but it's true. I don't remember a single simple ordinary scene where sex was simply a part of living, not an obsession. Not the coming together of healthy people loving each other. But rather there was obsession! Food, drink, drugs, fighting, sex, hurting people or animals, being hurt, all the possible obsessions of mind blind distortions. All of it is twisted. I felt so sad, you know. Most healthy citizens just stayed away. Of those who went in, some cried, some were amused." He was silent, letting Ben absorb that. "Then, Ben, and this'll be the worst for you. They're serving drugs as though they were refreshments. I think they thought to try to drug people into being interested. They have some remarkable new drugs, you know, non-habit forming, and giving people expansions of sensuality, rather than expansions of consciousness. And some people might not be able to judge, might not be able to resist, even."

Ben was numb, and his eyes could not move from the stone figure before him. He shook himself, realizing he was wishing to remove the problem that Tom was offering him. "Oh my God, and we just have to allow that rot in this town,. I never thought, never believed it would happen again. What about the children?"

Tom laughed shortly, and Ben was surprised that he showed no sign of anger, bitterness at all. "They took cae of that. They made it off limits to children under sixteen. It's good for business, you know. Makes it attractive, they believe, to adults too. And they believe the kids will be flocking in each year because they were refused." He was smiling a strange amused smile and Ben felt almost angry at that.

I can't see how you can stand there smiling at something that awful. What the devil are we going to do?"

Tom grimaced, his eyes only quietly thoughtful, "You should have seen this years crop of sixteen year olds. At first they strutted a little, being allowed in. But I never saw a more sober bunch when they came out. They didn't even stay long. Only one vomited on the pathway, the rest were talking about finding something really fun to do." He shrugged. "Oh, Ben, stop and think. If you went to see it, and you must, what do you think you would do?"

"I don't know. After all, I'm not immune to such feelings. I'm not that far from the old way." He righted himself, shrugged with a heavy frown, "Look at me. What you said earlier IS true. If I were even nearly free of such desires I would be indifferent rather than insensed. Except for what it might do to our young ones. And from what you say, THEY aren't interested!" He shook his head surprised.

" So your own fear is what's making you angry. You must go see it and then you'll feel the way I do." He laughed shortly, "It's not good but it's better than fear."

"Well, how is it you feel?"

"I ought to make you wait til you've seen it, but you look so miserable." He watched three children running pellmell across the path, leaping a low bush and falling in laughter and pummelling each other in the fragrant ground cover a few yards away. He smiled at them, remembering, and then said,"Ben, I was at first so angry I was livid, then I felt my own stirrings of interest,,and that scared me, so I was scared. That made me even angrier. I wanted to strike out, to drive them out. Then I took myself home and thought. Listened inside myself. Was still for a while. Then when I went back, I began to feel a strange over powering sense of disbelief and amusement." He made a rough sound like a strained cough, "I couldn't believe myself but I just stood there, a lot of little cubicles where people lost themselves in whatever their obsession was. I stumbled into a half open door and a customer lost in masturbating in his fantasy holo, but at least I saw no live people used as part of it. Believe me or not, one of our citizens though I don't know who. He was in costume. They do that too." He shook his head slowly from side to side,as if still puzzled. "Then I realized that I wanted to laugh. I wanted to laugh, Ben. That was how I felt. It was so - so- CHILDISH! That's it. I felt as though they thought we hadn't anything better to entertain ourselves with. It simply didn't interest me at all and the emotions it roused in me, when I actually looked at them, were so mild that I had no trouble refusing them. Though I did admit them." He stood a moment reflecting. "Even my anger was gone. I don't always respond with disinterest, but now and then when I'm standing clear of myself,I do."

Ben nodded slowly, his eyes bleak but a hope rising like a dim light in them."You think then? You think most of our people will feel the same way?" He drew his hands together, rolling them into hard fists, "Oh, God, I hope so." He was silent, letting it all sink in, "Well, it's a test for us I suppose."

Tom put a hand on his shoulder, shook him slightly,"It sure is, Buddy. It sure is." Then, sitting down again, he said,"I don't consider myself very Conscious, very enlightened or with a Heart as clear as most people's are. And so, I thought, if I can feel little more than amusement and disbelief, then most of our citizens will feel even less. Except perhaps sadness, Ben. I imagine many will feel grief that they're still trapped in that old stuff. I think that's what Rose would feel. Jane, I think, would cry. It would grieve her so." He looked sad himself then, realizing as he talked how others might experience this.

Ben stood, "Well, You're right, I must look it over and find out where I am. I suppose I'll never tell you if I find myself attracted. What would I do if I did?"

Tom said,"Well, I think I'd go to a Healer. I think that's what I'd do, but then how can I tell?" he joined Ben, preparing to walk on,"After all,we've been taught, Ben. We've been taught so well. But you can't teach people what their emotions are, they have to find that out for themselves. But you can teach what to do with them."

" And we have to know, don't we, or we are little more than self righteous hypocrites. So there it is!" They began to walk through the Archway of the outer Ring and started across the path through the playing and building fields. A clutter of kids worked noisily on a strange small house.."I'll walk with you. I've got to talk to the City Clerk. See if we can't get some equipment." He laughed, "Give our friend Henry some work to do." They were silent until they began the drop down

THE JOURNEY

into the residence valley between Centers.

Tom said softly,"I'll tell you one thing though, old friend,to relieve your heart. D'you have an idea of how many people have given them business?" Benjamin shook his head and Tom said, " We've done about the way Windhover did, after the first look,they're down to about thirty two people a week and some of them come from Denlock or Jasper." He was grinning." I think they'll go out of business.

" Benjamin felt a cool air through his body, a relief so great he felt briefly weak as he turned to meet Tom's eyes."Thank's. I didn't know how discouraged I was."

Tom said,"Only one thing really bothers me now, Ben. I don't know whether William could be involved in this part of their plan? Surely he's too fastidious, if nothing else."

"No! No! I'll never believe that until he tells me. He's too much of a man, actually, I think. He isn't dominated by his gonads, nor a twisted need for power because he has a healthy sense of power that he satisfies.But we could ask him about it. He'd have some ideas about the prevalence of it".

"Well, there's something else, though. The people we talked of, the discontented ones, they'll be customers, though I think the number will not be that great. The Healers say they can't heal anyone who doesn't choose Healing. They say they just have to wait and watch. We've been taught, people do have other things to interest them. But, what of the other matter? The thing Henry made us see. I'm not sure that I don't have some old desires for that kind of public power, that kind of indulgence of old fantasies? His kind, not this sick kind."

" Which is more sick?" Tom was serious, his face sad."Could I be persuaded by a powerful personality to do what I don't think is right? I don't know."

"Well, one thing I know is that I'm immune to any desire to control other people to the extent that they would be my servants, my field workers, etc. I never in this life will agree to being trapped like that. No prison is more awful than that made by one having to keep control over other people, or having to keep earning money to pay people to do work they aren't interested in. To keep having to be responsible for people's lives ."

Tom laughed, "You miss the point, if a person loves power, he doesn't care about that person's welfare and doesn't feel responsibity for his life,. He USES that person instead."They walked in silence for a bit and then he added,"But you see, we see that. We see because we are linked with one another, we know the nature of freedom -- that one cannot be free if others are not. And the ones who cannot link at all, cannot see that clearly, often see it at least intellectually. Ben, people, ordinary people are no longer ordinary. They won't tolerate what people did long ago. They think! They are beginning to realize! Some who don't realize much yet, like William, would fight for that right for others, even though they thought them only ideas, not reality."

"That's why I don't really worry too much about William. He's the most clear intellect in Altos, in my opinion. Or at least, equal to any other." He spoke with such strong loyalty that Tom grinned in sympathy and nodded."Don't let your own loyalty blind you, friend."

Ben looked at him, his throat tight, this matter about William had left him grieved more than he wanted to admit just then. He thought about that. Why? Then he said,"It does worry me about Will. I wish I knew how to understand him."

Tom's cheer vanished, "We know he's one of the founders of the Builders. We can't deny that he's very involved." He stopped to look at Ben. Taller, he must look slightly down for their eyes to meet. The muscles around his eyes tightened as he studied Ben's worried face."But Ben, this job I do gives me experience with a lot of different kinds of people, more than most of you. Mostly, people are experimenting, finding out about themselves today. Practicing some of the things our Teachers taught us and that we know, but haven't tried out. So many people are trying different life styles, new ideas, they protest, rearrange their ideas, trying to see what works, testing themselves to see how they actually react, feel about things. There's so much to learn about ourselves, you know. But these Builders, I've watched them, they are so narrow in their way of seeing other people. They're not the same."

"Why didn't you tell us before? Warn us? We might have talked to Will." He reflected on that selfish note and added, "Talked to all of them. You know Tom, we've lost Will. We've lost him and so I suppose we've lost the rest of our citizens who're involved. And why do I keep harping on William only?" He shook his head, rubbing both hands over his face, wanting to feel the comfort of that touch." You see? We're still so centered in our selves. Well, if it's true, its true, and Will IS part of us? I do know that there must be no 'us and them',Tom." He stopped, reflecting again," We KNOW that, and though we aren't free of feeling it, we can act to that knowledge."

Tom said," I feel as though we've lost something of our Valley? But how can we say we've lost them if we believe what we say we do. Every citizen has a right to create his own way of life."

"But they're serious, they really want to go back, to make life over the way it used to be, and they want all of us to go back with them. To regress! Except I've not heard of anyone refusing any modern technology. I'm sure they won't refuse the matter transmitters for transporting freight." He sighed, and they walked on, "Those were sad old days, people destroyed things, almost destroyed the Earth, lived in fear much of the time. It was a terrible world and no one seemed to realize there was a better way then. Not many learned that it was himself or herself who was making that world what it was". His face paled,"My God, Tom, how can we allow them to risk ruining things ?" Then he felt the twist of pain "My God, listen to me? I'm doing the same. THEY aren't ruining things, WE are. It's all of us! It's not what we KNOW after all. It's what we DO about what we Know!"

Tom nodded, "It boils down to how we live our lives. You see? Ben was not to be comforted, he paced, walking with his arms wrapped around his chest, his head stiff. Tom stopped, faced Ben. "As far as they're concerned we're at the worst dealing in witch craft at the best, we're involved in some kind of secret organization and leaving them out. They cannot know that we desparately want them in." He grabbed Benjamin's shoulders, his long strong fingers biting into Ben's thick muscle."Do you realize, Ben? Do you realize they don't know that partly because we haven't even told them we want them?"

Ben let his arms drop. His face sag into dispair. "Would they listen? I've withheld talking, we've all withheld, because we don't --we don't know much ourselves.But Jessie could advise us!"

"She won't, you know that. She'll explain, she'll answer our questions, but she insists that we make our own decisions." He sighed," Wow,Ben,old friend,,I'm amazed at how much resentment there is in me that they defy us, that they have made the demands they have and have begun to take what they want. To set up shops that -- " He shrugged then, "Oh, we've got to watch ourselves or we'll be right in their shoes, only on the other side, organizing ourselves to fight. And if we do that -- then we'll know that we've lost our vision, or that it was false to begin with."

Ben nodded, they began walking again."William's teaching attracts any of the dissatisfied,those who truly beieve the new vision is evil, or the talents witchcraft, but more, he is attracting people who've come to that uneasy place in life when they cannot find old meanings satisfying any more. They want something stronger and they don't know what. They have every thing they want, a good life, friends, family, what credit they need, travel, so much, and they still feel like something is missing. And they just give up in dispair. Because they don't see ahead, some decide to go back, to drop to their own lowest level and search for satisfaction, something, anything to obliterate the emptyness ahead. And they are the ones who might be able to wake up, to See after all."

Slowly Tom turned to meet Ben's eyes,his full of grief, "Benjamin, you probably don't know that there've been eight suicides in north Valley just this year. A number four times as large as normal.' He frowned,"Yes, dispair, real considered dispair. They leave notes that there is nothing more, nothing left to this life that makes them want to continue, and these aren't people like Henry, discontents, but people who've done --everything we think of as having a good life." He shook his head and they were silent.

Then with new energy,Tom's voice was angry, "We could help! Especially those who don't See what there is to live for. Those who have no personal experience of Spirit, of inner Life! The Teachers've given them ideals, an intellectual knowledge of that Life beyond what we've known, but so often they can't buy it. They see it as another chimera, an empty promise- like the idea of heaven used to be. But we do See, we could go out and talk to them, convince them that there is that Light, that possibility, and they can find it through something as simple as silence."

Ben nodded, slowly, turning to look at his friend, having to look up a little to meet those angry eyes. He almost smiled,the situation was a paradox."So long we've avoided preaching to one another, we even stopped talking of an inner life. Now we've begun to talk and we'll have to get back to making speeches to each

THE PEOPLE OF THE VALLEY

other, I think." He drew a deep sigh, Tom. There is time when people come to a brutal loss of illusion, a recognition of what we've been and that's is the beginning of dispair. If a person doesn't break through that barrier, doesn't See beyond it, then that dispair is unbearable." His eyes were full of his own memories, bleak and cold.

"It's only natural that they'd be attracted by a group that gives them a promise of something, that gathers together to find comfort in one another. It's only natural that they'd try to constantly distract themselves with things, a strong group's promises, a strong leaders convincing argument, work, whatever lusts can be stimulated, anything to refuse the dispair festering in them. And it's only natural they'd feel angry. And look for someone to blame that anger on." He heaved a breath again, then burst out "We've failed each other, Tom, we who begin to Know of Spirit, who wake to Vision, simply act as if its all a great secret, not to be advertized at all."

"How can we make that Journey Jessie speaks of, when we fail our fellows so utterly?"

Tom watched a young boy sauntering along the outer gardens, whistling, looking here and there, obviously feeling delighted with himself and the world. He said, softly,"We thought we'd better not stand together in silence, so a Builder could find us offensive. But we must! And we must explain to them why. We must talk, tell them, tell everyone about this recognition, this awakening that we know. What we - humanity - is becoming. We've got to risk that,Ben."

The boy had walked more slowly, suddenly quiet, his face alert, questioning, then suddenly, in one great blinding light,he was all around their minds, and then he was gone. He stood watching them and frowning. Tom's first thought was,"He's so young. How can it be."

But Ben cringed mentally at the blast and closed against it. Tom, met the boy's eyes, and then, the youngster flushed,"I- I'm sorry. I shouldn't have done that." He said softly, "But d'you realize how loudly you were debating? The issue isn't yours alone, but you don't have to blast it all over the gardens. Maybe a little shielding would help." He suddenly grinned and went on, whistling again, his mind tightly closed against their Touch."

Ben whirled, as if to run after him, and then, stopped, embarrassed, angry, then, as usual, amused at himself. He grinned at Tom, who stood looking utterly nonplussed,"It looks as if we're going to get it from those ahead of us and those not yet caught up. But we weren't even Touching! At least not consciously." He turned to Tom, his eyes wide, frowning,"It was our emotions! Damn it, these kids are aware of strong emotion and attitudes the way we're aware of sounds" He stopped, struck with the implications of that.

"And no one's been teaching them manners at all" Tom was frowning over an amused grin, "Shouldn't we get Jessie to do something?"

"I think she might say it's our job. And yet, look how we've failed so far. 'In the teaching, is also the learning'. Remember that old one?" He was silent,and they were climbing the slope toward the Civic Center, passing the clusters of

THE JOURNEY

homes. Little gardens projected from some of those fronts, others let their front doors open on rolling parkland. They passed one tall stone and wood cluster of four homes, and ahead, just through the trees they could see the next. Tom glanced professionally around, watching to see that things were as they should be here. He leaned to pick a few berries from a stout low bush. The air seemed to be filled with heat. Ben thought the light around them had gathered, was stronger, as though the day gleamed in on itself.

Tom said,"Ben, there's an example of the changes in us, right there." He pointed at a lovely, graceful cluster of four homes, back to back, shaded by a spreading beech."D'you know what people do when they fight about who's gonna get to live in a popular cluster?" Ben turned to look, shaking his head, interested. Tom went on, "Three families wanted the two houses on the south side of this cluster. One had petitioned a week earlier than another and they were moving in. The parents of another family came and refused to let them, saying the council hadn't been fair and hadn't waited for all the petitions to be in before assigning. It was a stand off." He watched Ben.

"Well, what happened!" Ben was irritated at his hesitation. "The first family, the whole family mind you. Just stood there, holding their furniture they had been moving, and then without a word, just a nod and a shrug, they took their stuff back into the floater. They hadn't even talked to each other, but their silence was - ! Now I realize they were Joined. I asked them what they were doing and they said,"It's not important. Where we live is irrelevant. They're welcome to this. We'll find another." The two men stood looking at one another, silent, for several minutes.

Finally Ben said,"It's that kind of people we live with now. And that's what's meant by detached huh? What happened to them?"

Tom laughed,"The angry family stood around looking ashamed, but they moved in. Then they came to me to find that other family a home. That's how I found out. By the time I got there, the first family were already moved into a new unit over between Industrial and Civic. They just smiled at me."

Ben just nodded, and they walked on, climbing higher toward the big central Rings.

Ben had stopped beside an orange tree winter-sheltered in the curve of a building to produce fine fruit. He reached out to break off a twig with a blossom on it. Huge bright oranges hung among the blossoms and a small basket stood beside the tree, half full. A young woman gathered those that had fallen, ripe and sweet. She smiled at them,her mind shielded, her eyes alert watching them and they both realized that she was aware of their worry. A feeling of being caught, of being invaded, wrestled with the knowledge that they had not bothered to dampen their Sending. She moved to them from around the thick branches.

"Exactly, you were Sending emotions like a clarion, the only relief other people have to that is to close down completely and that's not quite fair. To make us close so much,that is." She was laughing, obviously amused at their discomfiture. And then she relented,"Don't feel badly, Mayor Tom, it happens all the time.

Especially with older people.If you'd all talk about it, we might work something out, you know." Her face was serious, but her eyes laughed.

Tom felt taken aback. he hadn't thought he was an 'older person' but Ben laughed."You see? Tom, we've got things to learn from the ones ahead of us." So we can commiserate with those who must learn from us."

They walked on, silent,acutely sensitive to their own mental clamor and they finally they arrived at the wide field of fruiting trees and shrubs broken with small open meadows,beyond which the Outer Ring of the Civic Center curved. They crossed the field in silence, stopping to pull a ripe peach from one tree and ate as they continued. In moments they were stepping under the shade of the great archway and Ben turned to speak. "The dangerous part is that people like Will have power. They have power over themselves and they know how to use it over others. He's not to be dismissed as another fanatic. He has precise and excellent power over himself.If he decides that something is to be done, he can do much. And we've given them a potent tool. Our secretiveness is being used against us."

Tom nodded, touched his friend's shoulder then wiped his forehead dry of sweat. They could see people busily passing through the gardens beyond and they moved back out of the flow of pedestrian traffic. Both of them talked softly, but with shielded emotions, wanting no repetition of their earlier exposures."There is a difference, Ben. Just like Jessie said, we're not the same kind of people. But we're like babies having to learn how to live." His face twisted down into a dark frown, "You see? There's so much to learn, so very much!" He heaved a long hard breath, his face tight with thinking. "The children are more nearly what humankind is becoming than we are. And they've been talking to each other, they've Joined into an inner community, beautiful and tender. But we, we've got to learn how to talk, to them and to try to make things better for people who're - stuck there in our past." He let his face relax, now that the difficult thought was said,"What d'you think?"

Tom's voice had softened,and his face cleared, calmed with the final question. Then suddenly he was smiling , ruefully,as if at himself. Ben's head was bent, intent on the pattern in the brickwork of the path. Tom went on,"You see Ben, old brother, it looks to me as though all we've got is each other. We aren't any of us strong enough alone, but the gift this time is we have each other in a way we've never had before."

"Then we're growing up. We, as a people, aren't children anymore. We don't find interest in the old -- toys? We've lost interest in old entertainments? Is it like that?"

Tom cried out,"Yeah, I think that's it. Exactly! Jessie keeps telling us we're growing up and that's what she means."

Ben stood back, looked around,,then said,"All right, Tom, let's try this, let's try something we've never even thought to do. Let's Reach. Call out to our town people. See whether we can contact anyone together. Will you try?"

"It'd be like calling for help, wouldn't it? We wouldn't want to call for help when none is needed. Or it would disturb people the way it did those young ones."

"No, we won't call for help. We'll not Join, but couldn't we just Reach? A little contact! To see if we can find anyone? We'd know whether we did. We've got to begin somehwere!" They looked at each other, still standing inside the Archway, passed by people busy paying little attention to them. Neither had ever tried to Reach to anyone outside their family. Now filled with the pain of these gnawing questions,the hurt of confusion,they wanted to test whether they could find communion. With a slight nod, Tom closed his eyes, leaning back against the hard roughness of the stone. He felt Benjamin's hesitance, and then a fierce determination and then, slowly a quiet Reach that extended and gently their minds Touched, they knew each other and felt the fire of that. The increased strength amazed them both. They balanced, Joined, were together and then they gathered their attention to Reach out. For moments they seemed to find only resistance, then a bright acknowledgement here, there,- at each acknowledgement the Touch grew.

Then slowly, like a stream released from restraint there came many tiny touches that was like a flowing into deeper consciousness. The response became a deep resonance, a steady beat against their Hearts and in their minds. They had touched into a sea of response, Sea of mind?! Both men withdrew. Even as they felt their neighbors also shrink back. They were startled, frightened,,and filled with elation of wonder and delight. "My God, Ben, My God, we are -- it is possible., What it might be, if we actually all Touched together. And then, maybe we could actually JOIN. I cannot imagine. I wonder if we could bear that!"

Ben shook his head, but he could not restrain the laughter that rose through all his body, the delight of it. "Well, Tom, think of it. What we might be! But you can see the Builders have reason to be afraid of us. If they cannot Join us, if we can be as ONE people and they cannot know that."

"But can we ourselves handle our own strength? Handle what we are?" Tom swallowed, and looked off across the living riot of color around them,"Can we know even?" He felt such a profound love for the people with whom they had Touched. "As for the Builders, they wouldn't believe it!"

"Thank God they won't. They'd be furious to be excluded, I think. But they sense enough to know there is something and they resent that already."

After some minutes,walking on, slowly, not wanting to get to Tom's office and the problems of the day, Ben said, "If all the people of the town actually JOINED, it would be like a grand symphony, a grand Sound, a state of Being greater than anything we can imagine. I don't believe I could stand that. Just the Touch made me tremble, as though my very body,mind, began a vibration it could not bear."

Tom nodded,"It's true. I felt it too, all of us. We withdraw as if we were too close to something too great to meet. Yet! YET! Ben, we will though . There must have been Master Teachers drawn in to us. Now they know. Now everyone knows. We can talk when we want, as long as we shield the broadcast." He laughed. "It's been made public in the best way. No one can deny or pretend he does not know." He was suddenly exultant, "We'll do it, Ben, We'll do it."

THE PEOPLE OF THE VALLEY

For moments they walked on, stunned, their minds flooded with image and thought, Ben reached out one hand loosely seeking his friend's arm in comfort. As if he needed support to remember. He felt Tom's nearness like a raw wound, he couldn't understand the pain of it, the joy of it. Tom bent his head, his tall frame slumped a little, and Ben felt a faint trembling in his arm. His hands clutched one another. Finally he lifted his head and said aloud,"Ben, we've been together in a way we've never known. The walls of reality have weakened and broken to show us a larger reality than we could comprehend alone. We were on the verge of THAT. We were on the verge, and you could feel the young ones, there at the end, surging in, such surprise, such delight, like a river of Joy from them. They wanted to hold it, to make it last, and we -- we old ones, we couldn't.!" He felt a deep sorrow, and a desire to Reach again, but knew that he would not.

They walked, their minds were shaken, their hearts full to bursting, They both felt the desire to be alone, to seek a solitude in which they might understand.

Ben said,"I want to be alone, and yet I don't want to leave you, to risk being alone."

Tom nodded, walking rapidly now, as if anxious to be at home, safe in that familiar space."It was wholly unexpected wasn't it? I never thought it would be like that. Even just the Reach. It was -- so much. We were proud of ourselves, weren't we. We still are." A tear overflowed one eye and rolled down a cheek. An amazed smile pulling his mouth fitfully because that mouth wanted also to turn down into grief. "Why all these feelings? And yet, why not?"

Ben said, "Our Family heard,some of them. I wonder how I know, yet I do.It's hard to believe that we could Reach so far. At least a mile, if they were Touched. If they were with us, I wonder how they feel now."

Tom laughed, "I suspect some of them knew all along that we could, that we could make a whole Reach. And there was Jessie, so full of her special kind of Joy, I could feel that, and the Master Teachers,. But there was something else, Ben, something at the edge, something so beautiful, so full of a loveliness, that it was almost unbearable and it was what brought us to separate, I think. Whatever it was, I thought it was tentative, as if waiting for us to invite 'IT' in. What? Ben what was that. Did you feel that?"

Ben was walking faster to keep up with his long legged friend, and he didn't answer at once. When they stopped inside the inner Ring and found themselves nearly at Tom's office, he said,"I wonder whether the Monitors might have come near? Perhaps it was that. I've never known well how their power works but it's so great, they woudn't Join in, just be there at the edge, because they don't interfere,you know." He stood silent, then said again,"Perhaps it was the Monitors."

"I want to talk to Jessie, I think I'll come to the Farm today after I finish my work. Ben, I've got to talk to everyone. Would that be all right?"

"It's your home too, Brother. You come when you want. Yes, I need to talk to Jessie too. And I'll do it right now. Maybe she can help." He turned as Tom started into the office doorway,"I know I'll never deny anything again without serious thought. I'll never refuse to look,to listen, and to see."

Tom nodded, "Then until this evening". He went on in to his rooms where he could be alone and think, work, and set things into perspective a little.

Benjamin turned, the fragrance of the gardens seemed at that moment to fill him with a message of hope, of joy itself as though every living thing shared somehow in this revelation. He smiled at himself, but it was a lovely thought and he would allow it. A tenderness of joy gave him release from every question that rattled in his head. He didn't have to answer anything now. He could just enjoy. He could let the sense of what happened shape itself. And suddenly there was a clear thought."I never need again ask what that word brotherhood means. Here was a shaping such as they had never known as a people. The Touch of Mind, of Life Mind. Together they had felt Its power to teach the human race its song. Perhaps It waited to lift the entire human race into its own dimensions where Song was known. Where that song could be heard.Could this be the beginning?

He walked down the pathways, left the Center and kept on walking, his feet seemed to have their own direction and by the time he realized what it was,he was in front of Adwin's Temple. He went in, the great spires soaring far into the sky where clouds rode the high winds. Inside a good number of people moved softly to their chosen places. The flickering light of candles lightened a small table near the four Holy Books. From the center he looked around, looking into each of the seven chambers of the star that was the interior of this Temple. There were many people, more, he thought than usual for this time of day. He found a small cubicle, a place alone, and settled into the meditation that would allow him to stand at that highest point and from which he might see again, his own condition. From there too,he might call out to that highest power he knew, and ask for understanding. But most of all, he would simply enter stillness. Something had pierced the shell of his being, another bit of that shell had fallen away. He would never be the same.

He left the Temple when the sun was descending and the day was already slightly cooling. The evening light had already slanted across the fields by the time he reached home. The silence of the evening pleased him. He walked in an inner silence that healed and restored. He thought that great Joy, great Vision required as much adjustment as great grief or pain. He could not believe that one could know such Joy.It seemed a dream, it seemed to be what he could never have thought of. He felt great love for Earth, the path, the trees, the animals that ran across the Highway, deserted on this late summer day. The Festival would be begun this night, with dances,and singing, to usher in the morrow, but he would not be there. He would find his cottage and wait for Rose to come. He would not call her. Surely she must know, and would seek him out when she was ready.

What a day it had been, his holiday. Holy day? Yes, he knew he had already begun his Journey.

CHAPTER SIX

Summer Gather and a Sprinkling of Coins

It was only two weeks later, a hot dry spell in late June that Families in the Valley began again to call Gathers. There was a new sense of urgency stimulated by such talks as Jessie had begun in the Learning Centers, and by the questions Tom and Benjamin asked of anyone who would listen. An awakened north Valley seemed to be shaking its collective head and demanding understanding. The mystery of living, the harmony of life that held within itself all discension seemed to have begun to reveal Itself. And as a result,there needed to be immediate attention to the growing polarity of the people. For the Farm Family, the call went out one day, and as if everyone had come to the same conclusion, everyone arrived the next morning.

The sun was not yet visible over the turning edge of Earth, when the Family began to gather. An air car coming down from Altos drew near and landed on the small grid projecting from the roof of the hall. Rose was waiting, Ben was just coming out of the door to his cottage. The rest of the Family were finishing chores, or settling in the Hall.The swift soundless landings of Tom and Angy, riding belts from Adwin,, went almost unnoticed at first in the greeting of those from Altos.

Jerry Reached toward Ned and found him,just lifting off from town. Tom and Angela's son, Justin, was with Mary and her own son, Nathan, but the three had promised to be here in an hour or so. Steve and Rachel, arriving with their parents grinned happily,as the young Family members drew them away from their elders. Paul enthusiastically embraced everyone. His eyes were wet, and his grin wide, he had wanted this Gather so much. The Summer Festival was over, the excitement of those few days, always at the full moon of the month, seemed a fitting precedence for this Gather. He had seen the new kind of relationship among people this summer, stronger, clearer than ever before. It was time!

They all moved into the sprawling deck where tables were already spread with food and drink. It would begin as a party, just catching up, talking of every day living. Paul's longing to begin the talk of serious things, was held in check. He too wanted to make that loving greeting, the touching of one another, the renewal of contact with the children. It did not seem long since the last Gather. Why was this so important to him? To everyone? As if each hoped for something special this day. They heard the Temple Gong ring in Adwin as the Sun broke over the Mountain top. Turning, they watched, softly murmuring the Vagabond welcome to the Sun. Then Ben sang, his deep booming voice encompassing them all, and one by one they joined in,singing the songs of Dawn. Spontanious, it was a benedication to this day. Just as they finished, the soft thud of feet announced that Mary and the boys had arrived. The small scuffle of greeting was done and they settled to make their Gather.

Paul's happiness was made perfect by the fact that Will had come with Annette this time. Perhaps they could find a way to understanding between them all. William was dressed in a soft light grey, instead of his usual black or dark blue. Even in shorts and shirt, he was more formal than anyone else. He looked around at everyone, his smile full of genuine pleasure. This was indeed his Family and he enjoyed being home with them again. He beamed at the children, responded to embraces and listened with amusement to the songs. But he couldn't join in, he didn't know the vagabond songs and was surprised that everyone else did. He thought they sang well, their harmony nearly professional. He could hear Annette standing near him, her clear, sweet soprano leading, then carrying descant above the lower voices. It was a lovely beginning.

They gathered at the tables, got food, and went to sit in the low chairs. The morning was still faintly cool, the heat of the day not yet begun. Everyone talked, the low buss of many conversations seemed to Will to be right and pleasant. The sun slanted now across the fine polished wood of the deck, the shade of the great Walnut not yet down upon it. The weeping willow on the other side, swept the floor making a screen of long soft branches and the children had retreated behind that privacy. When the first burst of chatter leveled off, Rose looked around, then caught their minds with a gentle Reach. They were immediately silent, and she gestured at the tables, then said aloud,"We can help ourselves any time, but let's begin. I think it'll be comfortable here most of the day, as soon as the sun reaches mid-day, the Walnut tree will shade us and one joy of living on a hill is the rising breeze in the afternoon". Everyone seemed satisfied, comfortable and feeling that special delight at being together, the way Families sometimes do at Christmas time during Winter Festival of the December full moon.

She went on, "God bless us all that we've come together. I'm glad we've begun to have Gathers frequently. We'd gotten pretty careless. But today, we've a lot to talk about, to discover and to share. We'd best begin."

There was a brief stirring around, people getting final bits of food, or a full cup, some carrying empty dishes to the auto server, or drawing those left out of the sun. They pulled the chairs into a circle, bringing huge cushions to fill spaces between and everyone was there, sitting or lying in comfort.

Rose turned to Ben, her eyes asking and he came to sit in the wide chair with her. He said,"I'll begin. We've got some speaking to do, something from every one. We've got some confessions to make. Everyone of us. We need to clear our selves with one another. So that we can go on to the things we have to decide about." His eyes moved around among them, meeting every other pair of eyes, listening and opening his own mind to hear acutely. He was proud of the calm with which he did that. He did not Reach.

Rose looked around,, found Jessie sitting at one side, a little behind the others. Cassandra sat on a pile of cushions in front of her. They smiled and Rose thought how short a time it had been when they would never have thought to share their mind Touch, never have acknowledged their Talents. It had taken only a good talk together to correct that. Maybe this Gather would be as releasing. What is going to happen to us? Serious small fears pricked against her heart, wanted to swell and displace her joy. But she released them like bubbles breaking. With a lurch of recognition, she almost cried out the thought,'Especially Ben! He sits here, allowing us to see, to know of his feelings. He is utterly accepting. He's more so than I am. And a year ago last spring, such a terrible time between us.'

Benjamin began to talk to them. She realizeed that the others were focussed, attentive, listening with unusual attention. "We've got some real problems. We all know a lot of people are stirred up, angry, even confused about what's happening. So far we've been so secretive we made their suspicions worse. It's our own fault. We've got to explain to people what's happening. What we know. But even more, we've got to talk about the Vision we begin to See."

William was on his feet, his face flushed, angry, "Wait, surely you're not saying that you are willingly part of that mumbo jumbo that's been going on in the Valley? What of the children? Surely not they?" No one spoke, simply waited, nodding, and he frowned, a sudden swift look of terror crossed his face but was instantly repressed. "It can't be. You act as if it's perfectly natural, that it's a good thing." He looked around and they could see his disappointment. He shook his head, anger, fear, sorrow and a sense of exclusion warred in his breast.

"Will, we've tried to tell you. You didn't want to hear! Paul spoke quietly.

William gestured exasperated, "Oh, no, you didn't really say it out like that just now." At Paul's nod and frown, he went on,

" You must all know that I lead the North Valley branch of the Builders. That I am a full member of that group. Yet, you speak as though they are separate from the rest of us -- of you."

Ben breathed a long painful sigh. This had to be. This would have to be done first today. "William, we know that you are a leader with them. We don't want to separate ourselves from them, We want all Valley people to be one people. Surely that's been obvious to you all these years? But we think that the Builders don't want to be with us."

"I think it is the other way round. We see you pulling away, entering into activity that is evil, wrong, unhealthy. We know of the practices, and we know that even children are involved. Children! Ben. Surely it is not true of our own children.I've seen the town young ones in Altos using what you call Talents. I've been told they thin the fruit trees without using their muscles. Now, you know that has to be a lie. I am appalled that we let such self delusions go on. But even the Councils seems to think such ideas are all right."

"Why do the Builders think that is evil?"

"If they are doing that, if they actually move objects without their bodies aid, then it is an energy that is unnatural. That kind of thing is and always has been evil. What other energy could they use ?" He stopped, convinced he had said the last word. looking at them with barely supressed anger, he hesitated then went on."If it is not real, only a pretense,that seems worse. Why play with tricks like that? Those things are not natural, they are witchcraft, at their worst and self delusion at the least."

"William, think about it! People have created machines to do their hard labor, we did that with our minds. Now our children have learned they can do it directly with mind power. Why is that so different?"

" No! No!" His anger leaped across his face, he brought both hands up in harsh stiffness. No one had ever heard William of Altos lose his cool. None except Annette and she sat holding Tom's hand in a painful grip, her body rigid. Will caught himself, his flushed face draining to pale, and bent his head. His fingers had been moving in a rapid, nervous, fine flutter and he brought them quiet by closing his fist. He took a deep breath to everyone's consternation, and spoke as calmly as was his habit. They grieved, he needed to yell, to speak out his fury, his fear; they'd rather he had. "It's not the same. This is unnatural and I grieve to see it. In my own Family, but more" and now his voice turned stern, hard, "I'm appalled to see my Family DEFEND these very evils."

Benjamin saw that William believed what he said, he no longer questioned. His emotions had locked up his good mind. Why was he so frightened, so angry?

He let his eyes flicker to the others, a brief contact reassured him but revealed their pain. His heart ached to speak so to this brother. "Will, we can't stop our growth. These new Talents ARE natural to us. You must believe that. They aren't evil as far as we can know. We intend no evil use of them."

Tom spoke up then, feeling Annette's dispair, "William, we love you. You must know that,. You are our brother in every way. Uncle to our children. Yet, we must make this clear. For centuries people have known of these Talents beginning to crop up among human kind. There were charlatans who pretended, or who had a little Talent and used that little to fool others, to manipulate others. Yes, that's true. But most people saw through that and just enjoyed the play of it. I can't remember of any real harm being done, even then."

William, dropped like a heavy weight into his chair. His eyes bleak, a naked fear visible, but immediately, as though hiding that, they were flaming with renewed anger. He looked at Annette, their eyes met and he saw her involvement. He flinched, and she shrank, tears starting from her eyes that she must stand in opposition to him now. He said, "I refuse these powers, I refuse to believe that there are such things. I have not had a genuine example, nor have I seen true use of them. I say we must return to our old ways and destroy these temptations before they seduce you beyond reach." His voice had taken on a note of terror, and those listening realized that that fine, intellect, was not functioning. He was unaware that his terror was broadcast, or that the mental blackness around him was a cloud of fury, fear, self pity, and a desparate note of feeling utterly lost. What was this? Rose Reached to heal, wanting to know the source of such desparate fear.

He turned suddenly to her, as if the very Touch of her small Healing had irritated him, "You Rose, pretending to be a sister and suggesting that your Love is true among us. It isn't that love you offer, neither the personal love of yourself, nor the True Love that the Teachers taught us. You've betrayed us. We trusted you."

They could see that he was gone from them, lost and gone from his own sure reason. Will whose strength was that reason. He was drowned now in the habits of thought it had shaped. Now he would not question. This was unlike William, unlike completely. What was the terrible fear they sensed behind all these feelings and could not quite define? He thought that he acted now from pure caring. That this Family was falling over an edge into insanity,into foolishness at the best, and he must save them.

Rose bent her head, hiding the tears that wet her face. How could they themselves see? They too were lost in old emotions that blinded them. Jessie sent comfort, and she felt it,easing her pain, but she did not lift her head.

William went on,"Yes, hide your face in shame. It's fitting. You've betrayed your trust among us and you would have the Valley denied to everyone except those who practice these unnatural ways. You would deny the rest of us, because we see it's wrong."

Paul sighed, realizing what was tearing apart that strong man's heart. What he would not admit but what was beginning to be obvious. For the first time in William's life he cannot control any part of what is happening. Of course, that is the fear, he thought. But he did not speak.

Ben had leaped to his feet, reached up and took Will's shoulder in his great hand. Will towered over him,,tall and thin to Ben's powerful shorter body. Ben made no effort to hide the tears that wet his face and they infuriated William. He pushed the hand away, turned in a new fury,"You Ben, you can't control your women, your children. You've let things get out of control. Do you realize that. OUT OF CONTROL! Aren't we men any more? Can't we control our lives?"

The impact of the question brought sober cool recognition. That freed them from their own emotions and they looked at one another. Then at William. He was surely not the old William who would ALWAYS listen to a debate - argue on either side, explore every nuance of a new idea.They must see what had happened to close this eager searching mind. They felt hope, maybe they might heal him, if they could know enough.

Paul saw. Will was afraid that he was left out, that he would be excluded because he had no Talent that he knew of. He saw them practicing what he could not be part of. And he could not compete at all. He was - would be seen as inferior! He had regressed to very old social attitudes. Control his wife indeed! Paul felt a sinking of his heart. How could they heal that. It was the way William would take this difference. He wanted to speak, but dared not.

Ben chose not to answer Will's questions. He would get to the heart of this. "Will, it's time we talked of the City, I think. That's part of all this. Ever since you took that trip there, you've seemed different. What happened there?"

William squared his shoulders, as if attack had come from another direction. Annette nearly sobbed aloud to see him. He felt cornered, felt attacked from every side. She could not help him.

"That's another problem. There's no reason it should have made any change in anyone, and yet anyone can see Paul's different. Jennifer too." His eyes widened slightly, and his voice was strained,"Even my own wife!:" She's not been the same since that trip. It was a terrible mistake. I'm seriously disappointed in her. She won't listen to reason. She defies me. DEFIES me !" His voice had risen. He stopped, appalled at himself, drew himself together again. "I tell you Ben," his eyes were cold,his voice tight and low, "When a man loses a mate, and is losing his Family, then he must turn to others who see things as he does. People who make sense. I can't accept this fantasy of the City. It seems to be turning your minds to mush."

"Then you think that the Builder's fear of the City is valid? Tom spoke mostly to turn the tide of anger from others to himself.

He succeeded, William took off as if he had finally found a worthy opponent. "That City has got to be destroyed! Not just studied! No! It needs to be removed and forgotten! Yes, I think that its strange influence is a superstition but too many people have been caught in that superstition. If it were not there then people could get on with their lives and forget the notion that the Vagabonds have been feeding our children for generations."

He stopped, his eyes sweeping imperiously from one to another. He was confident again."Don't deny it. They have done that! It's been an evil thing. They've betrayed us too. We thought we could trust them. And you see how they've repaid us." He took a deep breath and went on,,his anger finally getting vented on something that was not so close to home. The others listened, keeping their minds shielded, their attention focussed. They felt the pain that was the source of these outbursts from Will.They did not want him to sense their dispair. They could see, hear, and feel the fire that burned in him. They had no choice, He broadcast without knowing it. He talked on a while, discharging months of anger that had built around that journey,and that City. The City that had made him feel something he could not define or accept. The City that had influenced others in ways he could not understand. Finally, he turned to his chair, picked up his coffee and drank deeply. Then settling down, he said,his voice quite calm again,"Well, now, surely you must see the facts are clear. We must make changes here in this Valley in order to make life worth living again. In order to protect ourselves!"

Rose said, "Will, it won't be possible for us to deny what we are already gifted with."

"If these -what you call gifts, are good, then why are there those without them? If they are not evil, why are they denied me?" The question had finally been asked.

No one spoke. No one knew how to speak of that. Finally he turned to Jessie unaware that she invited him."You Jessie, you're the cause of this. None of this was happening until you came here. I think you must know something about this. Why don't you speak?"

She nodded, "It's true, William, that some do not have these Talents. That some do not seem ready to Reach out of old patterns enough , or do not have

Mind development adequate enough."

Such a statement was bound to infuriate William and she knew that, so she waited."You mean that those who profess this garbage are more intelligent than the rest of us?"

"Oh ,no, William, not more intelligent. Surely you know that you stand forth among us all in intellect." The statement had an immediate mollifyig effect. But you see, there is another quality of Mind besides intellect, and that must also be developed."

"And what is that?"

It has been called intuition, it has been also called, Heart knowledge. That development of the Heart is absolutely necessary for these are talents to be protected from misuse." She watched him,and focussed steadily a streaming Love and healing energy that he absorbed unknowingly."What would happen if such talents were given to those who were not sufficiently developed spiritually, unable to know clearly the nature of Love Itself, of that True Love the Teachers taught you of?"

He frowned, intrigued, a debate he could hold his own in. "Yes,if these Talents exist, then that would be a danger.How can we know you, who people say are more aware, won't misuse them?"

"As I've said,they are a part of the development in Spiritual consciousness,what might be called a fourth dimension of reality. They are results of Soul Consciousness, of the raising of consciousness to its higher level so that a greater landscape of life is seen. But they are only part of an expansion of consciousness. You will concede that mind does expand? " At his puzzled frown but faint nod, she continued, "As for why some do not have them, we might as well ask why some have Talent as musicians and others don't. Why some can sing with glorious beauty and other only very ordinary sweetness. It is a Talent like any other."

He was silent for some time, "You mean only those you call conscious enough to be aware of Spirit would have such talents?"

" No, of course not.Such Talents've occurred in minor form for centuries. But a mind developing to consciousness of Spirit, the farthest reaches of Mind perhaps, seems to discover also certain other perceptive skills. Like a new set of senses, or heightened senses."

She smiled," But such awakening occurs simultaniously with the awareness of the presence of Love, such a person would have practiced selflessness, harmlessness. Otherwise, such a person could do great harm."

He snorted,"It's impossible. You make it sound like some natural process. But if it were everyone would be included! No matter what you say to try to prove differently, those people are dangerous. How can I know they are people of Loving Hearts? How can anyone know? It's childish to think that only the Good will have such Talents. Does that mean that those who do not have them are not Good?" He was furious again and his face black with frowns.

She patiently continued,"No, Will, for Goodness is not what I mean. There are so many, like yourself who are truly Good people. And they do not necessarily have the Talents, and their minds may not be developed to realize Spirit. But enlargement of perception comes from minds reaching out to farther dimensions of Mind. Such a stretch of mind reveals the validity of selflessness, and such people have practiced harmlessness because it makes sense. That is the logic of the Soul. Perception of reality is enlarged. A person perceiving from Soul Consciousness sees clearly that each of us in inseparate from every other and therefore, the Self includes all people. Remember that ancient cliche,'all people are selfish, but the result of their action depends on the size of the self.' Such people can be trusted."

" How can you trust such people not to invade another mind. To invade another's privacy? That is a sin."

"Surely it is. None who have that Talent can invade another's privacy.It's actually impossible,the way the mind works, but even if they could,they would not. Oh, we Send without knowing, our emotions, our attitudes, sometimes. We have always had people who could influence us, persuade, etc. They had to manipulate through playing on another's fear or angers or desires." She stopped, William was listening fascinated, as if finally he was hearing what he could listen to. Yet a troubled frown kept flickering across his face and his eyes were stern.

Jessie went on, focussing again that Healing current. "But these who begin to Know, to See,they are people of much higher perception.It seems difficult for you to realize that Soul perception makes these old small selfishnesses pointless. It isn't that such people are 'Good' necessarily, but rather that they see it's pointless to harm another,to do so would be to harm oneself." She paused, listening to the opening minds around her, aware of their joining her in this flow of Love and Healing to their brother."You see, William, That's why it's so essential that we Teach well. The children are beginning to be born with brains that can express such Talents if their minds are developed enough to use those brains. They must be taught how to use them rightly. They must have a highly developed ethical sense. And they do! Have you known of one person whose mind has been invaded against her will?"

Will stood wavering, her voice, her manner convincing him. She radiated truth, Love. He felt it,though he wouldn't have been able to speak of it.He wanted to deny that benevolent influence, and could not. It was clearly true that a radiance of Love surrounded her. He stood a moment,"What can we do. What can the Builders do to meet this danger? If it's true we cannot destroy it?"

"Will, why you do not have these Talents, in this life time, is something only you will be able to answer. I could never say you can't See, I can only say that as of right now, you don't! And this Seeing is not of the intellect. But of the heart. The Heart reveals its wisdom to the intellect if that intellect will stll itself enough to receive. We cannot know why one is born so and another not, just as we do not know why one is born a painter and another a builder. We do know one thing. People who are not Spiritually developed, in Mind and heart, do not have these Talents to sufficient degree to be effective. Also they seem unable to Mind

Reach. That is our safeguard. Only those vowed to selflessness and harmlessness will realize such talent. Those who See enough to realize the absolute presence of Love. Those who are ready to Mind Join."

" D'you mean that three year old children have made these vows?" his voice was full of sarcasm.

"Yes,I do mean that. They have made those vows from another life time."

"Oh, that again. Well, I have pretty well accepted continuous life times.It is logical,after all. And I suppose it is possible that such a development in mind could be." He didn't know of the collective sigh of relief that was breathed. He had finally reached that point of acceptance, approval and well being from which he could again think. He heaved a long hard breath, shuddering a little as he found some composure to his emotions. the release of his fury had helped. Jessie's clear statements of his goodness, his wisdom and his place among them, had helped.

Finally a different voice, a touch of loneliness in it, brought new tears to several sets of eyes."I want to accept these ideas. I can see that the fact that I do not have certain talents, does not diminish me, or my friends, but then, I seem to be interested in things you are not interested in. "He was silent, and finally said, "Well,I suuppose that's not so different after all. But I want to be part of this Family. Even though I still doubt you know or see what say you do. Maybe I can accept that, somehow." He sat, twisting his hands in a way no one had ever seen from William. Never had Paul known him so vulnerable in public. Perhaps he had seldom even been with Annette so, for they all felt her in-drawn breath and tenderness for him. "You say another life time might bring such a gift to the rest of us!" It was clearly a statement not a question. They relaxed.

Everyone waited, then Jerry said,"William,,you can never be other than part of our Family. You are, always will be, our Brother. No matter how much change goes on." He was grinning and William met his eyes, believing him.

Will sat straighter, his hands finally quiet,"I still cannot believe that a human being can be free of selfishness, of greed, of the need to control,to use their power for themselves. Humankind is selfish by nature! I can't see how people are free of that."

Jessie nodded, "That you can't see is the difference. But, as for that,look around you! You see a whole Family together here and you see their practice of living. Isn't that so? William, remember their lives, remember the way they live and act. You do notice those qualities missing from their lives." Her eyes went from one to another. Gently she Reached out and Touched every mind and gently they responded, even the thin, hesitant response from Steve and Jane, the wavering and resistant response from Silvia. Their faces slowly relaxed. The knowledge was clear. 'We Vow to selflessness. If we cannot hold true to that, we ask our Family to intervene and bring us strength needed to sustain us.' Will watched, felt a sense of power surge around the circle, a power so gentle and so inclusive that he misnamed it. Yet, he nodded slowly, he thought that might, after all,be true.

THE JOURNEY

Ben grinned wryly,"We vow to selflessness,and we notice when we are not. We pay attention to ourselves. Even though it hurts. Which it often does." His face was suddenly sober.

William studied their faces for a long moment, his own speculative, the anger gone."How do I know that one of you, one of these Talented people, will not use their Talent to harm someone who is defenseless," he heaved a great sigh,"one of us?"

The pronoun caught them suddenly like a sharp knife. They glanced at one another mentally but kept their eyes on him, and Jessie answered," "Will, would you? Would you, yourself? Do you think that you could or would harm others out of some desire of your own?"

He answered immediately,"Not knowingly. I am a man of honor. But how can I know that my ideas are always as harmless to others as I think they are? "He frowned harshly, exposing deep lines in that youthful face and they knew more of his suffering. "After all, how many of us have acted to effect another 'for his own good' and done harm?"

Ben couldn't resist a smile. This was his old friend and brother. He was confident his words were true. Will was, if nothing else, honest with himself. He said, "We ask ourselves that daily, William, just as any honest person like yourself does. It's your great intelligence, we count on, Will, and that intelligence has proven us right, because you've asked the most important question we know right now."

"And how can we be sure everyone will ask it?" His tone was sarcastic, but that they could deal with."

Ben felt the support of all the others, suddenly with him, making a foundation for his committment. He said softly,"Because we can do that thing we told you of, we can JOIN. And we begin to See. To see life from that large view, makes selflessness natural. It is true, William, it makes no sense to live for oneself alone,or even for one's personal loved ones. We do know ourselves, we cannot lie to one another very well. When one of us loses balance, we all support. And we are committed to balance as to life itself."

"It sounds like a mind control system." Will's voice grated now, but much less harshly, with both resentment and sarcasm.

Ben held his calm as carefully as his cup of scalding coffee. "It might be, perhaps, except that it is a Talent developed only among those whose ethics rise from an ability to see life from a high place. What we call Soul Conscious is referring to that ability to see from soul view. But we are together now, we see from the view of many, and that view changes our attitudes. We support and remind one another constantly". He stopped, worrying that he did not speak clearly. "William, there are built in safeguards that humans develop even as we develop greater Vision. For example the recognition that to harm another is to harm oneself, changes our world view, our social attitudes utterly,." His face intent, his eyes pleading that William understand, he felt his desire leap into his throat. "Society can never be the same."

"William felt the urgency in Ben, but he spoke as if surprised,"I don't understand why you think this change is different from normal growth. All of us must continue to learn and understand. We all are developing mentally. What is this difference?"

"I think that I mean an extension of awareness into another dimension, perhaps. It is of another quality of being. We've developed mentally, you know, for several million years. It is now we continue into an awareness of what we've called Spirit. And still, we only vaguely guess what that means. We are not just mental beings, we are spiritual beings also. From that level of awareness we know finally that Life itself is alive. The wonderful mystery that permeates the physical world, has become conscious to us through mind and now, it reveals itself in all its majesty through this quality of humankind called Spirit."

Rose said softly, all the time radiating the Love she felt, in as focussed a manner as she knew,to William,"It's the beginning, William, it's that awakening our teachers have always spoken of. The inner Awakening, that perception that leaps beyond our ordinary mental lives."

"You mean mystical experience?" His voice rasped.

She nodded, hopeful,"Well, that's one way it occurs."

"The results of such experience are illogical. Pure delusion sometimes and at their best, questionable."

"Yes, surely, that's been the assumption. But they occur after years of study, training of body, mind, emotions. they come as we lift our consciousness deliberately. They come from stillness of self." She stopped, bit her lip, could she ever explain? "At any rate, we haven't learned how to think about that dimension logically. It seems to have its own brand of logic that our brains haven't grasped, or language can't define.It transcends even the logic of fine poetry or of the highest mathmatics."

William visibly relaxed, he drew his chair closer to them and sat in it as though tension was gone. They had intrigued that sharp questioning mind. He would persue this all day if they let him. "You're speaking of that 'awakening to higher knowledge,' that our Teachers spoke of and that always seemed so puzzling. Are you saying it is a REAL experience for you? That there IS such a 'higher' knowledge?

Paul's clear tenor voice interjected, and Ben and Rose both felt the ease of tension."It is that. But it's only -mysterious - to the extent that we don't understand. Yes, it's a real experience and it's opening our whole selves,emotions, mind,heart, body, all that we are. It is REAL, William, and you must see that. All of us can't be delusional." He stopped,smiling faintly, glanced around, and then added,"You know that we aren't the same kind of people we were even in our grandparents day. We have changed from deep within us so that we don't think as we once did, we don't want, desire, perceive our world as they did. Look at the way we treat our Earth! Will, you KNOW that. That's true for every one."

He looked around, fidgeted. The whole family seemed too sure, too convinced. Surely they couldn't all be lying. He said, "So then, you can't deny . You admit that you have these Talents that are not -not - normal." His face was again strained, flushed.

"No! What we do is normal." Ben's tone was defensive.

Jessie signaled with a light shake of her head," Wouldn't it be better to acknowledge to William that what we do, what we're realizing has seemed to be not normal? In that sense, William, yes, we have Talents that are not normal to the old way of life." She was still with a quietness that refused him permission to rage openly. For William was a gentleman.

Finally he spoke again, completely back in control, relaxing, a little beginning of acceptance nudging into his emotions. "That is what the Builders resent. These -- things you do, these in-human practices, are not right. Not reasonable. We cannot help but resent them." His calm held, his voice steady but his eyes were naked with pain and anger again. They felt the exposure of that pain like a blow. Ben recoiled, feeling compassion blurred with pity that nearly demolished his own good sense.

Then, softening a little, William's eyes filled with a desparation that infused his controlled manner. He said," I might be able to accept that you are entering into a dimension of Spiritual consciousness, though I don't understand it. But these Talents! I can't get past the impression that they are patterns of evil. Psychic evil and dangerous."

They were silent, then Rose said,"Will, anything can be used for evil - if one does not know Love."   He glared at her, his anger at his mate included all women now." Love! Love! What is that? Another vague meaningless word. Surely you don't expect me to think you are capable of more Love than anyone else? Than us, the Builders, for instance?" He was staring angrily at Jessie.

"No, William, but we may be more aware of Love. Love present among us equally alive in every person. We may be more conscious of its power." She smiled unperturbed.

"You talk as if it's something other than our own feeling."

"It is, Will. Love is an energy, not just available but fundamental to every living thing. It is unceasingly PRESENT! But we must wake to that Presence!"

He shook his head, and frowned, standing again, walking again, his body expressing frustration that he could not convince them. They saw that they could not show him what they realized. Their insistence frightened him because he did not understand. Ben turned the conversation.

"Will what is it the Builders want?"

Will tore his eyes from Jessie, the appeal in them so naked she grieved and could not help. He could not bear to assume his Family had all become idiots. Neither could he countenance their ideas. Ben's question brought him down into an immediate matter he could talk about. The instant of plea to Jessie was gone, he was furious, ready now to fight. "We - and I include myself, want all the good things that life can bring, the beauty, richness of living, the enjoyment of pleasures of our sophistocated tastes, just what the Valley has already given us.

And we want new space, room to create a world that we can imagine for ourselves. For ourselves, mind you, not for every animal running wild." He eyed them thoughtfully a moment, his anger abated."I know all of you have contributed to what our Valley has become. Surely we don't deny that.But we want to extend those pleasures, those possibilities. We can gain more control over this world, this Valley. " He shook his head,"Can't you see that? It's no more than people have always wanted." He pointed one stiff finger at Ben, "You! You want the same, don't tell me that you will use your power for anything else. You want to wrest the power from those who cannot -- do not have the Talents. You would dominate all those who are without them. Who haven't developed into monsters." The last word was a harsh bark and they saw that his control was slipping again. For Will that was devastating.He would never forgive himself therefore he would not forgive them, unless they could heal that shame immediately.

Jessie's voice rang out with the subtle authority, the Sound of the Voice, they seldom heard, but did recognize. "You're right!" The agreement caught Will's attention as nothihng else could have."We want to know the beauty, the wonder of life. We desire the full flowering through humankind of that which is called Soul Consciousness. Therefore, you must see that to want dominance is impossible for us." Jessie knew well that such a statement would intrigue that sharp mind. He would not rest until he understood such a paradox.He could not doubt her. He stood looking at her, his face cleared, receptive."I don't see the connection. If you want these -- then why --? He shifted, "but then, what do you mean by Soul Conscious?"

She nodded, satisfied that she had deflected his emotional attention."That is the consciousness of what is beyond these desires you spoke of. Beyond them as the sun is beyond a candle. Those who have begun to See, to know of THAT which is piercing like a flame out of our very deepest selves to inform the consciousness of humankind, and that literally infuses our minds, are not as they once were. Among them there is no desire for control, for indulgence in -- pleasures of racial childhood. There is gone that overweaning desire to possess, to amass treasures, to demand power and to wield it over others. The pleasures of political life, of wealth, of goods, of the indulgence of the senses has so little attraction they seem to have dissolved from these who See. They do not interest us personally, but only in that they create a good world for all life". Her voice had the sharp decisiveness that even the Family had rarely heard . It surprised him. He had thought of her as a mild mannered little old lady who spoke vaguely and uninterestingly and seldom. He stared at her.

"Then they aren't human any more. How can they lose all their normal desires?"

"They haven't, not all of them. They stand between now, in various degrees of detachment, of release from themselves. Just as they are, to different degrees,aware."

For a moment he stood, his mind working through so many possibilities, then he said,"I don't believe you." He was back to normal. He had forgotten that momentary lapse that had revealed his terror and rage at that terror. Jessie saw that shifting of mind, rearrangement of memory, perceptions, rearrangement of thought, recognitions so that they supported again the old assumptions. Extreme new ideas distorted reality for Will and he could not bear the disruption. He deliberately surrounded himself with conviction. She shuddered faintly. How could one Reach through such a barrier?

"William, you don't have to believe her" Rose spoke so softly they were deeply quiet to hear. " Just be willing to allow us our fantasy if that is the way you see it. I know it would distress you to think your family is deluded. But bear with us. Group delusion is not common, you know. There must be something else going on. We at least, mean no harm to the Builders." Will drew his eyes from Jessie and turned to her finally with a look of calm superiority. His usual look! Rose grinned suddenly at him willing him to accept. Wanting that.

He nodded curtly, in that relief of acceptance,then said,"Rose, this woman, Jessie is not a good person for our family to include. I do not vote for her acceptance among us." The statement was so unexpected that everyone stared at him.Then with swift understanding, dropped their eyes and attention. A subvocal murmur spread among them, Will was so irrevocably distancing himself.

" Now," he said,his voice careful, full of his usual charm, bringing all his own powers to play, "We ought to see, Jessie, just what you mean. We can't any longer allow the fuzzy thinking that has been drawing our Family apart. I don't for a moment accept that what is called 'Soul Consciousness' is any different from pure reason, which is what I understood it to be when the Teachers spoke of it. What you speak of is like the idea of God, a notion that people use to comfort themselves with in times of trouble, or fool themselves with when they don't want to think. So let's put that aside. I would grieve to think that my Family was deluded by such fantasies. You're not fools and I have never thought you so." He grimaced,"It would have made things simple had I been able to believe that. But even intelligent people can get caught in emotional traps, I suppose. It is emotional, all emotional.And perhaps you need a good balancing with the Healers." He gave each of them a reproachful glance.

He stood silently for a long moment, then slid into his chair, reached long slim fingers to pick up his cup then stood and brought a carafe of bright green tea, with ice balls clinking again the glass. He poured himself a drink, then glanced around, and got several nods. He went to fill their glasses and found himself feeling in command again. When he was seated, he said,"Now, of course, it's not true that you don't want those very human pleasures and possessions that people have always wanted. After all, we're all human,aren't we?" He turned to Jessie, lifting his head in question.

She met his eyes, her own mild and gentle with a shining of Love that caused him to turn away. He did not understand that melting beauty and so mis- interpreted it. She said,"Will, that's a fair question. What is it that you think might PROVE whether we have lost interest in what the world's power -- or wealth - might bring."

He measured her thoughtfully with bright confident eyes. "Well, if someone made you an offer, gave you the wealth, the power, made it clear that it was a real power and wealth, then perhaps that noble pinnacle would seem less attractive. It is a pinnacle you've dreamed yourself onto. It isn't real. This offer is real. I will make that offer myself. If you Jessie, would leave this Valley, this family, go away and never come back nor contact them. I will offer you unlimited credit in the Valley banks." He hesitated, his own honesty affirming itself,"Of course, unlimited, with our rigid council, means only half a million Credits a year. But that's twice what anyone else has. Will you accept?"

His voice wavered a little. The offer was grand, he was not absolutely sure the dark One would go so far to rid himself of this woman.

The others were tense, watching the two. Their minds Reaching and then restrained. They would not interfere. Jessie smiled,"Your offer is generous -- tempting" Will smiled, as one conspirator to another.

Jennifer was transfixed, a wail coming from her throat that she herself did not recognize. "No, no, Jessie, surely you would not be tempted."

Paul slid an arm around her, drew her back to him."Shh, sweetheart, listen."

Jessie had not taken her gaze from William though he looked only at her mouth and would not meet her eyes. Now she nodded slowly, but said nothing. Jennifer spoke again, more softly,"There is power all around her, William. Can't you feel it? It isn't the same kind of power one feels around you. You know you do have a power, like a whip of will. While hers is -- like a brilliance of Light." She slid back into the curve of Paul's arm, an expression of puzzlement on her face. "From where did those words come?"

Paul said slowly,"From your own true Self, my dear. There is always power available, it is only a matter of being able to hold it."

Jessie nodded, flicked a glance at them. "Yes, there is always power. It is whether we know how to reach It. It is also whether we are open enough to receive it. It is whether we misuse or misunderstand."

"You could use it to give yourself whatever you desire? Fulfil those old deep needs that were left unsatisfied in your life? " Rose spoke musingly for all of them, seeing the temptation of it. Jessie listened, letting her mind turn, to look into those depths where such desires once hid, once stood in demand, were known and not denied until they faded into nothingness. The shadows of those desires grinned in mock salute. She smiled faintly. then suddenly, she laughed,"Could or would?" She shook her head,"It isn't like that."

Her face changed, she drew back into herself,,gathered herself,was still and deeply attentive. The silence was so deep that Will suddenly was uncomfortable, but he thought she had been thoroughly defeated. Exposed. And then, there was a faint,bright tinkle, a soft falling and a shower of gold coins fell all around them.

Silvia stooped to pick one up. "It's gold, pure lovely gold. So soft and so mild." Her voice broke, she was crying."Never have I seen such lovely gold."

Jessie was holding out her hand. On it was an emerald, the size of a small egg, it's radiance of green light pouring through the stone drew all their eyes.It was luminous with a beauty in which all human delight seemed held. They all began to move to her. Rising from their chairs and cushions, the children crawled across the deck, to pick up and examine the coins. They stared at Jessie, their eyes wide and troubled. Will was drawn too, as if against his will, picking up coins, touching, feeling them. Rose put out a hand to touch the stone, feeling its cool beauty.

Anna said,"You -- could bear this beauty. Could use it, have it for your own?" Her voice was full of pain, a strange grief rising.

Jessie stood bathed in the light. "You can take these. They are yours, to use or to keep. They are real. Hold this emerald in your hand. What do you feel?"

Jerry sighed, letting his hands fall from their reaching to her."Oh No! The gold is real. The stone has power. Look, it draws it, holds it. It's like a holy symbol, it's radiance pulses! Why it pulses with Love, Jessie." He stared at her,"Or perhaps with yours?" His face was full of astonishment and warmth.

Jessie nodded," It receives what it is given from us." She laughed. "Love is present, we project it, and the stone carries it. But feel the whole of it. Does it not draw else?" She gave it into his hand.

Rose reached out one hand, touched lightly the shimmering stone, her eyes dark, glowing, full of tears. She nodded slowly, falling back, her hands drawn into her waist tightly.

Anna shook her head,"It's not fair, is it Mother? Jessie? To tempt us so?"

Jessie turned and found Anna with her eyes, her look was like fire, but tender, alight." Who takes the gold and the stone, and is free of it? For the power of it is his own -- all his own. Who then has the courage to pour into the stone all her - or his - nature. The stone has no choice. Evil fills it as fully as does good. " She watched them, gently sad.

Ben woke as from a trance, "And all our evil rouses up to haunt us then. Our hidden desires are reflected back to us from such stones? Is this then the curse of the great jewels of history? Human lust recorded within them?" He moved as if released from prisoning. "And there are none of us without selfish desires. Without dark longings."

Rose leaned toward Jessie,"Please Mother, how can you tempt us so?"

Jessie smiled, her eyes moving from one to another. Jerry extended his hand, laid the stone into Jessie's. He said. "Not she, not she who tempts us but our own selves. And yet, there is such beauty there. See? The dark shadows shot through, that emphasize the Light. Such wonderful beauty!" His voice had a tone of sadness and longing but he smiled at himself.

Tom cried out, "Holy Mother! Let go. I will to be free of this." Coins slid, dripping softly from Silvia's hands, falling, a light sound against the floor, as if she had forgotten them.

Jane rose from where she had knelt to gather some, let them lie on her hand shining in the sunlight. "Only the utterly pure could be trusted with such power. Lead me not into temptation for I am not so pure." Her eyes met Jessie's and she burst into tears. But Jessie smiled at her and Jane felt a new sense of life spreading through her body. Through her mind, like a sweep of Light, waking something. She was absorbed in the changing flood within her, she felt no loss when the coins fell.

Rose nodded, "The answer Jessie - you've given us the answer and it is both yes and no. We are not prepared to know, to direct such energy as these or to have such choices.You can and do have that power, you can allow yourself and know yourself enough."

Jessie turned to Will. Her face stern."Do you see Will? The offer you make has no attraction."

He looked at her, then down at the scattered coins, shining coins, his face bewildered, anxious. Several shone in his hands, he cradled them. Then there passed across his face something that he would have sworn was absent from his heart. A thin cloud of simple avarice obscured her meaning. He was overwhelmed by desire, not for the wealth, but for that wonderful beauty of the Emerald. To have it. To own it. To keep it hidden for himself. He forgot everything else until his eyes met Jessie's and shook him from it's pull a little. he said,"Oh! Oh! yes, Jessie, I suppose. How ever, you have played a trick on us here haven't you?" He laughed and she slowly shook her head.

"It's no trick, Will. No trick. Try to understand the meaning. One whose desires are still immersed in possession is by that very fact also empty of that knowledge which would give him power to control. They are self exclusive. So life is protected a little from such evil."

He nodded, uncomprehending, still gazing at the floor of the deck then up again to the Jewel sitting on the table. He realized that he could not attribute this to illusion. He didn't want to. Jessie turned away to walk toward the outer steps into the gardens.

She said,"One who knows such power wills no longer from personal desire. That would be a great danger. Such a one responds to no voice except that of Spirit. Desires nothing and knows the Joy of that. Look." She turned,,stepping into the garden, extending one hand to indicate the Valley beyond them,, "There is the Glory. The radiant beauty of Earth Life, blazing out at us from every hill and meadow, catches our breath. Yet here is also pain and joy, uglyness and lovelyness, life, death, unceasing. Until we can stand apart and see it as it is -- and as it is not." She was silent then and they had followed her. Will, trailing behind, his brow furrowed, troubled. Jessie went on, softly, "You see, the power of the Stone and the metal too, focussing the quality that is drawn into it. Great good may flow from it, or great evil. Jane is right."

William bent to pick up the scattered coins and saw, still brilliant in the sunlight, the great flaming stone. He glanced up, no one was noticing him. He felt a great sense of rightness. He would be able to hold that stone without it's bringing harm to anyone. He was sure. He knew that his own rightness would enable him to keep that beauty safe. He lifted it into his hand,gazing at it in rapt attention. The others had walked on,their silence strangely disturbing to him, but he wanted now to go inside, gather his things and go home. To go home,this very moment, to leave his Family, his mate even, and be separate from them all. He wanted to be quiet with this wonderful beauty.

The others continued on their walk, and finally Jessie sat down on a small wooden bench at the far end of the garden under an apple tree. She turned to watch William, trailing now far behind, coming with such slow steps. Her eyes roamed the gardens, feeling the presence of every plant there, and then they rested briefly on each of the people, the three dogs and the two cats who had joined them. She glanced up at the clouds scudding across the blue sky, birds wheeling, noisy in the trees. Noisy? The summer heat had risen, birds were usually quiet then. She smiled, content.

William came near and she said, "William, do you see that the best way to rid the Valley of me is to kill me? There is nothing left for the Builders to do to persuade me to leave."

He stopped, startled, angry, his eyes swiftly glancing from one to another, and he saw as much surprise, fear, in the others. "That is an obscene suggestion. You know, you MUST know, woman that no person in this Valley would kill. Only our trained Hunters kill even for food. How could we kill a person?" He was visibly shaken and Annette wanted to run to him to comfort him.

Jessie nodded briefly and smiled, "That's right then. It's not just those with Talents who have grown and changed in these years. In all the Valley there are few left whose aggression is used against others violently. I apologize William, but I had to show you - and your family. And you are right about the Emerald, you probably can hold it safely. But note it's light, it's shadow and how they change." She watched him, "And note yourself."

He paled, then slowly, he smiled. Every person there relaxed with relief. "Thank you, Jessie. I want to stay here with all of you. For a little while at least." She nodded and they sat or leaned against the tree. She looked at them with serious eyes, her mouth slightly open, breathing in the summer air. It was past noon, but no one seemed hungry.

The sun burned against their skin, their faces. Jessie glanced swiftly to its position in the sky and then around the garden. "It's so difficult for us to see that we live in darkness on such a day as this, in such a garden. The sun shines, flowers bloom, the world seems full of life and joy. To these physical eyes, there is so much light. Look, clear your eyes, and look at one another, see the Causal body in which the astral Light plays, describing your individual nature as it is this minute. Brilliant, lovely and ever changing as you're Heart knowledge unfolds. See, and know that that is only a shadow to what is yet to be known."

When we penetrate out to that vision beyond these eyes, we know that this light is only a darkness compared to that. Just in the same way, it's only when we begin to realize that Touch of Love itself that we realize how small, how inadequate is the love we feel for one another. To be aware of Love is to be conscious! Soul Conscious! A great Soul, is surely conscious of the personality through which Earth's work is done. Then that person is able to participate in genuine Love. In that way personal love is emblazoned, a glory that propels us and fills us with Life. It shines with that greater Love within it."

She sighed, smiled apologeticaly and sighed again."Well,there I go again, lecturing you who know these things already."

Rose nodded, "Our Teachers told us that such Love is not an emotion but a state of being. I see how that might be so." She slid one hand across the thick lemon grass that covered this small circle, to take and close her fingers around Silvia's hand.The fragrance of the grass rose between them and her heart was comforted. The touch of another hand comforted the obscure loneliness she felt.

As if she felt the reflection of Rose's feelings, Jennifer said, " It's that! The loneliness that is less. The loneliness that seemed always there, within me, whether I was in company or not! And now! Now, I am not alone."

Jessie seemed to have left them, her eyes and voice far off, she shook her head slightly, but spoke clearly,"It's when our Hearts penetrate through the world condition and transcend senses into direct vision that we perceive the nature of relationship. That is a linking, a Joining of selves in an intimacy that makes all we have known of intimacy seem distance, loneliness. Then that condition called selflessness becomes real, for there is no longer any other than the whole Self. We see that we are not separate! There is ONLY one Self!"

Tom straightened, leaning against the tree, he stood slightly behind Jessie, but his eyes were dark with feeling."It's so. Jessie.Though I've not thought of it so. Only a touch of that have I known, but in knowing just the touch of selflessness, I realized the agony of selfishness, the loneliness of it." His voice was gentle with sorrow."I long to know that always!"

Paul looked around, struggling to believe this shared moment, this recognition that fairly infused them all."To share in this way, even a bit of it, Mind wide, Heart wide, is to know what I feel right now, a Joy so vast it aches through my body and through my mind. I have not known such a mind ache for completion. All the mystery of life has spilled out and infused us all in itself."

Jessie was nodding slowly,"Thus do we begin to know a little of what it is to be freed from darkness. What humankind is becoming. We are immersed in our lower natures as a root is immersed in mud and it is only when we are thrust forth in pain, feel the ripping of our hidden body so that we grow stems, that lift our leaves ,branches, consciousness, upward to break through that water of this dream-sleep life, into the air of the mental universe. Then, persisting in that growth, there will come the time when there will be another breaking forth,a ripping of ourselves into bloom, that flowering that releases the essence, the fragrance of our being. So we extend forth to fill the very universe with ourselves all together. And at the same time, continue as the flower shining in an earthly sunlight. "

Ned, who had been so silent spoke as if startled out of reverie,"What is the nature of that root from which we come? For surely the tree rises from its root as well as feeds from the sun."

Jessie laughed,"There, you've hit on the mystery that still must be known. Meditate on that, you will discover it." They sat then, feeling the growing heat of the day, but not wanting to end this time. Strength seemed to rise among them, an energy that was a power for each one.

Rose said, after a long silence,"Jessie, this is the beginning of something isn't it?" She nodded, then slowly,"And the ending at the same time!"

William stood watching them, he had not moved during the entire dialogue, his thoughts half attending. The ideas seemed to him to be interesting, but so vague, so far from actual experience, that he wondered. Finally, in the silence, he said,"Well, it's been a most interesting day. A difficult day, but I admit that there is a lot I've not thought about. I don't know whether you all do perceive something that I don't. You say you do, and I've not known you to lie, but you might be deluded. However, Jessie, whatever I've been told, whatever Greyson has said, somehow, I can't quite see you as evil." She turned to him and he held up a hand,"Not that I don't seriously question your influence here, but at least, I think my Family can make their own choices after all." He looked seriously convinced by himself and Rose suddenly wanted to laugh. William could be so self righteous after all.But he stood, a strange questioning in his eyes as he studied Jessie's face , his fingers caressing the stone in his pocket.Finally out of extreme reluctance, he said,"There is surely something I don't understand."

Jessie nodded, met his eyes thoughtfully, and then stood."I think it's time that we took some walks through these fields and then came back to have a bit of lunch. I need to walk.. How about the rest of you?" She waited and they began to nod, or to move off toward the edge of the gardens, down the paths and by twos or threes, they wandered away. No one spoke, as they threaded their way through the paths, and the children, ran ahead, released from the attention that had held them, their bodies crying for movement.

CHAPTER SEVEN

Andrew Stumbles

Several days following the mid summer Gather, Jessie walked slowly up from the big stone barn toward her small cottage. So early, sun only an hour up, and she was tired. Her body didn't have the endurance it once did. She stood quietly, gathering in the morning life, sending herself out into it. She relaxed in this moment, realizing this intimacy. She could see a very large flock of sheep winding across a high meadow. The predators had increased, wolves, cats, others, they'd hold the number down to balance the land, otherwise the meadows would be denuded in a few years. She tucked that knowledge into place like a tidy housewife going mentally over her household chores. The mountains off to the east, dark, with only tips of the peaks still white, seemed to her co-conspirators in a deep and fascinating game with life. She smiled at the fantasy.

The Farm Temple gleamed in the summer sun. The walls and the domed roof glowed with color and these colors seemed to move as branches of trees moved above it in the morning's breeze. The light wind from the west was not as cool as breezes coming up from the River would have been. Jessie felt the heat already and knew the day would be one to spend in the shade. She was listening to the steady beat of drums from inside, the rhythm intricate and demanding. Cassandra it would be with that rhythm. Jessie smiled, the unshielded feelings and images, the Reach of mind of the little girl resounded against her attention. She held her mind closed to them as one turns one's eyes to give privacy to a child who has not learned modesty. Jessie stepped inside and instantly Cassandra's mental noise was shielded. The suddenness startled her, then she nodded, pleased. "Of course, that one could do that. Nevertheless she needed to learn a new etiquette.

The interior of the Temple was suffused with a clear green light like new grass, here and there intermittent shafts of grey trembled and then faded,. She studied the stained glass panels -- family artist's conceptions of the Teachers. Buddha and Christ faced each other across the center of the open Hall. Mary, Krishna and Kali, Mohammed and Gandhi, Teresa and Marta, all were portrayed. Jessie let her eyes linger a moment on the abstract representation of Marta. She, the one who brought a teaching that revealed the power of the conscious 'Will to Good'. The one who taught the fusion of Love and Intelligence into that higher possibility of wisdom that was cresting finally in this Valley. Yet, she had died at the angry hands of traditionalists. Jessie was only a baby when the "Lady" died, but she remembered her parents grief. She had been puzzled that their grief was as much for the people who destroyed her as for the loss of their Teacher. She herself, as she grew older, had spent a period wondering why they were not angry.

THE JOURNEY

She turned to go back to the court outside, waiting there, she looked across the land, then studied the light shining through the Temple. It was like a benediction for her. She was drawn from reverie by sudden silence. The light faded, and only the sunlight striking color through the walls was left. Jessie turned. Cassandra ran, shouting her pleasure to see her. "Hi, there Jessie, I like you to come when I'm here. You bring harmony." She fairly danced as she reached to hug this new grandmother. "We're going swimming, would you like to come? Jessie looked down at the River, the glittering water below seemed to her tempting.. It would be pleasant, but she shook her head,"No, Dear, I've got some things to do. Maybe I'll join you later though."

Casssandra eyed her thoughtfully.? "You're worried about the fields the Builder's have taken? The extra ones the Council didn't give?"

Jessie frowned,this child knew everything, would she be worrying too much? "I think that must be dealt with, Cassandra, yes, but there's also -- " she hesitated, just how much DID this child know -- "those shops, the entertainment places that're opening in Valley towns." She watched the little girls eyes change, the frown and then the satisfied shake of her head.

" Don't worry about them,Mother. They're -- they're silly in my opinion. We tried them out, you know. My friends, and I. They're no fun!" Her condemnation seemed final.

Jessie smiled then, nodded,"It's a comfort to know that." She studied the child."How do you know what they are?"

Cassandra grinned,"Oh, we looked it all over and sampled things. They didn't exclude kids at first you know, and they didn't have anything to drink except beer and wine and the only film they have is sex films. Funny ones, ugly! What for I couldn't figure out. If a person want's to know about sex, he finds out at the Center. We have good films there. But these were -- " her face twisted a little, half grin and half frown, "they made me feel bad, sort of sick, in fact. But Jimmie got mad. He saw one where they were hurting people. We didn't stay. I don't see how they're gonna make any credit. "

"Were many people there?" Jessie wondered why she herself had not visited the place. She ought to see, know what was there herself. She wondered whether old fears had to do with that avoidance.

Cassie was shaking her head,"That's what I mean, every time we've gone by, there's been only a few people and they don't seem to stay. Like they're doing what we did, looking it over and then leaving." She hesitated, frowning and searching Jessie's face carefully."Well, I think a few do go back into the other rooms. But most just left. It's really not much. Not interesting." She studied Jessie's face,"You don't have to worry about it Mother!" Her voice was almost that of a mother comforting a child.

"I don't"? Jessie was amused, but pleased.

"No, we hear talk, people feel sorry for them. Go in sometimes just because they know they aren't selling much. I went to the Center and got out old films of the old days and watched the ones where they had places like that, entertainment houses, with all kinds of - stuff - going on. I couldn't see how anyone would make a living. People just don't drink enough now, and the rest - well, just see what it's like. You'll know. People talk about it, and they just aren't interested. So I'm afraid they won't last long." She looked concerned at Jessie, wondering whether this was good or bad for her Grandmother. She was relieved to see Jessie smile. Then she frowned deeply. Cassandra was an honest child and she knew that there was more."There were a few people who were excited. Some who were gathered at the little tables to gamble, and those who went back into the back rooms. Those stayed, Jessie. But only a few, you know!"

"Well, maybe you're right, maybe we don't have to worry too much. But we'll have to find something else for them to sell if they don't succeed with this."

Cassandra nodded briefly, "Well, come with us if you can," She ran off, down the slope to swim. Already Jessie could hear the shouts of other children there.

Jessie turned to the Hall. Something there needed attention. She quickened her stride. She was hungry, she had spent the past two hours in the barns aiding the birthing of lambs. Animals born here with the Family often came home to give birth, especially if they were out of season as these were. It was too late for new lambs. They must find out how this happened. But the flock remembered this barn as a place of safety. Rose had helped, between them they had seen the lambs born healthy. The mothers strong again. Was it wise. The balance must be kept in its own way. But she shrugged, as long as Anna or Jane found them coming in they'd be helped.

She could hear shouts now and then from the Hall and she hurried. The heat had settled on the land. The shaded pathway helped, but the winds carried heat from the Valley below. Gathering her attention and bringing balance to herself before she entered, she stood in the stillness, the morning quiet. Not a bird called. She sensed the roused feelings, the turbulence of emotion and was not surprised. That it had not happened before was the surprise. This family could sustain it's balance, she told herself. This family must! A faint shadow crossed her face, rippling like a frown, shadowing her quiet joy. So much depended on how they handled things. She must not, however, allow herself to be drawn down. That wouldn't help at all.

She stepped onto the wide steps of the deck and heard Andrew's voice. Immediately she tested the strength of it, the tone, and felt a brush of fear. Yet that fear was melted away instantly by the steady calm of her knowledge. To absolutely know that they would meet these things, to absolutely sustain steady trust, was her task. Andrew must meet this problem. It had been coming all along. The testing was always part of growth.

When she entered Andrew was shouting,"I MUST go Dad. I just can't do anything less. What kind of a person would I be if I didn't?" He was dressed as a Vagabond, green and brown with silver slashes across shirt and sleeves. She recognized the clan and nodded to herself. He stood defiant, feet wide, head high, one hand on his hip. So typical of youth in rebellion that she could not restrain a smile. She responded to Rose's beckon and entered.

"Steel, the Runner, that's who. He's meeting me at the bottom of the hill at the crossing of our path. His clan's not with him. They've --" his eyes fell briefly, then rose again to meet his father's, "they've refused him, and I thought loyalty was a Vagabond trait". Andy's voice was full of contempt.

"Who said they had?"

"He did!" At the confession Andrew saw the implication and hesitated,"At least he feels refused, so it's the same."

Ben struggled with his own anger, he felt it pushing against his throat and swallowed."Exactly what does that mean,Son? Refused him? They never abandon their people. For any reason."

Andy grimaced and Rose was more grieved to see him shuffle - turn as if to leave, then hold,"They just won't listen to him."

Ben nodded,"Or is it that they won't agree with him?" He was quiet now, the anger brought into check. His eyes held the fierce glint of its presence but he must contain himself -- he saw the reflection of that anger there in his son.

Andrew plunged on,"How can they refuse him, refuse him support at least." Andrew was shaken a little by that recognition. Jessie went to Rose who drew her in a hug and made room for her beside her on the couch. Jessie felt the sadness in Rose,but there was no fear. She nodded. Andrew went on.

"Dad, the whole Vagabond way of life is at stake. You all know their reverence for the Silent City! These Builder's are going to attack, literally attack and they've got equipment - bombs, I hear. Dad!" His voice rose,"That's not something we can let happen, is it?" Ben heard the appeal, the demand."I don't understand why you adults are letting it happen."

Andrew was near to tears suddenly, his own conflicting emotions and his outraged sense of justice, combined to literally frighten him with their power. But the worst was his recognition that he was out of balance, not wanting to be, not wanting to admit that. He prided himself that he knew how to balance ANYTHING. Some part of him didn't want to balance, wanted - - to be part of this excitement.

He stood a moment, looking from one to the other, then said, a little more calmly,"They've got an agreement through the Valley Council that she be taken off limits. That no one must visit her at all until they get their investigation done. Investigation! What they mean is to bomb Her because they can't get in any other way."

Jessie couldn't help a smile and that puzzled Rose who's face reflected a growing worry. Steel says they're going to attack from an air car when no one knows." Andrew's face reflected his contempt and anger, lines drew themselves across his forehead and around his mouth, his fury darkening his whole face.The tall, thin dark body shuddered with his dispair. "Don't you realize all this? I think you're all crazy not to help us." He moved suddenly, his body jerked as if some inner conflict activated it. Jessie followed his thought,the tensions and the quarded mind. To be able to guard in the face of this much emotion took Talent. She was impressed. She drew herself in, focussed, and saw the quiet wisdom that waited behind that excitement, that emotional surf. Could he bear to be so torn? So cut from his own understandings? Then strangely she felt a relief. Surely it was because he needed to learn, needed to know something of the rebellion of youth too. He was so young. How could he know without the trial, and yet, it could be so dangerous. He had to know his capacity.

Benjamin felt his own retort, sharp and angry and he caught it before it made sound. The flood of emotion he drew into balance could throw this meeting away. Lose him his son. If he could not balance, then how could he expert Andrew to. He knew and steeled himself. Took a deep breath, knew that his son was beyond the reach of reason. He could see that Andrew was nearly a man. He quailed, why hadn't he noticed before. Would it have helped? What kind of a man was he becoming? His heart sank, but he kept his voice quiet, betraying none of his roistering feelings. "Andrew, have you thought of the consequences?" Ben felt acute frustration that Andrew had closed him out. He could not Touch him. How many years he had denied and in those years he might have been able to offer. Was it too late?

Andrew saw the glimpse of pain in his father's face. He read the troubled surging of emotion and the self criticism. The recognition was enough to drive through his own turbulence, to check for an instant the fury that seemed wild within him. It left him trembling on the edge of compassion. Jessie read the inner scene and knew relief. Rose only felt a sudden fear.

Andrew hardened himself. They must stand steady. His friends had told of parents who would try to defeat their purpose. He must remember. They were right, they must resist persuasion. But he knew the nagging weight of another point of view. Reason will serve whatever idea is foremost, just now, this conviction of his friends was foremost. Andy said, "We've seen the consequences of the Builder's actions. We've seen the filth they peddle, and the land they've ruined. Now that they go for the City, that's the end. It's enough!" His face had smoothed in a hardness none of them had ever seen in him.

Rose spoke and as she did he turned to her slightly so that his body softened a little from the terrible ramrod-defiance ."Son, Steel intends to lead the forces that are gathering among the young? Isn't that true?"

Andrew bristled at what he heard as criticism now."Yes, it's true, mostly we're all young. There are few old ones who have the courage." He glanced at his father but Benjamin did not flinch. Ben's eyes were wary, puzzled.

Rose persisted, "And is it that they intend to attack the Builders because they see them as intending to destroy the City?" He nodded, wondering what she was getting at, already uneasy. Why was she repeating things? Then she said,"Then they are attacking the Builders to protect the City. Each is doing the same, each is attacking the other's idea of what is right? Isn't that so?"

The surprise of the question, the softness of her voice, caught Andy off guard for a moment, it looked as if the rigidity of his attitude would be penetrated, the higher, brighter point of view gain ascendancy and reveal the flaws of this one he clutched. But he rallied, stiffened himself literally and said,"Mother! No! What you're saying is talk of people who like to sit and talk rather than act and as a result they let the important things of life be destroyed." The sentence was so obviously a quote from Steel that Rose caught her breath. When did this son not think for himself? Andy hesitated, his arms suddenly moving, lifting up, swinging through the air,"It's what our ancestors did. They let things be destroyed!" Ben and Rose heard the rote quoting and knew that that would seal him from reason again.

But Ben stood then, hoping once at last to break the barrier to his son's own reason. "They did the opposite, they fought each other and destroyed because they could not listen, nor could they compromise. But more, because they would not find a better solution than violence" He took a long breath, because Andrew seemed to listen,"They would not consider other ways than violence because violence is exciting, it releases the furies, the rages of our frustrated power. It takes a people with great courage to trust and to listen to one another. A people who have learned to Balance not just in themselves, but in their nation. Such we have not had, but now -- " He stopped, Andrew's eyes had dropped, his head slightly turned away. Ben felt desparate to reach him to break this strange attraction that had gained power over his son."Surely Son, you see that there is merit in both positions, ours and theirs?"

Andrew wavered, he felt his body tighten with a desparation to run away, to refuse to listen longer. Somehow the argument that sounded so strong and right when he and his friends were talking the past few nights, did not seem strong now. His confidence was shaken. For a brief instant he felt ridiculous dressed as for a play. The shame fed his anger with Ben, with himself. That anger gave strength to that quiet voice that nagged so persistently at the corners of his mind. A voice that had told him much what his father just said. Gently he heard again what he did not want to hear. His family brought confusion, made what had seemed so real suddenly vague. He was too honest not to acknowledge his father's words."All right Dad, maybe what I said isn't exactly accurate. But it's still true that somebody has got to do something now. We can't let the Builders destroy our world." His confidence returned, this was the key issue the boys found as an anchor in all their disputes. "We aren't going to HURT them, for God's sake."

Rose spoke softly, her eyes holding his,"Why?"

"Why? Mother! You can't be serious! Certainly you see why. Or have you closed your minds again to what you don't want to meet?" The accusation was like a knife through his parents hearts. Unfair, and cruel, it was accurate. "Doesn't the Silent City mean anything to you? I've known Her all my life. She is the Light that shines all over our Valley. For the Vagabonds she is a guiding star. What do you mean?" His voice had become hard again.

Rose saw with a clarity as never before the power of her son. She recognized finally that he was entering manhood and that he had amazing strength. She feared certain attractions would turn that strength from the selfless path. He could do good in this world. He could do great damage. She must not secumb to her fear. And then she saw something else, the power behind his words, the need there, the need for that closeness, that excitement, that raging conviction of doing what was right to protect his own. To be a part of the gang of which Steel, the fiery charismatic youngster was leader. Andrew had pushed every other part of himself out of sight, and his anger was as much because his parents were threatening that precarious control, threatening to reveal him utterly to himself, to make obvious the Self he hid from and who waited with its infinite patience. Waited for the inevitable acknowledgement! Would it be too late this time? Rose saw the dilemma with a sinking heart. Andrew, her OLD Andrew would have been the first to have seen. Where was he?

Rose's eyes moved swiftly from Andrew to Jessie, She sought courage, but Jessie watched with only a mild expression of interest. How could she do so? Didn't she care? A swift cleansing anger swept through Rose, and with a struggle she relaxed, drew herself from its grip. Surely the knowledge was there, waiting for her to see. No one came to this kind of power, that power her son had, without also having the knowledge to know its danger. No one came to this, without having within him an equal power of Love. And now, he twisted his vision to imagine that Love was the source of his need to protect. He was locked in, cut off from Vision.

She focussed her attention to Andy and was astonished at the clarity with which she saw. The denial with which he held his own knowledge at bay. The way the residual passion rose up to claim control, it was a crude denial, insufficient. But, feeding itself on those ancient passions, it had overwhelmed Andrew's balance. Rose felt Jessie's calm, knew that she must keep her own or sacrifice much. Would her son be lost? Would that great Heart be able to stand before this inner struggle? Then she knew, even as the words formed in her mind, that this was the real struggle of the Valley. The danger that threatened was what lived within themselves, not what struck from without. How could they meet such an enemy?

Could they all, even she and Ben, be brought to this lowest common denominator? Lose their Vision? The possibility brought cold unease to her stomach, settled there sharp and hard. Why these young ones? Were they not the hope of the land? Without doubt, she knew. Lust for adventure, for excitement, battle, surged through young men especially. Atavistic, Yes! But real. A lust that had been fed by civilizations and beliefs for millinania. They must meet that ancient tug finally, all of them, meet and bring it to heal.

" Andrew, you haven't answered my question. It's not like you to answer questions with questions. Consider Son, there could be people hurt, even killed, not just young men, but the old, children. Do you want that?"

Swiftly emotions played across his face revealing the inner loosening of his determination. Guilt, anger, resentment, fear of the loss of this excitement, and a strange trace of animal glee, that frightened Rose as she had never been frightened before. But it seemed to have penetrated his attention too. A look of profound grief such as she had never seen in him, followed the surfacing of that naked desire. "Mom, you're jumping to conclusions. No one's going to HURT anyone. We're going to prevent that. We're going to keep the Valley SAFE." He spoke with exaggerated conviction and she knew he hid himself behind it. She could see that none of his friends had spoken of the possibility of death, of wounding others. His eyes were bleak for a moment, and for that moment, she thought he was going to ask that they Join with him. But with a straightening of his body, he said brightly, "It's just that if we stand up to them, they'll see that they have to stop their attack. They'll see they can't destroy things. No one has stood up to them yet!" He had succeeded in justifying his position by denying part of the facts. Andrew had learned not to do that long years ago. Or to admit it when he did.

She asked,"Will you Join with us, here, Son? Now?"

Exasperated, he shook his head, as if she had trapped him, and she felt the fear that burned up against his control. Ben was conciliatory, waiting for a moment when he could Reach, perhaps Touch. He said quietly,"The City can take care of herself. We don't need the death of our young men to save her."

Andrew gasped, angry again, here was the blindness Steel had warned them against. In his own parents! Well, what could he expect, how long had they lied to themselves? He said bitterly and both Rose and Ben quailed to hear that bitterness,"You refused us for so many years, you would not let us Touch you, and now, you tell me you know better how to go!" His eyes flickered with pain at his own statement, pain at the hurt he was causing them. He drew a long breath as if rebalancing,"You don't understand. We are the protectors."

The look of pride and innocent trust disarmed Rose and stopped her reply in her throat. Jessie bowed her head to hide a smile,, but no one noticed. Rose's mind raced, this was not her son, not the boy she had kissed good night just yesterday. She knew her thought had reached desparation, "Couldn't we take these things into the Temple,couldn't we meditate on these things?"

Andrew jerked , his body straight and stiff, feeling the impatience he could not refuse."We've done that. It only reinforced our convictions. I'm sure the Builders visit the Temple too, and each of us is just more convinced of the rightness of our position. The Temple cannot help.God cannot help. This is a matter for MEN." The last word was a cry, a wrenching loose from something that had almost touched him. "After all Mom, Dad, there is right and wrong here!" The faint question in his voice gave them hope.

Jessie stirred, surely there was a testing here, a severe test of these parents and so far they held stedfast. She was aware of her own tension. She released her hands deliberately from their tight clasping. Surely this was the primary issue for the Valley, If these could not meet it, how could any others? She said,"Must there be? Right and Wrong? The dicotomy on which humankind has excused its private lust for ages? Is there not a third way?"

Her words touched him. Somewhere he knew the answer. Her voice roused some memory, some wakening to that depths of himself that he had closed successfully. He struggled and with a shake of his head, he denied it. "Yes, of course, there is the way of the coward." Then, with a jerk of his head, he frowned and they knew he had to flee. Jessie had touched on that firm wisdom that he denied in himself. Like an animal fearing a trap, he shook his head back and forth then cried out,"I can't waste any more time. I have to meet the others. Steel will be ready. I'll talk to you later." He turned his eyes from them, looking with that strange longing and relief toward that Valley beyond the windows,. He flung himself across the hall, though his father stood to detain him. But Andrew was gone. Across the deck he ran, leaped ten feet directly down into the lower path, and catching himself like a dancer, he rolled across the ground, stood and raced away down the hill.

Ben turned to the women, his face a mixture of pride and pain. "I don't see how we could have avoided this. What can we do? Oh, my God, what can we do?" He sat down again, straight and stiff as Andrew had been. "Could we get enough people to go there, to the City, to know her strength, listen? Perhaps find a way out of this?"

"Ben, we've got to consider that to some degree they don't want to negotiate. I'm afraid they feel the lust for battle. For humankind, battle has been exciting. Daily life can get boring." Rose frowned, then went on,"At least it might for those who don't - - who haven't yet begun the Journey. When that begins, there is nothing more exciting, actually.But when one thinks one has exhausted what is to be done in ones life, then,-- why a battle rouses the blood."

Ben was nodding,"It may be so. I've always thought that ancient lust was satisfied in the old industrial world by a battle over economic differences, in the struggle for world position etc. testing oneself against opponents, proving oneself in that endless political conflict. It was not so bloody, as the old way, but no less cruel." He drew a long breath as if bringing his courage into use. "Our world is so different now. But still,we should've known some would be caught by these needs." He raised his eyes, his face a twist of pain, "But I'd never have thought our Andrew would be." He was silent then said,

"The boys, the unconscious boys've resurrected the old needs. They imagine romance, drama and themselves as saviors."

The Builder's want this conflict, as much as they say they don't. We must be willing to admit to our old fascination with violence. There was for one moment, a look on Andrew's face and I knew that he felt that - that urge to throw his great strength out against a foe." Rose's voice sounded heavy with defeat.

"But my dear, we have the Olympic Games, we have the Races, the wrestling and all the martial arts. They practice for every Festival! There are other ways to bleed that physical urgency off." He was irritable, angry that Andrew did not use those safeguards prepared for this period of his life.

She nodded, slowly, "They have done that, they do , as though their lives depended on it sometimes, but this, this Steel, who ever he is, and he must be a Vagabond,since the boys have adopted clan style clothes, has led them to more exciting ways."

There was a silence, a long painful moment when they could not Touch, and

THE JOURNEY

each felt more lonely than they thought they ever had. Finally Benjamin said,"If he is Vagabond, then, two to one, he's not able to Reach at all, he's not AWARE!" He nodded slowly, realizing, "So they lose one too now and then, after all!" He bent his head, absorbed in his sorrow.

After several minutes they turned their eyes to Jessie. They seemed to her to be children now, their young smooth faces, so different, one brown, round and smooth,the other narrow, white and furrowed in a terrible frown. She met their eyes briefly, then turned from the grief there, turned to look out the long windows. They knew more than they were admitting, she thought. Old habits of denial pressed them. She breathed a long slow breath, and turned back, "As for help from the City, it's true that energy is great. It flows equally through us all,the blind as well as the Seer. For those who are aware and tuned already to Touch Her, it can be used for good or ill. It is not separative but whole and inclusive. But this is a time of transition and so a very fragile time among us. However the energy cannot be refused once enough people have become aware."

Rose nodded,"I think we knew that, Jessie, but we're grasping at straws now. The energy is what brings fear in people like the Builders, those who do not See. Yet there are some of those, who know no fear but rather feel deep devotion to that beauty they do not quite grasp. Now, you say, that even among us,, we who do See, there can be wrong use of energy."

Jessie nodded,"It is the choice each of us must make. Knowledge, usually results in our choice made to the side of Love, of Humanity and the welfare of all life, but it is not always so."

"Oh, My God, I didn't know that. I didn't know that there could be any other choice"! Rose's voice hurt in her throat.

"It must be so, otherwise there's no choice. You don't think the People of the Way have been devoted to less than that? That energy the City focusses is powerful. Her promise of Life is grand. And they have taught their children, all of them, whether they See or not. They don't pretend, they admit they have children who cannot see beyond the ordinary mind. They train them ALL. But Learning Center Teachers were training only those who asked until we began the new lectures. Can they have been so careful they brought harm?" The reprimand was not lost on them." Each of you know people who attract, and people who repell. You know people who have that wonderful quality of deep, intuitive PRESENCE, that seems to speak without language. Annette begins to express that energy. Some just feel good in her presence, healed even, others feel uneasy, as if something they cannot control at all, emanates from her. It is her stillness. No one can control another's stillness. But stillness releases that energy of Love, genuine Love, selfless and pure. In that state she has been able to bear the conflict in her Mate. That Love she radiates, carries both of them through much. But for William, it is threatening. He cannot name or control it."

"Then, that's how she endures all that she has had to endure? She's beyond his reach, yet she continues to love him and to stand within Love before him." Ben shook his head, wonderingly.

"Do you mean that this is what all of us must do?"

"Ah, Rose, how can I say. It's your own choice." Jessie felt the tide turning, the swift lift upward and she was at peace.

"Well, this whole business has made me feel a new fear. What Andrew said knocked me off balance." Rose felt her throat tighten again, speech impossibile.

But Ben nodded, thoughtfully. His anger subsided, grief loosened, he said, "We can't do that, Sweetheart, we can't just say 'our son' and not include every son and daughter in this Valley. It isn't this way for us in the Valley anymore. Steel is as much my Son as Andrew. I cannot separate my thoughts from him, my Love from him. Else I deny everything I know to be. We have only to be aware of our own feelings, our own Balance. We've trained ourselves through the years, now is the test to find whether the training took. Now we will begin to find out how Self Aware people meet problems."

Rose swallowed, let her feelings subside, drew herself free of them with effort, and said gently,"Only if we can sustain Self Awareness! Otherwise we just repeat the past. So much is asked. Of all of us. I suppose we must say that we ask so much of ourselves. That Power that floods to us from the City, wakes the spark of itself in each of us, that Power of Love, is the source of it. It may frighten the Builders, but it demands of us. Demands that we live to our highest Self, to our greatest knowledge. And personal love may be a trap that will turn us into fools" She turned, sighing with tears overflowing her eyes.

Ben said,"The Builders are people who can't understand because they do not See. They know of certain change in the Valley, yes, but the Knowledge we have, the Vision, is unknown to them. Language has to be invented to carry concepts of what we begin to know. We manage to shape into words our theories arrived at through math, we invent words such as a 'Unified Field', we see the double nature of matter, both particle and wave, we recognize the interrelationship of the observed and the observer. But now, we See beyond the questions and we can't speak sensibly of what we See. Because what we See includes this physical world but extends far beyond it. I think we've transcended our own senses, begun to experience through further senses for which we have no name.". His eyes were distant, taking this problem into consideration, as if ready to spend some hours in persuing it. But he shook his head, looked fiercely at the two women and went on.

"So we cannot teach it directly. As always through history, Teachers have pointed to what they realized, experienced and could not speak of. You say Vagabonds have always answered the questions of their non-Perceptive young. We have failed our children in that." He stopped, amazement flooding his face, "You see what that means? We have no power with people when we can't explain. When there isn't a mutual realization. We must find a different way."

Jessie sighed with relief that they had seen that." They don't hear or see as you do." Her voice was gentle, almost tender in that relief. "Their polarization came from the same kind of regression as did Andrew's lust for adventure -- his need for a 'gang'. But his need cannot overpower wisdom. He Sees, even though

THE JOURNEY

he battles himself now. They don't!"

Ben was adamant,"Even Steel was taught. All the boys were. But do they See?" He was silent,shook his head,"Well, we don't know. But surely they will remember before harm is done."

Rose nodded,her face wet, grief drawing into sharp visibility the first faint lines of her face," I am afraid, Ben. As you say they've been taught the convictions. Their emotions overcome reason or rather twist it to their aims. Andrew has not only been taught, he Sees. And yet, he is able to at least partly shut himself from what he Knows. They feel the power of the Silent City. She makes a good rallying point. What we do with that power decides what happens to our Valley. It is not one group that destroys, but all of us, depending on what we choose." She turned to stare across the fields and hills, pressing her hands together. She said finally,"What shall we do? It's Spirit Itself that we must call to, isn't it? And that Spirit reaches out from within ourselves - together?"

Jessie nodded, " We have a lot to do. To contemplate and to understand. There are, of course, those who are truly innocent, whose lusts have not wakened, neither do they See. Only half conscious, they're unaware - but they love people and all living things, because their hearts are pure. They live here too, you know."

As if not hearing, Rose spoke,frowning, "We could have done better. At least done what the People of the Way did for their children. We were so stiff necked, so afraid in ourselves. It's our own fault."

But Jessie persisted, "The Vagabonds did not raise their children to be innocent, for the innocent often fall when that innocence is destroyed. No, they taught them to know their innocence, to honor their pure hearts but to ask questions beyond them. because they lived with difference they taught them to know difference is neither good nor bad." Jessie studied them, these two must bridge their own lacks, their own recriminations this day."Look to yourselves, you've been taught that guilt is not a healthy guide. "

Rose was nodding," You're right. We're getting bogged down in dispair at our faults and failures."

Jessie spoke again, "So where do we go?"

Ben spoke suddenly,recognizing finally, " My God, it's true! We want to control people, to make them accept our Vision, even when they can't see it. Yet we never tried to teach them what we saw. We've a lot to learn from the People of the Way. A lot."

Jessie nodded, Ben's body literally jerked, as he felt the in flow of energy,"My God, Jessie, I keep on doing it. I keep on denying. What's to become of us?" But then he settled down, allowing himself to receive, along with Rose, the blessing Jessie gave them.

Finally Rose said,quietly, accepting, "Must we then even see death ? Death of people by people? Death of the innocent?"

Jessie nodded, "Even that, if there's danger we might stand apart, imagining ourselves 'higher beings' controlling the 'lower ones'." Then she smiled at them,.

"Don't be dispairing, Do you honestly think your young ones would actually kill?"

Rose looked startled, for a long moment she stared at Jessie and then turned deliberately to meet Benjamin's eyes. "I would have said no, they could not, before this day. But now I am not sure of anything they -- we might do." Her voice broke, the admission was a recognition in itself.

CHAPTER EIGHT

Tom meets with Builders

Summer Gather began a time of communication such as Valley people had not known. They began to talk openly of their differences,even the Talents. But most importantly, of their aspirations. The hopes of the people must be at least known to everyone, whether they subscribed to them or not. When Tom got word of Andrew's flight and absorption with what he termed a young gang, he found himself worrying, searching other activities and watching as he had never done.

Tom waited for his visitors with misgiving. What would they want? How would they respond? He had spoken to two other small groups of Builders in the past weeks. Things were changing. Their confidence was high. He thought they didn't hear him at all. He felt a deep persistent sorrow as if something was lost. It was not new, it had hounded him all summer, but now it was stronger. Something loomed there before them, something he wished could be avoided. But he told himself he was borrowing trouble. Now, he had another opportunity to try.

A tall broad shouldered man was in the lead of the little group when they arrived. His heavy mane of grey hair shining in the morning sun, dressed in a dark blue, tightly woven, cotten suit, under a loose yellow plasilk cloak. He was splended. Tom admired his flair, his confident walk. Behind him came a woman, tall and slim, dressed in a very fine, pure green Senna dress, like a cloud of mist around her body. Atop it was a short coat of blue linen. With her height it looked fine, the colors complimenting one another. Tom wondered why the sartorial display on this already warm morning. They walked with an odd rigidity and he thought of mannikins, displaying their wares.

They were all smiling and he felt his spirits rise at the friendly look in their eyes. The woman waved to him and he heard the soft murmur of their talk. Behind these two older ones were younger people, a man with very fair hair, familiar tunic and trousers of light grey with green trim. The woman was small, round bodied person who walked with a delicate grace on small feet and wore her pale rose clothes as though they were a dress of state., He smiled, feeling suddenly better. They seemed such good people obviously intelligent, friendly and willing to talk. The morning should not be a trial. The other group he had seen last week had been belligerent and he had struggled to contain himself. Surely these folk would not test him so.

The tall man stepped on to the deck where Tom waited, his hand outstretched."Goodday, Mayor. I'm John, Ethan's assistant -- shoemaker, you know? You know Ethan, I'm sure." At Tom's nod and handshake he turned to the others, "Let me introduce Ethel" But Tom had stepped forward to catch Ethel's hand and smiling they exchanged a hug. John nodded,"Ah, of course, you would know our chief chemist, and perhaps you're familiar with Machinist apprentice

Larry?" But Tom shook his head, reaching to shake the young man's hand and at the same time taking the younger woman's hand to draw her nearer.

He said, "Ah, Amanda, It's been so long since I've seen you. Where do you keep yourself in this town? Your new facilities have my books here so fast I seldom have to visit the main library at all." He was smiling, enjoying himself and feeling at ease. He helped them to a group of chairs at one end of his deck under a spreading beech where the shade was deep. A small table held a big pitcher of iced tea and a bucket of cold juices in bottles. Plates of tea breads on each side, offered variety and looked good. It was breakfast time and Tom intended to enjoy it. They chatted lightly as they settled into their chairs and Amanda and John pulled bottles of iced juices, the others choosing tea. Already the rising heat made the shade welcome.

John took the lead again,"Tom, we've come to talk about the requests of our people for land. You remember the petition that we sent you?" Tom nodded and he went on, "We're confident that request won't run into difficulty so we're not here for that. We want to apply for time on town Vidio to advertize a product. We'll pay the usual fee but we want to air our ad every day for a few months." He took a drink then a deep breath, and Tom could see he was nervous, then realized he too was not at ease. What was there about this man that unsettled him? John continued, his voice a little louder, trying to appear in command of himself. "Good advertizing's been neglected, needs to be brought back. The Market Screen only says what's available, we can tell people why they should buy. We want to --" Tom could see that a long discourse was in the offing and he felt his attention shift from words to the man himself.

Then he interrupted," I'll get you an application before you leave and you submit it today. I think you'll have time this week. But I'd like to know what plans you have for the land you asked for? That was not clear, you know. Council will decide this week and we need more information."

John looked at him obviously annoyed and a swift anger made flickers of muscle movement in his face. Then he brought his face to calm as if shutting down that anger. Only a hardening of the eyes told Tom that he had an adversary here to be reckoned with. "In the hundred acres along the River, we plan to plant a new strain of Matta. We were lucky to catch this batch of plants before Altos discarded them because they exactly suit our purpose. One of our people works in the Domes and told us of its potential."

"That's odd, Altos always informs the Valley towns of every product."

Ethel spoke. "It wasn't an over sight. They produced it attempting to get a strain that would grow in the cold country farther north. This is one of the trial strains, it tolerates cold but its fiber quality is weaker. The fabric made from it does not wear well. They thought it a discard and are still working on it."

Tom nodded, and turned back to John who was moving his hands in impatience. "We want that hundred acres of wild meadow along the neck just north of Adwin. We could extend it by opening up the land to the River through that five acre strip between the low hills. We'll build a small dam and flood the land running inland beyond the opening to the River and make a new swamp. We could increase Adwin's production of Matta by fifty percent in two years." He was back in good humor, smiling.

"How could you do that? A hundred acres couldn't produce that much more, Surely?" Tom was wary.

"Oh, yes, we'll clear out all plants but Matta. Clean up the fields so that only one crop grows there. It's more efficient, you can see that?" He looked penetratingly at Tom, willing him to agree.

Suddenly Amanda spoke, her mild voice a pleasing change from the very deep growl that John spoke with. "Tom the system the Valley uses, strip planting every crop with companion plants is inefficient. And that further business of leaving hundreds of acres to wild growth, -- well, even though that's the way we get all our Matta for the mills, it's a terrible waste." Tom was listening carefully, interested, and she gained enthusiasm.

He waved his arms at the surroundings of Adwin, "Just look around you. The Master Farmer seems to want to make all our farm land into a wild meadow, letting grains grow together, or vegetables compete with wild ones. Our ancestors never did that, you know. We can harvest faster if we plant and control single crop fields and the crop would be cleaner." She smiled, meeting Tom's eyes.

Tom felt a signal go off in his mind, an alert. This request was not the usual one. There was something here he did not expect and yet he knew. Had known. "Why would you do that? The Youth Gatherers have no trouble harvesting, and the use of companion planting has been taught by every plant Wizard in Altos for two generations now. It's essential for the health of the plants, for the balance of the land." He felt mild worry escalating.

There was a moment's silence, a glancing here and there and then John spoke. "Of course, but you know that those poeple, you call wizards, have us doing things that aren't always good business. They're dreamers actually, Tom, you must see that! They've got control of who does plant breeding and won't let anyone in who isn't a member of their -- group. We've got to correct that."

Tom broke in,"But they have the talent, no one can do what they do unless they have the talent and no one WITH the Talent is excluded." He was genuinely puzzled.

John frowned, looked at the others swiftly as if gaining approval." That's what they want us to think. I think that talent business is a clever way of disguising their control system. Whatever they do can be learned." He stopped, glanced around again, met Ethel's eyes briefly and then shrugged. "That's another matter. But as for the harvest, we need efficiency. We plan to have adults harvest. The young ones ought to be busy with their study anyway. The way people used to do. We can raise two of these cold resistant crops on the land each year and that will double our harvest." His voice had dropped to quiet persuasive tones, and Tom recognised them at once. No one would have remained Mayor in the Valley for a week were he not sensitive to such tones. He felt himself tighten. He smiled, then frowned.

"Well, that's a valuable accomplishment. Countries too cold for our old Matta can raise it now and have fiber for fabric. I'd not heard of this. But I'm still puzzled, John." He included the others with his eyes, "What use has this Valley for more Matta? We've got all we need and of high quality. Even our export trade is sufficient."

This time Ethel spoke and stepped a little forward as if she would take leadership for a change. Tom saw the dark shadow cross John's face. " That's the beauty of our plan. Why we need advertizing space every day. We intend to market it outside. We can even increase the market here. We can gain a greater demand in the Valley if we use the Video rightly. You might want to see our advertizing plan. We think it will convince people they ought to buy new rugs and upholstery, maybe drapes too, that haven't been changed for years. Sometimes for generations."She laughed, glancing at her companions. "We can do that with proper visual material, the way the old ones did. It's an expansion of marketing, new jobs, new sales. " Ethel spoke eagerly, her eyes sparkling with these,her ideas.

Tom was bewildered,, but an increasing unease tugged at the back of his attention. "What would you do with the fine rugs woven here and by the Vagabonds. Their designs are world famous and they last forever."

John spoke again, but Tom noticed a fleeting frown cross Ethel's face. "Whatever they pleased. Give them away, roll them up and store them - whatever. Put them in museums if they're really special. Their time is over except for ritual use. Why should we want to keep the same old patterns. You see the old ones always did it our way. They changed their entire houses every year or two, at least every five. And the reason they did was because they got tired of the old ones, and also because they wore out. It made for a lot of business. We can't continue having enough business if we sell such durable goods for the low prices we now sell them for. The Vagaband rugs can be sold for much higher prices. We could show them how."

"You plan to tell people that your products won't last?" They glanced at one another but were silent. He frowned, "You really think people want to spend their lives in mills? Making more and more rugs when they could make just enough good ones and go on about their lives? You really think that's a way to live?" Tom heard indignation threading his voice, and swallowed, brought balance to his emotions. He wanted to think they had not really thought this through. He said quietly, "It was our choice, remember, in the beginning of the building of the Valley, to make things that last and make them beautiful enough that we do not tire of them, but can enjoy them for generations. Such household goods, and clothes too, were to be the finest for everyone, not only the special few. The Matta we raise is a fine fiber, but tough and strong. It resists wear well. Zenna, plasilk, our cottens and wools too." He calmed his urge to laugh, the idea seemed to him ridiculous. He said seriously after a moment,"I see you've done careful planning. But I doubt whether there is a need for more fabric. Our weavers have all they can do now. They've not used all last years crop and this years crop is still in the field."

They looked at one another again and John signaled to Amanda. She spoke, her voice sounding small after the strong voices of the others. "Tom, we've done a careful study. It's just as John said, I searched the records to see how the people did it in the old days." At his start, she held up a hand,"Oh, I know the practices of the old days are anamatha to us in many ways, but we've got to get over old prejudices too. They did have good ideas, you know." She laughed and the sweet sound woke again in Tom the affection he had known for her in years past. "We found that they didn't use fabrics that would last for years. Only the rich could afford such things. The common folks liked to change things around, to buy new, change colors and designs frequently. And the business world was stimulated by all that buying. They also used styling in clothes, designing certain styles for different years so people discarded last years to buy new ones. We don't do that. We have a hundred different styles made all the time and people choose but don't need to change them. You can see how we lose business. We have no control over things at all" She smiled a radiant smile, confident that Tom would see her point.

He leaned to her, interested, curious, but hardly able to believe that she meant what she seemed to mean. "But surely you don't -- wouldn't want to change our durable fabric for something - poorer? Everyone can afford the best under our system. Everyone lives with beauty. Isn't this better?"

She sighed but John took over again,"She did the research Tom. We want to build a new market, we must have fabrics and rugging that wears out fairly soon if we are to have a continuing market. "

Amanda's clear ringing laugh did not reassure Tom. She turned to Ethel and that lady's serene smile reassured him a little. She was a very sharp lady. "We've got a fiber that will begin to shred after a year or two . It combines well with other fibers but it takes color more rapidly, so the whole piece is ready to be disgarded when those fibers fade out. We can get varieties of color we've never had. We can put up our own mill here in the north and make a really good credit, a lot more work for people, and it's good business."

Tom's mind seized on the pattern developing. He decided to give them the benefit of the doubt. "But I still don't understand why anyone would use inferior fiber if we have finer stuff? The whole Valley intention is that people do not spend their lives making things, over and over, but rather make enough enduring products that last and are beautiful. You all know that."He drew a deep breath."Besides, we've got plenty of work for everyone, and they have time to keep learning, to travel, to make music and dance and to spend time out in our mountains. Everything we know as important!" He stopped, it all seemed so obvious to him."As for limiting styles so new ones had to be bought each year, I don't think anyone would tolerate it. We've always chosen according to our own body, some styles don't work for all of us. We have to have many styles all the time." He couldn't understand the attitude of these folk and had begun to imagine they were making a terrible mistake.

They were watching him with smiles as though a secret waited. A secret they thought would please him. John spoke eagerly, "Tom, we think that's wrong. People like to make things. They don't mind making them over and over. Gives them something to do and they earn credit that way. And we've read that they liked following the style of important people, like yourself, for instance. Ever notice how many more men wear beards now?" He paused, his enthusiasm rising as he talked. "Besides, working people need to keep busy, you know that. We'll have trouble in the Valley if we don't keep the common folk busy enough now that the main building is done. People spend too much time at the Learning Centers today." His voice had an earnest ring that sounded false in Tom's ears. Where had he gotten such an idea? People were constantly busy.

Ethel nodded, and said,"We can convince people that they want these fabrics. That they want variety, that they want to change them each year, just like they did in the old days. We can make a market that way. All of us can get rich. Actually rich. And it's about time, don't you think?" Her enthusiasm sounded very true to Tom, she was genuinely convinced."Look, we've brought some samples to show you."

Dennis nodded, his face a round wreath of smiles and he lifted the little satchel he had carried up to set it on a table. He took out several bundles, carefully wrapped and handed them to Tom. Tom opened the first, unfolded a length of fabric, a shimmering silver and green, irridiscent combination of colors . The fabric was soft, tightly woven and looked as if it might be quite warm. It was heavy, too heavy for clothing but would make wonderful upholstry or drapes. He picked up another bundle, this was a tight roll of carpeting. This time it was a quiet soft grey, the pile firm,pliant, more like plasilk, than Matta, with a brushed web-like pattern in blue. There were two more, each different, both carpeting, one heavier. Each sample was cut into small squares of various colors to show their variety of color. The fourth was a wool mix, thick and warm. Tom sat holding them and for a moment didn't know what to say. These were in his opinion not superior to any Valley fabric in color or design and that was, supposedly, the strength of this new fiber. Finally he said,"I have to say I'm glad to see these, countries that have cold climates will be able to produce fabrics they can use until we can develop more durable quality for them. In fact, I imagine the villages to the north could benefit from the plantings. Surely you must have sent them word, and plants for a trial crop?" He let his hands caress the shining fabric, liking it. "The plant wizards will have this flaw corrected in no time.They can take the hardier plant and work with it until it is fully as durable as our present strain." He smiled, wanting to encourage them.

"Oh,no, Tom, you still don't understand. These are our own plants, we want to have control over their use because we want to build a good market up north. We won't sell them our plants." Ethel spoke as if explaining to a child.

John leaned forward then, taking command of this little group."Wait! You've missed our point. We plan to build a market! The income would be steady because the fabric wears out soon and people must buy more. We control the product because we bought it outright. Those lands can't raise this Matta."

Dennis pressed in eagerly, his face still shining with that light of the young devotee. He was so full of the conviction, Tom thought, like a religious, one dedicated to the higher Search. How could a man, even one so young, dedicate himself so to such a paltry aim? He said,"We'll go north though, there's the vast bowl of the old lake bed where swamp land could easily be developed and we could - -" John stopped him with a look and Tom, watching Dennis's face, knew the exchange.

John said, his voice a little severe as if in reproach,"The northern people would not want to raise this crop. They are too lazy, with most of their lives spent fishing the lake and hunting. They are a lost people, in my opinion." He glanced down at Dennis, who being younger and shorter, felt suddenly like a child. John added, "They've reverted almost completely back beyond the old ways even, they're forest people. " The last phrase was spoken in a tone of such contempt that Tom almost Reached to Touch, contacting this strange attitude. John sat up straighter,"Now, we've explained surely enough, We would like to know whether we can count on your support when the Council meets. We need to plan on the use of that land." There was a no-nonsense manner about him now, he wanted to close this discussion. Tom appreciated that, he had a busy day too. But he was full of a nagging worry.

Ethel spoke as if she wanted to heal the strained atmosphere, "We haven't told you the best of it. This plant has a highly colorful bloom that produces a high yield of nectar. We are going to bring in bees and set up hives perhaps fifty to each sector,as we get them planted, and because we can raise two crops. In south Valley, three. We can make honey and then a processing plant for mead. Mead sells well, you know. The samples we've made has a wonderful flavor."

Tom stared at her,"But two or three crops following one after another is too hard on the land. Planted as you plan to do, as one crop fields, it would destroy the balance."

"Oh, Tom, you must know that that practice must end. We've got to be able to USE the land." John had allowed a faint irritation to enter his voice.

Tom said, "But we've been producing all the mead, and honey too, that the Valley needs. All anyone wants to buy, at least. We have enough, or have you a plan to 'build a market' for that too." He kept his own irritation in check.

"Oh, Yes," Ethel said, "we can manufacture enough so that every tired worker whose spent the day manufacturing the fabrics, or working in the fields will have a relaxing evening in the pubs we have already begun to operate." She was smiling broadly, sure now that he would see the excellence of the plan. "We'd wean them away from the habit of always going to the Learning Center evenings. They'd be too tired."

Tom jerked into recognition. This was a webwork plan, it would cover the Valley with an insidious pattern. Feeding on itself, it could draw into itself the unwary. He breathed a long slow breath, bringing himself into balance. He must listen, must know. He said softly, a wry humor shaping his words, "Well, surely anyone devoting his life to earning your credits would need to inebriate himself at the end of the day." John's eyes met his, hardened but the others appeared only puzzled . Their conviction of their good idea was complete.

There was a moments silence then John, cautious, spoke slowly, "We do want to manufacture Mead, and we will sell it out Valley also." His deep voice sounded so reassuring Tom was surprised, then realized that it was a poor attempt to use the Voice. Where had he come upon knowledge of that rare Talent, one that only the Monitors knew?

Tom said, "Well, I like mead, one of my favorite drinks, but I hardly think the Valley needs more. Maybe you can provide a new variety but it'll never make anyone rich. People just don't want to drink that much of any liquor. My Winter Festival bottle is still not empty. And you see, you folks already plan to build up the wine market. I'm afraid you're in for losing all your work. We Valley people are not a drinking people, you know"

"And why is that? " John snapped.

Tom spoke gently,"We just have been too busy with more important things, so much that we have to do, to learn, to realize, in fact. We -- "

John cut in,"Yes, of course, and now the work's done. The building finished and people are getting bored, tired of the old things. We need something to interest us again and business, marketing, commerce, can be that thing. You must see that!"

Ethel nodded,"Tom, you must see that people have just been absorbed, working hard, now we can relax and enjoy life and these things go with that, the enjoyment of life, you know. We intend to be there when people discover that they need more. You could invest in these businesses, yourself,you know. You could also be part of it".

Tom nodded,"I suppose I could. I suppose I could. But you see, I've so much, so very much to occupy my time that I wouldn't be able to attend to them. I"ve so much to learn, so much to realize. To realize!" He felt helpless suddenly, as if they would not understand. They were smiling again, John too, as if they had given him a new and valuable incentive to agree.

John said,"Well, you've got the whole town to worry about, and with two wives at home,, and children, it's no wonder you're busy, but you see most people don't have much to occupy themselves." And Tom listened as he went on, still repeating much that had been said, but using again that deep resounding persuasive voice, that irked Tom, but that he felt little reaction to. He felt a troubling sense that there was something deeply wrong here. And as he listened, he realized that it was a fundamental difference. These good intelligent people really didn't understand why a man might not have an interest in that preoccupation with selling and buying that had obsessed the lives of generations in the past. Nor in that supply of liquors that eased the dispair, and meaningless of that world. For most of the people it had been a vicious circle. For the few, it had produced a terrible kind of boredom finally. Suddenly he was very tired, very discouraged. The world seemed to him to have grown dull, dark and threatening. He felt sad, So much for that detachment he'd promised to practice. He needed to go somewhere and sink into a deep meditation and find himself again.

He turned to look at his guests, they were so assured, so convincing, and basically, he thought, except for John, such good people. Then he caught himself, what was it about John that was different? Surely, it was a difference that triggered his own dispair. The Families of Adwin were going to have to pay attention to realize the very great difference between themselves and the Builders. There must be some way that these folk could find interest in life without depravity.

He drew himself to attend again, John was waiting for him to respond, "Well, it looks as though you're working hard to accomplish what you believe will develop into a better product for the Valley. I can't promise you my support now, I must give it some thought, but I will certainly consider all the things you've said." He sighed, then added, "Be sure to send your written plan to every member of the Council before next weeks meeting. We'll give a fair hearing, I assure you." He wanted them to go, to give him time to rest and think.

John said, "You realize Tom, that we have to make changes here in this Valley now. We've got to enjoy life, to have some fun, to get out and do things. The technology we've developed has made it possible to attend to our crops with very little human labor, most of our manufacturing is machine labor and that presents us with a problem. What do people do with their time? They need to have more work, more jobs. Well, we intend to provide that for them". He laughed, and Tom did not like the laugh. They gathered their samples and left his rooms, he saw them strap on their belts and then as they lifted, each went in a different direction. He waited until they disappeared behind the trees and then sat down.

What can we do. What WILL people do? I had thought there is so much to do just to understand, to learn, to prepare for the Journey. There is so much to do listening to the call of the Heart, reaching out to that larger dimension of Being and learning to live there, to be alive as that larger Self. That seemed enough to keep him busy for years. Now he must realize there were those who didn't think so. There were those who did not know there was a call from the heart. What would those people do? The sciences were always a challenging frontier, to interest a good mind, but those capable of working at the frontier were limited. What of all the rest?

He went into his house, made a sandwich and went out again eating as he walked, absorbed. There was the spark of Light in every person. Those who could not -- or did not want to -- be aware of it, were those who would not know the fascination of that beckoning universe of Spirit. Those would be like the blind in the land of sight.

CHAPTER NINE

Dean's requests approved. The rape of a field. Unexpected Gathers.

    A special Council meeting, called between the scheduled meetings, was not unheard of, but very rare indeed in the nearly ninety years of Valley growth. The members read the call to meeting on the Videonews with sorrow and eagerness. It was time! This meeting would be another test, but it was urgently needed. However, no matter how it turned out, the Valley would be forever changed. Rose and Ben, hearing the call in Rose's cottage, early on a early July day,felt a steady unremitting grief. Rose immediately, on noticing that depth of sorrow, paid attention to it. Was their attachment to the status quo so tight? Were they still resistant to the very nature of growth and discovery, distinct change? She turned to Ben, still lying relaxed from their love making. He had seen, he knew she must go.
    "Well, Love, there it is. And surely there'll be something forever changed. We can't expect it to be just as we imagine. It's the surge of Life in us that designs this changing. We've got to bend,fit into it." She sighed,smiled wanly," I was just settling down to enjoying our way." She drew a long sigh, letting him pull her close.

  The day dawned grey and warm. Light rain fell, a rain that was needed, but the lack of morning sunlight threatened to carry their spirits down. And Rose was not the first to notice that. She brought herself into Balance, sensing that others were doing the same. Then the air car from Adwin lifted above the clouds and the bright sun surrounded them. Rose laughed, delighted as a child with the sudden change. Others smiled at her delight. Dean had met the Car from his northwest mountains, Dana from Jasper and three other passengers on business trips to Santiago. As she talked to them, she felt a lightening of mood.
    Rose glanced up from watching the sunlight on the tops of clouds to meet Dana's eyes. Dana's face was solemn. Rose started to speak, when Dean, with that quiet courtesy and gentleness that characterized him, leaned to ask after their health. He was not smiling, his waving white hair shone like a numbus of light around his head. He had the kind of beauty that some old people manage to keep. She felt affection for him. She had known him most of her life, though not as a friend. He was a man to be trusted, firm in his beliefs loyal to what he held in honor.
    Rose said,"I'm fine today, Dean, I'll admit I'm a bit anxious. We've some vital matters to talk through today."
    He nodded, "It's so. The papers I'm bringing will demand some clear thinking." Then he smiled, and she felt herself swiftly relax, surprised at the effectiveness of that smile,"But not to worry, young one,we can come to terms. I

trust our system."

Dana pulled herself from her reverie to glance at each of them in turn."I admit, I'm troubled. I've surely done my homework, but I'm still not ready to vote. Surely there will be further information for us. The original request seemed very specific and should have a clear decision." Her voice openly revealed the anxiety she felt. Her small dark body seemed taut to Rose, but the flaming red hair drawn so smoothly back into two thick braids shook with the emphasis of her nods.

He met her eyes,"I think it's mostly clarification now. We know we're asking against a strong precedent and we know people must have time to adjust. We don't have illusions that it'll be an easy transition. But without change, stagnation occurs." He smiled again, his erect thin body full of pride and confidence, he settled back, closed his eyes and relaxed into the auto form chair. Rose thought he seemed tired, surely there might have been a struggle in his own district that he'd had to meet before he came. She was right, the vote had been in the Builder's favor but it was very close.

Rose reached over to press Dana's hand. Dana had seen much struggle in the Valley Council during her fifty five years of life. She was a child during the forming of the system that had built the Valley. She remembered little of those years of struggle. The building of towns and cities had occupied all her years of life. And during that building, there was little conflict. She had seen the Valley take shape, decide it's Convictions. They had proved to be life lines of safety. To shift, or question one now would not be possible for her. She remembered the pain and suffering of her grandparents, their dispair and hopelessness. Her parents had fought to bring the ideas of order that Valley Convictions were based on. During so many years there had been the confidence of a people who had endured much, finding peace.Then, in the past years,she had seen these times of change coming and feared them. Why couldn't things stay? Finally safe? Finally good? Her service on Council had continued long after the usual terms because there was great respect for her fairness . Respect for her was endemic through out the Valley. Her home town had persisted in persuading her to serve. Since she thought she had little to offer the growing town other than Council service, she had continued. Rose studied her face, turned now to the open windows. Then, without surprise, she felt the tingle of an opening Reach. Unhesitatingly, this time, Rose met the Touch. Felt it like a gentle set of fingers against her mind, felt the entrance of another awareness, other indistinct thought patterns then stronger sensations, images. In moments, through swift pictures, expressing, scene, idea, smell, feeling, Rose knew the evidence that worried Dana of Jasper. Her heart ached.

The Builders had asked to be given land. That in itself was not surprising. Many citizens asked to use land, could have its use for their life time if they chose, could even extend its use on to their children if that was desired. But the Builders asked for OWNERSHIP. They would do with the land as they chose. Here the old conflict between personal and public good came head on. But there was precedent enough to deny that. Surely humankind had seen how wrongly people had behaved when parents owned their children or men owned their wives or other men and women and could do with them as they chose. And when people untrained in community welfare owned land and could rape or use it to destruction . Community agreement as to the right and wrong of things did protect the helpless against individual greed. For that was what it sprang from, that wrong treatment of others.Each person belonged to him or herself. The land belonged to Earth only.

Rose felt Dana still there, these ideas an exchanging network, none so precise as clear thought, but the essence strong and defined. Was it true that humankind had finally transcended that old greed that had utterly dominated the life of their ancestors and brought about the terrible wars, then the terrible non-wars? The next few years would tell them whether that was true.

Rose wanted to withdraw, to settle into herself and brood. Instantly she was alone, loosened and felt the sudden release like something lost. She started, then smiled. It was like that. Yes!. She gave a last press to Dana's hand, then turned away, settling into her chair. Two thousand acres. Rose tried to imagine that much space. They wanted more land east of Santiago where they had already been given two hundred acres. They wanted land extending those fields, and also another two hundred along the river, for that new crop of Matta. She knew the site they had chosen would be distant from the Highway and no Vagabond would need to see the destruction unless they traveled from their Way. But the People of the Way always knew!

Rose had caught the worry about violence that Dana had transmitted, but she had not understood it. The fact of its presence pained her. She had flashed to Dana that Dean was not a violent man that he could be trusted. Dana had reminded her that any person could be trusted to do what he thought was right. But that right might not be the right for all. What Dean thought was right would shake the Valley deeply.

The rest of the flight was a somber one. Rose closed her mind and let herself think about the sudden emotional fires that had erupted here and there throughout the Valley in the past months. Surely they were only flairs, young people letting off steam..At least they - her friends- had comforted each other with that explanation. She herself, worrying about Andy, had refused to believe that he could turn away from Valley Conviction. She and Ben had watched him in the past week. He seemed absorbed in practice and Learning Center activities. Surely his friends had worn out their intentions. Could any truly conmscious child blind themselves, refuse to see what they didn't want to see. Such a blindness was the cause of so many terrible events of history. She shook her head, her eyes no longer seeing the Sun outside, feeling the light drift of the air car through the winds. Her own generation had been trained from childhood to pay attention to what was going on and to see what was there without flinching. Yet they had -- all of them-- denied so much. How could they meet this genuine test?

She drew a long sigh, was it going to be always necessary to learn? Was there never simply a slipping down into a settled knowledge of things that was

THE JOURNEY

enough? She longed to be able to rest from such eternal vigilance. Had they not rested from such vigilance while they were building their cities, their towns? It was true they had concealed themselves from one another. But they looked out on their world clearly now. Surely they were on their way to that Vision they had begun to glimpse. A Vision of what could be, of what humanity WAS! She let herself remember! Through the Light, into that stillness inexpressable, there was possibility. She knew it. Surely the balancing of consciousness between this daily living and that Vision beyond it, would not overwhelm their powers.

New energy blew through the Valley. A new wind of power increased in those who were transcending old perceptions. Would it not also increase in those who were not? Then what would those blind ones do with that energy, except turn it back into old patterns, because they saw nothing else? She felt an intense thrill of what seemed to her a revelation. Something that changed the order of her thought.She wanted to share it with Dana. Then turned - no, she would think it out more first.

Discontent, could it be called that? Discontent was a spoiling sickness, signifying some deeper lack, but the Healers were skilled at treating that, discovering it's source. The only problem was that one had to be willing to recognize the problem and ask for help. Would those who felt it nagging at their strength, their creativity, ask? Or would they blame it on someone outside themselves? Then she felt a great gratitude that Benjamin had come home. "How could I manage with out him. How DID I manage so long without him." There was a clear image of Jessie in her mind, so sharp that she might have been sitting beside her. It startled her. How had they managed without Jessie? Well, obviously they hadn't very well. So much hidden, denied and so many hurts growing behind closed minds.

They arrived. The slight jolt of the car as it settled, woke those who had dozed off. The clouds were broken here, sunlight blazed across dark forest or bright grasslands. They climbed out and went down to the Leaf Plaza of the Council Hall. Standing at the edge they looked far out over the miles and miles of Valley below. And Rose could see the vast network of 'limbs, branches, and leaves' from which hung the residences like ripe pears. All the passengers as they walked off,stopped to gaze out over the Valley,except one. That one was obviously a native. No one coming in to Santiago was ever able to just go on to their business, the view, the sense of being suspended there in this sky city was so different, so wonderful. Only two cities in the entire world were at all like it.

The Council was swiftly gathered. This meeting took busy people from work all over the Valley and they would waste no time. She saw Paul at his place as Chair . He Reached and welcomed her and Dana warmly and Rose was a little envious of his ease at that Reach. "Well", he said when they drew close, "looks like we're all here and we can begin.

Rose let her eyes move along the faces around the big,shining, round table. Clandor made, it was exquisitely inlaid with patterns and colors and then polished so that their faces were visible reflecting from it. She sensed alarm among them.

She heard Dana and Paul exchanging friendly comments. She found Grace's eyes and then swiftly a light Touch. She smiled, so new this confidence in that kind of sharing. Yet so tender, so trustful. She smiled her gratitude. Then she focussed and attended. In one swift Reaching from Paul, they began a Joining, Minds met minds, melded and Joined in a steady ring. Calm literally flowed from those two deep wells that were Edsil and Grace. Oldest and strongest in experience, two whose 'secret' had been kept through those early years when even the teachings had not prepared them for its actuality.

These two found the eddies, turbulences and knots that threatened this meeting and soothed them. Like a mother calming a child, Rose thought, with a wry smile. Surely, their age gave them that tendency. The flow brought a settling, untying, gentling until there was a long quiet sigh of relaxation. With that the Council, in one breath, spoke the 'Reminder'. "Let us act with Love, let us think with open minds, let us refrain from judgement until we have all the facts, let us keep our true balance." Then with a look of sadness, Grace added, "Let us recognize our own bias."

The Joining broke and they looked toward Dean who moved to stand for speaking. They saw his eyes, the old seamed face filled with a sadness they did not understand. And behind that brave courage, a glimpse of pleading that he determined not to let them see. Then, with a suddenness that shook Rose's calm, they remembered that Dean had not been of their Joining.

The reminder brought a painful swift shaft of shame. Dean looked to Paul, unaware of their consternation. "I've submitted my requests. You've all read them. They've been broadcast through the Valley news. I would like the considered response of this Council." They could feel the control he held, that he reveal nothing of his trembling. Yet they all knew for he could not restrain the broadcasting of his fear.

Paul said, "For the record, we have all read and thought of your request. We appreciate your sending it to us in advance and giving us the time for study." His strong young body held erect, seemed also relaxed. "In brief summary, The Builders ask new land, east of Santiago, near Central Valley. Two, the Builders state that no change is seen among children relating to what are called, 'psychic games.' They request a meeting with all Master Teachers. Three, the Builders report there has been no success with investigations of the Silent City. They will send their own investigators."

Paul cleared his throat, a faint smile tipped the corners of his lips. His blue eyes twinkled and Rose was disconcerted that he could be amused. The agenda seemed to her threatening. Paul said, "We would like you to explain why you need more. We gave you two hundred acres."

They all knew it was a formality, Dean had told them in his papers. He patiently repeated. That was only the primary plot with which we plan to supply the Valley, it will not take care of growing markets all over the Valley and out side."

Paul was quiet, "Do you have these markets? Will you attempt to supply the world?

"If the world requests it. Already we are developing advertizing to build Markets. We have set Valley Computer Marketing systems to make a report for us. After that we'll set up our advertizing campaign. We've been broadcasting our products on News Video and we should know soon." His tension was subsiding, he radiated a growing ease. Rose wondered if Grace had not Sent peace, Sent calm. Dean's eyes met their watching faces. Quietly he added. "I understand the Council has initiated a separate study of world market needs. Between the two studies, there should be final decisions in August."

Thomas raised his huge golden head, shook the hair from his eyes and literally stared, then caught himself and said gently. "Every country I know of already grows the crops for its wines, beer and other liquors. Or has a trade agreement set up with one who does. How can you find enough need?"

Dean was patient, though he drew a long breath as though trying to explain to slow pupils. " We believe that the market has to be BUILT. People have to be persuaded that they want more, can use more. It's a matter of convincing them , showing them how they can enjoy themselves in new ways introducing activities that need our product." He stumbled faintly, obviously not comfortable with that thought.

Paul sighed," We're exporting and trading already pretty extensively Dean."

"Ah,yes, we're deeply involved with world economies. But from what I understand, we've done almost nothing to push markets, products. We simply fill certain needs. We must begin building markets. All of us, the other industries must grow too. Most of them need to expand ."

Paul met Thomas' eyes. Rose was aware of their relief. their strange amusement -- something ! Yet, as she touched, she also knew their sorrow. Paul asked, with a long breath."Have I read your request correctly?"

Dean nodded,"You have. I wait your decision."

There was silence and then Grace's soft voice spoke hesitantly."First of all, let's correct a serious error. We know that everyone here participated in the Joining just now, everyone except Dean. We are concealing! That is wrong! We must admit that we are among those who engage in what he calls psychic activity. We must not deny -- anymore. Not ever in this Valley must we lie or deny to one another again." She looked around. A dozen breaths caught, the relief, such vast relief but with it the feeling of having been exposed. Then the shamed acknowledgement.

Dean looked at them, not comprehending. every person at the table except Dean knew that Grace was right. They were fearful of that fact but accepted it. He felt their discomfiture. Paul nodded at Grace and said, "Courage was always one of your strong suits."

The realization of Grace's meaning penetrated Dean's puzzled mind. He frowned, stared at them. a look of dawning comprehension on his face and then that replaced with one of horror .The changes in his expression were like a handwriting that no one misread.It was not anger or hate they saw replace the

THE PEOPLE OF THE VALLEY

horror, but a profound dispair. In that instant Paul knew that Dean was one who would eventually understand. He did not question that inner knowledge, unlikely as it seemed at the moment. Dean had said nothing. Paul thought, 'He does not know that anyone of us knows his deep feelings. He broadcasts without restraint, as so many like him do.'

Rose quailed, watching,"There is so much he doesn't know and how can we tell him?" She sighed, watching Paul, knowing he could see the blindness this man lived with and did not know of. No wonder he feared. He could not 'know' the honor and love of his fellows, their fear or hatred, but he could imagine the latter." Paul sadly thought it unlikely that he would imagine the former.

Finally Dean spoke and it seemed his body had shrunk, aged before their eyes." I have thought this might be true. I am grieved to know it is. I thank you Lady Grace for informing me. What now?" He looked around at them and wearyness dimmed his eyes. "I've tried to calm the young ones among our members, the older ones too, for that matter,but now, I don't think they will listen to me again. For they have accused you of duplicity and I have defended you." He hesitated, his eyes bleak, defeated."I will have to tell them, of course."

He was silent,his eyes wet. He looked far past them out the long curving window and across the open air to what seemed to be a vast curving dark 'branch' rising upward until it was lost to view in clear blue air. "They believe already there is a conspiracy against us. That is dangerous,as you can well recognize. They believe that those possessed by these satanic practices have already allied themselves against all those who stand against such evil.But the grief of that is the pressure among them to revert to the ancient ways of violence. Even as we try to hold that balance, they insist that the old ways were right. The Builder's plan for economic regression has hatched itself a sister. And I do not know whether that sister, political regression, can be persuaded to be gentle." He stood, his hands hanging loosely, his body more relaxed than they had ever seen it, but it was the relaxation of dispair. They knew that he had and still did, stand half way between two opposing forces. A painful place to stand.

Paul watched him,"It's our own fault, Dean. We ourselves didn't understand and we refused our own growing Talents. We denied to ourselves, not only to you."

"You denied? Denied that you were - that this thing you do, these that you call 'Talents', were real?" He was incredulous but Paul thought he believed them."Why"

"Because we were also afraid, and we could not believe ourselves. You see, Dean, it's not easy to discover that you Touch another mind. Not at first."

Dean looked all round, his astonishment had overwhelmed his dispair, his fine curious mind was intrigued despite itself."Tell me, what is this you do?"

Paul waved to Grace, determined that while the old man was present they would not Join. Grace nodded and said,"It is a Joining of minds. We Reach out, we consciously Reach mentally to one another. If we focus and sustain that Reach, we can Touch! But we must have found another who is sensitive enough to have made that Reach too. At that moment, we either recoil, or we extend and do perhaps a mental handshake. Say 'Hello', I suppose one might say. Then if the invitation is there, we Join."

Dean's voice was a whisper,"And what is that Joining?"

Grace did not flinch, she spoke softly, using that wonderful skill of Voice that all of them had heard from her. . But now it was couched in tender, terms, ones of Love and calm. "Dean, Joining is that wonderful entering into mental communion so that images and scenes remembered or created can be shared. For those more highly skilled, imagery and thought combine into a conversation that can do in a few minutes what would take hours in ordinary speech. However, now, most people only exchange pictures, images and are aware of emotion, attitudes. But so much communication can be done through imagery that it is probably more useful than language. But don't imagine we 'read minds'. We do not!" She stopped, realising that she was talking to explain to herself more than to him. She smiled then, feeling the loosening of his body, the slow beginnings of an acceptance in his mind. That in itself was a miracle. She met his eyes, hers full of appeal.

He shook his head, a half smile on his lips."Grace, I've known you most of my life, we are not of this new order, you are of my own time. I have never known you to lie, or even to bend the truth. So I accept what you tell me." He stood thinking, finding again the fear that he had lost for those moments, "Isn't this Talent, this Joining one that can be used to probe into the minds of others? That is what causes fear!"

Grace nodded,"Certainly that would cause fear. It is not true. No! Tell your people that that is not possible. No one can probe into another's mind without permission, but also without careful training of both people. Not only is it taboo, but it is not possible. Though even those with Mind Sight don't always know that. Please get them to realize that. It is true!" She was finally tense, insistent. They could feel her Reach to him."It's true we can pick up emotional states, general attitudes, but we cannot read anyone's thought without cooperation and acceptance!" Her Voice projected truth.

"But can you not tell what we think at all?"

Grace frowned, ducked her head a second, in apology and then, met his eyes again and said, " Not what you think, so much as what you feel - and your attitude. But so much of what people term thinking is sometimes projection of feeling that it may seem that we read thought. Yes, you must teach them that also. If they carelessly radiate their attitudes, their feelings, think with violence or direct them at someone without restraint, then we have trouble NOT knowing them." At his clenched fist, she stood, one arm reached out to stay his anger, "Wait! All you must do is remember to direct no strong attitude or feeling at another. Simply practice what we've all been taught, to Balance. We CANNOT read ordinary thought, Dean. Please tell them that! And remember too, Dean, it is our own absolute law, and we teach any child with these Talents, that even when we sense feelings projected,we must always turn mentally away, as one would to any person engaged in personal matters. We MUST NOT receive unless the person intends us to!" But her eyes were anguished, and he saw.

"But you cannot gaurantee that all will obey that Law." His voice had become strong again, but stern in his old way.

"Not yet. For we have only just begun to teach ourselves what we are doing. We have only just begun to learn what it is ourselves. You must have patience too. We cannot learn and fight a battle at the same time." Her voice almost lost it's calm, but she rallied, and brought herself to calm again. She watched him, the plea clear in her eyes. "Dean, old friend, we have begun to See through the physical world, to See into the silence of Spirit. Humankind is passing through into a new order, a new state of Being. Such realization opens our hearts to Love Itself. We practice selflessness." Her intensity reached him."Do you see, Dean?"

For several moments he simply looked at her, his face softening finally so that she breathed out a long sigh of relief. He nodded once, then he slowly shook his head,"What a burden it must be. How can you find the understanding? Surely, it will not be easy to explain these things to our people. I will, however, try." He looked around at the others, the quiet control evident in his manner,"I will surely try." Then he laughed a short harsh laugh, "But then, I wonder whether I understand well enough myself."

Paul said, "We would be glad to teach all that we know ourselves. we'd like to talk about this, we want no secrets!"

Dean turned to him, nodding, and sat down."Well, that might be needed, if I can arrange it. But now, back to my petition. What is done of that? Can you offer any decision?"

Thomas said,"You want to raise crops we do not think are needed, and build markets that we cannot believe are there."

Dean, on more sure ground now, said,"We believe that people can be taught to enjoy those things again. Our young men say that people must be convinced of pleasures that they have forgotten in the hard times Then they'll be needed." He hesitated as if reluctant to say these things. "I remember when such pleasures were misused, surely we all do, and that must not be repeated. Not even for profit. But, our people insist that the sale of these pleasures will bring fortunes to those who invest." He drew a long shuddering sigh, and they knew his heart was torn. He did not want to think now on his own resistance to all of the Builder's policies. "You can do little else than let us find out what we can do. If you don't believe this will work, you will not fail. We will. We ask only now, that we have fields for the grapes, space for building wineries and the use of River swamp for the Matta crops." He was amazingly adept at mental control, emotional damping, but he did it by repression rather than shielding. They did not feel the blatant radiation of attitude and emotion that they had before. He learned fast. If only the others could-- or would! But the years of teaching younger people to Balance, to be aware, must pay off now.

He stood again, a courtesy instinctive to him, to regard them. He wanted to go back to his people with victory, and then perhaps he could quell the riot of disquiet, the firebrands, the ones who would not reason. He dared not bring them knowledge of these - these Psychic FACTS if he had not victory. He glanced up, his mind racing, focussed and meeting Grace's eyes, deliberately focusssed these feelings at her. Sending them out on a stream of desparate need. He didn't know how, but he knew he projected consciously his fear. He could not let the Valley erupt in battle.

Grace nodded, her eyes full of tears,, meeting his and holding them. Her response was there in those eyes full of a Love that comforted him in an obscure way he did not understand. He felt angry at himself for trying to show his fear, but he thought that it had worked. She did know, realize his dilemma."Yes, Dean, you and I are old enough to have known first hand the stories of the drunkenness that ravaged good people. Even in our childhood life, there were too many, too much pain and hurt of families. I have never forgotten it. Surely you and I will never persuade others to follow that example, return to those awful days? Surely none of your people would build a fortune on degradation? It's such a good world we have now." Her voice was pleading. He met her eyes and the sorrow in them was a knife against her own heart.

"I cannot change what is. There is another kind of blindness, other than that of ones who cannot Join. There is the blindness of lack of experience. Our people have not lived with that degradation in their midst. They don't know. Don't know at all!" The words burst from his lips as if from a hidden place. He did not intend them. He bit his lips, looked down at his hands clutched together against his waist. Then slowly slid down again into his chair. His eyes again bleak."Finally he said softly, "I cannot know that all our people have pure ideals."

Paul watched, wondering how it would all come out.He was not disturbed yet. He could not tell the others. Their refusal to Reach in consideration of Dean, seemed to him foolish, but he accepted. There would be no such market. There was no danger. He knew, without doubt in himself, that the time for that was past. Grace need not grieve, Dean need feel no guilt. The vineyards and hop fields, improved varieties of each, produced the best wine and beer the world had ever tasted. There was enough! Paul believed with absolute conviction that the People of the Valley would not respond to such efforts to persuade them against their better judgement and their much deeper other interests. He KNEW! Yet, he felt also a faint doubt. What if he were wrong? The market research the Council had already set into action, would tell them.

Dean looked around at them all. They did not have to Touch to see the growing fear and anger in his eyes, he spoke loudly in body language. Seemed uncaring who noticed."Then you don't approve our request? "His voice was harsh. Too much depended on this. They saw his need, his precarious position among his people, his wrestling with the problem and with his desire for peace. He loved the young men and women of his village, his own grandsons and daughters, grand nephews and each of those not related. He could not bear to see them embattled. He remembered the stories of his parents who had seen first hand the horror of such battles. Images from his own childhood filled his mind and he made no effort to hold them to himself. They saw, because they only had to open their attention. He seemed not to care that they might know. They turned to allow him privacy, his mind pain so sharp it hurt them.

Paul said gently,"No, Dean we don't say that. Can we offer another solution?" Ignoring the unspoken courtesy, he reached urgently to Grace. She must name it.

She responded swiftly, without further Touch."True, I move that we offer the builders 600 acres - what they need for their experiment. If the land is well used and the growth balanced, and if the plant wizards assist in planning for companions plants, then they have the use of the land for the life of their vines. At that time, we will reconsider." She looked around, heads nodded, a few frowns. "As for the new Matta they want to plant. We want to wait until the market survey comes in to us. The Builders are doing one and so are we. If it proves positive we'll reconsider."

Dean sighed, a tremulous sound and controlled his disappointment, and his relief."And what of the other request? Are you willing that psychic evils be extinguished?" Suddenly they could feel his control waver, slip away, and he shouted,"This Council is unbalanced. There should be half Builders and half -- whatever you are! We can't have these Psychic -- you call them Talents, we call them evils, threatening our lives. Since you admit yourselves guilty, how can we hope for safety?" His voice was bitter, drawn with tension.

Rose nodded slowly, leaning toward Dean, "It appears there is no other way, we must investigate these Phychic Talents. We have been doing that at the Learning Centers already. But we must talk to your people of them. We have so much to learn ourselves, we know so little of them. We must learn about them together. We would be willing to tell you all we know. But it might at least dissolve the fears built on what is NOT true of them." She heard his indrawn 'NO'. but went on, "You represent rightful citizens, who fear these things, and we must learn together. How else can we make it understood?"

Paul sent her a silent faint warning. He said,"Would it be acceptable to you if we granted the request for the land, with the said restrictions and that we go on record that we will investigate these Psychic talents with the help of a team from the Builders themselves. You select a team to work with us? Then we will make all things we find public knowledge."

Dean started to protest, but Paul held up one hand, "Wait, we would also agree that on that land, in your villages, and your fields, no psychic Talent would be used . Not among your people or against them." It was a lame plan, no Builder would have any way to know. And it would be like asking people to close their eyes, ears, thoughts when around Builders, but be that as it may, it must be done. It was better than war! He held Dean's eyes, willing him to think, to realize.

Without hesitation, as if he thought it was vital to get this in, Jerome waved a hand, stood and said, "There is an old 'rule of Six.' I've heard of it. You must find at least six options, at least six rational ways to explain these things, then talk about those six. Then, people would know that there is no such thing as one 'truth' limited to human minds. Builders must come up with six, and we will also, before we meet again. Always Those six 'explanations'will open the mind to possibility of many more. Besides it makes us think before we argue? " He smiled at them as he looked around, the others frowned, stared at him, then slowly nodded. They would accept.

Dean finally nodded soberly, hope rising in him. Perhaps he could return with success after all. Perhaps they could preserve the Peace in this Valley he loved as much as any man or woman. "I think our people could honor that agreement. At least the thoughtful among us."

Edsil could sit still no longer,"But two thousand acres, because that's how much land they will have when the 600 is added! Do you realize how many lives that will disrupt? Destroy even? the fine sensitive face was haggard. The thought of such an agreement hurt him as if his own body had been struck. "Surely there must be time for the Vagabonds and the Wizards from Altos to clear the land of all life first. We can do that, if you give us time.! If this must be, then give us that time!" His face was full of the pain he felt.

Dean looked at him with a bemused expression,"I don't know what you mean by all that,but yes, if that's what you need then do it immediately because my people won't know what you mean either. "

Jerome asked,"How many people have joined the Builders? How many are there in this Valley?

Dean turned to the young man, obvious relief erasing the tension and the heavy lines about his mouth. "There are two thousand Builders in our membership, but more come in every day. As word gets out, we expect many more."

Jerome nodded,"Then to provide land for all of them to build estates, winerys, production plants etc. will take thousands of acres?" A slow burning anger had begun in him, the others felt it and feared for him.

Dean shook his head,"No, I think not. I surely want to keep the Valley essentially as it is. It is a wonderful land, surely, everyone knows that. We plan to live in large towns, and we will build as we always have here, units that use little Earth, for most of the builders want no separate farms. We plan apartment houses and business offices in units fifty stories high, but then, that will not be for many years I am sure. There is much to be done first."Suddenly he smiled, and the change in his face was like a light going on, "Perhaps we can build a city like Santiago, far above the land and harming nothing." He meant it as a joke, for no city like Santiago had been built in the Valley itself. In the present mood of relief, he went on, "We plan to build a great world entertainment center where holograms will provide people with environments of every pleasure. Where animals and people will perform constantly, and little towns that duplicate life in ancient history will be open to visit. You've read of the Disney lands that our ancestors built? Well, we will go on from those examples." He stopped, looked around, no one seemed to respond very well to those ideas. He frowned.

Thomas began to speak, then stopped. Disregarding the restraint Grace had asked for, Edsil Reached to him. His calm and his images were clearer than any had experienced from direct mind Touch. But he said, "Easy Son, he's mistaken, They all are. I don't know why I let it hurt me so. There aren't nearly the number he imagines. If there are a total of three thousand, I will be surprised. There just aren't that many unable to see, or unable to learn to Reach in this Valley." Then doubt crossed his face. "At least those are the percentages among our People of the Way. It could be town people are not the same. But you must trust, Thomas, we can't let his fear infect us, as it nearly did me." Each council member received the imagery and knew his idea except Dean. A small guilt rose, a new and uncomfortable feeling. It seemed discourteous yet they were not speaking against Dean.

Paul rose, stood confidently, smiling and Rose wondered at his calm. "Let's be clear then. We agree to present to the Valley Builders the use of a total of 600 acres for their experiment. We will consider use of more land after the Market reports are in. We agree further that we will begin a study of the Psychic talents being expressed and we'll do this with a team composed of both Builders and this Council " He smiled wryly, "It's time we did that anyway. we've denied our own Talents long enough. He raised his hand and let it fall, a gesture of finality and acceptance. "Is that about it?"

There was agreement. Dean hesitated, unwilling to believe that he had succeeded as well as he had. He could show the young men that he was still a valuable diplomat. That agreements could be reached with diplomacy after all. There was the third matter to be met. He started to speak, but Paul had caught his concern and said, "How about the investigation of the Silent City?" Again the smile touched his lips and he met Rose's eyes, and she felt confidence flood through her.

Rose said, "Shall we offer anyone who chooses the right to investigate and report on that City? Whatever methods you choose to use must be brought to us for consideration."

Dean nodded, "We have already sent two teams. They could not accomplish much. We don't know why. Now we want to send air cars, and skimmers to search the cliff faces. You agree that is acceptable? " He felt his breath almost held, it was too easy. there must be some trap. he couldn't believe that everything was working out. "Do you want to have some people also on that committee?"

"I think we can trust your team."

He felt a tinge of worry, "You too Edsil? You agree, your people will not object?"

Edsil , obviously thinking of something else, raised his head and said, "Huh? Oh the City. Yes, an investigation. that sounds fine to me. But you will not make efforts to bomb or attack without further agreement with us?"

Dean's eyes narrowed, he felt a false note here. Then, he thought he would simply accept. How could they let go their power so easily? Perhaps they were more ignorant that he knew. "I can agree to that."

The meeting was adjourned and the Council members went back to their affairs. Rose left the building slowly , catching Dana's mind, reminding her that they would meet at the Grid at six that evening. The fun of spending a few hours in Santiago's shops, and in contacting old friends would not be as long today as she had hoped. She met Paul, took his hand and walked to the edge of the leaf, they stood, closed to themselves, just enjoying each other's nearness. Rose felt a dread in her heart that there might one day be one who used the linkage to pry. Could that happen? Such a thing had seemed impossible to her until today. Was she being infected with Dean's fears? She remembered the teaching, "The Mind that can Link, is a mind that knows sensitivity for the welfare of others." That was the maxim taught to every person who finally went to the Master Teachers with the evidence of their own budding Reach. Now was it to be supplanted with suspicion? She shuddered, then righted herself. "No! It was not to be. Suspicion was not of the nature of the Sensitive. They must trust, must constantly Reach with Love alone their guide as they had been taught. Paul felt her unease and slid an arm around her waist.

Below they could see the dark green forest, interspersed with bright meadow and at the far right, long curving, patterned fields of crops, companion planting of several varieties together creating a variety of color in intricate patterns. Through everything the Great Highway wound. They could see here and there travelers, slowly wending their way to new places. Shrubs and trees dotting that Highway were already bright with fruits. The hills rolled, dipped down into valleys, the wide slow winding of the Green River gleamed, trees made designs,sculptural shapes against the dark meadows; the serenity, peace, beauty of it all, stirred her heart and loosened the fear that had lingered beneath it. We must keep this beauty, this wonder that is our creation of the Promise. She shook her head,"Paul, let's walk through the Market Halls. I need to be distracted with new things, with some of the products that artists have got there for sale. I want to buy a few gifts." He nodded and they turned to enter a curving 'stem' that ran across the vast trunk then branched out into several spokes on which were clusters of markets like great 'leaves' or small fruits. But Rose had her mind set on going into the clusters of small shops inside the hollow stems.

They walked down wide polished stairways into the tunnel of the broad branch, a few yards of walking took them to an intersection where several smaller tunnels broke from the Main Branch. There were openings onto clusters of leaf surfaces connected by webworks of passageway that broke into the entrances to pear shaped homes. Bright sunlight and air streamed through the endless tunnels. They chose one market tunnel and began to wander here and there. The wide strip along each wall of the Tunnel was transparant so that daylight brightened the colors. Small food shops, little specialty shops, displays of the work of artists from all over the Valley were arranged in a beautiful manner for sale. On a wall at one intersection of six branches, was a small Market screen. The World Market Screen with its accompanying cubicles was off across the vast Main Trunk in another section. This one, exhibited actual goods from world supply. People sat around small tables leisurely sipping drinks or eating and watching the display.

They entered several small shops. Sometimes a person worked at arranging things and answering questions for customers, or just talking to the people passing through. Often no one was there except buyers and Paul and Rose simply found what they wanted and checked it with their own credit at the kiosk in the center of the shop. They finally stopped at a coffee shop,where a display reminded buyers that any coffee made anywhere in the world could be found here. They selected drinks they had never tasted and went to sit in a cluster of little tables where they could see the big screen. People were chatting around them. Rose felt a sense of holiday. She smiled, happy suddenly, and they watched the display of world products ride slowly across the three dimensional screen. For no reason at all, she felt that all was well with the world. Without thought, she examined the feelings. Then let them be. She would accept that for now. It was fun to sit and sip a drink and watch the display. Perhaps something would come up they did not know of. Some one switched the display from farm equipment to household.

Paul laughed. "It's hard to create anything essentially new or better for running a house. The selection is meager isn't it?"

Rose nodded, but she said, "Oh, it's good to sit here and drink this wonderful coffee and pretend everything is all fine in our world."

Paul was smiling at her, his head bobbed gently and she noticed a few grey hairs among that thick brown thatch that fell to his shoulders and was neatly drawn to the back with a silver clip. She met his eyes and was surprised at the depths of his calm. She said,"How can you be so content? We've just had to break a committment to the very foundation of Valley life. We've just agreed to allow the Land, our sacred trust of land, to be used. Used, mind you as a means of satisfying human greed.To some cock eyed notion that -- that- won't work anyway." All the former well being was fading, her worry swelled. She twisted in her chair in frustration, frowning at him.It was a relief to say it. She felt anger at his quiet smile."Surely you can't simply not CARE." She sighed, relaxing again, she had swung all the way from contentment to dispair in minutes. She shrugged.

He reached across the little table and caught her hand, drew it into his own. "Oh,Rosy my dear friend, I care. I suppose I'm teasing you and it isn't fair. This is too important a matter." He was instantly sober. "I do care more than you know. But I think I've remembered something you may have forgotten."

Testily she asked,"What is that?"

"I think that you aren't remembering that the Touch, the ability to mentally Touch doesn't come to those who think they would LIKE to practice selflessness, but to those who practice it already. That inborn integrity is a quality of a linking mind. It isn't something we've trained ourselves to DO, it's something we developed into as we grew in consciousness. It's what we ARE."

He watched her nod, and she with drew her hand to lean her chin on both fists."Maybe we have to keep remembering, Rose, Love, we're a different people from our ancestors. We're not suppressing our hidden greed. I think even the hungers. Because they had to try to 'make' themselves put their fearful greed aside. We simply See differently. Greed has faded out of our stock of qualities. It's not gone, but faded. When we are uninterested in making huge world markets, a chance to make a fortune, or enslave our fellows in endless monotonous jobs, we're not suppressing greed. It's not because we've disciplined ourselves, or that we're better. We're not! We simply SEE, Rosy. We See how pointless it is. We have no interest in such a life."

His eyes flashed, his face taut, all his energy projecting from what he said. He needed to speak the fact he had discovered, not only to make it more true, but to remind himself as well as her. She nodded briefly, then was silent, not looking at him, letting her eyes find the rolling hills across the miles of blue air out the windows beside them. She could see flocks of birds, probably water fowl, lifting and settling around the small lakes that made bright glints among those hills. Along several hundreds of acres that comprised one ridge above a village thousands of chickens of every kind ran here and there, eating, scratching, making nests or calling their young ones. They lived a life little different from the wild creatures except no predator could attack them except people. She watched the tiny specks of color moving in scattered flocks. Then her attention returned to Paul.

He had stopped talking and was watching with her. Absently he murmured, "Did you know that's the only bird ranch left that sells fryers. The other two handle only eggs. The fryer business is also slack."

She met his eyes then, nodded, she hadn't known but was not surprised. She breathed a long sigh, feeling the anger drain from her."I suppose I do know Paul. I do. There is truly inborn difference otherwise we would not suffer so." She managed a wry grin. "But I'm sad at the losses, the misunderstandings.I suppose I'm still not clear of those old fears. Perception is not steady." She shrugged. "Well, thank God for people like you. And there must be many. Let's hope that they all give new focus to people like me." She grinned crookedly at him.

He shook his head, leaning, wanting to speak the thoughts that filled his mind, "But Rosy, you must realize that I didn't have this clarity at the beginning of today's meeting. It was something that happened when Grace and I - linked, so briefly, so swiftly and yet it left me as though - cleared. I was on the verge of fury, until then. It was as though she opened my eyes a little more. And that's what we must keep doing. Keep opening our vision and remembering what we KNOW. Remembering what we See beyond ourselves. We imagine we stand between a physical and a spiritual reality,but they aren't separate, they are inclusive." He stopped, his face changing in realization, "WE are included within Earth and all Life."

She nodded, her shoulders straightened," I like that way of saying it. It's true, a matter of remembering!" She spoke as if astonished at her own words. He watched her and nodded, realizing the wonder of it.

Paul sat silently drawing all this into mind, holding it there as if wanting it to imprint indelibly on all his thought. Then he said,"The new vision is innate in us,

Rose. We are a people who do care - we know of Love. We know of Its Presence and how it pours through our very lives and effects everything around us. We KNOW. It will be all right. You'll see."

She relaxed, sipping happily at the delicious coffee. Her heart lifted and her mind began singing outward as though a Joy had been released in her. Deliberately she focussed, shifted Vision. The land beyond the windows was so alive with Life. Life is alive, she thought, and her heart lifted. She looked at the faces around her, and each one seemed to her more beautiful than any she remembered. The life shaping the expression, shining through the skin and bright in those pairs of eyes, revealed to her the living spirit of that person's nature. She let thoughts float, unattached, conscious of the pulse of life in that room of people. She saw that she wanted to be convinced. To feel the safety of knowing that humankind was ready to sustain it's finest nature. She searched through herself, safe enough at this point of Vision to risk exploring the depths. And she found there that old anger, that old fear. She turned to look into it.

She said,"Paul, I know that what you say is true. But, I see in myself - " she flung one hand in a forlorn gesture that unnerved him - "old angers, such dark anger, and it isn't justified. I think it comes from what happened with Andrew. You know, I told you of it." Hurt and confusion were suddenly in her face and trustingly she acknowledged this streaming anger.

He was sober,"With all my air of confidence, Rose, I'm having to deal with a lot of feelings wrestling in me. But I THINK I've got them in view. They'll not get the upper hand. Just as they won't in you. We just need to trust each other. Support each other pretty constantly and refuse to pretend, to hide ourselves. We've done enough of that." He frowned. "We don't know what we're capable of, either our worst or our best! We won't until we see what we do."

She grinned suddenly, the Joy she had felt earlier sweeping away the trembling of fear. "Paul, you're wonderful. You couldn't have said anything to relieve me more. I don't like what I'm seeing in myself. I don't trust myself sometimes. I'm still ashamed of my fear, my angers, and I want to deny them. But I cannot do that. I must not. Don't let me do that Paul. Because unless I keep clear and in balance, I'll lose sight of what we have discovered. And it is our most precious recognition. We are Human, but we don't know the half of what being Human means yet!" Her voice had fallen to a softness that made hearing difficult in the busy bazaar. But she met his eyes and added," It makes me feel better to know you struggle too. One thing I know being Human means is that we are not separate at all." They drank their hot drinks, ordered an African pastry. Savoring its unusual flavor, Rose let herself sink into that pleasant enjoyment of simple body satisfaction. Warmth, safety, food and drink and good company. They watched the people coming and going, a quiet normal atmosphere, nothing to feed fear at all. Then they saw three people enter the shop.

Two men and a woman, smartly dressed, vigorous lively people who caught their eye, sat down at a table next to them. They all nodded toward Rose and Paul. Most citizens knew the faces of long term Council members . Rose turned to Paul,"Before we go home would you walk with me to the end of this corridor to the little glass shop. I want to buy the crystal bowls they have. I got two last year, but they are so lovely, hand blown with pure colors, I want to add to the set."

Paul nodded,"We've got over an hour before you must meet Dana." He started to get up and then stopped. The voices next to them were loud enough that they must hear. A man was saying, "There has to be something done. How can a man sit and let the Builders make their own rules even against our Valley Convictions?" His voice was full of anger and a pain of loss. Paul and Rose sat motionless. The other man, answered, his own voice quiet.

"Look Rod, You can't take the law into your own hands either. How would you be different from them?"

Rod snorted,"So what do we do? Just sit and watch?"

Paul Reached, tentatively, an invitation only. But he found no mind to Touch. No receptive opening. He shrank away, the knowledge of that fact more distressing to him than the anger in the man's voice. He stood, and Rose joined him, they began to walk toward the passageway. They were quiet until they were once more walking down the corridor between shops and she spoke,"I wonder whether they are aware of the difference among us? I wonder whether their loyalty would stand up before that knowledge. What would they, these who do not want regression, who stand for the Valley as it is, do if they knew about the Reach, the Touch and the perceptions that we've only begun to talk about?"

He shook his head,"It gets seriouser and seriouser, doesn't it?" But there was not fear in his voice,only a statement.

By the time they'd arrived at the little shop,, Rose had forgotten what she wanted to go there for. But when they stood in front of the display of cut glass, brilliant color sparkling from its prism edges, she turned thankfully to it,letting her mind rest in this beauty. She made her purchase and they left to go to the air car grid.

Paul said, as they left the tunnel walkways,"Well, Rose, there's another dimension now. I think we've got to talk to our own families and then plan a new Gather. He looked at her with worry in his eyes."First though, we must be sure the field clearing is done on the six hundred acres. Did you know Dana has begun to train people who are Animal Speakers ? I know nothing of them. But I would bet Jane is one. Whether she thinks so or not.. And I'm to ask my son, Steve, to find a Wizard crew to help prepare the trees and other plants. Preparing living things for death or for the loss of their homes is not an easy assignment, you know." He looked morose. " Steve'll not be eager to be part of it. But it's been done before. There's so much life there in that much land. We've got to finish swiftly because they won't wait. I think they don't believe there's anything to do and they assume that it's just a delay tactic."

She nodded, "They'll never know anything's been done either. Too bad we can't risk waiting until they're there and must watch." She stopped,hoping for a moment, "No! the ritual takes such concentration and is so delicate, especially if students do the work, we couldn't risk that much distraction. The Wizards wouldn't agree to wait. But the Animal Speakers, they're so new to us, the Talent is just developing and they'd just not be able to do anything. It would take a Monitor to do that with people watching. There has to be a few days for them to prepare."

Paul nodded,"I'll send our people as soon as Dana tells us the animal Speakers are done. There aren't many trained yet. She spoke something of Jane, though, did you know that?"

Rose was startled,"Jane? I didn't hear her. So it IS true! My God, Paul, Jane has enough to handle with her empathic Talent. But perhaps that's part of this Speaker Talent?" She raised a hand, thinking,"Paul! I heard Jane telling Steve that she'd found a Teacher. I didn't ask what kind. I wonder - "

He shook his head, "It's about time! She told me a Teacher had found her. It usually works that way. We need to talk to her about it. However, in answer to your question, Speaker Talent doesn't necessarily make one empathic evidently. Our Jane is just special". He laughed at his chauvinism, "But Dana'd like to train her for clearing too. I was surprised. We don't know our own family, I think. But she said she had a young man who is talented and he can help her. She seemed confident."

"It'll be quite a job, you know. Where will they all go. It's summer, new burrows are hard to dig, young only half raised,. It's not the best time." Rose frowned at the thought,the image of so many creatures roused from their safety, their lives, and made to find new dwellings. Yet it must be done.

She nodded to him as they reached the Grid. "We'll keep in close touch Paul. We must. You call us tomorrow about a date for another Gather?" He nodded and they stood waiting for Dana, watching below where a cluster of Vagabond wagons were drawn up into a clearing between groves of fruit trees. Their eyes were drawn to an air car gliding in and then to a Hunter's floating disc just behind it. They watched silently as it moved into the landing space above the processing plant. The Hunter stood above his kill, riding the disc easily with two deer and a huge young bull at his feet, blood still dripped from their wounds. Rose and Paul watched while the Hunter adjusted his great bow, the carrier for his arrows bobbing as he moved,then bent as the great disc floated into the door of the big plant. Paul turned to Rose,"That must be Archer Cliff, his colors are black and Green, though I couldn't see his face. He nearly always brings back what he sets out for. His Talent is amazing too.

She nodded,"He's working this time for private customers."

Paul glanced at her surprised and then grinned crookedly,"So you Reached to him? I didn't think of that." He shrugged, "I suppose that tells it on me. I am prejudiced, perhaps. I don't think of Archers as people who would Touch. How could a man who could kill - ?" He didn't finish. Stood silent, and then added, "It's obvious, He never kills without a strong ritual and he has a profound respect for animals. No one who ever saw him perform his rite of the kill would ever forget. It's truly moving even to other Hunters."

Rose nodded,"I'm glad there are wakened ones among them. They hold the

THE JOURNEY

standards high" She felt tired, a little dispirited now. The sun was approaching the high coastal hills to the west. She wanted to go home. They walked up the steps to the air car platform and saw Dana running toward them from the far side. Rose turned to kiss Paul goodbye and got into the car. She leaned back and closed her eyes. She didn't want to talk, or link, or think.

After some time, she let her head roll sideways, looking down over the land as they passed over it. She could see a band of deer grazing across a slope, Then a pair of foxes, crossed into a grove of fruit trees curved between Highway and forest, looking closely, she saw young ones bounding along behind, learning, in this their evening hunt. There would be grouse and pheasant among those meadows. She loved this world, this Earth where all creatures lived a better life. Just as people had a right to live, so had all creatures. Her heart was sad as she realized that the Builders did not see it that way.

A week later, on a day that dawned already warm, Jessie sat on the Deck, watching the sun begin to slant across the floor. She held her mind open, listening as though to the Valley itself and remembered Rose's report to the Family the week before. The escalating of the conflict was immanent. She need no longer obscure her powers so carefully. She could at least Send without restraint. It was time to begin action! Rose had reported the Council's decision, had asked for another Gather. Two in one month. Would wonders never cease?

Jessie began the Calling. There in the very early dawn, the sun just barely visible atop the eastern peaks, she stood looking out over the land. She Reached out. Visualizing Tom, picturing his home, his body and his face, she focussed and Touched. He was waking to his morning work and with a slight start of resistance, he was receptive. She asked him to come to the Hall for a Gather. There was need of one immediately. Would he inform Ned and his own wives and children. Everyone should be there if possible. He agreed, curious but not asking questions. He had little skill forming thoughts in that Joined state yet. He sent pictures and she smiled. They were more reliable. They all had much to learn before they would actually Send thoughts.

During the next half hour she Reached to Touch every member of the Family, finding them and reminding them of that meeting, but wanting mostly to let them be aware that the Touch was normal, that it was usable for ordinary matters as well as for crises. They had never participated in a Calling before and were surprised and pleased. With quiet determination she Reached to Altos and found Jennifer. She must let the others know, but she must also search out the relationship of William to the Builders, must know more. And she must support Annette and bring her to the Gather.

When she'd contacted all this Farm Family she began the same Reach out to Families in and around Adwin, Denlock and Jasper. In the next few days each Family must gather. There would be many Gathers in this Valley this week. Both Grace and Edsil would be making the same Calling. She could feel the streams of energy, the calls crossing in a network of silent energy through the Valley. People were Gathering.

She noted that some of the Family heard, responded and accepted their Talent. Others heard, knew of the meeting but did not consciously record how they knew. They were not openly receptive yet. That must be remedied.

She watched Rose coming slowly across the garden from the Temple and she knew that her heart was heavy. Rose came and sat on the low bench beside Jessie. She wanted unreasonably to put her head in Jessie's lap and cry, the way she had done with her Mother when she was a child. She smiled at the desire. In this moment she felt the grief of the world. Could the Family meet in three days? Summer full Moon Festival was over, the cleanup done, and the fields and farm work was mostly mechanical during this hot weather. Jessie reminded her that the Learning Center would be at its usual quiet period during Gather time. She wouldn't be needed. Rose looked at her with surprise. She still had not accepted the fact that so many people were as themselves.

Jessie shook her head,"You hid yourselves from one another and thought everyone did that. Well, perhaps most other Families were as resistant as yours, but they are no longer. It is a new kind of waking. Waking into public acknowledgement."

Rose felt the awesome power of this old woman. For the first time she began to realize how controlled and useable was Jessie's power. How precise the direction for that power. She recognized that she had still only touched on what Jessie was capable of. She felt a radiance from her this morning, a literal glow of energy. Surely Jessie had hidden her powers too, but from the necessity to allow others, not because she was afraid. It was different. She sat rigid, holding Jessie's hand, feeling the Reach, the steely fine thread of energy streaming from her to others in the Valley. Rose did not know the aim, nor the exchange, but she knew the power of it.

Then, as though a small branch of that energy turned to her, she felt herself Touched, felt her mind drawn into that webwork and there, she could see Grace's face, within the visualizing minds. Grace, and Jessie! They were of a kind! Of course! The thought,'How could I have been so ignorant,' woke to shape itself. The response came swiftly,'You didn't want to know. Denial is too expensive for us to tolerate." Jessie shifted mind focus and held Rose's hand for her attention. There, in contact was Edsil. Rose started, then nodded slowly. She said,"I might have known had I been paying attention beyond my assumptions."

From this quiet place in the Farm Garden she had seen in the two days past, as did most other Valley citizen, the Video cast of the clearing of the field. The Builders had waited, leaving it empty again as they promised. Paul's Wizards came to the field east of Santiago. Dana and her assistant had worked through one whole day. The slow task of making known to these small minds, these who barely sensed the presence of the human minds as they impressed on them the knowledge that they must leave, must go to other land. The reason was not immediate fear. An Animal Speaker did not need to use fear. It was with resistance the little creatures met the impression. But gradually, as the day went on, the creatures began to move. Larger, more conscious animals first, swiftly the foxes, a single family of Cougar, passing through from the high land. Rats, then slowly the badgers, coons, and skunks, all the rest of the rodents stirred themselves and began to move, to wake in rustling movement, their young following. They traveled far across the field and forest that was doomed to this invasion. And they began again to dig, to find new burrows, and during this time, the hunting was suspended. It was as in forest fire. None attacked others. They must first find homes. Dana wished she could persuade those indefatigable diggers the moles to dig extra spaces for slower workers, but she could not interfere with their normal ways. And as she watched, impressing, influencing in a gentle, flood of pictures and impressions, she thought that this was the way higher Beings must feel when they Touched human minds. Unable to do more than simply plant the impression. Then hope that the human mind would respond enough to function a little. The comparison humbled her deeply and she resolved to talk of it to Rose.

But slowly the job was done. The field was cleared of animal life. And never before had such a thing been broadcast on public channels. Who could deny now?

The Plant Wizards began the next morning. Dana looked across the acres to be cleared, thinking of the changes. She had seen it before. The first time, amazed and full of a disbelief. Plants already began to wilt. The great trees would begin to shed their leaves. They would withdraw their life, there would be no pain. Life separating Itself from those forms that were doomed. In the one other time she had seen this done, Dana had watched, more deeply impressed with the power of the Valley people than she had ever been in her life. We must act with Love, always we must act with Love, for our power is dangerous otherwise. She thought long of that day's activity. Whether the Builders watched the news, she did not know. Perhaps their denial explained the events some other way. But surely when they came tomorrow to begin their clearing they would have to see a difference. Or would they? It took a day ot two to fully wilt down great trees. Many would not notice,but the life would be gone. Dana frowned as she thought of it. How much did the assumptions she had lived with all her life effect what she saw, heard. She began to focus,, pay attention, and persistantly reopen her mind to discover, She too would apply the Rule of Six. There were many ways to explain any given event. She went home that day more thoughtful than she remembered being in a long time.

Finally the time for the Gather arrived. On that morning, everyone at the Farm was up and in the Hall for breakfast early. The sun had barely touched the Deck, the air was cool and pleasant. It was a lovely sweet,fragrant, quiet morning.One of those mornings when it is difficult to believe that any harm could come to anyone. But the day would be hot.

The news had come on the Video that morning. Plant wizards finished their work silently and unobtusively to the end of the acres given to the Builders.

THE PEOPLE OF THE VALLEY

Those folk seemed not to notice and were gathering their tools for clearing the fields, cutting of the trees. They would slice them apart with laser saws, thin cuts, nearly without sawdust, yet the tree would fall in pieces and be picked up by freight floats. Wood handlers from Clandor were there, ready to pick up the trees, settle them on freight movers, and carry them away to the mills in Clandor. The Builders sold the trees, and no one told them they did not exactly have that right. The numbness of the people who watched was too great to make a fuss about such a trivial worry. But the roots must be removed too, and the great earth moving machines brought out from the vaults beneath Santiago where they were stored, seemed like great monsters to the watching Valley. The workers noticed no running or scurrying of little creatures, no cries of birds in distress, no upturned nests full of young. For there were none. the fields were empty. And the clearing was complete!

Through out the Valley during the days that followed, the field east of Santiago was forgotten. It had been done. Thousands of people Gathered and planned how they might educate themselves and each other, how they might acknowledge their powers, how they might acknowledge those with power and those who were still blind, how they might include one another whether they could See or not. They must look to themselves, must look to the angry young men and older ones who could not understand what was happening. They must attend their own. The people of the Valley Gathered and realized a new time had come.

On that morning, the farm Family began their final recognition. Jessie said,"When I called a few days ago, some of you responded in kind. Some of you still refused. Do we have time now for pretense? Isn't it time to acknowledge exactly what our power is? If we have not recognized ourselves, we can harm ourselves and others. A power denied is a power twisted."

Paul sighed, pointing to the cluster of young people at the end of the room."There are our own children, already realizing and exchanging knowledge with one another. Let's acknowledge them completely. Rachel, I want to let you know that I, that we all know of your talents, and that we approve."He turned to face each young person in the room, to each he said the same. Formalizing the message. Wanting it to be very, very clear that they were finally acknowledged. He stopped as he met Justin's eyes, the little boy seemed to him to be mocking, a strange smile touched his lips but he said nothing as his Uncle spoke his acceptance. By the time he had finished, there were tears in most eyes and the young children were both laughing and crying. The older ones simply grinned in relief. But their eyes were shining. He finished, "Today we want to keep no secrets, but talk of our deepest realizations. We talked of much in our last Gather, but we have not done this."

Steve said,"Dad, It's a big relief. You'll never know how much. I've wanted so much to talk more, to tell you more. I was lucky that my major Talent was one that the Altos already accepted. Being a Plant Wizard has it's advantages." He turned to his sister, her eyes streaming, she looked around at them, Anna nodding to her, willing her to speak.

THE JOURNEY

Finally she did, "Papa, I wanted to tell you, many times when I grew up, because I didn't understand. If it hadn't been for Steve, I think I would have been crazy". She stopped as if even now she was reluctant to go on, looking from one to the other of the adults.

Paul said softly, "Tell us, tell us all, sweetheart. We do want to know. Late as it is."

The young girl looked to Jessie for help. She didn't know what to call her own perception. Jessie nodded, then said quietly, "Rachel is deeply Soul conscious and she is perceptive of that highest Mind level. She is the one member of this Family born in that state we used to call 'God conscious.' She sees beyond the mental plane into the Spiritual plane naturally, but she is not flawed as so many of the early Mystics were, often mostly by their social world. But neither is she divided so that she cannot live normally in this world we have made in the Earth. Rather she is CONSCIOUS and able to KNOW and then to think about what she KNOWS. She has stabilized the dicotomy of Self and self fairly well." She looked around at them, Rachel was finally nodding and smiling a little, shy she seemed, and yet she could not resist adding her own words now that Jessie had started things.

"I remember hearing you say something once, Aunt Rose, about the experience of Seeing the Light, and that Light being so deep and so great it frightened you." At Rose's look of astonishment, the little girl shook her head impatiently,"Don't worry,I never told anyone. You were alone and didn't know anyone heard. But I did and I wanted so to tell you. To tell you that that Light was just naturally everywhere and it lit up the garden where I walked sometimes.I wanted you to come and join me if you only would." She was crying again. Her face was full of a loving splendor that caught the breaths of those who saw. And for several minutes there was silence. Rachel went to sit near Jessie, placing one hand on her knee as if to seek comfort in touch. Then she added,her eyes distant,"Sometimes I couldn't see the garden until I shifted my vision to wake my eyes to Light."

Finally Paul said,"My dear little daughter, so much you must have needed to talk about and you could not. How hard it must have been."

She sighed, bent to conceal her eyes, then with a brave lift of her head, she met those sorrowful eyes of her father."No, Daddy, I didn't really suffer after I was five. I went to the Monitors because Martha came to me and told me to come. To Call her when I needed to. I - found - " She stopped, she could not hurt her parents by telling them that what she had found was a new set of parents. But Paul was nodding.

"I'm glad, Dear. Glad even when I'm jealous and guilty that I didn't know."

Jennifer said,"Oh, my little one, I wish I had known. But then, how can we help what we are, or are not?" She held out her arms in a gesture more to comfort herself than Rachel though she didn't realize it until much later, and the young girl ran to fold herself in them. For one thing Rachel could identify was another's needs.

"Then you've much to teach us. We seek what you stand within. You've much to help us know". Tom could not keep his voice from the slight tremor that told how deeply moved he felt. "Rachel, can you tell us, is it God that you See?"

She sighed, sadly, "Oh, Uncle Tom, there've been so many names, and none are any help. I don't know what that which people call God is, or Allah, or Buddha, except It must be Life, it must be Love, it must be Spirit Itself. I only know that beyond the Light we see, is what I cannot speak of. I don't think anyone could. Cannot even be thought about very well." She ducked her head again, full of the vision she had lived with all her life. "And there's a Knowing, beyond ourselves. It's where Time and space and everything familiar is not. There are no names at all." She frowned, shaking her head, knowing she could not speak her perceptions. "It isn't even a garden really, I just call it that when I'm not there."

For some time there was silence, the children settling, the adults one by one opening their minds, letting themselves Reach out toward one another. They felt that longing to Touch and as the moments wove themselves away, they did. Jessie said, "When I called you, I found several who could feel the impression of my mind, but who would not consciously recognize. Now do you see that danger? To be receptive and not to take responsibility for it?"

Silvia stared at her, frowning, astonished. "I never thought of that. Yes, how could we be sure the impression came from benevolent sources? Ah, I see, Jessie. I was just content to let the rest of you lead the way, I suppose. I was content to wait for your Touch."

Jane nodded, "I suppose that's what I've done. And now, I see another wrong. I see that Dana, the woman who risked so much helping the creatures escape, that she - she - does what I can do." She heaved a sigh, as if the admission had been all she could bear for the moment. She ached in her heart, to speak of it. How long had she denied, refused even her own evidence? She shook herself, suddenly angry. "I won't deny. She talked to me last week, just a little, to ask my help, and I refused. Even after all that my Teacher's taught me. I wouldn't go with her. I was rude to her. And now, now seeing her there on the screen, I know that I must learn from her, and do what she does."

Jessie nodded, "I'm glad to hear you accept that. We are going to need you, Jane." Then turning to Rachel she said, " Rachel, your way of speaking of Spirit is beautiful. Awareness of entering a garden lit with a glorious Light, has been a mythic story since time began. I think myself that entrance way is the illumined state of Mind. Perception becomes greater every time we lift to that place of Being."

Rachel cried out, "But it's not my place, Grandmother, its everybody's." She was frowning, worried. "It's inside me, and I am inside It."

Jessie nodded, "Exactly, and everyone who begins to See will know some form of it. But we have to admit, recognize and acknowledge that ability to See, to Reach to that realm of Spirit. You have to teach yourself, have to practice your own disciplines, learn to enter through utter stillness into contemplations where Vision becomes conscious. Where you stand at your highest point; Soul. Where you know the merging of Soul and person and are AWARE. It is the only way to know. What Rachel knows is her own perception, she cannot tell us of that Realm. Though when Rose talked of her own experience, Rachel recognized immediately, and so will we all. Spirit is another state of Being, or dimension, from this and cannot be spoken of in our language very well. It must be, as Mystics have insisted all along, experienced to be known. And to each the experience is different. I ask you to remember and to wait in absolute silence of mind and body, intuitively focussed at that point of attention to Soul identity, so that what you KNOW will begin to impress your conscious mind so that perception can be shaped."

It was a long speech for her, and the others listened as if hearing in a dream. For they believed her, they knew in themselves that she spoke the truth. Most could remember times of that Touch into that highest dimension, the glimpse of that depth of being and of reality. They had not waited there, however, long enough to step beyond that initial Light. But they knew a little of the pure wonder of Love Itself present within themselves. They knew that she spoke truth.

"Now, right now, practice the highest lift of mind you know. Just as Rachel said, shift perception to Soul consciousness. Right now! " The command was so forceful that each person began, most with closed eyes, to focus. Silence surrounded them, it seemed the sounds of life outside had faded, that no bird sang, no leaf trembled. Perhaps they were between the movements of time. And stillness grew. They forgot themselves in remembering Life.

Then gently, like a stream rising through rock, the flowing of awareness grew and they moved toward one another, seeking finally that Touch of wholeness that they sensed there together in this Gather. First Jessie Reached, and those willing responded instantly, and the pyramid was forming, drawing everyone in, spiraling into higher and higher energy flow. Lifting them as a group higher than any knew alone. Rachel, there beside Anna Joined with Jessie, Paul and Tom, firm in profound conviction. The others were coming, entering, conscious, and the Joining grew, until everyone was present within that vortex of Life. There they found one another, found realization that was LIfe, that was Love streaming through them and out again, like a River they must acknowledge and allow if all life were to live free. Finally Jane saw the harm her fear had done. She woke, accepted. Steve, saw his old resistance a burden and longed to let it fall away. And as he chose that direction, he felt the loosening of it and for that moment at least, it was gone. He entered finally whole heartedly into the Gather and the Joining.

Thus was the Soul Light shining through them all. Thus were they able to see through the eyes of the those whose intuitive minds were so developed that they could reveal to them their recognitions directly. The wonder of that filled their hearts, and they were healed of an old separativeness that had built itself on fear. For their individuality was the bridge between them, and was strengthened not weakened in this wholeness.

Then did Jessie lead them outward, still sustaining that inner focus. They heard suddenly, as if a release had occurred, the sound of Earth life, the rustling of the great trees, the birds, the distant call of a fox, of cattle lowing where they rambled through a narrow gap to bring their calves, playing at a distance, back to them. The two worlds were whole again, consciousness spanned the differences.

Finally they felt the releasing and the beginning of separation and they knew they could never again be separate at all. Softly they chanted an old prayer, one of those written on most Temple walls.

> From the Point of Light within the Mind of God,
> Let Light sweep down into the minds of men,
> Let Light return to Earth!

> From the point of Love within the Heart of God,
> Let Love sweep down into the Hearts of men,
> Let Christ return to Earth.

> From the center where the Will of God is known,
> Let purpose fill the little minds of men,
> The purpose that Great Teachers know and serve,

> From the Center that is called the race of man,
> Let Light and Love and Power complete the Plan,
> That it may seal the door where Evil dwells.
> Let Light and Love and Power complete the Plan of God in Earth.

They sat now, looking at one another, moved and full with the memories of that expanded consciousness they had so deeply shared. The fears and worries of their lives seemed as gnats flying about in their minds. Trivial and to be dealt with without fear. For some time they sat, attending to that immensity of realization and their minds ached a little with the stretch of it.

Everyone talked, describing the thoughts that filled their minds, asking questions, informing themselves consciously with words and the shaping of thought into sentences. It was a final finishing of the experience for which there were no words. They must try to find some. And then, they left their places, one by one, with a promise that this Gather must continue into the evening and that everyone could and would spend the night and there need be no hurry. Each went to walk, or to sit in the garden, or to swim in the River, or to plunge into the natural world as into a beautiful demonstration of revelation.

They walked in mint grass whose fragrance wafted into their breath, knew the hunger of their eyes for color, and the filling of them, clouds settling like great gleaming ships with dark and heavy keels in the sky, saw the wonder of bird flight, and each one came to wonder how he had walked so easily past such wondrous things and never stopped enchanted, until this day. In recognizing Light, they discovered again, wonder.

THE JOURNEY

The next few weeks were ones of practice, of eager, experiments of calling one another, of silent sitting in solitude, to quest more deeply inward and to find those strengths of Spirit they had begun to know about. Yet work went on as usual, each of those who had practiced Joining was more alert, more aware. The work of the Valley benefitted. It was not until they sat at breakfast in July that they were shaken from their absorption. Forced to acknowledge that this too was a focus with limits. Great as it seemed, it was nevertheless another level of self absorption. The self absorbed with the Self. Important as that was, they were drawn from themselves wholly on that day, forced to see that in these times they could not take years to adapt to unfoldment. They were getting together more than they had for years, talking of the inner changes, unafraid, delighting in that interchange.

It was a fine morning in July. Most of the Family were at breakfast together. Anna who ate hungrily, and chatted with the other children as if they had no thought for anything except for that good taste of food, stopped, looked around and said, "Andrew! Tell us, Andrew. What is it?"

Andrew was sitting absorbed, and at her call, he shook his head, "Turn on the Video News, Turn it on and you'll see." He sounded angry, his voice full of a pain they had never heard in him.

Tom leaped up and turned on the Video, and felt the knob turn even as he touched it. His eyes flashed to Cassandra and she nodded curtly, silently, and he said nothing. But the screen was there, showing the news. It was a scene of astonishing confusion. A mavarick group of Builders had begun that morning at a site fifty miles south east of Santiago, to clear more land. The reporters said they had decided to take two thousand acres in this unused portion of the Valley. They had begun to clear a corner of a great meadow. Creatures there had no warning, the trees were ignorant of their intentions. There was a diffuse sense of danger, but nothing living there knew its source.

People approached the huge oaks and walnuts, beech and gum. Old and revered trees, many of them already a hundred years old. Precious to every Valley citizen. A workman lifted a laser saw, slicing at one huge limb, two feet in diameter, it stretched across a wide fern covered glen.. He grinned as the limb dropped at his feet, then dodged as a branch swept by him nearly knocking the tool from his hand. He was careless in his exuberance.

The scene so astonished those watching that they felt numb with shock. Until Jane screamed. There, in their midst, she cried out in a high pitched thin cry that seemed to cut through that numbness harshly. Hundreds of miles from the site, she knew the pain more from the pain of those sensitives near by than from the actual tearing pain of living things.. Ben felt his own heart cringe, and the children set up swift defenses, shielded themselves with a prescient knowledge. Jessie saw that shielding and admired their control. The older folk had no such skill, but neither were they as aware. Here there were more of the huge earth moving machines. Where they had got them was unknown. Someone in that department must have belonged to the Builders. Someone who thought the permission to use them on the smaller fields was enough for permission for this. Even if they had Council permission they must wait until the fields are 'cleared'. They had not. That was the crime here.

Someone had made a terrible mistake. Or someone did not care. Someone, she thought in grief, who could be influenced subconsciously by that dark hearted man known as Greyson. Could that be so?

She turned to the screen. She cried out without thought, "What are they doing? What can they mean to rip life away like this? Her heart ached. A long dark ribbon of naked soil lay steaming in the sun. Rabbits, squirrels, other little ones were being turned out in that great breaking of the earth. Freight lifters picked up the fallen tree trunks, the debri was being piled against the edge of the field as a further barrier against interference. Their method of breaking and ripping roots up was especially brutal. For the roots were the deepest life of the trees. It was like ripping out a living tooth from a mouth,the machines caught the stub above ground and pushed against it until it simply ripped free. They watched in appalled amazement, grief sweeping through them, drowning every thought of compassion, every ability to reason. Anger prodded upward through that grief, and Jessie saw the shift, watched with held breath to see who would find strength to balance. Who would remember. When she saw the beginning, she turned with all her powers to Jane, shielding, Healing; and Jane closed her eyes as if asleep, finally shielded.

Rose, Ben, and Jerry, drew themselves away, closed their eyes and began the familiar ritual of Balance. They felt Steve slowly, wearily join them. Andrew stood up, paced across the floor as if refusing any balance, as if hugging the fury to himself. But he finally began also, leaning against the window, crying with vexation. One by one, they found the strength and began to recite the ritual silently, not even noticing whether others did. They could at least listen to this report. One by one they taught each other to Center their strength, to Balance to some degree.

Rose sat numb watching, such wanton destruction seemed to her barbarous, but worse, seemed unnatural for a citizen of this Valley. What had happened to these neighbors, these who had been taught as she had been taught, must know the same deep reverence for Earth life? Surely there must be something here she could not see. The Builders had been given enough land, more even than they could use immediately. Why did they plunge into this rich, good land between the River and the high hills, and ignore the basic laws of the Valley?

A young reporter for the Valley News stood at the edge of the newly broken land. His face intent, emotionless, watching with the absorbed fascination of one who must write this into the evening news. He said,"There's another hundred acres a little to the south that the Builders intend to include. They tell us that it is part of one of their member's farm and so has been given to them." He tried to catch a passing worker to ask questions but everyone seemed too busy to talk.

THE JOURNEY

The young face assumed the most sardonic expression it knew, but Rose saw pain in those grey eyes. He turned away from their view, kicking a little at the loosened soil at the edge of the field. Then with a visible sigh of reaffirmed duty, he approached a small group of people. He held his tiny mike out,"Can you tell us what your plan is here?" The wide chest plate cameras caught every expression and the fields behind them for Television Viewers.

They seemed eager to talk, to explain, as if some trace of guilt still gnawed. One young woman, fair, full of zeal and excitement, laughed up at him. "It's wonderful, finally we're getting started. The Valley will recover the greatness it once knew."

An old woman looked at the speaker thoughtfully, the memories of the past strong in her mind,"We will create a greater Valley. We will not make the mistakes of our ancestors. We know how, and finally we've begun." She looked with a peircing frown at the young reporter, "Young man, your task is to make it clear to the people, so that they will see that what we are beginning is for them too. This is our heritage as a people."

He nodded, keeping his voice passive,"And what of the Earth Life? We've all been taught --"

She broke in, angrily,"If I hear that one more time I'll be ready to forget the rest of the people of this valley. Don't you realize this is for humanity? For the people? We can't limit our lives for the welfare of field creatures!"

With a calm that Rose envied, and a smile, he asked,"Why not?"

Her look of exasperation would have deflated a lesser man. She sighed, seeing it had no effect on this one,"Young man, can't you see that without even asking? Obviously human beings are more important than rodents. It's a foolish sentamentality that insists on protecting every mouse that gnaws in the roots of the trees."

"What of the Teaching? The ecological balance? The knowledge that all life rises from one nature and Earth creatures are our brothers?" He felt as though he was repeating a ritual that was so familiar that it should not need to be spoken. "What about the FACT that to remove lives from a place changes that place. Do you know the damage that might do?"

The two women nodded, impatiently, but the old man with them only smiled tolerantly,"Son, you've just not lived long enough. Those are good ideas for the classroom and the temple, but in real life they don't hold. Think, Son, think! Are people not the dominant creatures of Earth? Surely we must take a higher place! It's for man to work his will upon the earth." He looked proudly around him.

The young woman spoke again, her eyes full of an anger that Rose thought was tinged with guilt."It's not worth talking of, Grandad, surely the people of the Valley will see that." Her eyes had rested on the little mike and suddenly she was acutely aware that people were already hearing these words. Their chance to influence the Valley citizens could not be better. "We intend to improve life for every citizen, and surely there will be no real harm to those lesser lives. They will find a new place." Her smile was obviously now for the viewer and Rose felt more sorrow at her assumption that the viewer was not astute enough to see through her ruse. What indeed did the Builders think of Valley citizens?

Well, they had a right to want to build their own world, their own life, to make their dream happen. Every town and city of the Valley grew from that dream. But what were the limits. When did thay have to be restrained from harming life around them for that dream. She glanced over at Jane, whose eyes were fixed on the screen. She seemed transfixed in grief, fighting with anger, but sorrow was so heavy it drained all anger.

The reporter had moved off to interview others, he stopped a man walking briskly past. "Isn't it the Basic law of the Valley that we do no harm to Valley life? That we build our cities so that we disturb little of natural life?"

The man looked at him with the amused tolerance of one sure he was right in his convictions, and now pleased with the opportunity to speak out in public of these convictions. "We think this has been repressive. We believe that as soon as others see our plans they will understand. That's why we've acted thus so swiftly. We think that our Valley people want change." He studied the young man's face quizically, his smile still firm, "After all, we've lived from a fairy tale, a dream that our Teachers have taught us, and perhaps it's time we ended that kind of Teaching too. It makes for weakness among us."

" You think then that the Teaching of the Valley has been false?"

"Of course not. Son, don't twist my words. In our beginning they were necessary perhaps, to give us hope, to give us courage after the Bad Times. Yes, they were, I think. But now, we don't need them anymore."

"You believe they're not true? These Teachings that human kind has the role of elder brother to the less conscious lives?"

The old man's smile faded, his look was cool suddenly, studying this youth who questioned him, his voice took on the tone of the lecturer, "Young man, human kind has a task to rebuild our world to far exceed the magnificence of its past. We must take of Earth's very body and use it to build star ships, train the strong and the bright and leave behind here those unable to see beyond their obsession with Earth's lesser creatures." His voice softened "Surely, most of our people will see that. Once they see what we see. Once they know they will agree that we must use the wealth of commerce to expand our empire, to reach out to the stars."

The young woman broke in, her voice full of a conviction that brought tears to Rose's eyes to hear. "Oh, yes, Don't you see? We must create world markets, earn money to build the future. It's so obvious, I know people will understand."

Nodding sagely, in a charade that almost made Rose smile, the young reporter asked, "But then, you think that people are still interested in lives of buying and selling, in having more things to store away, in constant body indulgence, in eating and drinking too much. Even though that once resulted in the starving of three fourths of the people?"

His matter of fact tone caused the others to miss the irony. The woman nodded, unperturbed. "Of course, people have always been interested in

THE JOURNEY

economic development. It's our life blood! What else is there? We do not intend to make their mistakes, however. They lost their balance, you know!" She looked at him with a puzzled expression for a moment, then almost absently she repeated,"But what else has life to offer?"

The reporter's face was calm, his eyes sad without a trace of anger, Rose felt her spirits rise just watching him. He said, as he turned away,"What else indeed!"

He caught another worker, busy and a little impatient,"Has Valley Council approved the work you do?"

The woman turned to him, still lifting the tool she had come for, a slight nervousness obvious in her forced smile,"Oh, yes, we expect approval completely. We want to present the Council with a fact , not just an idea. We know that when the people see what we are doing, they will all join us." Then, as if weary, the young man, turned finally toward the field,readjusted the camera that hung from his shoulders,and began recording what was happening. Discs floated above the high grasses, moved in and out among the trees, feeding information to the fine cutters, being welded by other teams. At one side, with an ingenious, field saw mill, logs already cut were being sliced into board feet with very little sound. Already two huge commercial floats were nearly loaded to carry that rough lumber to the mills of the towns and to Clandor. Their sales would provide credit enough for the next task.

Jessie still held Jane's hand, still partly doused the young girl's sense of anguish at the field. Jane's eyes were fixed now in dispair and pain. She watched as creatures, ran from the wake of catastrophe that swept ahead of the Earth movers, and as others did not run fast enough. She wanted to be there, to help. It was as though her own body ached with that anguish of those lives. At that moment the picture ended, news shifted to another Valley event. Jane's eyes tore themselves away, met Rose's. "Oh, Rose what shall we do? "The spoken words spilled the tears unfallen in these moments. "How can they be doing that. Even if they had permission, they should not rape the land. They don't need to do it this way! They don't need to!"

Rose Touched tenderly, not wanting to press her own presence into Jane's grief. She said,"This must stop. We cannot protect each other from ourselves. We must Reach, Touch and know. We must. If we are to meet the Builders, then we must help one another gain strength." She poured what Healing she could around Jane but with surprise, felt the flow of Healing energy surround herself as well, and knew that Jessie did not stint herself or fear to heal where it was needed.

Jessie said, " The Council is calling an emergency meeting. We must Gather. All the people must decide how to meet this!"

Then the others began to arrive, as though an urgency had permeated the Valley, had drawn them out of their preoccupations. Ned arrived first, impatience in the leap that set him down on the deck and in the movements that ripped the belt from his waist. Annette and Jennifer, with Rachel, rode in on Paul's air car. Tom's mate Angy and Mary's son Nathan, came within minutes. In half an hour the family was Gathered and sat in the wide living room, pulling chairs close up to one another, crouched on the thick rugs, wanting to be near each other. Anna, sat gazing with wide troubled eyes at Jessie,"Isn't this like the old days, Jessie. When you were young?"

Jessie looked at her with surprise, met her eyes and smiled, "You've been taught so much we only had begun to imagine, to write in our finest philosophy. For you this is a tragedy. For us it was common place and normal."

Jerry said,"It's awful, what's happening. After all we've worked to build, to TEACH. It's as if people haven't heard at all."

Jessie said, "Pay attention. Pay attention. Right now." And in that moment, everyone became aware of Jane's pain. As they knew of it they sobered, Reached out in question and found that Jessie and Rose together had already set up a healing screen around Jane. But they knew then it could not be done without Jane's full cooperation. She must acknowledge her own power, accept what she knew and realized. Then she could release herself from receiving. If this affected this sensitive so acutely, what were those sensitives doing who lived within a mile or two of that event?

Grimly, aware of the question, Jessie said," They're already being brought to Healing Center and are shielded. They're learning what we've got to teach Jane -- and ourselves!" She sighed, touched Jane's hand, met the wide grey eyes,"But few are as sensitive as this one. Few would sense the destruction this far away." She looked around at them. "Look! Here's something we must do now, immediately." She turned to meet Jane's eyes, where tears would not cease their welling over, "We've kept the worst away, my dear. It would not be bearable for you had we not." Jane nodded numbly, unable to speak. " I know Roderick has taught you what you are. You're more than a Speaker. Acknowledge! Accept now as you never have. What hurts most?"

Her eyes were unrelenting, her voice firm. Jane glanced up at her, then found those eyes irresistable, and met them with a long trembling sigh as if allowing herself finally to lean upon that comfort a little. Her body shook, "It had to be the Video pictures, the seeing of it. That's what it was!" But at Jessie's slight shake of her head, she cringed away. "No, it can't be so. What kind of freak am I? Roderick didn't insist on this. No one could actually 'feel' something so far away. None of you are troubled at all. I cannot be -- I cannot be - !"

Jessie said,"You tell yourself you imagine this, that you grieve at the pain and destruction because you THINK it senseless and wrong. But I tell you there is vastly more-- you FEEL that pain. It happens to you as well as to them!"

Jane's mouth moved, but no sound came, then, with a new start of tears, she said,"It's the sound, in my head, the crying out of pain, of dumb, helplessness. The loss, the terrible loss everywhere, -- the nest place, the young ones, the -- " her voice broke, and after a minute she went on. "There is the drowning, drowning in pain and a darkness seems to be settling over everything, as if -- as if -- consciousness drifts off - leaves, because the pain pushes it out. The helplessness, the terrible helplessness! Nothing to fight even!" Her eyes were glazing over as though she entered trance.

Jessie saw and caught her shoulders, gave her a slight shake, then redoubled her Healing effort."No, no, Jane. You must not follow them. They estivate to avoid the pain, but you are not there!"

Jane was twisting and turning in her chair, Steve cradled her in his arm, wanting to surround her with his love and protect her from this, but he felt the absolute refusal, that inexorable steel of mind pinning his own mind away. Jessie would not relent. She said "Jane, acknowledge that you experience direct knowing!"

Jane dried her eyes, her mouth tight, her eyes narrowing, studying Jessie's,"How can you know what I experience"?

The question and it's admission brought a deep sigh from Jessie and she relaxed but did not smile."I experience with you, my dear. You're sending loud and clear. There are several of us here who suffer from your suffering." She felt brutal but the facts had to be recognized. Do you acknowledge that you sense the pain of those any where near that raped field?" She was like a fierce,but gentle nail, holding Jane to the question.

For seconds Jane wavered, then with a crumpling of her face, she nodded,"I accept what I realize. It's true. Oh, my God!" Finally she loosened her gaze from Jessie's. Her body still trembling but her eyes moved about the circle. Then suddenly she seemed to let the tautness of her body relax. "Why it's stopped. It's stopped." Her voice was soft with surprise. "They're gone. Have I closed myself to them?" She turned to look at Jessie, her eyes widened,"Did you?" Jessie nodded. Jane was frightened and relieved at the same time. But dispair filled her. Jerry Reached to her and she flinched, feeling that Touch and recoiling. Steve wrapped his other arm around her, wanting to help, to comfort. His face was full of confusion, of a strange fear as he looked around at this Family.

He said,"It's true. We've got to end her pain.She can't go through this every time the Builders decide to rip Earth apart." He stopped his face a mask of grief and then began to talk slowly, as if feeling his way."How can she know? How can she sense the Earth life so acutely. How can any human bear that?" He swallowed, looked down and then, " We did avoid the Mind Touch. And we had to learn to respond. Now this! She isn't able to avoid at all! This is different! I thought the Joining was -- was enough! And now, there's this! She can't stand this kind of pain! DO SOMETHING!"

"How do you know she was in pain?"

"Any fool could see that! It could start again! My God, how can you not see?" Steve was angry finally.

"Stop a moment,Steve.She says the worst has ended. Close your eyes, listen, feel, attend carefully to what you know right now. How can you know the pain is so great?" Jerry was adamant as Jessie had been, his mind penetrated, held Steve's relentlessly. He asked,"Don't you see Steve? Can't you admit too?" Jerry felt inadequate, Tom ought to be here, or Paul. But he persisted.

For a moment Steve was silent, his body squirmed slightly as if trying to escape from his mind's attention. His face twisted and then slowly relaxed, but tears poured from his eyes, his hands trembled. "Oh, yes, Oh, yes. I do see. I feel directly from her, from Jane, my Love, that terrible hurt she feels. How is that possible?"

Ned sat up straight, leaning across his knees to stretch one long arm out to touch Steve's shoulder. "Don't you remember? Rose told us about Benjamin ? Wanting to Reach to him, and he wouldn't receive, wouldn't even admit? Then we all talked and finally we all found out we could,-- that we could Touch each other?" Reluctantly, Steve nodded."Well, don't you see, it's just another dimension of the same thing. We sense each other. We are tuned to one another in a way we never believed possible. It's a shock to us all, Steve. But we're not crazy. We suffer when one of us suffers. Humankind always has done that a little bit. Now we do it acutely. We are TOGETHER! We aren't monsters.

Jerry took up the effort, pressed on,"Look Steve, look into yourself! Put your attention on Jane. Focus! We love her. You know that but YOU love her especially, as a Mate. Listen to her, See what's happening. You can Reach her, Touch! Touch!" His voice had a soft insistence that urged Steve from his reluctance. He felt the others, Touching near, not invading his own privacy, but - there.

Steve's eyes were closed, tears streaming down his face. He took both Jane's hands, leaned to her, needing physical closeness and they both began to feel the energy surrounding them, lifting them, pouring a strange light into the darkness of their fear.

Jane let her head fall against his shoulder, then shuddered once and cried out,"Oh,Steve, Oh Steve!" Never had she known such a river of power available to her. It seemed to seep through all barriers, to stifle the very throb of pain she had felt in the air itself, that pain coming from the living creatures who responded as she did to that desecration.

Rose watched Jane closely, wanting to do more, to teach her to shield. To teach both of these who were recognizing more of their own natures. Their consciousness was breaking old limits. She felt an awe of discovery,and within that, she realized Jessie's Touch. In that moment of wanting to know, she knew! She could teach them. She glanced swiftly in gratitude to Jessie and said,"Will you allow us to teach you to shield?"

Steve nodded,"Yes, for God's sake, Help us!"

Rose felt the gathering tide of energy from the rest of the family, felt it focus, surge into a strong bath that inundated them all, felt it focus again to center around Steve and Jane.

With care they entered, and then they were led by Jessie's sure touch, handling that energy like a scalpel, using it like a tool, she showed them how to shape and to hold that shield against everything outside themselves. The peace and quiet descending brought Jane such relief that she fell limp against Steve's body. He held her. To know what she had dealt with was terrible for him, but now, to know himself how to cut that pain off, how to remove themselves from its unrelieved pressure, was a rejoicing. And yet, they were all aware that their shielding did not end that pain for those others. They knew the unceasing presence of it. Now they could think how to help!

It was as though a clear bright lightedness surrounded them, penetrated their bodies, minds, stretched through them all and united them in one nature. They could Reach with this new power, they could SEND! And as they realized that, they felt Jessie withdraw, felt themselves Joined as a Family as they had never before been. This then was one limited meaning of 'Group Mind'; many minds having made a choice to Join, extending themselves through one another and knowing what no one mind could know and remain sane.

This, being here, living in this space of knowledge, of perception, was to see Earth, alive and powerful. It was to see humanity distinctly part of that Earth, and still dependant on Her. Those who tore at her body, were like blinded children, ravaging their Mother in ignorance. They could not feel even anger - but only pity. The recognition stunned them all. Andrew felt his mind turning and shaping into new channels, felt the old fierce urges surface and reveal themselves for what they were. Anacronisms. He cringed and all the others felt his recognitions of these old needs, felt and sustained him as he let them go. But there was no naming, there was only a lighted acceptance. A shifting of that focus shivered through them, Tom was arriving, leaping down from the railing with out separating his attention from them. And they felt Paul's Touch as he sped through the hot summer sky.

Now, they could Reach with that power they knew as ONE. Would they do this? Could they Reach to the field and heal those hurt lives? No. It was beyond them, but unknowingly they were Touching against the minds of their Family outside the Farm. Such a fiber of connection had been built in the past weeks that they Touched without effort. And just now, the shielding must be made clear. Jessie guided them, lightly from without, she pointed out the direction. They felt Paul with them as though he were present physically. Rose felt awed by the power of it.

Rose and Paul, Tom and Anna, Rachel and Andrew, able to stand steady in that astonishing power they had created, showed the others the process. Drawing in, building round each a shield, closing out all else. Building that same shield around them as a group, then opening that shield, opening and closing, they studied the nature of the shielding. Each one in turn, in this protected state, practiced that shielding around him or herself. Until there was clear knowledge. It was not that they were unaware of the pain, but that it was no longer overwhelming. As long as there was pain, they would know of it. Earth life endured in both pain and contentment.

In this time, they knew what they had only guessed. That among those called Builders, there were unfilled needs, the hungers of an inner nature not yet strong enough to See, to bear the Vision of that which is beyond ordinary perception, and yet, longing for that very Vision. Unknowing, yet, longing, mis-interpreting, as humanity had done for centuries. They sought to satisfy those hungers with sensations, with possessions, with control of others, with -- whatever seemed to satisfy.

This knowledge, brought the Family a new silence! So! It was unquestionable. They could not despise people acting out of fear, out of simple inability to know . They were deprived of their base for anger, and that knowledge sobered them deeply. But more, they found compassion as deep as their vision.

Jane drew their thoughts back to herself. "What's happened? I feel such a quiet, such stillness, there is no pain at all." She met their eyes, looked all around,"It is this- this shielding that you've taught,isn't it? It's this mental process, like a door within me, opening and closing and I have the power of it." She probed back into herself, felt the edges of her mind, drew herself together, her mind closed around herself and she was utterly alone within that place. She felt the isolation and at the same time the power of it. She deliberately opened herself up to them again, knowing their sensitive presence, the Touch of these who were so deeply with her. And then trying, tentatively, she opened herself further, beyond them, Reached out to the larger world and cringed, for again the streaming grief, hurt, swept in to her.But they were with her, and they all felt it, knowing and stunned by it. Jane carefully closed that door, looking guilty "I can avoid it now, but then, perhaps I will ignore it too?" She looked around, accusingly, "Is this what we've always done? We humans, when people all around us were in pain?"

Jessie spoke sternly, "It is! When humanity killed for food, for pleasure, when humankind warred on one another, when such pain of disease and crippling as would have driven us mad, occurred, humankind managed to shield itself but we didn't know what we were doing. We didn't know we stifled our very awareness in the process of protecting ourselves. Now, we must learn how to open ourselves to one another completely and to close ourselves again by choice. But pay attention. You cannot close off that pain entirely, never again can you deny the presence of human pain and fear."

Jane nodded, gripping Steve's hands until they hurt. She absorbed the knowledge. But Jennifer turned to Jessie,"Is it like this with many people in the Valley? Do many feel-respond as she does?"

Jessie shook her head, "Not yet. Jane you're one of the most powerful empaths I've ever known and you know that the best of these work in the Monitor Stations so I've known several. Yet we've not found you. You've shielded yourself in your early years too well. There have been SOME suspecting of you." She smiled at the mild witticism. " I think you've lost your need to conceal, as you gained trust in this Family. Then we began the Joining and you came to us, you began to Reach and to Touch. You let yourself wake to your love for Steve. And you were opening to other people along with all that. You are developing rapidly now, my dear child. Just as you all are. It is the Time." She turned to glance at Andrew,and saw him nodding slowly. He seemed to be listening for something beyond,his eyes distant.

His voice was a whisper when he finally spoke."Jessie! It's because of the Singing, I think. The City is Singing more than ever before! And it wakes us in our hearts. That's why Jane can hear now."

Jessie watched him,"You call it the Singing, the way the People of the Way do?" Before they could answer, they felt the thud of feet against the landing grid and heard running steps coming to them. Paul, wind blown, sweating with his running, came reaching out both hands in his concern.

But Andrew still held their eyes, even as their hands found Paul's. Andrew nodded, the others looked puzzled at them. Rose frowned, listening carefully, She got up to go to the door, stood a moment listening there and turned, amazement on her face, "Of course. But it s no better outside. We hear with our bodies, our minds, not our ears." She caught Jerry's eye and found him nodding,his face lit in smiles. Steve watched them, his eyes moving from one to another. Finally he said, "What d'you mean? Surely you can't -" Then, focussing his own attention, he cried out,"Oh, yes, you do!"

Jessie made a signal with one hand, Andrew nodded and looked at his twin,their dark faces shining with smiles. Little Cassandra moved to sit near Anna who drew her close with one arm. The three Reached with Jessie. Rose met them, then Tom, Annette and Jennifer, then Paul and Jerry. Swiftly she gathered in the others, except for Jane, and Silvia who were suddenly closed. Silvia stood up, angry, frightened, and then sank down again. Jane covered her face with her hands.

Gently, without pressing, they softly and slowly surrounded the two women. Amplifying the sound. The sweet, fine song that could be heard within the mind. Gently it entered and began to untie the knots, to open closed doors, dissolve fears, give access to the known and the refused. It could not have touched the mind unable to hear at all. But these were Joined, and they sought that Higher Touch. These were growing minds, expanding beyond their previous nature. In their brains the electrical-chemical activity was a brilliant explosion, waking sleeping powers, waking nerves and tissue not yet used.

The Sound rose, penetrated and sustained itself, bringing them together as if tuning this new Joined consciousness. And the disparity, the strangeness fell away. They began to know this new communion and knew they could not have imagined anything of its kind. This was a condition of Mind unlike anything known.

Silvia looked around, at first with frowning refusal, and then, slowly with a gentle longing, she Reached and entered in, knew the Touch of that 'Singing', and accepted. There was a waiting, and then Jessie moved through this current to reveal finally that taut structure that had made Jane so vulnerable. Jane risked much, to turn mentally to them, to trust. But she did.

Her Reach was swift, a mind long able, waking. She must see and finally master that old and bitter fear. Jessie cast the light of her own mind on it, and Jane could See. Jessie drew back but Jane moved forward, took command of her own powers. She could bring them all in touch with life forms that , without her, they might not be able to reach. As Jane knew that, she was humbled, and full of heart lifting Joy.

Silvia felt them turn to her, felt their love penetrating through her own fading fears. "Yes, I know. I can know you. I do hear! Yet for me it is not a hearing as much as a fragrance, a sending through my body like a current. It makes an adjustment through my whole being. A finer perception, vibration of our own song when we enter into that Song." Her face was open now, her fine large eyes wide, her skin pale, but she was filled with Light. Together we can know one another and know - even more." She sighed accepting the Joy of it finally, reaching out her hands to Rose and Jerry who sat beside her."I am not afraid. I can 'know' with you all and it is all right." Then she drew her hands down to lay them rounded over her belly. A strange look of puzzlement on her face."I feel - I feel as though my little one Joins us here. How could that be?" Her voice was a whisper.

For moments they sat quiet, sustaining each other, listening, their hearts full. The subtle delicate shifting of their bodies, brains, was felt like a light running fire through them. A fire that burned then cooled. How much time passed, none could have said.

Then, Annette was there,she drew them toward her. Her tenderness was conscious to each of them like a gift. "William is not here. Nor will he be." She said no more and they were silent with her in her grief.Then they spoke within one another of William, and that he would come among them another day, perhaps another life time. He would not come to be with them, but they could be with him. The knowledge comforted Annette.

They drew apart, sitting in wordless communion, aware of that fine presence of the Silent City among them, singing through the air itself. They appreciated their separateness now but never again would they be alone.

Ben nodded, finally said,"It's been so hard for us, to come from where we were to here. Is it always so hard, Jessie? "

She shook her head, "People are so different, each group has its different resistances. But then, you must realize that the process is one of growth and cannot occur in a day. Even now there is much more to learn, much that is developing in you, and that will unfold as gently, as irrevocably as this has. We are no longer a people living in the land of the blind. Most of our citizens now can See. It is the minority who cannot. And so we will all begin and know our world in a new and wonderful way. This is a time of recognition. We See, we Know, what our parents could not even imagine."

Tom said, as if just realizing,"Reality has new dimensions!" He was elated, full of energy. Our ancestors were narrow, limited, blind, yes. And there are those today as unseeing as they were." He became aware of a smugness, a feathering of pride around his vision, that smothered its acuteness. He stopped speaking. The recognition was a sharp pain within knowledge. Self awareness was unceasing.

Ben stared at him, sensing something of his realization, and said,"The measure of our growth is just that, perhaps. Surely that old habit of clinging to what we think we know , to how we have always perceived things,can be our shroud. We will have to remind one another, because forgetting is our chief sin, is it not? Forgetting and seeking comfort of old habits?"

THE JOURNEY

Rose frowned,"This situation we're in now with the Builders, it's one where old habits can deceive us. We could refuse flexibility out of old habits. We could blind ourselves again. That one idea, the idea that they're wrong and we're right, it's the chief danger?"

Jessie nodded, "A danger, perhaps, but you See now. That can't be taken away. However, you must remember, remind one another, that the talents are accompanying a greater Vision,and that Vision is of what you do not yet See. That is the doorway in which you stand, where the Light blinds you at times, where you glimpse that vision of Spirit, of possibility   such that you cannot yet conceive. More and more of us begin to be conscious at that level."

And now they must turn back to act. They must attend to the event that was happening hundreds of miles south. And that attention would offer another test. A test more severe than any they had yet known.

Andrew went to sit near his father. Everyone was moving into small clusters, talking, visiting, comforting and he touched his father's arm, glanced at Tom, sitting with them and asked."How can we say we're more conscious. I've been really mad at the Builders, Dad. My friends convinced me they were right." He shook his head harshly,"No! I've listened to old needs. I convinced myself!" His face was a mask of sorrow and confusion. Ben felt an urge to comfort, but he was also relieved.

   Ben nodded, "It's true Son, but the important thing is that you see this. You see the attitudes that would result in selfish actions,even seemingly benevolent ones. We humans always justified our actions, even when we killed people. We convinced ourselves that it was sad that it must be so, but that it was the only thing to do." A sadness filled his voice, his eyes moved from one to another."There must be lots of people confused, must be people who really don't know what's happening."

"So what do we do?" Tom spoke impatiently, knowing that his job must be to act now.

Then Jane spoke out harshly, suddenly reminded,"Wait, there is something to be done now. Someone must go to that field. Someone must help the creatures." Her voice broke and she looked pleadingly at Jessie.

Jessie raised her hand, "Wait, the Council will send down a judgement! But look." She reset the Television screen so they could see the field being torn. Silently she pointed to two quiet figures walking unnoticed among the grasses. They moved with acute attention on the Earth. Around their feet there was a stirring, a rustling and looking closely, they could see that small creatures came from Earth, ran along beside them, swiftly drawn from their nests, their young following. Birds left the trees, the grasses seemed to grow limp, to settle and bend as if already giving up the life they would lose. The shrubs the quiet ones passed by rustled and some simply dropped their leaves, others turned slowly to grey as if life drained down from them. The Builders seemed not to notice at all. For the action was deep in the long grasses and those quiet ones knew how to make themselves unnoticed. Jane leaned to watch, "Oh, I'm so glad. so glad.

THE PEOPLE OF THE VALLEY

They will be all right."

Tom said," The Monitors! It has to be. But how? Who?" He looked at Jessie, she smiled but shook her head. They watched as the small dim figures disappeared through the far trees. Then Tom, said, "Listen!" And a man appeared on the screen who said, "The Elder's have made their decision. Everything here must stop until a full meeting can be held. That will take a few days. The Builders have agreed and are now leaving the fields." Tom sighed, he was frowning, looking at Paul, then at Rose.

Paul nodded,"I'll call Grace and Jerome, as Elders they will know as much as anyone. Must we all meet again? Or just the Elders?" He left the room.

Anna said," Have we finished talking? I think we ought to - there's more, you know! There're other things we do, that no one's talked about."

Jessie looked speculatively at Anna and Andrew,"How long have you two known that you could hear the City Sing?"

Anna met her twin's eyes, their dark faces solemn,"We've heard it all our lives. Lots of our friends have. But we didn't think of it much until the Vagabonds spoke of it when we were on Journey. Then we asked them about it."

Steve shook his head."It didn't scare you?"

Anna shook her head,"No! We loved it when it came. The City didn't Sing as often then as She does now."

Jane sat, remembering that quiet figure walking in the field. Finally she broke in," Who could it be, Jessie? Who are those who work so swiftly and so silently. How do they walk so nearly invisible there. Because no one seemed to notice them at all. How can they do that?"

Jessie laughed, "Child, one question at a time. They are Monitors. And they can sustain a quietness about them so that people don't notice them, they do that when they walk among us. One day, Jane, you will be able to clear a field like that too. Once when you have accepted yourself."

Jane met Jessie's eyes, and held them, her own strong and troubled but full of a new hope."Perhaps I could, Jessie, perhaps I could at least help."

"What you've learned today, what you've been shown and taught, these things are not easy to digest. You all need time to think, to absorb it all." Jessie waved a hand toward the door way,"Look, there's a lovely day out there, waiting for us to go and enjoy. It's near time for lunch. Perhaps we'd better move to the deck and eat a little." She smiled at them, standing and moving toward the door.

When they had made sandwiches and got huge pitchers of iced teas and bowls of soup, they settled themselves down again in the shade of the deck trees. Ben held his sandwich untasted, his eyes shadowed," Still, something has to be done. Something right away. The Elders can only hold it off a few days.

Well, what if they decide to use force. What if they gathered together weapons and fought? We outnumber them, we surely could defeat them in any joined battle." His face was stern, and she knew that he tested himself,"But then, we'd have lost, surely we'd have lost finally because we would have joined them. We would act as though we had no Vision at all."

Rose nodded,"We can't win unless they win, We are the ones who know. We can't blame them, because they don't know. We must be responsible." She closed her eyes foccused and felt with surprise the power of Jessie's sustained support. At one edge of her mind she was aware that Anna and Andrew were Joined with Jessie in that flow of energy. They need not hide their power any more, but neither would they make it obvious.

Tom nodded, "Yes, Ben, we could overpower them, we're the superior force. This time in history, our kind, conscious people, people who value the power of Love and Thought, are greater in number. So -- do we take vengence? Vengence for all the times in history when we were persecuted and destroyed by those unthinking forces who could not See?" He shook his head."Obviously we cannot. That is the whole difference between us!"

Steve and Jane listened in astonishment, listened as they never had before. Silvia however, said with an anguish they could understand, "What do we do with our own fear, our anger, and the grief of these devastations?"

Ben spoke quickly, turning fiercely toward her. "We manage ourselves! We know! We are aware! We can manage ourselves!" His voice softened,"All it takes Silvia, is to pay attention to that. Just as we are now. To act always with Love. To pray we can act with Love!"

She was shaking her head,"I don't know. I don't know."

"Then you can ask help. Ask it! It's availble to you if you ask. There IS help. You must feel it. Focus with Jessie. NOW!" There was a tinge of that power of Voice strengthening his words. He was startled at the energy rising through himself. He continued slowly,"Use your own power, Silvia, find it. Find the Spirit in you and will to be calm."

Silvia stared at him, stricken for a moment, then slowly her eyes softened, as she turned her head,fixing those dark, bright eyes on Jessie and accepted . She nodded." I only just begin to know, to be aware, and yet, I See as though a light floods my mind." The fact of it was awesome. She contemplated it, only half hearing Ben.

He spoke with unconcealed anger," Every violence we do regresses us all, doesn't it? Whether that violence be of the body or of the mind." He was staring at her, his anger like fine jabs of pain against her sensitive attention.

"No,No." She descended so suddenly from reverie that tears flooded her eyes. She was shaking her head,"I don't want any harm done to any person. Can't you see that I don't?"

Ben's face underwent swift changes, rage, to dispair, to anger again, but now at himself, then to disgust and finally softening into grief. He felt his shame rise to an overwhelming level. He wanted to walk away from the others, to escape this exposure, but he held himself, sitting now, watching himself, seeing his hidden fear, but worse his own hidden lusts. Slowly he was aware of the support, the Joining.

Rose said,"Surely we need no self recrimination either. We CAN balance. All of us feel these things, Ben. You know that. We must not pretend, or conceal old patterns because then we will undermine our very intentions." She reached out to Jessie's focus, felt the others follow and Ben's great energy enter in like a surge that lifted them all. They could and did Join in support.

After several minutes, Ben said,"I need practice. I was nearly lost." Silvia, not sure what had happened except that a tension had broken said,"I felt it. the strength of it, all of you were there with me!" Again she felt that strange awed delight. What wonder it was, to feel their combined strength. The comfort of it had been a healing. With a great in drawn breath, she said, "Well, maybe if we can help each other, we could practice that, stabilizing, healing. That's what you mean by asking?"

Several heads nodded to her. Rose turned to the children "I wouldn't admit that you were so able. My own children to be offering us so much now with Jessie." She sighed, "I don't know why I still refuse, but maybe I'm jealous. After all, you're only children. Why must I be so much less and I your mother?" The cry seemed to break from her reluctantly, and she took her own turn with shame. Then turning her attention inward, she focussed, began the ritual of balance and found that balance. "I see that power you offer, and neither of you is smug, you accept and you know without pride even. It's natural for you." The thoughts seemed to her to punctuate the new reality she finally was accepting.

Andy frowned then, "Mama, we forget too, you know. We forget. You must be ready to help us too." He frowned deeply then, "Maybe because our power is greater now, we must watch even more carefully. Must be watched even. I don't know how Jessie guards herself." He sighed,"I was aware of Dad's anger,I felt it too. I think I added to it. It's seductive, anger is. It pulled at me, something in me. Something I don't like to admit. I don't think Annie felt that at all."He glanced at her and she shook her head but dropped her eyes. Jessie nodded, relieved to hear his admission. "We'll have to watch all the time. You're right, the old patterns are seductive."

"If that's so among us, our Family, what of the others?" Silvia worried.

Ben turned to Silvia,"Sil, I'm sorry, I guess the worry of things got to me. I let myself get off balance . No, that's an excuse. The truth is that there is in me a lust for violence, for power over others, for making things come out my way. I feel it there, like a nugget of cold down far beneath my attention, except now,, as I speak, I see it rise to view. It's visible and it can't surprise me again. My God, if we can't control ourselves what can we control? If WE can't how can we expect it of anyone else?" His chagrin was obvious and the others nodded, no longer confident. Ben looked finally at Jessie and was surprised to see the pleased smile,sweet and radiant making his own heart lift. "Jessie, you look so happy!"

Jessie simply nodded to Anna and the young girl met her father's eyes, her dark face as radiant as Jessie's old and withered one."You see Dad, we've done it. We've swung back. We didn't fall into it. We can DO it?"

Andy nodded, relieved and eager, "And if we can, so can all our Valley people."

"We can do what?" Steve was utterly perplexed.

Jessie said, "We can balance, we can watch ourselves, we can keep a sustained Vision and we can know when we lose that Vision and seek help to reinstate it. We can recognize our lower nature and meet it when it rises to trap us in the old habits. We are AWARE!"

They all sat digesting this, each one more hopeful but each one a little fearful that he or she might not have that strength. After a little while, Tom said,"Well, we've got our own task set out for us. Now we also have to know how to meet these Builders and their devastations."

Ned snorted, "Think, Tom, think what we just said,"We meet it by meeting ourselves. We meet them by preventing our own fall into the traps they reflect in us. We KNOW. We are able to know and we cannot allow ourselves to regress no matter the provocation. That in itself is enough for just now, isn't it?" His black face was shining in the afternoon light, his eyes seemed deep pools of night, and Silvia felt that love she knew for him overflow in a wave that surprised her.

Paul got up, he said, wiping his face with a handkercheif, "Wow, it's hot!" He brought a pitcher of iced teas, a mixture Jennifer was making up in the kitchen, and refilled glasses. "So we have our task laid out? We must meet the Builders with the literal force of Love?" His voice was full of an irony that was not lost on anyone.

"No, we go apart, and we think on these things, we let ourselves find out how to act with Love. We let it lead us. I think we don't know how to act with Love. We have to be awake to Love and let Love act through us! Maybe show us how to act." Jennifer's soft voice seemed at that moment to penetrate their hearts, to speak for them all.

"You've stated it well, Jennifer. Fear is a power that the builders will use, and are using whether that is a deliberate intention or not. For most of them, it isn't. For a few, their leaders, it is deliberate. They know the awful power of fear. And we must see to it that we are not caught in that wash of dark power. There is NOTHING that can meet it except that Love we have Touched upon, that we feel rising in our Hearts. We must rely on that, keep IT in focus. If they could see what we do, they would have no reason for fear. But they cannot. So we must discover our actions as we go, as we listen to that highest voice within each of us." Jessie spoke resolutely and with that touch of Voice that made the words unforgetable.

Jane spoke as if out of deep attention to all that was happening, "We thought the six hundred acres would satisfy them. Now, they attack this new field. The death and destruction has been ended but by those we call Monitors, not by ourselves. We could not end it. And yet we are able, are we not? What will happen when the Council denys them? Will they ignore the decision?."

Paul settled back into his chair, letting his eyes roam across the brilliant green of the fields below, the bright acres of color on hillsides to the east, where wild legumes bloomed. Grazing herds created a pattern of dark on one hillside and he thought of their slaughter by the millions, if humankind regressed.. But then, people had killed each other by the millions too in those times past. He shuddered, surely not that. Not back to that! He said, "There has to be a way.

Surely, Jane, there will not be such pain for you again, because now you do know how to meet and cut it off. You must ask for help until you are proficient at that. But still, we have to respect the rights of every citizen, even the Builders. They have a right to their way of life too." He sighed, watching them, "That's what worries me."

The others were silent, what he said was true. Finally Tom broke that silence, "Well, I for one think that there'll be little real problem. Maybe there'll be trouble for a while. But what kind of market can they find? What vast number of people in this world will want what they plan to sell?"

Ned laughed, "Well, we'll surely see. We'll find what the level of world development actually is in these next weeks. Because the market evaluation has been started and the first shipment of that new fabric is already out. It's a test."

"In the meantime the Valley must suffer!" Tom stood and walked to the railing to look across the distant town. I feel such anger sometimes, and to balance that, I must do a lot of hard work. If that's my task, it's going to keep me busy." He turned to them, his face full of the pain he felt.

Ben frowned, watching Tom, "It's in all of us, like a fine sharp wire hurting against our nerves. Yet we know what we have to do. Maybe it's like when we have to let our children hurt themselves to learn. It's painful but it's necessary."

Rose and Jessie smiled at once. Anna studied her father with warm affection and Andy said, "Dad, one of these days you're going to know how great you are." Ben turned to him, pleased and puzzled.

In the silence, Rose said, "Maybe that's exactly it. We have to let it happen. Could that be possible?" Her eyes were wide with worry.

Jane cried out, "No, No, we cannot! " She shook her head, "We cannot allow the Valley to be destroyed".

"No, Jane, we can't allow it to be destroyed, but we may have to allow it to be made sick, to be harmed. We can't impose our own will on others, or we are not different from them. If the tide is to be turned by Love then I've some learning to do." Jennifer waited.

Andrew felt a strange hush in his mind, his body trembled for he knew there were thoughts and feelings he had not shared. He knew the Joining had claimed most of his self, but that a small part still held itself separate, and he trusted that he must attend to that small part when this Gather was done. He did not deny it was disception, but he told himself he would correct it. He dropped his eyes,,not wanting to meet his father's. Anna's small brown hand lay suddenly on his own, and reluctantly he turned to meet her eyes. He found such a serene trust there that he nearly cried out to her. She could not doubt him. He sighed. He realized that he did doubt himself.

Jessie stood up, went to put her cup and plate on the table. "We need to separate. To allow ourselves time to think, to bring all that has happened into perspective and find what our actual ability can be. We need to come together again soon. Then we can know how to act."

The others nodded, moving slowly, they began to stretch, move about, clear the tables, and one by one, to leave the Hall. The air car from Altos was first to leave, and then those from Adwin strapped on their belts and soared swiftly home. The family watched, a sadness and a hope sobering them. Andrew stood for several minutes with his parents, then suddenly impulsively hugged them and strapping on a belt, called out his intention to go to the Learning Center for the evening and leaped away across the hillside.

Finally Jessie stood alone, gazing with unseeing eyes out across the Valley. Her thoughts did not form words, but realization shaped itself to recognition and grief pressed like a minor chord into her Joy. A thought grew from that and swiftly she set it into words."Joy lies like closed fist beneath my heart,,sustaining,holding the wonder of Life within itself, but I, crouching in my narrow room, fear possibilities that might prevent its opening. I see all around me, blurring the edges of things, dulling color, chilling the warmth of noonday sun, that slow fog that drifts its way among us. If there is Light that will melt this darkness, it must rise from within ourselves. Can I trust that it will? Am I myself so dark that the Light cannot penetrate me and make its Self known? Can I sustain stillness deep enough that Love can flow forth undiminished?" She stood for a long time, finally turned to go to her cottage.

CHAPTER TEN

Monitors do a Teaching. Violence erupting. The Dark Watcher is seen.

The troubling of life that came of the illegal taking of the wild fields left a shadow through out the Valley. A profound question had been asked stirring people, waking them again from the tendency to assume all was well. Now a closer look was taken of everything, of their work, their life, the Convictions themselves and of each other. People did not want to nourish any tendency to suspicion, nor harbor doubts about their neighbors, so when they found themselves doing just that, they were troubled. Some went to have it out with their peer groups, talking and disclaiming gently or in loud worry. Until they had found some balance again. Others went to talk to the Healers and some were satisfied to enter into the new classes of the Master Teachers and to listen and to ask. But surely, the Valley was no longer asleep, nor was it apt to doze again. Something stirred the heart, the mind and illumined perception of the nature of things. Something that brought a delicate touch of joy to the heart, and at the same time, a recognition of grief.

After Summer Festival,with its lift of energy and excitement,summer days passed with a quiet peacefulness.The time of the July full moon would be the celebration of Adwin as a city. She would present herself, with tremendous pride, to the Valley as a completed city in a ceremony that would rival Festival,but it would be only a one day celebration.

When the day arrived, the town was full, banners and ribbons flew from every house top and from the high roofs of each of the Center Rings.Visitors from everywhere had come to walk the color- blazing pathways that wound in gentle meandering as though this town had little business at all to do. They came also to enjoy the fountains, to inspect the fruits and vegetables growing among the blooms, the pervasive fragrance and the broad Triple Rings that were the invention of Adwin people. Tom walked the gardens too, seeing it anew, realizing its beauty with a fresh eye. the presence of strangers or old friends, come to honor their work, gave Adwin people new sight.

Other cities honored the little town. Altos had sent as their gift twenty young trees new and already planted in May so that they were showing great blue puffs of bloom and a few fruits, still small and green. Both bloom and fruit would fill the mature trees through the growing season. The new trees were planted at the edges of the Temple court, they were a prize that no other city had yet. In a curving half moon, shaped by these trees, was a new fountain with figures carved in stone. Done by children completing a project 'Harmony in Relationship'in the Learning Center. It was proudly dedicated with the trees. Tom walked with pride beside its bright whispering water because he had suggested it be placed at the Temple plaza and he came on this warm, clear, morning to look again at its symmetry.

He wanted to sit a while, in this quiet place,but he could not take the time. His promise to be at the Farm later this morning meant he had to get an early start to visit the Temple and then to talk to a few people about town business before he left. He'd been up since three this morning, bringing into custody,(a rare experience for this Mayor) three young Builders who had been harrassing Vagabonds and had intended to ridicule their morning celebrations of the Silent City. Nothing like it had happened before. Tom felt a nagging worry. These weren't untaught young people, they knew better. The worst of it was he had had to settle two disputes between groups of young men ready to fight one another. The Builder's young and the --" He stopped, thinking of exactly who those others were. When he reached to them there was no respnse. He felt the pulse of their anger radiating all around them. The memory made him shudder, they were Mind-Blind youth faithful to Valley Convictions. They were so sure they were right. Regardless of the convictions they professed, they would solve problems by force. That troubled him enough that he was glad there was another Gather this week. He would present the problem to City Council for a more public solution but he wanted to talk this out with his Family. The worry of these sudden outbursts was an acute pain for him. Respect for other people was something every child learned, and practiced. Why? What had pulled them away from their training that badly?

He glanced up, the sky was clear, only a few small white clouds, and the sun was barely up. He could make it, even detouring to join Ned at the Industrial Center. He frowned, Ned was inspecting the new fabric shop the Builders had set up. Their fabrics came off the looms faster than any other product. The bolts piled up there on the loading platforms, waiting for freight cars. How could they make it so fast? Ned had promised to find out. Tom cut across a stretch of mint grass fragrant under his feet and on under fruit trees, fruit already ripening. He passed a clutter of children beside the curving edge of the Civic Center's outer Ring. They were picking buckets of berries to be taken to the auto- processer. Perhaps there would be berry cobbler at the Dining Hall for lunch today. He could hear their noisy chatter, their calls from one group of vines to another. They sounded cheerful and normal. His heart lifted.

He smiled then, began to walk more rapidly, and leaped down the trail into the residence area, crossed the creeks, wound about several clusters of homes and began the climb back to the farthest of the town's Rings. He reached the Industrial Ring just as the sun swept it's light down across the third story windows, gleaming a promise for the day. He nodded, accepting that promise.

He saw Ned coming down the covered walkway, the multicolored roof of the inner walks, not yet lit by sun, laid little light across his tall body, bright in blue trousers and a loose gold and brown shirt. But he moved without the usual joyous dancing stride that usually identified him as far as he could be seen. Tom sobered."What've you found,Ned,old buddy? You don't look happy."

Ned grimaced, then suddenly his face lit with that wonderful grin that seemed

THE PEOPLE OF THE VALLEY

to erase all troubles."Oh, it's probably nothing after all. They're producing fabric like water running fast." He frowned a little,"Traditional Weavers just working away, calm as you please. I felt uneasy at their -- good humor in face of this bombardment of competition. Tom, some of them actually seem amused. They don't have a competitive bone in their bodies, as far as I can tell. Maybe they're making a mistake." He sighed, as he swung along side his friend and they turned to the belt racks.

"I hope they're not refusing to deal with what might be bitter facts." He adjusted a package he'd clutched into his hip. "I got a few samples to bring to the Farm with us. Strange, Tom, it's really pretty stuff, but it -- it seems poor in quality,in my opinion. But that's not saying much. I'm no judge."

Jennifer and Silvia will be. They'll know.? What about the Taylor's Guild, are they beginning to use this new stuff?" Ned seemed preoccupied and he prodded,"To make our clothes, Ned. Are they using it?"

Ned turned his face so his eyes came to rest on Tom's face, but he was seeing nothing,"Oh no. They won't use it. They say it wouldn't stand up more than a year or two. They insist their fabric be durable and that when they make clothes for us, designed for us as they always are, that they last -- and last." He laughed suddenly, and his eyes were focussed, the Joy in him seemed to lift, to rush through him finally, to erase that dis-ease that Tom had noticed earlier. "Let's get the belts, it's too late to walk home." Tom glanced at him ruefully, it was barely sun up.

They lifted off a few minutes later and soared through the air. Ned didn't handle his samples well and suddenly they found the colorful materials streaming behind them like kites as they rode the morning sunlight across the fields to the Hall. Below Vagabonds were already moving along the roads. Some gathering in the Highway groves to pick fruits and berries to take on for the day. The two men could hear the singing as they rode the silent air.

Paul and Jennifer were already at the farm." Must have got here before sunrise" muttered Ned, catching himself on the deck railing and gathering in the fabric to roll it onto its spool. Jennifer stood laughing at them,"You made quite a colorful sight Ned. What's that you've brought?"

Ned handed her the fabric,"The new fabric the Builders are selling out Valley. They've already sent out several freight loads. I don't know whether it sells in Valley or not." He reached over to grab Jerry's arm, and laughed,"How's my brother? You look as if you've been fading out again" they ribbed each other about their difference in color, Ned's shining black skin, wet with the sweat of the ride across in the sun, did indeed make Jerry's brown smooth face look pale. It was their affectionate joke. Jerry only laughed at Ned, this time and punched his arm lightly.

"I think you deliberately travel in the sun just to make your self as black as Satan. You love to absorb the light." Jerry teased.

"Is it my fault that I can absorb more light? Bigger and blacker, stronger and finer, that's my motto." He preened as he chose a chair next to Silvia and his eyes went immediately to her belly, swollen now enough to push her a little farther from the table. "Ah,ha, my Love, that little one is aiming for the winter Festival I see."

She was sipping coffee and she nodded without setting her cup down. Her eyes met his, her face pale as a flower beside him. She was watching Jennifer unwind the fabric, letting her hands run through it, raising it up into the light, testing it through her fingers. Silvia reached out, took a handful and her eyes met Jennifers. A worried frown touching her smooth forehead.

Ned , aware of their interchange, turned from them to Paul, reached to take his hand and then Annette's. He slid one finger across Rose's cheek and laid another on Anna's shining hair, gently so as not to muss it."It's so good to be here again. If nothing else, trouble brings us together. He settled himself, then stood suddenly to greet Jane and Steve with great hugs for each. Finally he was quiet, watching now ."You realize most of the Families of the Valley are meeting every month now too? It seems we can't get enough of each other." He laughed.

Cassandra leaned against his shoulder, and he slid an arm around her, drawing her head to his. She laughed,"I'm glad you came Uncle Ned, you're always so happy."

He winked at her,"I'm just good at grinning, sweetheart. But,yes, I'm happy too. How could I be otherwise with such a lovely little niece." He turned,"Where's Jessie? Not gone I hope. Surely she wouldn't give up on us."

Ben came toward them, his plate heaped with food, his eyes soft with the loving between himself and Rose this morning. " "She's going to be a little late, we can eat and swap gossip til she comes." He hesitated, then glancing around he added,"You all must know she meets with other Families. She's been gone most of this week." He grinned, and Ned sighed, it was good to have the family in such a good mood, in spite of the way things were. He got up himself,went inside to get himself a plate filled with breakfast and sat again, his face smooth now, sober.

He said, "The Builder's fields east of Santiago have been planted. The vines came from Altos and they're growing so fast they'll look like three year old vines by winter. But they tell us they don't endure. Again, that same pattern. As though the builder's don't plan for generations at all. They'll have a small crop in another year. Give them enough to test their plan, maybe. I suppose I ought to be glad for them, but I can't help but feel sad. Something's not right. Something I don't know how to name." He was silent, eating for a moment and then," But the early crop of fabric plants were harvested and already they've used it up. The sales will tell them whether it's worth it to plant more. They're going to want to plant acres of it if that fabric sells. What's it look like Jennifer?"

Jennifer looked up, she laid the samples of fabric down on the table, folding it slowly so that it was protected from the wind.She shook her head gently,"Oh, Ned, it seems at first glance so pretty, shimmering as it does. The same with the rugs they're making with the new Matta they planted this spring. But then, you begin to feel that the beauty fades, it leaves me with a sense of something hollow, something --" She shook her head.

Silvia nodded,"The word, Jennifer, is 'cheap'. We've seen the Matta variety they're using, it grows in less swampy areas along the canal. It branches excessively and the stalks aren't thick like our old Matta.

That's where they got their first crops. We don't make fabric like this stuff." She picked up an end of the bolt and then let it fall. This one shimmers color because it's got a lot of plasilk, and there's some cotton in that one, but the blend doesn't make either durable. It's just not going to last, and the colors won't hold well either." She shook her head vigorously, her eyes sad,"It's poor quality and it's been made to be so. People will be tired of it quickly. Our traditional fabrics are beautiful and hold that beauty, delighting us in new ways each year we wear them. I don't know what's the matter with these folk."

Tom spoke softly, "I do. They came to talk to me, I saw their work. I already knew." He too felt a grief, a sense of betrayal.

Paul stood to refill his coffee cup and get a hot spiced roll. Tom told them of his meeting with the chemist and salesman from the Builders. Finally he added,"They used wild ones to try out their plan. Later the chief Wizard was worried about having given the inferior plants to them and he came to the Council about it. They've decided to refuse any more until there's a Council decision."

"What about the grapes? Were they rejects too? Nothing's grown for that quick a production before."

Yes, they were,they produce at an early age, grow very rapidly, but they won't last more than ten years. Same deal. Trying to develop vines that will grow in less perfect climates. In this case - dry. Most grape vines last nearly a hundred. These produce an inferior table wine . But there it is. What decisions do we make in a case like that?"

Anna looked at Paul thoughtfully,"But what's wrong with that? They can change crops can't they, if the vines don't work out?"

Paul sighed,"Honey, it's not the Valley way. Or hasn't been. We don't raise crops just to keep ourselves busy. We've worked to get plants that will live long, produce well, and even more than one crop a year. We want our crops to settle into their Earth place, create their own ecology and live with all the other forest and meadow plants the way a natural world lives. We don't replant. We don't rip the soil. More and more of our grains are perennial. Or they reseed themselves. Most vegetables, you know that." She was nodding, seeing his point.

"It's Earth balance then that you're worried about? The Builder's aren't concerned with that? " Her eyes held a hint of unbelief. She did not want to think that people would be careless with Earth.

Steve set down his fork with a clatter, "It's not even that, Sweetheart, it's that they don't care about the Valley the way we've always been taught. And they don't care about people and what they do with their lives if they assume they'll spend them replanting fields. They can't care much if they do these things. The Valley is - is - a living part of Earth, Great Valley is a living being for us." His face softened, watching the look of surprise on the faces around him."It's true. I've

THE JOURNEY

been watching and talking to a lot of people. They don't want our way. They plant fast crops to exploit what they call a new market, and to build and meet more new markets. They're very proud of creating those markets themselves. They want to make millions of dollors of credit for themselves and -- ". He sighed again,"I can't imagine what for."

"What about the balance, the Balance of Earth life?" Rose's voice came like a whisper among them.

"They aren't thinking about balances. They're thinking of profits to fulfil some dream that they remember from old romances, I think, of old land barons, of vast empires, of life as one great pleasure garden and all the senses played upon as the ultimate joy of life, the main game that of economic power shifts." His eyes were bleak. "I may not be able to Join very well with you all, I may not understand all you do, but I do know that Earth is alive, is very precious and that life in this Valley is beginning to be balanced as it never was since --perhaps since humans were primitive animals running among other animals. And I do not want to see this wonderful balance turned back into that awful imbalance that ruined Earth once." He was silent, frowning, glanced at Jane, then added,"After all, we ARE Earth."

Everyone was silent for several minutes, surprised and glad to hear his words. Then Paul nodded, "But the Builders see no value to the balance." His sadness permeated their previous joy, weighted it, but did not destroy it."They say that the wild creatures must be reduced to small clusters in 'wild life preserves'. They really think we cannot share the Earth wholly. And yet, our very life has been built around the creating of food plants that would make us able to live from fewer and fewer living things. We've created pasture plants to make grazing rich and nutritious. Animals have what they need, without bothering our needs. We don't plan our lives around eating any more. We plan it around another dimension of Being entirely." He was silent, they waited, "We are ourselves only beginning to learn of what is beyond us, out ahead of us. But we know for sure there is more there, another whole dimensions of possibility that we reach for today. Today! All of us. And the Builders don't know that. And we don't know enough to teach them. Even if they'd listen to us now."

Jessie's voice startled them, no one had seen her come but she had joined them and sat in cushions on a low bench beneath the walnut tree. "What you say suggests a new kind of thinking has become possible among you.. And a new kind of ethics to accompany that thinking. For perception of Life in a dimension that INCLUDES this one, makes humankind a single Mind, a single Being, and all of us one nature that is finding it's power, it's possibility. It is outside the realm of thinking as we have known it."

Paul broke the ensuing silence,"So we divide. We become a people divided the way the Cro Magnins put aside the Neanderthal?" No one answered the question. It seemed irrelevant now that he had spoken it. And after a minute he went on, "No,we will absorb our brothers just as they eventually did, by the replacing of lives through time, being born again in bodies capable of much greater perceptions? Is that it? Already people being born now, have greater Vision and receptivity to Spirit? Look at our own children. Are Mothers to bear no more bodies unable to express that great Spirit that we begin to embody already? " His eyes were troubled, questioning.

Essentially, that's it." She smiled happily at Paul, her gladness at his understanding obvious. Jessie was terse. Her eyes bright as she watched them, listened to their response.

Ned shook his head, his fork standing on its end, still holding a bite of food. "Sometimes I feel like going out and preaching, telling them how crazy they are, telling what a great life we have, that we don't need all those things they say they want. That we won't regress to the old ways. And somehow, I know it would be futile. I guess I just knew that, so I haven't gotten on the stump." He grinned, laughing at himself.

Paul smiled, "That would be something to keep you busy, Ned, and it might catch a few. A few might see the point if you could find the words. But I doubt if many could. It would take a philosopher such as Benedict, or Aurobindo, or Hegel with the silver tongue of a con artist to put the thought into words". He shook his head, "No, the Builder's want romantic dreams to shape themselves, they believe they can actually relive the romances of our Video rooms. They see themselves as empire builders and they forget that that life was dull, finally. That it lacked meaning. I've always thought that's why they had so many wars, to give them some excitement. It's why they created economic empires and played that complex and bitter game all over Earth, because they found no other excitement when war became too terrible to wage."

Young Steve looked at him, "How did that entertain, Dad? What's there in making money to satisfy?"

Some people played with it, had it, pleasured themselves spending it for luxuries no one else could have, for services from other people they could enjoy. But the real financiers liked the game of it, getting it, investing it, making new businesses, merging them, dividing them. It was a great gamble. It was a world wide game. It evidently engrossed them and they had tremendous power, you know. Lust for power is seductive, it controls men finally. " He sighed and shook his head, " Could it happen again?"

"You said 'men'. Didn't it control women?"

He laughed, "You've read history, Stevey, women weren't much included in those old games, you know."

"It's why the world took so long to make any changes. The part women were supposed to play was to support, reinforce and display male power. Women finally woke up!" Rose was laughing too, but a glint of fire in her eyes let them know she meant her words.

Jennifer stood up, Jerry and Anna, then Andrew all began clearing the plates and carrying them back to the cleaners. They moved as though it had been planned and with surprise they realized they had informed each other of the intention.

THE JOURNEY

Paul frowned, aware of the energy that seemed to flow through their gathering, the strength of it, the renewed pulse, as though a stream ran through them and linked them. Steve and Jane sitting together, holding tightly to one another's hands, yet listening with deep fascination, and growing understanding, knew this growing energy without identifying it at all. They accepted as Jane so often did in these past weeks, the energy that streamed through her body and mind from Earth depths. These two, were realizing themselves part of something, belonging so deeply they felt tears rise. Ben saw that. Jerry turned to Silvia, and Ben saw the look of deep abiding Love on Silvia's face as their eyes met. He felt relief. She was affirmed at last. They would enter into the ceremony of Mating in a week. Then Ben turned to Ned, who sat behind Silvia and Ben was glad that Ned did not notice that look she had turned to Jerry. Later, Ned would welcome it, but not yet. Benjamin felt a sudden Touch and knew that Ned felt his concern, but not his thought. He met Ned's eyes and they both grinned, but Ben saw the sadness flickering there.

Jane stood and began to clear the tables, her eyes following the movement of birds, of Rob who came to stand questioning among them for moments before he dropped heavily and tiredly against Jerry's legs in the shade. She knew that today this Gather would have a special quality. Jessie had planned something. She wondered what that might be, looked at her but saw no hint.

After a few minutes, Jennifer spoke,"I want to sum up what we know. We see new possibility. We've wakened to knowledge that we call Spirit. New knowledge - the stir of Life within us, of our pregnancy, as a race, a new Life waking through humanity. It's just that. Surely there's enough to do, enough to occupy ourselves, more than enough." She was staring now, far off across the fields, over the Highway where a slow caravan of Vagabonds were traveling and singing on their way. She let her eyes rest on the flaming spires of the Adwin Temple."It's as though a birth were near, not just Silvia's child, but another greater child, the birth of ourselves as a people." She was very serious, her face shining, her eyes full of a light few had seen except Paul when she was in the midst of composing. But no one thought it strange, they had begun to see the flow of energy, like a pearl colored light in the air. How had this come about? They were not Joined, and yet, there was a sense of deep unity. Consciousness was extended, Vision long and far, without mystery. It seemed as natural to them as breathing. This then was a hint of what that new 'way of Being' meant? Was this then a beginning of the Journey they must take?

Annette said,:"There you are! We reach an edge of such recognition, we stand at a doorway which is only slightly open and we see such Light, such a great Life - that we feel blinded by that very Light".

Silvia murmured,"Why don't we go on? Why don't we step across that doorway into the Light? Surely within that Light is new direction at the least !"

"But what is it? I feel it - - and I'm afraid, and at the same time, I long to go on." Jane spoke in a burst, as if reluctance had been overcome.

Steve pressed forward to draw her back to sit down,"It IS Light- and yet - it isn't. It is as though an illuminatiuon occurs in my mind, and I call that Light! I am aware, CONSCIOUS as I've never been! But while I stood in that Light, there seemed to be no experiencing, just Being." He hesitated, "And a profound sense of Love Present!" He did not see the nods among the others. His expression was perplexed,fear flickered in his eyes, but did not hold there. A tentative Joy shattered all other feelings, as if determined to wash across any barrier. "How can we realize so much?"

Rose said, "Because we are strong individuals, clearly honoring that individuality and at the same time because we are able to lift above it. To become one with one another. Together we wake one another further, give courage, make more possible, don't you see? Surely it's obvious we've got more to understand than we ever had. More to do, to learn. But that's because we do See, do recognize what the builder's do not." She shrugged, turned to Jennifer and said,"This, what we do now, is the beginning of the Journey." Jennifer, startled, frowned then relaxed and nodded.

Ned turned, wiped his nose, and the tears from his eyes," You've all missed the most astonishing fact. We're talking about that Light, the experience of being Soul Conscioius, almost as we still See. My head aches, my brain's been fired up." He stopped, the others nodded.

"We've never been able to speak of this while we're still so much in touch. It's true Ned, a new beginning."

After a moment Ned spoke again,"It's true, we change each other. I feel energy here among us that I couldn't have born even a year ago. And that's it. There's so much to learn. We still don't know the nature of Life at all, nor even of brotherhood. But right now, there's a new energy here, something more, more than just our Family. Isn't that so?" He turned to look around at them, looking at the air, the empty space around them, and finally at Jessie.

Jessie nodded, they all watched her, knowing something special was coming."It's time, I think that we recognize that there are always others, always those who help to guide our lives when we ask. Well, I have asked, because I thought you are all ready to know more of the nature of this Valley itself." She looked upward, into the air above them, nodded curtly a couple of times and then laughed. It was a light joyous laughter, as though she was so glad she could not contain it.

Instantly there was a gentle softness of bells, a lightening of the air, as though greater Light radiated through it. A profound stillness surrounded them, as they saw the forms of human beings take shape among them. These, once they were complete, seemed not different from themselves, except for that soft radiance that persisted through their bodies and the out-pouring of a sweet tenderness that disarmed wherever it touched. At the same time, a certain steely strength, a hard precision of being, that would not be set aside. The Family watched with bated breath, astonished and receptive. Jessie, stood, reaching out her hands to take those of these loved Teachers, these who served the Valley all their lives as Monitors and Teachers of young ones becoming enlightened. Estella and Jedro smiled and embraced her, their eyes sparkling with a mischief that seemed odd to those watching. How could these play - laugh - at themselves?

Jessie, drew the two new comers to the edge of the deck. Found them chairs, and asked them if they would not like a drink. They accepted happily, all the time smiling around at the members of the Family. Jedro sipped and then said, "Yes, it's such a lovely day and the gardens here are full of fragrance. It's a pleasure to be among you."

Estella nodded in agreement, seeming to enjoy their astonishment. "I see Jessie has not told you of our means of travel. She does not reveal her secrets at all does she?" She was laughing, and Jessie nodded. But Estella went on, suddenly more serious, "It is time! It's time that we talked to all of you and to others of the Valley, that we too reveal our secrets. Because there are things you must realize, that you are ready to realize at least intellectually. And then, gradually you will wake to these truths wholly. In the past, we always took those coming to these realizations off to our Stations and trained them carefully away from their fellows, But now, the stations are full of students, more than ever before! The very level of energy and consciousness itself has risen in this Valley.

"The people are AWARE," Cassandra, irreverantly sighed, "But you are enlightened ones, aren't you?"

Jedro laughed and in the sound was such delight, such joy, that they smiled. He looked at Estella and she was grinning with her own pleasure. She answered, "Oh, now. How can we use a past tense ? There isn't anyone who is not in the process of enlightenment, and we are certainly in that process. It does not end, you know. There is no past tense for enlighten." She smiled.

They all sat, no one said anything, so awed by these two were they. Finally Jessie said, "I think perhaps they don't acknowledge how much they know, but " she turned to Rose, Ben and then others, "remember, these are our Teachers, and are human like ourselves. They are not to be feared."

Rose shook herself, "But you are amazing to us. We have always heard of Monitors, and we've thought of them as beings of another world, almost. Knowing that you are always there, far above us in the Stations, even though some of us have visited those Retreats, you still remain mysterious and far above our poor human powers to understand. So forgive us if we are astonished to see you."

"Yes, just two old people, soon to pass beyond this world state." Jedro spoke with laughter in his voice, he was enjoying this visit. "But then, do you wish that we will Teach you? For Teaching is never given if not requested, and although Jessie has requested, we must also know it from yourselves."

They all nodded, Several voices spoke "Yes, please teach us to understand what's happening in this land." Paul said, "We've known much of what is going on, or thought we did, but now, I realize that more has been happening than we realize. But most of all I don't know what we must do. How can we understand? We have seen and known the Light, we are aware of the Presence -- of Love surely, but we are helpless before it." He frowned, "We're afraid of our own wrong action."

They nodded, "That's what we're here to Teach. Jessie cannot do it all. She has taught so many families of this northern Valley. I'm afraid we demanded very much of her." Estella smiled at Jessie, and Jessie frowned. Estella bowed her head a moment, drawing her own thoughts together and then suddenly looking up, she began to speak and her words were spoken with that Voice that made them carry the weight of understanding. The listeners received these teachings as if they were being printed into their receptive minds.They would not forget.

"As we learn to efface and obliterate out of our consciousness, ourselves as the central figure in our life drama then are we able to truly serve that Vision we begin to See. Then are we able to begin to perceive the Whole." Estella's voice seemed to be directed to each one individually, each felt him-herself with a loved Teacher. "And that does not mean that we reduce the power of individuality, but rather enhance it".

" There has been a gradual revelation of Love among you. What that means is that you've chosen to learn how to Love. And you know when you are separated from Love. But it means more. You participate in conscious living. You've offered yourselves as channels for eternal Love." It's never been successful to exhort people to morality,or to better living. It's a shift in identity that brings possibility."

For a moment there was silence, Estella paused as though listening, her head slightly bent, a faint smile on her lips. You must reaize that selflessness does not erase selfishness." She looked up, met their eyes, looks of relief. "I see that surprises you. Stop to think. You practice selflessness, living from Soul Consciousness. This takes no effort, you simply have changed the size of the self. We continue in our self interest, but now, self interest IS Earth-interest. Humanity-interest. You're aware of the difference between self and Self, the expanding identity, because you See! And THAT is changing your world. YOU efface yourselves from center, and understand Life is the central factor in all Life." Estella smiled now, a bright joyous smile that seemed to make the air brighter.

"In this way,, you made a choice. Thousands of people have made that choice. Have begun to feel Its influence and to be aware of Its power within themselves. It is Love that makes possible that Joining that you have begun to practice. It is Love that clears the minds and the sight of people so that you can realize how very precious each human being is, and realize equally that you are one, single, humanity. Individuals Joining with conscious choice."

"So now, there is also beginning that revelation of the mind. For most of you that comes at first as though a literal Light were blazing there at the edge of consciousness - as though a real veil broke past that point beyond which we had previously not been able to push. Beyond which you cannot imagine thought yet."

"To begin to percieve ANYTHING at all beyond that limit of ordinary thinking is fearful. Rare human beings have pushed at that interface through generations and you have called them extraordinary, you thought that they had genius,beyond yourselves. Spiritual genius! I suggest that they had persistence and courage beyond most. That they had retained the awareness of childhood and developed it, rather than losing it." She looked around, her eyes penetrating as though she could see to their hearts.

"If a person looks steadily into that Light of stillness, that seeming nothingness at the edge of consciousness, that person may even recoil with the thought that this is alien, not normal at all. The mind at first distorts what is seen either with a cloud of fear, excitements, or with overpowering adoration. For we have called that blazing Light at the edge of consciousness, God. We've called that recognition within Stillness, the Eternal Spirit and worshiped and sought no further." Her voice was stilled, the Family, caught in the power of the words, was motionless. Not one among them seemed to have trouble understanding.

Now, another voice began and so smoothly was the transition done that for seconds the difference was not registered. Jedro"s deep voice carried all the gentleness and strength of his nature.," You are all aware now that it is when the mind comes to rest - is at peace and is quietly willing to See -- when the Heart has offered a listening ear, a willingness to know of that which is beyond itself - that realization can begin. It is the power to trust and to persist, to hold steady attention in that Light until there is a knowing that echos from the wakened Heart through out the mind .Each of us, those you call Monitors, have had to stand at that point and to hold and to open ourselves so that that Light could flood into our entire beings and waken in ourselves that flickering flame that waits in us all. The flame of Soul Consciousness, of Spirit!" He looked around,"We can talk of this because you have wakened to know, and all we do is shape into words what you know!"

" To have courage enough not to be overwhelmed by that blinding first glimpse, means you have subsided into watchful attention and acceptance. Many of you are ready now to enter into the ranks of those who live beyond physical limits. You practice that utterly quiet state that is the state of meditation - the condition when the ordinary mind can allow and receive knowledge which comes like an impression from beyond itself. We can talk to you now because your vision has expanded and includes impression of that greater reality."

" Humankind has called that impression intuitive realization and by other names. But you must know that it is the MIND Itself, not the ordinary mind but that Mind that is so vast and extensive that it includes all our minds in itself. Includes all Earth, for Earth is living Mind. These are teachings of a living Earth." He stopped, letting them absorb, nod, realize that was true out of their own intuitive knowing..

"It is the wakening of Intuition, of inner knowing. Thus, for you, these early impressions seem to come from 'outside' yourselves, and it is not until later on that you realize that they are simply part of the fullest, true nature of Earth itself." He stopped and again Estella's sweet voice spoke, again with that resonance that they both used so well, that sound called the VOICE.

" This point of greater perception, has seemed so alien to your ancesters that when they touched upon it, they called it the touch of God. We prefer to say, the Touch of Love. It frequently was distorted into purely human assumptions. Whereas had they stabilized themselves and held firm to that point of perception they would know something of the truth. The Truth is too great for human minds to hold, but something of it can be glimpsed."

" Humankind has known through its rare people that we called mystics that we could receive impressions or realizations from beyond the mind's known limits. Those people also knew that the inventions, the great discoveries of science, arts, genius of all kind, that seemed 'magical' or unexplainable 'gifts' were actually glimpses from beyond that edge of personal consciousness. So were the truest philosophies that guide the human race. They are results of having pressed consciously for long and long against that interface, searching for that which was unknown. They are the Vision into what we called the 'beyond' but what was actually the impersonal Mind, the true nature. What we call God, the Divine, Spirit, etc. That is beyond! But at the same time, Spirit is what all things are, in themselves too! And so what was once strange and unnatural, now is perfectly natural for those who truly seek."

" Today's science shows us how to meet that interface consciously. How to choose Love, to choose to live Love. Indeed the science of consciousness and of Spirit, recognized publicly in our time, is the major training of our Stations. Those of you who have been there at all, know that. We all began meditation as young children, that is the opened door. We learned to quiet the mind at the interface, to end thinking, mental chatter, and listen because we we could see there was something beyond that chattering mind. Then we could pay acute attention and finally begin to realize, as water seeping into a sponge, what had seemed beyond us."

" When we practice this, the little personal mind extends itself and there is greater consciousness, that which is of Mind itself, infusing itself into those narrow, familiar limits and this can actually be painful, frightening at first. For after all, we are dealing with, persisting in holding our attention to, the truly UNKNOWN. This greater consciousness is what your Teachers have called the Soul. It is the SOUL nature filling this personal self now, claiming its own, and it stretches that self beyond all it ever knew. That stretching is the process by which ordinary consciousness is opened into Soul consciousness ."

Through the years you've practiced and you've opened your minds to such vastness, to reality so unlimited that you cannot find language to describe, to even speak of IT. People often think of the experience as one of Light, fiery energy, as God, as a power of Love that literally drowns the senses, and you must be prepared to hear any of these responses when you work with your students. Because once one has entered into that state of consciousness known as Soul consciousness, any person who comes with questions is a student."

" Gradually you will --in fact some of you already do - absorb perception enough to shape into idea, and then gradually idea is brought down into language as thought that can be shared." She stopped, looking around at each of them again, "It is what we practice at our Stations, bringing that Vision into language, and into daily living, or as the old ways had it, Spirit into flesh. For you, there is perception as it fills you." She smiled then, her eyes seeking the mountains, resting there for long minutes.

"Always we begin to balance again. All your lives you were taught to 'balance'. That was the skill that all children must know, how to balance emotions, thinking, action, and physical experiences, sensation, all into a harmonious healthy personality. Now there is another greater balancing. But you already have the basic skills for it. You know how to balance."

" To Balance the inner life with the outer life, the greater consciousness with the smaller consciousness, the personal life with the Soul life, that is simply an extension of that familiar skill of balancing. Listen, listen carefully to your self and your Soul. Listen and pay attention so that you stand at that interface and know. As you do, you will find the way to balance."

She ceased talking. There was silence for several minutes during which no one spoke,so absorbed had they become. Estella and Jedro looked at the gathered people and the quality that radiated literally from their presence, their bodies and minds, had no name, but it included utter acceptance, and a penetrating intensity that seemed to enter itself into those listening hearts and minds.Jedro continued after the silence.

"Estella said that wonderful thought, 'when we can efface and obliterate from consciousness ourselves as the central figure in the life drama then we begin to See.' that is a guiding principle for Valley life in the future. Extreme as it sounds now, it will become obviously true as you live it." His eyes found theirs, tender and full of a stern power, something that woke their very will to Know.

" Don't forget it's in Solitude that the Soul reaches down to our familiar nature. It's in solitude that the greater Self can speak to the personal small self. It is then that the impression is made into this mind from that great and unlimited Mind. Then ideas begin to form from that impression. Thus from Mind to mind, comes a renewal and a gradual recognition beyond anything we have known. Some still describe that as the Touch of the Divine, and for us it does seem so. Others say it is a Voice heard, others that it is revelation, enlightenment, expansion of all senses and an awakening of new ones, so that all the world seems to have changed. In that moment, everything is brighter, clearer, more precious. One's heart swells with unexplainable Love. Love is a lighting of the inner self, an exposure of the depths where Joy lives." His eyes were full of a light Rose had never thought to see in any person. She gazed at him, listening, hearing with her whole mind and she knew the others did too.

He had stopped, looking down at his hands, clasped quietly in his lap, then he went on ,"However the Light of Love is ruthless in its clarity, it also exposes our darkness, even until we are full of great pain. Such knowledge of the smallness of our poor nature seems to be nearly unbearable to the newly awakened mind. All of you must know by now that if we awaken and know the greatest GOOD, we become clearly aware of suffering, and we sometimes confuse these things with EVIL. But they are not evil, though they might lead to such if we followed downward into our own darkness rather than upward into our own light. One is acutely aware of one's own shortcomings, ones own capacity for harmfulness and selfishness. But one knows too one's capacity for selflessness and harmlessness. One begins to learn Right speech and Right action. These grow out of balancing. It is a true Remembering! Awareness comes full and complete, not in parts. And for the first time in our lives, we know of CHOICE!" He smiled at them, and the radiance of that smile erased their worries that they could never be what he was. He said,"Real choice does not come until we begin to KNOW ourselves. Then our errors and mistakes are truly serious, because we KNOW. Those who err from simple ignorance, may be more quickly forgiven. The Builders are ignorant. You are not!"

He hesitated, turning to Esther, and she nodded, her eyes sweeping around the room, catching each one instantly in their fire. "So you must deal gently with those coming from that darkness gradually into that wonderful Light. Some have said the wonder, the realization of the utterly beautiful is harder to bear than the exposure of ourselves to uglyness and suffering. Others say that only that perception of the highest consciousness and beauty makes the recognition of our darkness bearable. It is for you to decide that. You must learn to deal gently with yourselves as you do so."

" To sum up,then, my dear friends, we want to remind you that from the edge of sustained stillness of mind comes a perception of mind shaking Light, or it may be realization, indescribable and inexpressable. It might be called a message from God,Allah, Buddha,Krishna,Kali,Mary, or Adana, which ever name fits. But it is a glimpse from the Source of Life.

This is the beginning of the Journey. It is happening to all of you! It is utterly new, changing the very meaning of life, of things. Purpose shapes itself out of that vastness, no longer out of this small self centered world. Purpose begins to include, not exclude, until all Life is within that purpose. It is upon that mind-stillness, through the Stillness, like a quiet pool of water, that revelation is written on the mind and that revelation is the direction for Humanity. It is our task to learn to stand steady enough to receive that impression, and then to listen deeply enough to know and to discover that direction." He stopped .

The two of them standing there in the sunlight seemed to fade a little. Then they turned and to everyone's surprise they went to fill glasses with iced Tea. Then turned back to the Family with smiles and that old look of mischief in their faces."You didn't think we could or would share your world so much?" Rose had risen, Jennifer and Paul all suddenly struck with the thought that they had not been hospitable. Jedro waved one hand,"Don't be disconcerted. We enjoy visiting and sharing among our friends. Please remember that we too are human."

They sat then, ate and drank with the Family, talked a little, answered questions that came with hesitation at first but then grew easy as everyone began to accept these two. They joked about the restrictions of life in the stations, but at the same time, they made clear the wonderful community of that life. The challange and dedication that each Monitor knew in regard to the Valley and to its people."We think we're as dedicated as the People of the Way, at least". said Estella laughing. "They are such wonderful carriers of the wisdom and their songs and dances are the perfect perveyors of that beauty within their hearts. Such a people. We have many among us who came from their ranks, just as we have many from your own town people."

"And from which did you come?" Paul was curious.

They looked at one another a slow smile spreading until finally Jedro said,"I was at the Station before the towns were built, though I was only a child. You were building Clandor when Estella came to us. She too was barely out of childhood." No one spoke for some minutes, imagining their age, belied by their youthful appearance.

For an hour more they enjoyed the companionship and conversation, talked to the cats and to Rob, and walked out among the gardens. And then, they said goodbye. Smiling again, in that attitude of mischief as though they enjoyed surprising people, they simply faded away as did the Cheshire cat,in Alice's adventures in Wonderland.

Anna stood as they faded, her face filled with a longing as though she would call them back, tell them something. Ask! But then with a sigh, she stepped back and droppd into her chair. Her face only thoughtful. Jessie watched silently, knowing something of the future direction this young girl's life would take.

Andrew stirred as from a deep meditation,"They weren't holographs! They ate!" He shook his head, his eyes wide,puzzled. Then with a softer voice he asked, "They do have families, those folk?" He turned to Jessie.

"If you mean do they mate, bear children, etc.? Yes, there are some who do. It is perfectly possible. Some come to the work later in life when their child bearing years are done, as I did. But those who come in youth, may of course fulfil what their personal life demands as well as that greater life they live."

" Then,are all their children born to that service?" Andrew seemed to be asking for his twin, as much as for himself, for he glanced at her searchingly.

Jessie smiled, shook her head,"No, Son, they are not, but through the years, the parents of such children have learned how to teach more fully than even our Master Teachers. So their children learn swiftly. Now maybe we'll bring their Teachings down into our Valley for those whose natures don't give them great perception. Every person must learn to understand, to realize difference and know no shame, nor fear. And they do so. Those children sometimes stay and work among the Monitors as helpers, sometimes they return to Valley life and live as all of us here, visiting their parents as they choose."

They were silent then, letting the Teaching of Estella and Jedro settle in their minds. Wanting to realize all they taught, and knowing they must give themselves time to absorb. For several hours they wandered through the land, into their cottages, to write, to make music or paint, to think, whatever recorded their deepest responses best. Then, late in the day, they came together again and the foremost question was what they could to do to meet those who threatened their Valley life.

Jerry asked the question, " I begin to understand something of how to go on with the search,the inner journey. But surely I can't understand how I can 'obliterate myself as central figure in the life drama' without destroying myself and all myself stands for."

Jessie nodded, "It is an art indeed. But one not learned except through practice. It seems paradoxical to most minds. But you work on it, Jerry. And talk to us about your discoveries." Her face was intently serious, but her eyes smiled as if with secret mirth, and he nodded.

After a moment he shrugged and said, "Right now, I keep remembering all the problems. My mind is stuck on the problems we've been having, the trouble among us. Even with all that they gave us, this morning, --- " He frowned, then began again,"I suppose it's just what they said. This -- meeting of the problem -- IS the practice. Seeing it impersonally, -- seeing ourselves impersonally -- in fact - What we're doing. Paying attention. How can we do that?" He was silent, they all listened then several nodded. Some just looked down at their hands, a feeling of impotence. So much asked. For long moments no one said anything and finally, Jennifer decided to go back to the specific issue they must meet.

"Would it help to know how the Builders began feeling this separativeness?" Her face was desolate. "We might find out whether the people of the Builders learned Meditation and practiced it deeply in their childhood. Perhaps that's a difference among us." Jennifer stared at Jessie, hoping some explanation might come of this.

" And you think explanation might relieve some anger?" She looked around."To listen inwardly, to wait upon one's Heart knowledge, one is freed from much trouble. As Jerry suggests,one is detached a little, and therefore can See better. Where are we reacting instead of responding? Where do we feel attacked? But if we know they are not able to Reach into a higher place, we might, first, have sympathy, second, correct our Teaching." She watched them, saw which eyes widened, who heard.

Ned said, "Every child is taught these things. I believe they practice too. Every child!"

"Yes, but do they continue when they have gone from the basic Teaching of early years. Older children do not study with the Master Teachers unless they choose. Has the inward seeking reached far enough in young ones that they have Touched upon that power that fires the mind, wakes the heart so they seek on their own?" Paul was thoughtful, determined to investigate how this came about in Altos.

Annette nodded, "We can find out, look into it through the Learning Centers. We have asked the Master Teachers why some people haven't understood our intention. They told us how we neglected them, failed to wake their hearts. We do know!"

Tom stood up, walked a little, moving up and down the deck, touching the leaves of the great Walnut hanging down before his face. "After all, we've only begun to blink back the darkness of our yesterdays, we still don't know whether we can Love,can stand at that point that we See, and hold steady. How can we teach them when we don't know enough ourselves?"

THE JOURNEY

Annette said,"There's a lot of fear among us, there's shame, there's anger. And the habits of thinking we've lived with aren't gone over night. There's a dangerous tide building, if we don't pay attention it'll sweep us in."

Jerry turned angry eyes on them, "It's not fair you know. They're attacking the Valley, not us!"

Paul nodded slowly, "We ARE the Valley. They are part of 'us'. We feel guilty. They remind us of that guilt."

Jerry nearly shouted,"What can we be guilty of? We're not guilty. They've made the first attack on this Valley!"

Paul met Jessie's eyes and nodded, "We can see, They can't! We denied what we See. The Light itself, wonderful as it is, we denied. Love Itself, frightened us in the beginning! So vast and all inclusive it is. But we began to see what we are, have been! And we have a gift we think we don't deserve, one they don't have. How can you say we don't feel guilt?" His face was full of a mixture of sorrow and anger, then a clear realization smoothed it, he spoke with conviction. "And yet, I repeat, it is not they who threaten us; we are all one people, it we who threaten ourselves!"

Rose studied them both, her eyes first worried then amused,"Yes, well said! We can begin arguing, can begin escaping into our own anger, our fear. It's just that easy.! Doing exactly what we know not to do. Estella said we must practice." Both Paul and Jerry looked at her with resentment that faded to recognition and then sorrow. "We feel superior, we've got a heavy dose of it". They were looking at her, letting that thought settle. Several heads began to nod, Anna's face paled slightly and she ducked her head. Admission hurt.

After a few minutes Jennifer said softly,"Surely it was at first fear that tore my heart when I saw that there was so much, so much of knowing, that the Silent City had wakened in me something I had denied. There was no pride, only fear, nothing else, then. But now that I'm losing the fear, pride replaces it. I imagine myself something special. Yes, I don't deserve this gift, this perceptiveness, anymore than I've 'deserved' the Talent for music that has made my life so joyous and given me recognition in the world. Yet, do I feel guilt because I can create a symphony and others can't? No, I don't! Not for that talent. But for this? Yes! I can see I must feel sorry for those who cannot See. And that creates guilt in me." She sighed, "Maybe because Musical Talents, or Talents in other arts, or sciences, have been accepted, are familiar. But this new Talent has some quality that transcends what we accept as normal." She shook her head,"I don't know."

Annette nodded, leaning toward Jennifer, wanting to shape her thought, "There you see? I think maybe we begin to See something new. We stand in a doorway that is only slightly open,but beyond is such possibility, such wonder already, like a great Light. LIFE seems to pour through that door - Life that is promise. How can I have that, and not everyone?" Her eyes were wide in realization !

" But we are refusing to step across that threshold, we're resisting acknowledgement even now. We don't focus our lives enough to stand there in that Light. How can we think ourselves special?" Jerry was still angry, still almost contemptuous of himself, of them all. "We're still absorbed in ourselves."

Then Jane ended her long silence,"But it's there! I feel that absolute Beauty. I will not deny! I will keep my attention there and I will enter into it." Her determination was so strong it shook them to hear it. Jessie nodded to her, her face a wreath of smiles, delighting to hear that clear voice. "Standing there, aware, I am as worthy as a tree, or as a leaf, of the sun's light. No more, no less!" Her eyes were soft, she drew a long tremulous sigh, a gentle sadness seemed to cradle her.

Steve reached out one arm to draw Jane back to him, "It's true, my darling, and that you and I have just begun to know, but these others, have known so much longer and they might see it better." His expression was perplexed, fear flickered in his eyes, was gone, and a dawning hope lay there naked to them all."It IS Light, isn't it? It comes from a 'beyond'. There is more than I've ever imagined, and I realize that." His voice finally carried the awe he felt. "We are aware!"

Jessie met the eyes of the others, looking at her they reflected their chagrin. Then she said,"Do you see? They, the two of them, just born, so to speak, just waking, have set us all to shame. They see without our own years of doubt and fear and denial. And so shall our children See. Perhaps our own children here have suffered from those refusals and fears, but none in the future will need to. Neither of these two have guilt, but simple acceptance, because neither of them feel pride. For them, it just IS".

Steve and Jane themselves sat trying to understand her, gradually seeing the difference but not impressed. The others saw the flaw and sighed. Finally Ned said,"Well, there's nothing that'll make us feel more defensive than guilt can. We could learn to hate Builders because of that guilt. Blame them for it. Unless we acknowledge it, without pretending. "

Andrew spoke softly, his perception of his own feelings visible in his voice,"Well, it's exactly what our Master Teacher taught us last week. He must have known what we'd be feeling." He got up, walked around to get a cup of tea, then set it down and pulled a beer from the ice bucket. He found this distressing. What had he said to Steel? To his other friends? Had he stood firm at all in his own knowledge? He must remember because he had known their anger was rising.

The evening light was delicate, rose and purple across the hills, long shadows lay along the land, the air blew in small gusts rustling the leaves. It was cooler now, so quiet, that faint sounds could be heard far away, a howl of a wolf, distant, the baa of wild sheep up in the rock cliffs, out of reach of predators. The Valley lived and breathed all around them. They felt it fill their bodies, their hearts and were comforted. But the delicate melancholy of evening hovered over their spirits.

Paul met Ned's eyes, then Rose's. He moved his steady gaze among them, "Well, there it is. It's going to take some getting used to.It's time we did some

THE JOURNEY

thinking for ourselves."

Anna raised her head to look at the adults as if in apology, "What did Esther mean by harmlessness? Because if I were harmless I would feel no pride, and no anger. I would know no jealousy, and no resentment. And I do. She said we must -- must -- 'obliterate out of our consciousness ourselves as the central figure in our life drama'." She spoke the words of Estella with perfect memory, and hesitated,. " But oh Jessie, how can I when I am always forgetting! Harmlessness and selflessness! I've been taught that all my life, and it's very hard, very hard even to understand. But when you speak of guilt, that feeling that somehow I'm better, or that I am given what I don't deserve, then, it's true. I do feel guilty at being aware of what other's aren't. And I'm aware that that's harmful. And it isn't a matter of deserving at all! And so I have to re-balance. And that's interfering with the practice." She was silent, thinking, then with a wry grin she said,"Or maybe that IS the practice!" She saw Jessie's nod and was silent.

"So now we're all going to get caught in the trap of feeling guilty about feeling guilty, Huh?" Jerry was restored to his usual good humor. He laughed, and everyone relaxed. "Well,I'm not. I accept that I am. I won't justify anything. I'll do what your Teacher also taught you, Sweetheart". He looked at Anna,"To watch and pay attention and quit hastling myself all the time, but never deny either." He was frowning then, as a realization broke through his thoughts and claimed him."Just that, to think even, is to be trapped, except we have to think. But to remember that thinking is not the - the Way. Thinking is making all we realize available to us in another way. We have to come up out of ourself, enter into that Light, into stillness until we know! Then bring what we know back to ourselves. Isn't that it?" Others nodded, looking with surprise at this young man who had so obviously begun to See. To respond to that inner Self.

"And then, remembering, until it's out here, in this everyday conscious world like everything else. That's why we always think later." Anna was amused at herself, but then she frowned, began to look around, to know with growing attention the wonder of this evening, the Love that filled her heart. She forgave herself, in those moments, and knew she would need to do that again. But the humor of it lightened her thought. She could learn to stand in that lifted awareness that was Love, she could because she had done that. And in that place, she knew no self disgust, nor could she harm. Lost from herself, she was selfless because she was unaware that she was other than that streaming of Love through her. They all absorbed her words, her realization as if receiving it from her into themselves. And again they were silent for a long time.

Then slowly, one by one they began to stir,to stand and walk around the deck, to lean to pick a few flowers from the blazing color around them. Laughing again and murmuring to one another. Thought and attention shifted, was less focussed, inclusive. They separated so that they were isolate among one another again. Words seemed superfluous now. The magic of the evening drew them from their self absorption, poured them out into Self awareness and Earth.Afer a while, they drifted back to the deck, looking again at one another, embracing now

THE PEOPLE OF THE VALLEY

and then as if suddenly wanting comfort before the overwhelming Love they lived in. And finally, they began to clear the tables, move toward daily tasks.

Tom said,"Hey, before we break up, there's something I've got to tell you. Something that'll give encouragement to us all." He picked up a sandwich and perched on the deck railing while they stretched, moved about and then settled to listen.It's this morning, the Vagabonds. You just can't realize how wonderful those two were."

"Who? I heard there was some trouble,,some kids harrassing them again?" Ned was passing cold beer,tea and juices around again. The evening air was still warm, enclosing them.

Tom liked the experience of being the one who had great news."How I'd love to have seen Deborah and Adam. They're quite a pair,you know. They met that mob. They were great!" His grin spread,remembering.

"Tell us, you oaf. Don't keep us in suspense." Silvia shouted at him.

" I feel happy just having heard it. It's made my day." He was risking their patience, "It was from your own daughter, Paul and Jennifer,that I heard it. Rachel's with them, that Family, you know." They nodded, looking a little worried,"Well, she told me that the kids -- that gang - came last night, about eight of them, and began demanding answers about the Silent City. Demanded to know why the Vagabonds worshiped Her. They used that term. Pure harrassment. What right did they have to demand. I'd have sent them off in a hurry with a paddling perhaps." He laughed again aloud, enjoying the telling."But Deborah simply went to them, invited them in to the camp fire. To Rachel's surprise, they came. Adam served them drinks, and they quieted. There's not any kid who hasn't been on at least one Journey, you know. Deborah's courtesy seemed to deflate their boorishness, Rachel said. She said their rudeness made her so angry she wanted to send them on herself. Little slip of a girl, I bet she could too. She's an adept at martial arts, isn't she?" At Jennifer's smile and nod, he went on.

"I was surprised at myself when she told me. Proud of her readyness to approach them, run them off. Just that same pride that we've all known. It wasn't until later that I realized I was proud that she hadn't. I think she lives a lot in the Light." He bent a puzzled glance on Jessie and then went on, shaking his shaggy head, his long hair swinging against his shoulder. "Well, Deborah got them talking, asking, the derision still loud in their voices, but Deborah began answering as if they were really interested in knowing the answers. They made fun of her, emptied their cups in the fire, then stood up and yelled at her. Then Rachel said Deborah just got very quiet and listened to them. Rachel said it seemed that somehow she was Reaching them after all. She was in the Teaching mode, Rachel said, her voice very penetrating and clear. You know how it sounds. And Rachel thought Deborah was Touching too, Touching their minds just very little,but enough to quiet their fear. Rachel thought they had planned to hurt those folk, to do literal violence there. But Deborah got them talking again, talking as if they hadn't been able to talk before. Talked of their anger, their hate,

THE JOURNEY

their fear finally. Deborah and Adam there encouraging them, and all the time doing a bit of Reach, a bit of Sending of that wonderful Loving energy the People of the Way know how to Send. Although how they keep their love flowing in some situations, I don't know."

"But you know, those boys finally just left. Didn't do any damage, and stopped their rudeness. Then next morning they came back, they'd camped down the Highway a little way. When Deborah was doing her morning greeting of the Sun, they were back making fun again. They had wine with them, drinking already, for courage I suppose. Or rather a loss of healthy inhibition. The Family had just made breakfast and were waiting for Deborah.

She didn't bat an eye. Just went on with her prayers as if they weren't there. Then when she was done, she turned to them, that robe hanging to her feet. You know how she dresses, her long wonderful hair curling down to her waist, she held out her hands to them, open, her arms ready to embrace. Rachel said she couldn't see how the boys could resist. She was lovely and so full of love. Her face was full of smiles, her eyes were shining like she had just seen God. Rachel said she'd never seen Rachel look like that. Her own family too were surprised, watching her as if something special was happening. And those young men, they watched, her, they were suddenly silent, watching. Adam came up behind them, but they didn't know that. The two of them had the young guys between them. And then Deborah began to sing. To sing mind you, before all that.

And then Adam joined her, and you know their voices, great, powerful, full as the very best. No one said anything, but the rest of the Family joined in. Rachel, said she held back, not having their quality singing voice, though they wouldn't have cared. But she wanted to see. She said it was as though a Light began to pour between them all, catching the gang in between. The light poured out like a stream all around them, literally. Rachel said it was like a flowing visible light. You know Rachel's one who could see that Light. She felt the power of it and she said she began to cry, it was so moving."

"The boys yelled at first, trying to stop them, to laugh at them, but they just kept on, and gradually the yells began to fade, their voices lost in the wonderful singing. And then, - this'll get you, They stopped to LISTEN. Couldn't resist, it was so lovely. And when the family singing stopped, they just looked at each other, as if to ask what were they doing there. They began to walk off toward the Highway. But Deborah and Adam came after them, "Wait", they said,"Come join us for breakfast. And sing with us. I've seen some of you on Journey and I know some of you sing. Come join us ."

"Do you know they did! Ate with the Family, even sang with them, began to loosen up and enjoy themselves. Rachel said she even got to like them. When they got ready to leave, one of them hung back until the others were a little way off. Rachel said he looked puzzled and angry, but a little ashamed. He stood there a moment watching the Family, watching their departure. He finally said,"You must know that worship of the City is insane. You must realize it must end."

THE PEOPLE OF THE VALLEY

Deborah nodded and laughed, "Yes, it would be crazy to worship a city. If anyone did that. We only honor Her. We don't worship anything, except the Eternal Life."

He actually looked relieved, as if he had accomplished something after all. He went off quietly then.

Adam called after them, "God go with you." and that was the end of it. By the time I got there the family was all talking about other things. I had a nice visit and then came here. Tom was still smiling. Rose laughed.

"Tom, you're a great story teller, but so is Rachel and I'd bet she told it just that Way." He nodded, still pleased. "There must be something more, you look so happy"

He turned to her, nodding. "It's those two, Deborah and Adam. They just give so much. they Give -- Love -- that's what it is. Makes everyone around them feel right -- right. It's just that." He turned swiftly to Jessie, met her eyes, her understanding. A joy shone in her face to hear Tom. He said softly, "Just the way you do, Lady."

The sun was nearly down by the time everyone left but the long summer twilight would keep the Valley lit for hours yet. A thoughtful, bemusement filled them all. Time to think, a search of the heart seemed crucial. Jerry set out to walk. He turned toward Adwin. His mind racing, his thoughts not yet in order. One part of his mind noticed the trail, the trees, vines, meadows on each side of the pathway. He brushed his hands across the tops of bushes catching a handful of berries, tossing them into his mouth. He could see on ahead a scatter of young children, the first age group for helpers. They would be about ten now, he thought, and their entrance into the Gatherers still a couple of years away, but they would be serving as the pickers of small fruits and vegetables. So they had worked this afternoon, and their buckets were nearly full. He caught himself in mid thought. Their families would be Gathering, some of them this day, shouldn't these children be home? Surely if the Monitors came to his own family, they must be coming to all the others.

He shook his head. It wasn't his affair. They would keep touch with all the people. He had other things to attend to. He could see another gathering, a larger one, in the fields below the Learning Center. The main playing fields beyond the half dozen tennis courts, just finished this summer, still had the banners and flags left from the Summer Festival. This July full moon celebration would include two tournaments of Three Ball. Jerry knew Cassandra and Anna were playing. How did they get down here so fast? He could see Anna across the nearest field, running with that easy grace she had, though her body was not a rummer's body. He thought of playing a while with them. They might not welcome him, but they'd be polite. Then he realized they wouldn't. They'd tell him they had to practice. This tournament was with players from Jasper and Denlock and the mountain team from the villages up in the west asked to enter. It was an unfinished game left from the Summer Festival and would culminate in the final Autumn Festival. They played at nearly every Full Moon celebration. He saw another team, as he

THE JOURNEY

walked closer, already playing on the far field. There was an exhilaration to this game, a pleasure of body and mind joined in mutual delight, in a harmony of movement and attention that was real pleasure.

Watching intently for a moment he realized that it was Bangor they played. The new game, an intermingling of three teams, and one he thought you had to learn as a child. These kids had grown up with it. The competitive games of the old days were either gone, or so modified they couldn't be recognized as the same he had watched on old tapes. Times had changed! The long twilight would let them play for another hour or more.

He walked a little on, looking through the treetops, as he passed them, he had a clear view. Andrew played another game at this side and he could recognize Steel and a couple of the other boys Andy had been seen with a lot lately. Something stirred like a warning in his mind, he shrugged. Turned toward the other game. He stood now between the two fields, a third field beyond these two, was being prepared for even a different game. But Anna ran into view just below him, racing to kick one ball and at the same time her teammate leaped to catch another. Jerry followed the kicked ball, and then his eye caught the thrown ball, leading the team away, so that suddenly with a swift catch in the crook of an arm, he sent it on even as he ran to intercept the kicked ball. The players shifted direction and another boy was receiving the kick, playing all the possibilities and keeping track of everything seemingly without effort. He sighed. Even games had become more complicated in the last few years. Or was he getting old?

He began to walk on, but was aware of the utter intensity, the absorption as they 'Mind Touched'to communicate their intentions. How could they do it. This Touching among team members, at the same time aware of much the other team intended as they could pick up. They shielded as they tried to adapt their plans and share the changes with their own team as it happened. It must take mental contortions unheard in his own youth. Not so many could do all that. He laughed seeing the fierce looks from one boy who had missed Anna's thrown ball, She was grinning, circling, Sending loud and clear, and yet with a curious edge to that Sending, and he realized it was shaped to be clear to her own team. How did they do it. Most adults couldn't shield even, and to do it with some kind of selectiveness -- !" He shook his head.

Then Anna's teammate, never glancing in her direction, sent a kick accurately to her feet, or rather to where her feet would be when the ball got there. Jerry was impressed, no wonder he never had played Bangor well. Then, suddenly he felt a change. The boy who had looked so fierce, anger rising, was bringing a depression of energy into his team's unity. There grew a flaw in the harmony, in the fabric of the game. He could sense it, and stopped, wondering at himself, more than at them then. The high joy of the game faltered, sank a little. A wild surge of competitive fury pulsed through the angry boy, infected a teammate, who charged into another. Coordination was off. Jerry watched. Emotional imbalance could throw a team off badly. Could they recover?

Anna swung her attention toward the sagging mental hole in the team play, she still held her own focussed attention steady to continue, lifting, sending energy and intently seeking balance within their fabric. She was tiring, nearly missed a ball but caught it with an ankle. Then sent it on. Two others Touched her with their attention, so aware of themselves, of their group interaction that they perceived the whole picture together. The three met the disgruntled player, supported him, swung an envelope of power around him. Jerry could FEEL that. It struck him as an amazing act of Love. How could they do it? He knew some members of the other Team aided in that re-balancing.

The ball sailed then from his hands and flew off too far, the other team recovered it, but the imbalance had been met and the Team was back in harmony,.The recovered boy found the ground ball coming at him as the opposite team roused from attention to his energy depression and focussed again on the total plan. But he had recovered enough and caught it with a swift turn of the ankle and sent it hard and precisely timed back and into the goal. It was obvious to Jerry that at that moment the unsettled player was still being held in balance by his team mates, and though that took their attention a little from the movement, it didn't seem to disturb their skills that much. It was all one thing to them, all of it was the GAME. Jerry shook his head thoughtfully as he walked on.

He said aloud to himself." And it was clear that boy didn't feel shame that he'd lost balance. He'd have done the same for any teammate had they fallen off. They enter into this as though it's all perfectly natural and yet -- -?" As he walked, he knew that for them it was. How could the adults of this Valley hope to learn? And yet, there must be young ones who couldn't either, who didn't respond to that Joining. Were they unable to play those new games? Then he stopped short, but how had he himself realized so much of what was happening? Were his own perceptions sharper since the Monitor's visit?

He found his thoughts began to take shape, remembering all that happened this morning, remembering that there was still so much to learn. He stopped at the edge of the hill top, just before entering the gardens of the town, to look back. Seeing the patterns of the games from here, noticing the almost rhythmic movements, the sweep of players , he sat down to watch a little while before going on.

Ben strapped on his belt at the Hall and waited while Tom made his farewells, kissing all the women goodbye. Ben grinned. Such a lady's man, Tom. Two wives of his own and he still loves all the others. Tom came out grinning and Ben watched him tighten on his belt,. They walked to the edge of the deck and went up the steps to the jump stand. It was easier to get altitude if the flyer leaped out over some drop off. They pushed off into the air, activating their belts expertly as they went. The evening was very warm under a clear sky, except for piling of clouds over the western hills. They moved apart, watching Earth, the fields, the people below. They saw the game and Jerry watching, so they hovered a moment, watched the activity to identify the game. They waved at Jerry. then they

THE JOURNEY

swept swiftly over town, down into the entrance to Tom's cottage.

As they removed their belts, Ben said,"Well, Tom, it's going to be a lot of work. I feel as if I've been given an injunction to rebuild the universe. There's so much I don't understand. It seems almost strange to see everyone going on with normal life, the kids playing games, Jerry watching, every one going home as if it's an ordinary day."

Tom nodded,"Yes, Ben, but an injunction to rebuild ourselves as well as the universe! Or is there really any difference?" He looked at Benjamin,with a thoughtful smile then shrugged. "Well, we might's well get on with things but I feel as if I want to settle somewhere and just let it all come together in my mind, and yet, it's as if some part of me is already doing that, behind the daily worries. So much is happening Ben. I got a call from your cousin who's living at your Dad's old place south of Santiago, and he says the Builders've finished their planting there, got the fields all in and the vines are leafing out well. But he had a question that seems to be the usual reaction most people have now. He asked,'Where the devil they going to sell that stuff? No body wants more.' I thought that too, Benjamin, but I've not taken my own thought seriously until then. I honestly begin to think maybe they'd made a mistake, that there is no market out there at all. Wouldn't that be a come down." He sighed,collecting some materials he needed then the two went out again to the deck. "Shall we walk to my office?" At Ben's nod,he added,"You'd better keep your belt, you'll need it."

They set out, the short distance through the bright fragrant gardens, dipping their fingers into the fountains that splashed clear water into the quiet air as they went by. Tom said, "People seem to think that the mayor ought to be able to do miracles. They give me these problems and seem to assume that I'll just solve them all."

Ben nodded, feeling no sympathy, "Well, just where do they say they'll sell their new products?"

"They're convinced that people really want more, want to have more parties and bar time now that the building of the town is done." He glanced over at the thoughtful Ben."What d'you think? D'you really think after a Teaching like the one today, that people're interested in those old pastimes? "

Ben shook his head, "No way! And I think I agree with Janco, my cousin. 'Where the Hell do they think their stuff will sell'?" He grinned, then suddenly frowned,"I really do think they're making a mistake and when they find out they've judged us by standards that're no longer working, they'll be angry, but worse, they'll be much more afraid. We'd better be prepared."

Tom glanced at him, walking slowly now, thinking about the problems of so many citizens disappointed and angry,wanting to blame someone. "It doesn't look like much of a future does it?"

They were silent, arriving at Tom's office they went inside and he began listening to the messages the auto sec had recorded. Ben sat, sunk into the chair as though he'd done a day's work. He felt a tiredness weigh him. And yet something in his mind nagged to be given attention. He turned to it, thinking of the morning, the radiant look of those two -'people'? - who had come to talk to them. Could they be called 'people?'.

Tom finished perusing his messages, turned to Ben,"We've missed some of the Builder's talks at the Center, and I missed on the Video. But Dean's been telling people , he's been explaining their plans. He was silent, frowning. "William too, Benjamin, Will's been talking to a lot of people ". Both making speeches up and down the Valley. Will was down as far south as Black Rock country this last week. He's getting around. He's never done that kind of travel in the Valley before, has he?"

Ben looked at his hands, locked together between his knees, he shook his head,"I've avoided the talks, I didn't just miss them. I just have trouble seeing William involved so much. And I like that old man, Dean. I hate to see him in over his head. I don't think it's going to work, Tom. I think they're both in for a terrible time." He frowned, Somehow we're going to have to find more for them. More than building meaningless markets."

"You mean if the survey convinces them there's no market?"

"Exactly! We've never thought of that. What will interest them? How can they live in our world. We're focussed on an inner life they don't admit to." He frowned, touched a button, so that a cello sonato began to fill the room then took another chair and turned to Benjamin,"We don't know for sure they're meaningless yet. But shouldn't you be at work? Won't you let this all get to you too much if you've nothing to do to keep your mind off it?"

Ben laughed, got up, "Yes, I should. I'll be there most of the evening. We're doing some changes in our hours so we can work while it's cooler. But then, I never seem to get any rest during the day either. We're setting up labs that will give the young ones real experience. We'll be nearly as sophistocated as Santiago by another year. Our young ones will still go to study elsewhere, but the kids from other towns will come here. We'll know each other." He was smiling, thinking of his work. But the frown didn't leave his eyes."Tom, the whole thing is getting like those games the kids play now. About three levels of activity, body, emotions and mind all having to be balanced at once. Here we are, trying to keep the daily life going,, and yet, inside us is that furor about how to meet this disruption that threatens to tear apart our life. Then underneath it all, so much deeper that it penetrates everything else ,is the knowledge of Spirit and the way of living that rises through that awareness. What the Monitors talked about. We haven't met that knowledge yet nearly as openly as we must." He shook his head again, spread his arms wide, his powerful shoulders bent slightly then straightened as if he saw himself taking up the task."We've got to do it, Tom,, we can't avoid anymore. Not anything!"

Tom nodded, his long lean body bent to look out the window over the sloping hill side below his house." Yes, but Benjamin,there's something wrong in our Valley, something dark, something that's not just the Builders. Something Cassie said to me, that her friends talk about, that they seem afraid of. A kind of darkness, that seeps into things now and then. She told me that they have to

Balance much more often, that they feel depression weighing them down and have to pay attention to that a lot. Can our Monitors be unaware of that?"

"I've felt it." Ben said, "A strange reasonless depression that makes me tilt toward -- anger, fear, all kind of negative emotions, and like the kids, I have to catch myself and balance carefully. But what if it overwhelms someone before they are aware?"

"That's it! Just exactly. It's insidious but we've got to meet it, Ben. We've got to learn what it is and talk about it. No secrets, they've caused enough trouble." He didn't look hopeful.

"Then you've felt it too?

"Damn right! It's like some subtle pressure that's coming from where I can't imagine, to push us off balance and assist the Builder's intention." He sat, finding his pipe and adjusting it, filling it and taking time to get a bright spark started inside the herbs that were burning. Then he said, "I don't think it's what Dean and Will talk about? What they're up to isn't evil. This thing seems evil to me. And I don't say that lightly." He drew a long breath, "Someone's going to have to go to other cities, Altos, Clandor, find out. If it's the Black Lodge where the center is, then we must go there."

"I agree, Will and Dean are, in my opinion, wrong headed. They're ignorant actually, ignorant of what we know. But this, this darkness, it's something I've never known in our Valley before. It takes the breath if you get a real touch of it. I think that's happened to me. Because I've already been there."

"What's that?" Tom was interested, leaning to his friend, "When, what'd you find?"

I was traveling south, had to go to Clandor a week ago, and that's how I knew Will was going. I rode a car over Black Mountain resort, just to see their development, and there was a wave of something -- something I've never known. It was not the same kind of fear I knew when I kept denying the - the Reach, when I was afraid of Rose's Touch!. Nothing at all like it. That was strange and so unfamiliar it seemed unnatural, so I resented it. I couldn't explain it in my own terms so it made me mad. But THAT was an underlying Joy, a promise and a sense of vast LIFE. THIS was different! It was as though a terrible gulf was opening, dragging down everyone, as though there was a sink, a pit in which dispair lived and grief was a bottomless lake. When I got over the mountain into Clandor it subsided, but the effect of it weighed on me. I couldn't shake it all the time I was in Clandor. I asked my friends there how things were going. I spoke of my experience and they didn't deny. They said it's subtle, it's insidious, and it does effect them. They have to keep steady attention or their own fears, angers, jealousy can build until they lose their balance. They said the town Council's even brought it to a vote. They've made an agreement to watch each other. And an agreement to listen when they're told they're slipping, because the very reminder can enrage one whose lost balance." He shook his head, tears in his eyes. "My friends were very aware. They've alerted the Master Teachers, started asking a lot of questions. They think only those who were able to Reach, who could SEE, were troubled by it. Other people just get depressed or angry and blame it on someone or something." I don't know whether they're investigating the source of it, Black Mountain, yet, but they were planning to."

Tom watched his friend, "Wow! It's already begun then. And we haven't realized the seriousness of it". He frowned, stood to l ook from his window, his eyes resting in the green of leaves and grass. Then with a worried look on his face he came back to sit down again. "I think I'm not as sensitive to lots of things as you are Ben. Maybe that's why I can be mayor. But I need your reports of things regularly, you know. I can't imagine what you describe, but I believe you. I'll investigate. I know a lot of people in that area." He was quiet, letting his thoughts gather," But then, you know, I did meet someone whose presence gave me something of that sense you describe. Man named Greyson. As though a dark wrongness were afloat among us. He literally gave me chills. Yet, there was something amazingly attractive about him. Charismatic in fact. He's attracting a lot of listeners. I couldn't bring myself to speak to him at the time. Now, I think I should have." He stood up, restless again, Come on, let's talk while we walk. I've got some work to do."

Ben got up and they went out. The evening was cooler, the gardens smelled of mint and apples. "What was he doing? Where? "

He was here, in Adwin. He was just standing in the learning Center inside the central Ring,beside our Library entrance watching us. I had come to pick up research papers for Mary. I felt the power of the man, Ben. I felt it! And I'm not sensitive the way you are. As I sat on the fountain sorting Mary's papers, I watched. The kids came out, under that vast oak, you know, beside the colored fountain, I felt him Reaching, a steady stream of energy it was. But also, some quality that roused some kind of wish, desire, old emotions. I had to balance fast! He surely isn't mind blind. They reacted, those kids. Some started toward him, then they would shake their heads, stop, look puzzled and turn away so rapidly I was surprised. Others, others seemed to feel what I did, pulled their jackets around their shoulders as if it were cold. But there were some who simply went to him as if drawn like bees to a flower. They seemed to just be pulled. I couldn't avoid the analogy.It worried me. " He sat silent, lost in the memory.

Ben stared at his friend,"There were some though who refused him wholly ? And he was right here in our town?" His anger blazed, but he held it carefully before his attention, recognizing its source.

Tom nodded, slowly, walking rapidly as if working off that restlessness. Reliving that experience."He was here! And some did refuse, without hesitation! Surprised me. There were some who stopped, looked at him as if they were fully conscious of his intentions, his darkness, knew very well what he did, and they sort of shrugged their shoulders and walked away. One young fellow, sent up a mental shout, such that I felt it even. It was surely a warning. The man whirled, the inner shout had penetrated, that was sure. He looked all around but the boy was walking on as if nothing had happened. His mind closed. I looked too, and the man nearly turned to me, I think because I was so obviously surprised, but I managed to shut down. What leaves me hopeful is that he genuinely was not able to find the source of the shout."

Tom was frowning now, the telling bringing back the worry he had originally felt and then ignored. "You know, I hadn't thought of this, but I wasn't sure at that moment just which child it had been. He screened himself so well. Ben! That's it. I didn't remember until later myself. He had that kind of power and control. It took amazing self control too, because that man, that watcher, was not an ordinary person at all." He shook his head , puzzled, "Where do these kids learn how to do these things? Surely it hasn't been from us. Who teaches them?"

Their eyes met, questioning, "Oh, Ben, old friend, we've been standing in the dark. We've not known half what is going on. The children are far ahead of us and we don't know enough to guide them. What will become of us? Do we have enough wisdom to guide them at all?

" To every one with that kind of control, that kind of perceptiveness, there are still many who know but who have not learned to balance emotionally and mentally that well. There are also those who are mind blind. So there're always those who need you and me."

Ben chuckled, "We'll let people like Jessie and Estella and Jedro manage the ones who're beyond us." He smiled, "Maybe those'll be the ones to help US".

Tom nodded absently,"Yes, I wonder if Monitors haven't already been working with those kinds of young ones. "He nodded sharply, as if dismissing the problem."Well, surely they have guidance somewhere, and you and I have people like Henry to deal with." At Ben's quick frown, he nodded,"Yes, he's been wondering around lately talking a lot, dissatisfied and catching young ones sometimes to talk. They're usually too polite or inexperienced to escape. He may be a danger."

"Wait Tom, before we talk of Henry, I'm worried. What kind of man would let himself get pulled into such anti-life ways. Or would have that kind of power? "

Tom shook his head,"Beats me. But if we've recognized that the Monitors have been traditional Watchers for the Good of Life, surely it would be reasonable to assume there might be Watchers on the side of wrong and harm." They let that thought settle between them. "But I've decided to find out. I've got to get on that today. Why've I waited at all?" He was doubly worried now at the question.

Ben frowned,"Are you sure you haven't been affected by him? Tom, it's not like you to be so slow to get into an investigation. You know how to do it. What's stopped you?"

Tom stopped, looked at his friend, a dawning horror evident in his face. Ben felt his Touch, questioning, asking. He responded and met, then Touched Tom's open, unresisting mind. What he saw there, felt, knew with hard clarity, shook his confidence. But with Ben there, illuminating, Tom saw too. That natural reluctance to hold a man guilty until proven so, a virtue and a vice in a law man, had been used to prevent his action. That quality, drawn into place, screening his equally natural caution. Both men sat in astonished horror,"My God, Ben, we've got to be more than careful. Who ever could do that to me could effect the minds of anyone." He thought of the boy who had walked off. "Almost!" Then, frowning he said, "Well, nevertheless, we've got to alert people. He'll use us against ourselves, then against each other. We've got to guard ourselves from that kind of power." They walked on more slowly.

Ben spoke in sad, dispair,"Why? Why does there have to be such. They seem to work with the darkness Itself. Could such a being, I can't call him human, affect our own children, that attraction Andrew feels for his cronies, for that boy Steel, could it be -- that he's pulled off balance enough so his desire to 'save' others, his feelings of responsibility, becomes a chain to bind him? " He was sick at heart.

Tom shook his head, "Ben, remember, Master Teacher Harold was just reminding us last week of that Teaching rule. 'If you would know the sublime, then you must be prepared to know evil. And evil descends below human selfishness in its intention to anti-Life. It USES what qualities we have, greed, desires, any things it can. It is the CONSCIOUS choice to descend.'" He was silent reflecting on that thought. Then he nodded," Just as now we make a CONSCIOUS choice to know Love, to seek the Light. Heretofore, we've been ignorant, and now we are not. So the choice is profound." He walked silently for several minutes, and they approached the center Ring.

He turned to Ben and said, "We've been taught about the negative in ourselves for most of our lives. Now we must understand the darkness of humanity itself. The qualities in us as a people that've brought about our wars, we allow ourselves to be convinced there is no way but war. We've been conned into approving official periods of torture such as the inquisition and the burning of witches, we've literally built tyrants by bowing to their power. The weakness and the fears of us as human, the qualities both great and terrible of ourselves as a people." He shrugged, "Awful as it seems, we've got to know whether we are capable of intention to do evil. Evil that is far beyond petty human greed and distorted lusts. It's my opinion that an intention to do evil is to use fear as a tool to manipulate people, it's a will to deny Love. "

Ben sighed, "It's surely a different kind of problem from poor Henry. There's a person full of fury, jealousy, and ridden with all kinds of fears. But he's not evil." He turned to look at Tom, "No, he can cause all kinds of harm, be cruel even, or kind, but he does not intend evil.

"You think Henry might actually hurt someone? Might do damage in town?"

"Yes,I do. He actually likes that job we got for him, but he's been attending Builder meetings and just getting more suspicious. He seems crazy with rage. He can't find any reason for all of us to act the way we do. He's beginning to be suspicious that we have some evil intention against him. A man like Greyson could use that anger, push him to act."

Tom nodded, slowly, "I ought to see it. I think I keep denying, because it doesn't make sense to me either. First of all, he's somewhat of a fool, harmless in himself, but led by evil intention,he could be dangerous." He tightened his lips as they turned to the office of the attorney he must see." We could throw him out of

THE JOURNEY

town.." He turned, his eyes twinkling, a faint smile curving his lips.

Ben knew the impossibility of throwing someone out. But he asked,"Why not?"

Tom nodded, he didn't take it as a question."Yes, were we to do that we would cast our own doom. How would we then be different from those who seek to control and to rule through the power of fear? "He dropped his head, studied the floor, "The danger is that he is ripe material for such people as the Watcher. He can be used, maybe already is being used. He seems so much more furious than he used to be."

"So WE'VE got to begin to Watch too. We can't go on in this casual trusting way. We must pay attention to these things. What's the weapon -- or rather the tool to use against such fear? Jessie says it's Love itself. I think she would tell us we must powerfully focus that Love we begin to know until its all round him." He shook his head, "How can I be capable of such Love? How can I even allow Love and do nothing myself? I'm afraid I haven't the strength. We've got to alert her!"

Aren't we being guilty of a kind of arrogance? We are going to ask, with all our hearts, for help. We are going to have to seek that Source of Love" He was silent, realizing the demand of that. "If we don't begin to focus we can be the next tools of that Watcher and never know it, You realize old friend, we could be used easily and fluently.I don't know that I'm balanced enough to be aware of myself. Nor do I imagine that I'm able to Love enough!" His face twisted in dispair, "But we've got to keep trying. We know of Love, we can -- can pray, and we can hold our own intention only in Love." He clenched his fists in determination, "Let me act in Love, Let me act with Love." His eyes were bleak.

And what of us? Can we stand? He's harmful. And I agree? We can't let him destroy all we've built."

"But we forget to notice it when he wakes fear and anger in us, then we will destroy all we've done.All we dream of now." Tom was thinking rapidly, consciously sustaining balance ." It will be ourselves who destroy. He won't have to act at all, except to press us to act for him. After all, Ben, we're no different from other humans, except we Know. We See the difference between what we are and what we are becoming. We must risk Henry's fury, his fear of us. Let it be. If we get caught up in opposing it, we are trapped as surely as if we joined him. We need to ask for Jessie's help." He was silent, then a hope brightened his face, he repeated what he had said, "Surely, she already knows."

They were suddenly shaken from their talk by the sound of running footsteps. Three young men came to the door. Andrew and two others. Tom searched his memory and found the name of one, a tall, powerful young man ,Steel, an athlete, who had won the cross country run last Festival and who won the triathelon two years in a row. He was doing his final training as a Master Weaver in the Skenna Mills in town . The other boy was Dave, youngest son of the Master Farmer and a boy surely to fit that task some day. Both were exuberant, confident, more than a little arrogant. Tom thought they might need a sobering soon. But now he felt irritation, it surprised and put him on guard.

Andrew Reached to him with careless disregard for his reception. Pushed, in fact. Tom accepted and nodded to each in turn. They quieted, sobered a little. Ben joined him,less willing to be courteous, but waiting. Then Tom said,"Well, boys, it looks as though you have something that can't wait for telling." He suddenly broke the severity of his tone with an engaging grin.

Andrew glanced at his friends, tempted to blame them for their refusal to wait. The older men saw this, then saw him douse the excuse , amused and ashamed of himself. Andy said, mildly,"Dad, Uncle Tom, Pardon us for interrupting, but we've just come from the Temple. You know what's happened there?" The three looked at them in surprise,"You don't know! How could you have missed it? Just in the last half hour they did it."

As though he were flinging a light at Tom and Ben, Andrew Touched their minds with a picture. A picture of violence, of a red flame of dispair and fury combined with the wrestling to control them. Tom felt Andrew's strong desire to retaliate. He spoke in the stern, unyielding voice they all had heard before, "We were very seriously busy. Now, quiet your own mind. Get control! You know better than to allow yourselves to be so overwhelmed by another's emotions. " He waited a moment and then said,"Tell us!"

They glanced at one another, rebellious, but quieting. Steel and Dave not sure what he meant,but after a moment, accepting, they settled their emotions into a fair balance. Steel spoke first,"Tom, they've done what no one would have believed. They've bombed the Temple. The one place that - that - " He turned, tears in his eyes, to conceal them. Then suddenly with a force of released anger, he said, "It's absolutely the worst. We can't allow that to go -- to go -- unpunished. You see that, don't you?" He twisted toward Andrew a moment, angry, then back."Andy insisted that we come to tell you,, to give you a chance. I wanted to go right on, to see they learned they can't do that." He frowned at Tom's calm face,"So now we've told you, now I say we go punish them well."

Ben felt the blood drain from his face, then he righted himself. "It's bad, Son,yes. It's seems inexcusable. "He wanted to give them time, to drain some of their fury, to balance. He wanted to comfort them. "Tell us, the whole thing."

Steel nodded to Andy, who began in a tight voice, absolutely controlling his own anger. There was little balance evident. "They did that, they blew out well over a dozen windows. Maybe even tried to bring the main spire off balance. But it's build too well. It didn't even budge. Or else their bomb skills are poor. They hurt PEOPLE Dad! Several people were hurt. You must have known when the healers came?" At Tom's head shake, he went on. "They ruined some of the finest stained glass ever done in Adwin. And the inside of one whole section is a mess. His eyes were full of hurt,"Oh, Dad, to destroy something so beautiful. For no reason. How did it hurt them? And it was something we built ourselves!" Ben felt amazed at their tears. These big, tough, powerful young men had helped build this town. They loved it too. He felt gratified, relaxing a little.

"We do build well, Son. And the Temple has -- other protections. Who was there? Who saw what happened?"

"There were a lot of people there, at meditation. The walls are scorched, torn in places. It's an awful thing." Dave was speaking. His eyes losing some of the anger as he talked," I can't believe they only hurt three people, the place was full. The glass fell all around, you know and the stone splinters too. It was as if the glass fell in between people." He frowned, shook his head, "Couldn't have happened. It was impossible."

Tom was nodding, he wanted to run there, across the fields to the Temple. "Why didn't we know, know before you came? He looked at Ben," Why? Why didn't we -- we FEEL it?" The heat of emotions flamed like clouds around them. He stopped. Maybe it was the source of his worry about evil! Maybe, misunderstood. But that could wait. He had to do something now. Now! For the first time in his life he raised his focus, Reached with every ounce of power to call for Healers. He could feel the force of his Reach and was surprised.

Andrew shook his head, put out a hand as if to stop the Call. "They're already there, Uncle Tom. The repair crew already too." He looked curiously at him."How come you didn't feel it?"

Tom shook his head, feeling sick. He looked at Ben, nodded again swallowed his hurt and said, "Well, there it is. We've thought it might come. Something's blocked us."

Steel glared at them, angry and making no effort to balance,"You're both cowards, afraid to even condemn. Why? Why can't you act like men? We've been attacked. We've been damaged by fools, by incompetents. Are we supposed to sit and let such people destroy our town?" His feeling of urgency to act, to do something, was so great his body danced in response. "Why do you let it go? They did it! They did it! Everybody saw!"

Tom frowned. "Stop-!" His voice was fierce. Pay attention to yourself! What brings you to such fury?"

"What they did, dammit."

"Are you sure? It was a gesture! They didn't want to damage much. If they had it would have been much worse. Although they have no idea of the protections around that Temple. Surely any good chemist in the Valley can make powerful, effective and precise bombs. You all must know that. Especially you Andrew. You could yourself. That proves to me they didn't want to really harm anything. I think it's a cry for help!"

Ben found himself agreeing with Steel. Felt his own fury rising. He had worked so lovingly on the building of the Temple. Every citizen, even the tiniest little ones had done something to make it partly their own. He cried out,"No, NO, they're right Tom. Those who did that must stand responsible. We've got to bring them here, interrogate them. Find out."

Tom's voice was anguished," Not you too, Benjamin. Not you! Pay attention. You must!" Dave had swiftly turned as if to carry out his bidding, but Tom threw out one hand,"NO! No! Not you boys. We'll do no lording it over people less able." He surprised himself with that last sentence. "We are being led astray. Led from our best judgement!" He felt tears rise to sting his eyes.

At the comment, the three boys stared at him, recognized and dropped their eyes. It HAD been what they wanted. To lord it over them, to prove themselves superior. They stood reproved. Tom nodded, to see them accept that.

Andrew said, "Wait - wait - it's true. It's what we're doing. I do feel pressure, a pull to what I know is wrong. And it's in me. The desire is in me. But that pressure uses it, uses me." His face twisted, his eyes dispairing. He turned away. Then, after a moment, he righted himself, drew himself up, met Tom's eyes and both held that gaze. Slowly a smile replaced Andrew's tortured frown.

"Let's consider! What are we afraid of? We're not handicapped! We can See. How can we know how much pain those who can't must endure?" His voice was urgent. He had regained balance. His mind reached out, sought contact. But Steel held himself taut, anger blocking any possible Touch, and -- what? There was something else between them. Some thing Tom saw and feared to see. There! The old lust - lust for a fight, for violence itself, for hurting. It was there in all of them. Only Andrew so far, could see it and acknowledge it. Tom felt it in himself, the real enemy. The ancient rage to revenge. He watched Ben bring his own feelings into balance, draw their energy into focus. Then, the two of them, minds focused, tried to Reach, to Touch, the closed minds before them. Suddenly they felt Andrew's presence, then his voice, crying, "Dave! Steel! We've got to bring ourselves to Balance!" The tremulous shine of Love broke through the darkness in them, flickered and penetrated, held and was hidden again by that ancient urgency. Tom caught the edge of the Light, held there, crying out in his heart, "Tell me how to act with Love."

"You sound like the Teachers. They weren't out there looking at that damage, I noticed." Steel's voice was full of contempt, an arrogance creeping in again, and animal eagerness that Tom recognized for what it was. He had met and battled with that old lust for long in his own youth. Could this boy bring it to bay in time? He thought he might not have done so at Steel's age especially with this provocation. Steel was not awake, could not Touch or take strength from that wisdom. There it was, the difference. Did Steel have any Talent at all? Or was it only repressed?

"O.K," Tom said quietly, "So he's talking like a Teacher. That's never been a fault. It's true what he says. We've got to hold or lose everything. Everything we know." He was silent, watching them, their refusal and their taut attention. He tried to remember how he'd felt at that age. What would have reached him? "We are NOT threatened. Do you hear! We aren't the ones being threatened." His voice was loud, yelling at them, trying to Reach behind the barriers they had both set up, barriers fed with that lust to fight.

Steel heard, with ears, not mind, but he heard. He stopped, let the doors of his mind open slightly, tentatively he held himself, struggled toward balance. He turned tortured eyes to Tom, then Ben, saw the quiet of their faces, their trust. It tipped a balance he never knew was there. He felt something as Tom's Reach met Andy's, the locking of their minds and then, Ben's Joining. The three steady,

THE JOURNEY

so calm, he felt that calm like a tide reaching for him. He wanted to be there, to enter in and know that comradeship. But he wanted this excitement that tore at his guts too. Dave looked at him, his own resistance weakening. He turned from Steel, and met Tom's eyes and then he saw the rightness of their quiet. There was no demand, only a quiet invitation, a stillness like a surge of power. But Steel held himself out. His intelligence battled with the knowledge that he could not longer avoid. HE KNEW, yet he was desiring something that his body remembered, something old and half hidden in these years. He turned away, felt the snap , the pain of that turning. The sense of loss was sharp so that it almost stopped him, but he gathered his will into desire. He ran. Ran and did not look back. Andy's cry,"Steel!" Rang like a bell of grief after him and Steel heard and swayed and stumbled but he ran on. They heard his forlorn but angry cry,"I'll do something if no one else will !"

    Andrew dropped his head, crying and unashamed,"We've got to go. We've got to find the other boys, talk to them. Steel's lost himself." The two boys drew their own minds from the linkage. They were powerful enough that together they could have forced Steel. Could have caught him and drawn him in and they knew that was no holding at all. They could only invite. They knew and grieved at their helplessness. Steel must make his own way.

    They left, went back to town and Ben and Tom began walking rapidly down town to look at the damage and hear the reports from officers who would be there now. The sorrow they felt rippled like a questioning through all their convictions, but only like a brief mist, it drifted and then faded before their knowledge.

CHAPTER ELEVEN

William meets Felix

William did not know why he came. He reflected on this fact as he climbed the slow way to the ice caves .The path way wound steeply through the peaks above Altos. They were carved by the perpetual fall of water through fissures in the rock and by the slow grind of ice through endless winters. People came during summer to climb and visit the fascinating chambers carved so smoothly they looked polished. William loved the climbing, and he had not climbed this trail for several years. Indeed, people seemed to have forgotten the ice caves in the past few years, he was surprised at the realization. Why, he could not imagine. They had been favorites when he was a young man.

He loved the climbing, the cold and utter whiteness of the high snow. Storms in the past days had sifted another coat of white over the highest passes. He had no intention of climbing further than the caves however. Trees to either side, already stunted and bent with the winds, were rich green with summer growth. He sighed, smelling the pines and fir. The twisted little squat shrubs that bore a smooth, round, blue, pear, nourishing and tart, clumped themselves together in clear spaces. Their fruit had given strength to more than one weary climber. He smiled, reaching out a hand to pick one fruit. The contributions of Altos to this Valley, indeed to the world, were every where evident. His city! He was partly responsible for these accomplishements. He stopped a moment, breathing slowly, adjusting himself to this altitude.

To the north the Great River wound, a silver thread through rocky, narrow canyons, but to the south it spread, wide and winding, sparkling through field and forest. He could follow its lit passage for so many miles.It was for him, equal to the Valley itself in majesty. Before he turned again to his climb, he reflected on the urgency that had brought him here, too late in summer for skiing. He had told himself he needed to get away, to take a vacation alone, away from the worry and the pain of the estrangement from the Family. He shook his head, as if dislodging the worry. He need not think of that now. This was a time for peace.

He began again the steady climb, his lift belt buckled around his waist, gave a measure of reassurance. He must be home before dark, which meant that unless he started back in a few hours, he must use the belt. And that would be fine. Depended on how he felt when he left the caves. But when he arrived at the familiar entrances, the brilliance of shining ice inside, green, blue, white, catching the mid day light, he knew this was not where he had to go. And that thought reminded him of his earlier question. Why had he come anyway? And alone? He'd never come alone before but with a laughing, party of friends. He stood looking into the wide entrance, frowned. But where, if not here? There were no caves higher that he knew of. A sudden surge of fear ripped past his control.

THE JOURNEY

Then he felt as though a hand passed over his forehead, a quieting of thought. Shrugging as if to be free of that hand, he found himself searching around for a path that went on, but the familiar trail ended here. And then, a few yards beyond a fall of boulders, he found a narrow trail. Animal trail surely? What could be up there. It looked as though there was only snow and cold rock, not even stunted trees. He might as well walk a little way on. His chest felt tight, uncomfortable.

For a moment he stood, frowning, then as if comforted, his face smoothed, bemused, he began to walk slowly up the steep incline of the trail. Once he began the climb, the tightness in his chest loosened, he felt that this was right. But his mind also seemed released and he wondered what pulled him. But as though guided by an unseen hand, his thoughts veered to settle into a new direction.

Curiousity, stronger than any he'd known for years took hold of him. Something about this trail, he had to see what was there. After about fifteen minutes of twisted climbing, he cut off the trail, climbed through a fracture in the rock, extricating himself from several tight turns and suddenly was out, beyond the rock fall. Directly above he could see a smooth wall, fairly glowing with reddish light. It must be the mid day sunlight gleaming on the ice there. Then he saw there was another cave. One he had never known. The ice walls were shining with their light summer melt and a cold clear little stream ran noisily down among the rocks and disappeared beneath them. The caves faced directly north, the ridges they penetrated ran east and west and little sun entered their cold cavern. Now, he could see the light gleaming, blindingly on the blue ice. He bent his head away.

It was when he stood at the entrance that he realized as though a revelation dawned in his mind, why he was here. The idea was like a sharp stab of recognition. as if he ought to have known that all along. There was someone here to meet him. Someone with tremendous power. Real power, such as he had not thought possible. He felt shrunken almost in that awareness, as though it towered far over and beyond him. He felt fear, vindication, terror, excitement; an eagerness to see that suddenly drew him inexorably. Here was power that a man could look to. He could share in that power!

He found his energy renewed, his feet hastened to that rendevous. He went into the opening of the cave and was disappointed to find no one there. Nothing except large strangely shining caverns filled with their own cold light. The soft colors ran through the ice, It was truly magnificant. He walked deeper into a branching tunnel that made a sharp turn into darkness. He drew his hand light from his pocket and switched it on. At once the light shattered into a thousand colors, shards of brilliance filled the air, rippled over the smoothly curving walls. Why hadn't Altos capitalized on this beauty, bringing travelers who came to see their fascinating city, up here as added inducement?

They could build belt lifts, they could enlarge the ledge make a flat broad porch before the entrance. Remove the boulders that hid it. They could -- . He stopped. Grinned at himself. Already I'm trying to make a business out of this. But he knew, deep inside his mind, he knew why Altos, why no one, had tried to make a summer attraction out of these caves. He couldn't have spoken the reason, but they were not for ordinary use. Again he wondered briefly at this recognition.

He stood transfixed as he walked inside, They were so much larger than the familiar caves below. They were like a cathedral, a Temple,in fact. There was the same hushed quiet within .Then a renewed urgency caught him, like a shrill sharp pain, as though a hook caught in his heart. Drew him to relieve that pain. He ignored all rational objections and went on.

He walked, rapidly obedient, and entered a polished corridor, between blue walls and he had no more need for his flashlight. Through these walls, light streamed, settled into the walls, puddled there, and far at their end, he could see a bright globe of red light. He walked rapidly, sure, his direction clear. Beyond, there would be an end of pain. A strange pain he did not try to explain, it wove through his body like a whisper, relentless.

Light grew. Strange, how could there be red light here? Everything seemed wholly strange to him. Surely, no one could live here. Yet, there seemed the quality of a place occupied, a place used. Somewhere deep within William a tiny resistance, held, tried to lift to his mind, and was drowned.

Some excitement began to fill him, something he could not name, roused in him that urgency but stronger. It reminded him of something, something he wanted to push away, and yet, he couldn't remember. And then, all thought was wiped away by the sound of a whispered voice. As if it occurred in his mind alone. There seemed to be no sound needed. A sibilence, whisper in the air. cold as the frozen cavern. He hesitated, a terror gripping his heart, a refusal and at the same time, a terrible desire. Then the whisper shaped itself into words, " Will? Yes! I'm here! Come swiftly. We've not much time, if you are to be home by dark."

William felt some obscure sense of comforting at that seeming concern for his welfare. That knowledge of his condition. He was puzzled at the desire, the almost uncontrollable yearning that had caught at him, that drew him now. These emotions were not familiar. Nor was that shaft of desire, of WANTING that pierced him , held him as if he were impaled upon it, stuck there. The thought ripped at his comfort and tore it but he shook it away. What he wanted seemed to grow to fill his mind, shudder through his heart and press out all other feeling.

He stepped forward, moving as if the air had become thick and he must press against it. A dull pervading fear,born from some deep unconscious sense of danger rose, pulsed through him,stung in his bones like a sound vibration. He stopped, surprised. He had an over whelming desire suddenly to run, to escape. He felt pulled viciously, his equilibrium gone. He thought he heard Paul's voice, Paul's cry. Did Paul need help? Why would he call, how could he call from so far away?

Then the pulling ended, snapped as if cut. The relief was so great it made him feel victorious. He righted himself, drew his resolve together and brought into focus a life time of discipline. He stood stiff and straight as he began to walk toward a waiting figure. He could not see the face, hidden in the shadow of the cowl that covered it's head. There was only a pool of darkness within it, as if no

THE JOURNEY

face were there at all. Then the figure moved, and a thin shaft of light slid across that darkness, revealing a wide mouth tilted in a strange sardonic smile. Willaim felt himself waver. The distant cry, he had heard before seemed now to return, a muted voice though, like many voices gathered, calling, a thin, desparate cry. For a moment he thought he saw Annette's face flickering there, and then it was gone, the voices dissolved as though a wind had brushed them away.

    He felt rooted, as if he had found what he sought. Had finally come to the source of desire. He wanted to stand closer, to touch, perhaps this One. Walking the intervening space, he stood beside this tall, thin figure. Surprised at the height, he looked up now into that shadowed face. With a gesture , a liquid movement, bespeaking a fine tuned exaggeration of stealth, as if mocking William, the figure threw back the cowl and stood revealed. William caught his breath,unable to move, to shift his fascinated, frightened attention from that mesmerizing face.

    Dark it was, lean and straight nosed, handsome in its way, but possessed of a depth of darkness, a drawing of energy that seemed to impell William into itself, into those narrow flashing eyes. For a second he thought he would literally be swallowed by them, his mind, his emotions even, perhaps his body, the pull was so devastating. He managed to right himself, as if for a second the man had released him. The strength of will necessary to sustain himelf separate had been appalling. It seemed to his watching mind that he watched himself through a long tunnel, that he was being cut off from himself. A thin thread of panic spun itself through that mind and was caught and obliterated in the soft darkness between. He shook himself,and focussed on another thread, one that drew him here, frightening as it was. It was something to do with identity. He felt a great weariness rise from his feet, spread through his body, and he wanted to sit down. With all the power left in him he held that weariness at bay. Held it there, beyond himself. Yes, that was it. He must maintain identity. Somehow before this one, He must not forget who he was. The idea seemed acutely important though he could not think why.

    The one thing William would never have guessed of himself, that he would forget himself,seemed now to be reasonable. He shook his head, with an act of will he broke eye contact long enough to drop his eyes and the separation seemed an infinite relief, but a splintering pain also. "Who -- who are you?" His voice came out rasping, weak. The sound of it angered him and he stood on that anger, using it.

    The sardonic grin widened, a cruel glint shone in those cold piercing eyes. What was their color? He glanced, needing to know, and felt relief that he had passed his gaze across them without getting caught again. A grey-red steely color seemed to move within those eyes. It seemed to William there was no other color, no white, just hard flowing depths of dull red. Was it only the reflection from that solid red light that wove bands of itself through the opaque ice around them? He glanced behind the man, wanting to know, to see, where the light rose, but could not. And he dared not look again into those eyes.

THE PEOPLE OF THE VALLEY

"I am what you have spent most of your life denying." The laugh was short, without amusement. Then suddenly William felt a 'flame' of merriment gusted from that dark form. Yes, it 'flamed' so that it was clearly visible. William's mind raced, he knew, thought and yet, he could not doubt. He felt a lightening of the atmosphere, as though a strain had released itself, a taut holding inside himself. He felt grateful but afraid, for it was as though he had been 'allowed' release."You are a strong man, William. Strong enough to stand before me. I appreciate that. I can use you."

William tried to speak. The demand he heard in that tone terrified him but he was at the same time filled with a strange elation. A promise that he might also stand beside this One. Then he drew into himself, holding himself firm. He would be no man's pawn. Stiffening his resolve, holding himself tightly as though to keep terror at bay. He said," I don't understand. I don't know what I've been denying." The admission seemed suddenly a failure to him, as if he'd been caught out. He wished he could retract the words.

The man before him turned then and beckoned,"Does anyone ever know what it is he denies? But come, let's be more comfortable. Now that you've stood well before me, we can relax a little. No?" He laughed this time, uproarously as if the joke were real.

William followed, bemused, unable to do otherwise. Even still his mind was alert,free enough to wonder at that inability. "Sir, you seem -- you seem - ", he wanted to say,'not to be human' but he said, "strange". Yes, impossible as that is -- you seem something - - Other! What gives me that feeling?"

His guide laughed again, waved one hand and continued until they had passed another series of bends in the tunnels. Then he slid one hand against a wall, the wall silently rotated and there before them was a room, comfortable, full of furnishings of casual living. William was too astonished to speak. His guide turned to invite him in, that sardonic smile wider, a dull, flash of red in those eyes, he said,"Just like in the adventure stories of your youth, William. We enter a secret place." He laughed again, taken with his own jokes.

Then when the door closed, there was warmth, blessed warmth, and Will sank gratefully into a chair. He stared around. A plethora of equipment, a wall studded with various screens, lights flashing and rippling on and off. Every kind of communications device Will knew of and some he had not known of. A jeweled cabinet set only slightly out from the wall in which there were video screens of sophistocated design. Where had he gotten these. They were not on any market Will knew of. Doors in two sides of the room opened out to other rooms, wide, lit, finely furnished, they blazed with jewel colors that were enhanced by actual jewels set into lamps, table tops, and hung as decoration against the walls. Will thought that light that gleamed from those jewels was malevolent, full of a tart intention for his own harm. But their beauty caught at his heart, drew him and he longed to have such beauty for himself.As to their malevolence -- he thought that idea itself must be a result of the strain of this whole event. He must watch himself, he could begin to imagine and ruin all his chances. Chances for what?

THE JOURNEY

He was surprised by that thought, that question. His own mind was absorbing, working on its own, seemed cut off from him again, but now, in a different way.

He looked around, seeing the pure luxury of the furnishings, the paintings that hung on the walls, the sculptures, the rich carpeting, wonder of chandeliers, sparkling like diamonds in the clear warm air. Tremendous wealth must have built this place. So much, so much he could not take it all in.

He could hear sounds, as though mechanical devices of high complexity murmured to themselves, cut off and then on, etc. He felt a momentary desparate desire to flee, to race back down those corridors and fling himself on his belt into space beyond this ice cave, this mountain. At the same time, he felt a longing for this kind of luxury, this kind of power. He quieted himself, watched the man take the long cloak from himself and hang it. He reached out and William took off his outer parka, his cap. His hosts body was so thin that William wondered at its ability to sustain itself. How could a man live -- he cut off his thoughts. There were other more important matters. Why had he never spoken his name, introduced himself? Who was he? Taking on the trappings of - of a Satan, a mythic god of evil. Surely, it was effective. But why did he speak of personal matters? Yet unable to resist, he continued, wrestling to bring a little composure, "Tell me, if you know? If there's anything at all that I deny?"

The man turned then, his face closed, harsh, that cold light again in his eyes. He studied William, "Come, Come, surely you can do better than that. You're talking nonsense. You're denying right now. Don't you know that?" Sudden amusement pushed away the coldness a little, warmed slightly those peircing eyes. Will was silent and then he took a long, steadying breath. He closed his eyes a moment and realized the confusion of his previous thought. He said, sharply. "It's true, you've got me off balance."

The eyes flickered, "Few have kept balance so well."

"You enjoy that!" Without waiting he pressed on, "If you called me here, how did you do it. I got no message. And yet, yet, I thought I must come." The wish to be relieved of his fear was great. He waited, knowing that something was wrong with what he had said.

Taking his eyes from William, the man sat down. Leaned and clapped his hands. A figure appeared in the darkness of the doorway, then without words, turned to bring immediately a tray on which were steaming cups of brew. Sweetmeats and breads in gleaming silver trays and generous slices of meats, gave off aromas that reminded William of his hunger. His host gestured that they should help themselves and said, First, please sit down, and we can talk." He picked up glass and sipped. "Now! What do you deny? One: that I exist at all. Two: that I can influence your actions." This time he waved aside William's protest and went on, "No! Pay attention! Look at me. I am not this --- this poor body you see, this bit of bone and flesh. I use it and I will use you just as easily. But your use is important to the Valley, that is why it is of value to me. You are a man building a great Valley, You have plans, plans that would transform that Valley below and perhaps it's people. Isn't that so?" Thus, appealing to William's dream, his pride, and his loyalty, he set his net carefully.

"I do, I want this growth and the development of our Valley. Of our people. What Valley citizen doesn't?" He knew he was avoiding the myriads of questions crowding his mind. Knew they led only to madness. He would accept what appeared, and ignore what created the appearance. To do otherwise, led only to madness, to what was intolerable. The breath of it stung against the back of his watching intelligence, thrusting to probe, to ask, and he denied that thrust.

With a sigh, like a disappointment, his host relented. The intensity of his manner softened. He saw that he must take a little slower path with this one. "And that is precisely what I want. Development. But that development must be in the right direction, must it not?"

William nodded, puzzled, aware there was more here than he could grasp. But something drew so magnetically at his attention, that he fell into its sway, an attraction, promise of fulfillment of a need within himself, tantalizing. So close! He clung to that promise, unspoken, but so sharp. His host went on,"You are right William, your understanding of the problems has merit. You recognize the danger of that City. You and a few others. It is necessary that you teach that fear to your people before they fall also into danger."

William was caught off guard. His previous questions, fears faded. The soft, smoothness of this voice, so different, persuasive, relaxed his vigil, relieved his fear. "What is your name, Sir? I need to know how to call you?"

The man smiled again, his eyes flickered with their grey red light and he said,"Some call me 'The Dark One'." He watched William closely, and saw skepticism in his eyes. He grinned in satisfaction and added,"But that is not true. I am merely hidden. As are the hearts of the people, as are their dark selves. Hidden! As is your's Will." His voice had become almost tender, gentle, and his eyes swept gently over William's face as if in caress. "You must call me Felix, Lord of the Ice."He grinned again engagingly, a friendly amused grin."Yes, that's it. It sounds fine, doesn't it?"

William nodded, accepting. Surely, any one who called himself Lord must be suspect, but the manner of this Felix, this One, gave William no doubt that the name fit. He thought of dreams some of the Builders had voiced, and shook his head. He had not shared them, had he? Now he said,"Then, Felix," he almost added,"my Lord" but shook off the impulse, "Then you have ways to influence our people? You were able to call me here without -- messengers?"

Felix hesitated, evaluated quickly and shifted his plan."No Will, my senses are perhaps sharper, and even yours Will, are sharper than most". It was with that he turned to point to a carved shape of wood and gold, a sculpture, a work of such perfection it brought a sigh of envy from William as he moved to examine it more closely.

"It's beautiful. Utterly beautiful!" His eyes were soft, pleading, desire burst through him, desire that no jewels had ever wakened to this degree. He suddenly wanted such a piece, a thing of utter perfection. Felix nodded, a faint ironic smile turning his thin lips. William contained himself,"But I don't see how -"

"Of course, it's a device I developed myself. I can send to any mind there in the Valley that has sufficient strength to receive. The message is not one of words, more one of intent. I have not -- used it yet for words, for precision." He started to say more, then stopped."

William nodded, satisfied. His eyes still moving jealously over the figure in which lay this wonderful ability. Machine and art, welded into perfection. He longed to hold it in his hands, let his fingers slide over the perfect lines. He shook his head, All Altos metalurgists searched for such a combination. He asked,"What good then, what good if it does not --"

"It brought you here."

" Then there have been others?" He felt another kind of jealousy, a bitter prodding, that surprised him.

Yes, but few with your powers, William. With your kind of mind!" Felix watched William swallow that bait without hesitation. The pride he had in his fine mind would serve well, he thought.

"Yes, but then -- " The power of it, the insidious power of it hit William, and he sat down abruptly. "It not only influences but it controls. I could not resist. I didn't know why I was coming, nor even where. I came as if compelled. I did not think, I simply came!" He was looking down into his clasped hands, feeling a great ball of anger building in his chest, anger tangled with a fierce longing, and that longing to be so owned, so cared for, so held, dominated. It fought and then swiftly -- as if refusing the grossness of battle, sucked out the anger and won. He was utterly lost to that now waxing longing. His eyes lifted, fastened themselves on that now sardonic face, the bleak promise in those ageless eyes. He no longer cared. To be so possessed, and to possess such wonders as that sculpture. He thought surely Felix would give it to him. Give it! As a sign of his favor. He no longer allowed the shreds of doubt to lift into consciousness. He stood,"My Lord Felix, What shall we do?"

The arrogance of the question amused Felix. But he hid his amusement in a frown. "You are wise! There is not much time. There are those in the Valley who would open the Seal of the Silent City and bring its strength to flow. To open that Seal would bring devastation down on you. It would release into the Valley forces you could never escape. It is your strength, William, your eloquence, your power with the people that is needed to turn that tide. To interest the people in things that will give pleasure, happiness and bring back that control over the Earth that they used to have. You can shut the doors on those emerging evils that you have suspected and that are infecting your enemies."

"My enemies? You mean those who court the City? The ones who begin to play with the old psychic powers?"

"The same, some may even be your own Family. And you must stand firm, even in that pain. You have that power, William, it is evident that you do."

William felt a great swelling of pride. He repressed ruthlessly the sudden burst into view of anguish of something lost. A terrible loss that had no name. He would -- could-- help. Save even his own Family. He could be the emissary into the Valley. The thought made him happy. He looked about quickly, noticing things, seeing the room anew, feeling himself set apart and honored, a part of this power. "Is there no companion devise to this one, by which I could call you or hear your own call more clearly? It was most faint,,you know. I had to -- respond almost unconsciously." He did not hear the naked desire in his own voice.

Felix nodded, "Yes, you respond unconsciously,you respond from within where you have hidden yourself from yourself. That is right. But there is another device. It is yours, it is slightly smaller, but it is exactly a replica. It will send a message, and it will receive mine. I think with a little adjustment it can send spoken words as well." He got up, went to a small cabinet, and took from it a duplicate of the figure. Gleaming, softly radiant, it nevertheless carried an aura of darkness. Will wondered suddenly like a shaft of reasserted questioning, who the figure represented. What ancient God had had such a form? Felix settled in his chair, watching the transformation of William at the moment. He had thought this one would be able to stand firm at least this long and he had been right. He had estimated him well. The sculpture was as good a focus as any and William need never know that the 'divice' was amplified by the Talents of Felix himself.

William held the small form, jewels worked into the form like bright light cutting through shadows, made it brilliant with color. He held it reverently,,his palms slightly sweating with the avid satisfaction of having it. He tore his eyes away, and turned to his benefactor. "Then I must go?" The fact seemed clear. He stood.

"Yes, you must go before it is too late. You wore a belt, use it, you won't have time to walk home." Absently will strapped the belt on. Felix touched the wall, and great doors swung back on the other side of the room. Surprised, William found himself standing at the edge of the trail down. He stood on a little apron of ice, notched for foothold, and still gleaming in the evening light . Felix stood a moment, watching him and then the doors closed. William was alone before the vast panarama of the Valley below. The beauty of it made Will catch his breath. How many times, he thought, and yet, it is never the same. He adjusted his belt, set his thumb on the power switch, shuffled his feet, in a strange reluctance, and then cast himself off into the evening air. He cradled the small figure in his deepest pocket with one hand curled around it. A great passion of direction swept through him. A fierce intention. Then far beneath, nearly crushed to silence, a soft weeping for a terrible loss.

As he fell lightly, shifting his direction so he could see the ski slopes, he watched a lone cross country skier passing through a clump of pines. Then he was above the city slope, empty at this late time, it's lower fields green with thick deep grasses. His mind turned back to the interview. He grimaced at the memory of his 'Felix, my Lord,' it repulsed him suddenly,but justifying, with the logic with which he would formerly have searched his own divided mind,he refused the senses that felt repulsion. With that refusal came a new hope of comforting that pushed deeper the objecting voice. He wanted to accept. He would not search himself.It was a relief to accept so.

His fingers found again the form in his pocket, the exquisite treasure and all shame swept away. Then without expecting it, he rememberd with total recall, a flood of images, that visit to the Black Mountain Lodge. Greyson! Yes, that was his name. Greyson was somehow like this one, only not so -- perhaps a little less. No much less! But they both had that quality of power that he felt drawn too. Relentlessly his reason pushed forth the knowledge that he also shrank from both men. But he shut off that thought. They were both attractive to a mesmerizing degree somehow. He wanted to know how to develop that same power. He wanted to have that power. And from these two, surely he could learn.

He felt a conflict rising through his mind, a question that insisted on being spoken, a doubt that rubbed itself raspingly against his pleasure. He shook himself. It was not time for such thought. He could and would resist it and free himself of such conflict.But he had been educated in the Valley and though he had control enough that he could choose, he was ignoring the fact that he had also been taught never to ignore a question that persisted through strong emotion. It was necessary to at least give it thought. Right now, the elation he felt blinded him to his avoidance. Perhaps Felix would have approved in this instance, of William's use of denial.

The next morning, in Santiago, in a room in the great western trunk of the city which stood like a wall against the green of forest around it, men and women gathered. The massive stone-steel walls of the supports of this sky city were like cliffs that resembled grey slabs of swiss cheese, full of the round and oblong holes that were windows and narrow dark openings running along the edges of each upper floor to supply circulating air for all of this massive in-trunk world. Hundreds of rooms and halls, runways for transportation, and manufacturing plants, filled the vastness of the foundations of this astonishing city. Rooms here were easy to reserve for meetings and so Greyson had arranged for this monthly gathering, to inform his people from a dozen towns around the Valley.

They came in the early hours, slipping in silently, filling the seats, getting drinks and a hot roll or small cake, from the Auto Serv and settling down . Their talk was quiet but continuous, a gentle hum through the carpeted room. Outside the day was hot and dry, people sought the shelter of the globe buildings and the canopied 'Leaf' plazas where the high city felt the breezes even when the ground level was left breathless in the heat. But in the room where the people waited, the air was cool and fresh.

They had waited no more than a few minutes when Greyson himself appeared. He entered swiftly, as if hurried, but his eyes swept from face to face, smiling, greeting, making contact and giving each person the sense that he personally was touched. The talk subsided, and by the time he had reached the small table at the front, it was quiet. They waited.

There were twenty men and ten women in the room and they seemed not to mind the wait as Greyson examined swiftly the boxes stacked near the walls behind him, then began to look over some papers that had been placed on the table by a small man in brown . The man stood, his hands clasped in front of him, a posture of adoration almost, watching the 'leader', himself pleased to be in this presence. Greyson nodded to him, reached a hand tentatively then withdrew as the little man went to sit down.

Softly, so they had to be utterly quiet to hear, Greyson began to speak. "You're all here to pick up the materials for your town meetings. We've not had too much difficulty getting these new holoroom projectors, or the films, but we need more than we have. Every town ought to have such equipment and so far our supplies are limited, so we want you to invite nearby towns to share these. The task now is to get as many people as possible to hear you, and to get more of our people on your town councils. That's essential. Through government you will have power. Mostly, today I'm interested in your problems and questions." He paused, his eyes flicking here and there, touching as if alive against the faces, one by one, and each touch seemed to knit a tie, a recognition. He smiled, a thin calculating smile, and his eyes narrowed.

"We need more of our own people active. Have we new members lately?"

"Yes, we've got invitations and information on Video News every other day for two weeks. We've got new people coming. There'll be more." He smiled broadly, confident. He didn't mention that out of all who came to find out what the builders taught, few signed themselves members.

A man stood, his face flushed at his own temerity, "I've been watching the people in the south west, I'm from Toppletown, near the lake, and we see too much of the work of those witches. We've vowed to weed them out, but how can we do it alone. We need help. They're already settled in the councils and they have positions of authority in the industries, but worst of all, the very teachers of the Learning Centers are such and I'm not only referring to those called Master Teachers." He hesitated, his eyes far off, frowning,"What THEY are I don't know, but I suspect they're witches of another kind." His face squeezed in a tremendous frown so that it was darkened. "Surely, you must know they're in every town." His voice peaked, splitting its sound until it was a rasping squeeck. He looked around, wanting affirmation and saw several nods.

Greyson, raised one hand, then let it fall, and his smile didn't change."You're right, Donald." He appeared not to notice the man's surprise at his use of his name."It's that that we're here for. The videos, and holorooms in your town will help. People will begin to come to spend time there, they will enjoy, and find pleasures they've never known. That pleasure will bring them into your reach. And it'll also wake them up to what's wrong among us. Those who're already obsessed with that witchery you speak of, will be known, those who aren't, will join us." He was so calm he seemed cold,as though nothing threatened at all.

The man Donald, waved a hand, then still frowning, cried out,"How can you be so calm about it. Don't you see the Valley is getting more and more lost to us? I see these people every day and our very Convictions protect them. They prevent our action against them."

THE JOURNEY

Greyson, frowned, briefly, then replaced the frown with his smile. "You're very anger is what we need, my friend. Your anger will help to change things. You must remember that through history people clung to such things and were defeated as soon as those who saw their fault gained strength. It takes time. You will find yourself in those position of power. You deserve that!" His smile was sending an approval, a stamp of recognition that at first puzzled then pleased Donald so he finally shuffled awkwardly for a moment then pivoted and sat down, a smile on his face.

For a moment there was silence, then swiftly came questions, angry demands, fearful queries. Greyson listened for several moments. A large woman, exquisitely dressed, attractive, obviously intelligent, and with jewels that sparkled around her neck and wrists, stood, "My partner and I have a tavern already built at the intersection of the Highways between Barnes and Cedar City. We've begun to gain customers, but not enough. Why can't you help us get more business?"

"Ah, you've done very well!" His eyes gleamed in approval, and she looked around smiling, Then he asked, "The Vagabonds haven't resisted your presence there on their Highway? "

"How can it be called theirs? It's a public roadway, isn't it?" She was nettled. But she added, "No, they actually ignore us, and we thought they'd bring us business."

"Then be glad they do, just now. Later, business will come. They could have made much trouble, you know. You're doing well, just what we all must do. Get control of the Highways. Remember the Highway has only been Vagabond territory by common consent, not any legal control. They can't prevent your business." He looked thoughtful, "However, you've got to have patience, the business will pick up soon when we get these holorooms set up and people learn. They've forgotten how to enjoy themselves. We've got to give them options. Then there will be business for such Taverns all along the Highways." He bowed slightly to her, smiling expansively and she raised one hand toward him as if to touch him, then, flustered, sat down.

A big, thick set man stood, cried out in a booming voice, "When can we begin to build the new weapons you showed us? All we have now are old guns, a few museum pieces, no missiles, flying fighters, etc. We've no modern equipment such as those we saw at your Black Lodge Fair. How can we get them built? There's only one gun manufacturing plant in entire Valley."

A dark haired young man leaped to his feet, whirling toward the speaker. "What would we use them for? Attack our own people?"

"Why not, when they're practicing evil?" That was a shout from a big man in the back of the hall.

"They're our people nevertheless!" The young woman turned to stare back at him with defiance. "You can't hurt people. We're not like the old ones."

"The old ones had good sense, they'd never of allowed things to get this bad. Nor would they've let such as witches live among them."

The heavy man lifted his arms, nodding vigorously, "That's exactly right!

They're the ones we've got to run out of the Valley. The 'Light Heads 'we call them. They go off like idiots, looking off at the air as if they see something there, or hear it. You never know when they're going to fade out. Its a good name." He laughed and the others smiled, nodding. The dark haired boy started again to speak, looked unsure, then frowning sat down.

They began to talk more to one another, calling out the names of those they feared, questioning, recounting stories that prodded their anger. The whole group drew into a fierce unity. Greyson watched and nodded. They needed no more of his own energy to keep them going. The talk turned finally to the Silent City and that brought increased angers.

A fair young man stood up,shook his fist, "We'll blow her up, we've got a plan. We'll not have it any longer. People don't know the evil there and it's got its power down here in our Valley." He turned to the dark haired young man,"You, you don't want to hurt anyone, well, if they listen to sense now one needs to get hurt!" He turned to look around at the others, "What are the rest of you doing? To many sit on their fat asses and let the crazies take over everything. A man hasn't got a chance of getting anywhere. Jed's right, we need those weapons, Mr. Greyson. How can we get them?" He stood, defiant, frowning into Greysons face, his hands grasping the chair in front of him, so his burly arms stuck out akimbo. "We've got to fight, understand that? It's a word we've got to get used to. This Valley is a place of fools, too afraid of each other to fight."

Greyson only smiled, which naturally infuriated the boy. but before he could speak again, Greyson said,seeming to calculate his words to inflame and yet to control. "It's a pleasure to see a young man with such fire, Edward. You'll help this cause more than you know. You keep talking about it, just the way you are now, it'll bring other young men into the work." He nodded satisfied as he saw Edward's pause, frown and then pleased look. He went on,"But Son, if you're to accomplish much, you might want to be more subtle around our enemy. It's not time yet to create trouble is it? We need to be stronger before we speak out this way."

The boy bridled,"I'm tired and my friends are tired of holding back, of always being so careful. Why should we be? What's to be lost? I say arrest those Light Heads. Arrest them and make them get to a Healer, or -- or " he seemed at a loss for alternatives. He looked puzzled at that fact.

"It's the devils own work there. Something evil there without doubt." A woman, turned to Greyson,"But it ought to be first. How can these new holorooms get that City emptied out? Or stop these people who do that thing called Mind reaching. That scares me."

He shrugged,"They can't, except to make people want something done about it. If enough want it done it 'll be done, you know. We've got to get people's minds on something more real, more human. Down to earth. You each have a set of this new equipment here in these boxes. You've got your credit chips already for them and you take them home." He laughed,"They're not just to teach, mind you. Just as I promised, they'll make you money. A lot of it." He turned to the woman who had the tavern already built,"Gladys, just get this set up in your place, I gauarantee there'll be business." He was about to speak again when an interruption in the hallway made him turn.

Greyson nodded to a man at the back who went to open the door. Tom stood there with a young man. Both looked very serious, Tom stern. Greyson was annoyed,spoke curtly, "Your business?

Tom nodded, glancing around the room, came to rest on Greyson at the front, his face showed no mark of recognition. But his heart hammered and was immediately quiet again. Tom knew well who Greyson was, but he wanted to deny what he knew. No man could be what Greyson appeared to be. He drew a tight breath and said, "Michael from Denlock and Gary from Adwin. They are here." The statement brooked no denial. He looked around, and nodded curtly to his deputy, Monroe, a young man with hair so white it shone silver- gold, and eyes like blue jewels. His narrow angular face hardened his beauty and made it masculine. He drew a breath, visibly ill at ease and then, resolutely strode forward to two young men who had stood when their names were called. Monroe spoke without a trace of nervousness, only his Teacher could tell he trembled. "We are sorry. We must arrest you for the crimes of bombing the Temple in Adwin and that in Denlock, and for inciting riot among our folk." He held out a hand in which were two sets of handcuffs.

"We incited no riot", Michael said, angry, his fear showing little, "The damn fools wouldn't even fight with us. Wouldn't do anything but stand there."

"Ah, No, Mike, you forget the ones who went into the fire. The two boys and a girl, walked right in they did." Gary seemed still shaken by that sight, though it had been days ago."

"And proved just what we've been preaching against." Michael cried out, encouraged now by the deputy's calm, questioning face, "If you want crime, look to them. Nothing natural about that. That fire doused itself right where they walked, just went out like a river had poured on it. Nobody but a witch could do that. They're the ones you ought to arrest." He turned with an angry face to Greyson, "You Sir, you said it would be effective, that it'd wake the people up to what's wrong. Now tell the mayor, we'll not sit in any jail for nothing."

The faces of the crowd all turned expectantly to Greyson. He stood immobile, taut and seemingly calm. Finally he said,"If you break the law, boys, whatever the reason, you suffer the result. It is so for us as well as for them." At their swift hard intake of breath, he held up a hand,"The work of reform has its own suffering, and those who suffer are those who are martyred to the cause, with special rewards later!"

Tom spoke then,"You are not martyred for small cause, Lad." He cast an angry eye at Greyson, so the man HAD instigated this. "Haven't the Temples been damaged? Thanks to those three young ones they're not hurt as bad as they might have been, but you must know that there's one death attributed to that bombing at Denlock. This boys, is not a little thing that can be repaired or healed. It's murder!"

A horrified whisper loud enough to be heard in the silent room,"Not in the Valley, no murder in years!"

For several moments there was a stunned silence. Then Michael whirled and cried out, facing the crowd now, he yelled, "You fucking Light heads, that's what you are, you, Mayor and all the others. You're ruining our Valley. Then when we try to do something you make it worse. If you hadn't started that witch stuff, it'd never've happened. You want to put anyone who fights for the Valley behind your fucking bars. Never allow a bit of change. Well, we won't have it." He drew a deep breath, "You're afraid to live like men, you live like women."

"The women I've known in this Valley, it would honor us to be like them." Tom said quietly, but Monroe took hand cuffs, turned to grab Michael by the shoulder and whirl him toward himself. His fist was clenching then unclenching, unable to tighten but his face was full of anger. Michael, as if relieved, swept up his fists covering himself with one, he hit Monroe's jaw with the other. Monroe staggered back, his arms both reaching -- one fist clenched hard. Then, suddenly as if a cord had snapped inside Monroe, he dropped both arms, his face fell, the anger draining out. He turned to Tom. "Thank's Sir. I really missed it, didn't I?" Tom's face was impassive but his eyes twinkled,"You never closed, Son, you received my Reach. That's not bad recovery." Then he suddenly grinned, went to Monroe, picked up the cuffs, caught Michael's wrist with one hand and drew it behind him to catch the other wrist. Michael, struggled, but Tom's movement was so fast he was caught before he fully realized. Mike yelled,"God damn it, somebody do something. Are we to be caught like rats right here in our own place? Isn't there any justice? "He nearly sobbed out, "Don't you realize we'll be charged with murder now? After all, we did it for you!"

Greyson shook his head,"Not for me, young man, not for me, but for the Valley and your own people."

But Tom shook his own head, " Calm down Son. It was not you who killed them, it was their own effort to quell the explosion. In the Denlock Temple, a young woman was there, and felt the detonation readying itself, and she ran to stop it, with mind control and -- she was not fully trained, she stopped much of the explosion but not enough. It killed her." He stopped, "I don't know how the court will decide as to blame. It was her choice. But it was your cause."

Gary's eyes were brimming, he shook his head to clear them, angry at that, grieved at the death,after all, he had been Valley trained a well as any other. He cried out,"No, No! There was to be no one harmed. No one harmed." He turned in accusation toward Greyson and Tom did not miss that movement.

But Greyson's eye was turned away, and the people in the room were looking shamefaced, or frowning in defiance at one another. No one looked at the two boys arrested, except Monroe. Greyson turned finally to look at them, an ironic smile on his face, his hand raised as if about to say something. Tom's eye met Greyson's, his own instantly filled with question, then attraction, then, as if discovering something, with astonishment that faded to compassion, to sorrow. The change brought a black fury to Greyson's face for a moment, brief, passing and immediately in control again, he looked quietly smiling.

Michael drew what seemed to Tom a terrible ragged breath, his face flushed, his eyes were darting from one to another and finally he held them steady, looked at Tom, straightening,"You! You don't hold us guilty?"

Tom's eyes steeled, penetrating, but the boy held firm, and his eyes softened, "You could not have known the danger or you would not have done what you did. What you're guilty of will be found out by the courts."

In a voice rasping with hesitance, Gary said,"Then for our ignorance you'd forgive us!" It was a statement, accepted with surprise. "How about the girl -- her family - surely they -?"

"We are her family and we mourn, but her personal family mourns greatly." He was silent, reflecting," Perhaps a judgement of us?" then he frowned and said, "But neither we nor they seek further mourning for you, so I know they think as little of you now as possible. Their loss is great. Perhaps at this moment they have even little pity."

The two young men, standing with bent heads now in the silent room, seemed girdled with a heavy burden. Greyson, moved, began to speak, wanting to break this sympathy, this guilt. But Gary raised his head, met Tom's eyes and asked softly,"How can we understand such thinking? How can a man who thinks so, feels no fury for revenge, be Mayor -- do his job anyhow?" he wanted absolution, wanted to free himself with their hate.

Tom held his gaze, though it sought to leave,"How can any Mayor think or feel differently? You all are our people."

In the instant of silence that theatened to last long, Greyson broke in,"Well, there! You will not be deserted by your own people and we will bring defense for you." They didn't look at him, but turned as Monroe began to guide them out.

Then he added,"Don't resist, accept the law. We will have the law to ourselves soon. There is nothing to lose and everything to win. Remember that we will be with you."

They left and the room was quiet for some moments, then Greyson calmly began issuing the boxes to each one, helping to set them on carryalls to be taken to their flight grid. No one had anything else to say.

CHAPTER TWELVE

Beginning of the Journey

    A week after William's secret journey to the ice caves, Jessie stood in the garden that surrounded the Hall. She surveyed the scene before her, cluttered with autumn leaves. Chrysanthemums and late annuals bloomed in brilliant splendor, the rose garden was fragrant, and shrubs, some fruiting and blooming still, were littered with the leaf drip from the trees. Indian summer would come in another month when the frosts of September would give way to the final blaze of warmth and color. But now, these early leaves, bright and drifting dry in the air, would have to be raked or blown into containers and carried to the compost circle. On this day it had been cold in the morning but it was warming rapidly in the clear sunlight. Clouds hung in great white piles here and there to the east. It was a time when the breath of winter whispered against the trees of that grand time of sleep during heavy storms of winter. Light shining through the trees and vines of the pathways, still heavy with multicolored leaves, reflected and magnified colors in the rain washed air. It was the great beauty of the dying time. So much beauty that people sometimes found themselves bemused, lost in it. Sometimes even, there were those who must close their eyes against such beauty, its overwhleming splendor an aching of the heart.

    Yet mostly it poured into the eyes and nose, rousing joy and it lay upon their minds like pure delight, even though it might touch their hearts with melancholy. In these days the very Soul seemed at times to have loosed itself outward in the softly echoing dance of the universe separating and uniting so delicately that its farthest stars echoed into the smallest balance, pure and fragile, yet strong and unrelenting. It was as if the instant of its call hung between time and eternity and questioned them both. She thought, 'Great beauty of Earth lifts the mind, even as it fills the heart so full it is a sweet pain.'

    Jessie knew that there was much to understand, much to be brought into balance, and she must this day hold herself ready, be available for those who would come. She thought she would busy herself with clearing up, making order out of the lovely garden chaos. Winds of the night had scattered leaves over the land. Now the golden willow leaves fluttered like tiny slivers of gold through the still air and walnut leaves drifted, reflecting sunlight through their veined shapes. Large black oak and maple leaves fell faster, orange in the light. Jessie wore low boots and thin tights under a simple garment that fell below her knees and gently drew in at her waist. It was a soft grey blue, made of very light fibre of wool and plasilk. It seemed now to float around her as she moved.

    She began to slowly and carefully rake the leaves into piles, clearing the patio, the stone and the beds of flowers, straightening and lifting the heavy heads of chrysanthemums until they nodded gently back and forth, free of weight. She felt the impact of these autumn colors on her mind and body. She enjoyed this work, felt the nourishment of its energy. The odors of drying vegetation, of recent rain soaked into old stalks, of the flush of autumns final bloom, of the air itself, penetrated into her body, her flesh. She breathed in deeply, enjoying pure pleasure of this moment, the movement of her body with the work of raking . Then she heard footsteps behind her and a long heavy sigh.

Jessie did not turn. She waited and went on with her work until Jerry called her. "Jessie could you help me? I've got this strap hung up and I'm going to have to take the whole thing off again. But if you'll just pull this through here -- " he guided her hands with his voice ."Yes, there, through that. Now, I think I can get it. . Thank you."

He was dressed in knee boots into which his bright blue trousers had been tucked and a blue shirt and bright gold jacket of double weave material designed for warmth. He was planning to spend an hour riding the sky. He met her eyes as they finished and stood back."How do I look? Like a daring sky raider from the children's stories?"

She laughed and nodded, "Yes, you do. But if I were going to be that high, I'd want a hat to keep my wits about me."

"Oh, I have one here." He pulled a soft, warm toboggan from his pocket. I thought to stop at the Temple before I go, but I'll do my best meditation in the sky." He frowned briefly, then his face cleared in a smile."There's so much to think about, so much to balance. I need this solitude."

She nodded and turned back to her work. Later she heard a small puffing sound as he left the Temple to begin his flight. She turned, watched the small blue and gold shape ascend, like a brilliant leaf falling into space. He stopped his climb, tipped his body a little in a salute and then with a final wave, soared in a ninety degree angle so high that he was only a small dot there against the blue. He drew his arms and legs tight against his body , dipped and turned , rose and fell, lay out flat on the wind then lifted again and dived through a small cloud. He was playing, enjoying the wonder and silence and movement. She felt a moment of envy.

She remembered the near obsession that her own contemporaries had felt with these belts when they were first made available to everyone. How they had all tried themselves on them. It had been dangerous because there had been few good rules at first and no training. Children now had to pass tests before being given their cards. She shrugged,she had spent enough time in the air one way or another to do her. Now, the leaves must be raked. Thinking could be done here as well. As she worked she began focussing, aware, intensely aware of her movements, her surroundings and listening to silence to see what rose to view. In a clear stillness, she breathed, a mind breathing, a heart breathing. No thought interfered. She was an action of movement, she was the leaves before the rake, the rake itself, the sky, and she was all that was around her,being.

Then, shaping like fireflies in a blue evening, thoughts came. They were the action of a small part of her attention. She saw an image, of what she knew had not yet happened. In and out, a rhythm that ebbed and flowed,she was her thought, the leaves, the plants uncovered and making a final bloom before they shrank back from winter. And then, she drew herself to one stream of thought to discover where it led.

Jerry would be ready for the Journey, the knowledge was clear and welcome. His spirit, his blithe joy and courage cheered her. There were others ready too. She felt a secret exultation swell her heart. They would be ready when the time came.Then her thoughts increased and began to clump, and she turned to them. William, and all those who walked unknowingly in his path, would not be ready. So, although there would be many who would be making the Journey and there were many who already had, unknown to their fellows, there would also be those, enough to bring sorrow, who would not even know there was a Journey. The sorrow of that leavened the joy. She reminded herself that eventually every human alive would join their fellows in that upward Journey, even though it might take several more life times. Through such absorptions of being alive in a material world, and then later, in more subtle worlds, life prepared itself for LIFE.

She went on working,content. Rose was in town with the Council again, distrust seemed to be seeping through the hearts of people. Too much distrust and there could be imbalance. She frowned, then brightened., Trust must be held inviolate within herself. She must meet what was, not what she wished to be. She stopped finally, resting with one arm on the rake handle, to look up again for Jerry. He was hanging now, as if sunk in the atmosphere , drifting, drifting, his body rising and falling in rhythmic response to the wind and his balancing weight. The power unit was on maintainance. and he was lost in an atmosphere of sky and light. Lost in Silence!

She knew how powerful that could be. How stimulating to consciousness, to awareness itself. It would awaken other qualities in that young man. Intuitive mind dominated in that stillness, its open end expanding into Mind itself to allow experiencing that would have stalled the thinking mind. Awareness, acute and all understanding, could develop there in that quiet. Years of meditative practice would yield Jerry's mind to what was beyond it's ordinary attention. These new minds were strong two fold minds, integrated with that Higher Mind that she knew as Soul and that drew the fledgling consciousness into Itself, beyond familiar limits. She smiled, rremembering the hours of teaching for each of those families for whom she was responsible. Now she met with individuals, Jerry was one of those she must make time for. Perhaps today --. And Steve too. And others, she had not seen alone lately. She frowned, impatient that she sew up all the loose seams. Then she laughed at herself. She must not worry. There were many like Jerry who deliberately chose to seek greater awareness for clear vision. They would know what to do when the time came.

There in that reach of attention the intuitive mind was prepared for receptiveness. Jessie had seen the young children playing with these skills in games taught them by Master Teachers. They practiced it to find their 'Reach', and their control of their mental capacity. When she had been young, the greatest urge had been toward physical risk. Now, that same urge to danger, to touch against danger, was one of mental risk. And so both were joined in sky games, in games beneath the sea, even in games far in space. In this Valley, there was conscious willingness to risk oneself in spiritual recognition. In possibility of consciousness .She sighed, there had been so much growth among human kind . People felt a sense of power they could not have named. But that power inflamed their hearts, their minds. It cleared their vision to see one another as individuals precious to themselves.

    Jessie reflected on those debates, fiery and sharp that she had heard among young people. Debates about the nature of life, debates about possibility , and including obvious knowledge of intuitive skills, perceptions.The remembrance comforted certain nagging worries that she could not seem to quell. Because she was one who worried. She smiled at herself. In the past few months the Master Teachers had worked to repair their neglect, to educate and guide those rapidly expanding minds. To openly ask for questions. They were doing good work. The children were bombarding them with questions now. Asking had become important and right. It was common among them to take off on such flights as Jerry's into that absorbing sky. They KNEW what they sometimes could not express well in thought. And it was a conscious knowing.

    The piles of leaves had grown. The wind, so far quiet, could scatter them all again. She must get them bagged. She glanced at the sky, and saw a thin band of clouds riding in from the eastern mountains. Weather changing! She stood a moment. She always hated the time when the bright leaves must be stored away to rot. But left here, they would rot anyway. She leaned the rake against the wall and turned to get the bags from the storage shed, when she heard whistling. Steve came from the Hall, tossing an apple in the air as he walked. He came near when he saw her, "Jessie, the leaves look so beautiful and now you're worrying that they have to go in the compost?" he grinned widely.

    She laughed, "Yes, I suppose it must strike everyone the same." She glanced up at the brilliantly laden trees."There'll be plenty more for weeks to come."

    "I don't know about eveyone but it always seems a sadness to me. The easiest thing is to get it over with. Besides you'll notice the weather's changing. We'd better be quick, I think. he took a bite of his apple and stood a moment regarding her. "The wind won't be here for a while and I'll help so we'll have it done soon."

    She felt glad of his willingness. So now, Steve was here and it was time for their talking. "You have time to help me then?"

    "I've just finished with the job I was doing, a sitting job inside at the computer. My brain is tired. I'd like to do this. My body only lets me sit for so long and then it refuses." He took another bite of his apple,"Maybe we could have a talk   after?"

    She nodded,pleased,"Or perhaps while we work!"

    He shook his head, serious, "No,Jessie, it might not work. What I want to talk about is too serious a matter to talk about while we're working. It needs focus. "

He held out his half eaten apple and said, "If you'll hold this until I get the bags and the vacuum unit, we'll have this done in no time." He went off to the storage room behind the hall and she turned to look over the Valley.

The Green River flashed among the yellows and reds, lavender and blues of the trees and fields. Autumn wild flowers were scattered through the meadows. Many crops were already harvested and those fields lay softly rumpled with the thick stalks and leaves left from the taking of grain or fruits. Companion plants, raised with every vegetable crop, were still green but bent, their own fruits gone. This heavy plant fiber would be rotted into the Earth and cushion the coming rains. She could see along the pathways forking out from the Highway a group of children and Vagabonds gathering fruits and nuts. Vines covered two stone huts along this end and children crawled over the flat roofs picking that harvest too. She smiled wondering whether the Vagabonds helped with harvests for the sharing of food, or for the pleasure of working with town children each season. Surely, they were a wise people. They knew that isolation and strangeness had bred the misunderstandings that led to battles and wars of the past. Such work built understanding. People of the Way were not dependant on town help, ever. They had resources of woodland and field that Town people ignored.

Jessie remembered with a sigh when her own children had served on the Harvesting gangs. They had seen it as a lark, another game. making fun of it, singing, vying with one another to do a crop better or faster. That had been so vastly different from her own youth when work was done in silence and separation. Now she heard the music, and a group of dancers moved from behind a low hedge . Musicians and dancers kept the workers entertained when they worked with the Vagabonds. Sometimes workers stopped to dance a round, or exchanged with one of the players. It was a time of laughter and fullness. Since learning was life long, no one was pressed to 'finish school' as she had been. Any one of these children could earn credit enough for a basic living by the time they were twelve. But they wanted more, and would go on. She watched with a trace of sadness. This kind of beauty, of joy, would soon be lost to her. For Death was another way of Being where such was not.

She heard Steve return. He carried several bags and power units with their long funnels. He gave her one, and they plunged the funnels into the first pile of leaves. Softly the little power unit whirred, drawing the leaves in, pulverizing them as they filled the light transparant bags. When the bags were full they would empty them in the compost piles inside a circle of raspberry bushes.

Jessie worked steadily with Steve, aware of the lithe movements of his body, his power. After a while she said,"Steve, I know your life is full, but I've wondered whether you want to mate again." They carried bags across the gardens into a circle of bushes, lifted one over the edge of the netting that held compost together.

He glanced at her as they spread the contents into the fenced circle."Well, that's a matter I'm still deciding. It's part of what I wanted to talk about. " He hesitated ,letting his thoughts shape. "You know, Jessie, I've finally regained my

THE JOURNEY

interest in women. Jane's responsible for that. She's so gentle, so aware. I know it's been a long grieving, it's been eight years since Cassandra's mother died". He stopped, frowned, but did not turn away as he usually did on mentioning that tragedy. " She was my true Mate, Jessie." She had never heard him speak her name. "I thought I'd never get over it. Never! But I've recovered enough so that women tempt me." He frowned, drew another bag into place and began emptying it. "But Mating is something else. Sex is no big deal, you know. Mating is!"

"Tell me, Steve." She felt the tension in him as they drew the last bag into the compost circle and began letting the bright fragments pour into it. She wondered when he had last talked of these old griefs.

"You know, the old hungry cock. It's not as insatiable as it was when I was younger. It's settled a bit, doesn't harass me the way it once did." Then he laughed. He had seldom admitted as much. Strange that his tongue seemed loosened here with Jessie. He didn't wonder why, that it had was enough.

Jessie nodded, reading his recognition. "It's natural, Steve that you would relax so." They wet the leaf mulch a little, pulled covers over it and walked back to the neat garden. Jessie's eye roved over the area, a sense of satisfaction filling her. "Well, now it looks as good as it did a month ago and the flowers are not weighed down with debris.

Steve said, "You said it's natural. What's natural?"

"For that hungry cock to grow less demanding. His energy rises to other things -- now that you grow more aware. And now that the weight of grief has lifted a little. But then, too, you know, there are hungers that rise from a higher level. Hungers that are not so basically physical, perhaps."

He looked at her frowning, puzzled at the meaning of her words, yet knowing very well what she meant. He finally nodded. "It's true. I've denied that. I've not wanted to admit -- a lot of things. Every physical urge was so much a part of my life in those years. But it adds up, my life has turned to a new direction and I didn't plan that, you know." His voice became soft, "If I did choose a Mate, if perhaps Jane -- if someone were to decide that she was true Mate to me, then that would be part of this new direction. I think, Jessie, and I feel a little guilt saying it, that such a Mating would be as wonderful, although so different, as that one with -" he drew a long breath - "with Minna." He was silent, his eyes soft. Then, "If Jane and I should truly mate, I would want to give her a child too. She wants a child, you know. But it's true now that the fire in me is dimmed, the energy has lifted above that sexual fire to other higher fires and they begin to blaze up, damping out the lower one. But it doesn't take much to spark a child." He smiled.

"Are you sorry the blaze is dimmed?"

"No, No, I'm not. Actually. Surprises me . I would have thought I would be. I feel relief. There's so much more - so much happening. " He laughed again, short chuckle. "It's like a new beginning, to learn to live here with everything the family's waking to, that I'm beginning to realize myself. The learning about the Mind reach, and that wonderful Touch. I've still to really enter into a Joining wholly, but I want to do that to. The glimpse of such unity has filled my heart with an eagerness I've never known before." He was cleaning the vacuum bags and handing them to her one by one to be replaced in the storage shed."There's so much happening, Jessie. Jane's realizing -- things about herself. Were I not able to realize with her, I'd be utterly alone, you know, because Cassandra has already moved beyond me. No, I'm not at all sorry."

Jessie laughed too, softly as if remembering,"It's true, Steve, a lot is happening."

Steve deliberated, It IS Jane, Jessie. Jane is the one person who might be true Mate to me. And I hesitate to ask her. She's younger, you know. But she does love Cassandra and Cassie goes to her the same way she goes to Rose. For mothering." He shrugged, then looked at her with a surprise that made her smile. "Why of course, Jane would be my mate, wouldn't she? " He stopped, turned to look at Jessie,"I'd be afraid to ask her. If she said it was not so, how could I continue to work,to live here?"

Jessie nodded, "It's always a risk. To ask for anything is . Always. But then, you do love her. Living here would make being with her at least as good as it is now,wouldn't it?"

He sighed, "You're right,but now I've admitted it, it's as though the longing floods my heart. I think as long as I denied, it was easier." He was silent, frowning, then said," I've got to know. One way or the other." He was pensive, silent, then "Oh, she knows I love her. As do all of you. I've not kept it to myself at all but to be a Mate is so much more."

Jessie looked at him musingly, "For you it's a deeply important matter,isn't it? You can't approach lightly such a decision?"

To admit that I loved her that much, that we were -- might be -- mated, seemed a betrayal of Cassie's mother. "Softly he let himself murmur her name, "Dear,dear, Minna. Minna my life! Would you mind Minna? Would you mind if I found another Mate?"

Jessie went to sit on the wide stone bench among the blooming autumn flowers. She drew him with her and he sat without being fully aware. Presently he said, his voice gentle,"It's true, Jessie. How'd we ever come to this? It's not what I'd thought to talk about. And yet, it's changed everything. It's just right!" He laughed then and hugged her,an excitement running through his limbs, his skin, that she felt." I think I wasn't actually sure what it was I wanted to talk about,and so,perhaps it was just this and I didn't know. Here I am talking like a tape left running."

She turned to reply, smiling at this burly young man, eagerly sitting now, turned to her like a boy. But there was a sound at the edge of the garden where it bordered the deck. They both turned. Jerry was descending,hovering over a bed of late blooming roses. He breathed the fragrance, wrinkling his nose at it. He hung there, as if lost in thought for several minutes, then he settled on the walk and loosening his belt,came toward them.

Jessie watched the soft and inward expression of his face and knew another needed to talk.She said,"Come sit with us here, Jerry, in the sun. The high

THE JOURNEY

altitude must have chilled you."

He nodded, absently, set the belt aside, then took off gloves and hat, and clasped her hand tightly. Jerry nodded to Steve, his eyes wounded. He did not shield them. His face so naked in his need that Steve turned away. Then matter of factly, Jerry said,"It's really a great place to get in touch with things you avoid thinking about most of the time."

Jessie nodded,"The way you do it Jerry, it is. The wonder of flying, the danger of it, the stillness; all of it prods attention awake."

Jerry looked up,"Danger?"

"Yes, there's danger in Reaching so far, unless you're ready."

He nodded thoughtfully. "I never thought of that. Danger? But, yes, it's true."

Jessie'e voice was soft, as if she wanted to protect the attitude with which he had returned. "How was it this time then?"

Jerry sighed and smiled, then he was deeply serious,"Yes, I'd like to talk a bit about it." They were all three silent for moments. the sounds of the Valley, a bird call, the lowing of a cow to her calf somewhere among the foothills, were very clear to them. Then Jerry said,"There is a silence there, A great silence, broken by nothing at all, even my own body does not break it. I can sometimes hear my heart beating but usually there is nothing and the drifting suspension in that wide blue air draws me to a point of awareness that is -- well -- it is too much." He was silent, remembering and he swallowed, then said intently as though he needed to be sure they understood."It's as though there is a strange opening inside myself, I've known it before but haven't really looked at it. It's as though I'm just about to --to realize something, and yet, it's as though my body, this brain, perhaps, cannot -- or will not -- hold it. Hold -- what I, myself, am. That's it. It is my Self after all that I'm recognizing. my Self there, beyond this. Whatever this is. It's very clear to me up there, in that Silence, that it is my Self. And so," the breath shuddered out of him, "it's as though, I cannot bear all that I am."

For several moments after that, they all sat silent again, Jerry ruminating on his words, the sound of them, spoken, he felt somehow committed to the facts they gave shape. Steve nodded slowly watching Jerry intently, as if something in his words might reveal what he himself needed to know. Jerry sat up straight, his eyes now looking back into the hills that rose one on another behind the farm land toward the northern mountains. He finally said, as if he wasn't aware he had stopped,"And then, even with the small self, that I think of as myself, up there, there's something in me that goes beyond everything I've known. And it's through this very small self. Deep within me is that which is beyond me." With an expression of wonder, he shook his head. "That cannot be. And yet I know clearly that it is so. I am a door way into far more than I know." He shook his head slowly, trying to speak the experience,"It's more like a vastness, a vastness in myself, and that -- that's what brings me fear. The possibility!" He was silent again, searching their eyes this time, looking for encouragement, acceptance of these strange ideas.

"You've spent time in the deprivation chamber at the Center? " At his nod, she went on, "How is this different?"

"Oh well, Jessie! That's artificial." His eyes moved from one to the other, asking something they could not define."When I was a boy it was facinating. Something different. And we didn't spend much time there. At least I didn't. I thought it really didn't have much to do with life then. It was just something to know about. I think a lot of us did that. But now - I've chosen to pay attention.To hold myself at that point of awareness that brings me closer to the edge the Teachers are finally telling us more about. And you see, it's the whole sky, the heartbreaking beauty of Earth that I'm inside of, not an empty tank. I think that must be the real difference." He was silent,and when he spoke again his voice was little more than a whisper.

"I'm just that, Earth too, I belong, I'm like a leaf, a tree, a rock, a part of Earth. " He grinned gently, "A loosened part that can fly off a bit, maybe, like a bird, but no less a part." He was silent and they waited,"But there's a difference isn't there? I 'think'! I know! I'm aware of being what I am. And how does that fit me into all other life forms?" He shook his head harshly, as if shaking something from it . Slowly, he added,"I wonder whether we, human beings, are not Earth thinking?" He did not smile.

"It's a little as though we are - I am - at the edge of something so great it doesn't have a name,, not for me any way. It could be what people used to call God. Maybe. This grandeur, this intelligence. Love,that we see only a shadow of, is beyond personhood. Is that Earth? Or Humanity? And what is the difference? It's beyond human conception of it anyway. It's obviously something being perceived by me, so it's not EVERYTHING, but it's - so strange. Because I realize so much, that I can't even tell you. He was shaking his head, struggling to find words. They listened. "For just a second up there, a second that lasted - forever - just a brief moment maybe, when I decided to focus attention, to really listen, to pay attention utterly, there it was. Far within myself or beyond me,I can't say. But it was an unceasing presentness, a stillness of Presence - and of PRESENTNESS. If that makes any sense. " He turned his gaze back to them, "I could never have imagined any of that. It must be real".

"Then what would you say God is? If it is not that?"

He sighed, "Everything! All of this, and yet, so much more we can't even conceive it. God is - must be - infinite and I'm very finite. Even Earth is finite." He did not smile at all. His face looked sad.

"So that is what you were dealing with up there today?" Jessie spoke matter of factly.

"Yes, that's what I was dealing with. It literally hurts my brain. My brain can't think about it actually. It spills beyond thought. My heart feels stretched. I want to cry." He grinned crookedly, then bent down to put his hands in his hair, rubbed his temples with his thumbs. His expression was infinitely sad,yet a glint of something else flickered in his eyes when he raised his head to look at them again. It was as if he avoided the Joy that flickered there.

Jessie wanted him to balance these realizations, to realize it all. "Can you say more Jerry? Say more and perhaps the pain,the misunderstanding will clear a little. Sometimes it's the resistance that hurts."

Jerry laughed, a short, sharp sound," It does hurt, doesn't it? I hadn't admitted that. And you're right again, I am resisting,but I don't know what. It's as though I hang on to the edge of that point beyond which I saw such --" his voice dropped, "wonder! Isn't this what you've talked about, what Rose's talked about, seeing, knowing of? That wonder of what we are? Humankind!"

Jessie nodded, glad that he could go ". "Most people experience that opening into themselves, into that doorway beyond themselves, differently, but essentially, they notice it's much the same."

"The Teachers taught us so much. Even though I didn't really understand at the time, I must have absorbed a lot, because things keep coming back to me. Teachings! I begin to understand! I wasn't so afraid, or so overwhelmed as I would have been had they never taught us. "He laughed again, his eyes meeting hers again,"But Jessie, it's truly amazing, you know. There's something wonderful about it. Like, like, " he bent his head, as if unwilling to meet their eyes, heaved a great sigh, to prepare himself and finished,"As though such Joy as I have never imagined possible rises up through my heart, and saturates my mind. It's just that, truly Jessie, Steve, even though that sounds somewhat mad." Now, braving their imagined ridicule, he looked at them, a little defiant. But they stared back at him, their faces quiet,Jessie slowly nodding."That's what I resist. It's so -- grand!"

"It's that that I sense in you. The Joy. And you hadn't spoken of it. Only of the quality of fear and being overwhelmed. Pay attention to that Joy, Jerry. Let it live in you, let it be acknowledged." Her own voice was filled with the Joy she knew so well, and the two men watching her felt that over flow, that bridging between them of that slow, deep Joy.

Jerry said, softly, nodding, accepting her words, the tears finally filling his eyes."It's there, absolutely impossible Joy. It's like a welling up, a presence of Itself filling me so I think I might break apart. As though it's been there all along, and I didn't notice. There seems nothing more to say, it's like something so powerful it's stirring up my whole life." He stopped and shook himself."Oh, I couldn't bear it alone. I couldn't recognize it until I shared it, until I found someone to know of it with me." His face was shining, but his smile was gentle, musing, as if unable to express that inner sweep of power.

Jessie sighed, knowing that he did not know."You realize that it is also a gift you give. Every time anyone SEES through the limits of our ordinary life, realizes that Presence you spoke of, they offer all of us a wonderful gift when they tell us. And Jerry, you can -- you are able to bear it. Even though it may be beyond understanding right now."

He was nodding again, as if the realizations were just finally coming into conscious recognition. "Yes, it's so, isn't it? I was able to bear it, though I pushed it away until I found you two." He was silent, Steve, suddenly aware that Jerry included him, felt amazed; he felt a total outsider here, of no use to either of them. Jerry went on, "Whatever -- I was able, and I am now. I feel as though I have been burned out, the way someone said not long ago at a Gather. I feel as though I am emptied out, hollowed, and there, up there, the wind was blowing through me, swelling the size of that hollow straw that I am. Now, remembering, I long again for that recognition. The memory even, seems precious beyond saying. But then, at the same time, I shrink from it." He took a deep breath."It was finally after I had gotten myself quiet, still actually, and just accepting, just being aware, that the resistance faded and the Presence was -- was knowable. I won't give it a name and so decrease it. I finally acknowledged what I knew. That's as clear as I can speak of it now. Speaking of it makes it live a little more in memory." He shook his head with a reuful grin, "Even as it brings it down into little human terms. Reduces it! To have talked and to have formed words to try to hold something of it, is your gift to me, you know!" No one spoke, so he finally said,"Then, finally, I recoiled, before it all, I backed off, as though I closed a door, and dropped down into myself. I,small and afraid - and full of wonder! I am utterly changed. I will never be the same, you know!"

He stopped then, his hands lying flaccid in his lap. He seemed to have exhausted the search for words. After some time Jessie nodded, gently placed her fingers on the wrist of his right hand, then she looked into his face. Soft with memory, the Joy now leaked through his smile, pooled in his eyes, and glowed through the skin of his body. She smiled, watching, seeing much.

Steve took a deep breath in his turn, glanced at them both, then looked away over the Valley. "What you're saying seems exciting to me.But it also seems terrifying and I don't know why. I remember Rose saying once that she felt fear when she met up against that -- that kind of thing. At least I think it's the same, because while you were talking I felt that same old feeling of wanting to escape from listening. Why? Why am I angry? What you're saying fits in with our talks lately. "He flushed, turned his head, then as if taking up his courage, he said,"Is there anything to be afraid of? I see you all entering into something -- realizing something that I don't. Yet it doesn't hurt you, it makes you look so -- so full of Light! And makes you seem to see beyond me. I want to see what you do! "He frowned then a bright grin flashed to light his face."I guess I don't want to miss anything."

Jerry nodded, smiling at him,"You mustn't, mustn't miss any of it. It's worth more than you can guess, even though it's fearful sometimes." His face was washed by tears that rolled down unheeded and without fuss. He went on. "When I've listened to Rose, or to Paul sometimes, and to you Jessie, I've felt that wish to run away. To deny! But something has touched me, Touched my mind and stung me into an awareness that I never knew before.And that's never stopped. I think once we begin to See, we cannot ever cease."

"That's it! The experience exactly, as if my mind's stung, jolted awake. But there's something in me that -- demanded that! And there I am!" Steve spoke with a tinge of wonder in his voice.

Jessie watched them, saw their minds waken and saw them explain to each other what began to know. They were not offended by their mutual disclosures. It was so much better than at the first of this year. Vastly better than a few years ago when she had watched them groping toward their first recognitions. She began to talk softly, "Remember, remember as you understand, as things become familiar, then fear fades. You know that. Listen, watch and identify with that great Self that calls from your own hearts."

Jerry shook his head,"You know, Jessie, when the Teachers taught us the ideas, I never imagined anything real. I never could have thought it would be so very, very REAL! But now, what I experience as Soul threatens everything I am, or thought I was. The idea always seemed comforting, but the reality seems absolutely to turn everything upside down. To think that there's more -- more than this small self has been able to know, that universes of stars are only a physical manifestation of unlimited other universes, beyond our knowledge or even our conceptualization just now. The little worrying troubles of our mutual world antagonisms seem petty in that frame. Pointless! We've spent centuries fighting each other when all THAT waited there, here in us to be known. That is what can test our capacities to their limit. Something to discover that is beyond our very dreams. It's easy to see why we fear. Everything we've tied up into our comfortable world view, is radically changed. Nothing is as it seems! New perceptions that tell us little more than that THERE IS MORE, is enough to push us off balance." His body fairly danced as he talked now, released, full of his delight, possibility.

For a time they sat, silent, watching life around them. Jerry's eye was caught by a drop of dew, still balanced on a leaf that was so shaded the sun had not drawn it into the air. The gleam of light in that drop, the slow movement as the wind caused the leaf to bend sliding the gleaming drop toward the Earth. It's movement so slow, it seemed time stood still. As it finally reached the edge and fell, Jerry watched it flatten against a dry small willow leaf and form itself again. An ant, near by, came to it, then, plunged its mouth parts into the shining round drop and drank. The drop held its shape, its own form intact. Jerry shook his head, as if released from another world, and then said,"It's as if I'm dying -- dying away from what was my life. I think I've lived in a shadow of life, only a reflection of something greater, that I now glimpse and want to know more of. And here it is, right here, around me, just the LIFE that I've taken for granted, looking through it, looking carefully AT it, I begin to SEE what Life is - what it is after all." He nodded as if he had found something of a truth he might consider."It's as if I'm losing myself, have maybe already lost myself inside a greater Self." He was still, then whispered,"And that Self is LIFE itself, I think."

He sighed, memories were persistent,"But now, I want to find that Self again. There where that Vision draws me. I feel lost" he shook his head again, dislodging something, clearing his vision. "But at the same time, I am found." His voice had fallen to a whisper, just realizing as he spoke. "I begin to find out something of what humanity is. More than I ever knew we are." His face was soft with realization.

They were silent again. Each taking in this confession. Then suddenly Jerry grinned,"No wonder the Builder's are terrified. There is really something to be afraid of. Our old universe is being yanked out from under us."

Jessie smiled, glad to see his sense of humor back. "Except the Builders are not experiencing anything like what you are. That is their fear. They don't know to be afraid of what might lie ahead, but rather that there is an unknown they must deny. They don't guess at inner change." She stood and went to press both her hands at the rough bark of an acacia tree, stood then, her fingers white with the pressure as if taking strength from that strong,life.

Jerry said, "The Master Teachers have told us that for some it would feel like a kind of dying. Giving up our old perceptions and old patterns would feel like death to our minds. I thought it was a metaphor, but it is actual". He got up and walked about, stooping to pick two roses, and hold them to his nose. "This fragrance, for instance, so lovely, points my attention toward something more. Everything we realize is only an edge of what is ahead."

Jessie watched him, smiling faintly, turning from the tree, she sat down again."There is such a simplicity in the way things really are. They are not the intellectual complexities we've devised to explain them. The reality you begin to See, must be lived into. Not something one can think up and decide on. It's a slow process but it is inevitable once we begin." She laughed and pointed to his rose,"Follow your nose, for instance, know all there is to know of that and what it points to."

The two young men nodded, lost again in thought. the sounds of the day grew around them. Leaves muttered in the thin sunlight and Jessie glanced at the eastern sky where the high sheet of white clouds swept like a fan across the blue air, below them, rumpled and bumping against one another, a dense field of cumulus clouds, harbingers of new rain. It was needed, weeks had passed with no good rain. Perhaps it would come now, and before the sun set clouds would cover the sky with their grey,black bottoms. They felt the chill of the breeze and Jessie wrapped her arms around herself.

Jerry turned to Steve, a resolution firming in his mind. "Steve, you said this kind of talk shakes you, makes you uneasy. Would you tell us, now I've done so much talking, what it's like for you?"

Steve gave an incredulous look but the request fired his desire to tell them. "One thing I've found out, it's easier if I do talk about it. It's a relief and I never thought it would be. My Peer Group always insisted that, and I didn't believe them. But finally, I began and I could see it was true." He sighed, his eyes moving from one to the other, then satisfied that they took him seriously, he looked far afield. "But I didn't think it applied to things, things like this."

He stopped, frowned, let his eyes rest against the color of deep blue petunias and then went on," For years I've felt two battling forces in me. Since I couldn't understand them, I denied them most of the time, except sometimes when I was alone, or meditating in Temple. I felt as though there was a demand being made on me, as though something IN me is demanding something OF me. I've refused to believe this could be so and explained it as old griefs, or whatever. But the demand would not diminish, no matter how I denied it. There are times when I feel unbalanced, as though I live at an edge of something. You both know how I refused all you were realizing! And I couldn't really deny you were, but I did deny it. I wouldn't talk to the healers, I was ashamed that I'd failed to balance myself adequately and yet, ashamed of that very shame. I justified things by telling myself that I could work this out, and that I'd go to the Healers later on. But I know now that it was because I didn't want to know what was happening in me."

He looked at them both one after the other, searching their faces. Seeing no censor there, he smiled a strange lost smile,"I remember Rose telling us something like that, the battle in herself, and it did help me to hear that, though I didn't say so. At first I resented it because she thought maybe she was going crazy and if she was then I was. But then, still it gave me courage, because I could see that Rose wasn't crazy and no one thought she was. Then later on, Jessie, you talked to us a little and I began to trust that maybe there was something very reasonable that I could understand. I didn't but maybe I COULD. Then when the children, began to talk to us and I saw that they were realizing what they spoke of as LIGHT, or as an actual presence of LOVE -- well, that threw me off a bit. Kids couldn't know things like that!" He looked around at them again, his face deeply serious,"After that, Jessie, you said that to perceive beyond our physical world, to See through the surface of things, was a gift; that we must listen and watch and pay attention, and I finally realized there was something to all this and that my battle must be given attention. I couldn't deny things any more. I felt exhausted in my heart, inside I was tired trying to hold off what was so imminent. I could well understand that old tale of Noah and the whale. How he ran and ran so as not to hear what was right there in himself. I couldn't believe how accurate that was for me."

He was silent for so long that they thought he had finished but then he drew a long breath and said, "I thought that I was doomed. Actually I must have made life hell for poor Jane.Bless her heart. If it hadn't been for her --. She seemed to accept me whatever." He turned to them again,"Well you've seen me refuse to accept possibility of that Reaching. But when everyone did that I felt myself Touched I responded. I felt tyour Touch. It was as though my brain had opened, broken a sealed place." He sighed, looking away.

After a moment, taking a deep breath he went on, "Then later, alone, I felt that deeper level of myself, as though what was in me was trying to Touch me the same way we did one another! Then I couldn't deny. Mind Touch! That was like an earthquake. I KNEW! For the first time. I knew what it was I was denying. Then later, in the times we Joined in the Gathers, I saw that my fear was not there when I participated. Only when I refused was there fear. The whole things was a lifting, a growing outward. I know now that there's really nothing to fear and everything to discover."

Jessie leaned to him,"Steve, how did you know that this voice within was a Right one, not something that you should refuse?"

He laughed softly, got up and began to pace back and forth "Because it was so beautiful, it urged me toward a goodness of action and perception that couldn't harm, not even me. It didn't ask me to DO anything but to BE. Yet it was so powerful it scared me. I knew it was rising out of a Love that I thought I could never allow. It had the color and brightness of life but it demanded that I rise to that possibility."

He stopped a minute, looked at her and added, "It never did suggest any personal benefit to me. It was - for life instead." He turned to them again, then turned away, walking to the tree, touching it with his hands as if unaware that he did.

"All this isn't new, you know. All my life, I've run away from that inner knowing. I tried everything, you know. I fought to deny it totally. Went to sea, got drunk, got busier than I'd ever been in the daytime and drank at night. I even joined the war games for a short time. That was awful, unbelieveable that human kind could participate in such brutal activity. And yet, I did! I found out something of myself there. Something I didn't want to know." He was silent again, his mouth down in a bitter frown, he sighed, "I needed to do something to cleanse myself after that. So I went on jungle search to find plants we could develop for medicines and for other uses. I thought I helped there a little. I could escape that way, doing good for humanity. I thought I was running away from memories of Minna and I suppose that was part of it. But I know now I was running away from myself." He realized that he had spoken his mate's name twice in the same day after a silence of years.

He came back, sat between them, his hands dropped down between his knees, "It wasn't until I came here that I became a little resigned to her loss. I did get to the Healers finally. I thought if I didn't do something I wouldn't be able to be a good father to my little girl. I did everything I could to avoid but the Healers saw at once. They at least made me see that the fear was in myself, and that I must look at it. Then gradually, with our talks, Rose's talk, sometimes, I began to see that there is more, an Inner Self. And that I must meet it."

He sat still, his eyes on the paved pathway. I had begun to gain a little insight but then's when I stopped seeing the healers. Everything that battled in me threatened me and they wanted me to bring all that to look at. They wanted me not just to acknowledge the fear but to steadily look at it. That was too much. I quit. " He twisted his hands together, shoving his palms against one another then up and down the surface of his thighs, as if calming the tautness of his muscles there. Never had he spoken these things, never had he ever really thought them out so that they were articulate. But now, he knew that if he were to heal himself, he must tell all of it. Jessie seemed somehow to make it easier, she healed as she listened and accepted. He felt a fierce flow of tenderness between them and marveled at its healing.

He went on, "I ran away. After I left the Healers I had nothing left and a kind of panic would grip me now and then. Before that, even though I was haunted, I felt in control. But now, acknowledging that fear, I see I was losing control. That great strong inner Self, like a quiet stream of -- of wonder, kept presenting itself before me and I couldn't any more deny. I have denied with tremendous power. I see that now. I tried to resist even a Monitor but--", he shook his head, grinning ruefully," Monitors aren't routable. They know too many ways to be there regardless of whether you run or fear." He grinned, looking at Jessie." At least I learned how to be there for you all, for other people, but I could not be there for myself at all. And so it was because you were so much there for me that I began to take courage to look at myself."

"What do you think changed that"? Jessie's voice was soft.

"There were two things mainly. One was the pure wonder of our Family. Never had I known such closeness with anyone other than Minna. Never had I been in the environment of such unconditional Love. That was it. The Love I had never known, except with Minna. I never knew such love could be., I thought only Mates could be so for one another. But the other thing was a change in myself that I couldn't control. At first I thought it was a breakdown of my mind. Things occurred that seemed so full of transcendant beauty, of JOY. As though Life itself had permeated everything all new."

He shook his head, the memories coming fast, this speaking of these things bringing them into coherence and acceptance finally. I began to know something in myself that I couldn't believe, a deep Soul Love, of Love in myself, as though I was worth loving, worth that Joy. How joyous that love is, it is never not present. And it was with you all that I knew it to be real. And then -- then -- there was Jane! She was so gentle, for I don't think she intended it at first, but she led me to that personal love that seems now to radiate like a rainbow through the world. I refused that too. Up until this moment I've continued to refuse to some degree. What a fool I've been!" He shook his head, his eyes wet. So I suppose I could say that in one way or another, it was love that drew me back and allowed me to have courage to look into myself a little."

"What strength you gained from that massive resistance. Holding it." Jerry was reflecting,"They say nothing is lost, every experience is a learning." Then he turned to look directly at Steve," Jane, she is an extraordinary woman,I think, Steve. She has loved you for so long, and whether you returned that love or not, it would continue." He hesitated,"Right?"

Steve nodded,a look of such misery crossed his face that Jerry could not define, then he said,"It's true. I've not been kind with her sometimes, I think."

Jerry shook his head vehemently,, "Oh, no, Brother, you can't think that. You have kindness as a trait. It always works in you, even when you're at your most thoughtless. I wish it were so for me."

Jessie had been listening to this interchange, she laughed softly,"Well now, Jerry, You're not exactly a brutal man yourself, you know."They all smiled, feeling a sudden lightness, a waking of joy at being thus with one another.

Then suddenly, as if the closeness opened something in Steve further, he said, an angry note in his voice,"You folks never seemed to notice that difference among us the way I did. I hated it. I knew that there was something - something I

THE PEOPLE OF THE VALLEY

couldn't or wouldn't understand, admit, accept. Whatever! It's why I can understand the fear of the Builders so well. It must be terrifying to them. And now, this talk of our going to the Silent City, it's brought everything back. I've never even flown over Her, never had any contact, and yet, I've just assumed that I'd never go with you, that I'd be left behind. I think I tortured myself a little with that." He managed a rueful smile. "Funny how a person can almost court misery sometimes." He was silent, then "I plunged into the farm work, helped Jane, just found myself really enjoying being with her, especially with her. If I kept busy enough I could forget everything, Minna, the differences in us, everything! Then lately, with the new Gathers things changed, we began those talks, and now this! Like a knife slid between me and peace of mind, it opens up all the old wounds and so much more that I hadn't ever looked at. You see, there's no place to hide, and my own brain won't let me any more. I can't fool myself. I have to recognize what's happening."

They sat together, supporting each other. Jessie and Jerry Reaching gently, lightly, to Touch against Steve's mind, Touch only with reassurance and Love. Jerry was full of wonder at Steve's words, so strong but full of a private pain they were. This then was the darkness that always had lain in Steve's eyes, the pain that stood behind his jokes, and his good humor. Jerry extended a hand, one finger barely touching then withdrew it. He said, "So that's how you know the Journey is the right direction."

Steve looked up, his eyes returning from a great distance. He spoke out of wearyness, "Well, I've learned one thing. There must be some kind of step ahead. I trust Jessie, I hear you Jerry when you tell us of the recognitions you experience, and so, I know there has to be another way .I tried everything else, work, fun, play, sex, politics, fighting, whatever I could throw myself into, and nothing worked. It would work to numb me, but only for the exact time I was immersed in it, as soon as I stopped for a moment, there it was, that thing that haunted me, that drew me as though I had a magnet within myself, seeking its mate. It won't quit. And there is just a glimpse, a memory of something so full of beauty, of wonder, that it broke my heart a little. It must be good, something must be. I'm tired, I don't want to run, to fight against it anymore. I'm willing to stand and look, to see whatever it is you all insist is there. Whatever is in me. It's hard to believe that's good, I'm such a poor excuse of a human." He shook his head, a wry smile relieving the nakedness of his eyes. He hid nothing now.

Jessie chuckled now, "I can see that you've made it pretty hard for your Self. Pretty hard. But no Self can be denied in the long run. Because it's your Self, you know. And with no difficulty I see the beauty of you, the very goodness of your nature shines out like a beam of light. I SEE you Son, more clearly than you know."

"Oh Jessie, you see goodness in everyone, surely there's little in me. " A tone of hope and anger mixed in his voice.

That's probably your great pain, and task, right now. To acknowledge your own beauty. Your own SOUL. It's the part of yourself you fight to deny, isn't it?"

He looked at her, denial there in his eyes, but a dawning recognition, that pleased her, With a sudden gesture of defeat, he slowly nodded, embarrased, "It might be so. I see it might be so! It's just that I can't wholly accept."

Jerry nodded, "Then what Jennifer and Paul've told us meant a lot to you?"

"It did. I could see it was of the same familiar stuff. The same feelings woke in me. I had trouble denying what they said." He allowed himself a small grin, "That's why I got mad."

After a moment, he turned to Jessie, "It all seemed to go round and round. My arguments seem now to be an endless maze in which I'm lost. Is there no way out?"

She nodded thoughtfully, "Well, there are other ways to travel to understanding. But one embarked on the way of the mind finds that the human mind is a circular thing unless it lifts to a spiral. Though the circle grows larger and larger, unless there is a constant pull upward it may form no more than a whirlpool and stagnation. It looks as though you negated that pull upward as hard as you could and so you got into a stew."

"All right! I think you're right. I see and hear all of you. I have felt a little of the Joining, I have known it's power and the wonder of that. It's possibility. I can see there's no way I can refuse to acknowledge that power in me. I feel a longing to surrender to it, Yes! That's what it would be, a kind of surrender."

"Yes, it is, Steve, and for one so long fighting, it is more so. But if you begin now to listen to your Self. Just stop everything and risk listening. You will discover your own way out. The courage to listen to yourself, to quit the fight and listen. Accept something of it at least, enough to listen. You will see how to Join with yourself, to see out of that dark stew where you feel only confusion. That which is in you will guide you out and into a singleness of being. A balance and integration that will relieve all this pain."

"What you say makes sense Jessie, right now at least, while I am listening and aware. The sense of safety I feel here makes it possible for me to listen to you, and maybe I could begin listening to my Self in your company. Perhaps?" He looked at her questioining, a request clear in his voice.

She smiled at him, her own mind Reaching, Love embracing him palpably, "Can you feel that which we offer?" He nodded, not meeting their eyes, "Do you see that that inner Self is also of that quality of Love Itself? That what you refuse in yourself is seeping through your very nature all the time, what makes you the most loving man most of us have ever met? Why do you think Jane loves you so? She feels it too. It's your mind that won't accept. There is finally a jump that must be crossed, one the ordinary mind can't follow, one that feels like a split in the fabric of one's consciousness, until after the jump is made and then -- then, it feels like the normal condition of living and why didn't I know this before!" She was silent, looking out across the mountains toward that Station that was home to her.

Then, stirring as if remembering, she went on," The place of recognition and greater life seems so natural, once that jump beyond what your literal mind can grasp. What art, music, beauty in all its forms, the loving between people, all these have taught you all your life, silently and in their own way. Such a mind, willing to step across that gap in consciousness, sees farther than it's thinking. Sees to that beauty, and knows that it is REAL. The Teachers have taught all of you,but for you older ones, it's just harder to absorb the reality, that it is not just IDEA. Your daughter has no such struggle as you have had. Her HEART leads." Her voice had fallen so that they leaned to hear, then she broke into a smile that lit their faces as well as her own.

Jerry nodded slowly,"Understanding doesn't come in a logical manner. We realize something, realize, KNOW, but we doubt because we can't prove it mechanically. It's our human weakness. Isn't that when we must take that jump". He was silent and then,"But Jessie, our Teachers have trained our intuitive minds, that intuitive faculty that makes it possible to see beyond thinking. Why then all this denial of what the intuitive mind knows."

Jessie nodded,"The Valley people have done just that. Why do you suppose you are at this place of recognition. The training does not mean that there will not be resistance to that inner knowledge. It means that the inner knowledge is finally available and it is. That's what makes you suffer as you do. The knowledge that your trained mind is realizing what your rational mind has fought to deny. The whole matter is a greater mental consciousness."

"I think modern physics has reached into that realm of Soul but just never named it so. The unified Field theory, the search for that Unified Field, for the wholly inter-related structure of everything, has drawn us far toward that. If the times of trouble had not torn the world so apart, we might have discovered this way through science, perhaps?"

Jessie shook her head,"Maybe, Maybe not! Science got stuck in its own rut too, you know. Mathmatics might have catapulted us out of that, a new young mind, able to see with that tool. But perhaps that is happening right now, and we don't know that yet."

Jerry was nodding, "We begin to perceive what we always thought could not be. And we cannot talk of it well,but we can share it and perhaps we will find language, or perhaps we will simply go beyond language."

Jessie nodded, "Perhaps. Who knows what will be. What is! And you must notice that we have discovered the way to make matter transmitters work but we don't know why they work. It's like electricity, for centuries we used it and didn't know what it was. And so, we have that energy called Love, and we don't know what that is either, yet it is the most powerful energy in our world."

Steve frowned,"The energy of Love? Useful? How?"

She was short,"Oh, Steve,you know. It's in our own hearts,it's what we use to power our entire lives, and don't know it. We've sought its reflection since time began. It's Love's reflection with which we link up with our mates, our love for our homes and children, our land, our world, all that he hold dear. It's the foundation for all relationship, whether negative or positive. That's why when we touch upon IT, get a glimpse of Love Itself, we don't recognize it. We feel the power: we are afraid. It's like a blazing sun before a match compared to all we have known of love. Love ITSELF is flowing through and around and within all life, all that we call LIFE. Nothing can stop its flow except our own denial,, our own refusal, our own greed, fear, ignorance, lusts and they are based on fear." She sighed, feeling weary suddenly, as if their talk had touched on old refusals, resistances against which she too had had to push.

Then she relaxed, smiled, felt the release within herself and the renewed flow of that very Love she tried to speak of. Energy poured through her, she felt light and strong. She looked steadily at Steve, her eyes like fires blazing through his very consciousness. His heart lurched, a spasm of joy, so great it hurt and then a slow persistence of quiet well-being seemed to flow through his own heart. He thought, watching, his mind numbed with the experience,that he had never known such clarity, such vision. His face filled with a radiance that reflected in Jerry's and for moments Jerry thought Steve might Reach spontaneously. On his own.

But the moment passed, Steve was aware, his eyes met Jerry's, he smiled and nodded."Yes, give me time, Brother. Give me time. I have to think, you know. Even though I know my mind is reluctant. I See so much today. I See and I cannot forget or deny what I am seeing now. But I will never go back to what I've been." His voice was soft, tender. And then like a gift to them, they felt his mind Reach out, Touch so gently, so tentatively, like a flicker of a moth's wing, and he was withdrawn. But it had been there. Steve was giving birth to himself.

Jerry nodded, tears in his eyes, but he looked at Jessie, smiling so he thought it would stretch his mouth. Unable to lessen the smile, his delight so great. Finally he let out a long sigh,"Oh, there's so much, so much! And we're living in the middle of it."

Jessie laughed, watched them for a moment. She reached out a hand to Steve. The evening was growing chilly, they had been sitting too long on the stone bench. They heard a sound of laughter, several young people rounded the Temple and came down the path toward the Hall. Andy and Anna and their friends, arguing about an air game they had just watched that day above Jasper. They were searching for Jerry to get his opinion. He heard their calls and got up to join them.

The two left there watched the group move into the hall. They sat reluctant to leave, Jessie drew her robe closer around her and then, Steve stood. He touched Jessie lightly on the arm, meeting her eyes and smiling, then he left her. She sat a little longer, reluctant to go into the house, though the clouds had fulfilled their promise and had darkened the sky nearly across the entire Valley. Hang globes had come on along the pathways across the fields to town. Here and there along the Highway the soft glow marked passage. She stood, shivered a little, went along the path to her cottage under the bent pine. It felt good to open the door. To enter into that place of safety and familiar warmth. She could perhaps call out, call out and talk a little with her home Station. Maybe even the Touch with her Beloved there. She smiled at this indulgence. Joy was present. Pleasure waited. A good book that she had been waiting to read,the soft patter of the first drops on the roof, the sound of quiet, and aloneness. She felt a luxury here. There was even some good fresh bread and cheese, some hot tea, a slice of ham . She had never lost her pleasure in a bit of meat now and then, though she knew that appetite was almost an anachronism today. She settled down, opened her curtains wide, and indulged in the luxuries of all the senses, of all the feelings of warmth and belonging and Love that she might Reach to.

CHAPTER THIRTEEN

Further Preparations for the Journey

The August Festival of the Full Moon was over, a brief, one day affair, it did not take the time and energy that the big Seasonal Festivals did. There was a weight to the festivitiy however, a dulling of the celebrations, that worried Tom. The Valley had been rent by the struggle with the Builders and their assumptions that they could take land without the vote of the people. The bombing of Temples weighed down the spirit of the people even though, since the arrest, that had stopped. The news that a delegation of Builders had set off to find access to the Silent City,determined to find its secret for themselves and to defame it, had little effect. No one had heard from them since they left, two weeks since.

On this lovely, autumn day, Tom went out to do a round of the town, to see that everything was in order. He had kept up a close vigil in the past month, more watchful, more aware of where people were and how they acted with one another. He deplored the knotty pain of subtle suspicions that strove to claim his attitudes. He would not let that happen. Suspicion, for Tom, was a ground work for trouble. He would trust the people of his town, but trust them only to be normal people.

On this day however, the world seemed in balance with itself and everything living in it. The nagging irritations of living,little snags on which good will may lose itself and disturb the whole current of the day,,seemed more flexible and easily loosened. As he walked, talked to people, looked into businesses, Learning Center or Civic Center, he thought with relief, that things seemed in harmony. It was his job to know that seeming harmony might be false, and his frowns now and then chased the good humor from his face.

Benjamin had spent the day in Adwin working at first at a new labratory in the industrial center,to help set up new equipment for the design of precision tools that would be used in world communications centers. Once the design was satisfactory, the first sample encoding device must be built in the plant in Adwin and given its trial run in their own world Marketing office at the Civic Center. Then Adwin's small plant would bring a healthy new credit to Adwin. Benjamin was elated and sure that they would have the finished plan in days. They had not yet paid their town debt off to the Valley, he hoped that the added income would free Adwin of major debt by the next five years. After lunch, he went to meet with the town Council, to prepare for the welcoming of the new students coming to study for the winter. Some were Vagabonds, some were from other towns, a few from out Valley. The Youth Centers would house them adequately, but they had sent requests to work with certain Teachers, to study in certain labs, or factory or in a particular business office. One would learn town government with Tom. Tom had already arranged housing and food for the students. There was left only assignments. Finally it was done, the schedule looked good. He was relieved. He could meet Tom for a visit.

    The student exchange program was one Tom had initiated when he was barely sixteen and doing his own apprenticeship at learning to govern a town. He had suggested the idea of having students travel, fostered by more than one town, study with different teachers, get to know their neighbors, and share knowledge. He was proud that the whole Valley had adopted it finally.

    The two friends met finally at the junction of the outside Ring of the Civic Center and the pathway to the north, which also branched into the way to the Farm. The western hills were lower than those peaks of the east and so the sun still shone making long shadows across the land. Benjamin watched his old friend, smiling,"Being Mayor is what you like, isn't it Tom?"

    Tom turned a beaming face to meet Ben's eyes,"We've done a good day's work Ben. I've got two kids coming to ME. Thought there was only one, now another. They plan to study the way to govern a small community." His pleasure was evident, he loved his work and liked nothing better than to wake that love in others. Trees, rustled with leaves brilliant in the autumn evening. Their feet scattered fallen leaves. Ben took a long breath,"I love the smell of the leaves, the crunch of them underfoot. It's the finality of it, I think. The promise of winter."

    Tom laughed,"Promise? Usually the promise is of spring."

    Ben shook his head,"Ah, no, it's also of winter. The quiet time. The still and solitary hours in a warm place, or walking in the deep cold. I like the barren cleanness of the trees, the rain dimming distance, closing us in on ourselves, and the silence of snow. Winter is a a good time, when our people are all safely housed, Tom, and we've food enough for every one." He drew a long breath again, The air smelled wonderful. His good feelings over flowed. He slapped his friend on the shoulder , "Let's go have a beer or two before we go home. At Nin's, perhaps. It's close here."

    Tom laughed,"Whatever it is, it's wonderful. Haven't seen you so happy in a while. Will you share the joy?"

    Ben nodded, still smiling, but Tom had stopped to look at his watch. "We'll have to have that beer at the Farm because we'll be late if we stop here."

    "And you're a punctual man?" Their eyes met. Tom shrugged.

    "I don't like people wasting my time by being late so I don't waste the time of others. One of the things my students learn early!"

    Ben nodded, "I don't know exactly what it is that makes me feel so happy today, Tom. Actually maybe it's just because I'm alive and things seems going well. Even the Builders have finally calmed down and are causing no more problems. The World Market report has to be in this week, and yet they seem to be absolutely sure that there's no problem there." He shook his head. "I don't agree, but that's not my worry now. There are days I feel depressed for no reason, things seem not to be 'right. But today, well, it's just a lovely day, a day of luxury, a day when I feel rich, wealthy, full of the wonder of living." He laughed again. "When I'm depressed, I used to try to search out the reason and end it. But when I was full of Joy, I would just enjoy. Now, I think I treat them both the same.

THE JOURNEY

Oh, I inquire as to the source a little, but mostly just experience either." His face had sobered, but his eyes danced.

Tom was walking rapidly to the steps that descended the hillside. He nodded, almost absently having to slow his long stride so that Ben would more easily keep by his side. "Well, that's a talent, I suppose, to do that. A balancing."

Ben shook his head, stooped down to pick up a shining piece of Jasper from the path, rubbing it with his hands to bring the color out. "Well, it's just two different ways of being. One's as good as another I suppose if you think only of experience, but I enjoy feeling happy more. I can't always stay so centered that I don't get mired in a depression. But usually, someone helps me lift out. I remember trying to figure why I didn't 'get mired' in feelng good. Decided that something in life always serves to squash happiness, but equally, there's always something, or someone, who can delight and erase gloom. I think I didn't learn all I needed to when I was young."

Tom turned to look down at him, his eyes squinting in disapproval, "Ben, you were like the rest of us, not quite ready to understand all we were being taught. But I'm glad you're talking about it now. I don't feel depressed much, but Angy does and I never have known exactly how to help. Even though the Healer told me once. I keep a fairly steady level, not into heights and depths as much as you and she are."

"Life is just one long clear understanding to you, eh? You don't sink into dispair like other mortals."

Tom laughed, looking at the distant hills where late sun still poured a thin light. Shadows gathered here along the Valley floor. The ancient melancholy of evening touched him and brought memory. "Well, Ben there are days I endure that are dark in my soul. I endure them, knowing they will pass. But then, that's what we were taught to do. And they never last. Gloom can wear itself out if you let it." He was silent, Ben walking faster again to keep up. Tom sensed it once more and slowed a little. "Why is it so many of the Teachings are coming to mind lately? I remember so much. I've noticed how those old practices fit into living in these past months more than for years. " The bantering tone was gone, he was serious. They were both tired and the fast walk was making them aware of that.

They crossed the highway and waved to a camp of Vagabonds fifty yards on. They started the climb up the hill to the Hall. They could see little figures moving there, on the way to the warm, soft lights through the wide windows. Everyone would be coming in from the day's work. The gardens were still full of color, the leaves raked and cleared, and not too many fallen since. The major harvesting was in full swing, only the early light harvest was done. The town larders were not yet full, but were rapidly filling. Tom felt a surge of that melancholy joy, familiar to him at such moments of great beauty. The sharpness of the feeling made him catch his breath. He stopped walking and looked around, savoring the moment, alive to it.

They bent to the hills steepness and climbed it . The wide deck was empty, Jessie appeared in the doorway. She turned to walk toward the cluster of deck chairs. Light still lingered in the cherry tree, and among the yellow leaves of the weeping willow. They both turned, let their mind's Reach, making a contact that was as delicate as a light kiss. She smiled, drew up chairs and sat. They went to join her. No one spoke, the welcoming had been done.They were together.

Long shadows ran over the dark boards of the deck floor. The scatter of bright golden walnut leaves seemed lovely, rather than just something that needed sweeping up. Tom said,"It's good to be here Jessie, to finish a day's work and to sit with friends watching the day die."

Jessie nodded, she needed to search out the hearts of both these young men,bring them to talking so that she might know their readiness for that Journey they must make. She sat waiting. Ben found a chair across from them . He felt good about his day's work, the sense of accomplishment that gave him a 'right' to sit now and rest. He thought of that old habit and smiled. For some time they sat, no one speaking. Benjamin felt Joy growing in him. He was immensely grateful. He didn't want to question it,for fear it would fade. He sat grinning like a cheshire cat,just enjoying himself. He poured himself a cup of hot tea from the pot Jessie had brought. It tasted fine. He felt the delight of the moment, the company, the resting, the brilliance of color and sky, the feeling of life, so awake, so vital in himself.

The leaves above them slowly lost the light that made them golden as evening fell. He thought he hadn't seen anything more beautiful in his life. Thoughts swept through his mind as if drifting from some lower realm. He knew that Rose would soon come, the rest of the family, the anticipation gave him a new subtle pleasure. All around was utter stillness as if all activity of life had ceased,so that this moment could hold itself briefly still in beauty. His smile faded, but only because his face relaxed completely. His joy was serene, still. His very consciousness seemed to extend, to reach beyond him to that vastness of beauty. Joy trembled as though with a sudden upsurge of that unceasing sadness that lay also at the bottom of Ben's nature. He found himself muttering words, grasping for mental hand holds to comprehend the experience. He glanced at Jessie, aware of her light Touch.

"That light is here again. And it floods through me,, through my mind, my sight. There is pain and grief and I know it, but around it all is this unexplainable Joy. I am so 'full'". He drew his mind into a focus of attention, held it centered. Easily he sustained stillness, aware. A thought drifted by threatening the magic moment and he ignored it. As he held himself simply aware, he felt again the lightness, the raging flood of Joy, rising like a fountain that over flowed and spilled to everything around him. He thought the others must feel it too, and glanced at them and saw that their faces were all alight as though they too knew what he knew. The evening light in the leaves that hung silent, moveless, seemed to him to hold his mind as still as they were.

"It's a kind of contact", he murmured,only half aware that he spoke aloud. He was aware of the family members coming out to join them,he was aware of thoughts flickering, moving past his attention and drifting off, unattended. He

THE JOURNEY

knew the extending of his consciousness as if he had become elastic and could invade the universe, as though he himself had gone beyond this person and lived within everything , through everyone. Light permeated everything, and energy moved, flowed like currents in an endless sea that washed around them all. A sea, yes, a sea of -- of that glowing energy, that energy that nourished them with Itself. And what was It? His mind tingled, as if cells, tissue of flesh, loosened, shifted and came alive. Gates opened, long closed gates that had hidden possibility, worlds that lived inside that sea of energy. A wash of new vision swept across his eyes, perception intensified, and he heard his voice say,"Why of course.! Why of course!" Meaning was so obvious to him, he could see the depths were barely touched, possibility seemed endless.

He wondered whether he could bear all he felt.Knew that it was stretching him, every fiber of his being. He felt willing, with a profound sense of surrender, as if he gave up all resistance finally and accepted. Accepted what? The question came like a sharp nail cutting itself into consciousness from that point of his watching self. He wanted to share this knowledge, the wonder he realized at this moment. He didn't know how.The tree had done this.The tree had triggered this entering, through the beauty of gold light and the extension of all his senses.That and that tenuous faint Touch-push from Jessie.

Again, like a wave, Joy threatened to inundate him. He felt it, wondered if he could bear it. And in that moment of question he knew it faded and felt a deep gentle loss. Suddenly he knew the source of a grief that had lain below all the joy of his life. He was losing consciousness, falling into that half consciousness of normal life.

His brain-mind clamored for explanation. The recognition was unlike anything he had ever known, unlike the joining with the trees that he had practiced so many times. It was vastly greater. How could he describe this? He realized suddenly in the torrent of questions racing through him that he had retreated to the small and very tight limit of his personal self. To Ben! He smiled sadly.

How could he tell them? Jessie and Tom? It seemed it had been such a long time he had been gone from them,. Surely they must have noticed. But they seemed lost in their own wonders. He spoke then, finding words."Jessie,I'm here. Tom, I've --I've realized something. I am, I was-- through the tree there, the golden leaves, the light and the wonderful air this evening, and you. Yes, you too! " He realized he must not be making sense. Tears flowed over his eyelids, wet his cheeks.

Jessie nodded, watching him gravely, "Yes, Yes, speak of it. Don't hesitate, Benjamin,we'll hear." She seemed intent, he felt the flood of affiirmation from her. It eased him.

"I have always denied my Self." He nodded, his eyes turned toward the cherry tree, the slim clean dark limbs carrying their banners of flaming leaves. Only those at the very top still caught the sun. He sought again that lost moment when he had stepped through into that heightened perception. Why could he not sustain always such vision? He felt as though a bridge had been built in himself, by the touch of poignant beauty, a bridge through himself to that Vision. Understanding opened before him as though a curtain had been drawn. He could see events, causes, their effects, that had been invisible. The Valley struggle took on a new dimension, was something accumulating and building itself. He saw the way the knots and anguish of his life fit into a larger pattern. He sighed a long tremulous sigh as if releasing himself finally.

Then he felt again the Touch, light, feathery, undemanding and he swiftly, eagerly responded. It was the first time he had so decisively Reached. Between them a Joining began. He gave himself into it knowing without reluctance the vast extension of mind that Joining made conscious. Things began to fall into place. And he shaped images of his realization for them to know.

Great relief shook him, relief and residual fear. The fear faded, snagging on its own edges. He shrank instantly, small, limited, separate, and felt the awe-ful lonliness of that. He had drawn out of that Joining, receded. For moments he contemplated the separation, knew it for what it was. Knew he had choice. And then he extended, Reached and entered into the greater Seeing that the Joining gave. And for a long moment they knew one another!

Then, without fear he felt that Joining fade, the withdrawal and the contentment of being alone. He looked at them, his eyes seeing them anew. "Sometimes in a day's living there has been this Touch, this entering in. I have felt it and torn myself away as though I touched fear itself. Among you, I have skirted the edges of our Joining. " He wiped his face with both hands and moved his body to bring himself around to face them."What is this Jessie? What is this Joining?"

"It still carries fear?" Her voice was comforting, full of that tenderness he had felt earlier.

He nodded, his throat full of tears, that pushed also against his eyelids. He was angry at himself. He hated the feeling of vulnerability, the descent into hurt. He felt himself tighten, refuse the hurting. He thought his brain could not meet the energy of these Joinings."It's an energy that uplifts, that tears us away from old limits, old patterns and they bleed with memory. He saw that he was watching that old, frightened, self, still cringing from such amazements. He said aloud,"Why do I get so scared? And why do I get so elated?" The question, logical and sensible, comforted him.

Jessie spoke to him from outside the mists of that emotion."At first, it is sometimes too much. Especially if we have lived many years before we begin to SEE. Before we accept that we CAN See. Tom, you know of that, speak to him." Tom, watching Benjamin, a worried look on his face, nodded slowly.

"It's true! I know that fear too. A fear that I cannot bear all that we're beginning to know." He stopped, smiled thoughtfully. "Do you remember, Benjamin, one of the prayers we learned when we were in first training? I remember it now, as though it was just told me and I haven't thought of it in years." Ben's eyes held Tom's, willing him to go on. "I think it goes thus -- 'I, standing at that highest point of consciousness, focussed; I, Soul, standing at that place of awareness of the Cosmic Light, individual among Joined individuals, know the fear of the litle self trying to understand. I know compassion for myself'. There, that's as near as I can get"

Ben nodded, "Sounds about it." He shook his head. "It's a wonder to me how we learned and only now the meanings come clear." He was silent.

"It seems natural now, natural and Right and I cannot -- will not deny it again. I have born that fear and felt the veils tear away even farther. So I know I can. But each time as I realize more, I think I cannot. But I do! I want us to speak of it now, you give me courage,old friend. I know that there is fear and even hatred in this Valley, but they both dissolve when I See. Neither hatred nor fear survive full consciousness. But how can I bear the stretch that is the dawning of Love." He sat stunned at his own revelation. For some time he was silent, letting himself absorb what he realized. The others, joined enough, shared.

Finally as if accepting, Ben nodded, turning to meet Tom's eyes again,"Always in those times when we tried the Joining, I followed. You all brought me in to your center. Now, I want to initiate the true Joining."

Tom grinned,"About time,old friend. If you try you'll do it! Just now, when you drew yourself into that focus, we could feel it. We were with you as deeply as I've ever been with anyone." Jessie watched the two of them, waiting. Tom went on,"You gave us a gift you know. It was you who plunged to those depths. We just joined you." Without turning he added,"Look Rose has known of it too."

Ben turned, startled, and saw Rose coming through the Hall doors. Swiftly she came to take Ben's hand. He looked at her in surprise. She laughed,"But my Darling, surely you would realize I'd know of a Joining right here in my house! Especially one led by my own Mate!" She was smiling proudly.

He shook his head,"I hadn't thought. It's so wonderful, and so new. But I'm glad that you did."

Tom said,"Tell her Ben, what you've told us."

"I think she knows. I think I don't need to speak of it" He looked at them, then shrugged and said,"It's just that I think now I know what you meant. Seeing through the surface of things, I see that Life is shining through all lives. I actually SEE it Rose." His voice again had the hush of awe. Then, trying to pinpoint what it was he saw, he added slowly,"I think, mind you, think, that it's Spirit itself that shines through things, that it's literally like a Light and I CAN SEE IT. Not just know of it, but See with my mind's eye as clearly as I see with my physical eyes." He laughed shortly and shook his head,"I never would have believed that I would say something like that. After all, I'm a scientist."

They laughed, and Rose drew his hands into her own,"You're doing pretty well, my Darling. Better than the rest of us, I think." She reached out one hand to take one of Jessie's and then Tom leaned to set a hand on a shoulder each of Jessie and Ben.The physical connection felt good. Rose said,"Well, Tom, Ben's talked to us, spoken his experience, maybe you could do that for us too."

Tom frowned, a startled look crossed his face,"I was just then, denying that

I'd realized anything unusual at all." He shook his head at himself,"Old habits die hard" He was quiet, thoughtful. "I know now, after all our talk, it is the touch of Soul Itself. Consciousness expands far into what was once subconscious. That's why Ben could see how fear disappears." He pressed his long fingers together, held his hands before his chest, and finally rubbing them softly, dropoped them into his lap. "I remember when we met at Spring Planting and each of us said how the inner life seemed. That was a beginning for me of paying attention and acknowledging. And I've begun to understand that shift of perception. I'm more and more conscious of the Light -- a mental Light, not a physical light, that emanates from everything alive, comes without expectation. Just at odd moments, unexpectedly. If I try to bring it about, I just get in my way. If I can stand out of my own way, then realization occurs. It illuminates everything and clarifies every idea.It's like seeing things from a great height, and all the bits and pieces fit, things begin to take a new shape that I'd never have thought of. Sometimes, when I sit silently, blocked because I've thought out things to my limit,mental weariness quiets thinking utterly. I am still inside. Then, like an elevator rising, perception lifts and seeing is from a vast point of view. You're right, Ben, fear or hatred, neither work anymore." He made a gesture of impatience. "Oh, don't you see how hard it is to speak of it?"

"Unless we do we're always going to be avoiding. Because we are still human, becoming aware of Soul. Soul does imprint mind with at least some shadow of its vast Vision. It may only be a shadow of the real, but it is at least that. And it IS hard to describe." Jessie spoke quietly, as if to herself.

He nodded, still focussed in the effort,"Well, it's really just paying attention, paying attention to being alive. If I do that with intention I just move beyond myself. And then, the shift -- the shift of perception occurs and I am aware!"

Rose nodded,"To explain always leaves a person who's never experienced it baffled, and yet we must learn how to speak even if we have to make new language. Because there're children coming who need to be taught better than we were. And people who're still denying. We need to be ready."

Tom grinned at her,"Always the teacher, eh, Rosy? But you're right. For our own sake we want to understand." He had gone again to sit between Jessie and Ben, Rose settled into the bench next to Benjamin and leaned into his curving arm.

Tom said,"You know,it's easier to talk now than it used to be, so we must be doing something right. And we know how to lift perception in a very useful way. Yesterday a man came to see me furious about the open market. He said he wanted a lower price, said they were making prices too high for the average person. I told him he got his share from our fields just as the rest of us did and the people who sold their goods would charge what they thought the products would bring. No one can go hungry. But he glared at me as if I'd insulted him. He said that we'd agreed on a socialist-democracy and everyone should have equal shares of everything. I told him that we'd also agreed that applied only to the basic needs and opportunities for a good life and resulted when a person worked enough to have credit. If people want to increase their credit with extra work, that was their business. But he wanted something to satisfy his own need and wouldn't listen.I explained that if the products don't sell the price comes down. It adjusts itself. I knew I had to find the real thorn in his flesh. But I was angry at him and I didn't think fast enough."

He was staring across the gardens, looking out now toward the distant lights of the town, the moon was just beginning to rise, far to the west, clouds around it white and pink with its light. It was growing chilly, they'd have to go in soon. "Then I remembered to focus, just as we've been taught all our lives. I saw my frustration and resentment of him. He was making my job harder. Messing up my orderly day. I was resenting what I saw as his obtuseness. But thank God, I noticed that, and stopped. I focussed and lifted awareness. And miracle of miracles, it worked. I began to see farther than the two of us. I was lifted out of myself a little. From there, I could think clearly. I could see how he fit into the whole system we've got and that he had to have his place too. Individuals must be honored regardless of the cost. That's why our towns and cities are kept small. At least one reason."

Jessie nodded, "Notice that mind gift. You chose! You chose, Tom. You were more conscious! Once anyone does that, he sees farther. And it's good." She stood up, it's getting cold and we'd better move in, even if the moon is just up. And so beautiful there on the foothills." They took their cups and plates, moved into the Hall where the solar furnaces had warmed the air.They settled down in the big chairs of the Gathering room. The hot drinks Tom got for them tasted good and warmed their chilled bodies.

"What was it you saw?" Rose was interested.

"He grinned, "He needed to have some outlet that gave him options for making money. We checked the help wanted notices and we went to visit a small craft shop that needed a buyer because business was growing and the owner couldn't do it all anymore. He was interested. Then he confessed that his wife and he together had been making carved kitchen utensils and that they did it as a hobby, so we arranged for some of them to be brought to see if they'd sell. He was satisfied by the time we finished. Went home to get his wife." Tom was grinning, content.   Ben said, "What puzzles me is that when we sit here thinking and talking we don't seem to reach that same degree of perception. Thinking limits me, I don't know why."

Jessie laughed,"You want the same high balance that a deep meditation brings you even when you aren't in meditation? Well, there's an art there too, you know."

"What? What is it?" Their voices sounded like one voice.

"It's a matter of learning how to open and sustain openness of mind, to stand at that Soul level constantly, to live there, and then the perception is constant. The thinking mind does it's thinking, but you shape thought out of a greater frame work of meaning."

"It's true! We think about what we already know, so we need new language to think about what we are realizing. I don't know how to BE conscious and THINK about being conscious at the same time. It's like we have to be silent, to stop thinking to SEE. It must be a matter of balancing on a mental level. Again, a new learning." Rose smiled ruefully.

Ben looked surprised," You have to keep trying to understand then shape language to hold perception. That makes a door through which we see more. It's like pressing up against an interface long enough,and accidently we discover an unknown door opening, showing us. It's that way in mathmatics, push at the farthest equation long enough, intensify the effort to See and then -- rest. In the resting suddenly there is recognition. The way hundreds of inventors of things and ideas, the latest being Grishold with his finding of the Star Drive and then Denforth with the Mass Transporter." He was silent, thinking. " Constant discovery in subatomic physics, biochemistry,and genetics, astrophysics, all the other sciences. This is breaking through into a consciousness we call Spirit." He looked in awe at this realization.

Jessie was looking around at them, wanting them all to see that."It's time you noticed that. People are practicing that system, that conscious use of the intuitive faculties, pressing against that interface, as you call it, purposefully . Pay attention! We've Reached out into a greater degree of consciousness,it is larger, deeper, we break through old perceptual limits as if our very brains flamed to life. Surely our Hearts have. We are participants in this greater consciousness, we ARE that consciousness, all of us." She spoke with that powerful, soft VOICE. They could not doubt! Finally they would notice!

Ben ducked his head,"No man likes to see that he's been sticking his head in the sand!" He looked at them, his face hard, and then as swiftly relaxed,"Oh,it's no use, of course I see that. I don't know why I hold out. It all depends on our ability to trust. I think." They were silent, contemplating this.

Rose finally broke that healing silence,"I used to think that if such Joining could occur it would be only between two who loved so deeply they were united through out their beings. Two so close they were part of one another. Could even be friend or parent and child, as well as lovers. But now, I see that is only the easiest way. All those who know the inflow of Love Itself, are connected enough that Joining can occur."

The others absorbed this idea, then nodded, thoughtful. So deeply attentive to the sharing of thought between them that they did not notice the coming and going of the rest of the Family, or those who stopped to join them. The darkness had fallen, the heat in the house felt comforting and good. A brisk wind had come up and the first thin mist of the coming rain had wet the windows.

Tom said softly,"It's a lovely thought. That Love brings us this Joining. Then those who cannot Join, or do not, might be those who have not become fully conscious of Love?"

Ben studied Tom's face, as if absorbing that idea took time., then he said, "Life grows out of Loving. One's open to one's beloved. People know of Love through that initial attractive need- love."

THE JOURNEY

"But then, a person can be open to every living thing. To a leaf, a breath of wind, an insect, people who are strangers, wholly open and absorbing of their Life essence, and then there is that awareness of Love. When it's like that, we don't say only that, 'I love' but also, 'I am aware of Love'. Even the enemy, seen with eyes illuminated, is not separate." She shook her head, "It can be disarming, you know, in regard to an enemy. When you perceive the needs that drive him to that battle, what he is blind to, his fears." She was silent, then rueful, "As long as any lust overpowers us, we can avoid perception." Jessie spoke her words carefully, trembling at their ability to understand, at her own desire that they perceive this recognition.

Rose nodded," I remember the Teachers telling us that 'Love is the river in which we live. We have only to open our Hearts and know it.' They used to say that we drink it's nourishment every time we are aware enough, when we love someone, or are touched by a great work of art, And we know hunger as long as we do not.' All that was simply a lovely idea then, now it is real."

Jessie smiled, "Have you watched the children lately when they do their 'attention' exercises in the gardens? You know how they are sent to sit, sometimes for hours, just really giving all their attention to a leaf, a tree, a stone, a frog, whatever caught their attention first, the way an artist does. They really See, but they also focus, pay attention. And you all know what happens. They make a connection. They begin to See so acutely that they do not want to be disturbed. They become fascinated. They discover! Then, though they don't always know it, Love has Joined itself in awareness through their lives. They talk to their Teachers about how 'changed' the object has become. They feel drawn to that object as though it has become more alive, more meaningful to them. It isn't until later that they realize that it is themselves -- their perception that has changed."

Tom was watching her, "All this is also of Love? I hadn't tied the two together." He was silent.

After a moment, he said, "It's amazing. It actually makes sense to me. And yet, surely Love is not limited to this."

" You have heard often, remember, that one of the characteristics of Love is that it is unlimited." Jessie got up, went to the dining room and found there Jane and Silvia, preparing the table for dinner. They looked at her questioningly, "We thought since everyone's so absorbed, we'd just get a good dinner for us all."

Jessie nodded, grinned at them, "Looks as though we'll be ready. Thinking makes one hungry, you know." She filled a cup with hot coffee and returned to the small group by the windows.

She sat down in a deep silence, the rattle of dinnerware, the soft voices of the two women in the kitchen, seemed loud in the quiet. Then Rose said, "We have so much to learn."

Ben nodded in agrement, settling himself deeper into the chair with her, reaching to take a sip of her hot drink, "How can we learn to live like that, so it is happening all the time, so we are 'in Love' all the time?"

Jessie nodded, relief and joy showing in her face,"It's something you practice, just as you've practiced balancing for so long. That practice made you ready for this one. You could not even ask the question were you not already practicing the art of Loving at the same time."

"And how?" Cassandra asked, settled between her knees, and listening with a grave attention.

"Pay attention! Pay attention to everything. Your own actions, your thoughts, your manner of being, all contact with any life around you, no matter how alien it may seem, how disgusting even, then soon you will DISCOVER through yourself. No one knows of Love by trying. Love is something you discover to BE when you pay enough attention. Love is inevitable, because it breathes our very lives. We just have to be aware, cease denial."

Rose nodded, a peculiar look on her face, "We've been taught that too. More times than I know, yet we didn't hear, did we?"

Tom shrugged,"Oh, we heard! Old habits of thought drowned what we heard. But we've been practicing, and the Vagabonds have reinforced it constantly, every time we make contact." He turned to Rose,"You've known so much struggle within yourself, so much pain, Rose. You must see that the Teaching was always going on in us."

She nodded, their eyes meeting and holding for a moment. "If I'd been one who could accept once I see the way Jane can then I would have known less pain. I've begun to understand, it's been a battle royal between intuition and intellect for me . I thought I had to choose. I couldn't see that a larger view would hold them both."

Tom shook himself, moved around to sit straight and stretched his long thin legs across the carpet,"I want to LIVE that way. Consciously aware of Love." His voice had risen, and he was speaking with an intensity that verged on anger."I don't want to go on as I've been all my life, only half alive, only half conscious." They heard the note of pain that came from that knowledge . To be half conscious is a punishment". He got up in his turn, walked into the dining area, where Silvia suddenly threw her arms around his neck and hugged him as though she sensed his dispair. She filled a cup with hot tea and he returned.

Jessie broke the silence that had fallen,"Remember these intermittent stretches of mind and Heart, are after all stretches. They do not happen all at once, or you might break. As you let go of your fears, as you practice the art of loving- which to some extent is the art of being aware, that will make you more receptive. Then you will live more and more within IT." She met each of their eyes, the children who had come to listen, sat attentive, fascinated."It takes courage, you know, to remind yourselves to do that. Valley children begin to think, respond, in a way their parents have not taught them. They are finding their own truth. And so are you all." She watched their faces, saw them realizing those ideas.

"Remember there are some who don't know of Love. Who aren't Soul conscious. But humanity has been practicing in small ways for centuries. We are all becoming conscious. " Her eyes became sharply bright, her gaze so inward she seemed gone from them but she Reached and they saw the mind-picture, the image of Valley life, then and now. So brilliantly, it was a shining recognition.

Jane had come in, her apron hung to her thighs, and her hair was loose and gleaming around her shoulders."Jessie, I felt that. I was with you all, seeing too." She was excited, never suspecting that she could be included in such a manner.

Jessie, laughed, taking her hand and holding it in both her own a moment."I'm glad. You are surely one with us, you cannot be excluded."

Rose roused herself from thought," I want to live so. Without forgetting!"

"LIFE is!" Jessie's voice was strong, penetrating their awareness. "It's our capacity to REALIZE life that limits us. And it is understandable that you long for those limits to be removed. But the longing itself is wrong perhaps. I will tell you a story. Once there was a woman who was imprisoned in the dungeon of a great castle. She had been there for many years and the only way air could get in was through a slim tube that was thrust down from high above., She could feel the air entering, and she could directly breath it at that point but she never felt there was enough. She could not see the sky, she could not know air was plentiful. Finally one day she was set free and taken up and released outside on Earth. She could not accustom herself to the fresh air, the wonder and joy of it. She kept feeling that she had to catch hold of the air and draw it to her mouth in gasps and hold it there. She built herself a larger but similar tube because she felt she must have it to be sure the air would not fade. People had to come and help her to learn how to just live and breathe the atmosphere in which she constantly lived.

" Jessie stopped and they all nodded,Tom said,"It IS the way we live. As if we're starved for that Love we won't let ourselves accept." Then he asked,"But Jessie, what of all those people who've learned? Who do live so. There must be such! How can they bear so much, alone. To be aware of so much must be very painful -- more than we've ever known?" He sipped his drink, already growing cool . Silvia came then bringing a plate with tiny sandwiches with delicious filling and neat small sticks of fresh vegetable. Another plate offered thin, hot, crisp, filled rolls, smelling wonderful. They each took a handful, not wanting to leave this moment. Jane poured a light white wine and served the glasses as if she thought the others daft. But she was smiling.

With her eyes twinkling, Rose Reached, and suddenly they bombarded Jessie's mind with appreciation, the flood lasted little more than a second and she was startled and then laughed, appreciating the joke. It was amazing to her that they COULD joke in this way.

"There are those. There are those among us, but they do not-- rather they have not commonly lived among us in our daily life. We send such children to the Stations. We call those people our Monitors and I doubt if many have asked just what-- or who they are." Jessie sighed, remembering, "But never imagine they are ever alone. They value and deeply seek solitude, but they are not alone."

" It's true. We just never talk about them,as if we haven't wanted to know.They are beyond us,people out of sight. But they are also present, and they have visited us, you know!" Benjamin drew himself out of the chair, stretched and continued nibbling on his snack. He could smell dinner in the kitchen and his stomach rumbled.It was going to be one of Silvia's special creations and a treat.

Jessie nodded , "They do, they're here more than you know." She took a bite of the tiny sandwich in her hand , shook her head admiringly,"Silvia,you're amazing, These are delicious and so tiny they only whet our appetites."

Ben moved to take a new handful from the plate and sat again on the edge of his chair,"I feel like a child who knows the doors and windows are all open but who will not walk out of the house into the light of day."

Anna had come to sit near him, "Daddy,,that's just it. Maybe we're all afraid to go out."

Silvia and Jane began to serve the dinner, everyone got up to arrange the table and take seats. The smells were delicious, and a deep sense of well being filled them all. Benjamin said,"Strange, how just being together and having a safe warm place with good food sweeps away a lot of worry."

"It's not hard to make people content, and I'm wonder whether contentment is more of a danger than a blessing." Jerry grinned."It's just what I need right now."

"So then? When contentment gets to be a rut, a stuck place, then its dangerous? Is that it?" At the nods around her Anna shrugged. It didn't seem enough to her. She wanted much more than contentment. She wanted adventure and excitement, new worlds to enter. Not the least of these being the worlds within. She was thoughtful as she ate. The preparation for the Journey was part of that Journey, she thought.

They were silent, eating, enjoying the fine food, the excellent wine. Silvia grinned at Jane as they complimented the two of them. "We've earned ourselves a reputation, Janey, we'd better be careful or we'll be asked to cook every day. You can all come patronize our restaurant." The moon broke from the clouds briefly, like a sudden benediction over the gardens outside, lighting the room softly for several moments. The wind rose, but those inside noticed little of it now. The dinner was late and they were all tired from the long day.

"There's always so much to think about. I need more time just to sit in my own rooms and put things into focus." Silvia said as they were finishing their dinner. Andrew stared at her, frowning deeply.

"Aunt Silvia, There's always too much to absorb. I think I can't ever get it all into order." And they laughed, and talked of those things while they began to clear their table, sending Jane and Silvia out, telling them they had done their share. Finally they began to leave one another, as if a quiet was settling, a need to be alone again.

Jane and Steve left, to go to her cottage He had much to say, he was eager to say it. The children left too, gently touching others in a silent goodnight. Tom went out to belt up and Ben went with him. Within a few minutes only Jessie and Rose were left, sitting in silent meditation listening to the wind.

Finally Rose said, "Jessie, what is happening to us?"

Jessie nodded seriously, watching Rose intently and tenderly,"You're on your

THE JOURNEY

way, my Dear, on your way." She smiled then,"It doesn't seem normal, these changes?"

"Good Heavens No! It seems as though our world is uprooted and can't get together again . I suppose for you it means something different than for me." She moved to sit on the stool beside Jessie's chair, her hands folded in her lap, she sat studying them. "There's so much ahead. But at least, I think we're no longer afraid."

"And what else?"

"It's also the longing, such a deep, bone deep longing, Jessie. I've never known anything like it."

Jessie chuckled, her smile a reassurance,"It's so, Dear. That longing will not cease.It is part of that knowledge that there is further to go. To have touched against Soul at all, leaves us deeply longing, and often, we don't exactly know what for." Jessie took her hand, brushed it softly with her own and held it.

Rose frowned,"I can remember when I was a child, and my brother was crying and I had hurt his feelings, and I didn't see why at all. I thought he was a fool. I dispised his weakness. Little as I was I made fun of him. I didn't see any reason why I should consider his feelings, although my mother told me I must." She turned to look out the windows, feeling the sense of safety that the warm room gave against the dark. "It seemed so obvious to me, that he had no reason to be hurt.The difference didn't seem to fit a child mind. Then, for no reason I know of, nothing I can remember, one day, I saw! I saw how another person might feel something I didn't. I could even share that feeling FROM them, and I was amazed. It was a revelation." She was silent for some time, then began to speak slowly.

"That may sound simple, yet it's the same, a stretch in consciousness. It wasn't something I did, but something that resulted because our teachers taught us to pay attention. Yes, just paying attention, I began to see what I couldn't reason out at all." She looked at Jessie with a great desire for her to understand. Jessie nodded, seeing how these reflections might illuminate another perception.

Rose laughed then, a brief harsh laugh with little amusement in it. "I do know that I can't ever go back, be what I was. I have no choice now but to go on. And I don't know where to!" She wiped tears from her eyes, absently.

Jessie said, "To talk about what it feels like makes it more real. To tell the process to one another will make it more possible." She laughed, and shook her head, "Oh, it's never done, my Child, it's never done. But there are stages of growth one completes and then there's a new understanding, before beginning to journey toward the next. One stands upon Mind itself, and travels intuitively, consciousness pierces beyond itself."

Rose looked at her, curious, drawn suddenly back to this everyday world of the trees and the land, the Hall and its warm shelter from weather and darkness. "Jessie, I didn't realize there was something to get ready for. Is it -- for all of us? Must we all be ready?"

Jessie nodded, I think so. I think all of this Family, and other Families in the

THE PEOPLE OF THE VALLEY

Valley are ready, or will be. Some already have begun, you know."

"Will all of us go, on this Journey? We wouldn't leave anyone behind, would we. Anyone of our Family that is?" She was aware of the selfish quality of her question, the limited perception asking it, but she accepted that.

Jessie laughed at her thought," There are those who are not ready now. Who may not be in this life. But everyone eventually will enter into that journey and make that step."

Rose sat nonplussed. What had Jessie just told her? It seemed so strange, so real, as if all her longing to go on, had suddenly been accepted and she must prepare herself for more than she had- bargained for.She shook her head, suddenly almost sad that Jessie had told her of these things.

Jessie said, "Well, you can handle it and you all need to know. It won't be too long before we must go. Before the winter becomes too cold." With that enigmatic statement, she stroked Rose's hair lightly,"It'll be all right. You surely aren't going to worry about this are you? She was smiling.

Rose suddenly bent forward and rested her head against Jessie's knee. Their silence was so deep that Jerry and Silvia passing through the other end of the room, hesitated a moment and then went on. Jessie watched as that inner union grew closer, that Rose the person and Rose the Soul, the greater swept slowly around and encompassed lovingly that lesser self so that there was not fear. Jessie thought it was as if two lovers met after long absence.

An owl hooted, so close to the house that they started. What would an owl be doing out in the rain? Then they saw that the winds had blown away much of the cloud cover and the moon again lit the earth. Its light fell into the room like a soft spread of pale paint. After a little, Rose raised her head, met Jessie's eyes and held them with no hesitation. Jessie returned her wan smile, glad and relieved that Rose consciously trusted her.

They sat listening to the night sounds, the world seemed so full, so alive, so much just there,, beyond the windows, here between themselves. Was there even in this normal living almost more than humankind could realize? Perhaps it was not at all different after all. What Rose imagine to be another world, was simply an extension of this. Everything took on a greater Life, a deeper reality, and yet was as it had always been. Here within what was, was all that was to be discovered. Rose thought about that, and wanted very much to talk to Benjamin, perhaps when they woke in the early dawn. She took her leave and went to his cottage. Jessie sat a little while alone, then she too went to her own rooms. The moonlight fell all around them, brightening the Earth and making a magic lovelyness everywhere.

CHAPTER FOURTEEN

The True Joining

Autumn had become a time of reflection. It was a busy time and the harvest was good, so it would have been easy to put the troubles of the summer aside. To forget the demands and the resentments of Builders. But those very conflicts had wakened people, caused them to pay attention as they never had. Jessie must increase her preparation of those who would Journey. Through all northern towns, she went from place to place, She must continually respond to the calls from the heart wherever they might be. But most important, she had begun the first of the Journeys! Families who were ready went silently off with her and were gone several days. The folks at the Farm missed her, but knew nothing of her Journeys with those already meeting that greater initiation into awareness.

Though they knew little of Jessie's labor, they found themselves caught up in times of silence, sudden and sometimes strained, as though the flood of thoughts and recognitions rose unbidden, demanding inner focus. Insight sometimes would not come to clarity, or would edge out of sight, then swim back at moments of silence just enough to tantalize, inform a little more and keep alert the questioning of their Hearts.

Jessie said this self absorption, this practice of heart listening, was a common phenomenon in the Valley in these days. They all knew they were not struggling alone, but they could not grasp the extent of realization through the Valley.

These were people who were meeting something in themselves and in each other that they knew they must accept.

Greyson, having assigned overseers to the Builders in the large towns or cities, traveled among business men, officials, met with teachers, sought to convince and so persuasive was his method, that he succeeded in bringing hungers long forgotten, into life. For most, this was simply another recognition, to pay attention and acknowledge these parts of themselves, but to remain unattached. For others, it was arousal, a reminder of something lost and of desires quelled unwillingly. These he brought into his following.

Jessie knew these things, and she knew that her own work must simply continue and be well done. She was familiar with the wrestling of those who could not make the decision, could not willingly choose yet. She did not demand, nor insist. Most students at Stations went through these times, but faster, with less turbulence. She waited with patience and love. She trusted that all these would make the Journey and step through that open door.

By the beginning of September when the first change in the autumn leaves brightened the heavy green of summer, at least in Adwin and other northern towns, Family Gathers were endemic through out the Valley. So engrossed were most people that they were unaware of how universal this awakening was, or of the continued activity of the Builders. So the division between them grew wider, and though Jessie saw and grieved, she could not disturb this period of gestation the people must endure. New Gathers were needed, time for a full unlimited Joining and therefore for that final recognition. The knowledge of the Journey!

The activity of the Builders seemed to them to be confined to the fields they had either been given or had taken. They waited the results of their market study. No further pressure toward more land had occurred after the middle of July. Their Gatherings, their Video programs encouraged others to join them, their calls for membership did not cease.

On a Wednesday afternoon in the first week of September, Silvia waited in the main Hall,, restlessly moving from chair to window, to gaze across the Valley then to the chair to sit again. Finally, she sighed a ragged,angry sigh, flung herself again into the chair, her small body almost hidden in its soft depths, and said aloud,"I don't know what's wrong with everybody. This whole thing is like volcano erupting among us and where are they? Off to town to do the usual work, business, visit, or whatever. How can they do that?" She was silent, tracing a finger across the arm of the chair through the thick fabric, refusing to settle her mind, or even to focus it. She felt a fierce rebellion toward everything and wanted to shout at someone. All the old familiar family safety,the wonderful family security and calm was gone.

With a jerk of her head she said ,"We should have all taken vacation time, all of us. This is important!" Now tears were in her voice and feelings of loneliness and confusion brought her close to self pity that threatened to drown her in its depths. She realized that and drew herself out but was left with anger again. She sat slumped, her eye fixed on the carpet, her legs thrust before her, the mound of her belly a great distortion of that once slim, delicate body.

"Did you tell them?" A soft voice spoke from the couch near the window. Silvia looked up in surprise, Jessie was settling herself there, arranging a large pan on her lap and another beside her. She began to string a large bag of beans. She glanced up from her work at Silvia's heavy frown.

Instead of answering, Silvia said irritably,"Jessie, why'd Jane plant those old fashioned beans? The processors can't string beans." She laughed, I suppose she thinks the flavor's better?"

Jessie smiled, "No, I think she just had the seed and didn't want to waste it. But she has plenty of the new variety too."She met Silvia's eye and gave a curt nod."Well, did you?

"No, not yet, but I will." Silvia felt anger and fear flooding through her, she could not bring balance to herself. She spoke harshly, unable to find relief."You, Jessie! You're not at all what I thought. You've changed too. You're not the little old lady I thought, not at all. Why you're a - a powerful woman!" She looked accusingly at Jessie."I've always just liked you,because you're like that sweet loving Grandmum I've missed in my life. I'd gotten to -- " her face opened, vulnerable, a trace of self pity naked upon it. "I'd gotten to love you. Yes, I had! And now, you scare me. Actually scare me!"

Jessie glanced at her and smiled. But Silvia did not notice, she was intent on her own discoveries , her own amazement."Why, you're just a little old lady no bigger than - than I am. Everybody towers over us, and yet, now, you seems to be six feet tall." She shook her head,"Why Jessie? Why? Who are you really? " She shook her head, uneasy. Had she overstepped her privileges with this strange woman?

Jessie finished a handful of beans and tossed them into the pan, reaching for others with the same motion. She looked up, her eyes were serious and sad though the smile remained, "As you said, I'm a little old Grandma. It's true, I am."

Silvia got up. Impatience and distress energized her muscles so they wanted to dance, to run, yet she held her self quiet. "No! You know what I mean, I'm sure you do. You're something much more than that. I just don't know how to ask. How could you do the things you do. How did you take the money-- gold money, right out of air, for instance."

Jessie sighed, that trick always brought repercussions. But now and then -- a sharp sound in the door way, caused them both to turn,"She's the one who Teaches and we're the ones who learn." Jennifer entered the room, went calmly to sit in the chair opposite Silvia. Her face was tired, but a peacefulness seemed to emanate from her. Silvia felt it and was envious ,jealous, then finally receptive. Jessie smiled, relieved, she had begun to think perhaps she was wrong and Jennifer would not arrive. She needed time with these two.

Silvia nodded,"All right, but what does that mean. And where did you come from, how'd you take the day off? Everyone's always so vague, saying things that can't be taken simply as they are. I can't understand always and it leaves me lost." The last sentence was spoken softly, she hesitated,then with a strong angry voice again, she said, "It's as if something's happening all round and I'm not sure what it is." She stood straight and as tall as she could, her eyes flashing, demand in her whole demeanor. "I've always thought that we were different! And now, I know of people everywhere who're talking this way. Just like the rest of you, and I'm the one who's different.She stared at them both from wide puzzled eyes, a strange hurt visible in their depths. Jessie thought how lovely she looked. What a wonderful mother she would be. Jennifer watched her, glad that the moment had arrived and that she was here. She saw that Silvia was meeting herself in a way she never had. And it was time,surely, before the baby was due. Silvia's blue,black hair, smoothly hanging about her shoulders, gave her the look of a little oriental girl, until one looked into her eyes. They were unmistakably the eyes of an angry woman.

Jennifer looked expectantly at Jessie but Jessie went on quietly stringing beans, nodding and smiling. Jennifer frowned but said," Silvia, I just arrived in Town and belted out. I think it's time we 'took vacation,' " at Silvia's gasp, she grinned,and went on, "And as for your next question, isn't that very difficulty in understanding,and the demand to understand, what makes us seekers?"

Silvia sighed, tears in her eyes, she felt she was treading close to a dangerous place. Jennifer, used the word Seekers, as of someone searching for something lost, or for a treasure - it shook the little calm that anger had brought her. She felt a rush of sorrow, wanted to deny it, saw that and then bafflement. She understood her fears, but the sadness,, that strange and deep sadness that literally hurt, and had become greater lately. She knew it had to do with those long talks of the Gathers, the talk that fascinated her but that left her unsatisfied. More, left her confused. The moments when they practiced the Reach,especially that astonishing Joining, had been enough, though she accepted that. But this, this talk of a Journey worried her. A great upwelling of grief surprised and caught her off guard. It was as if a barrier had broken, and grief rose from a long choked source. She spoke so softly they nearly did not hear."Oh, what can I do? What have I lost that is so precious?"

At these words Jessie looked at her, stopped her work and met Silvia's shifting eyes to hold them steady."My dear child. You will discover that it isn't as far away as it seems."

Silvia nodded then, tears streaming down her face,she ignored them. For moments she stood, looking without shame from one to the other, feeling that she was foolish, but refusing to accept that feeling. "Then,that's it? There's something we've got to find? Something we've missed somehow? Is that right?" She watched them intently, demanding response.

"That's part of it, surely. The Builders -- it's different with them." Jessie watched her narrowly, wanting her to say it.

"They don't KNOW there's something that needs to be found?" she asked. "They think there's something wrong with us? But all the time we've come to a place where we must go on, on to something -- someplace where we might -- might find what we seek?" She drew a long trembling sigh, "And I don't know what that is. I don't know what it is I search for! But whatever it is I've GOT to find it." Her eyes cleared, and she shuddered, as though the tide of grief threatened now to flood forth. "I've never rightly realized that before! I don't know why it's so sad for me." With a stifled sob, she shook her head, "I am going to my cottage, I need to be alone." And she ran from the room, swinging her heavy body more gracefully than most woman could have. She disappeared down the pathway through the garden to her cottage along the north ridge.

Jessie had gone back to work, her eyes on her pot of beans. Now, she looked at Jennifer, a great smile brightened her face,their eyes met, and she said,"I'm glad you're here."

Jennifer nodded,"You know the necessity, Jessie. I've only begun to know. There's so much I don't understand. I sympathize with Silvia completely. But what I need is to be here, to feel the love of the Family close,the presence. I need your help." Jessie nodded, and Jennifer felt that giving, that strength that flowed to her. Instantly she was aware that she had been closed and with deliberate choice,and surprising skill, she opened herself to receive. They sat so for several minutes, then Jennifer said,"I've worried, Jessie. Early this summer all of us began to realize a lot; we knew we were at a point of crisis within ourselves and yet, that was the time the Builders created all kinds of trouble so that we turned from our own needs to attend to those problems." She saw Jessie's nod, "Now, I think we're doing the opposite, ignoring what's happening out there, for what we're realizing in ourselves."

Jessie said,"It's all part of the same thing, isn't it?"

Jennifer shook her head,"I suppose so, but I can't see it now. I only know that when they started clearing those meadows near Brandhover and were ripping the trees out without plant healers to help, most people didn't even notice it was happening. Then they kept what acres they'd cleared, even when Council denied their request for the whole field. The Council hasn't reported on the Market research yet,but they've begun planting that stolen field as if they're absolutely confident what it'll be. People just aren't paying attention. And look at us! Silvia needs time, and attention, I do too. I know it."

"Jessie watched her, continuing with her work steadily, "Valley laws don't enforce behavior. People are free to try things. Would you want to change that? "

"Absolutely not!" She sighed, frowning with the effort to shape her mixed feeling and thought into words. The terrible part, I think, is our assumptions. Do we really think that we're beyond such selfish greed? Don't we still have that longing to stand one above the other, to possess more, to command and to control?" Her voice was strained, as though it hurt to speak. "Have we transcended any of our old desires?"

"You think then that it was only in theory that we have changed? That human aspiration has not truly risen? It is only in THEORY that we see others as of equal importance to ourselves, for instance?"

Jennifer frowned, searching for an answer,"No,No! I know there is real change, in our hearts. In our attitudes towards others, our values. There is real change." She was thoughtful,"It seems to me that it's more so in this northern country though."

Jessie nodded encouragingly at her. "The quality of Good Will, it's strong in us. It's what makes it impossible for us to look at life anywhere and not be concerned with its welfare. To see human beings and know they are OURSELVES. Do you see that?

Jennifer held her eyes frowning, then with a quick toss of her head,"Yes! Yes,I do. I've seen that very few people I know look at life otherwise. So why do I worry so? " She was silent, the afternoon sun filled the red and gold leaves of the trees,making them bright. There was the long plaintive call of mourning doves, sweet and sad. The day seemed very still. Jennifer said,"But that's not completely true, of course, there's William. I always saw him as the wise one, the benevolent one - and now, I don't know." She looked away.

Jessie said, "It is a disappointment to you, isn't it?"

Jennifer nodded, "And more so to Annette. But she has accepted. She says that he is truly kind, benevolent and wise. She says that he simply must be so within his own range of vision. I think she's right. He cannot recognize the differences but he can't completely deny, because he respects people who speak of them. To begin to suspect there might BE a difference and feel himself unable to realize what others speak of, must be terrible to an intelligent man. At least one like William who wants to know everything!" She smiled sadly.

"If he has courage, he will insist on studying what others say they realize, at least."

"But I think Will has lost courage. I think he has grown resentful. That his work with the Builders makes that resentment stronger. But then, I can't say that there is much more honor in me. I know, I See with all of you, at least a little. I have known the glimpse of what is before us. I do KNOW. I cannot doubt. For me life in this Valley is absolutely precious. Under no circumstances can it be dishonored, or abused. Yet, with all that, I find various fears assaulting me. I have ignored the rights of others, subtle rights, perhaps, but I knew the difference. I am not as wise as William, nor as intelligent. He is actually a very brilliant man, you know."

" I know that brilliance of mind has always been a matter of high regard among your people, and that William has trained his mind well. Yes! Perhaps that's why now, he cannot discover these truths through his trusted method of careful reason. He refuses what he calls non-scientific, or sloppy intuitive reasoning. He says since he is not an artist, or a woman, he has no need for intuition. Since he does not See for himself, he has no experience to think about. To use as his medium for research. Does he not ever trust the experience of others? Surely he has not had reason to question Paul, Ben, you, Rose? Surely he knows all of you are capable and to be trusted?

"He used to. In the beginning, when we would talk of the few recognitions we knew. When we talked of the Spirit. We could talk mostly from an intellectual point of view. But when we began to bring intuitive perceptions, or experiences that were unexplainable in traditional terms, he -- well he began to dismiss those things by saying that we were unbalanced. He actually thought that! But if he'd simply paid attention, he'd have seen. All of us couldn't - " she stopped, frowning, unwlling to go on.

Jessie nodded slowly, "It was after I had been here a little while, I think. He could justify that by seing me as evil influence. No?"

Jennifer nodded, sheepishly, "We didn't think you knew that, but of course you would. Oh, Jessie, William has changed too, you know, since he began working to gather all those together who are mind- blind." She frowned, "They hate that expression. They say it's superstition." She sighed, "He won't tak about numbers. He still thinks a large majority are as he is."

Jessie nodded, "He cannot bear the fact that there is something he cannot understand. Something other people speak of as you folks do. His intellect is very sharply honed, but his intuition, his Heart, has been neglected. Now, he fears what he cannot understand and since he is accustomed to understanding whatever he sets his mind to, it drives him to that for which he himself would have felt only contempt, denial, and accusations of superstition."

THE JOURNEY

" Yes, I think that's why he is so angry, to. He does see that, when he will admit it to himself, then Annette says he feels a self contempt that drives him away from its cause. So, his anger just increases." She worked silently for a moment, then glancing at Jennifer, said, "Builders all have the same attitude, don't they?"

Jennifer curled her body deep into the chair, nodding, and silent in her turn. Then she said, "Well, I too have my moments. I want to go out and fight against the Builders, force them into different attitudes." She shook her head smiling grimly,"But, of course that's impossible. Impossible. Fighting is not the way, Jessie.I know that in my heart"

Jessie, finished the big bag of beans, got up to carry her pans and bag to the kitchen. "There're enough here for dinner and for a couple of other dinners this winter. Let's run the ones we don't need now into the processor. Jennifer got up to help her, carrying the empty bag and the pan of stems and strings. Jessie poured a large quantity into a kettle that she would cook later, and the rest they cleaned in clear water, dropped into boiling water for a moment and then poured down the spout of the Processor, setting it on 'bag and freeze'.With a sense of satisfaction they watched it register and begin to obey.

They went to the Hall door, walked out into the autumn evening, the odors of ripening fruit mixed with the fragrance of harvest and late flowers made the air a perfume. Jessie breathed a long deep breath. "How wonderful it is. Jennifer, I cannot imagine how any human being today can be sad or dissatisfied, and then, in the next breath, I know exactly how we can be. We are animals whose greatest strength has been dissatisfaction with the status quo. And our greatest grief also." She laughed," But you see that there are other ways to change things besides violent ones.

Jennifer nodded, pleased," Well, they have no business taking land not theirs to use. They have to see that!" Her voice had little anger.

Jessie stood very still, listening, her eyes far, seeking that Station that her mind already had Reached to. But Jennifer had no knowledge of that. She waited, watching the evening begin to settle around them, the shadows lengthen . She could see People below on the Highway, and someone far down in the Farm fields, riding a disc float over the crops. Probably Jane, she thought, testing whether it was time to harvest. Jessie said softly," You remember the task of the Monitors is to watch. They see and will help Earth. Just as they did at the stolen field."

Jennifer looked to the west, where the Station was, too far to even begin to see, and the northern Station, behind them, though much closer, was hidden by rock. She looked back to Jessie."You lived among them, didn't you? Are you one of them, Jessie." the question was hesitant, as though she feared asking.

Jessie met her eyes but instead of answering, she said,"I was trained there."

Jennifer stared at Jessie. " I didn't know. I never have known much about them, Except that they are there. They keep so distant. Why!"

"Do you think that had we all known of them, people whose powers are so great, then would we not all have begun acting as the Builders are toward us? Or we might have wanted them to play parents to us."

Jennifer was silent for a long time, finally she slowly nodded her head, "I suppose it might have been so. We are afraid. We are - were - mistrustful. And we've also sought powerful people to take care of us in the past. Surely we might have -- who knows?"

Jessie sighed, moved slightly toward the rack on which belts were kept. "It's still early, let's go take a look at that field we're so worried about." Jennifer stared at her startled at the idea, then nodded."Why not? We could see for ourselves."

They took belts, strapped them on and leaped from the deck rail platform into the clear air, and climbed high until it was a little chilly. They descended swiftly into Adwin and found an air car that would leave soon and whose route passed through Brandhover. The town was not on the hourly routes, but the car to Clandor would stop there.

Across the land they saw the movement of people and animals, the clusters of fruits trees along Highway and fields. Discs floated among the groves, young people harvested pears and plums. The harvest discs did the job rapidly. It took only a couple of hours a day for these young ones. Several varieties of apples were ready. Others, with late pears and Pomagranates, Applecots, and about half of the grapes would wait at least a month for harvest. Within the forests, there were great open meadows with small clusters of fruit trees among the wild grasses. The floats made it easy to bring them out. Variety and companion planting was essential to the health of the land. They looked with the interested eye of farming people at the land below. Soon, they could see the flat land, grass country, with scattered interruptions of small forests and with dense strips along winding streams. Literally miles of grains stretched like a band of gold around Bend. The fields were ripe, the grain golden in long curves, alternating fields of different wild and domesticated grains or beans, created patterns from the air. At intervals dark green ridges of shrubs bearing nuts and fruits, divided the smooth sweep of the grain. These, along with the high stubble and discarded straw, held the soil, kept the harvested fields from being empty and unprotected from winter winds. Winds could be fierce here. Jessie mused again at the wisdom of the Master Farmers, their deep caring for the land.

Now, near by, Brandhover appeared from behind her low rolling hill country. Small lakes, teeming with water birds, some of whom would soon be harvested, dotted the land. There to the east, in land left to forest and field, was a dark, newly opened field. The soil was bare,dark, no crop visible from the air, but when the two women leaned to look closely, as the car dropped to land, they saw that there were new vines planted there. They had cut into and ripped out part of an old deciduous forest. Here had been the old sweet acorns from which flour was made in the early years.

The two women disembarked and went to the Belt racks. They silently strapped on belts and lifted out to fly the short distance to the new field. No workers were visible inside the protection of the force field. Jennifer sighed, standing beside the remaining forest that surrounded the field."They cut into this, this wonderful forest. We've always thought of it as a kind of shrine to our early Valley people. It got a lot of people through those first years." She shook her head, frowned and then added,"Well, so long as no one touches Tilling's Field, I suppose we can survive. And they did stop, when the Council gave them its decision."

Jessie nodded,"It seems so senseless. Much of what they took was old meadow, only one grove of the oaks were ripped out. The meadow is nearly gone here, the few yards around the edges of the field won't give enough space in this forest to keep grass clear of young trees .They guided themselves easily over the field."Look Jennifer,they've planted straight as a dye, as though nothing at all has been learned about how plants grow best. Not a plant of any kind in the rows between, the soil looks as if it's been raked out. They actually did it the way the old ones did." She laughed suddenly, a laugh of amazement and pain, "Why, the little vines are growing well, but they won't be protected by companion plants There is nothing here in all these acres but Vines." For moments she stood looking at it. "It took us so long to learn from Earth how to grow things, and now they would forget." She had only sadness in her eyes.

Jennifer nodded,"It's for the wine they plan. For the wine, Jessie. And the results of their market research isn't in yet. They don't know whether there will be a market at all."

But they are so sure. They say it's absolutely logical. That people being what they are, there'll be markets. They insist that that technique, borrowed from our ancestors, advertising, will convince people that they want more than they think they do." She looked at Jessie and said,"You are remembering!"

Jessie nodded,"I am, Dear. I remember the last of that. People were already ignoring those persuasions before the Valley was built, aware of the distortions of fact.. In the very first years, when I was young and mated and had my first child, there was such a to do. But even then advertising was being looked at with amusement. More and more subtle methods had to be used and I don't think these folk have that skill. We had distinguished between making full information available and insidious persuasion, but assuming people can be made to want what they don't, finally became something of a joke. I don't know why they haven't read of that in our history."

"I think they have. People've always been able to convince themselves of anything we want to. Look how hard the Teachers have to work to make us aware of that tendency. We aren't so far from that time. But we must not regress!" Jennifer's voice was a cry. Jessie glanced at her, but the young woman smiled sadly and said, "Jessie, let's go back into the forest, let's see whether we can find how the little creatures managed."

Jessie nodded, and they flew in among the great spreading trees. The shade beneath was deep,for this south land had little cold until December. They walked a little while on the deep forest cover, thick with leaf mold, with fruits and nuts already falling from the scattered fruit trees, oaks, english walnuts,and pecans. It was obvious harvesters had been here, there were few on the ground and little rotted fruit. But most acorns still clung. They did not fall early. The patchs of conifers blazed dark green here and there among the bright color of the deciduous trees. The forest seemed so still, so immersed in itself. Jessie listened, touching individual trees, sliding her hands down the rough bark, and once pressing her body against one very old oak. In this way she learned much. Jennifer moved here and there and finally, coming to a small dark pool at the center of a small meadow, she sat, stroking the fine grasses and picking a few tiny blue flowers that grew on them. "Oh, Jessie, the forest seems to me full of peace.I don't feel any fury or old pain here."

Jessie came and sat beside her,"There is none. There is acceptance. The trees torn from Earth, have been mourned, the little ones are safe among the roots, and the normal life of wild creatures has been resumed. The forest will abide."

Jennifer stood looking outward, through the trees to the dark field. "They planted those vines as though they were unconscious."

Jessie laughed," Few but an Altos citizen and mother of Wizards, would speak so."

"Jennifer turned to her, "Well, it's true. The straight rows, no companion planting, every row so far from another. It is not natural for a field to be so."

"We know that! They do too, because they've been taught that knowledge, but they refuse it because they want to return to the old days, remember? They exagerate the difference."

Jennifer nodded slowly," Yes,they do know."

" They want to get back to where they feel safe again."

" I'll ask Paul if he's seen this. He may have. He wouldn't have wanted to trouble me, I think , to tell me."

"Well, Jen. Let's go on down to Bend and see what people think." Jennifer agreed and they lifted off, soared through the autumn air and directed their belts to Bend, across the flat grain land.

They dropped down finally at the midway outer flank of the great Stadium City. The city that was built like a vast mile wide football Stadium,rising in a circle of grey and white from the brilliant colors set in many shades of green of the great garden park down in the circle at its center. The city rose around the park and when they drifted down to stand a few moments at the lake in the center,they looked up. This great wide park seemed surrounded by gleaming, slopes of mountain. But Jennifer wanted to be where people were walking along the broad roadways that circled every residence or business story. So they lifted again and landed on the avenue that ran outside the markets. Trees and flowers bloomed and fruited along the edge, people walked and worked in the high air of their stadium city. Jennifer had been here several times but always found the visit exciting. She walked slowly, looking into fascinating shops where goods of every discription were displayed. Robot clerks greeted her in their monotonous tones, but she smiled and went on. Here and there a human clerk smiled and waved.

She thought she would buy some thing, something different for her children. If she could find --but Jessie caught her arm, and led her back to sit on a bench were several other citizens were taking the late sun."Please, let's look at all this later."

A man walking slowly as if lost in thought, suddenly swung around, looked at them penetratingly and then with a broad smile, came to them."Jessie, I'd not thought to see you here. You've been gone some time. We've missed you." He bowed slightly and Jennifer remembered that the people of Bend practiced a kind of ritual of manners.

A woman sitting near came to them, she too bowed and reached a hand to Jessie and then to Jennifer, simply touched with a warmth that surprised Jennifer."What brings you here, friend?" She was a tall woman but too thin for Jennifer's tastes. She had flaming red hair and dark green eyes, and wore clothes that any Vagabond would have envied. Jennifer found herself wondering what weavers did that kind of work and resolved to ask. The woman's name was Linda and the man's Justin. He accepted their invitation to join them and went to get them all drinks. When he came back, carefully setting their glasses on a small table that he pulled out from the wall, he asked."Yes, have you come to stay?"

Jessie shook her head,"We just came to look at that field the Builder's planted. "

Justin grimaced,but said nothing, Linda asked,"You seem troubled about it."

Jessie met Linda's eyes, saw the depths of knowledge they held,the warmth and humor behind them. "To be blunt, we want to know what you folks think of that action. The people of Bend, how have they dealt with it?"

Justin groaned,"It got a lot of people ready to declare war, at first. Especially in Brandhover" He grinned, "Maybe I ought not to use the old word, it does seem a little dramatic, but some people were furious. Some people didn't seem to notice, until some of us made a protest and brought it to the Town Council. Finally, now that it's done, they're going to discuss it this week." He shrugged,"That's it, both reactions, some very angry, others seeming not to notice."

Jennifer sighed, "Democracy is slower than tyranny, you remember. But then, everyone knew, didn't they? Shouldn't it have been on agenda right away?"

"Some people said that's not really our land so we're not responsible, some said that the Builder's were a phenomonon that would just end of itself. Others just seem to --- to turn into themselves and to ignore what's happening around them. Bad business, that. Maybe we've begun to be smug, to think nothing of real trouble can happen.We've been so sure of ourselves here in this Valley." Linda was herself troubled, though her eyes seemed to shine with a bright knowledge that Jessie wanted to plumb.

A young man sitting near by, finishing a paper he had been writing, leaned toward them,"It's unnatural, what they've done. We've got to replant the forest. We don't need vines there. Did you see the way they planted?" His voice was angry, indignant. Jessie noted a tone of self righteousness in it. He closed the brief case on the papers he had written, and stood, "We've got to find the people and punish them." His head bodded emphatically.

Jessie turned to him,"Do you think many feel as you do, young man?"

He bowed and said,"Reginald here." Then he came near to them.

"There are a lot more than most people think. I met with twenty ready to take action just last night."

Surely you'll wait 'til the Council meets?"Justin did not seems surprised at the young man's attitude. He seemed confidently to think the Council would solve all problems. Jessie wondered what his reaction would be when he knew the extent to which people like Reginald would go. He met her eyes and she Touched,and knew his thought. "The boy's a minority. I don't believe there are extremists here."

He said aloud,to Reginald,"Why would you punish them? Any citizen can choose his way and is given help to do it."

The young man frowned,"But taking without asking, it's right that we ask! You know. They didn't find out if it was right for the rest of us." Jessie noticed that he did not say,'for the Valley'.

Jessie and Jennifer stayed for another hour, listening to the discussion that began to grow around them. They heard two others who thought as the boy. Surely there were not many, but those few were loud. They were indignant and angry. They did not realize their own hidden wishes to do as the Builders had done. Or to control others. There was a subtle jealousy rising from that.There were others who were quiet, listening also, whose minds filled with worry, and a few whose minds radiated calm humor. Jessie noted them all, Jennifer saw only the outer manifestations.

Finally Jessie got up, and began to say her goodbyes. Jennifer stood, filled with an eagerness to be gone. True to her promise, Jessie turned to walk through the bazaars and stores. Jennifer chattered happily about the amazing displays. Much of it she'd seen on the Market screens at home, but seeing it here was special. They bought a few gifts, one gift of Jennifer to herself and after about an hour, both wanted to leave.

They walked in silence to the air grid and stood beside an empty air car. Jennifer took Jessie's hands in both her own, searching her face, nodding. Jessie Reached gently, Touched faintly into Jennifers mind and after a second of resistance, was received. Jennifer shuddered faintly, willing herself to meet another mind again, willing to stand firm in the power she felt growing around them. This was not just an ordinary Joining. It seemed as though a great bell of power and Light surrounded Jessie, moved steadily outward to surround her and then, sank slowly and astonishingly into her very mind. She felt it, knew it and was shaken by it's revelation there. She stood firm, the muscles throughout her body felt as though an electric current ran though them, she frowned, focussed, then knowing her desire for that Touch, she wholly accepted. Her body relaxed, receptive. The power of it staggered her. She had not known the beauty of it could be so great. Jessie's Touch was not as Paul's, or Rose's, or even the whole

Family. It was clean, pure, like a golden light, a radiance of awareness, that sang through her mind, opened it, made her own inner consciousness available to her. She wondered how she could deserve this gift. Understandings flooded her mind and she gasped to realize so much. Then, in reaction, she closed away, but her mind was once again stretched and would never be the same.

The beauty brought tears to her eyes, but the power frightened her and she had to employ all her will to stand firm, steady and to KNOW. As she relaxed, she knew the possibility of Joining as she never had before. It was not simple mind Touch, sharing of imagery, thought processes, it was infinitely more.

When Jessie withdrew, Jennifer felt immediate, terrible loss, and then instantly a great relief. She opened her arms to embrace Jessie, and said,"I See." Knowing that she could not have said all she understood. She must take time to absorb all this. She said, "I'll take a car on home from here. Goodbye Jessie. We'll come to the farm soon."

Jessie nodded, kissing her and turning away. They went without further words. Jessie watched as Jennifer's car lifted off. When she arrived at the Farm she was tired, feeling that this old body did not always take all she asked of it with peace. She came into the hall and found Ben sitting in a big chair with Cassie on his lap. She was snuggled into his shoulder as if seeking comfort. Steve arrived just as Jessie did, walking in beside her he smiled happily at her.

"It's been a good day, you know. But the tension's not letting up at all. I found Jane, of all people, in the tool shed. She'd forgotten what she'd come for. That's surely not like her." He laughed and dialed himself a hot cup of tea, nodded at Ben, stroked his daughter's head as he passed and said to Ben, "How can you drink a cold beer this late when the evening chill begins?"

Ben shrugged, and continued to sip at his dark, cold bottle. But Steve was looking at Cassandra, feeling the tension in her body, wondering whether Ben realized that. For minutes they were silent as Steve and Jessie settled themselves. Jessie drew some knitting into her hands. Ben smoked his pipe, the habit almost an anachronism, but the herbal blends smoked in the Valley were healthful, created by Healers themselves.

Rose called from the kitchen, "Shall I arrange for dinner. Will you accept what I choose? They could hear her laying out a menu on the kitchen auto-dial. Jessie sent her a sharp agreement, not wanting to talk. She sank gratefully into her soft chair. They heard Jerry coming in the back way talking to Rose.

Jerry came into the Hall, his dark face almost lost in the shadows until he stepped into the light of their lamps. He flung his bright blue jacket on to the chair he sat in, "What's happening?" he asked perfunctorily. Rose came in just as he asked, changed from her town clothes, she wore a long soft green gown belted at the waist She curled up beside her brother , throwing a kiss to Ben and Cassie. They sat, silent, divided.

Finally Jerry said, "Something's been pounding at me all week. I've got to talk about it. See if I can find it out. It's like, I feel as though we're related in some way that I've never known before, as though we're already Joined, so that when we consciously Join we're just acknowledging being conscious of what's already true." He frowned, searching out how to say what he meant. He looked from one to the other, their tired faces giving him little help. He went on,"It's more than the fact we're a family. It's as though we're together, part of one another. Not really separate at all." He drew a long ragged breath, determined to finish what he had begun."I've begun to think that we're a lot more than I thought. Than I ever imagined I could be." He shook his head, looked at them with a lame grin, then doggedly began again,"Don't you see? Does it make sense? I feel as though I can't speak of myself unless I'm speaking of us all. And that doesn't make sense to me, it's uncomfortable. I don't want to be less than myself, I want to be ME". He thought their faces registered so little interest he felt defeated. he finished,"I guess I can't say what I mean."

Rose leaned over to put one hand on his arm."You do make sense. What you're trying to say isn't so far from what I've felt too. You said it as well probably as it could be said. After all, it's a new concept, a strange and impossible idea, even. But, maybe we've got a case of over load. We've heard and realized so much lately. Besides,that idea, whether we all think of it or not, is a scary one. We ARE individuals, after all. Can we lose that? In this Joining?"

He nodded, his eyes shining, "That's it! That's what I worry about."

She was silent, then as if from deep within herself she spoke," Let me try, maybe it's like this." She drew a breath, frowned, "We are together in consciousness. We are together in Joined consciousness. And that means then that we are one person on that level?"

Jerry was nodding, his face eager, his eyes lit."Yes, Rose, it's something like that, actually. And it sounds crazy even though you said it. But surely we're not less, we're still individuals who've come together by choice!" His voice had dropped to a whisper.

"I don't like that." Steve broke in. "Makes us sound like some kind of octopus, or a conglomerate, not really people."

Jerry nodded, determined to get to the bottom of this,"Yeah,I know Steve. I thought that at first. At first I felt like I was losing something, myself maybe. But then, as I realized it, realized our Joinedness, it began to feel right after all. Because I choose to Join. I don't ever Join unless I choose to! I separate myself when I choose. The Joining is inside us, deep beneath what makes us persons." He waved his long arms trying to shape the thought with his hands,"Don't you remember the Master Teachers telling us some time about something called Group Consciousness? Well, I decided this must be like that. Only just us, so far. Like maybe we've just begun to learn."

Jessie looked up from her work,then down again, Rose ran her hand up and down Jerry's sleeve, wanting the touch of him. She murmured out of memory," ' Humanity growing conscious of Itself as an entity, Joined within Itself as One Being.' Yes, I remember that. They did teach us that. I didn't absorb it at all then."

Jerry was impatient,"I want to tell you the rest. I thought of those old teachings and then, remembered they said that Love was the quality that made us become conscious. Made that Singleness real. That Love drew everything together and when we knew that, realized that kind of Love, we would be becoming what Humanity IS." He stopped suddenly feeling accomplished, he had said all that he had thought except the most important part. "And if that's so, then it means we're learning what Love is, learning to be open to that energy! There, how does it sound, I've been thinking all week about this."

Ben stared at his brother-in-law. Cassie blinked her eyes and frowned. Rose said, "We keep finding that the word Love fits into everything that's happening. It's as though we're fish in a stream. All of us thirsty and yet we don't drink. It's like Love is all around us and we take little drops and think that's all there is for us." She turned to Jerry, her brown face shining with her smile, her dark eyes serious. "But then, maybe that's part of the fear of Joining. I've worked out the 'idea' of it. What a blow this is to the ego. I, as a person, fear loss of myself. I, as Soul, patiently wait for me to be conscious there is no loss." She stopped, trying to realize, and find words to fit."I think that it's natural to feel afraid, as though we are finally aware of the danger of losing ourselves in that greater Self that we are becoming? That sounds like the teaching too but it also sounds like what we've experienced. At least, most of us have, haven't we?" She looked at Steve, aware of his restlessness, wanting to leave, to escape and also wanting to stay, feeling he MUST stay.

He said,"Yeah, it's true. That feeling of something not right, and yet,- yet, so very Right after all. When you all Join I feel as if I'm about to be invaded." His expression was so mournful Rose could not repress her smile.

There was a sound at the door and they all looked up. Silvia was there, leaning against the wall, her small face white in the frame of her black hair. She came to them then, slid melting down into a graceful heap on the floor. Rose thought how remarkable she was, eight months pregnant and she could move like that. She leaned on her elbow, gazing far off."I know exactly what you mean, Steve.It's just that for me. The sense of being a part of something, not myself alone." She twisted about until she leaned back against Jerry's knees, her legs straight before her. Tears spilled over, ran down her face.She had spent a long and difficult day, struggling to understand and to take some risks within herself. Her face seemed pale, weary. She reached for Jerry's hand above her shoulder and held it tightly. "It's as though something's happening that I can't control,. As though I'm changing and I didn't decide to." She wiped a hand across her face,"Look at me, Here I'm crying and I don't really want to. I don't know why. As if some part of me is crying and the rest of me is not." She shook her head vigorously, as if to shake off the strangeness.

Jerry leaned over and kissed the top of her forehead, wrapped both hands around her's and gave to her consciously a streaming of comfort. He loved her with his whole being, right now it seemed to him he had never loved her so much. He felt himself shaping that Love around her, and around their child.

Rose said softly,"Your child is not separate from you, and yet he is not a 'piece of something'".

Silvia turned to her angrily,"It's not the same. He's growing , becoming something for himself, SOMEONE. Separate and individual. It's altogether different." She was silent then, thinking, her face softening, "It's true, a child always is physically a part of it's mother - and father too. Always,I suppose."

"Even though to grow up, it must free itself,must live an individual life." Rose watched her."Then, it is free to choose to become Joined again. And so to become whole."

Silvia looked at Rose, then up at Jerry, who smiled tender encouragement. She frowned suddenly, as if irritated at that tenderness. Then said,"That's what the Master Teachers said, isn't it? It must be what they meant, when they said that only the strong ego is willing to die. At the time, that was sheer nonsense to me."She turned in appeal to Jessie.

Jessie nodded to her, "There must be strong individuals, learned in their own inner disciplines who choose growth,-Love, the way of realization. Then these can bear the knowledge of that Singleness of Joining. That singleness of Humanity Itself even."

Silvia nodded, her eyes locked on Jessie's, "I think I see. There must be discipline and strength,because Joining threatens our very identity. We must be clearly sure what and who we are." She was silent, not taking her eyes from Jessie's. And Jessie did not reach, but let this conversation do it's work. Silvia had been taught as had every other child of the Valley, She would understand. Silvia finally spoke, looking away, and speaking slowly,"It's the little self that's afraid. We learned that. I'd completly forgotten. Now we've begun to know the possibility of life that extends beyond what we've been. Reality is so much more." She was nodding her head as if she had told herself what she needed to hear "This personal life is a small part of everything, it's not at all what it seems."

Silvia was absorbed in her thought. "So all of us, coming together-- knowing one another as mental beings, that's a step toward- what's more real? She stopped nodding to herself. "So this - what I've always called my 'self' - this is a small part of what I am? Of what we are?" She was nodding steadily, lost in the thought and the understanding.

Steve broke in then, "Ah, Silvia, you've said a lot there. I think maybe it means something for me now. It's a new beginning, we are becoming what we might be?" He sighed, taking that in.

Rose laughed, Jerry was stroking Silvia's temples gently, he focussed his will and attention to send Love as forcefully as he could. Rose watched, knowing, and turned to do the same for Steve. They must be bathed in Love until each was separately aware of IT. To allow that flow unresisted, they would need help.

Rose said,"It's seems right to me, Silvia,Love. It seems right that we're conscious that we're becoming what is possible."

Silvia looked around her, at all those in the room, meeting their eyes, feeling their Love, She reached to Cassie, and knew that Cassie knew as she knew and more. Yet Cassie was so young. Her heart leaped, there was so much yet to learn,to know."Then this is all of that, that the Builders fear? This knowledge , this Joining?" She was suddenly aware that the old familiar thorn of being left out, of being ignorant of something the others knew, was gone, faded as though absorbed.

Benjamin answered slowly,"We've known of the Joining for such a short time. They don't know of it at all and wouldn't believe it if you told them. We've said before, the Builders fear what they don't understand. We've been paying attention to ourselves, looking into our own hearts. We've forgotten them. The Builders have actually not done much harm . The harm is their attitude that it is all right to harm others, other lives, however small or large." He looked around, a growing worry on his face,"That could esculate into something as terrible as the times of Trouble. Because that's what caused that world wide devastation, you know. That attitude." He breathed with astonishment, never having realized that before.

Silvia nodded, realizing more than his words. Her frown deepened, wrinkling her smooth,soft face. "Ben, we aren't immune to wrong doing. To selfishness. Look at us, so self absorbed now we think only of our struggle, our own awakening. For those who See even, those who CAN Join, there's temptation. Such Vision, such perception could be used -- for selfish ends. It's a powerful tool, for good OR harm!"

Benjamin turned to Rose, his eyes bleak, for he knew they had avoided that fact. Finally he nodded, Rose refused to speak.He glanced at Jessie and she too was silent. He said," Silvia, you so often hit the mark exactly! We've got to pay more attention.It's a powerful tool,or it's dawning realizatioin! We've assumed all of us are dedicated to Love and responsibiity. We know that might not always be so." He sighed, leaned back, loosened his body with a shrug, and said,"Jessie, you've taught us, and the Master Teachers insist that unless a person has begun to realize the presence of Love, selflessness, at least as an ideal, that they are not lifted enough out of their personal natures to Touch. They might just begin to Reach, feel a little of that possibility, but a true Touch comes with compassion, and some integration of Soul and self."

Rose met his eyes, "Once that happens, we're not the same person. Once that happens, we see and realize each other as of one greater nature. It's true, we're Self absorbed, inclusive, 'other aware'. We have to watch ourselves though. We are capable of harm, always we are capable of wrongness." She frowned, looked away then back at them, her eyes flaming, "Tell me! Tell me if you see me falter, if you see my actions don't come from wholeness. We must always be alert for any one who uses these Talents selfishly. Look what's happened to that man called Greyson. He's one who is aware and has CHOSEN to turn from the Light."

Jessie said,"You're training through your lives was designed so that you would be responsible by the time you were able to perceive and to Join. You've practiced meditation, the entrance into perception and Love since you were children. In these ways, we are taught, and ready." She smiled, "A strong sense of responsibility is part of that realization. Some of you let that get out of hand too." Her smile was merry, laughing at them.

They looked at her, relieved, but still feeling a nagging worry. Cassie suddenly broke in, her high little girl's voice startling in the quiet. "Some of my friends are afraid anyway. They feel like life is so -- so BIG - that there's something inside us that -- could explode." She sighed,"I feel that too, that I'm more than I thought I was. There's a me that cares about people and there's a me that wants to do whatever I want. If I care too much then I might miss out on things I want." She fidgeted, wriggling her body as she got out of Ben's lap and stood,her face composed,suddenly she seemed older than her years."I think it's too much to understand. But -" she smiled a grimacing smile, a look of perplexity coming over her face, "There it is! Just the way Rose told us." She turned to look around at them. "But we're not always - always aware of the Light. Some of my friends say they're afraid. Not when the Light is around them or when they see it in someone else, but when they think about it later" She was silent for several minutes, but everyone knew she had not finished. "Or when we forget."

Rose almost held her breath, wanting this little one to speak. Finally Cassandra said," But we can't really forget, you know. It keeps coming back. Every time we pay attention. It's as though there is more than me in me. It's like that, you know. And when I pay attention to That, it only makes me happy ,not afraid."

They all laughed with relief, wanting to comfort her. Cassandra added,"In meditation -- then I always know the Light. Then it's all right!" Rose got a distinct impression SHE wanted to comfort her adult family.

Jessie nodded, smiling with Cassandra now. She focussed her own energy, drew from sources to which she kept connection and sent streams of Love into the group. Now she said,"You've said what it's like for some of the rest of us, Cassandra. It's different for each, you know. Most people find the first contact with that greater Self a bit of an adjustment." Watching, Jerry wondered at her merry smiling, as if this were somehow all a joke.

Silvia slid down on the rug,to lie on her back, more comfortable for the mound of her belly." I think it's just as well we don't fully trust ourselves. We can get mighty self-righteous, you know.

"We have seen and known, we will not let each other forget!" Rose spoke with a sudden firm joy, as though she felt a rejoicing to so speak at last.

They heard another young voice,were surprised to see that Anna was there, sitting alone, listening." Well if we'd just admitted sooner, hadn't denied because we couldn't explain things well enough, we'd been better off. Mom, we've been as stubborn as the Builders, you know. We didn't want changes. We liked the Valley the way it was, our lives the way they were. You all know that. How can we judge the Builders ?" She cupped a hot cup of tea in her hands, sipping now and then, watching them, a look of clear question on her dark, young face.

Rose watched her daughter, pride and wonder struggled in her face,"It's true Dear, but we know our denial now. We know we must keep watch on ourselves.

THE JOURNEY

But the growth in us is deep and powerful. No matter how diverse we are, how cohesive, demanding, resistant, disparate, resentful, separate, loving, angry, and all the rest, we know that we all are TOGETHER. We know that now!" She let her eyes move to each face, and added,"We have to be conscious to take that Journey, you know!" She was silent, as if debating, then burst out,"I think it must take great singleness of mind to enter the Silent City."

" Three things we had to acknowledge. That we are still corruptible, and that we can demonstrate we are Mind Joined in Love. That we choose to be. But that we have two natures, the lower and the higher, and the lower must give way to the higher, enter into it." Benjamin spoke so slowly it was like a judgement." For minutes they were silent. Then he added."Now, we know something else: that we must Journey to that Silent City."

This was the first many of them knew that the Journey was specifically to the Silent City. They stared at him speechless, then turned to Jessie. That woman did not answer, because suddenly there were rapid steps on the Deck. And Andrew burst through the door, letting in a gusting autumn wind. He looked around swiftly, his eyes finally resting on his mother with an accusing look. His sister was hidden from him by the backs of two chairs."Mom, you didn't call! You didn't tell me you were meeting like this!"

Rose's expression was mild pleasure,"We knew that you would come. That you would feel us here and come. I wondered how long it would take, Son." She said the last teasingly and laughed a little at his outraged expression. After a moment, while his eyes swept the room, he shrugged and went to sit on the floor.

Suddenly there was a soft chime, repeating itself from the Videophone. It was signalling and Ben got up to switch it on. Paul and Jennifer were crowded into the screen, anxious looks on their faces. Paul spoke,"Well, we were right, we both knew, that we must call. We didn't know why but we knew that we must." He looked apologetic. "I guess there's no emergency after all."

Andrew laughed,"Well, Uncle Paul, Aunt Jenn. You heard too. I'm not surprised, they were Sending loud enough. I was surprised that I felt them in Adwin. Wow! It reached all the way to Altos! That's a record, I bet."

Ben stood looking at them, "My God in Heaven, Paul, you two actually knew -- that we were together? Actually 'felt' us?"

Jerry frowned, disbelieving, but seeing it might be."How could they? After all, it must be coincidense. Tom and Ned aren't here, they haven't called. And what about Annette?"

Jennifer said, " She did know, she called us to find out whether we knew. " She seemed to want to emphasize that. She added,"I'll call her and she can come here."

Rose was laughing, a Joy rising, filling her heart, an unreasonable Joy. "It's unbelievable and yet it's so believable. Wait, as for Tom and Ned, listen, Listen! She focussed and there was silence,"Jerry, you're wrong, they're on their way. Focus, you can Touch for yourself. It's something -- something I'd never have believed either a few months ago. But if we're Joined, if our family is mentally sensitive, then -- of course. We're tuned to one another, aren't we? It would be so, wouldn't it?"

A moment later they heard a soft sound outside, and then heavy stamping of boots. Ned landed, pulled off his belt and opened the door wide to look in at them. Tom just behind him, quiet, listening. Ned said,"Well, I'll be damned. We were right after all." He grinned, white teeth flashing and came in.

Tom said, "I called Ned and he was calling me. Our phones jammed. We knew we just had to get here, and I'm relieved it's no trouble. We thought it must be. Rather I did. Ned said if you'd had real trouble you'd have split our skulls." He glanced at Ned, now sliding his great body onto the floor. Kissing Silvia's hand, smiling happily into everyone's face. His black face shining with the light sweat of his hurry to get here. He touched Silvia's belly lightly,and said,"Hello, there little fella!" Silvia smiled at him, blew him a kiss, he was the only person who always greeted the baby, though Jerry talked to the child often and she thought, 'Two such men, to father him.' her heart sang with the thought.

Jerry spoke, sighing the words from a full heart,"We're truly Touching,finally!"

They were all suddenly silent, then after some minutes, Jessie said, "Listen! All of you. Listen to your own hearts. Refuse the clamoring of your thoughts right now. Listen!

Ben watching her, was aware of a flood of questions. He wanted them answered, but moved his attention above them, held that focus and Listened.

As they all did this, a quiet ring of power began to form around them. Paul and Jennifer and now Annette too, included in that ring. They could feel it distinctly now. More than they ever had. Some knew it instantly, others gradually. For long moments they felt that clear flow of energy moving among them. They knew it for that power called Love, and were astonished at how great it was. How very present! And the radiance of it swept on, far through the Valley. They were not even a Family alone. They were a people uniting, not yet complete.

After long moments then drew away, their attention fragmented. Ben's questions demanded attention. And he turned to them, "What is it? This, this moment, we've been immersed, - yes, immersed, in such a great power of Love that, I -- I have trouble finding myself. " He shook his head.

Tom said,"Is that what it was? Or is it the easiest name you could find?"

Benjamin turned to him without rancor, still bemused, "I don't know. It's true, I keep seeking a name. I feel as though I have to have a name. I suppose it gives me some feeling of control. I don't like the feeling of such unlimitedness."

Silvia sighed, then suddenly spoke, a note of anger in her voice." I couldn't bear to listen any longer, Jessie. I couldn't and yet, it was so, so wonderful. I don't know why. But then, how can you call that Love if it can make us afraid?"

"Because it's so powerful, but it brings everything together, Love unites."Ben looked surprised at his own answer, then he reached out both arms, a gesture of inclusion and question." Would you be able to realize what that kind of -- Love -- if that's what it is -- would cause us to demand of ourselves? Would insist that we BE, just by it's own very nature? " He looked around, dropped his arms,. " To know such as that is to know what we might,-- might become! But what a demand that is! You can see Sil that it could make us afraid at first." His face was full of awe that he was explaining himself. "We talk about ourselves as a Family,that means we're Joined in many ways. The Love we've known in the past, resembles need, you know. A need of each other, not this kind of Love. And so I wonder. Can we realize that Other." They could hear the capital O of the word 'Other'.

Cassandra had gone to sleep.It seemed to her the adults belabored obvious things. Anna sat watching everyone, a rapt expression on her face, she looked from one to the other. As they sat, Jane appeared in the doorway from the deck. she moved slowly, a look of surprise on her face. " For nearly an hour I've been feeling as though I ought to quit my work and come here. I kept insisting it was foolishness. Lazyness, in fact. But ten minutes ago, I felt shaken,I HAD to come, like some absolute demand pulled me to you. And now, here you all are!" She stood staring at them. Steve got up and went to her, drawing her into the room with them, She moved as though in a daze, started to speak again, drew a deep breath, and met Jessie's eyes. She nodded suddenly and sat down.

Jessie was watching the little ripple of movement to make room for Jane. She waited. Her face luminous, her eyes clear and bright. This family was growing more sensitive, they were AWARE of one another, of themselves. Everyone of them had known of this uncalled Gather! Her heart lifted, they would be ready before the winter snows.

Andrew lifted his head from the soft edge of the chair where he had been lying with closed eyes., He twined his hands together, drawing them in and out from one another. His words came brokenly, slowly, as if feeling his way. "What I know -- know NOW - " He drew a long breath, " is that right now, I'm connected to every one of you. That's never happened before. Never! We're together here. As we've never been before. We sent no outer message, only inner messages. Yes, maybe pulling and resisting, but together. Do you feel that?"

Ned and Jennifer both started to speak at once, they waved each other on, both together, and both stopped again. Everyone laughed, lightening the air. Jennifer said," You first, Ned."

Ned nodded, the laughter had loosened tension. but then, his face went solemn. "The amazing thing is that everyone is here. Every one of us is here!" He stopped, letting that be for a moment." And I have to admit that there's been so much waking up in me lately. In my mind, In meditation, it's like everything's expanded beyond thinking, beyond feeling, and I have finally known the Touching, far, far beyond myself, that Rose talked of long ago." They had seldom heard Ned so solemn, everyone listened intently. "You can see my eyes have opened." At that he shook his head. marveling and a little embarrassed. Joking was his usual way of talking of important things.

Jennifer nodded," You've almost said it for me, Ned, Love. I've been afraid, didn't want to talk about all this. And now, there's a split in my vision. So much Light comes through it shines even while I think. And Paul and I have wondered how we could think and SEE all at the same time. Well, now we're doing just that.

How can that be? But it is!" She looked around, her fingers sliding into Paul's hand. "Don't you see? We all came. Just as Ned said, we all came here and yet, no one told us to."

"All right, it's true. But how do we explain it?" Benjamin frowned again, "I want explanation!" He gripped his hands together, restless.

Tom shook himself out of a brown study, "I don't see why. There's no need to limit by a label, what we can't even encompass with our minds yet." He rubbed his face, looked around at them, "People've always tried to find names, like God, Spirit, or Prime Source, around all that we realize. People've tried that for centuries and always come out poorer. What is beyond us, what beckons us now, what we begin, faintly maybe, but begin to Touch upon, sings with such beauty, such wonder, such Love, whatever word we use, that it deserves to be left open. Open so we can follow on, find, discover. How much more there is out there!" He was silent, a look of surprise,"Or in here." He touched his breast.

They sat silent, Tom's words struck down some field of fear, of need for grasping the whole into names. He had released a barrier and beyond it lay stillness.

This time they smiled, but no one laughed. Paul glanced toward Jessie, sitting so quietly among them. He saw there a smile so sweet, so disarming that he was struck with a great sense of tenderness for them all. Her love seemed to pluck the strings of his own, send it radiating out beyond him. He said, "Jessie! You've been so quiet. What d'you think?"

She spoke quickly, "I'm enjoying myself, listening. To know we will all make that Journey gives me great Joy. And to have seen your response today, your ability to know of one another in this way.You have grown in awareness and you all know what that means. And now you are able to bring that awareness down into that ordinary thinking mind and speak of it. More than ever before. It is wonderful. I have worried a few times in these months,but I do not now." Her smile touched each one. As though a finger had touched a harp and drawn sound through it's various keys. They felt a leap of response , a release of something fine as though a note of their own hearts, so plucked, had sounded. She said, "Let's try silence. Let's sit in whole awareness of one another. Setting aside fear and embarrassment. Sit in trust."

Several audible sighs sounded, shuffling, movement of bodies into more comfortable positions and then there was a silence deeper than they had ever known.

Paul watched himself, as though looking at something separate. He wanted to see if he could think what was happening as it happened. To be conscious of being Conscious. He felt his mind Reach, Touch against and meld into that greater Mind, and he knew himself small before it. This was paradox. He was watching himself aware and knew he was also that Self. The realization wavered.

He could not hold it. He was unfocussed. What he was, extended far, inclusive but vast.He saw that the focus was greater, so great he had to release every previous attitude of reality, release his limited controls,in order to begin to focus here. Everything seemed opaque because he held on, but he could not let go. It was like being a drop of water in a vast sea, and if he released the tension that was his own identity, he thought he would simply dissapear within that endlessness. Yet the tension separated, limited him.

Perhaps he could just stretch himself, be, all that was. He felt a strength from the Family around him. A thought shaped. Were they enduring this same dilemma? The thought instantly dissolved. But the strength helped him. There was all around a kind of Lightness, a whiteness of Light. It seemed now to flow everywhere, through himself, as though he were translucent. He was conscious simultaniously of that vast Self and this tiny personal self, Paul, and he felt himself filled until he stretched beyond Paul and became that which was nameless. He was a drop of water entering a sea. The drop of water broke and Joined. He was with Life.

The fire of white Light absorbed him, caught him up and fed him such nourishment of mind that he was limp with amazement, but not unbelief. It was real. It was happening and to him. He - Paul - was aware of this invading consciousness and KNEW clearly of the nature of things. "I am the eye through which God sees Itself!" The whispered thought startled him. Silenced him.

Suddenly it was all gone in a flood of fear that washed him, tightened like a string, identity shrank. The Light faded and he felt lost, he could not find the Family, the Minds that had bled strength into him. He felt caught in a tide of his own fear that was sweeping him away from them. He wept terrible tears from his Heart to lose that, to lose them, to lose the wonder of Light. He was caught in a knot of darkness.

He found resolution, a focus of attention held in a relentless act of will. And in that focus he found a bright point within himself, and focussed himself from it. He WOULD find himself, Reach to them. Recover. Like a finger of Light, they reached to him, Touched and he caught hold. He steadied, the backwash fragmented and fell away. He swam into the circle of power again. Felt it draw him, felt it's tension strengthen. He, Paul, could choose. Could decide to BE within this. He felt a balking, a spasm of fear woke, pulsed through him like a searing pain. DANGER! To continue - to sustain Joining might erase Paul. What then would he be?

He, Paul, could be lost in this greater LIfE. This which was him Self, and included himself. The paradox jolted in his mind and tore through membranes of division so that that great Mind was flowing into his very being, becoming himself, including himself. Then he realized he had it backward. He -- Paul was flowing out, entering into that Self, just as that Self had filled him earlier. How could he distinguish which filled which, except that the larger began the flow, the smaller stretched its identity beyond recognition.

Then, at that crucial moment, he knew the others, the rest of the family, supported and sustained each other. They together let their own identities loosen enough to know the OTHER. To know themselves as THAT. And the knowledge did not terrify them, for Jessie was there. They could feel the power of her vast perception helping them, sustaining their identity as a group. They felt her Love like a joyous laughter, an intensity of being alive that flamed like a fire in their minds. Their Hearts sang, and the song would not stop, as though it was caught up in a greater song, so far inaudible. Then Paul rallied, and as he did, so did every other member of the family, little by little, supporting one another, they held firm. They consciously knew themselves ONE nature. Paul agreed to know him Self, as did they all. He let himself go, fall away into that which was inclusive.

Joy ran like a wire of cool fire through them, flooded their bodies, their minds, their hearts, and released them. To live in a flood of Joy, what extravagance, and yet it was only natural here. For Love underwrote all Joy.

Paul sensed that the fabric that was their Joined Consciousness was strained at certain points. His own firmness, his decision swept forth, firming, helping. He too could offer strength. He laughed and heard the laughter of others. He attended to the Otherness of their group identity, was aware of the Presence of them. In this, Being was Single, yet they were all distinctly there. Each one, identified also there. He marveled, knowing them, loving them.

They had met one another beyond their personal selves. Small traces of fear flickered, was known, met and allowed to fade. Tom, reached this point of Touch, having plowed through fields of resistance and finally entered into that open water of surrender. He felt freed. ALIVE! He had known panic too, felt himself shrink, fade until the panic and shrinking grew, until he was cut off from that Source of LIfe that had filled him and he was lost,enshelled,dark, alone. But from Jessie's heart he felt a call and found himself Reaching. He could make clear choice. He knew Paul,Touched, and instantly a knitting began that was like the knitting of waters into other waters. He too felt that Self surge everywhere around and through him, inundate him and then stretch him as it entered in and broke down the barriers of his fear. Broke down with the steady healing of Love every spine of fear that stood between himself and that greater consciousness.   They felt the power around them grow, the Joy of it. Utterly amazed at how 'limited' the old Tom had been, he explored this new Self. Knowing. A playful humor, a sweet laughter as though at a wondrous lovemaking.

Gradually a great tough life was forming, growing in the way a collection of single cells eons ago, drew together and began to create a multicelled creature whose possibilities were so vastly more. But there was choice here, Mind melded to minds agreeing to give themselves to that greater Self. There was no question of 'what could it do? What could it accomplish? Such questions were irrelevant within what they WERE.

Tom Knew and his heart swelled with joy. Here was Paul, Rose, Jerry, Anna and Andrew, every one, all the members of the Family, present, with him. They blazed with light. There beyond him, acting as catalyst, was that fiery Light that seemed so familiar and yet so unknown. Slowly he knew that unwavering Light was Jessie, unseparate from her own greater Self. Joined, as she worked with them, and offered them strength and recognition.She too had made the choice, probably long ago.

He knew that this choice meant a demand upon him to be all that he could possibly be. To be wholly responsible. He knew the only thing he sacrificed now was self indulgence, for this -- THIS promised what could barely be imagined. Could not be shaped yet into thought. They were giving themselves up to 'becoming'. The difference shattered old fears and old desires into shreds that fell like glass broken. They no longer had meaning. They could accept this inevitable growth that was upon them.

They felt Ned, drawing and ebbing, the pull and Reach of his mind. They felt him Touch against their combined Mind. He saw them as a pure white flame into which he must enter. As the flame approached, he retreated, then felt an unutterable longing toward it. What else could be worth anything at all, if one had not this? He felt a powerful attention of thought sweep him, lift him, and he stood suddenly left, waiting choice. He wavered, watched himself, watched that SELF they were together 'becoming' and with a sudden leap of pure, clean joy, he made the choice and felt himself Joining. He felt his entire being stretched through pain, stretched until pain broke itself and he was beyond pain, free, entering into what throbbed with Life and Light.

Jane swayed, felt the power of Earth beneath her, felt that wonder of her own many reaches into Earth, into the Life of Earth. And yet, now, there was something more. She felt it through the others at first. The conscious lives of Earth were so gentle, so accepting. Here there was conscious life and in it was power, and questioning. Fierce questioning! She knew herself part of that questioning.

She saw Light rising like a fountain, falling again to enter into them all, a flooding of liquid Light. Darkness rose then, separated her, made known to her the fear of losing herself. She would refuse this vast consciousness that was Soul Consciousness, a group consciousness beyond her personal control. It denied her self, beckoned her into its extinction. She shuddered. No! With a kind of fury, she desired to be all of this herself. She could. She would be Earth Life herself and inviolate. How could she Join with those not as knowing of Earth, not aware? She sighed, long and sadly, so that sadness drew from some deep well of grief. Sorrow swept through her in an illimitable river. Such sadness she had never imagined could be. Such Grief, of life in Life. '

Among living things, only the human must endure such dispair in order to enter into such inexpressable joy. But she didn't know that then. Slowly she learned, and through her the others learned. They held, lifted and sustained her in that grief, taking it into themselves also. Earth bore their Grief, their Joy, their Life beyond ordinary human comprehension. Jane, Joined now with her people, very faintly Touched an edge of that unknowable life that was Earth Herself. She saw the illusion of desires exposed and faded. She could bear only an instant of Earth Touch! Such Life was incomprehensible! How could she have thought herself equal? How could she offer herself? How could she be acceptable?

And what was Earth then? How could she - they - participate in Earth Life?

She felt response, a roaring of fires, of thrusting and changing and building and falling away, of eroding and creating in endless measure. She saw the thin green Light and surrounding that, the blue,that was a halo surrounding that vast round body floating in the dark sea that was space.She knew that in that great body she lived, it held her, gave her birth. She was of itself, she was a fragment of living Earth. So were all other life forms. Together they breathed Earth Light. She was a part, the whole was incomprehensible.

Finally she knew a humbling that tore ego pride like a cancer out of all the interfaces of her body. The pain of it was excruciating she gave thanks for those who bore that pain with her. She wrenched herself finally free, hollowed and broken, listening, Reaching finally. And then, at that last moment, standing alone, to finally make that choice. The choice, for her was instantanious, eager, and she entered Earth Consciousness as one come home at last.

Her mind reeling with the thought, her heart drawn almost to terror, she knew this vast Life was only part of infinite Being.

Steve was held in the swaying currents of these waters, aware and watching, willing to listen, willing to know. The struggle of the others informed him, taught him and he turned finally, weary of that, to offer himself, offer his conscious self, wanting to know as they knew, wanting to be part of that Joy they radiated and that he could feel as if it were an Earth sized shout. As though with an eye wide as the solar system, he could see the many nets that were creating themselves out of Light that streamed from the Families of the Valley. He felt this one strengthen and glow with its own LIfe.

He moved toward it, moved and stood there, knowing the fear,the danger that Jane knew, and he caught at her, then swiftly let her go. She must choose freely, and so must he. He could not see his daughter, nor the others. There was nothing to see, but only to Know, in this blinding Light beyond which he would eventually find another kind of Vision. He knew that as he knew his name.To make the choice was for him a relinquishing of dispair, of loneliness, and fear of pain. For he knew that the choice would take him into pain and through it, would carry him beyond pain. He knew and yet, he hesitated. He had known so much pain. And as he knew that he also felt the sustained Reach of his chosen Family and he knew that he had made that choice lifetimes ago. He knew too that they would bear that pain with him. They would not stand apart from his release. He could choose.

Silvia drew close to this moment, listening, hearing and knowing more than ever in her life.She could feel the power of her unborn child, feel his exultation as though he knew, more than did she, the moment's wonder. The creation was now in process of being born. He, sensing the Joining of single minds within greater Mind, glimpsed something of what was being born of this wholeness. He longed to be part and to bring this mother along with him. But he knew she must make the choice for herself. He retreated from her, entering into the Family's vast and strengthened Life, and waited.

Silvia, felt the Touch, light and real, the offer. She heard the Song, strange but penetrating into her Heart, like some winged bird that would lift her soaring

THE JOURNEY

beyond everything she knew. And she exulted also, with her son, knowing a little of his Joy. She loosened herself, looking at her fear. How strange to thus look without being drawn so inexorably into it that she could not rise out. She stood, watching herself, and as she did, instantly she knew her Self. But the recognition terrified her and for a moment she was lost in that fear, shrinking down into herself, dark, alone and safe.

Then, there penetrated a thin wire of Light, thrust down by the reaching of her own Heart to the Family. They could receive her because she Reached to them. She felt the surge of Love following, a surge that bathed her in relief. And the dark fell away as water does from a rising hill side when the Earth thrusts herself up. The knowledge revealing itself was a shaft of Light that sped like an arrow outward, upward, lifting her in its wake, and she expanded with it. The delight of it drew her on. She felt awe, pure joy, a stillness that rose around her, expanded through her, and Reached her outward through itself into the others. She felt their coming together, and knew that she was willing. She felt Joy swell within her, as they Touched, the joy that drew her into her Self. She knew she had chosen. The transition made her physical body faint. They held her freely, among them, sustained and quiet. They let her rest from this grand step into Life. And while no time passed, they were one life.

Slowly they drew down into their little personal minds, into the focus that was for each a separate identity. That too was choice. Slowly they recovered identity, with a kind of pain resulting from that shrinking back into what now seemed infinitely too small. But never again would that identity be limited to its old self. For some time they sat, their eyes turned inward. Knowing the stark beauty of memory. Suddenly not sure how to balance themselves, how to sustain this physical density, how to tolerate within this smallness that open edge of Being, through which they saw endlessly, they knew themselves persons of dual nature.

Jessie watched them, saw them fumbling back to 'normal' and was content. With a mild gentle pride, softened by her own knowledge of herself, amused at the necessity for such careful discipline of her own self, she saw their Vision clarify and take its place in their stretched and flexible minds. She knew that they could, and would, Reach to one another the entire length of the Valley now. That they had gained power.

Finally out of long silence, Paul asked, "Jessie, what do you call that? The Master Teachers spoke of something called 'Group Consciousness', as though it were a real thing. Is that what we've just begun to know?"

She smiled at them, and her face was radiant with Joy. They felt that Joy like a benediction, a further nourishment. She said, "Words are useful. We have to have them, and that one will do. We are together as one life. That is our reality today."

They sat back, those on the floor sat up straighter and there were unnoticed tears drying on their faces, their bodies were relaxed, as if the very molecules that made up those myriad cells had shifted slightly into a finer substance.

Anna studied her hands in her lap. Andrew moved his eyes silently, serious, from one to the other. He got up, went softly from the room and up stairs. They heard him, at the piano, beginning, speaking to them in the only way he knew to say what his heart realized.. They listened, the sound was at first hesitant, then it gathered confidence, the notes clustered into a music that told of an awakened heart. They listened without speaking until he finally stopped, the music gathered into him to be made into a symphony one day.

All their faces were full of stillness, a patience of quiet that was new. Finally, they began one by one to turn to Jessie, nodding, giving her the answer that they thought she needed. They told her they were fully accepting of their task, and of their Journey. Rose said,"To realize that other dimension shook my mind apart, never could I have imagined what we might know together. I could not have born it alone."

Paul coughed and they turned to him. His mind raced, thoughts forming and fading,desires blossoming and demanding. It was as though a powerful stimulant had charged his thinking. He thought that he must find the wonder again, focus, recreate IT, keep it for himself always. He closed his eyes, wanting suddenly more than anything he could remember to find that same absolute beauty. Why must it fade?

He drew himself inward, Reached, with a longing that hurt, and then like a blossoming of knowledge, a piercing thrust that informed, he knew. This, this Reaching, trying within himself alone, to recover what had been, could be nothing except an imitation, a dead thing. That which they had known so briefly - WAS! It could not be imitated, recreated, it must simply be acknowledged. His arrogance, his desire to be the creator, shamed him, then made him laugh. What foolishness! To Be- just to 'be' in that Presence of WHAT IS was enough. He knew he must wait until that moment re-occurred in its own way.

Rose and Ben both got up and began to replenish cups of hot drinks. They went to the kitchen, got sandwiches , little cakes, soups, from the auto-kitchen, brought them to the others. They were all quiet, waiting, wanting to rest.

Jane ate slowly, methodically, as if simply feeding her body. Her eyes were distant, and finally she set her plate aside,"There's just so much, so much that we've realized. How can I -- absorb so much?" Her eyes moved to the others, her arms suddenly flung out, palms up, in a gesture of wordless beseeching. Then she let them drop, one on Jerry's shoulder. He reached one hand up, took her's and brought it to his lips in silent empathy.

Ned shoved his plate back on the table beside which he sat. leaned his forehead on his fists, elbows solidly planted there. The only word that fits, the only word that I can find to describe anything, is -- is Love. Yet it's so beyond every kind of love I've known. What I've known as love, must be a small reflection of THAT."

"Well, surely now we're committed! There's not much doubt of that,is there?" Anna looked questioningly at her mother, wanting Rose to acknowledge. Rose remembered that look with a twist of pain. For it was that way her child had looked at her through those long years when she had in exasperation been unable to know what Anna wanted from her. In those years Anna had learned dispair, loss and longing, but she had also learned tolerance and patience. Now, suddenly, Rose knew, she met that look directly, ready and willing to offer response. She held Anna's eyes, nodded, Sent love and acknowledgement. "Yes, my Darling, Yes, we are committed!"

She saw the look of relief, vindication, and then joy that came to Anna's young worried face. She thought, 'all these years, and I WOULD not know. Oh, dear child, how painful it must have been for you.'

Anna smiled now, nodding, then shook her head. She was not to worry. It was all well now. And the others saw too, for they were not concealing anything at all.

Silvia looking from one to the other, said, "Then, we'll discover something in that Journey to make things more clear. Is that true?" There was a note of sadness in her voice, but stronger was that sound of eagerness that they had not heard before.

Jessie nodded, "The Journey is one of discovery. It is Self discovery!"

There was silence again finally broken by Paul. "And my heart grieves for William, but it grieves for every citizen of our Valley who is not able, who cannot just now know what we have known. There is not one who is not our own brother or sister. Not one! Even Greyson and all like him are part of us."

Steve nodded, "I can't understand. If I can realize these things, if I can overcome my fears, my resistance, then surely Will would. He's twice as smart as I am." He looked at them, "Could I go talk to him? Would it help?"

Paul and Ben looked at one another. They knew that they would go again to William. There was a long silence. Then a gradual quiet settled about them. A melding, a quality of peace? Acceptance? Rose searched their faces, wondering. Anna was watching her elders, Andy had returned to them and he watched Anna, a slight frown building, darkening his brown face. Anna's expression of sweet serenity and loving stillness somehow troubled him. But for others, it seemed to erase fear. Ben looked at her, his daughter, and was conscious of a literal emptying of fear. He was himself calm. He thought he ought to be afraid for William, for others like William, but he was not. He too frowned.

Jessie said, "We are together, we must know that we are together. We are able to be and we are learning how to be, each day we live. But we must know that and make a purposeful intention to bring every life of the Valley into that stream of Love that you feel now. It is present and available and we only have to empty ourselves of fear and wanting in order to know it. She smiled then, a great wide sweet smile that radiated that Love she spoke of, focussed, even as they began to realize it, through their midst.

She went on, "Love is present, as you see, it is available to everyone who pays attention and who opens his or her Heart to it. It's NATURE is to fill us, to nourish us, if we accept. You've seen that, felt it. So you know it's true!" They nodded, and she went on, "There are those who cannot consciously stand upward, or outward into that Light of Love, but we can surround them with that focus, and they will respond unknowingly, for Love is powerful. It is like the atmosphere, it can be breathed. There are those who cannot Journey now, with us, or any other Family. But their turn will come some day. It is not our task to demand of them what they are not ready for."

The others listened, understood and with a sadness, accepted. Steve shook his head,"Then there's no use trying again with William?"

Ben shook his head, glanced at Paul who nodded. "We can Reach to him, we can do everything we know. We can continue to love him. But we must do the same for every person who does not already Join. Unless they have a glimpse, at least an instant of experience, they know nothing but theory and that's not very real for them."

"So we're to be compasssionate, kindly, nice people relating to the handicapped?" Steve's sarcasm was heavy in his voice, his face was tight.

"Not unless that's the only way you know to relate. "Paul was hard, his voice stern. He saw Steve's sentiment as a weakness that could demolish his strengths. Visibly relenting, Paul said, more gently,"We can love them, support them, but WE cannot change them.They, all of those like Will, have to make their own choices. But then, they have plenty of greatness, plenty of power and value just as they are, you know. We know that they are as we are, no less. Whether they know it or not."

Again there was silence, Anna got up and went to Silvia. She placed her hands on Silvia's rounded belly, closed her eyes, smiling. Reaching, knowing that Silvia tried to follow her, she Touched that life within her friend. Silvia watched her with a sudden jealousy."I wish I could do that." she said, then the jealousy faded, and only a plaintive longing remained.

Anna whispered, leaning to kiss her cheek. "You are here with him every day, you know. You are his world too just now. Closer than any of us." Then she turned and left the hall, closing the door lightly against the chilling night air.

Gradually others followed her, going to their cottages, or alone or in pairs. They left, until Jessie was alone again. She picked up her knitting and began to work, quietly, a small smile on her lips.

CHAPTER FIFTEEN

Jessie meets with Vagabonds and Town Council

The hours and days of work, meeting, talking, bringing about the beginnings of Joining,told Jessie that Valley people were making the changes of unfoldment consciousness. The crisis that threatened the whole of that unfoldment, rising from the yawning gap between groups, could not be prevented. She must hope that they would be ready for that important Journey. Conscious enough! After the first of the True Joinings, that awakening to wholeness that occurred the first week of September, the powerful energies flooding the land increased and she knew that a careful balance must be held. The tension grew, she felt her own frail body taxed to its limit. But she must continue.

A few days after the seemingly impromptu Gather, in the very early dawn before the light of the sun had broken over the edge of the eastern peaks, when the air was still pale and silvery cool to breathe, Jessie set out to walk to Adwin. The Silent City stood sharply etched against Her cliffs, even as Jessie looked, the light increased and the City seemed to fade so that she must focus very carefully to separate the spires from the grooved marks on the towering cliffs behind. She nodded, satisfied. It was thus that the City did not impose Herself, was in fact barely visible much of the time.

She continued on her walk. She enjoyed the solitude of these early mornings, the silent house , the barely waking life around her. Here and there she could see returning night creatures loping home from their night's hunt. An owl, late this morning, mumbled and ruffled its feathers before it settled down inside a great hole in a standing snag. She could feel her own energy rising as she walked.

Morning bells chimed in Adwin,bright in the clear air. The path was dusty with the summer's travel on it, but grasses bent thick to either side. Berry vines, long since picked of fruit, hung heavy, their leaves beginning to brown at the edges. Logan bushes, heavy with their round,olive sized berries, were turning finally red, would be ready for harvest in a week. The leaves were already falling and the berries stood brilliant and thick over the half bare branches. One of the most fragrant of small fruits, already the odors hung heavy where the path wound into them. She picked one, tasted it's slightly sour sweetness. It was not fully ripe, her mouth puckered slightly. By the time the young Gatherers came they would be ready. She extended her awareness, delicately, into the lives of creatures among the bush. "So fine, so delicate and fine, these small consciousnesses. So delicately they absorb themselves in their lives. So many, like an underlying purr of being, the billions of tiny lives. Their mental sound was not so different from the physical sound of myriads of insects humming and singing a steady rhythm in summer. That insect hum was already beginning as the sun broke over the peaks and swept in a wealth of light over the land. Shadows drew themselves long and dark, Jessie stopped, caught in breathless amazement at the beauty of it. And it happened every day!

A fox, late at getting her kill, swung round an outcropping with a pheasant dragged beneath her. Pups clustered against her legs, nearly grown now, they would be on their own in days. Jessie watched, wondering if this might perhaps be the last meal the little family would eat to gether. The male, stood, watching, still alert for danger around them. Yet, in that early dawn, far to the east in a field where grasses stood yards high, drying and seeded, there was sadness in the pheasant hen, calling for this lost mate. Yet, mercifully, she remembered, memory was short for such little ones. She would not suffer long by human terms, but that time would be long for her. Jessie reflected that she must not make the mistake of generations of humanity and assume the simple creatures did not suffer. She frowned, such an assumption was a denial that excused responsibility so that persons were once able to insist the poor did not feel, were not as sensitive, as the educated and rich. "Well, " She said aloud,"Suffering is a part of life, common as pleasure." She listened, heard the unnumerable sounds of Earth life, the rise and fall of consciousness, of hunger and of satisfaction. Death and Life enveloping one another in their endless rhythm.

Earth flourished, extended Herself outward toward that brilliant sun, now flaming between two greying cloud banks. Jessie knew herself part of that exuberance of life reaching upward, and she could participate in that Reach. Her life radiated its Joy, while all around her, gentle but persistent, rose and fell the waves of sorrow and joy, little distanced from one another.

Here Sun met Earth, Light met the Dark, and in that union, was all physical life. Yet, through the oceans of air and Light, there was another universe of Life, non-physical, and that too, could partake of other unions . She focussed her attention on that flame of Life that swept through the Solar system, the energy roaring silently through empty space to bathe the planets and give them their various forms of life. She stopped a moment to watch the sunlight enter into the tops of the low forests, gleam through night's fading shadows on dry grasses, finally to catch in a sharp glint of silver along one long exposed length of the great River. Day had come.

She descended the final twenty feet of the slope down from the Farm. The Highway lay before her, much of it still in shade, but the sun caught the colors of a few scattered dome cars far down the roadway. The People of the Way would be up to greet that living Light. Jessie began to sing a little folk tune the children had sung last evening before dinner. One created by their friends and being practiced for Winter Festival. It cheered her, and brought a fleeting sense of happiness. The wide forty feet of tough short grasses, roadbed of the old Highways, was dotted with shrubs and trees, gift plantings from Altos. She looked up and down the Highways to see if any Family cart might be moving near. She held attention, focussed and nodded, satisfied. Then she saw the Low Cart of a large Family moving out from behind a thick edge of forest to the east.

THE JOURNEY

The Highway ran through Adwin's River forest at this point and she waited, eager to greet them, glad for this perfect timing that they should find one another again here.

She let her mind Reach, felt the absorption of some Vagabonds with their morning songs to the Sunlight. Of some to the beauty of Earth, and of some to their own worries. Then, as if her own Touch was a match striking fire, there were three swift flames of attention directed to her. She could see them now, their faces lifted, looking to see what their minds had already seen.

Several young children and an old couple walked on past her, nodding their greeting. A man stood in the cart, working a piece of leather, fashioning tools as he rode. A woman rounded the opposite side of the cart, running to stand smiling and spreading her arms wide in greeting. The man looked too, his face a wreath of smiling, but he did not put down his tools until the cart was exactly beside Jessie. This piece must be finished this morning. Leather was rare for working, the Hunters saved and cured all they took, but it was not a great lot. Boots and shoes were made from fabrics created from polymer composites tougher and better breathing than leather and people had begun to find it also good for carving and staining with color. He put the piece down, then he climbed out, leaping like a young boy, though Jessie knew he was at least sixty. The cart stopped. He caught her hands,"I am Douglas. He drew her toward the cart. But there was a third! Where?

She walked closer, drawn by what her senses told her and looked into the cart. There was a woman lying there on a soft and embroidered couch. A robe of warm, light plasilk, it too, richly embroidered with this family's designs, drawn up around her shoulders. She looked thin, tired and very old. Jessie sighed, for the People of the Way were not ones to continue life into such extreme age. They held a farewell Gather,then within three days, composed themselves in a quiet place and died. But she knew, with a certainty that brought tears to her eyes, why this one had held herself in continuance, long after her alotted time.

Jessie's eyes met those brilliant, deceptively young grey eyes. Smiling eyes, full of a joy to see her.Then, as if she had held herself in abeyance until this moment, there was the full intentional Mind Touch. The others waited, wondering, for they had never seen Jessie in the flesh either. Now, they felt unexpected shyness. They realized then, that this was the one their grandmother had waited for. This was one of those meetings that the old One had held on to life so long to impliment. She must bring this meeting about, she must Join with them here at this particular time. And they knew and understood.

The old woman, sat up slightly, then the man and woman came to lift her, draw cushions behind her to ease the pain they knew she endured. She was smiling, as happy as a child. She need not continue after this day, this one, Jessie, was the last to be found and seen in the flesh. They caught her joy at completing a task and the joy of the meeting itself.She reached out a slim,work hardened hand, to take Jessie's. Their mind's enwrapped, they informed one another of so much, the others could only sense a blur of brightness and of rolling thunderous sounds that barely touched their awareness.

Then, with a lighter air, the old One spoke as if the speaking were a ritual wherein the younger ones could enter. "We have held the faith, there are not many of us left among our people. Our time is done! Your time is here! Of all of us who are Guides, none are young. Most of those of my generation have left Earth. So we are few along the ways." Her face seemed so radiant now to Jessie that she wondered that she had thought her old. She squeezed Jessie's hand,"We have held -- and taught -- the Vision."

Jessie nodded. "We know that. We have watched and seen that Teaching flower among you. You have prepared the Way. We heard many of your students who talked with strength and wisdom at the North Country 'Gather of the Way' earlier this summer. There, I learned of your waiting, and your work." Jessie was nodding now, filled with a Joy that she had seldom known since she arrived in this Valley. She was aware that that Joy multiplied itself through the four of them and exalted them in the process. It was a Joy that seemed to come through them from everywhere at once,it had it's source within them all, but it also flamed up from every living thing within miles of that spot on the Highway. Had Jessie looked around, she would have seen the rest of the Vagabond family both ahead and behind, now about to catch up, standing suddenly watching in awe that Light they could see blazing all round the cart their old grandmother was in. They wondered and thought that this person she had come to meet, must be quite some lady.

Jessie laughed, ""You have prepared the way and now it's up to us. The rest of us. For me -- my time is also near." And the two of them grinned at one another as if comparing a great joy they both knew was immenent. Jessie glanced around at the two others who stood by them, "But there is enough time. We will bring the task to fruition. Surely you know that?"

The old One, nodded, smiled at Douglas, who sat beside her, then glanced at the two younger ones and said,"These two, Martha and Warren, they have returned from study at the Station and are committed to our Ways. They are ready and they will continue."

Jessie, nodded,"I can see that. Margarita, I can see." She turned to look at them, so strong, probably not over forty five, a depth of knowledge in their eyes that delighted her. And she said,"It is a true gift that you give us. We thank you!"

Warren nodded, his eyes shining, held by Jessie's gaze, he said,"The gift has been given. You folk who teach, Margarita, and you, Mother, and your fellows who have taught us, that is the real gift."

Margarita laughed, "Whose gift is greater , is irrelevant, what is important, Jessie, is that the seed is within us now. The children are being born, already in two generations they have bodies able to KNOW, able to SEE. We recognize them coming among us and they seem to absorb the Teaching as if it were milk." Her eyes were shining now, and surely she looked years younger. But Jessie knew that the strain of this meeting would leave her weaker in body, and stronger in Heart and Mind."It's with such a joy that I recognize you and your kind here among us finishing the plan, preparing for the Journey. Already many have taken

THE JOURNEY

that Journey have they not?" At Jessie's nod, she went on, her voice a little weaker suddenly,"I have sensed it, seen them passing through, known their destination and have rejoiced. That knowledge has kept me alive until I fulfilled this longing to meet in the flesh those who taught the WAY." She shook her head, clinging suddenly to Jessie's hand again,"Now, I am prepared to leave this old body and Join those who have gone before."

Martha nodded, worried a little that the talk was wearying Margarita too much, yet knowing it was alright anyway."It's time! We know that! And we are ready! We listen, we are grateful and we will continue when you have left us, Mother. We will continue!" She spoke as if she feared she might not be believed, but Margarita smiled happily and sent a spill of that happiness out to surround them all. Martha's face smoothed, all worry faded but sorrow stayed.

Margarita sighed then, a sadness flitting across her eyes, and then it faded into that resounding Joy. She was looking far through the sadness, through the Joy itself, and that had been her practice for many years. To see through the grief, to keep vision pure. She sighed again however, "It would be good to stay a bit and see the coming of it all. The shaping of the new generation and the wonder they will create." Her eyes met Jessie's and a faint frown touched her forehead,"Or am I assuming too much. There will be problems even in this time, No?"

Jessie smiled, "When have there not been, beautiful One? But they will be problems to be met by those ready to meet them. All war is internal war, war for the claiming of the minds and hearts of humankind to lift into that sweep of possibility barely realized. There is much yet to learn, much to endure of adjustment." She nodded,"But your task is done, you are free, you have prepared the fields, now the seeds are planted and the human race will grow beyond everything we have dreamed."

Margarita was smiling again, her eyes clear,"I am ready to turn over all that is to be done to those we have taught. There are many among our people. And these two are of the best. So now, I must prepare myself. I will have my Death Gather within the week. Perhaps you will Reach to us?" At Jessie's nod, she went on, "My eyes are already filled with that Light that is shining everywhere through that thin, so very thin veil. I will not wait!" Jessie nodded, and looked into Martha's tear filled eyes, full of a knowing that Jessie recognized. They smiled slowly, Warren came to stand near, touching their hands. Jessie withdrew hers from Margarita and leaned to kiss the old One gently. Then the cart began to roll softly through the deep grass. Jessie stepped back, waving farewell, letting her thoughts linger among them for some time.

She thought about them as she walked on, the way the People had taken up that task, had practiced, as they traveled, the Teaching and guiding the Love of Earth for all Valley children. Where had the earliest Vagabonds come from? No one could say. They'd simply gathered, come from everywhere, as if planned, begun their endless life of Journey. And Jessie suddenly understood why few People of the Way made that 'Journey'to the City as her own people did.

THE PEOPLE OF THE VALLEY

They lived a life of Journey, of practice that never ceased and revelation that reformed itself every day.

She doubted that there had been members of the Builders coming from these people. Those Vagabonds who did not See, or Reach, were taught how to meet that lack, taught what Reaching meant, and honored for their other gifts. They did not deny! That is the way it should have been in our towns, Jessie thought. She turned once as she climbed toward Adwin, looking out across the Highway where it wound into the eastern foothills. She stood watching the bright cart with its now invisible people disappear in the distance and caught the thought that was flung back to her from Margarita. "Remember, Jessie, that our people choose, all our people, which includes the people of town and city. So those who do not want to remain traveling in our Way, have left us to live as towners. That is also why we have no Builders .It is not entirely because we Teach unceasingly."

Jessie nodded as she returned to the climb. "That is the way of Love then. The allowing of others to choose their course, and to honor their choice. It is a Valley Conviction . It's contributed to the teaching that has brought us to this readiness for the Journey. The Vagabonds have been like glue, a yielding glue for the whole Valley. The running stream of their influence through every part of life." She nodded again, was silent, feeling the smiling acknowledgment from those departing friends.

She began to climb in earnest. The sun had climbed higher, the day was growing already warm. She must be at the Community Center in time for the Council meeting. She would sit as a member this time, and she felt honored to do so.

The town is not different from the Family at the farm. The town is a collection of Families who prepare or have already made the decision and the Journey. They struggle with the growth. They see so much, begin to see what they struggle not to see. What they cannot avoid now. The Vagabonds have taught so much through their dance, their songs, their music and their art. Symbol and myth, metaphor and story, carried the Teaching for so long. Now it must be spoken, Heart recognized by intellect. Acknowledged in words. All minds must Join in knowing. Somehow, even a mind that cannot KNOW directly, can know indirectly through beauty, through art, as William so deeply does. Yet, those often cannot admit what they know.

Her thoughts continued, affirming her understandings. Aloud she said, "We are ready to begin finally. To begin the final steps. We must be so careful. And I think there is one more test waiting us yet this autumn." She went on climbing, this last few yards where the path was steep, and the work of it took her breath and all her attention for several moments. But she was smiling to herself and nodding. The morning seemed complete.

As she topped the rise, she found a man standing watching her. He was smiling at her exertion. "It's a hard climb. I don't know why you haven't made use of a belt, Grandmother."

She nodded, pausing beside him, "If I were to do that, soon I would not be

THE JOURNEY

ABLE to climb, now would I?"

He laughed, agreeing ruefully. His eyes followed the path down and then up the farther slope to the Farm."You've come from the Farm yonder?" At her nod, he said,"It's one of the best here abouts. But there are strange stories going around. Have you heard of them?"

She was serious, her eyes still full of laughter, but he didn't seem to notice. "I wonder what stories you mean."

"You come from there and don't know? Well, I suppose that's the way it'd be. It's the ones in the middle of things that don't know, sometimes. And it's not just that farm, there're stories of others nowadays." He mused, glancing down the path again. Then he turned fully to her and said,"We'd as well get on into town. I've work to do and you must have too." They began to walk rapidly toward the outer Ring of the Civic Center before them. "I'd not be honest if I didn't tell you that people say there's those at the Farm yon, who're opposed to the Builders. That some of them even have unnatural habits." His voice fell. "I think the Builders seem sensible. I don't hold with the foolishness about what they call the 'Psychic' but I think they've gone to far at times ."

Jessie said,"What is it about the Builder's teaching that you like, Ronald?" Her use of his name without having been told, did not seem to surprise him, he didn't notice.

"It's their idea of keeping the Valley for ourselves, not letting the outsider in. And the idea of using the land for more crops, selling them out Valley. We've got one of the richest valley's in the nation. Why we could all be rich. I agree with that." He was silent a moment."You know it'd not be hard to defend this Valley. She's surrounded by Mountains and a few air cars, and a few troops with good gun emplacements, anti-aircraft lasers etc. up there, we could keep any one out." He seemed to enjoy the idea. Jessie knew suddenly that he had spent some time in his youth in the War field - he would have called them the 'Games'. As far as she knew there was only one nation in which the War Fields still continued.

Jessie said,"Who on earth would attack us? This is not a world where war is a choice. You must know that." She hesitated, "Wars of physical fighting at any rate. We have several wars still being fought within ourselves and even within our cultures for the life of our planet."

He looked at her puzzled, then his face cleared."I should've known. You're one of them. You don't believe in progress, in building up this Valley the way it could be." He didn't seem to take offense that she didn't agree with him, which comforted Jessie greatly.

They passed through the great Archway into the first Ring Gardens and walked slowly through them toward the second Ring. There were lights still on in a few places where people had come in before dawn. But the sun was already up and no lights shone in the upper stories . Ronald laughed suddenly,"It's just that you women are soft hearted. It wouldn't be wrong surely, if we were attacked, to defend ourselves. That's our strength. to be ready. We'll see to it, Mother. Don't you worry." And with a wave of his hand he went off to his business.

The huge world Market screen was already on and products were being studied by a small crowd of watchers. She walked the winding pathways through late chrysanthemums, myrtle bushes full of color, calendula, pentstamen, petunias, huge bobbing marigolds, and here and there, rose bushes that were a mass of color and perfume. The mild, fragrance of autumn leaves filled the air. The path wound in a twist, demonstrating that Adwin people felt that getting where you were going was no more important than the way you got there.

She walked slowly now, enjoying the color, the soft murmur of fountains, the simple loveliness of this series of varied gardens and lawns. The Arch way through to the Inner Ring was before her. She could hear people chattering as she passed, looking at the foriegn and domestic goods displayed, meeting for social drinks in the small cafes. It was a quiet pleasant morning as though nothing of any importance was happening in this Valley at all. Nothing that would harm or cause any problems to anyone. She walked through the Arch way and approached the steps into the Civic Center Hall where Council meetings were held. Under a wide spreading maple,much older than the town itself, were stone benches, a low table and a small pool inside a stone trough. People stood about on the paved square, some sat, it was a favorite meeting place.

Jessie entered the Council chamber. It was not a large room since, except on special occasions, few other than the members themselves and the usual small group of watching students were present. She settled in a low chair at the round table. There was silence, several already in meditation. She quieted her mind, her emotions, and entered with the others into the stillness and acute attention that enabled her to the focus receptively.

Presently there was a single note, sounded on a chime. It floated through the room, bringing them gently back to the time for business. Jane sat across from her, she nodded briefly. Two others she knew well, the elders of this Council, Emery,and Virginia had served on permanent status for several years. Younger ones, she knew less well, but nodded to them all.

A gaunt woman, in her fifties, Matilda, Reached to all who were there as if it were second nature. So delicate was her Touch that anyone not able to Touch would only have been roused to attention. Jessie was impressed at her finis, until she reminded herself that Matilda was a Healer. Her abilty to focus was probably better than most and she would have no unsettling fears. Her Touch was light and sure. She said,"Main business today has to do with the study done for the Builders by the Communications Center at the request of Valley Council. Well, today is the day! Those results are ready. They'll be announced through Santiago broadcast Station in less than an hour."

Then Matilda grinned, some unspoken amusement in her eyes,"I'd say the news will be announced several times during the day and maybe again tomorrow. Everyone must understand the results. Of course all Elders will have received notice by now." There were no other questions so she went on, "We've already got the vote on the local election for making Market screen extenders available to home computer centers. There was a lot of resistance to that, as you know. The

THE JOURNEY

final tally will be sent in to us any minute. Some say we'll hole ourselves up in our houses and never come into town, if we keep inventing new ways to do things at home. Half our people already do their business from home offices and yet we seem to have a constant crowd in town too. Others say that busy people need to be able to get information fast."

George, a soft voiced black man frowned as he looked around ,"I don't think there's any danger we'll lessen community involvement if we include every kind of communication and business equipment in our homes. People need solitude as much as they need company. I think systems should be built in when we build new homes the way we've built in cleaning and food processing devices. We've always installed basic computer links with library and Learning Center. We do that! Why not the rest? If we're only involved with one another because we can't avoid it, the problem is not our technology. People need people! We'll never lose that."

Jessie smiled at him, she knew instantly that he was broadly telepathic and was using his voice less and less. Needed to hear very little, and felt bombarded by the cacaphony of thought flung freely through the air. She Reached, and met that remarkable shield he had built for himself as protection. But he was aware of her touch, her sensitivity and turned to smile.

Matilda nodded,"I agree, if our coming together is business only, then we as a people have failed."

Lowell shook his head,"The Learning Centers have failed if that is so. Surely the fact that they're constantly busy, day and night, with people of every age, must tell us something. I vote that the extensions be installed."

Matilda nodded. Jessie watched, realizing that every Council member this day was Aware. Then Matilda turned to the board beside her on the table. A faint hum suddenly erupted into a series of little clicks. She read swiftly and raised her head. "The vote is 'yes'. So now we have to decide who's going to pay for them. Any town funds to be used? David, what's Adwin's credit now."

David stirred slightly. He was a large man, over weight, ruddy of face, vigorous and good humored. He said,"Credit's good. We've kept up payment on our building debts and we've been taking in a growing profit from the Industrial Center for nearly five years. If we keep our other costs down, no citizen travel except for study, for instance, no new homes except the apartment circles, for a couple of years, we could afford to pay a percentage. But I vote that individual extenders be bought by citizens as they decide they're useful enough to them to make the investment. It's not our affair."

Others nodded in agreement and it was so voted. Other issues were town guest housing. Now that winter was coming students coming here for exchange study would need some warm quarters and that was town business. David offered to find out which rooms needed improvement, the cost, and to report next meeting. Then it was agreed Adwin participate with the other north Valley towns in sending a letter to the Builders to protest their taking of land near Brandhover without Valley agreement. Matilda said,"It's a formality, but it needs to be said.

Most towns and cities in the Valley have already sent their protests."

The next issue was presented by Clyde, the Master Farmer of Adwin. "There are fields no longer needed for the farms especially in the South Valley. We've learned to grow food more efficiently, we get more nourishment from what we do grow, and we have a good supply of food plants in the forests and wild fields that are doing well. So Adwin could give back to the wild at least fifty acres. If every town does something of this, we could replace the land the builders are claiming."

"Which fifty?" Jocelyn, chief nutritionist, asked.

Clyde grinned,"Well, actually, I was thinking of the fifty that includes the little Hazel nut groves, the new planting from Altos, and the twenty acres of meadow with peas and Accra tubers. They're both doing so well, they'll take care of themselves and we can harvest both if we have need. The hazel nuts are not quite as sweet or as big as the newest variety people farther north are planting, but there'll be enough for every family and lot of wild creatures ." He frowned, looked around with a wry grin, "I suppose you'd say it really isn't giving back to the wild when its a wild crop that will be harvested, but then again it is. No force fields will protect it. Already we haven't been harvesting the whole crop."

Jane asked,"Is there any town needing nuts? Most plant their own groves, don't they?"

He nodded, It's true, but we could ship our surplus out to the south land for trade." He laughed, "Maybe the town that makes the extenders would trade us."

Matilda shook her head,"We'd have to sell and buy, that town has its own groves too." She was thoughtful, then asked,"What's the combination of food plants there?"

Clyde answered with a nod,"The Accra have good companion plants in the indigo peas, the nut bushes give intervals of shade. They nourish each other and both make good forage for wild creatures. I pulled up a tuber last week and I think they're better than sweet potatoes. Surely they're bigger. The peas were harvested this summer and have a very different flavor. Something really new in vegetables, both of these. We'll have all we need just letting them grow on their own. Both have high nectar and colorful flowers, our bees make a good honey from them and we don't need to harvest until long after the flowers are gone. The three crops support each other, Insects avoid the Accra and the peas fix nitrogen for the others." He was grinning at their expressions. It had never been known that Clyde gave up land without making sure it was at least available in a time of need.

Matilda nodded, "So we can give up fifty and yet keep the value of them after all." She gave him a calculating look. "As long as the fields don't hold wild life out, and as long as the land balances itself from now on, I agree it's a release of land. They took the vote, and asked a letter be sent to Bend Council of their decision. Lowell protested,"But won't the Builders simply ask for more then? Once they see we're offering land back to the wild?"

Matilda looked around, and without a word,their minds met. The Touch was instantly made."Wait"! All regular members of Council Joined. Student members

THE JOURNEY

and those outside the circle, government class students, watched. Jessie felt a satisfaction. And they knew together that the Builders might do just that. Depending on the results of the marketing test. It was then that the results were tapping away at the board beside Matilda. She looked down at it and Sent them the results as she read them. When it was done, she looked up. George said,"I'll be damned. That was world wide wasn't it? And there wasn't enough interest in more wine anywhere?"

Mtilda glanced at the listening students,"The results were clear. Survey found little response. No new markets showed themselves."

Joclyn laughed,"I could have told them that. We've done more tests than the vota-test people ever have. Besides, I know something of that test too. They brought in large quantities of really good wines, not only the product of those fast growing vines they planted. They offered them in a hundred communities and the Builders them selves designed the strong advertising program they wanted. They've had months to study this, you know Maybe they're just not good enough at it, but it got almost no results. A few people bought a little more,, but it only lasted a day or so and then dropped back to old demands. "

George sighed, "Well, I don't know anyone who'd want more. We have what we want. We aren't a people interested in drunkenness."

"But what about parties? What about the new bars they've opened here, in Adwin. That was supposed to be the way they'd build their markets."

He shook his head, their looks invited him to go on. "Well, I don't necessarily consider myself a test, but maybe I should. I suppose I'm average after all. I went to the bar to see what it was like at first. I liked it, they've got a pleasant environment and now and then I go with a friend, but people are drinking other things more than they are beer and wine. They just don't want to lose alertness. Then it must be the same in other towns."

"Obviously it is. So all we had to do was wait. Just as Jessie implied to us. They turned to her, and she felt their gratitude. Some had been urging strong action at one time. "Well, Jessie, it's true. Things're different from the way they were in the old days. People wanted to use alcohol to decrease alertness. Life was full of too much pain for them."

"From my study of history, I'd say it was the other way round. Life was too monotonous. People didn't have built in systems for involvement with one another, the way we do. They weren't INTERESTED in enough". Joclyn sighed, "At any rate, I'm not going to worry about the Builders. I don't think the whole thing will matter enough to fuss over." Then she turned to Matilda,"Did we get results on the fabric sales?"

Matilda shook her head,"Not yet, but it'll be the same. People have what they need and more than enough to do to want to get involved in cheap products. But the results will be in soon."

Clyde looked frowning at her,"It's too early to be so sure. We've got to do something about that blatant breaking of our laws though, the way they did at Brandhover. After all, this is a law abiding land too". He closed his hands together before him on the table, looked around.

Joclyn frowned,"Law abiding, yes, Clyde, but we don't oppress people with the law."

He looked abashed momentarily, then grinned. "Of course. I didn't -" then he shook his head and said. "Maybe I did!" The thought silenced him.

Joclyn said,"It's a mark of our difference that we are proud to be able to turn land back to the wild, the old folks were forever trying to take it away . They could not bear to produce less, even if it wasn't needed.It's taken us years to rebuild the prairie land and we still raise enough grain, corn, wheat, etc. there to supply other lands who need it. We keep permanent prairie strips running through the thousands of acres of grains around Bend, for the land requires such care. Every other grain farm does the same. But best of all, we've learned to harvest wild grains and they're producing nearly as sell as our domestic ones. That is the Altos varieties of wild grains are."

Clyde laughed, glancing around, amused,"Can they be called 'wild' when Altos gets through with them?" He frowned then, his eyes moving from one to another, then he said thoughtfully. "I think they can. After all, Wizards work WITH plants, not on them." He nodded to himself,"It does mean we need very little disturbance of Earth, little digging into her. Farming is a new science today. How can we go back? We've just begun to learn how to live with our Earth?"

The others nodded, knowing that Clyde could talk for hours on that subject,and interestingly too. His Teaching hours at the Center were well attended.

"What about jobs, Clyde, work for people to do. Don't we need farming jobs for those who like that work?" George spoke frowning, this was his worry.

Clyde turned to Jocen, "Well, that's your field. What're the facts.

"There's enough work." She spoke passionately, out of grief for a past where humanity limited itself too much. "We involve ourselves in different things. Everybody gets hours of physical work every week, enough for health and energy. Everybody is INTERESTED ! That's the difference, you know, interested in something or other. We spend a lot of time learning and improving our town or farm homes. We ALL do that, children and old folks too! We like to make things, all kinds of things." It was as though she must convince them, convince herself."

Then she was silent, frowning, her head bent, suddenly she looked up, her eyes piercing. Her voice became soft, "But mostly, I think we are involved in an inner search. I think that's what takes our lives out of old patterns the most." Everyone was quiet, it was as though she clairified things for them. They listened to hear what they had wondered about for so long.

Nodding gently, slowly, as if summing it all up, Matilda said, "And the search demands we add things up for ourselves. We've no time for old world games of power, or war, or wealth, or one-up- man-ship. Economics isn't the only way of life today!" She let them sit in silence for several minutes then, looking around, finding them so intently with her, she nodded curtly and went on." We do talk a lot, about ideas, we explore new sciences, arts, dreams and visions, and maybe especially, human relationship. We've four new centers for training of animals, almost any kind you can name. Sales of race horses and cats have increased but they're bred for intelligence before all else. And I've not mentioned space technology at the rebuilt Space Centers in Florida and California. Already we're talking of building a Valley spaceport. That'll take a lot of people. Then there's travel or dozens of other fields of search. Don't the Builders see there's more to do, to think about, to explore than humankind has ever had? It's why we've been able to explore all the outer planets so well. We've got time now, you know, time and energy for almost anything. Surely, George, you must already know that. It's our way."

They were looking solemnly at her, nodding too, and finally began to talk a little, sharing either agreement or questions. And the talk shifted to general news, events, plans. a cheerful friendliness surrounded them, they felt lifted by these accounts of their accomplishments. Finally Matilda called the meeting to an end, all business done. And then, Joral, a young student member, doing his first trial year, asked, "What do I do when friends want me to influence a vote?"

Someone chuckled, another smiled, and he was surprised. It had taken courage for him to even ask. He'd thought they would be incensed. A voice said, "D'you think you could?"

Jocilyn said, "Son, you must do what the rest of us do. Listen to their needs tell them you'll represent them. And do so! Don't imagine you can sway us, manipulate us. You can't. Don't waste your time trying underhandedness. We're experts at recognizing that." She drew a long sigh, shaking her head, "It just doesn't work anymore. Another of those old anachronisms that the Builders try to bring back, I think." Jessie read the sweep of anger among them at the Builders and it's immediate resolution into acceptance.

The boy looked at her with wide eyes, a little awed, and she realized that he didn't understand. With a wince of pain at the necessity, she explained, "Joral, we're not a group to be persuaded against our will, nor for profit. It just doesn't work, you know. How could it? And don't imagine that you're the first who's been asked for illegal help." She deliberately Sent him a swift and powerful Touch. He recoiled and then turned pale. "You see? How could we not know, or see through such motives?"

Matilda spoke softly, realizing that he was chastened, "If they have a request that is at all acceptable, even though others don't share it, we can often grant it. Even when we know it as an attempt to manipulate us. The people of the Valley are just, Joral, and even generous, you know." She was still, turning to look for a moment at the students sitting silently behind the Council members. Then she turned back to Joral, "Surely you have learned from your Teachers at Government study that you must pledge yourself to bring to the Council any pressures made upon you. You don't have to give names. Just ask yourself who tries that. Who wants your interference? I would imagine they might be people without that talent to Touch even, people who do not know that the Joining makes impossible such subterfuge." Her voice was stern, now, tinged with anger. The watching students seemed suddenly restless. She glanced at them,"You know now, all of us, acknowledge the Mind Touch, and that it is not evil! If there is one who has no Mind touch, then we teach that one the wrong of things and the right of them too." For moments silence held. Then two or three heaved great sighs of relief. Another frowned and bent his head.

At that moment, a blocky, gentle looking man named Tomito spoke for the first time.,"It's the same son. we all have to face that. We all have responsibility to never play in secret with the public trust. We each can be bribed, if we have needs unfulfilled or if we are afraid. That's why we talk to each other here, report such pressures. It isn't as hard as you think to do that. But it makes a free and fair Council that you yourself can count on." He stopped, looking off into the distance out the windows of the room."You remember history. People could be bribed because they were so deprived in some way, greed grows out of feelings of deprivation, whether for love or power."

"How deprived? Those old ones? How'd it happen and why aren't our people deprived ever?" A woman student leaned forward as if this were very important to her.

Matilda nodded to Jessie,and smiled, and Jessie turned to the watching students and said, "They had millions of babies who were unwanted, or too much trouble to be given the kind of care they needed. They also had young parents untrained in parenting. That is never - NEVER true today. Even if it did, either Healers or Monitors would locate any child so neglected and correct the flaw. Provide! Because such a parent would be an incomplete person too. Both would be immediately brought to a Healing center."

The students listened fascinated, slowly nodding, they sat back, satisfied.

After a moment of reflection, Tomito went on, "In the old society sometimes secrecy was part of government itself. In a society where peoples needs and wants are taken seriously, where individuals are honored seriously,greed fades. It is not a power among us. We fulfil our needs and the needs of each other, both materially, emotionally and mentally. It is our creed, you know, because we know where danger is sprouted. He stood up, and placed a hand on the boy's shoulder," I think you aren't able to fully Join with us. Is that true?"

Joral flushed, looked embarrassed, then shook his head,"I get a feeling, I sense something. Like a few minutes ago, when Matilda, Matilda looked at me,I REALIZED -- its like that! but -- I think it can't be what you mean. I'd say I don't - do that."

Jessie breathed a sigh of relief that this was now spoken. Others looked surprised, they had not paid enough attention,had not noticed. They felt a swift flush of shame, of serious carelessness. But Matilda, Jocelyn, and George nodded, meeting Jessie's eyes.

George turned to Joral,"We can and will protect you Son. We mean that. When we say you must bring it to us, we will both protect you and help you, so that the threat becomes empty. Don't doubt us. You can at least understand what Joining is?" At the boy's hesitant nod, he went on, "Do you see why it might be

THE JOURNEY

hard to fool us? We know even how to deal with gambling debts and some one desperate to do illegal business, or pressures that you know little of yet. Personal fear is not something we hold against a man or woman." His voice was so serious, convincing that Jeral began to relax. George went on, "The Valley's not perfect, but we are working hard to help each other, not punish. Just bring us the problem. We won't embarrass your friends either. We are rather skilled in these things now, Son. I think you can trust us." He smiled then, a great wide smile that warmed the boy's heart."Besides, if you got anything at all from Matilda's Sending,, then maybe all you need is training."

Jeral drew a long sigh of relief, then he too smiled. His face seemed full of light. "This Joining, I"ve heard of it. My Mother, has talked of it, but only once, then my father, my father was angry and she didn't anymore. I didn't understand just what she meant but I want to know more of it. Why can't I do that? What is it like?"

Your Teachers are teaching any student willing to come and learn about it now. For two months now they've had special classes. Go and learn, Joral. They will show you." Matiida held his eyes until she thought she felt a promise there. He would go far, be an asset to the town, she thought. She would contact George, would remind him to pay attention to that young man. This might be one of his . The meeting over, people rapidly scattered.

Jessie left the chamber and turned to go home through the outer Rings. She heard a call, and a tall grey haired man walked to her."You are the Jessie who lives at the Farm? The one who is the Teacher?"

She nodded, bringing her attention to acute focus, but she did not reach. He made a curious speculative search of her face and then said, "We've got to do something to bring the Builders back into Valley order. They've attacked our way of life two times now."

Jessie nodded again," You want to bring them to order? What is your plan?"

He snorted, impatience wrinkling his face,"Good God, Mother, aren't you Teachers supposed to offer solutions, plans? You seem to do nothing at all!" His anger rang against her tired bones, she studied him, but he went on."So! We've stood for non-violence always. Yet shall we destroy nearly a hundred years of work, for the whim of fools? You saw the destruction at Brandhoven, the other fields east of Santiago, before they were given land hold. But what was worse, their insane bombings, of Temples. That comes out of ignorance, out of a self centeredness that is criminal." He was venting anger, and knew it, and he didn't seem to care that it splashed over her.

She watched him sadly, didn't he see his own reaction was only a reflection of that of the Builders? She said,"Ignorance has caused wars in my own parents time. Even a refusal to see the whole truth of a thing, has done it."

He drew himself visibly into balance, a frown telling her of his recognition that he was out of balance. He said, "But Mother, this isn't your time!" He drew a long breath. Finally he had a Teacher's ear, he'd say it all."Surely, we've done our part! We allow them to learn the only way they can -- don't we? We've let them try out their ideas to see what they can do --- so that they can fail! Isn't that it?" She sighed in vast relief, perhaps this man was able to keep the trust after all.

"You think they will fail?" she needed to know how he thought.

In a tone of exasperation he said, too loud, "Jessie! You know! Everyone who thinks, knows that we don't need more wine. Or mead either for that matter, though we could use a little more of that. Already the market is flooded, we've been trying to sell our products from the South Valley winerys, and last year, the board began to make plans to refit the buildings for other products. There just isn't any further desire. We produce enough for all our people and sell out Valley. And they haven't the sense to see that!" He stopped, frowned darkly and said, slowly loudly, as if breathinhg a litany. "We've - got - better - things to - do!"

"But then, how can they be helped?"

He shrugged, a bitter grin playing for a moment on his face. "I think I don't want to help, but to punish!" He grinned at her, his face softening, his eyes finally taking on a twinkle."I'm venting some old prejudices, I'm afraid." He walked a few minutes silently, his eyes down, a self deprecating smile touching his lips. Finally he said, "After all, they are citizens. I suppose we can't let them lose too completely. We'll probably have to cut our own production a little, in order to give them some market, but within a few months they'll see the campaign to persuade people doesn't work. People know what they want and they aren't to be persuaded by somebody's idea of what they ought to want. No matter how attractive the method." He grinned again, this time a sunny friendly expression, "I studied the system when I went into business, thought maybe we could borrow from those old methods, and believe me, Mother, we did tests, we did several studies with a number of cities out Valley, and trying to persuade people, even subtly, just doesn't work on people who think. Our advertizing consists of simply educating people as to what's available and its quality. Maybe if we'd done the studies in the Valley, the Builders would never have tried."

He was nodding vigorously to himself,"It will end, end if we don't blow a lot of wind into that fire and make it worse. The way I've almost done!" He looked at her, "If we don't descend to that same level, bring our own miserable lower natures into taking our power from us. We know better,Jessie! We've been taught." She was startled at this seeming about face. Here was another person with inner conflict. She let her self Send gently, Reach out to Touch lightly against this good mind. There was no response, none at all, he was mind blind. She frowned, puzzled. "You have no fear of that 'strangeness' those qualities they call Devil practices, of which they speak?"

He laughed and his round oriental face was more relaxed, "You know, there are so many who are different now, I know that,you do too, and yet ---" His voice dropped as if secretively, "People like myself must rely on minds built to think but not to Join,-- Oh, I know the difference. I've gone to the classes, I understand there's a difference. We see enough evidence, even in our own children, and I for one will not deny it. I can't make music, but I don't deny others can. We've all been taught how to live, to contain jealousy, envy, to live according to our own capacity. We've all been taught. We know the time will come, in another life, when we will return with bodies able to Join, and maybe even more. We can live with out fear," He stopped, his eyes thoughtful, "If not without envy!"

Jessie felt a great happiness at this man's insight, balance."I'm so glad you think as you do. Can you help others to understand these differences?"

He nodded, looking away, "I do, there are many of us who meet,and talk of the necessity for balance and for cooperation with those who Join. No, we're not the problem, we've got to deal with the Builders before they harm our world."

"So you think the best plan is to let them try and fail? On their own?" He was grinning at her again, his head bobbing in agreement. Jessie nodded, then asked,"But then, what do we do with them?"

At last he was quiet, his thoughts expressed,"Beats me. I actually don't know. We can't give them the power and the credit they seem to want. But they'll have to find other things to entertain themselves with. Maybe we could send them on journey's to the other planets. Those trips aren't too costly now and maybe they could create their way of life out there" He laughed, but she knew he meant it. He turned, "Well, I've got to go, It was good to talk to you." He walked rapidly away, around the curving side of the central building. She turned and thoughtfully walked through the gardens toward the middle Ring Archway. She suddenly wanted to be at home in her cottage,to think and to rest.

A loud whir startled her, and she turned. A flock of quail broke out of dense shrubbery, whose leaves were already tinted with color. They swept up as one body into the open sky, scattered and landed on the trees around. She heard their soft calls. The flights south would begin for many birds soon. She looked down at her feet, feeling the autumn closer upon her, the winter ahead, that she would not live through. She went through the Arch and out to the gardens that led her finally through the outer Ring and onto the path to the Farm. Standing at this high point, the farm was directly across, the Highway down between , she looked out to the eastern mountains. There high peaks were already capped with early snow. The air was a breath cooler. She could see the City, gleaming in the bright light of this mid- afternoon sun.

She stood, breathing quietly, letting her thoughts calm. She thought that it was strange how the City changed. Before sunup, she seemed so distant and misted, then in the mid day, she receeded out of sight nearly, and finally as the afternoon sun fell against her walls, she was sharp and clear as if she were only a little distance away.

She could see a large flock of blackbirds, hovering and dipping, then circling about. They finally landed on one tree, making it look as if it had suddenly fruited black fruits.The sound of their chattering was like water running, a bright, tumbling sound. She smiled, when they took off again, as if suddenly decided, and flew straight toward the City. She imagined they were messengers. She watched the flight then lost it in the distance, her eyes lingering on the bright walls of the City. "City, you are the finger pointing, you are the synmbol of our task. And we do not forget. You keep our eyes focussed. We humans need something from which to take direction." She looked down at the path, and began to descend. Above her a fairly busy traffic of air cars swept across the sky, going in every direction, from town to city to village. Harvests must be gathered, traded, stored in town and village for the winter. Traders were busy at this time of year. Like other creatures of Earth, humans stored their food for the winter.

She reached the Highway, watching a scattering of travelers, two low carts, many walking, and two on horse back. That was not common,she thought. There must be a Gathering ahead somewhere.She reached, but received only friendly distant response. They were too busy and so that comfirmed her thought. She began the climb to the Farm rapidly, feeling suddenly more energy. As she went, she could not forget that clear image of the City above the Valley. She stopped finally where the path twisted in a sharp curve and looked toward it. Memories crowded, full of both Joy and sadness. She wondered who kept watch there now. Who walked through those glorious gardens, along that clear,pale lake. She longed suddenly to breathe the perfumed air, to feel the power of that place where she knew Life kept vigil.

She stood silently , knowing this Family was ready. She knew their Journey must be soon. So many others had already completed that Journey, and her eyes swept across the Valley floor, past the northern towns toward Santiago. The pools of Light grew broader everywhere. She whispered softly, " There are so many now whose lives do their teaching." She stepped slowly on, tiny tentative steps, as if feeling her way.

Her thoughts raced, finding explanation as she always seemed to need to do. "Surely humanity is ready."

Her mind drifted to silence, no thought intruded, She stood, in a stillness that was complete. There was a fiery burning rising through her, sweeping through her mind, leaving her Heart empty, still. A power like a wind sang through her, loosening that tight furniture of her nature , setting her a bit more free. She felt and knew. the air around her seemed to shine as if diamond dust filled the air, caught at the sunlight and radiated it everywhere through itself, doubling it's power. She saw the Life energy streaming through every living plant or animal around her. The brightness of that Life, the endlessness of it. It was as though some single song was being sung, and every shape, and form, a note of that song. It was as though she had shed another layer of darkness and could hear.

She stood for a time that had no extension. She felt as she did so often now in her life, that nearness of Presence, of what she knew to be an entrance into the realm of Spirit. It's beyond thought, beyond imagination, it's another dimension in truth. Laws of this world do not apply there, but are encompassed . Even yet, she could not walk there, could only glimpse something of that Wonder and feel her own being draw at her Mind as though to purify, polish and make clean. Her heart was full and nourished.

Gradually, she drew back into the Valley world, limited herself. The job was still to be done. She felt infinitely more ready to complete it, to Teach. She walked slowly on toward the Hall, feeling again that deep abiding Joy upon which

THE JOURNEY

she could have lifted herself, could have ascended this hillside without once touching the Earth. She did not. There was not much time left here. This body was wearing out, it was ready to lay itself down.

CHAPTER SIXTEEN

Ned and Silvia finish a water fall

In the same week that Jessie attended the Council, Silvia and Ned were at work again in the Industrial Center. The gardens between each of the the three Rings of that sprawling huge Center, had much room for work. Trees were growing, shrubs,and perennial plants, most of them also providing fruits, nuts or tubers for the town people, made a rich canapy of green and a tapestry of color. North east, outside the OuterRing, was a work field. It was surrounded on two sides by a wide strip of tall hedge roses, and an eight foot high wall of wild berries. Across a half acre of work space, where machinery was assembled and repaired was a ten foot high arbor covered with grape vines. They provided shade for work and food for town. The inside rings of this Industrial Center were finished and busy with manufacturing, but Adwin gardeners were not yet finished with their shapings.

The work still to be done, was the delightful work of making individual gardens, sculptures, fountains, pools and walkways. Young art students worked at some of these, especially pathway mosaics, and two of the fountains. But experienced artists created the major works. Silvia and Ned had undertaken to build a complex waterfall and pool at the southern end of the outer Ring. They had plenty of room in this far end where the oval Ring stretched for forty feet between Inner and Outer Rings.

While Jessie talked with a worried citizen before the Civic Center, in the late afternoon sun, Silvia moved a block of dark stone with an antigrav belt. The late sun played through the colors of the glasteel roof covering the wide walkway behind the the striking dark 'mountain' they had fashioned. She was beginning to feel tired from a long day of work on the stones face over which the water would fall. The 'mountain' was a tall,latticed triangle, twenty five feet high, ribbed with scattered open sections through which inner grottos could be seen, and which would later be planted with water-shade plants, They had only the broad concave top to seal and a few stones yet to be lifted in place. At the very top small trees already emphasized the look of a mountain dell and a still pool would flood and pour down from three sides to crash over rough rock and sluice ways below. There was little left to do and gardeners were already planting trees into the outer edges of the empty field.

No water fell yet through the raised pools or down the ridged sides. Easy access to its heights was made possible with stepped ponds staggered harmoniously about the dark, cratered walls. Children would soon climb naked or in bathing suits over these pools and splash in them happily. Workers might strip down to shorts and cool themselves in them during a work break. Neither Ned nor

THE JOURNEY

Silvia gave thought to that now. They had the carving of the stone, the placing of these massive pieces, and the decisions about where paving around the falls should extend.

As they worked they could hear the sounds of work, soft hum of machinery, busy movement of people coming and going over the walkways. Sometimes pausing to watch their work for a few minutes. One of Adwins main textile plants faced the Waterfall and the Master Farmer's office and laboratories were opposite in the middle Ring. A small winery fitted snuggly into the three story Ring building next the Textiles plant. And between it and the town brewery, a small bar blazed with bright colored lights to announce its presence. Across from the color spangled bar was a small dance hall and restaurant. It had been open only a few weeks, and Silvia was curious to visit. She hadn't gotten back after going home to change so far. But as she glanced at the garish doorway, painted with strange symbols, and lurid color it seemed to her to have a menacing look to it. The thought surprised her and made her frown. True, it was not bright and inviting as was the familiar bar and dance pavilion in the Civic Center, but surely she went too far in imagining some menace there. Now her curiousity was roused and she asked, "Have you been there yet, Ned?"

He glanced over, sensing what she meant,"No, I haven't, I've heard a lot about it though. I suppose we ought to go find out for ourselves."

" What's that mean? Sounds as if you've not heard good?"

He sighed an exasperated sigh,looking at her,"In the first place, Silvia, I can't believe it's right, no matter what you say, that you should be here working this far along with your pregnancy." At her look of protest and impatience, he waved a hand,"I know, you've told me. But I can't help protesting. But to your question; what I heard, was that it's a place for- for -" he looked at her a moment, "for enticing the worst appetites, if you know what I mean."

She stared at him,then finally said,"Well, it wouldn't hurt to be tested, find out what appetites we've got that we've denied." She was grinning, but he frowned.

"I suppose, Silvia,I suppose. I've heard of similar places in other towns lately, even though those cities have been finished for years. So it's not just something that comes to us when we've got our main building done, It's something that's come to the Valley recently, along with the Builders." He frowned again. "I suppose that smacks of prejudice, doesn't it? But I can't help being impressed by the coincidence." He drew a long sigh, laughed at himself, then flinging both arms out in an embracing gesture, he said,"Ah, if prejudice is there, I ought to acknowledge it. And you're right, we'll surely find out about ourselves." Then the smile faded, his good humor with it,"But what if, what if, we aren't able to keep our balance. I don't know whether I want to find out that I am attracted to -- to some things."

His eyes were following the progress of two students carrying musical instruments into the small factory where such instruments were built, and repaired. It reminded him of his own guitar which was there now to be picked up. Silvia watched him silently a moment,"O.K. Let's go then, let's find out for ourselves. I don't like to go on heresay." He nodded absently and they returned to work." Anyway, Ned, I'll keep a close eye on you." Before he could laugh aloud at her, she added,"And you keep yours on me."

They could hear the murmuring voices of three gardeners working on the other side of the triangle. They seemed to be explaining something to a young woman from the Learning Center Art dept, doing an apprenticeship. Silvia listened with a wry smile, remembering her own days of helper. She felt the strange melancholy that always accompanied the ending of a job for her. There was excitement to see it all finished and functional at last, and there was sorrow of that ending. She was contemplating this when she heard the three workers moving inside the main grotto. They were plastering the insides of the stone frames that would hold the plants and the water routes that would carry water in a cascading, intricate pattern through them to the raised pool in the floor. Water would be carried up again only to fall in sheets out over the black outer walls, breaking here and there, pooling in another place. A twisted small tree planted into the stone itself, already grew leaning against the walls. Then the talk stopped, silence broken suddenly by singing. She felt exasperation, "How can they get any work done!"

Ned laughed at her. "Sil, lots of people work better when they're singing. And they've got great harmony. Must have selected their student with care." Then they realized the song was the 'Ending Song'. Composed by a member of the Stone Carvers Guild, it was one sung often at the ending of a job. Those three were also feeling the sadness and elation of this day. Silvia hummed a little with them, feeling strangely drawn to join them. Then she knew. These were Reaching, even as they sang, Reaching invitation to them to join in. She stopped,angry,feeling somehow invaded. It was one thing to practice this mind Reach at home with the Family, but here in town, it seemed to her improper.

"Ben!" She cried out. "Why's it happening everywhere, that Reaching. How can they imagine we could enter into THAT so easily?" Her voice carried panic.

He shook his head, wonderingly, "Maybe, Sil, maybe they've already made the Journey." He looked at her, his eyes wide.

Silvia frowned and drew herself to balance. With a long sigh she relaxed and said,"I feel as though I'm at the edge of a vast sea. But the place where I stand is about to crumble, to fall away so I am in danger of falling down into that sea. What would happen to me if I give myself into that -- that -- " She stopped, the word that wanted to be said was 'yearning' and she denied it. They were silent, moving the finished stones up into the craggy top, beside the shallow bowl where a pool of quiet water would soon reflect the sky. Together they finished the placing of the final oblong carved stone, and stood back to look at it. The height gave them a view across the roofs. Three stories here,the roof line jutted up to another story around the curve of wall, but from their vantage point they could see far across the River and north to the Farm.The late sun glinted on the dark stone that completed the pocket in which the pool would sit. She slid her hand down the polished sides ran a finger into the deep grooves of their carved designs.

THE JOURNEY

Ancient runes of magic and good will, stood out dull against that shine.

Ned said, "We might as well climb down, Sweetheart. We've finished up here." And lightly, slowly, as if reluctant, they wound down through the little breaks and pools to the court below. Silvia sighed deeply, leaned against a great shaped block that would be left as a place to sit, on the equally polished pavement. Her thoughts raced. She could not ignore their insistence."If I let go, fell, then I'd be nowhere. Nowhere at all. Nowhere except further into myself.And I don't think I dare go there. Any farther!" She slid up onto the smooth surface of the stone bench, chin in hand, she studied the work of their past weeks."It's like this whole sculpture, it's got so many parts, and it's got dark and hidden places where water pools, then comes rushing out, in white spray, and pools again, or falls sheeting over stone, gleaming when the sun hits it like silver.

Ned looked at her, listening silently, then when she was silent for several minutes, he said,"It's frightening to give yourself over -- to lend yourself to others so completely."

She looked at him sourly,"WHY?"

He glanced over at her, saw she was serious and said, "Well, I don't know except for me it seems dangerous, as though I might not keep myself intact at the same time. Can any human trust so much? Ought we to? That last Gather - Sil, I haven't said this to anyone, but, I felt then, as though I lost myself - in all of us. At first I could feel panic and nearly withdrew, then, the sense of a whole, a greater Self was so r eal, I felt -" He shook his head, "felt only a sweet joy." He was silent, remembering, then, "But my memory keeps that moment of panic too. Maybe I'm afraid I'll fall too far into that giving away." He was grinning, because he felt unsure of his response. He was glad she was talking. He knew she needed to and that she usually didn't. "Trust can be seductive, you know!"

She was startled by the statement, looked at him penetratingly, then sighed deeply, her almond eyes opened wide and he thought she looked frightened. The black man beside her stood, towering over her, and stretched his aching body. She glanced up at him, then back at the stone walls, "Well, there's a lot on my mind, and there has been ever since we talked last, at that accidental Gather. It's as if we all knew, came together without having to be called. That was enough to make me uneasy. But then," She added in her necessity to be honest,"It also makes me feel wonderful." She was shaking her head, unable to understand.

Ned lauged then, "I have some trouble with all of it too, Sweetie, if I let myself think of it too much, I'd get indigestion of the brain." She glanced irritably at him. His jokes weren't always to her taste.

She began to collect her tools, picked up a sweater she had dropped earlier and put it on now. "Jane taught me something that helps. I just flatten my whole body against the Earth, let everything in me run out. She says Earth can absorb anything. Even when my mind feels like a thick soup, and won't digest into meaning." She looked at him again, he was sitting as she was on another stone and studying their work."Sometimes I just get a belt and go up into the sky, floating there. It's as if all the questions float out, just drift away. But I know it's only a rest, that they'll come back." She was silent, glancing at him out of the corner of her eye,"Sometimes, rarely, I get real insight there, when it's so quiet."

He shrugged, serious suddenly,"I've tried that. It works for me too sometimes. Othertimes I'm completely out of balance and I can't settle. None of the practices our teachers taught us seem to work. It's true, it's like some thing raging inside me, something that won't settle. And then sometimes, it's the opposite, as though great stillness grows. An utter stillness to measure things against." His smile was gentle, he looked at her, "Maybe all this is just having to adjust to the reality of what was so long just theory." He sobered,"Maybe this is what Jessie means when she says we are aware in a new way. Mental awareness is one thing. Spiritual awareness is another."

"They can't be separate, can they?"

"I don't think so, but then, what do I know". There's a lot of difference but whether it's difference in degree of awareness or in quality, I don't know."

Silvia moved slightly, her chin in her hand, gazing at the air."Ned, about Jane, have you noticed she's changed a lot. She's practicing things I never knew she could do. Since she started seeing that man, Roderick, you know. I only saw it once, but it was strange and beautiful."

"What'd she do?" His voice was soft, wondering.

"She was out beyond the lower fields, I'd gone to find her, and there she stood, looking up at a whole flock of geese flying south. I could hear their calls, even the soft whisper of their wings. Jane began to call, the way the geese did. Then she raised her hands, lifted them toward the geese as if wanting to touch them. And she stood like that, silent, for several minutes and then, Ned, believe it or not, that whole huge V of Geese simply swerved, curved themselves back around and silently came settling down there all around her, like a billowing white pond, they honked, whistled and mumbled around her while she talked to them. Ned, I couldn't hear a thing she said, but I know she was talking." Silvia frowned, but went on. She knelt down among them, reaching out toward one great white gander who was limping badly, and he stood while she went to him, stood there! Ned, these were wild! Wild geese and they stood. Then I could see she was doing something to the gander's foot, it was hurt someway. And she got her first aid kit from her pack, I don't know what she did to it, but then, they all began to mutter and honk again, as if talking it over." Silvia shook her head. Ned was fascinated, his eyes fixed on her face.

Then they began to arrange themselves and by twos and threes they flew away, swept up high into that grey autumn sky and went on, making their V as perfectly as before. I was stunned. I couldn't talk for a while. I waited to go on to where she was." She was silent. Then,"But I didn't tell her that I'd seen. I wonder why not!"

He murmured softly,"She's grown aware of herself!" Silvia felt angry, and knew it had no cause." Yes. Aware! That! It's the word that describes so much. And it's what we've all been taught! Well, I'm having trouble. I think I always thought it would be so easy . The ideas sounded easy." Her voice softened, a tone of wonder coming in it."But you know, Ned, It's true. What we learned is true. The waking up brings a real battle, but it also brings wonder like that with Jane. To us to, you know, Ned." She turned to him, as if seeking comfort." And all this with the Builders. My feelings are so mixed up! I always thought the idea of battle was a figure of speech, but it's not at all." Tears came suddenly, wetting her eyes and making them look larger than they were."I'm afraid it'll only get worse."

He nodded,"Don't worry, it will, worse - and better!. But we've got help. I remember hearing Ben talk this way once years ago. And Rose too. But they didn't talk much of it. I think they suffered it out alone. Not talking, that's been our major sin, I think. But they survived! Remember? Ben running off for months at a time? Rose dissappearing and staying for days in her cabin? They had to struggle by themselves because we didn't have Jessie."

Silvia nodded, engrossed in the memories, "Yeah, I remember, and how strange I thought they were. Had no idea what was happening. But there was so much work to do then, a person could lose herself completely in the day's work. Now, so much of it is done, we have more leisure and we can't escape as easily." She laughed ruefully, reached out to touch his hands, then swiftly withdrew.

Ned met her eyes, sat very still, with a shrug she continued,"Well, I'm accepting now. I really think that I understand something of it all. I listen to our Gathers, and I listen to my friends now too, there're a lot of them who're doing a lot of realizing. I believe what the Teachers say now. I think that I have to admit we're literally waking up to another measure of ourselves, another state of consciousness that we humans are naturally gifted to, but that we've denied, or couldn't reach before. Our brains are able to key into more than we ever thought possible. We have the equipment, it's just doing it. Just putting our attention out there where we've never been."

They sat silent for some time. The singing inside the Triangle had stopped, they could hear the others preparing to leave for the day . They must do that too, but they did not move.

Finally Silvia asked,"Ned, why've we been so afraid?"

He shook his head, no grin on his face, made him look almost strange to her."I don't know, Sweetheart. I think maybe it's that we've all been sure this entering into another state of consciousness would be something we could imagine, could think of, think ABOUT. We couldn't imagine that it would be something beyond imagination. Something utterly different and UNTHINKABLE. It made it too strange, too unfamiliar to be born. We have to trust enough to enter into it and then find out what we discover."

She said,"For so many years, we've known the idea of transformation, the IDEA of what the Teachers called Awakening. But we all had our own personal notion of what reality is, what that Awakening would be like and when it's not,it's like a betrayal."

" We thought we could transform ourselves, didn't we? That our personal ideas of what we would be, what humanity might become, was what was real." He laughed as if at a great joke,"Well, we got our ears pinned back for sure, didn't we?"

She was nodding, her understanding growing, she watched his big shining face, her love for him transforming his ruggedness into beauty. "I think we assumed, without thinking about it, that we could THINK it into reality. That Soul Conscious would be what we imagined it would be. I never knew I must wait in that silence to find out, to discover what I could never have imagined."

"There it is again," his hand waved and both his arms spread out embracing the air, "that same old thing. The Teachers told us that, that we must DISCOVER, that it could NOT be thought up by our ordinary minds." He sighed, sat down nearer her, "They also said it would seem to us like something 'OTHER' and so it does, something alien. That state of being is not familiar at all." He paused then, "Silvia, I stand in awe, absolutely in awe and it's the first time in my life that I've ever felt any real sense of AWE."

"At what, Ned?" She felt an intensity and solemnity she had never seen in Ned.

"At what we humans appear to be coming to. What we ARE. Silvia, what we ARE! Soul Conscious beings, not the simple brainy animals we have been. But something so much more we can't imagine it at all. That's what I've begun to glimpse, that we are becoming something beyond what we've always been. We've got so far to go. Just accepting the possibility has taken us so long, and is so hard." She sat lost in the power of his thought. "We do glimpse that, when we've been Joined, at least. For me it's happened a few times, but for the others, glimpsing THAT is not so new. They KNOW, and I see it there, shining in their minds, even when I can't quite understand. I glimpse something and only begin to realize that what I glimpse is also myself!" She was shaking her head in full disbelief, unable to take in that idea, that thought that she had heard Jessie speak of. That she had finally begun to see for herself. " Yes, I do glimpse that, but I think the others, See it clearly."

He stood up, his long arms reaching here and there to gather his tools, he said, "It's absolutely different, that way of being. It is actually. The Spiritual substance is not material substance. Neither is it mental substance. At least not the mind we're used to. That's the problem. It just isn't. But we're only used to experiencing material and mental substance, so we can only glimpse that finer, purer substance we call Spiritual. That dimension is out of sight for us, so to speak. It's beyond what we've known so that our brains balk at perceiving through that level. It's as different as the thought of Love is from Love Itself. As totally, essentially and innately different."

"And yet, one dimension opens to the others, just as lust, crude as it might be, is a beginning toward love." Silvia was enjoying the talk now, they were shaping ideas, an effort to explain and to understand - and that she could handle. Talk was easy. It was the EXPERIENCING of Spirit, that overwhelmed her.

He seemed to have caught her thought, for he turned to her, tying up his tool kit. "My brain feels like its buzzing, trying to understand. And that's strange, because when I am simply quiet, really still, when I hold my mind steady in that stillness, then there it is! There is the Light growing, present, the realization lighting my mind up like a revelation. I KNOW that power rising through my consciousness. I am more. More! I am AWARE of everything here and -- and elsewhere! Aware of so many assumptions, habits, patterns that I've taken for granted and that I see now are all only that -- limited perceptions. I try to figure out what my poor brain cannot really understand after all. I SEE so much, and all that is has multiple facets, so many dimensions. Strange that you can be aware of what you can't understand. It's in stillness that I know, not in thinking. When I think, I have to choose a couple of sets of assumptions and use them as points from which to judge. When I am simply aware, whatever is, can be." He paused, arrested by that realization. It struck him hard and he could not speak.

She nodded, watching his face, searching out what had just happened, and felt his Touch, so gentle, so unsure, but real. And she Reached also, wanting to be there with him.

He frowned, letting his fingers slide along the pattern in the block he sat on. "Funny how I do it. I see a wondrous Light approaching me and instead of accepting, enjoying, I dodge everywhere trying to explain it." His lips were tight suddenly, he glanced at her, reached out to take her small white hand into his great black one. He finally confessed, softly, "I can't really ignore myself -my SELF anymore, Silvia. That inner voice grows so strong. My frantic brain can't explain, but I am ready to accept without explanation because I KNOW, through clear experience, what is so REAL it makes a fantasy of everything else I have known. And my rational mind simply shudders sometimes."

Silvia did not shift her gaze, she blinked, frowned, said, "The decision that we will make that Journey, it's settled then?" she expected no answer, "At first I thought I'd not be among you, then, it was as though a far memory, a deep inner calling began in me. I realized that I must be ready too, that I must be with you all.

Ned laughed, "You bet your life, you'll be there, Sil. We need you as much as anyone." He was suddenly very serious, "I know I must go, I must -- enter into that place, stand where the power can Touch me and relieve me of these doubts." A wry, puzzled grin drew his mouth up, "It's the way the kids just accept, no doubting, no questions, they just seem to -- to KNOW."

"And you're jealous?"

Glancing at her mocking face, he withdrew his hand, "I suppose I am." He saw her relenting look of apology, "Or else I'm afraid for them. For them!"

She was nodding seriously, "And my child! He's going to meet all that too, I suppose. I tell myself that it might harm him, and I know it's a lie, it's an excuse when I feel uneasy and want an excuse. He won't be harmed. Neither will the other children. I do know that, Ned. I do know that!" She met his eyes, "Our children, Ned, they're extraordinary!"

He shook his head, "For the new times ahead, they're ordinary. We're the ones not up to it." His voice sounded a little plaintive to her. She laughed.

They finished putting things away, and stood, looking far across the gardens. "You know, we've made a wonderful paradise for us all to live in. I wonder what we're doing seeking more? I wonder how we can need more." He sighed a long tremulous breath."But I know. Nothing is enough now that we've begun to know, unless we go on into that universe we've begun to glimpse. Our hearts won't be still."

"It took me so long, I tried a lot of things to distract myself, flying, a moon trip on the shuttle, agreeing to work on this sculpture, spending hours in the Learning Center film rooms, reliving, just letting myself be distracted with whatever was there, and even went to the Builders Bar in Santiago" She grimaced, "They've got a fascinating decor, and music, changing light, fragrances, they're using everything, and it worked, with a little wine or good whiskey - - for a while, it did work. I could imagine that there was nothing different. That the world was the same small familiar place. I could shut myself off." She went to pick a late rose bud and to twirl it between her fingers while she smelled the fragrance. He waited, watching her.

"It's true. Much as I denied it. I've tried to hide just exactly that way. Just the way Rose used to do. And I'd never have believed it. But being aware of one's Self, makes a person admit there is more than we thought. Even now, I'd like to take a belt, and escape in the sky, play among those big lovely clouds there, get wet even, and yet -- I know it won't work anymore. I feel such dispair when I try to understand. Nothing works to keep me from knowing of that inner pull.Nothing at all. It's the way Steve said it was for him. And lately, I searched through history, and I read of St. Augustine, how he fought to avoid the touch of Light. And of course, the classic case of Jonah, and Arjuna. Everywhere you look, there're examples of people who resist the knowledge." She breathed deeply of the rose, then said,"Unless I acknowledge -- ". Her voice faded.

"Acknowledge what?" He almost held his breath, wanting her to tell him.

"That I, as myself, am empty. As Silvia alone! I can't hide from my Self, I can't distract myself from my Self. That's in ME, this longing, this knowledge, it's what subconscious means, I think! Bringing the subconscious up to consciousness. And we call it Light, Ned, Light making visible what I've denied. That I know I must accept." Her voice fell to a whisper and he saw that she was working it out, saying what made meaning for her. So he was still.

Tears spilled over her eyes and ran down her face and she seemed not to notice. He knew that she needed him then,to listen, to reflect."When things began to lose fascination for me, living began to close to a halt, the whole work of our Valley seemed to be more a game, a great play we were all immersed in, then I had to stop and take a new look. I felt as though the bottom had dropped out and there was nothing for me but grey dispair. Not even an interesting misery, just a kind of nothing. But, you know, Ned, even before the last Gather, I was sitting on the deck at home, listening to a recording of the Ashley Cello Concerto, and watching birds gather for their autumn flights. I felt drawn out into that beauty, all of it, the delicate smell of Earth there, of decaying leaves after the rain, of -- everything, and I knew again that same quality of pure Wonder, as if -- as if--" She shot him a glance, saw his absorbed steady gaze, and went on, "in a moment more, I would step through it into -- into Beauty itself. Or something from which Beauty came!" She turned fully to him, catching his arm,"Do you see?"

He nodded,"I do, Sweetheart. It's been like that for me sometimes. I understand finally what some of the others tried to tell us long ago. The pain Rose lived through, you know, for instance."

They stood for moments, leaning against the smooth hard stone, feeling the coolness of evening gather around them, unable, unwilling to move, to end this strange wonderful moment. He said,"There is an attraction, something that pulls me, to that point, like a Lighted place, and I long for it. Then I feel afraid, and then a sense of Awe fills me, Sil, something I've never known, a power that I can't resist. Then LIFE is suddenly so pure, so alive, so Real, that I feel surging JOY. I know that LIFE is right HERE waiting for me, if I can have courage enough to enter into IT. And I don't even know how. And then, there I am, alive in that LIFE. Aware !" He breathed raggedly, "And I didn't do anything to make it happen. Awareness was just occurring as I paid attention."

"She nodded, absorbed in his passion, realizing how it expressed her own."Well, we've got Jessie, Ned. And now, some of the others seem to have an idea. Maybe together, all of us, we can find the courage."

He drew her over to settle down on a bench far enough so they could see their stone sculpture whole. They sat, letting their eyes roam over it's familiar parts, wanting to do a little something here, there - and then he said,"You know, Silvia, it takes some work , some pressure, some pain and some fear, for a baby to be born. For a mother to open herself enough to permit that. And it takes pressure, pain and work for a universe to open Itself, ours especially that we've got so tightly closed, explained, finished by our limited standards. When it does open, it lets in new light, new questions, new wonders, but it upsets all our careful explanations. The explanations have become our prison, limiting us to themselves. So it's no surprise that we long to push on, into that further Vision, the one that frightens us."

She nodded, "It helps me to have you talk about those things, Ned. I think you see more clearly than I."

He seemed not to have heard, he said,"Sometimes, then, when I do what you described, just listen, just sit in stillness, pay attention through myself, then a strange quiet filters through me, dispells my dispair, beckons, as though there is something there -- just beyond myself -- that I've not realized. And then, sometimes, that other event, that sense of having everything, the trees, the Earth, the sky, everything, laughing at me, and wanting to include me in the great Joke. Joyously laughing, and me sitting there, wanting to see the Joke too. And I can't. And I feel so sad as though I've missed something. And then, suddenly, like a brilliant glimpse, I DO!" He leaned close to her," And I want to laugh too, to laugh at the wonder of the Joke. Then later, I can't remember what the joke was, only I know it was alive with joy. Does that sound crazy to you?"

She shook her head, her large dark eyes full of such love he turned away. Then she said,"It's what they said in the Gather, isn't it. Pretty much like that. I think you're just beginning to discover what it's all about. I wish I were so near to it."

They were silent, his arm slid around her shoulders, and they were comforted by each other's warmth. Finally she stood, looked over at him, perched a little above her, "It's nearly evening, we ought to get home. We've done all we can do and there's not so much left anyway. I like to leave something for tomorrow. And tomorrow, we'll be turning on the water and we can see it finished." The delight in her voice made him grin." You know, I NEED to feel there's something for me to do nowadays." She laughed, cried, then picking up her tools, turned away. He followed her.

"It's time to go home, Yes. I want to visit some friends this evening. We're going to try out the cafe by the River bank, where they say they have a great show." He shook his head, grinning, "Well, here I go too, Sil. Looking for something to take my mind off everything. Maybe I ought to just go to Temple, or out to the Farm and talk to Jessie." He was silent, waiting, "But I won't. I'm looking forward to this. What we realize is everywhere, in the simplist and most ordinary things."

They walked on past the unfinished gardens, through the great Archway and out to the outer Ring. People were beginning to fill the walkways, going home, finishing up their work. There were those who preferred to work at night and they were drifting in to the Center. It was seldom that the factories, and mills were not operating. Here they must part if she were to go on to the path behind the Civic Center and home. He lived in the residences along the edge between the two western knolls. They stood a moment after they passed through the last Arch and were looking across the tops of roofs where cluster homes dropped down into the sloping saddle. Trees concealed most of the residences. Silvia looked at the cluster houses on the rim, one of those directly ahead was Ned's. She sighed, she had known some wonderful, dear hours there.

She kissed him and watched him walk across the winding paths. She did not turn toward the narrow trail that would carry her back to the northern edge of town. She stood, letting her fingers smooth the edges of a branch. Her gaze fell on those fingers, watching silently their movement, the still hardness of the smooth bark. She felt a sadness penetrating her body, a feeling of essential loss, loss of what was supposed to be. The idea of life, the fantasy. Here, now, in this place where evening cast long shadows across the Earth. She recognized that loss, stood quietly accepting, conscious. And then, the stillness deepened, gathered around her as if some permission had been given. Her thoughts whirled, drew at her attention, but she felt too tired to attend. There was something so still, so POSSIBLE. She held her breath, then slowly, let it pour from her. All the worries, fears, struggles and refusals she had known, seemed to gather, spin there, like a top, grown heavy with its own resistance, and finally to fall and cease, to enter also into this stillness that encompassed her.

Her fingers still smoothed the patch of bark, it seemed all that there was in existence, it seemed all and everything. The universe held itself there, at that point, and she felt herself cast through that endlessness, looking at herself, at the point that her fingers touched. Here in this timeless awareness was Life itself. All that was seemed to tremble through her. Then she shifted to wanting this moment to continue and she lost it. It could not be kept. Like a bubble bursting, it was gone.

But she felt alive as she had never felt herself before. Alive and suddenly recognizing Life for what it was beyond all limits of explanation. She caught her breath, Joy threatened, and she sought to grasp the knowing of that Joy. It was gone just at the effort to grasp it. A grief throbbed in her heart, but she was smiling, knowing that somehow Life had touched her. Or she, herself had Touched against Life?

The late sun touched the hills behind the Farm. She must hurry. The trail wound in comforting familiarity around the far edge of the knoll. She would cut across down this edge and then over to the slope behind the Civic Center Knoll. That way led to the crossing of the Highway below the Farm. She walked without giving attention to anything except to the tenderness of her feelings, her acute awareness of the living things around her. Life offered Itself, promised Itself. She felt a stir within her body, another life that curled there safely and peacefully waiting. That life was changing too, changing rapidly and in ways she wondered at. She felt her heart swell with Joy, a reflection of that Joy she had almost known earlier. But this joy was enough for now. This joy, her child shared with her. She knew without doubt.

CHAPTER SEVENTEEN

Benjamin meets Dennis - Jessie's test - and the Hunters call Ben.

    Neither Ned nor Silvia spoke of their realizations the next day, wanting the time to think, to absorb and to allow those realizations to inform their still questing minds. Benjamin saw a difference in Silvia when she came home late and tired. He opened his mouth to speak of it, more than once, and each time, he waited. It was hers to tell. The next day, he was out early, into Adwin and attending to the daily work. The questions of his Heart held for a time quiet.
    He walked out of the front office of the Adwin Business Machines Inc. and realized it was nearly mid-day. He smiled in satisfaction. The young business was going finally, two new products were selling both in and out Valley . One was his own work, a filter for the weavers,designed to completely clear the air in their work rooms. He'd worked with the biochemists to develop it. Living organisms that literally ate the dust, fiber, etc. Mechanical filters had not been totally efficient, ninety five percent clear air had been thought adequate until Anna,went to do an apprenticeship there. She had complained loud and long to him. He was glad to know of it. The regular workers had not complained so no one had done anything. However they had genuinely blessed the creators of this system, insisted they felt better. He turned to look at the name printed above the door: Adwin Biomachines, grinning at his own pride and delight in it.
    Things were changing, now the whole industrial complex was finished. New business and industry had been moving in, most of the warehouses were at least half full. The work rooms were occupied profitably. Adwin was not only basically self sufficient, but making credit for itself finally. People were able to begin improving their own homes, their lives. Adwin's debt was manageable, indeed the Council had sent word to Santiago that she could begin offering a small credit for new towns. The first time that had been possible since they had started the long years of building. He glanced up at one of the ware houses built into second and third stories. The huge sliding doors were open, wide windows brought in sun during the cold months and a narrow edging of balcony offered benches outside so that workers could enjoy the air and sun. The low sound of light machinery humming away was a pleasing sound as Ben walked on.
    He threaded through the gardens, the outer ones nearly finished, and stopped to admire the growth of a young almond, nuts already gleaned. He picked a few that still clung, then catching a flash of color around the curve of building, he saw masons holding their gathered tools. The 'Mountain' was finished and workers stood watching the flashing water race down into pockets and through green tumbling vines and small trees over the many waterfalls. He knew it was designed and built by Silvia and Ned. He watched a few moments, mesmerized by the play of water and light. Then turning he saw ahead people on

THE JOURNEY

their way home. He walked fast to catch up. When he reached the group he said,"Well! You've finished for the Winter Festival, after all?" He grinned.

Most of the group glanced at him, nodded and walked on, but a short powerful man still in his working overalls, stopped, then caught stride beside Benjamin."Ah, Ben, my friend, we've so nearly finished I feel that we come only to rub a little polish on our final walls. The big Water Fall your Sister and Brother did, sets the tone for all the new gardens. All we had to do this morning was to polish a couple of the grottos inside and turn the water on. So there it is, Man, something else finished and we're out of work." He shook his head ruefully, even though he smiled.

Ben laughed, looking at his friend's face, seeing the wearyness there - and the great pride."It's been hard work, eh Dennis? It's good it's coming to an end. All our people have worked without much vacation time now for years, and this city is something to be proud of. We're going to take an extra week at Winter Festival and celebrate. Everyone who was a builder must have a name carved into the Temple walls."

"That'll be about ninety percent of present citizens." Dennis smiled, but sorrow was in his eyes.

Ben bent attention to his friend, and realized belatedly that Dennis's face did not reflect weariness from this loved work, but from something eating at his heart. He rejoiced that he could realize that and accept his knowledge. He asked,"What's the trouble, Dennis. You've got something on your mind besides the ending of years of work."

"You've given us a name I'll not accept at all, Ben , though I know you meant it kindly."

"And what did I say?" Ben remembered backwards, and added,"Oh, you mean speaking of you as builders. Then what angers you about that."

"That's the name of a bloody lot, a beggerly bunch who'd try to tear out all we've lived for. We PLANNED this town, our farms, our land and the forests,and the fields, we PLANNED it to be as it is. How can they ask to tear it apart? They built this Valley too! And they're our own people. They had the vote like all the rest of us. Why are they complaining ? Damn them all!" He clenched his fist and stopped walking to look at Ben with an angry face, but a terrible hurt in his eyes. Then suddenly, his face relaxed downward, spilling the angry look and leaving only a confused worry. "I suppose I'm not much better,am I. Getting so angry that I curse my fellows. The same as my father would have done. Oh, he never did hesitate, and I think his curse harmed some. But I'd never let mine stick. I'd not do that." His voice had fallen, a tired, sadness claiming him. He laid one hand on Ben's arm and after a visible fight in himself, his eyes shifting back and forth for a second, he met Ben's eyes squarely,"I've something I've got to talk of."

The sun splashed peacock colors down through the over hanging roofs but neither man noticed. Dennis lived in the saddle between the two western Knolls and it would be a little walk to get there. Ben nodded,"We do need to talk. I can hear it in your voice, my friend. It's been too long anyway."

THE PEOPLE OF THE VALLEY

They crossed the edge of the down slope into the residence saddle west of the Industrial Center, and began the slow winding walk down through these lawns and gardens. A clear small stream ran through the narrow rocky creek bed at the bottom of the saddle where it pooled here and there. Children played, making dams between the pools though the evening was growing cool. Dennis said,"It's my son,Benjamin. He's got in with them and he's been a problem to me since his eighteenth birthday. Ah Ben, children aren't easy to raise." He shook his head, smiled ruefullly, "But they are a wonder too and I'd never've missed a moment of it." They walked a bit further before he spoke again after a long sigh.

"But this! It was so unexpected. We had no idea he'd got that way. He was always a decent lad, he'd taken to the Teaching so well, thought a lot of the Convictions and though he had no Talent for Healing he was going to study medicine. " Ben wanted him to get on with it, to tell him the terrible offence, but he swallowed his impatience,"What started it, Dennis?"

He could see Dennis relax, walking now, with the quiet ease of a man with a well cared for body. "It's what we've asked ourselves, Maud and me. We've come to the notion that it was when he fell in love with the little Marilee,. She that lives just across from us in the Cluster behind the apple and apricot grove.She's a good girl, never troubled her folks that I know of. The two of them were always together, and naturally when they got older, he just naturally fell in love with her. We thought it good. We liked her. If they'd mated we'd have been glad."

"Then what?"

"Well, she said their love is not a mating love. She told him she couldn't be sure. She did say she loved him, would always love him, but she wouldn't do more. He thought he'd give her time, so it was all right for a while."

Then they weren't mated?"

My son wanted that, he said she was his Mate. True Mate, you know. I've never been sure just what that means. I used to think it was the same as being in love, but now, I know it's not that at all." Maud and me were wed before we knew of such things. Merilee just couldn't agree. She said it wasn't right for them. Maud and me both knew that they loved each other. We just had to watch, wondering how to help. Then, because we'd kept waiting for Jackson to develop -- to show signs of - of Reaching, of making a clear Touch, we finally realized what was wrong. We saw that she could Reach, could Join even, and he couldn't. We saw that she'd Seen through the rift into the greater universe, that some folks call the Spirit, the Inner Vision. She'd felt the pull, the reaching beyond herself, until she could See. He didn't! There is no longing in him, no desire to wake the Spirit. And we knew then that she was right." His voice dropped and was filled with grief that Ben knew was not based on his son's loss of his first sweetheart. "We'd hoped he'd grow into it, but he hasn't and it's too late to keep hoping now. He just doesn't have any perception of what it is about"

Ben didn't need to ask, but he knew he must. Dennis must speak it all out."What was it he hasn't grown into, Dennis?" He wanted to comfort this father, remembering his own recent grief.

"Ah, you know it, Ben, old friend. I know that you do. But I'll say it out. He has no inner voice, no inner sight, or hearing, he's one of the old ones, the ones who are Heart and Mind blind. He just doesn't know. Even though he knew the theories when he was taught them. He believes in the IDEA of an extended universe. We've taught him of Spirit, of the Heart's wakening." He turned agonized eyes to Ben. "Now, he realizes that she sees what he doesn't, that she knows, realizes in ways he can't. Finally he told me! He spoke of it! Said it's like being born blind, but not knowing it until you finally realize other people are aware of things you're not." Dennis turned and they continued slowly to walk through the autumn trees, seeing and nodding to people they knew along the way. Passersby saw Dennis's grief, looked with sympathy as they passed. This was not unusual in a city where people learned to talk of their griefs and fears as very small children.

"He knew then that she'd never Mate with him. He saw that there was something he didn't know, couldn't know. He saw that perhaps she was right and that this was only a first love and he didn't know the difference. You see, SHE knew the difference. She knew it was first love and willing to let it run its course. But he only knows enough so he sees the difference between them and he can't abide it. It's like a young boy my mother told me of who was intellectually retarded just enough that he saw how much less he was capable of than his friends. It was the cruelest kind of lack. And Ben, Jackson can't abide it." He stopped, his voice choked. His eyes swimming again.

Ben saw the tortured look and said, "My God, Dennis. You never talked of this to anyone at all? Not even your own peer group?"

Miserably Dennis shook his head. "I don't know what's happening with your family, but in ours, we haven't talked of such things much. For years we didn't admit we saw what our parents didn't. Even Maud and me, for so long we didn't talk to each other even. We'd only begun to accept the fact we could Touch, but then the Master Teachers started bringing us all in to practice, to acknowledge, and it's all coming out. We've known the Touch itself. With one another! We can't deny! But I've hurt so badly that I didn't want to admit. I suppose I felt ashamed for my own son. Ashamed!" His face twisted into a terrible grimace, the pain of his confession more than he had thought it would be.

Ben nodded, suffering with his friend, "Do you know many, Dennis, many who lack the Talent?"

"I know a few, I think. They don't seem to have any sense of it at all. So unaware they suspect nothing and so they don't suffer at all, except sometimes -- they seem to notice a silence and think we're odd. They seem happy enough among us." He threw out his hands, "There, you see? It's as if they're AMONG us. As if they're different!"

"And so they are, Dennis. We've not admitted that. And we must. That doesn't mean they are less at all."

Dennis frowned," It's not what people'll feel, Ben.. Just wait. We human's aren't as kind as we might be. We haven't been a people who've been understanding of those who are different." He stopped, thoughtful for several minutes. Ben reached, Touched and smiled slightly when Dennis said,"Although that's actually not true of us any more, you know Ben. We are tolerant, we are -- accepting. It's just that we -- " He stopped, jerked his head suddenly, and then said,"I thought we were the only ones pretending. But I've found out at the new meetings with the Master Teachers that most of us have been denying. It's as if we feel guilty, or afraid, or can't believe what we actually know to be true. But there're people like my boy who sense something, who see us doing things,and we talk of these things with him. So he knows and he knows he can't. When our children began learning the Convictions and the Teaching, I could tell the other children KNEW, that something had waked in them, like the Teachers say. We were certain with them, but with Jackson, -- well, we thought he was just coming to it slower. He studied with the Master Teachers. He learned the words, he could talk about the ideas, but it didn't mean the same. Not at all. It was never real to him."

"It's not uncommon,Dennis. How could you be sure?"

Dennis shook his head, letting his tears fall unrestrained. He sobbed now and then, the release of emotion tore at him, but he knew he must continue. He stopped at the top of the ridge past the civic Center Outer Ring. There below them was his home,the eastern house in the four joined homes of the cluster. He could see the lights already on in the upper rooms. His mate would be waiting, perhaps sensing his pain and worried. Ben did not want to Reach, it was not his right. He knew that Dennis would.

Benjamin asked,"Does Jackson know of Joining. Does he know there is something more than the Reach?"

"Thank God, I think he doesn't. Oh, he knows the idea of it now. It's been taught to him.But the real knowing can't come without experience. He understands that we somehow Touch, mentally, And we thought he was accepting that. Because we thought he'd soon be with us. But now!" He shuddered, "Any more than that is probably inconceivable to him."

"When he goes to the seminars what does he say?"

Dennis nodded,"He won't go any more. Says there's no use. He's a bright boy, Ben, intelligent and he realizes finally what it means.Some days he looks so black that I hesitate to talk to him. Maud does better. We would like him to see a Healer but he won't".

"When he enters medical school he'll have to do a heart study and they'll help hm, whether he intends it or not."

Dennis turned sharply,"I hadn't thought of that. It might really help. That'll relieve Maud's worry, I think." He stood nodding his head, his face relaxing within its sadness as they stood silent for several minutes, the color gleaming through the radiant leaves seemed to cast a benevolence over them and to nourish and heal them. Benjamin leaned against the rough trunk of an old powerful walnut tree. Slim, golden leaves drifted here and there through the air. He caught one, pressed it into his palm,"You know, Dennis, we've got a lot of work to do. The Builders have to learn to accept us and we've got to accept ourselves."

THE JOURNEY

Dennis felt the gentleness of the afternoon, the lovelyness of the moment, through his pain, "Accepting is hard. We've not done too well. How can we expect it. I feel all this fury at the Builders and I can't lay blame at their door. They're there for my boy, that's all. They speak to him in his own language because I don't. But too many of them are angry, Some even hate. I fear that Jackson might learn to hate, Ben!" A sob broke in his throat, but he swallowed it and said,"I suppose it might have been possible for him to accept things, knowing that it's all a matter of time, another life time will make most all humanity aware. But his pain over Merilee, was too much. It threw him off balance."

"But we've got to count on that, that he's learned how to balance his emotions just as all of us have. He did learn that, Dennis and will return to it."

Dennis was quieter, his grief subsiding,"Well, there've been changes in this Valley. Healers used to hide their Talent, pretend it wasn't real, study medicine and hide it within their profession. But now, we search for Healers right in the first few years of a child's life. And we've got some of the best in the world."

Ben nodded,"We've grown up a bit, Dennis. Our children are already ahead of most of us. They've seen that Light, met the wonder of their own inner awakening. They are already Soul conscious, while most of us old folks are learning how to be. They stand without fear or righteousness. I stand in awe of my own children sometimes Dennis. And I grieve at our family members who are mind blind."

His friend nodded,, absently,"The two of ours who do See, yes, I am amazed at them, their patience, their Love for their brother that has made them behave so circumspectly all these years, knowing, when Maud and I didn't" He shook his head, has face calm now, a quiet and peace entering his eyes as they met Ben's at last."They are a different people, Ben. When I was a boy even, there would have been too many of us standing braggart, making fun, lording it over a sibling or friend who was -- was -- retarded. A strange word to use for such an intelligent boy. Nearly genius quality mind, and yet - he's retarded spiritually. I hope there're no longer people who would make fun of someone left less fortunate." He didn't finish,, but Ben nodded.

"We've got a lot to learn, but it's true, Dennis, we're a different kind of people. Not just the young ones. They're more fully developed, in most cases. But we are different too. We have to notice that. You can notice the KIND of awareness they have that makes them unable to hurt anyone who cannot know. A fine brain didn't make that difference, but a great heart, filled with Light, does."

"The Builders are like my Son, like him and hurt with their lack. And you see how I've acted. How angry I am? Why was I so furious at them? I don't act as though I'm any different."

"Ben laughed, touched his friend's arm, drew him on into the path to walk to his home,"Oh! Yes, Dennis. You know and are ashamed of your feelings against them. You know. You are aware of yourself!"

"Maybe! I hope so, Ben. If I can keep my balance. Otherwise we could have a civil war here in this Valley. A civil War. How terrifying to think of that."

"And that's why we won't have one. We may have a lot to learn, we may not have balance over ourselves yet, but we do See, we do KNOW, and we will help each other stand firm with our Love, rather than our fury."

"But they want so much, the Builders. They want to make more money, to plant, raise 'livestock' as they put it. Who in this Valley who's conscious will raise animals only to be killed? There're only a few farms that do that today and those raise only fowl of one kind or another, or rabbits. Ben, we've Touched their minds, Ben, we've felt their Touch, their simple trusting Touch against us. They're thinking beings, that simple thinking that makes them know of the possible pain, the possible hurt we can give. And the possible Love too. How can we eat such sensient beings?" Yet the Builders can't see that because they don't listen to them, don't Touch against their minds. Builders'll make more money, more than most of us even want to make, it's true. But then, why not. if it makes them happy?"

Ben sighed, turning at Dennis's entrance way," Did you know that they refused the findings of the World Market survey? The survey found that there's not enough market for increased production of liquors or poor quality fabrics.. But they deny that and are going to go to the work of doing a survey all over themselves. It'll take months. I think they want power,Dennis. I think they want to run things, and to just keep collecting things, because having things is a sign of power, and wealth. It makes them feel that their lives keep developing. At the same time most of us are shedding things, wanting less, in fact. And it's because they can't SEE what's beyond everything. I can't blame them at all!" His face was full of grief. "After all, we've seen something far more interesting, more exciting even."

" But they aren't willing to allow difference. that's where we'll run into trouble. It is a sorrow, Dennis, a great sorrow in me that they cannot understand and that they persist in demanding." He felt the weighty grief of that, coupled with the grief for people like Dennis, and took it into himself, feeling the shape of it. Knowing it must be met.

Long shadows lay over part of the hill side, but much was already in shade. They moved past a high hedge and two tall slim young golden oaks. A few great fat acorns were left on the ground, all the others had gone to feed the town's bakery stores. Ben turned to Dennis,"I can't come in, Dennis so say hello to Maud. And tell her, we'd like to see her soon. Both of you. It's been too long." He extended all the Love he could, knowing Dennis was wary, vulnerable still, and then, Dennis extended his hand."We'll work on this, Ben, we'll work on it and perhaps it would be good to get together again."

Ben nodded,"You can count on us, Dennis. all of us. Your friends are here. Just don't keep it all to yourself anymore." He smiled, "Your daughter, Glenda and your son, Joseph, are both ready to help, I think."

Dennis smiled a wry smile, his eyes clear and calm now,"They are, Benjamin, have been too, but I wouldn't allow them to Touch me. I think I've been ashamed, and unwilling to admit the facts of this. Thank you, old friend. It's helped." He was thoughtful as he drew away to go in the house, "You know, Jackson's calmest with Glenda. Of all of us, he seems to feel right with her, and yet, I think she's farthest ahead, farthest beyond him of all of us."

"Stands to reason, Dennis. She knows how to accept, be with him without assuming anything. Just love him. He feels that. There'll be young ones like that. Jessie's like that, you know, and she's been trained as a Monitor. And she was born in a time when her Talents seemed as bizarre as anything we've had to deal with." He shook his head, he hadn't realized that before. How difficult it must have been for her.

Dennis sighed, "Yes, that's the other problem we have, you know. Gloria was offered the training. Monitor training. We didn't say anything. It's her choice, I know, but it'd mean she'd be gone so much. So many years it takes, you know."

Ben nodded, "Yes, but then, when they start their world training at foriegn or South Valley Learning Centers, they'll be gone a lot anyway. It's just part of growing up, to lose our children out of our lives. That's why it's good to love the children of our friends. Some of them might stay around." He laughed, knowing it was not actually a joke.

Dennis nodded, they stood a moment and then Dennis said good bye and turned to his door. Ben went on, walking rapidly to the grid. He thought he wanted to take a belt home. To get there, to find comfort there.

Suddenly he wanted more than anything in his life to Reach to them, to find and be with them mentally, to Join. He just couldn't, could he?" He got a belt, strapped it on, his mind pulling beyond him, kept seeking that Touch. He lifted off, then without restraint, Reached with all his strength. Wanting to know that he could, that he might celebrate this wonderful power, rather than hide it.

He arrived on the deck and could see the family inside the dining room,, already bringing dinner to the table. He saw Rose move away from the rest and come hurrying to the door, throwing it open, she ran into his arms.." Ben! Ben! You were loud and clear! We heard you and we were so delighted. But you were so intense Sending you wouldn't give us room to enter. So we waited for you." She stopped, studied his face, "Maybe that was wrong, maybe we should have -- "

He laughed, swung her lightly up, hugged her until she squeeled and then he set her down. "No, No, I was so busy sending I couldn't feel your Touch at all. That is amazing, but I was absolutely doing it. I knew you were all here."

They sat to eat, and he felt the depth of warmth and closeness, the power of this Family around him. He was utterly included. Then he told them briefly of his talk with Dennis, his pain and grief. "You know, we've got to prepare. To decide. We've got problems among our own as well as among the Builders."

Jessie started, "Ben, your words are dangerous!" he looked at her mistified, "As soon as we start polarizing, thinking of someone as 'other' than ourselves, as separate,, then we create danger. It is our knowledge that we are not separate. All of the people are 'our own'."

Seldom did Jessie speak so forcefully, or with such demand. He stared at her, and then understanding spread over his face,"You're right. I wasn't thinking. Or maybe I was, thinking as I used to. Not paying attention to what I KNOW."

Andrew swallowed a mouth full of food, frowning," But we can't ignore what Dad's saying. There's a lot of hostility out there."

Ben met his son's eyes,"I know Son, I know that. That's what I want to talk about. Unless we all understand, and unless we can meet that without reacting, how can we assume any other family can?" He looked at the food on the table, shrugged; he couldn't eat now. "After all Jessie's right. They're Valley people, our brothers and sisters, in fact. They have a right to live as they choose, to plan what's important to them."

Rose listened numbly,"I'm not much help. I still want to make them stop doing the things they're doing. Go back to study economics. The world economy today won't pick up their tab. It won't work, and no one can tell them that. By the time they've had to admit it, thousands of acres of wild land will have been destroyed." She frowned miserably.

Jessie chuckled,"But finding it out that way will be irrefutable. They'll convince themselves! What damage they do can be undone. The pain of it is bearable, as long as we don't imitate their methods."

Jane came into the Hall, her eyes wide with wonder, she looked at all of them silently for a long moment,"I can't believe it. I just can't. I thought to Reach. Just trying myself out,because - because - I wanted to practice a little. And I sensed you all here as clearly as if you'd spoken. I felt you - all." She shook her head. They all laughed, and Andrew stood from his chair to hug her.

"Jane, that's right, it's astonishing,isn't it?" His eyes were shining and she was surprised that her Reaching, her Touch had been so important to him.

Jessie said,"We've got some things to understand. The time of the Journey is near for this Family. There's a lot to do. We have established that we can See and hear, that we are aware of a dimension of Spirit. Humankind has persistently glimpsed that realm, but fought over the interpretation of what we glimpsed, for centuries. We,these generations, KNOW of further dimensions, Life extending everywhere! We as a people know it as a fact. We must acknowledge that." She looked around, The rest of the Farm Family were coming in for the evening , she waited until they were sitting and then asked,"What exactly do we know?"

They stared at her, forgetting to eat. Finally Benjamin cleared his throat, "Jessie, we're becoming what the Teachers called Soul conscious. That means--" he hesitated, feeling strangely lost in this question, "that we - do realize the nature of things, the fundamental Heart of Love present within every living thing, in ourselves. We know of Life Itself, beyond us and of us. We do realize that Life itself is alive. Just as truly as we realize that bread is good to eat. It is as normal as that." He sighed. "Although the implications of that, Life as alive, resound too far for me to follow."

Rose took it up,"Yes, Ben and we stand consciously in that Highest Light. We know, are aware of that power that is the Light within Life. We See through the astral veil and know that in that dimension too there is illusion. But we notice the astral and the causal worlds seeping into this one we've limited ourselves to, and this one seeping through into those. It's a breaking of old barriers." She stopped, looked around, wondering if anyone followed her. She felt lost in her own thought.

Ben watched her,"Go on, Sweetheart."

She looked at him as if unseeing, absorbed, Well, we've begun to distinguish somewhat between illusion and reality. And that shows us that we've not learned to See accurately, that we too can be caught in new varieties of illusion and in our own logic traps. But we know that we have already entered into another dimension of consciousness within which we are learning how to live fully as Soul Conscious Beings in Earth." She breathed a deep sigh, knowing that she had repeated some of the Teachings recently taught in the Learning Center. She knew however, that those Teachings were no longer only ideas, only theory, but reality, to them all.

Jessie smiled at both of them, Jerry took up the litany, for it was becoming such."We can't think as we used to, because our minds reach out, our minds merge outward into that Mind substance that informs us. It's beyond traditional thinking completely. thinking only blocks that informing. We have to be utterly still. Then we ARE perceiving a greater Reality than we've ever thought possible, even in all the Teachings. No one ever thought it to be the way it actually IS." He too stopped, wondering where all this understanding was coming from. But the impulse to speak of it was strong. He went on as if impelled.

Frowning with the effort to speak what he realized, what he hadn't thought out at all, he said, "You see Jessie, we KNOW too much to think as we once did, we have been Touched to deeply by Love Itself, we can't feel toward living things as we once did. We've realized that there is a universe of Spirit, as real as the universe of Mind. We have much to learn, our whole body, mind and heart natures are changed, unfolding, to express that Spirit waking in us." He looked around, aware that his voice had been strong, sure, full of a strength of conviction. Now, he wondered again where that clear understanding came from. He searched himself, and found that he drew from his own Heart, without working it out in thinking, what he so deeply knew. His face reflected the awe he felt in these revelations. The voice of his Heart has risen up and was crying out its JOY.

For long moments they sat, absorbing and understanding. Then Jessie said softly,"So we are no longer as we once were. Then what do we do with those whose minds, bodies, hearts, continue to be as we once were and who have not reached these realizations?"

Anna was nodding, her face too serious, as her mother watched, wondering how such a child could look as she did now. Then, instantly she knew that Anna's childhood had not been as had her own. And the knowledge saddened her. She heard Anna say,"It's not much different from the way we teach the children, is it? Those who are still learning, still ignorant of certain things?"

Jane stood, anger flashing from her large grey eyes, "That's terrible, to call those people who don't realize things 'children'. It smacks of arrogance, of snobbishness and you've got to admit that." She looked around at them, their still faces, then sat down.

The others waited for Anna to respond, and she was shaken a little by Jane's anger. Visibly steadying herself, she met Jane's eyes. She could not restrain that look that had in it a faint pleading which was part of being a child. "I don't want to do that, Jane, I don't want to be arrogant. Truly I don't. I don't think I feel that. I FEEL as though we're together, all of us. I do.!" Then her face smoothed, lost all touch of pleading, was strong in its understanding. Rose felt her heart ache for the young girl who seemed at that moment so wise. Anna had taken a deep breath and tried again. "Maybe we could think of it this way. What I'd like to say to all of us. We're already so different, one from another, each of us. Every one of us is unique, we all would agree on that, No?" She looked at them all, "I can't paint a fine painting, my paintings are those of a child, and so as far as any true painter is concerned, I must be taught as one. But there's Andy, he's my age, and yet no musician would teach him as a child. He realizes too much. A teacher teaches him as an artist. It's all in where we are. We don't think any the less of me, or of Andy."

Jane softened, stared at the young girl, whose dark brown face held such a melting look of love that Jane could not meet it long. She said, "Well, yes, I see. That's a good example, Annie. I don't think, I've ever thought you arrogant, actually." And Jane's face lit with a smile that healed Anna wholly.

Jerry said," Wait, only a percentage are disturbed by our differences. And those by differences that are minor. None of those who do not see have any idea of the real difference. So far the Builders have picked at the things that don't matter."

"Yes, going on with my analogy, what do people complain about in artists, sometimes, their complete lack of interest in what a social adept would see as important, yet put that artist in proper clothes, washed and smelling good, and no one would know she was an artist. And no one would complain."

Yes, and to go on. The other side of it. No matter how carefully the artist tried to explain a great painting to a person devoid of that sensibility, the student would remain only a little less ignorant than before. He would never SEE what the artist sees. Though he could learn the ideas, and what to look for in a painting. It's the same with music, with gardens, with the Tapestries of the Vagabonds. We've never been able to equal them or see what they see. It's the same with all art. " Rose was excited by this metaphor, it helped her own grasp of the problem.

"And so, we're not so strange after all. We simply perceive what some other people don't and we can't tell them what we perceive until they develop an eye, an ear, or a sensitivity that will open their consciousness to what we see." Jessie summed the ideas up. "Now, we have to decide how we will meet those who not only do not perceive that greater Life, but who want to regress backward to old patterns of human living."

Jerry studied her face, knowing that she wanted them now to think this out. "Maybe we'll have to let them regress. Maybe we'll have to let them try. Try out their convictions. People learn best through their own mistakes, don't they?"

Rose said,"At least we ought to try. For those who can imagine that we do See and know that they don't and who accept that. There are some, you know. Who are not even jealous, anymore than I am that Jennifer creates music that I can barely understand, let alone perceive for myself." She stood up with a need to touch her child and went to put her hands on Anna's shoulders," There're some people who do trust the Teaching, yet who've never had a single glimpse of what we now KNOW as real. These might be our greaest help."

Jerry sighed, "We've got to do some good thinking now. And then talk again, I think." Right now, I want to eat." He smiled.

Ben sagged wearily in his chair, tired from the day's events, longing for a time when problems were not so constant, he bent his head and let his mind empty, quieting him, relaxing his body. Instantly he felt the others there, supporting him. Felt his body relax, his heart lifted. They could eat dinner, talk and laugh again as though the world was not changed irrevocably.

It was two days later that Jessie left the Farm for another of her journeys into the Valley. But this time she told no one where she was going nor how to reach her. She took a belt into Adwin, stood very early in the morning on the air car grid and selected a small car that had not been scheduled for use this morning. The sleek little body seemed just right, not much bigger than herself. She started the motor, heard it purr softly, and with a deft hand, she moved it off the grid and into the air. The sky was cloudy but the sun lit the rooftops of the town below. She swung north, passing over the Farm, seeing people walking along the trails, in the heavy shade of the thick clouds. The last two days had been stormy, and it would take time for these clouds to clear away. She deliberately circled the Farm, Sending a message for whoever was attentive. Then she swung east.

The sun broke through clouds there, gleamed on the City in the cliffs. Had she not known, she might have thought there was nothing there except beautifully chiseled stone cliffs. Her thoughts tumbled in her mind, chaotic, jumbled. She paid no attention to them and they slowly subsided. Her mind lifted, held itself free. She had done enough thinking, the Silent City would give her direction. It was time she clarified her task here, knew the exact dimensions of her work ahead this fall. There were still so many Families who had not yet become conscious of that inner pathway that they must follow toward their own realization as a group. There were some who had done so. She rejoiced to remember those few. But the rest, these she thought she might not serve well. Something seemed to cloud her best efforts lately. As though her very power was snagged on something within herself. Something she did not see.

She had thought of returning to the Retreat. But she knew that they were very busy now, especially with new students coming from out Valley as well as from within. Those who had made the Journey,,whose minds were opened, whose realization clear, were going to the retreats, to meditate, to talk to the Monitors, to give themselves a new balance. It would be so for all the ones making that Journey. They would need new balance.

No, if she went alone like this, entered without any purpose except to be informed, then there would be help. She could see ahead, the City was visible from here, like a rainbow playing over the mountains. From out of the City those colors came in spirals, arching over to rain down into the Valley below. She watched, startled, her sight opened, the energy fountain ,that she already knew poured down into the Valley ,was, for her, finally visible. She laughed, happy, suddenly as at a gift.

Then she turned to look far down the Valley, hundreds of miles into the clear air,she could see beyond Santiago and after a moment of adjusting her sight, she could see Clandor. She could not see the physical form or either City,but she saw the energy pattern that each was, and she saw the City's Light raining into each. Then she saw the deep darkness of that Pit in the Black Mountain, that place of unlight, that place where energy pierced downward from that festering sore of evil. How could Earth abide such within Itself. And she knew that Earth was all of these. That all of Earth was dual and inclusive of good and evil. And so, there was the Black Lodge. For humankind was an expression of Earth, and something in humankind fostered that hungry seeking for itself.

These energies seeded themselves in the hungers and fear of humankind. Without that hunger, that fear, they would have been melted away in the pure Light of the City's out flow of Love, of that Will to Good that she was. But the City lived from the powerful consciousness of those members of humankind who had gone before out of this physical world, into that universe of greater dimensions. They who persisted in nourishing that deep will to Good that lived in every human heart. The City was a pathway to Life. She had stood here too long, stood in steady balance,, never letting that unlight possess the life that was under Her care. Something there knew Light must slowly absorb the darkness, fill it, make it one with Itself.

Jessie felt a moment of doubt, a shaft of fear rose in her heart and instantly she knew the power of those arching needles of unlight. With a gasp of recognition she wrenched herself back, back to focus all her attention on that City. She was a target today. She was a target for those who denied the Light because she served the Light. She knew the necessity of focussing on that City now, for she knew the power of that Pit and accepted her own strength for what it was. She needed help. Doubt stirred again. Could the City hold? Was the great Heart of Humanity strong enough now to withstand the seed of greed and lust that sucked at its new found life? Could the people of the Valley maintain their new found Vision? Could they stand in Love recognizing Life? She resolutely refocussed, let the doubt fade like dew in the sunlight.

She felt anger with herself for that moment of doubt, for having given way to that Source of dispair. She knew that dispair was the gateway into that dark realm. Her mind wavered, she felt her eyes avert and then with a clear controlled act of Will, she snuffed out the degrading thoughts and was still.

THE JOURNEY

She thought,"There is in me that which can draw attention from that darkness. There is fear, doubt, dispair, hungers, old desires, still clinging against my memories. These not yet dissolved act as points to which that unlight can catch and cling. Otherwise I would be untouchable. And so I will hold fast to that Light , I will stand firmly at this point of Light within, this Soul consciousness springing from that Light, born out of and receptive of Love. She whispered,"Let Love and good Will fill my mind, my heart. My Being. Let no remnants of old dispair and unsatisfied needs give permission to those shafts that dispell and suck away the Light. I See the Light! I See the greatest Light!"

She was silent,then, feeling all tension eroded, fading as though it drained out and fell from her. She began softly to sing.

> I see the Light
> I am the Light
> I live in Light.
>   Love is Its nature
>   Life is Its Gift
>   I will to stand in that Light.

Then she repeated the words of an ancient chant.

> I am Soul, Love also am I,
> I will to lift this little self
>   Into that Light Divine.
>   That which desires to lift,
>   And that which calls out for lifting,
>   Are One.

Over and over she sang, her voice true and sweet. She progressed on that journey, her back to that darkness that sought to claim her. Her attention focussed at the highest point of her inner consciousness so that what was lowest in her be given no attention. She knew she herself was the center from which her fears might rise. That dark power would seek a seed of response in her and finding that single infinitisimal point of old desires, spread itself through all the suffering of her life. But she was calm, holding attention steady in that Light she knew, saw, trusted.

Thought formed in a small part of her mind, and she realized,that if she could be so nearly trapped by that dark power, then those with less skill, less knowledge of the forces pulsing from that terrible Pit, might be overwhelmed. They must know. They must learn their own strength of Love. If she could not stand wholly aware, then how could she help?

Clearly another thought formed itself there, like a writing on her mind. It is equally true that there is the seed of Good within me, that spark of a divine Love that has through lifetimes, sprouted into true Goodness. So she had the choice.

She could pay attention to that choice, she had been taught and she taught others to know how to distinguish between the Dark within herself and the Light. She knew that Dark was master of pretense and could make a longing, a desire appear to be good, right, when it was only another step in that downward journey. Let her thinking mind be caught in efforts to explain, to judge, fallen from that absolute trust of Light and she could be captured by her own shriveling darkness. As she entered into Light, she must take her darkness with her.

Jessie had drawn herself up out of that darkness more than once, had fought against the urge to give herself over, sink into satisfactions of the self, and she knew much of its method, its means of enticement. But she was wise enough to know that she didn't know enough. She must keep her eyes fixed steadily on that Light, that point where Love lived throughout the universe.

With practice, holding attention at that point of Light, that dark seed within herself would wither from lack of attention and die away. The Builders might be prey to that power of the Dark Pit, perhaps, their little lusts and needs lay them open to its energy. But she knew too that their very lack of consciousness, their very limited awareness, gave them a kind of immunity. For as they could not hold much Light within themselves, neither could they absorb much of evil. Petty selfishness was about the limit of their evil. And that could do great damage, but not the massive harm those who had once dwelt in knowledge were capable of. Realizing, she held firm to her direction.

She refocused her attention, feeling the stream of Light flow through her body-Heart-Mind, felt it link together her whole nature. Already she knew she had passed the danger point. She could respond to thought rising from knowledge. The focussed will of years spent practicing and honing her own Will to Good paid off. She said,"That darkness comes from the terrible fears of humanity. Perhaps we ourselves create the evil that hounds us through our very fear, our terrible need for survival, which is natural,and a necessity."

" For Evil cannot be outside the ultimate Good. We have created those fears of death, hunger, fears for survival itself, which gave birth to those needs for recognition, power, adolation,and unlimited control over those who could either give or remove those needs. We want with an absoluteness that is unlimited and to fulfil that terrrible wanting in ourselves, we create all the evils of humankind's history. But that same powerful wanting, leads us toward the Light Itself. Love lives through us too, impells our creativeness, impells our absolute love of life, impells our power to progenerate, all that grows, all that gives birth in pain and joy, and yet these two, Evil and Love, live, undiminished in us, until we begin to reach that point when we can KNOW and so Choose. And I think that evil is the absence of Love." Thus she explained herself to herself.

The task seemed to her at that moment painful beyond endurance, for what was not revealed must be yet unbearable to look on. She had sought so long to know the 'GOOD',so long to stand in that Light. Was it not enough?

Before her, her sight magnified by Astral as well as physical vision, was the City. Seen with this greater perception,it was a great lake of Light. Energy flowed

THE JOURNEY

as from a fountain, pure and shining white, threaded through with Gold. The Light pulsed revealing an aura of Love that reverberated through her, touching and finding response from that flame that burned now brighter within herself. She was astonished at the pain of it, the stretching, wakening of herself. At the same time, she knew an absolute almost unbearable Joy. Such Joy, she realized now, she had only previously tasted. This - this spun through her, rose through everything that existed, through the Earth Itself and she knew suddenly that her small body, its firm hand on the steering mechanism, was long since forgotten. She stood, out beyond herself, living in other subtle bodies more capable of the Vision that she sought.

She drew near the City, was aware of the creatures living along its walls, the coming and going of life protected by its benevolence, but never interfering with its natural course. Forests grew in bursting health, smaller plants bloomed and fruited in abundance. Small streams fell through the land, gathered in clear, shining pools and reflected the sky, the passing of birds, and the trees. It was a narrow, highland of beauty and health.

But then, the Valley itself lived in the Light of this City. the Valley was blessed too by this steady flow of Love and Light. How had it come about? Had the intense and focussed ideals of the Valley Founders brought this power to them? Or was it that the City herself stirred these ideals, stimulated life within the Founders minds? Jessie knew with surprised certainty that the first answer was true, but the second followed it. The Founders, focussed in that commitment to Love Itself, had sought the Way and had drawn to themselves this Gift. The power of the City could not give unless asked. Just as they, those same Founders, had eventually created the Stations and entered into them as the first of the world's Monitors. Thus had the Valley been given its birthright.

As her little ship neared the shining walls, she felt the tug of another question at the back of her mind. She wanted to focus on the scene ahead. She could glimpse the color beyond the walls, the shape of buildings, sculptural forms. But the question could not be ignored. She formed it aloud,"What of those who are not conscious and cannot see the possibility of humankind?" She let it sit there, in mind, The grief of it pouring around her, but this grief was not of darkness but of the Light. It was born of the compassion that the Light ignited. It was born of understanding. She bent her head, murmuring an old prayer a favorite during her long years.

> Let us See the Way.
>   Let us travel the Right Path.
> Let us not be blinded
>   By the astonishment of our own Vision.
> Let us distinguish between
>   Desires of the person and desires of Soul.
> Let us recognize always Love.

THE PEOPLE OF THE VALLEY

The prayer comforted her and steadied her mind again. She could set aside the vague backward pulls of body and emotions toward that world of fear. As she stood free again, realizing that she could avoid recognition of both dark and brilliant depths in this immersion in immediate scenes and thoughts, she sighed. "I will not avoid, I know that this Journey is bringing me to them precisely. I must know myself fully." The little car crested the walls, crossed the smooth surfaces of their tops, and she floated in, over the lovely gardens.

She was so close. The fact registered and she remembered the belief among Valley people that none could enter, descend so close. Her little ship brushed the upper leaves of stately blazing trees. Fragrance wafted all around, she moved so slowly the ship seemed to stand still. Trees here seemed so very 'old'. With the girth of giants they towered nearly to the heights of the snowy walls. Now, she saw that the walls were laced throughout with color, minerals veining them with rose and here and there a thick blue band jutted out like a design cut into the smooth stone. The effect was lovely.

Vines climbed inside the walls, here and there where they could gain foothold in cracks or around sharp outcrops.   They cascaded color downward. Below, smooth fields of grass, and wild flowers, wound among blossoming shrubs. The whole scene was of a garden of indescribable beauty, but utterly natural. An air of life and vitality seemed to make every leaf stand forth fresh and clear. Were there no voracious insects here? No disease, no harm? Or was there simply a profound condition of Balance?

Jessie piloted the car lower, threading her way through the trees into the meadows and then, passing a clump of fruiting trees, she saw buildings. The first was low, wide, curving grey stone, set in with gleaming windows. The walkway around the building edged the shores of a clear blue lake, from which a stream ran lazily through the garden. At the front and to a side of the building, a long broad plaza, extended and then dropped with wide low steps down to the waters edge. She could set the little car here, perhaps. But she hesitated. Could she profane this beauty so?

Then she heard music. It rose as steadily as the fragrance, but was soft, so that until she opened the car's windows, she did not hear it above the light hum of the motors. It seemed a welcoming sound, full of harmonies, then subtle discords, threaded into a strange and fascinating pattern that drew irresistably. She knew she must land near by.

The music rose, melodies within melodies mingled and designed into an order that pleased her. The soft sound of the motors melted into that larger sound and the beat of Jessie's heart seemed part of the song. She felt herself joined into this Life that pulsed through out the air. She was full of a Joy that was penetrated with some subtle fear.

Held there in that fear, like a conviction, was herself. She could not leave this place with secrets. Here she would be utterly, finally exposed - to herself! That revelation frightened her. Here there was no place to hide. No subtle comfort of self delusion. She sighed, what could be left in herself that she had not already

THE JOURNEY

seen, recognized? In this magnificence she would lose herself. She felt so drawn into that sense of absolute Love breathed by this garden and knew that she longed to give herself into it, to be wholly a part of it, and yet, she resisted as if threatened by fire itself. Wise from years of self knowledge, she saw that was the signature of unfinished business.

The ship lurched upward,she had lifted it up out of the influence of these pulsing energies. Had done that as an animal leaps from danger without thinking. She breathed deeply, knowing with a powerful certainty that she must listen. That she chose to stand firm in this power. The music again surrounded her, comforted her and the fire within burned in a clean steady flame, tears poured from her eyes. She held fast to the bars of the ship. There was no where else to go. She must decide.

With a gathering of will, bringing together all the power of her nature, a focussing, she drew herself together. She would choose.

" How can that be," she asked herself," that Love can be so inseparable , so present in everything?" She felt the bonds of herself loosen, resistance fade,and she herself expanded beyond what she knew herself to be, for Love entered, saturating mind and body with its Life. She heard herself say,"Why that's it - Life IS Love." The choice was innate in her nature.

Thought wove itself from music, thought her mind could understand, as if something in it had been wakened, made newly conscious. The sound gradually shaped itself into words, and she heard a question."What is your choice, Jessie of the Valley?"

Her heart leaped in her chest, her mind utterly still, opened itself the way a flower does, unfolding. She was conscious of herself within that greater Self. There was no separation. With a wrench to respond, focussing her will to whole response, she said,"I choose the light! I chose to serve all Life. To give myself up to that service."

It was that - the simple speaking of choice, that ended the pain, the tearing within her. She knew a filtering of darkness falling away from her, descending like a dust. She knew the tightening, the strengthening and a great joyous lightness that dissolved doubt. With sure knowledge, she set the little ship down on the smooth radiant pavement confident that she belonged here. As she sat, unmoving for long minutes, she said solemnly,"I choose to discover what shadows still haunt me. What I am."

There was a rustling sound within the music grown so soft it was an echo beneath everything. Then, from the high towers, slim and tall, there came a shower of bells ringing, tiny sweet bells first, then clear firm tones of larger ones and after that the great deep toned bells joined in. The sound became for her like a gentle laughter all around. A joyous delight. Jessie listened and thought she had never heard anything so pregnant with Life. It was as though Life Itself lived and was daily being born through these sounds, these fragrances. But then why not? Life Itself is alive! The realization made her breath catch.

She stepped out of the ship, the sounds grew soft, and she looked around this new world. The land stretched away on all sides, more vast than she could have imagined. Fields and groves, the sparkling lake, the little stream, and set into all, were the buildings, the temple spires, reaching like echoes of one another high above the trees.

Birds flickered in the trees, small animals ran here and there. She saw that they must know how to enter and leave this place at their desire, for there were deer, foxes, wolves, great cats, rodents, and then she knew, without seeing them, that dogs, cats, horses, all the creatures of the Valley passed through this place if they chose. It was as if she saw days and days of living passing before her, watching them happen to her here.

She walked down the steps to the little lake, the water, blue- green, light waves splashing against huge boulders that lay along the banks, or sat half exposed in the clear water. She looked into the water, It was shining, as though a powdering of diamonds saturated it. She breathed a deep long breathe, and the air too was bright with shining, so that it filled her, tingled through her body like a fire at first. And as she stood there, she knew the presence of Love as she had not, could not, have imagined it. She realized that Love was the fundamental substance of everything that was.

She walked a while through the land, marveling at the beauty of it, the intensity of its life. And finally coming back to the plaza, she saw again the little air car, sitting like some strange creature there, so alien to this land. Then, with a swift recognition,,she looked into it, saw the smooth working parts of it, fitted together, a work of art, indeed. It was then a gift of humankind, a creation of humankind. And a pride grew in her, accepting.

She knew that there were people here, somewhere, invisible for some reason, or inside the great lovely buildings. She dared not enter any to find out. Turning to the little lake, she suddenly felt a great urge to enter it, to feel that wonderful water on her body. She let her clothes fall to the ground and stood naked, unashamed, that this little dumpy, old woman's body was there exposed. It was her own and it was good. She stepped out into the water, feeling the grainy sand under her feet, the cold, the electrical tingling of water on her skin. She went on until she lifted off the bottom and began to swim. She thought she would swim to the other side. A great surge of energy filled her, she reached out and swam eagerly. Gradually she tired, but she willed herself to continue. A cloud of small birds came down and dipped as they drank then were up and away. Fish swam in this deep water, small ones bit at her, searching out this strange intruder. She twisted away, and saw the shore near, found her feet on sand and stood to look around, breathing deeply.

She drew her hand through the water,,making it curl up and break over in the sun. She had never seen water so crystaline, so pure, so filled with Light. Far in the depths she could see small plants moving, the memory of herself at twenty five when she swam in community contests, came like a longing. She looked down at herself. This body surely was not the young lithe body that she remembered. It would be a joy to be so again. Her body sagged, was thickened,

THE JOURNEY

and her face had a netting of lines, wrinkles, the marks of a long life.

She thought,"I am no longer beautiful, nor even pretty. I am old, and shriveled, and soon to die. The thought hurt, and she was surprised, for she had thought herself untroubled by personal appearance. She remembered the pleasure of seeing others admire her, seeing men she liked look at her with interest, even desire. She remembered the feelings of running, dancing, leaping in the sheer joy of youth. She looked down at herself, surprised at how strong the desire was to be so again. Perhaps the water would give her youth.

She was an old woman. Ugly? She had never thought of that, never thought the lines of age were not themselves beautiful, but as she looked, she knew that something in her did see age as ugly. Some part of herself she had not acknowledged.

A ray of brilliant light from one of the needle slim powers fell on her, burned faintly against her skin. She looked down at her body in the water. Astonished that it was suddenly youthful, slim, smooth skinned and lovely. Yes, she had been a lovely woman She knew a strange feeling of unfairness, as though something had been stolen from her. At the same time, she was aware of a deep, almost hidden sense of amusement that this would matter at all.

But the water rippled around her. She felt delight at this gift of youth. She turned and leaped from the water, watching her lovely breasts push through, sending a rainbow of shining colors out before them. She splashed through the crystal water, the Light followed her like a bright pencil in the air. She stood again, moving her hands caressingly through the water, looking at the smooth lovely skin of them, the loss of those aged brown hands. Then ruefully she laughed.

Stepping closer to shore, she stood looking down at herself, smiling on the beauty of herself. She laughed again,"No! No I don't need this again. It's part of youth not of age. I have not use for such an appearance. My old body will do." With that and a rising sense of amusement, she looked up through the pencil of Light, saw the window from which it came and through that window the movement of 'others' through the room. She sighed,"Oh, dear, so many here and I am naked." She began to walk from the lake up onto the shore.

She sat on the thick grass, not worried about her nakedness, eating a yellow fruit. She thought,"What have I done? Perhaps that is the gift here, the gift of youth." Then she reflected on that."No, No, it is not a right gift. I've lived my life learning, struggling. For those years to be visible in my body, is right. I am all that I've become. She hardly noticed that her body was again old and dumpy.

She sat quietly reflecting," In those days I had a great desire to be holy." She smiled sadly at that youthfuyl self."Do I still want that?

"Well, it's at least a more appropriate desire for an old woman." She was smiling again as at a joke. But she stopped, serious."No, there again, I have sought something, always. And was it holyness? What is holy? I do not know. How would I know if I were such?" She bowed her head, looked across the lake at the little air car shining in the sunlight. There was someone there looking at it. Someone tall and radiant, wearing long snowy robes. She racked her mind to find

THE PEOPLE OF THE VALLEY

how they were familiar. Then she remembered, "Of Course, that is the way we robe the students when they come to be trained at the Stations. Their robes are not long, though they are snowy white." But that one --!" Now she gasped, as the being moved around looking the machine over. "Surely that must be one who is holy."

The figure turned, looked across the water at Jessie, standing there. She reached out her hands, wanting to be recognized, wanting to be called by name into that company. The 'holy one' walked toward the water, touched the pile of her clothes, there was a flash of green light and then it turned away. Something in herself trembled with eagerness, something wanting to be as that one was, Holy and pure.

And yet, another part of herself held firm, bringing to her eyes the humor and the questions that marked her life. With a patient tenderness for herself, she bent and squatted on one knee. A most unlovely position for a naked old woman. Watching the figure, she saw it waver, a trembling of her vision. She sighed. Grief welled up, spilled out her eyes, she was weeping for an old longing, that she knew now was empty. "That wasn't real. It was my old longing, to be an angel, one of those pure beyond others." She thought sadly, and then with amusement, that she could be only what she was; an old woman.

A small creature crawled across the sand to wriggle into the grass at her feet. She slid down to touch it. Watching it sadly, weeping in a final helpless loss she released a sorrow she had not known she had. The little salamander lifted its head and turned penetrating eyes on her. She felt suddenly embarrassed by its scrutiny. Was there intelligence in that tiny head? The thought did not seem foolish, but began to please her, amuse her.

Jessie watched the lithe smooth body turn, felt the beauty of it. Recognized suddenly the perfection of its form. Without thinking she heard herself say, "You are a holy one then?"

With a swift glance, it turned away, slid back into the water and she watched its swimming for a long time. She said finally, "There it is! The Salamander is part of the nature of things. Part even of what I am."

She stretched, felt the warmth, peace and quiet of this place. She picked up another fruit, an orange one, and ate it. It tasted delicious, it fulfilled her, satisfied. Perhaps this garden heightened one's senses too. She ought to return, to get her clothes and go home. But a reluctance held her, it was so wonderful here. She would stay. She curled up in the grass and fell asleep.

When she woke the sun was low. A great heat seemed to have risen all about her,. She thought to get a drink. Water. She needed water. But the lake was not there. There were no trees above her head, no fruit, no deep grasses, no lustrous fields of rich growth. Only a dry sand. and a place of desert stillness. Heat radiated from the white towers and the endless walls of the city, flowing down upon her, it burned against her bare skin. She needed shelter and there was none except for some great boulders leaning against one another to the left. She crawled into their shade and studied her situation. How could this have happened. She had been in a paradise of beauty, and now, she was in a hell of dispair. Had she imagined the garden? Or was she imagining this? Surely it seemed real enough.

Fear like a dark wave inundated her. She felt it draw her down. then, with all the strength she could muster, she stood free."No! Fear is its own weapon. I will not accept the direction of fear. After all, I have lived a good life. Even if I die here, imagined or not, real or not it will be no great loss. I do not need to live longer. Except -- except that I imagine that my work is not yet done." That thought troubled her. But if it is not, then I will not die. No matter what the conditions." She felt reassured. She sat contemplating her dying time. She had no fear of it. In fact she looked forward to that time of leaving this state of being, of entering into that further one, where she would not be burdened with this heavy, limiting body. Dying was not important even now.

Jessie looked around. This could not be! And then she shrugged. It was! She frowned, said softly,"What have I done with my own powers? How have I let myself be seduced into those sweet pleasures? Or have I?" Doubt of herself grew. She shrugged again,"Right now I need water." She crawled farther into the rocks, finding a slightly cooler spot. Then, focussing, she searched Earth. Feeling, sending her senses deeper beneath the sand, she found an up-welling of water. It was near that low depression where the heat shimmered and seemed to twist objects around it. Vaguely she could see the air car, it looked burnt, it would be an oven inside it. But she must get to it, open the doors, there would be shelter, shade, and perhaps water. She began to move, taking a deep breath, she slid from the shade, out into the hot beating sun. The sand burned against her feet, she could feel them blistering. But she went on, descending into the empty lake bed, she began to cross. The heat sucked at her, seemed to draw her downward, weigh against the heavyness of her head. She felt herself sinking into the sand, pulling herself through it was slow painful work. The drag against her body made the walking a terrible work.

She knew that whatever water there was in her body was evaporating from her too rapidly. Her tongue felt huge in her mouth, she caught herself, fighting against the compulsion to turn back to the tiny shade of the boulders. The desire and the refusal stopped her suddenly in mid stride. With an act of will that took more of her waning energy, she won the fight. She would go on. Walking now was little more than dragging one foot through its slow movement so that her weight could settle on it and the other foot begin its own slow pull forward. She did not think. She moved with steady determination, willed herself forward, not even trying to see ahead, her head was bent, hopelessly trying to avoid the burning sun. Her feet tore on sharp rocks of this lake bed.

She felt suddenly a great tenderness for this old body. It would persist. However, if she did not have it she would not need water. The thought amused her. She felt a little lighter, One must do what must be done. The old axiom was one familiar to her life.

Then she could feel the lake bed sloping upward and saw she was nearing what had been the shore near her car. The shining stone of the steps lay ahead, their whiteness hurt her eyes. She could get her clothes on. They would protect her a little. Near the clothes was the spot where she had been aware of water. She must dig a little, to be sure, but it was there. Her confidence reasserted itself. Her attention focussed now on that water, she could see it, cool, clear, a life giving pool. As she drew closer,she felt her body gain the energy of hope.

Then with exasperation, amazement and chagrin, she stood still. Where had her mind been? She focussed energy again, drew it into a small kernel inside her, attended. Smoothly, easily, lifting herself, her mind steady,,using its own energy,,she floated slightly from the sucking sand, moved across it and carried her body up to the first step on which her clothes lay, She put them on, then walked the few steps up to the plaza where the little car waited. Her feet left bloody footprints on the white stone. She fell exhausted beside the car. She thought she could not open the doors, could not move. She wanted to drift into sleep. But now was that amused self watching, watching and undisturbed. As though this were not a life and death matter at all. She was angry. Then willing herself again, focussing her attention, she sat up. "To forget yourself, is inexcusable. USE YOUR POWER!." She spoke aloud, a dry whisper. She looked around, what could she gather water in if she found it? A small jar without a lid, lay where she had dropped it with her clothes. She had brought tea in it.Now it was empty. she picked it up.

Gathering herslf again, ignoring the pain and exhaustion, she moved to the point where the sand lay smooth and dry beside the plaza, there where she had sensed water. She gathered her resources, focussed again, and began to press against the loose sand. The swirling energy bored into the sand creating a deepening spiral, made a hole that grew deeper and deeper. Then with a gust she blew the sand around the edges away. There was left a deep depression. There in its bottom lay a clear little pool of water. She bent, buried her face into it, drank, filled the little jar. Then she washed her face, neck and arms and hands. It felt good. It restored her. She bent to look at her feet and then lifted handsful of water and poured it over them. Then slid them into the pool, as they sank into the sand she enjoyed the pleasure of relief. She drew them back out and wrapped them with torn strips of her scarf. The heat beat at her, she drank again,refilled the glass jar and crawled back to the shade of the car. Lying still, letting the pain of her feet dull to a throb, she rested.

What should she do. What were the rules of this condition? What would return her to that lovely garden, for surely it had been real -- as real as this at least. She could open the car, find food, even leave this place. But she knew that she would not. There was something here she must learn. She turned, focussed again, pressed with mind and hand against the panel of the car door. She felt the panel slide and then the door opened . It had been cool inside, but the heat filled it instantly. She waited. The air car would fly, surely.

She sat very still, listening, letting the heat throb through her. It seemed finally to be unimportant. The drying of her body seemed to her to be a slow silencing of inner demands. She felt sympathy for this body that suffered, drew it back as far into the shade as she could. Dipped her fingers into the water of her jar, then drank a little. She slid down, half reclining against the wheel of the car.

There was a movement along the edge of the plaza, Then, from the shade of the low wall along the plaza, appeared small people, twelve or fifteen inches tall. She thought,"I must be hallucinating. They can't be real. But my mind seems clear. This is not a place where ordinary rules apply. They must be as real as anything is." Then, as they moved toward her, she said,"Perhaps if I call to them, they will prove their realness, or not." She called out, and they stopped, staring at her. Then, after glancing around at one another, they began to move toward her again.

Among them slid several lizards, two snakes, as if familiars of the little humans. They came as a group, giving each other courage. Curious, peering at her, they came to a stop several feet from her. She felt a surge of fear and recognized it, but put it aside. She didn't need fear here. she said,"Who are you?"

At the sound of her voice, they startled and stepped back, then one, broader of body, with dark thick hair over head, arms and legs, stepped forward and said, "We are the People. You are the stranger!" His eyes glittered, He drew back his shoulders, then with greater confidence, a malicious grin spread over his face. He had decided she was not to be feared. With a wave of his hand, he set the whole tribe dancing, circling her, darting in now and then to pinch or take quick bites at exposed toes or fingers. She felt revulsion sweep over her, their dance was growing more lascivious. They exposed parts of their bodies, thrust themselves forward, bent to project bare bottoms at her, whirled and caught one another in obscene movements, and laughed raucously at her look of bewilderment and revulsion. Was she creating this event? No! It was too real. The thought of their fierce little teeth fastening into her body made her cringe. She drew back, glad she had her clothes on. She heard herself shriek,"Get away, you ugly little demons."

The fury, revulsion,,fear rose in her, spiraled, snagged at her control. She shuddered, fighting with herself. Taking a deep steady breath, she righted her attention, focussed her energy, caught her balance. The calm compassion her life had taught her, rose to the surface and saw the revulsion as false. " How can I find revolting what is alive?"

Then she caught herself. "What revolts me? Their difference? Their littleness? Because they seem to combine human and beast? Beauty is not form itself but the inherent life of form. How can I recognize the presence of beauty or uglyness until I know the whole? I've judged again from assumptions. Am I never to learn? My idea of beauty is an assumption. I must wait and allow beauty to become visible to my attention."

The thoughts quieted her. The self-counseling brought a new confidence. Her balance restored, mind cleared, she turned her attention back to these awkward, posturing creatures. She saw the heat rising from the hot sand, thought of their hard life. She saw the barren country side, their staring eyes, as they leaped and danced around her, already keeping further away, not nipping at her, as though her own calm had effected them. She thought of their fear, their need for water, survival and she lay, Reaching, absorbing fear, lifting up that sense of desperation that they carried.

But her shout had startled them enough that they watched her now with cunning care. This interval of her inner attention had not essentially changed them. They saw she did not move to threaten and their faces became gleeful, fierce. The snakes lifted their heads high,,swinging back and forth to a rhythm she heard only faintly. Old childhood fears surged, froze her thought, her awareness and threatened to blank it out. Poor people living in a tent city,breeders of snakes with whom they told fortunes -- and frightened children. Memories crowded. But she watched her own process push at her calm.

There was a drum beat,coming literally from Earth itself, and that beat met their rhythm in a syncopation . The dance was driving them to greater hilarity, greater obscenity, stronger dashes to nip and pinch. She drew her body close into itself, protecting fingers and toes. Finally, she moved, with a swift roll of her body, she stood out from the car's shade and into the blazing sun. If they were to reach her, they must do it out here.

"Stop!" Her voice was a rasp in her dry throat. She stooped and caught the jar from under the edge of the car and drank. Then with sudden suspicion and a needling worry at their immaciated bodies, she dripped a few of the drops into the upraised faces of the watching dancers. The effect was startling. The one on whom the water fell stood holding his face still, as if afraid to move. His neighbor caught his face in her hands and licked the drops swiftly, before another could. The others finally realized what had happened and leaped to grab the two. A scrambling fight ensued. but was over as soon as they realized there was no more water. They turned back to Jessie, fear and hope on their tiny, deformed faces.

She smiled. "Surely you aren't without water?" She turned and walked to the depression where the pool stood again clear and pure. They crowded around it, uttering cries of wonder and awe. They looked at her, then at the water. They were not drinking, they seemed instead to touch it, gently as if it were holy. As if it were something wholly new.Then, with a movement like a releasing of a spring, they were crowding, shoving and pushing their way into the water, drinking, dipping their hands in to bring up handfulls to drink and lick from their hands. They seemed afraid there would not be enough, but when they had all drank, and there was still as much water there, they stood around the pool, gazing in awe at its shining surface.

The leader, his hair slicked back and wet from the struggle, came and bent down before her. She slid down to sit before them watching and at ease. She felt once again, calm. She marveled at her self, at her own quiet. The little man was trembling, he said,"Forgive us. We didn't know. We didn't know!"

She wondered what they didn't know but nodded. "For whatever forgiveness is needed, I forgive. And I ask that you forgive me. Now, tell me who you are."

THE JOURNEY

Again, he shook his head, puzzled,"We are the People. There is nothing else. Who are you?" The question was asked now softly, with a gentle fear.

Jessie looked at them, their shiny small eyes, their drawn tight faces, more nearly the faces of toads than of human beings; she felt a pity, and then curiousity that dismissed the pity. She told them of the Valley from whence she had come, the land of Rivers and lakes,,of many people like herself, of forests, and fields. She felt great nostalgia in telling of the land,remembering the beauty of it. A sadness grew in her. Would she return to it? Would it be the same? Had she only imagined it as she had the garden that was gone now?

Then she looked all around. Of course! She had forgotten. Where was that Garden? Where had these people come from, how could they be locked away in this desert land, denied all that either the garden or the Valley offered to life? She looked at the little wizened faces around her, she felt a stirring of -- what grew beyond pity. a budding compassion. There in that burning heat of the relentless sun, she felt a change in herself. A return to her own power. A waking of something deeper than she had known. " Here is myself I look at. By which I am revolted."

She stood, lightly, with movements of a young girl, and her old body began to dance. She thought surely that she must dance for these people, that in the dance, her body would speak, to them, to herself. She focused her energy, willed movement,yielded to the heat, danced.

The little people watched her intently. Jessie felt the dance take her body into itself, lift, whirl her and she laughed with delight. With realization. Sweat streamed down beneath her clothes, dripped from her face. The watching demon faces saw that water dripping with renewed awe. As Jessie danced she felt her own strength growing, returning. She heard the beat from the Earth, the steady power of it, renewing her own power.

She discarded embarrassment, lost herself in the movement and the sound. Her body was the same, old and heavy with its thickened flesh and yet she felt it lift, move with grace,delight, and a forgetting of its fragility. Here in this dance was possibility and here was Joy. It seemed to her that the land itself watched. The Earth lifted through her body, dancing to itself. Those who watched, silent and entranced, had lost hope, denied hope. The inherent impatience she had lived with, had striven to erase, wrestled eternally with hope. And she saw that hope was persistently unbalanced by dispair.Now, wanting to See, she danced that hope, The sun wrapped around her body, drying the sweat that cooled her.

And what of dispair. Surely this whole destroyed garden was dispair. She then, had nourished this? Had denied Life? Out of her impatience she thought she must make the world aright. Must turn it to renewal? Must save what helpless lives burned here alone? A refusal to trust in Life! Her dance spun through her, took her into itself and danced her life out of Earth.

In that moment the burning of the malevolent sun lessened. Earth Reached through her, through her dance, called out to the sky, extending the call through all of Earth and the sky focussed the call toward that sun from which the Light and the hope might come. Burning now, wrapped in a drying that invited death, she called for compassion and Life. She was willingly a sacrifice. For she could not imagine living beyond the heat radiating in her body, as if she absorbed the heat into herself to cool the land. And the hunger for mastery crumbled, broke like tears from her body. There was time for all that must be.

The little people went to the pool, filled their hands with water, brought it to fling over her body. They leaped to pour it over her head. Their actions were full of a necessity to save her. Their attitude had turned around. They knew her offer, knew her death must not go unnoticed. Some became frantic in their effort to save her, others watched, with a dawning sadness. The snakes twined themselves, swayed with her rhythm. They lifted themselves literally on their tails and leaned into the sound, straining all their energy toward those clouds that had begun to gather above them that would not bring rain,, would not give their land life.

Jessie danced a dance of the old world. Her body was loosened from its weight, wrinkled skin stretched and dry, was shining now with the last of her body's sweat. She focussed her entire attention upward, higher and higher she lifted herself, finding at last that place of sheer Light in which she could see a brilliant white star shining. And with deep utterly focussed attention, she lifted her consciousness to respond. Then she was of the Star . The light of the star shone through the physical world, transforming it to all human senses. Without doubt she realized the universes through which this Light drew her, the passing through, the entering into more subtle dimensions of reality. She was in that Light, shifted from form to formlessness from thought to awareness. She carried the plea of all humanity that Life renew Itself in Earth. Her presence was that plea.

Light streamed in a steady flow out of that point she sought to reach. The desert faded from view, she knew only that point of Light. The beat of her feet rose through her body resetting the clock of her life, retuning her attention. Dispair dripped away, dried in that Light, even as hope lost its meaning. Life WAS. It would always BE. The dry air moved, rose around her, became slowly a wind, that pressed also upward carrying her hair and sweeping bits of dust upward into the gathering clouds. Her thoughts circled still there in her brain-mind, still beseeching. If the Light could be reached, Touched by a focussed human consciousness, this small finger of humanity Itself, then, perhaps that terrible shrinking of life, this dispair of the heart, could be bridged. The desert that hid the life of the garden must be caused to reveal that life. The life of the garden was the source of Valley hope. She who had allowed even a small part of this desert to live within herself must be forgiven and must be able to forgive.

She was unaware of the rain that had begun to fall softly, all around, causing the little creatures to turn and reach hands out, feeling its coolness with awe, disbelief, and then with utter joyousness. They knew what it meant. They saw the land growing dark beneath that rain, the water entering into the land to give life to it.

Jessie danced on, unaware, sustaining awareness far beyond

speech, beyond thinking. Higher and higher, Reaching as she had never known that Reaching could be. Then, she knew herself within that 'Touch', the powerful, overwhelming Touch downward of that to which she Reached. The Star had Reached down to her cry, to her dance. The dance became a rhythm of Mind and Heart. Jessie, the woman moved in silent rhythm,,softly, her body moving slower and slower. Mind and Heart became the entire dance, lifting, participating in that vast dance of the Star. That fire that was Soul, burned through Jessie, the woman, there below in the land. It lived through her, blazed in a Joy of Being.

To know her Self she had necessarily transcended her self. All things were possible. Fear and dispair had become small flickers within her and there was knowledge that transcended them, included them. She held the point of attention, that identity, focussed and rejoicing. Her body, overwhelmed, had slid down to rest on the Earth, to lie still, to receive ministrations of the little people. Compassion was a recognition for all that lived. Then, as the rain fell, as Jessie lived beyond that place, they began to slip away, into the boulders, returning to their sheltered dens. The land was changing, the heat softening, but Jessie did not see.

Her body slept in the gently falling rain. The little pool rose higher, began to over flow and to run steadily down into that basin which had once been a lake. But Jessie walked in a vaster universe. She held steady in the Light, walked without fear toward it. The Light that had once blinded her, beckoned now. She stood within the blazing doorway and looked beyond that Light. Her sight cleared. She could See beyond everything she had ever known as life and there was 'Life'.

This 'Life' was of further dimensions. Human thought could not shape words to fit. Thought was of wordless, liquid harmony. It was a fluid knowing and needed no voice. Her Heart received it directly and was filled. She felt finally like one who no longer watches, or reaches for Life, but as one who participates wholly in Life. Hope and Dispair had become meaningless bindings loosed from her and fallen away.

Now, slowly, she was aware that she must return to that small self lying against the Earth. It was like asking a mountain to shrink itself into a cup. She had become expanded to horizons slapping against shores beyond thought. She brought back with her consciousness of that universe of Light. She returned to live in the narrow limits of a person. Her Heart in its illogical way, was stretched between the two, would never separate from all it knew.

She felt the pain of it, the shrinking was a grief, for she began to wake. Slowly she knew herself again, a woman living in this land. She roused herself, lifting her head, bemused by all that had happened. She was not surprised to see the garden as it had been when she arrived. The trees whispered softly, the water shimmered with that pure diamond light. The grasses moved in a liquid breeze. She reached out to find a fruit, slowly drew nourishment from it and sitting up, felt energy course through her, a new energy, alive. Reaching out one hand, she extended it to the water, and a bright yellow fire shot from her fingers, touched the surface and created a small geyser of steam. She laughed, playing with energy that was precious, and to be used only with careful wisdom.

For a long time she sat reliving all that she knew, realized, was. She knew that the Light was forever within her, that she lived in that Light that she had so long sought. She must Join with all humanity. She must stand steady in the Light. She must hasten to teach all who can See the true Joining so that all humanity know that Light with her. Together they might be able to know of the vast Knowledge of that Light. Alone, they could only realize the idea of it with hardly a brief glimpse of its brilliance. Together they might guess at that Eternal Life that was the Source of all that was.

She prepared to return, taking the seed of the fruit she had eaten, gathering a few others. She would plant them there, at the Farm. Perhaps they would grow and give the Valley a new nourishment. She stood, looked a last time over the gardens, and then, got into the little car and lifted off. The journey home was without event.

------ ------ ------ ------

Ben walked slowly back from Adwin even as Jessie was preparing herself to leave the Garden. He had just heard the decision from Santiago newcast. Valley Council had sent word that all Learning Centers must begin training children openly whenever any psychic talent began to appear. The new teaching was good, but not enough. They must train all younger children as they grew, finding those talents even before their owner knew. Just as they had always done with the talent to heal. He shook his head. How strange that was, that no one had ever fought with the decision to train Healers. But these new talents, frightened more than pleased. But how would they train such talents? Or even detect them. Already his team at the physics lab was recruited to discover technology to help both detect and train. He shook his head, actually, the biotech labs were more suited. This needed to be living equipment, cellular technology.

One thing they knew surely, that old practice of sending children out to Look, to See, and to Discover, the foundation of all Valley teaching, might even be strengthened. It taught them to be aware! It could not wait. He smiled, remembering his first time 'paying attention'. He had been adolescent, and it had changed his attitude to a lot of things. He walked on, remembering, then, the events of the day pushed out memories of the past. So much was happening.

This morning the Council members had spoken directly to the people. Grace, Jerome, Edsil had spoken on Valley wide network so no one missed the decisions. People were finally confronted with a reality most of them had avoided. Only one Council member had desisted from agreement. He felt supremely relieved and at the same time worried. He did not know Dean personally, but had heard Rose speak of him.

Ahead on the path he saw Jerry walking home. He turned at Ben's shout, waited, his eyes troubled, distant, so that when Benjamin reached him, he thought Jerry was grieved. Ben said,"You've heard? and at Jerry's perfunctory nod, he sighed. "Well, you look as if you don't want that kind of training!"

Jerry shook his head, turned to walk slowly beside Ben up the slope."Oh, no. I'm glad it's finally here, out in the open, talked of. I just don't know how it's going to work."

"It will! Just wait until we get some work done to identify talents. We've been developing some techniques for some years, but without much use of them. Oh, the obvious ones'll be no problem of course, except the training of them, but there are much more subtle Talents. The Reach and Touch are so subtle no one knows you do it unless they receive and the person to whom they happen, unless she's trained to some degree, doesn't know what's happening. Now we can go ahead, all our young bright minds involved. A new direction, and an acknowledgement that makes for possibilities of thought. People can't think of what they deny, you know!"

"Well, at least the Healers've devised tests, biochemical and molecular-magnetic that even I don't quite understand yet. The old tests, the ones by which we've tested every living child and adult just don't do the job. It'll take some time, but no one'll doubt where he stands. Then what?" He frowned again, turning to look directly at Ben.

Benjamin chuckled, "You've not heard even the last survey? Monitors are down among us, living here with us. Started this week. All over the Valley. I didn't know either until today. They've been teaching the Master Teachers. They've been doing some testing of their own. I don't know how they do it, use their own methods, but the results are -- are startling to say the least,Jerry.

"They came to the Learning Centers, Ben. I saw them, some of them, and they -- they didn't LOOK any different from the rest of us but" he shook his head, "there was something -" he shook his head again and was silent.

Ben looked at him darkly,"They are, Jerry, no doubt of it. They're -- they radiate some kind of -- of Presence. That's the only word that fits." He was silent, thinking, and than with a look of surprise and amusement, he added,"Like Jessie, in fact. Yes, like our Jessie. We've never really 'noticed' her either!" The two men walked silently for a little time. Then, Ben heard the ring of his belt communicator. He frowned, seldom did it call him. He opened the receiver and said,"Benjamin here."

A voice said, "Yeah, Ben, we've got a kill. Two other Hunters called in and we need a carry all. Can you bring it?"

Ben felt the sudden surge of excitement he always felt when the Hunters called for help, and instantly following it, the sudden slump of distaste. He both liked and hated to be involved in the killing of intelligent creatures. Even though he knew that they were the lame, the old or the too numerous. The Hunters did their part with predators to balance the Valley life. He said,"Where are you?" He listened and then said,"We'll be there right away. It'll take me fifteen minutes to get to a floater." He nodded questioningly at Jerry and at his nod, he said, "I'll get Jerry to help me." He signed off and the two men turned to hurry back to the Civic Center. Jerry had spent time in the morning with the fishing teams and said an empty floater stood waiting at the warf. The day's catch was in, unloaded and being processed. They went like children racing toward a new game, down the hill and onto the floater.

Jerry handled the carry all easily. Ben always admired that, he managed any machine as if he had some rappour with it. Briefly he wondered whether that might be one of the talents the Monitors had uncovered, and if so, what would it be like? But he did not have time to think about that. Jerry asked him, "Did he say what they'd got?"

"No, just that several Hunters were in the territory and needed help. Why they didn't take their own machine I don't know."

Probably took what they thought they'd need and something happened they didn't expect." Jerry was matter of fact.

"You're right, I'm not thinking. I'm still at the lab. We've been debating the new testing. It's not just the kids, you know, it's us too. To devise a proper test we've got to understand a lot we never have. Some people are really disturbed about it." Ben looked at his brother in law and grinned, then his eye caught the gleam of white in the distance to the north., "Look, the setting sun always blazes so on the City. It lights it up like a sheet of glass."

Jerry turned, he nodded silently, his face seemed to be lit with the white light of the great cliff face. He started, did a second look and said, "Look at that. A car! Coming out of the City! That's impossible."

Ben leaned to see out the side window, "By God, you're right. There it is, a little one, single occupancy. Who on Earth ?"

Jerry said, "We could Reach." he met Ben's questioning eye. Would it be an intrusion. They were not used to such a way of communicating. Could it be right?"

Ben thought, "Sure we could. Whoever it is doesn't have to respond. We won't intrude." He felt an excitement as if some ban on a delightful possibility had been lifted and he could practice what he had been denied.

"Maybe it's someone who can't, who won't --" he hesitated, not liking to admit to such difference. He finished," doesn't know how to accept a Touch."

Ben shook his head, his face at peace. He said quietly, "If that person could take an air car into the City, if the City would receive her, then the person can Join." He looked at Jerry and their minds met.

"You think it might be Jessie then?"

"Worth a chance. Besides who else?" Together they Reached toward the tiny craft. They felt a block, then a sudden lift of the block. Jessie acknowledged their Touch. But she did nothing more. They smiled in relief.

"What do you suppose --?" What could she be doing there? How could she have gotten in, no one else can!" Jerry laughed then, knowing it was none of his business. "Well, we shouldn't be surprised.. She's told us there's a Journey coming up for us. For all of us. Maybe she had to arrange it." He spoke without conviction, not believing his own words. Ben heard the sound of his longing, his heart's question.

Ben said, "You know, I went there. Flew over. I suppose you've done it too at one time or another. I couldn't resist. Just felt drawn to see, to get close to Her.

All the years I've traveled with the Vagabonds, they were so devoted, so sure. I wanted to know and so finally I did it." He stopped, was silent so long Jerry asked,"So what happened?"

Ben grinned , "There's so little to tell actually. I went in a tiny car by myself. I couldn't fly over at first, just around, near the tops of the walls. Do you know those walls are wide enough to land a car on? The City looks so fragile from a distance." He was silent again, his eyes distant,"Then, Jerry, there was some kind of a shift in things, I don't know -- but I just swung the car over the gardens, right above them. That's what it was in there, a vast, wonderful fragrant garden, Jerry. And there were buildings, fragile looking spires that caught the light like fairy towers. There was a lot I couldn't make out too, down below, like it was misted a little. But I saw a couple of small lakes, blue as the sky is. But I don't know. I've wondered if everyone sees something different. " He was silent again,"One thing I was sure of. It's not an ordinary City. It was generating, radiating some kind of energy, the power of it could be FELT. It seemed to actually lift me up. I knew I could not land. After a little time, maybe twenty minutes, I just felt like I had to leave." He was silent, absorbed in memory.

"How'd you feel when you got away?"

At first disappointment, then afraid. Yes, that's what I felt. I dreaded the idea of going again. Yet, I wanted to go so badly too. Remember what Paul said about his trip? I understood him, even though I didn't tell him at the time. I felt terrified somehow, pulled one way then the other." Jerry turned the carry all directly south and the City disappeared from view. Ben shrugged,"Well, that day changed my life. I've never had such a jolt." He glanced over at Jerry. It was after that that I started traveling, you know. Going off on those long trips, hunting for -- something -- someone -- who could tell me what I needed to know. Someone who would recognize what I sought at least." Jerry was adjusting a slim bar that protruded from the instrument panel, Ben watched him absently."I don't know why, I couldn't ever talk about it at home. I didn't know what I was looking for."

Jerry glanced at Benjamin, his heart full. With all the years, their closeness, Ben had never told him of this. Perhaps he'd told no one, except perhaps, Rose. "I'm glad you went,Ben. We used to miss you. But every time you came back, there seemed to be -- more of you, Ben. It was that, you seemed to be more there."

Ben was solemn,"I've asked myself since,why I never tried going to the Stations, to the Monitors. I know now they would have taught me, given me what I needed. But maybe, I was stubborn, had to do it my way. Besides, we didn't talk of them, didn't admit they existed almost, in those days." He was shaking his head,in the sadness that memory roused.

They had reached the site where the Hunters waited. Below they could see several people moving around. Hunters were usually loners. They liked to hunt alone and a fierce but friendly competition existed between them. But they were as fiercely devoted to their guild members. Jerry leaned to the door, watching the descent. "Three men and a woman. Wonder what they've got that's drawn them

THE PEOPLE OF THE VALLEY

together like this. A great giant of a man came up to them as they settled on the ground. His face divided by a great joyful grin. Obviously delighted at their catch, he waited for them to step down. Jerry looked him up and down, grinning too. This man was Randolph, a Hunter who stood half a foot taller then himself, so that put him at seven feet at least with shoulders to match. He could carry a full grown deer. He remembered that Randolph was known for his good nature and he felt grateful. Ben caught Randy's arm in a swift arm embrace, the two of them grinning. Ben looked like a boy beside the giant. "Well, you finally got here, Ben, old boy. This time we've really got something ."

He stepped back and they could see the others. They all had the usual Hunter calm, with detached, poker faces. Randolph waved one huge arm toward the others and said,"Benjamin and Jerry from the Farm north of Adwin. Then turning to the woman, a small person, standing beside a small man, he said, "Sybil, the finest archer in the forests today. She could hit a leaf falling off a tree fifty yards away." He seemed to be enjoying this role as host. "And this here's Billy, and yon's Bart." Jerry turned to nod to Bart, a man about his own size. Hunters fascinated him, but he firmly didn't want their jobs.

They began to work, dragging the huge body of a great black bear into the carry all. They lifted the car to the other bodies. Jerry touched the heavy black fur of the great bear. He turned to them,"How?"

Sybil nodded,"Arrows. No guns for me." Jerry noticed that one of the other men had bow and arrows, another a gun. He knew the clannish divisions among Hunters.

"It's not usual to kill a bear. We don't see them often." Ben was trying to find words to fit, that would not offend.

Then Sybil laughed, transforming her face into beauty. Jerry watching thought she had had to teach herself to be dour, to meet the tradition of the Hunter at least in public. Her eyes sparkled and it seemed to Jerry that she held Joy in her.She said,"No, they aren't easy to track. We don't hunt them, unless they're over breeding. But this one was hurt bad. A rock slide caught his leg and crushed it, he couldn't move and was in terrible pain. He'd've simply died of it there. I heard him from about two miles away." She spoke softly, glancing at the other Hunters as if uneasy at her confession. Jerry was startled. She drew nearer to him,the others were still loading. "Jerry, you must know that I'm a Listener. I work also on Monitor Service for accident patrol." She grinned again and then was without expression. The huge animal was settled, then three young bulls and an old cow. She would provide soup for those who still ate meats. A pair of male deer, their newly grown antlers already scraped and scarred, testifying that they had been fighting. Too many males this year.

"Well, you've done a good job, here. There're some folk down there going to welcome all this." Benjamin wanted to ease these dour people, But Jerry wondered whether others might be like Sybil. More complex than they appeared."How'd you get them all here together?"

Sybil laughed,a short, light sound,"Randy had the communicator and when we called for a loader, he told us to gather here. The lift belts could handle everything one at a time except for the bear, that's why everybody met at my kill. We don't usually find so many needing killing in one area." She spoke the word sternly, no euphemisms hid reality for these people.

As they loaded on the last carcass and prepared to lift off, the dark giant, Randolph, said,"Wow, I seldom see the City from this point of view. The evening sun lights her up, doesn't it?"

Sybil turned and swiftly made the ritual motions of the People of the Way. Gestures across breast and forehead, and soft spoken words. Jerry silently repeated them with her.

> Let the Sun light our lives,
> Let the Sun leave us,
> And return always, shining on our City
> With the promise of Life awakened within us.

Ben studied her face a second then turned away. She had the look of mischief as though she with held a joke. Randolph reached a hand to her. "It was fine work Sybil. I don't know how you manage to find the cripples like you do, But there's not a better job. We don't have to know of hurt creatures suffering in these hills."

Jerry was pleased to hear no trace of envy in the big man's voice. They crowded on the carry all. Sitting on the dead beasts. Then flew with ease directly north. The City again shone before them. The small man, Billy, turned toward her and said, a tight resentment audible to one who listened." There's the blight on this Valley. That - there! That what you call the City. I'd like to see those that admire her tell me what's to be admired."

No one spoke for a moment and then the mild voice of the rifleman, spoke, "She don't do nothing to me, Billy. If some want to worship a white cliff, that's nothing to me." He shrugged then a trace of a grin apppeared in his bearded face. Jerry was smiling at him, liking him, wondered that he had not met him before.

Randolph, nodded, "Maybe that's the best way, live and let live, I say."

Ben felt the draining of tension as they sped on. The silence of the Hunters was natural, Jerry was lost in thought. They settled down rapidly over Adwin, landed on the grid above the main dining hall and the entrance to one of the Food Processors. The Hunters each took a belt and were gone, lifting over the town to their homes. Their job was done. The food staff would take over now. Hides would go to the tannery, the edible meats would be taken to the freezers, and the rest disposed of in dryers for the composts.

Ben and Jerry hosed out the car, and left it at the City Grid. they picked up their own belts and began the journey home. They were getting hungry, maybe someone would have made dinner.

They did not speak until they were nearly home, then Jerry floated near to

Ben, took his arm to keep them together and said,"You know, Ben, we aren't the same kind of people that we once were. We just aren't like our grandfathers. Did you see that? Those Hunters? They hunt as much out of compassion as out of any other urge. They see themselves as husbandsmen of our world, our Valley. They HAVE killed healthy mountain cats, or wolves, or other predators when they threaten the balance, but they don't hunt for sport. They hunt knowing the animals, feeling for them. More deeply perhaps than we do."

Ben laughed,"Jerry, brother, you sound as if you're convincing your self. Well, I can understand that. People have assumed that Hunters were a lusty breed of killers. And I've known for a long time that they aren't. The Hunter corp weeds out any who go into it for those reasons. We don't think the way people once did, our attitudes are different. I think we're more civilized, in fact. But some might argue with that. At any rate,we've still got problems.And they're coming to a head,I'm afraid. Though I can't say just how. I feel some sense of impending trouble."

Jerry sent himself a little distance away, they set down on the deck landing platform and he said,"Well, I hope that's not so, but right now, I don't want to worry at all.I want to go in and enjoy, just enjoy seeing my Mate and my Family and eating a good hot dinner." He laughed, and they went to the Hall.

CHAPTER EIGHTEEN

The Clearing of Tellings Field

For the next few days the Valley seemed to drowze in the quiet of autumn stillness. The people listened and watched, divided in their expectations. Those not aware of the carelessness of assumptions, relaxed, sure that the period of disruption was passing. But those whose attention held ever vigilant, knew that danger was at its peak. They watched with troubled sorrow, and with compassion.

On a bright day only a week after Ben's talk with Dennis, Jessie stood beside the Highway, watching the slow movement of the Low Carts carrying the People of the Way toward the River. They would spend time along these northern banks, fishing. It was the time of warm days and cold nights, the autumn air was full of the fragrance of change. Frosts had whitened the fields two nights ago and the tall grasses were heavy with seed, gold in the sunlight. She idly nibbled at a late apple she had picked on her journey down the hillside. She knew the Valley had reached a point of crucial change, a moment that would decide direction for many years. Her heart was full, both with joy and grief. All her senses were alert, watching, waiting for the signal that would tell them where the critical event would occur.

Then, knowing a difference, she watched an approaching troop of Vagabond families, several together. Children ran ahead, it was early in the day and their energy was high. She smiled at their foolishness, then frowned as two running behind caught the two ahead and wrestled them down into the thick grass, pummelling and rolling back and forth. It looked so much like a fight that she Reached out to them, sending steady calming and doing so, she found that they wrestled with no desire to hurt. They glanced up at her, even as they rolled, strove to catch the other in an unbreakable hold and grimaced in their efforts. Then as suddenly, they were on their feet. She felt their attention, penetrating her Reach, eating up the calm she sent as though it were so much breath they must breathe. She sighed and then laughed. Who were these then, aware beyond even the usual wakened Vagabond.

She watched them a moment longer, a they turned from the rough play as suddenly a children do, silent, utterly absorbed in another interest. They sat or knelt there, in the grasses, as if entranced by the hanging beads of grain. Jessie knew instantly that they were wholly aware, seeing beyond the surface dullness of things. And doing so, they found the graceful heads of grasses, golden, swaying lightly, a great delicate butterfly resting on one slim curving blade, full of dancing color, mystery and fascination. Slowly one child lifted a long stem, gently broke it and continued in a smoothly attentive movement that brought the heavy crown of seed up level with her face. She looked at it there, silhouetted against the still blue sky. The others waited, watching too. Then with movements as carefully acted out as a ritual, she bowed her head, then bent slightly to touch the bending tip with her lips. For these children, life seemed to be gathered there, filling the moment,carrying them into its boundless distance. They were so still they might have been statues, and the adults passing by them barely paid them mind.But Jessie knew that a deep relationshp was honored in those moments of silence. A recognition of Life. She smiled.

Adults, drifting along inside the lead cart, were working on the fine embroidery of a large tapestry, its heavy folds already rolled away along one side, brilliant with color. Their attention was as wholly attuned to their work as the children's were to theirs. In the other cart, several sat at work, carving the soft stone scuiptures they loved or fashioning musical instruments carefully from the fine woods of Clandor forests. Several teenaged children worked along with them, learning and practicing. Jessie took in everything with approval. The Vagabonds were about their business of life without upheaval.

As the lead cart came near, she waved and they looked up to nod and smile. The cart slowed and a husky dark man stood from his work on the Tapestry and climbed lightly over the Low Cart to jump to the ground and walk to her. The carts stopped, the people were still, the children walked now toward her and gathered round her with wide and curious eyes. "Mother, it's a pleasure to find you. Will you have tea with us?" He bowed slightly in a gracious gesture of welcome.

Jessie smiled, "I would enjoy that, if you have time, friends."

A woman laid down her tools, slid from her place beside the heavy fabric of the tapestry and with one smooth leap, was out of the cart and by his side. She caught both Jessie's hands and smiled welcome. The children came then, turned from their absorption and brought cups to fill from the tall glass tea maker. Jessie looked curiously at the great carafe. It was, as were nearly all the few things the Vagabonds owned, a work of art. How could they bear to risk such a lovely blown glass form to this less than delicate life? She grinned at the question and dismissed it. Her host had reached out a hand, palm flat and held sideways, and she laid her own palm against his, letting the first finger and thumb wrap slightly around each other in the formal greeting. He said, "I am Nelson, and this is my Mate, Avelda, our people have sought to speak with you again. It's good that we meet." His grin was wide, and merry, "Please come, sit with us in our Cart. We'll talk a while."

The people of the other cart were setting their work aside also and coming to join them, Jessie saw an old man and two old women, a younger woman with three teen aged youngsters, very blond, very slim and grey eyed. They could not be clan with these first two. Nelson laughed at her, knowing much of her puzzlement."They aren't, Wise One, they are the people of our son's betrothed. We travel together to know one another before the wedding time." As the others came, he introduced them, Grandparents to themselves, Jason and Merilla, Grandmother to the in laws to be, Aletta, and the parents to the girl, Genessa and Gideon. The young people, stood, listening and serious, studyiung Jessie with a curiously distant intensity. Gretta will be our son's Mate, and this, our son, Dilon. He indicated a young man with raven hair, deep brown eyes and the young woman, as golden blond as her mother and with eyes green as her fathers. They smiled, then reached out their hands to meet hers in solemn greeting.

Jessie nodded, satisfied,"Then you travel to finish the summer with gathering fish for the winter?"

Avelda laughed, "We only do that because we are near the bend of the River. We came this way wanting to talk with the people of these regions. We're searching out for our Councilman Edsil, the mood through the Valley and the work going on to keep the Balancing intact." Her face was serious now. "You've surely known the problems the People must meet. And we teach our young ones daily. The Cloverleaf centers are full during these days, children coming back to us, the new Teachers coming from -" she stopped, meeting Jessie's eyes, then with a curt nod she went on, "from the Stations themselves, Jessie. The Monitors are among us as the ancient teachings have told us they would be. It is the time of wonderful events, but also of danger."

Nelson nodded, his shining black eyes cheerful as if they could not imagine a thing worth worrying about. "Well, let's drop the steps this time, clear over the tapestry into its holder and settle here in the sun to have tea together. It's a cold morning and even this dawn sun has a little warmth." Small benches and chairs rose from the floor and they all sat. Gretta brought cups of steaming tea and Dilon set a plate of small cakes before them. Jessie took a seat against the edge of the cart, watching the smaller children, three blond and one dark, settling into the grass along the side, to play mumblety peg and listen. They played the game with a knife and two polished carved rods six inches long and she wondered what rules they used. She had never seen it played so. But her attention was taken back to the adults, when Avelda said,"Mother, tell us how the people here are meeting the changes the Builders seek and also how the Families are coming to their seeking of the City. We who travel see much, but we often talk little with the town people unless we seek them out or they are on Journey time with us and that is mostly the young."

Jessie nodded, noticing how they took up their cups, drank deeply and refilled them soon. They ate as if they had put off their morning meal. " The Builders are uncomfortable with the way the people of the Valley meet their demands. There is little resistance. There is nothing for them to fight so they are divided. Some suspect a dark plan against them. They cannot understand this quiet acceptance." She drew a long breath, frowning, "Others see the calm as helplessness, as weakness against their stronger convictions. They do not fear, but intend to hold us at that weakness."

Jason nodded, his white hair, thick and long, sliding along his shoulder as he talked animatedly,"Ah, yes, Mother, and the Families continue to Gather, to meet and to learn?"

Jessie nodded, and suddenly, happily, projected the image. Like a wind that cleared the skies, swept old veils from eyes, these people were looking out, aware, awake, and searching with decision to know."Yes, they have been steadily meeting at Gathers. They come together in great numbers to the Learning Centers to teach and be taught . They are aware of the hesitations, fears and denials they've lived with and they dissolve them in new awareness. They acknowledge their Vision, my friends. They begin to accept their own inner knowledge."

"And all this time the tide of fear grows among the Builders? Marilla spoke sadly, her old wrinkled face brown with long turning to the sun, but her eyes were bright and clear.

Jessie nodded and went on," Yet they too are divided and some have a great confidence that they are already the victors. They tend their new crops,they gather everywhere, in houses, learning centers, public halls and they listen to one another and talk and their leaders speak to them with great persuasion. We see that and hear their constant call to the rest of the valley people to listen and to join them."

Genessa, put one hand on the arm of her daughter, Gretta, and drew her nearer,"It's as our children tell us when they Journey into the towns. They hear the constant calling from the Builders. Gretta says that the Builders cannot understand why more have not joined their numbers. They have had no new recruits for weeks and those who suspect us, insist that it is because we have put some evil fear in the people so they cannot come to them."

"And all the time it is because the Valley has so few that cannot Reach, and even among those who can't, there are fewer who feel such fear that it creates the need to regress to safer times." Dilon spoke from his place beside his betrothed, his hand clasping her's in her lap.

Jessie nodded and her eyes moved among them, studying their sadness that the Builders must struggle so. She was satisfied. These people felt little anger, no fear, no desire to oppress. She said,"They must try to do something to get our attention. Our lack of reaction worries them more than our anger would. So we must be ready, we must expect such to happen. What it will be is unknown."

Several heads nodded, eyes dark in frowns. Finally Avelda said, "I rejoice that they don't rouse fear and lust to match their own among our people?"

"They haven't!" Jessie smiled,"Too many have gone or are prepared to go on the true Journey. Too many have become consciously awake and aware. They know and See without doubt. Old lusts lose their attractions when there is so much more ahead. The old hungers fade."

Avelda spoke again, and the worry was evidence of her own doubt."Yes, but fear could destroy the Valley. Destroy us! We speak with such hope and yet it is here in us, we all have that capacity to fear and it could be roused yet, unless we are careful to watch."

"I doubt if any who have taken the Journey could be brought to such an imbalance. But there are many who have not yet made that conviction and the wakened perception that it brings." Jessie spoke slowly, thinking of the work yet to be done.

THE JOURNEY

In a voice so soft it was almost a whisper, Gretta spoke and Jessie, meeting her eyes, was aware that here was a young one as conscious as any she had met. Surely her Heart was great as Anna's, her vision could surpass Andrew's. She said,"And what of the Monitors, Mother?"

Jessie saw Dilon's eyes meet Gretta's, and their Touch was deep and full. She said,"The Monitors have moved into our lives at last. We have known they would, for the ancient teaching told us so and now it is at hand. I have seen them walking among us as themselves, not as ordinary citizens as they used to do, but acknowledging what and who they are. They meet with the Master Teachers and teach them further, and the Master Teachers do not wait but prod the people to ask for their teachings." She saw the look of relief and hope in the eyes of the travelers. They nodded, and they were silent. They talked a little of the autumn beauty, of the coming winter and the work yet to be done. Before she left, to go on her way, Jessie looked to meet each of their eyes,"We will meet the greatest test now. We must be ready." Sadly they nodded, knowing she spoke truly. The People of the Way made their farewells and went on their way. Jessie went on into town, spent the day with two Families who had gone on their Journey in the last week.

But a time of testing was upon them and it became evident that same evening. At the farm, sitting at evening meal, laughing and talking of the day's events, they stopped in the midst of the enjoyment. A curious weight settled among them, a sadness. And Jerry went to turn on the news video. Something was beginning. The Builders were moving equipment to the South, no one knew exactly where, but it was certainly the same earth movers they had taken before.

They looked at one another. Jessie stood, her breath held a moment, wanting them to respond, to See clearly. But she would not interfere now. Ben said,"We've got to know! That's the first thing to do. Tom we've got to KNOW! What the news tells us isn't always complete. Let's you and I go. We've got to be able to tell folks here what's happening. Andrew had been watching the video screen with a look of such pain and fickers of anger that Jessie frowned. He looked around. Would no one stop this? Would no one prevent the desecration of their land? His torn loyalties, trusts, were stretched to a limit he had never had to endure. But now, this impossible action was proving his young friends right.

Tom said, "No, Ben, you stay. Go into town and find what the people are saying, find out if there is reaction, because we must not react we must respond in a manner that holds clear of old habits." At Ben's nod, he went on," I think Paul must go with me because he's near William and may have some knowledge, but also because he can bring word to the people of Altos. Word of a citizen who has seen."

Tom turned to them, his eyes full of sadness, but his face quiet. He stood, just inside the room, feeling the presence of them all so acutely he knew that there was need. Swiftly he emptied his mind, cleared thought and Reached. And found there the others, waiting, Jessie held steady, receptive and centering for the whole. Their Joining, held, not one member of the group withheld. Then, with

THE PEOPLE OF THE VALLEY

steady control, Jessie urged them toward the Valley beyond. "Let us Reach beyond ourselves, let's see whether we can at least Touch other minds in the Valley." The idea was a spill of fluid energy among them and they shivered and responded.

The Reach was true, and far it extended, entering beyond their known capacity. They found and Touched against another gathered Family, a group focussed and lifted to its highest point of attention. And over all, there the bright, shimmering mental net of the Monitors, so steady it was as though immoveable, as though unhurtable. And the Farm Family felt its protection, its energy from which they could draw. They must strengthen their quiet understanding. They were able to send the message that Tom and Paul would go and report back to the people of the north.

But there was, far beyond their effort at preparation, another grand gathering being called. Jessie knew she must go. She said little, but took her leave, strapped on a belt and began her journey even before she finished her dinner. For the first time in long years, for the third time in their service of the Valley, the Monitors had called out, had gathered among their own. They would Gather at the Teaching Station because it was farthest from that Black lodge from which came the pull into descent to dark places of human nature . Now that pull was at its strongest. The Builders were creating the field, a field on which this test would occur. What would it be?

And when Jessie arrived there at the Station the evening sun still spilled light down on the cooling fields around the Station. The people stood outside on the great meadow, students and Teachers alike, and they gathered the students, young and old, into the center circle, so that there were three rings formed and they stood there around a great star shaped by white mosses in the field. Forming the outer circle were the adepts, the Teachers and those soon to be adept.

They reached to take hands, touching body-mind- heart. Then slowly, they Joined in a pure white light of energy, that created, had there been any to see, a light blazing up into the blue sky, a fire of brilliance and those within the circle of that Light, felt that energy Touch, waken, reveal. Knowledge was like another light within their minds. The understandings that had previously hidden behind dim veils, and would not clarify, were as though swept clear and obvious. Their minds stretched, opened, receptive, and the understanding descending into them came because these months and years had made them ready. But the gift was not ordinary. This was a time of need and the Teachers had gathered to meet that need.

And so they 'Gathered'. They Joined in a masterful point of attention to which they drew the energy that waited, waited always for such as this. They stood in the great meadow deep in thick soft grasses and slim delicate wild flowers, a double circle. And they waited. A Gather such as this was not unknown at all. Often at Seasonal Festival times, the Monitors Gathered and gave initiation to those ready. But this was a Gather obviously special to the times.

They heard nothing, their silence was like a resounding wave, rising, spreading, engulfing them in its energy. The apprentices closed their eyes, striving to sustain balance within this powerful flow. They felt their very minds assaulted, driven, opened, the Teaching they had been practicing for their year or two of training, seemed to each of them to be revealed in simple clarity. Tough knots of understanding untied themselves and were clear. They felt a surging of the Tension among them all. Then, they opened their eyes , knew the Presence of the Old Ones. For moments they saw nothing, then they practiced the shift of Vision, and there, in the center, among them visible, were the Elders. Clothed only in astral bodies, they seemed to shimmer with their inner light. To see them took focus, attention, and these apprentices willed themselves to focus.

    They almost never saw any Elder, those who did their work far in the background of the Stations. They had come, and that itself meant this was a special Gather, for the old ones could not bring their old bodies, too fragile and ancient to move from their home Stations. The students felt their hearts lift,they knew the power those Elders could give. They literally felt realization grow stronger, their vision clearer, their thoughts more focussed at that Soul conscious point. Supported by this power among them, focussed to lift themselves to that bright point, they stood, joining those in the outer circle, Soul conscious. They attended.

    The pain of the lifting was great for it ripped away old patterns, flushed out half discarded remnants of thought and feeling. But pain subsided as they responded and offered themselves. They were aware beyond the limits of their old thinking so that flaws in the old patterns were exposed. Their brain-minds infused, filled like small ponds inundated by waves from the sea. Then the permeation drew each out into Soul identity, turned inside out the self to Self, brought them conscious beyond themselves. They knew intimately that which they had begun, even in childhood, to know faintly. Now that faint knowing grew, and they extended out into that sea of Mind, they WERE the powerful waves crashing through consciousness. They woke, realized themselves beyond that personal self, a part of what woke and filled it. Impersonal awareness was a point of view from which all things were perceived as from unlimited heights. They were stretched further into a Knowing that their Teachers lived from. And because their training had made them ready for such perception, even as the Valley itself was nearly ready,the unfolding was rapid and true.

    As the old legends had long promised, these, the Elders, had come in shining splendor among them, some came wakened from long sleep and bodyless lives, from their work within the frame of dimensions unknown. They brought the next gift. a gift to be given to these new lives unfolded into KNOWLEDGE. They would be aware of that new state for humankind. The time of understanding among humanity had come.

    They felt that power build among those shining Elders, they felt the strength of it, and they knew, even as the brilliant Sun came shining down illuminating that sea of Mind it brought something utterly new, something as different from mind as mind is from emotion. They felt the wakened spirit within them blazing

THE PEOPLE OF THE VALLEY

out and drawing a further influx of Spirit Itself.

Entering, like Light does, shining down through the powerful mental currents, these small mindpools, inundated, were now gleaming with that penetrating Light. Not one molecule of mind that was not filled with it. For it filled and left no weight, added no size, it simply filled and transformed. Mind, utterly infused with Spirit, was transformation, and so their Vision broke through thought and entered into Knowing. There was no word spoken, no thought sent, no need for Touch. All that was was JOINED in a single Consciousness and all partook of that larger nature, transforming themselves.

The Elders Joined together in such an offering, would have seemed to any one watching like a great sun shining in the midst of this circle of smaller suns. But there was no one to see, for ordinary minds would have quailed and failed of consciousness in this power. These minds, trained for years, supported by one another, prepared in Joining were united through Mind strength to hold consciousness of what was beyond itself. It was an unlimited Touch of Light and they stood firm before it. They sustained themselves through a condition of their natures that made receptiveness possible; the condition of Love Itself.

Then slowly the Gathering ended, the Elders visible now to everyone, turned eyes that held the terror and wonder of Love of LIFE Itself upon their fellows who waited their blessings. The circles were broken, the Monitors, new guardians of the Valley, mingled in talk and reception of those blessings.

Jessie, joined thus among her kind, felt those eyes on her, felt the powerful presence of Jedro on one side of her and of Dolores on the other. She looked across the circle and saw there, John, leaning his incomplete body on a carved cane. He smiled across at her. Her heart leaped in a Joy far greater than any she had ever known. Literally, it surged through their circles, sang through their bodies like a taut harmony of multiple notes, like a stillness of silent dance. She felt her body shudder, adjusting itself to the energy. And she turned to Jedro,

"It's true! The time has come., The Valley is ready, whatever the pain or the Joy of it."

He looked at her, his eyes still filled with that brilliance of realization. He nodded,"It's true! We can help more directly now. The People are moving toward their own recognitions. We can help now. "

"If they will hold fast!" Her voice seemed to waver slightly, and he laughed, a rumbling sound that startled her to realize her doubt. She nodded then,"I understand, Jedro, it is our task to sustain the power for them, know without doubt, to offer help wherever they ask?"

"And they know enough now to ask. That has been in part your doing, Jessie. Remember that. But you too must not forget to ask!" He smiled.

A novice, her eyes wide with amazement, joy, fear, all the emotions held in balance that this amazing Gather had fostered, came to them, stood, simply absorbing all she woke to. Then after a little while, remembering, she looked far off across the miles of distance and asked, "What, Jedro, what of the Black Lodge? I"ve felt it! Like needles of many fears. They trigger mine." She looked

THE JOURNEY

away, but they saw the flicker of that fear. "It creates a net, doesn't it? A net into which we lure ourselves." She sighed, her face, again shining from the wonder of this Teaching Gather, shifted slightly with a frown of worry. Then consciously, steadily guided, returned to its former awe. She could choose and she could rebalance even when the pull away was great.

Jessie and Jedro turned to her, their minds melded into agreement, but Jedro spoke. "Focus your attention, child, focus. Don't you see that the energy from the City is to the power of that Black Lodge like a River beside a little creek? It must eventually flow into the larger. Don't you see the only danger possible in the Valley now?"

She met his eyes, receptive, "Ah, yes, it's myself, the narrow self who is afraid, who desires so much. And now, because of our Gather, I stand Soul conscious. It's not what's outside I need fear, but what is myself." With a long relieved sigh, she added, "It always has been. And I will to sustain Vision." The firming of her resolution was like a light around her.

The two elders nodded, Jessie reached out to touch the young woman, "Always remember you are not alone. Ask! Remember there is always help." Jedro smiled, "You're greatest task just now is to remember!"

The Monitors met with one another, a little more, some eager for that physical touch of another friend, some merely enjoying the touch of eye, the fragrance of presence with another, and some sustaining throughout their number the literally singing silence, that taught their minds the wisdom of the HEART. They each watched as the diamond brilliance of the Elders gradually faded, the meadow was again simply a bright meadow on a summer day, and they began to gather to the long tables to enjoy a feast together. But their Hearts sang, were great with realization.

During this time, the Family turned finally to one another, knowing they must discover their own possibility. This time, they must prove themselves capable, and they Reached, willed the Joining and drew into one.

On the roadways below, the Vagabonds felt the stir in their bodies and minds, they drew into a focussed attention. Then hundreds began the long trek to the southern end of the Valley. Leaving off their fishing, their visiting of town folk, what ever had caught attention, they turned from. Down the Highways they streamed, coming out of little mountain roadways, where they'd been gathering winter herbs, picking up children from Journey time in the towns. What danger was focussing in this Valley now? What new threat? Was it the Black Lodge wakened and firing its own seductive energies among them? Or was it something they had not known. Dolores, Monitor and mother's sister, to Marian, was walking with them now. Others of their kind would join them when the Gather at the Station was done. These people could feel their presence among them, guiding, acting as a strength they could borrow. But now, Dolores would give them understanding. And so they trekked, joining each other along the Highway so that their caravans were like great bright beads on a green strand. The evening light played softly over the land as the sun went down.

THE PEOPLE OF THE VALLEY

As the Joining loosened and faded, and those of the farm began again to think and wonder, they found fear still there, lying like a shadow that darkened the earlier recognitions. But they were aware of it for what it was. They took thought and were not caught into its net. Later Rose felt that pressure rise. Felt it as she never had. She felt a wash of darkness, that seeping pull of the dark energy needling through the Valley floor. Rising from the Earth through which it passed, it touched, drew, persuaded, as it caught against her own questioning self and took hold to grow into a heavy weight that would not lighten. She knew herself divided: a lifted soaring of Light, sustained wonder, Joy, and against it a heavy darkness of old dispairs, of desires and needs. She could feel them fed by that hungering darkness, pressing doubts against the Light to ceate a clouding. It was clear that a crisis had been reached. She called instantly for Paul's help. He called Tom, and then Tom called Ben, and each together began the journey to the farm. Jennifer and Annette left their work, drew the children to them, and joined Paul. William could not be found.

Tom called to the Ocean City where Margo worked, then to the two boys, Justin and Nathan, each studying in different cities. He asked them to come home. Angy heard, felt, knew, and came home before he called. Jessie was gone, they must meet this together and each would be needed.

The time of recognition was at hand, no one could deny now the innate qualities awakened finally to conscious recognition. Resistance rose and fell, understanding grew as people listened to their inner hearts. Each Family Gathered and the strong gave visible evidence to the weak of the threads of darkness, the lust of old hungers pressing against thier intentions. They found those with uneasy balance, drew them back, visualizations passed mind to mind, exposed the dangers. Ben held himself taut, sustaining his greatest understanding and said, "Our enemy is what is in us, not what is out there. We are able to stand firm or we are not! It is that simple. "

Tom came with a noisy landing on the platform. He shook himself, shook off the water that beaded the pure plasilk shirt, and saw it dry immediately. " There's fear out there. You can feel it like a dark cloud, that conceals the sun. A small cloud, in comparison, but able to blind us. We ARE able. If we keep balance and lift awareness. There's only one question! Will we lift ourselves beyond that cloud?"

Benjamin stood beside Rose, his arm across her shoulders as if he needed to protect her, he said,"It's exactly that, people are realizing now. We've waked up, are awake, perception is acute among us, Tom, all of us. We know that!" He felt excitement, finally able to speak of himself, his knowledge, and surprised that the words came so easily.

Rose said, "The folks from Altos are on their way. We would not have needed to call. Annette! She knew! Why not? The energy rises here in this Valley. We're preparing and I'm not sure for what." She looked around, the youngsters lounged easily on the cushions, Anna reading, Andrew plucking absently on a mandolin." Why isn't Jessie here!" The cry was like an accusation.

424

THE JOURNEY

The touch of That which Is, had awakened comprehension. The Gathered energy of the Elders swept out into their lives. They knewthrough their own minds the breath that filled their hearts and that was the Source of their very Being. The People of the Valley were waking to Spirit, themSelves,to that fire that pushed aside the limits of their lives and flamed into possibility. The Farm Family sat gathered in their Hall, wondering, aware and more alert than they had ever been.

Then the Video News suddenly blasted on. They turned to watch the screen, amazed. The Citizens alert went on automatically only once or twice in a year. Yet why should they be suprised, this was a time of marvels. The news told them that something was happening at Tellings Field west of Clandor.The old meadow that was a landmark, a living laboratory, a field of deep ancient loam, matted roots of vibrant grasses and surrounded by ancient trees, undisturbed for centuries. It was a place of study for ecology and biology students, a place where agricultural students learned of the balancing of Earth with Herself. Of the way plants and animals adjusted to one another's lives and complimented one another. A thousand acres of land undisturbed for centuries, mostly meadow with a few groves of trees here and there. Forest bordered the field on three sides. Clandor children camped there, went there for parties. Many had done their adolescent solitary 'two weeks in the wild' in the sun warmed groves that stood like islands within that sea of grass. Fearful as it had been at first, they treasured that disciplined touch with loneliness.

News traveled fast, Video reporters sped by air car to the site. But even as fast as people got word of it, the destruction had already begun. Builders had flown one machine, their people, into the land and before the sun had set, began actual cutting of the soil, the clearing of the ancient trees.

World news carried this event, and people watched with deep interest what was happening in the Valley. Would there be battle? The thought terrified, grieved, or delighted people of other nations, depending on their understandings and development. Few were indifferent.

Paul leaped first of his family on to the deck at the Farm from his small air car. He was filled with a strange exultation, which he did not trust in himself. He shook his head, to bring calm,and went to take Rose's hand, grip Ben's shoulder, meeting both their eyes in consternation."What'll we do?"

Tom came to them, "We'll go there, you and I at least. We don't want too many people. But there're laws that prevent this kind of rape." His voice was calm, but a flicker of anger darkened his eyes. Rose nodded, turned and walked to the windows, outside sun light slanted through the evening, clean and bright on the hills to the east. She pointed out at the distant Highway,"Look, the People know of danger. I've never seen them go so fast." Now the setting sun seemed to make grey her world. Wind rattled the bright leaves that were left on the trees, many falling now in the gusts. Then she went to them, Paul waited, knowing somehow that she must decide."

"I agree, Paul -- Tom, you must go there. Find out, for us all. See what can be done. They'll not do more today. It's late. But maybe you ought to leave in early morning."

Paul started to speak, then frowned, anxious, fear threatening balance. He swallowed, righted himself. "In the meantime, can't Valley Council stop all action pending a meeting?"

She nodded, " Grace's already contacted us for permission to call the emergency five members tonight. They're meeting probably by now."

"In the meantime, all of you meet, listen, wait for Jessie. Surely she'll come. Practice Joining! This is a time to Reach to other Families. We've done it with Jessie's help. We must do it also without her. Now, finally we must learn!" Paul was determined, they felt his urgency. Yet his voice seemed to them calm as one without a single worry.

That night Paul's sleep was uneasy and full of strange dreaming. He and Tom left the farm early, in the cold before sun up. The rest of the family promised to be alert to their Sending, to Reach to them as one. It was a subdued and thoughtful group that was left standing there as the two men climbed the steps to the grid where Paul's car was parked. Ben would go into Adwin with Anna, find out the temper of the people there.

Tom and Paul arrived at the field in grey dawn light. Several miles east of Clandor, and with no towns near, the number of people there surprised them. People stood scattered around the north west end of the Field whose thousand acres lay in a long flat between forested hills. It was home to a variety of plants and wild creatures that could not be found anywhere else in the Valley.It had been named for an old, old man, after the people had just begun to return to these lands. He had lived there, and had exacted a promise that the Field would be protected and never cropped. Since then it had become a precious part of their heritage. The idea of its destruction brought real pain to the hearts of millions.

Float tillers and seeders hovered over the broad sweep of the grasses and intermittent clumps of shrubs or small groves. They were looking over the job, deciding the best approach. To the west were low hills covered by spreading oaks,walnuts, ash,sumac,alder and many others already older than any other living thing in the Valley, except coastal or mountain redwoods and some of the coastal pines. through those trees people of outlying villages were coming. Then, above the old trees, bright green in this southern land, came a big earth moving machine. It floated clumsily as it came in from Santiago.

Paul and Tom circled the field, watching the activity below. Their trip down had been nearly silent, with occasional mutters and exasperated expressions of "I can't believe they'd do this!" And "They didn't even file a petition this time."Then he said,"I wonder if they really intend to rip the field up or if it's just a threat to get some action out of us."

Finally Tom said softly, as if the thought puzzled him,"Paul, we've got to keep calm. We've got to listen! I could legally arrest the whole bunch, but if I did, wouldn't that be just what they want. An incident to strike the match to the feelings in this Valley?"

Paul had glanced at him, finally nodded, frowning at the anger he felt."Funny how self rightious a person can get when he thinks he's right. I was doing just that." Now, hovering over the field, his anger rose again,he cried out."But they'll ruin the field, Tom. And it's priceless."

"We've got to keep cool, Man. We could percipitate trouble ourselves."

"What the hell d'you think they're doing now?" Paul shouted suddenly, releasing pent up emotion. He let that anger drain and drew calm around himself. Then he said,"The mayor of Clandor broadcast their plans this morning. Said the Monitors knew their intentions. Probably a lot of other people near by do too. They weren't trying to keep anything quiet. Shouting at one another over the fields, on Video phones, discussing them all the way from their various homes to this field. You'd have to be mind deaf not to have heard. And of course, they are. They actually think there's no problem at all. That it'll be all right just as the other fields were given once they took them." He was silent, shaking his head, lookng down at the busy workers. " But this field. This Field! How could they do it, don't they love the field too?"

Tom was very still, his eyes distant, holding himself balanced,keeping intact his attention, listening and focussing.He said," That's not what's bothering you actually Paul."

Paul looked at his brother-friend. He felt quieted just from the glance. Tom was so quiet. Was that part of being a law inforcing agent,to be calm in ANY situation. Paul felt glad he hadn't learned, he felt better from having shouted. "It's their effrontry. It's their ignoring of everything but their own wishes. It's their -- Tom, the very heart of our culture stands on the Conviction that we attend to the welfare of others, of the Valley itself, of the life here. It's what we've built on. This - this is old world stuff, it's an attitude that's supposed to be dead.. An anachronism. It scares me that it can be so alive here."

"And what else, Paul?" Tom was adamant, his utter calm beginning to irritate Paul.

Paul glanced again at his friend, his hands gripping the controls of the car, keeping it steady, then hovering over a stand of great dark trees. Then with a short barking laugh, he said, "You never let up , do you? That's what makes you good at your job." Then his laugh was real, it's release lessened the tension and he felt himself relax. "It's true. I'm afraid my own Convictions are all being drowned under my anger, my fear. Another Conviction equally important is that one about honoring the rights of every person and I can see I'm about to break it." He met Tom's eyes, seeing the pain there.

They were silent for a few minutes, then Paul said,"It could leave me no less self serving than they are." He took a deep breath, then shrugged,holding his palms flat together before his chest in a gesture of great sorrow. "At any rate, I think I can balance myself, Friend. But I'm going to land and you do the talking. You've kept your cool well."

Tom grinned,"I just haven't dared let my self think about what I feel yet. But right now, yes, I've chosen to keep calm. We have to find out the facts." He

THE PEOPLE OF THE VALLEY

hesitated, meeting Paul's grief filled eyes,"Maybe we need to do just that. Focus! Locate the Center until we stand in Love. We need that help!" Paul nodded, mute, his eyes waking to new hope. They set the flyer down, and sat, silent, intent, their eyes closed for better focus, seeking that help. Softly, each murmurred the familiar words, "I lift up my consciousness into the Light of the living Love. May I keep that connection during these hours." Feeling a little more stable, they got out.

They had landed the car in a tiny meadow some yards back inside the forest. They walked out to the meadow, through the people coming now in greater numbers. It seemed to be a day of celebration, picnic. People chattered excitedly all around them. As they watched they were horrified to see one of the huge earth movers settling down into the thick turf of the meadow. It dug its powerful teeth into the Earth, a faint high drone sounded as it moved, leaving behind it a yard wide trail of naked dark soil. There was not a trace of plant life showing as it turned this skin of Earth under, exposing the dark loam. What about the animals living beneath this thatch of meadow? They saw small shadows dart through the tall grasses, racing for their lives, tumbling and frantic. But he also saw the torn bodies of those who didn't make it out of the path of the teeth. Deliberately Paul watched, bringing his emotions into balance, his thoughts into harmony and stillness. He watched this desecration without denying the shock of it.

Tom went rapidly to an empty hover disc. Started it moving and swept rapidly toward the busy monster. Already it had cut a trail of dark glistening soil, densely webbed with fine grass roots, nearly fifty yards long. He swung the disc near the operators cabin and gestured vigorously, sending with all his might but not expecting reception. The power of his Sending might have helped the meaning of his gestures, because the operator stopped, opened the cover over his head, and looked questioningly at Tom.

"What's the trouble, Mate?"

Tom asked, "Do you have authorization for this work?" His face was quiet.

"The Boss does back there. I just do the work." He grinned, good naturedly. "So if you go talk to her, I'll get back to work."

Tom wanted to ask him to wait, but knew it would be pointless. He turned his disc toward the group of people the operator had indicated. They sat under trees, picnic baskets clustered near by. The thought that they were making a holiday of this angered him more than anything had done. He acknowledged his anger and landed his disc. "Who's in charge here?" A woman moved from the group around the tables and came toward him. "I'm the Ag. Tech. here. If that's what you mean." She drew closer and then recognized him, "Oh, Hello Tom. This isn't your jurisdiction, what're you doing here?"

Tom stood easily, waiting for her to get nearer." Darrell from Clandor was at a meeting at the undersea city, Costeau. He'll be here within the hour. He asked me to meet you." He recognized the woman, Marie from Clyde. "Actually you're a little out of your territory too, aren't you? Do you have Valley Decision given to the Builders for the use of land here?"

She shifted swiftly, her body and face took on a quality of defiance that startled and dismayed him. "We do not. We've decided the Valley belongs as much to us as anyone. This field isn't being used and so it's fair for us to use it."

"Well then --" Tom heard the fury rising at the edge of his voice,they had no right, the nerve of them! And he felt the same sadness at himself that Paul had felt, but he also felt the powerful background of a greater awareness steadying him. He drew himself into balance with difficulty, then with ease. he said, almost tenderly,"I have to ask that you stop the crew. We've got to bring the matter to the Council before you can proceed. It is the Valley law. No one can change uses of land without the Council approval, you know that well, Marie. " His voice held a plea, his mind Sent his great need to her that she comply.

"Sorry Tom, we'll not do it. We've made the decision already. William of Altos has told us it was right. He's handling the legal end of it. We'll go ahead unless we get his order to stop. And I don't think that will happen. "She turned and went back to her friends at the tables.

Tom stood a moment,stunned with disbelief. Then the dispair of it hit him. He wheeled his float and rode back to where Paul waited.

Paul had watched the interchange, for a moment,then been distracted by a woman who walked slowly, silently and with a purposive manner through the field beside the furrow the earth mover cut. The operator shouted at her to move off, but she seemed not to hear. She moved steadily, as though she studied Earth as she walked. Paul was stung by a sudden hope. He lifted his head, Reached with all the power he had. And felt reception!

She swiftly informed him." I am Claire. I monitor this land, these living ones.I must take them to safety before the mover destroys their lives. Let me be!" Then she raised her head, turned briefly to him with a warm smile,"You take care of getting this stopped, Paul of Altos."

Paul felt his mouth drop open. He'd never seen a Monitor in action so close up. And she'd come so quietly. Soundlessly, seeming not even to be seen by the other people. Her presence comforted him. He drew his attention to Tom's disc, coming swiftly to him.

"Paul! It's William! William gave them permission. William! Our Will!" His voice was full of tears, chagrin, pain. They said we'd have to talk to Will. My God, Paul.It's come to that!. What'll we do?"

Paul was silent for several seconds Reaching, wanting to Touch Tom in a comforting. Never had a Family member torn himself away in this manner before. There had always been complete trust. They both felt as though something had been torn from their own bodies. They stood together several minutes, while the great machine ripped away across the field. It was slow, awkward, in fact. They weren't meant to be used for farming at all. They had become mostly museum pieces kept in Santiago. Paul said softly,"We talk to Will."

In those few moments they each felt the surge of their emotions, the rage, grief, helplessness, the desire to use force to make these people do what they should. They watched this current of emotions run its course. They waited. Then they lifted their attention, lifted their point of focus above those currents and allowed them to subside. To an onlooker they seemed entranced. They seemed to stare at the ground beneath them, or at the trees across the field. When they had together allowed the last of the fury to drain from them, they felt a softness, a strength, and a clear understanding. They knew what they must do.

When they lifted their eyes to look around there were three people watching them. Two men and a woman. One of the men said,"What's wrong with you two? You're acting strange enough. Dean told us to watch out for anyone acting like that, acting like he's 'tranced. That's the sign of the devil in him, Dean said. We've seen it before."

The woman nudged him, "Wait, Benny, they may mean no harm. Maybe they don't know why they're taken like that. It's purifying they need. Not harshness."

"Two full grown men taken by an ill at the same time? It's not likely!" He was silent, then unconvinced but wanting to be fair he said, "Well then. Will you come for the purifying? Do you know the Devil's in you?" He searched their faces, his eyes narrow and grim. Tom did not think he held much charity in his heart.

Tom, ever the diplomat, nodded and smiled. "Well, we do feel a trifle distressed. Maybe we'll go to our own Healer for advice." He started to turn, catching Paul's eye, telling him they needed to return to their air car. But the woman spoke, hesitant, a hint of fear making her voice strident. "Wait, you'll not get help from them. They'll try to turn you into it. They're half sold to the Devil themselves. We don't go to see Healers any more. We've got only medical Docters to take care of us. It's best if you let our people do the purifying."

Paul shook his head, bemused, watching the slow steady progress of the machine. "No Ma'am, we've got to go home. It's important!" With that they turned and sprinted to their car, leaped in and were air born before the three could speak.

"You realize they could get an awful lot of that field ruined before Council can make its decision or send out word to stop them?" Tom was thoughtful, steady in his balance "What the devil can we do? We have to do something fast."

Paul said, "I've got an idea. You've heard of Barry from Denlock?" At Tom's nod and look of beginning of understanding, he went on. "He can stop the works. He could disturb the metal in the engine. Stop them dead, both of them. Enough to give us a couple of days. That would be enough I think. Shall we do it?"

Tom nodded, a grin finally brightening his face,"On to Denlock. Barry! I will not ever ask anyone to use their powers for self service,but this isn't that. It's Valley service, It's protecting Earth." His face became grim again. He felt through himself, watching the flow of emotion and found little trace of that glee of battle in himself. He had seen that in the face of the woman who refused to stop the work. The old unconscious urge to destroy, even to kill. Paul, watching,thought of that even as Tom did. He was glad it was not there in Tom's face. No one who was aware could avoid seeing that in themselves, if they'd lifted into Light enough to See at all.

We've denied the powers that have been emerging, but we've also denied the old lusts - even this one, the lust to battle. But I've felt it. Paul, I know that I'm not clear of it. We're admitting the new Talents, the new Vision and there is no longer any room for those old primitive lusts. Even though their energy may be the foundation for some of our new Talents. He tensed, then let out a sigh,"I hope we're not too late."

Paul turned all his attention to his flying. If he pushed the little car to its limit he could get to Denlock in half an hour. Although that might be a record. Half an hour to talk to Barry, then half an hour back. It would not take too long. Finally,he said,"That may well be, and we've got to correct that. But right now, aren't we about to do something as presumptuous as they're doing? We're planning to get Barry to stop their motors and we don't have a Council permit either." They sat in silence.

Finally Tom said, "You fly as fast as you can, Paul, I'll Reach for the Monitor Station. I think there is emergency enough to call for help." He settled himself. Closed his eyes and felt the lightness of Reach. It was as though his body was left behind and his mind flew far ahead, carrying him along, consciously extending. It was as though a hand lifted him, carried him more swiftly than he had ever known his mind to leap.

Then, without warning he felt the Touch of another Mind. Swiftly he was drawn into a Joining. Drawn into a power that amazed and filled him with wonder. The Joining at the Station, shaping itself before dawn of this day, had spread out over the Valley, like a great net of mind it shone for anyone who could have seen. It gave them clear vision of the Valley everywhere and when Tom Reached, his Touch was instantly felt. He was lifted into that net, carried along its mental threads to that full communion. He told them in swift visualization what was happening, what he and Paul had done. He felt their power, like a -- power station. Of course,their retreats were called Stations. And so it was. It was a deep center of energy held in control and used.

He felt their response, their listening. "Your plan is to stop all action for a few days? You ask us to use power to interfere? We cannot interfere. But we CAN speak to them."

" No use! They'll have the thing done before talking can happen. Talking takes so long, you know. A century of life ruined, a priceless heritage gone."

Then we must enter their ranks and try. We have other ways to work, you know. Would you use power for personal gain?"

"It's Valley gain!"

" Your personal idea of Valley gain. You will have to do what you will do just as they have. But pay attention to your motives, to the harm in yourself of that action. However, destroying life is wrong, it's true. To stop the action of the Builders may well be only delay but might not be harmful. You must decide concerning your own action.

"We are sending Speakers to them. Some of our Speakers live and work as news people in the Valley. They will inform them of the law again. After we have done this, we will wait your call."

He felt the release, the spring back to his old self. The sudden smallness of himself. The fact that he could literally hear and know in his mind their thoughts, as sentences, as ideas. It was not telepathy but something much more refined, complete in knowing. He felt astonished at the power there, the Valley wide power. Why should he worry. But they had their laws too. He thought that he and Paul must act now according to their own laws. And he sat lost in thought about that tendency in humankind. Was there such a thing as 'right and wrong'?

"Why haven't they dealt with these faults in us? Why didn't they tell us to teach our children differently. Why didn't they do something long ago?"

" They cannot interfere!" Tom shook his head, this wasn't the time to debate the past. "I got the impression they felt remiss. Maybe they make mistakes too, you know. They can't or won't change now. But they've at least Gathered, all of them, Paul. What that must be like. To be there with such Wise Ones. They see beyond all we see. Surely they'll plan a way to help. Jessie must be with them. That's why she wasn't at home."

"They have the power to Reach this entire Valley. Obviously! They've always had it. Why didn't they use it before to warn us?"

"They could have, surely. They had such a rigid rule that they must not interfere. At least we've asked them! Maybe now they'll do it." He was silent a moment, then turning to Benjamin he said softly, They could have even Reached to Steve and Jane and Silvia and all the other beginners among us. They could really wake us up! Why not?" He was shaking his head, realizing the wish that that greater power would take all this burden from him. After several minutes, he said, "Ben'll be fit to be tied by now Good thing he didn't come with us. I doubt he could've held himself from a fight."

"He's come so far this year,I think he's got a lot more balance." The sky they traveled through was nearly empty. Few air cars dotted the blue. "People must be home Gathering;people must feel as concerned as we are."

Tom laughed,"I had to ask several to stay home and let me check things out before we acted." He was silent, "But probably they would've done as well as we are."

Benjamin nodded, then started with realization,"Oh, Tom, what about people like Jane. She must be in pain right now. Even though she's that far away. The lives being destroyed, that have already been destroyed.It'll hurt her. "

"Remember, Jessie taught her how to close, to shield. She'll be all right, Paul. And maybe the Monitors could do something there too." He grimaced,"If we had sense enough to ask."

Then Tom turned a swift glance to him."That's what I saw, there in the field. While you were talking. There was one, a lady, a Monitor, she looked like a worker. Never would have guessed what she was if I hadn't Reached. She was caring for the little ones as the ripper did its work. I wish I could go a little faster, but I think that this is the best we can do."

"We'll be there soon. We're doing the best we can. Paul. D'you think we could try a Reach to him? Maybe we could let him know the need before we get there and he'd be ready."

"We can try. Somebody might receive for us anyway." he shrugged,"My God, just a few months ago I would have been horrified at such an idea." He grinned.

"You know, I got the feeling that the Monitors've decided it's time to accept things differently too. They've come into our lives. They're beginning to contact us. They're not hidden!" Tom's face was full of a hope he had not felt before.

Paul's voice was impatient,"Try Man, try! I can set the car on auto for a few minutes. Together we could do it." He leaned back, set the controls and with an audible sigh, relaxed. Tom did the same and for seconds they could feel the density of space around them,the feel of distance when mind Reaches, the push of attention out of the dimness of ordinary thought, and through that grey light that preceeded full Light. There was literal resistance which puzzled them both momentarily, then the push through into clear. echoing silence. The Joining was a feeling of expansion, of depth and an entering into perception that seemed to extend far beyond thinking. They had never tested their abiity to Reach out of a Joining! They did not know it's extent. They felt fear because the Reach seemed to gather them up, cast them out of themselves, as though into a realm of Mind itself. There seemed, just at the edges of their consciousness, someone else, perhaps more than one, others out there, aware but not Touching. Supporting? Were they being tested as well as testing themselves?

Merging their minds finally, casting away from all fear, knowing the need so great, they finally melded, they were one mind. Then, there was recognition that they were alone with one another, Mind was beyond, around, within them - everywhere, but not limited. And yet, it was as though a clear barrier stood between them and that vast sea that was Mind. They understood finally, as though an image had formed itself before them, that this was the unconscious human shield learned through millennia of fear, honed during years of having a Talent they would not acknowledge.

The recognition was a release. Tom felt Paul draw himself into balance, thrust away the edge of that shield, appeal to him, Tom, to do the same. To thrust unreservedly OUT. No! It was an allowing of all that existed to enter into them. He saw Paul setting aside old patterns, old emotions, old systems of thought as gently as if they were bits of fabric covering a naked body. He smiled at the metaphor. It was a kind of nakedness, a new unity, unknown, this Joining of focus toward a single goal. Tom joined in that setting aside of himself, thrusting through himself, seeking beyond. His own fear, habits, fell away. Excitement, pleasures, thought were released and he felt the barrier dissolving, fading out and they were conscious. But they knew they were still limited. Vast as was this sea that was Mind, what they knew was only a finger extending from a vast and relentless hand.

Then taking hold,accepting this focus of attention, they Reached toward Denlock. Tom thought fleetingly of the monumental energy involved. Or was it simply a skill one must learn. The Monitors must do this effortlessly, out of long habit. Then, they were aware that those who had seemed near were clearly all around, watching, offering strength, ready as parents are when their baby begins to walk. And then comforted, more sure, they touched another mind. They held steady, Touching, and they found her, knowing automatically that it was a woman named Janice, in Denlock. They had done it!

Her energy throbbed, untrained, flickering with shards of fear, but determined. Willing! They caught at her Touch, she withdrew, hovered, scared, then Reached with abandon. They drew her into their Joining and held. She did not shrink, she was there with them,quiet. Paul thought the whole experience resembled a dance, he and Tom, and then finally this new one. But he knew he must focus, exclude all thought. The message must be sent.

They felt her reinforcement, their strength amazingly greater. With her, they could surge ahead, as if on new, powerful mind patterns, She realized swiftly as they reached for Barry,their images sharp and clear, she saw the condition there in Telling Field. She caught her breath with dismay, but her mind was utterly steady. She was not Earth Sensitive, but she knew those who were. She recoiled at the thought of Reaching for them. She had once accidentally Touched their pain. Then,together they turned to focus on Barry.

Barry recoiled so violently they were shaken backward by the push of it. Steadying themselves,they tried again, but this time,the tremendous fear he felt at their Touch was so real they abandoned all effort. "Wait,"Tom thought, "He isn't ready. we've got to reach him physically. Talk!" They held the link steady with Janice. Paul found he could attend the air car, direct it at the same time. The fact astounded him. Then they were there, settling in over the house Janice directed them to.

They landed and approached the house, but a man stood already on the porch, a look of anger, distrust souring an otherwise handsome face at the top of a great powerful body, the biggest man Tom thought he'd ever seen. Then he remembered that this Barry was the one who won all the contests for strength in North Valley. He smiled, walked confidently toward him and knew instantly where the anger came from.

Barry leaned against the railing of his wide porch, his hair blown across his forehead and over one eye,. Chestnut brown,thick and unruly, it shone in the sun. The muscles of his body beneath the brown skin seemed to move in oil. His every movement was graceful as a dancers, This was no muscle bound one. "Wait, I don't know whether I want to talk to you. My father warned me about people like you. It WAS you, wasn't it?" At that question he faltered, his eyes dropped briefly, A tall thin man came out the door, stood behind him.

The thin man said,"It's two of them. I can tell just by seeing them now, Son. They ain't to be trusted."

Barry stood straight, his eyes meeting Paul's then Tom's. A visible shift occurring in his own."Wait, Dad, What's wrong with these two. They aren't the kind you talk of."

"I'm telling you they are, Son." Paul spoke rapidly, "Wait, please, Sir. What is it we're being accused of. It's only fair that you tell us."

The old man said,"You're the kind the Builder captain told us about. One of the Devil possessed."

Barry kept his eyes on them, a look of incredulaty passed over his face."Daddy, how do you know. Daddy how -?"

His father interrupted,"I just know. There's those of us can spot them. We're gonna be the corporals . Spotters'll have more rank, get some special treatment.!" He grabbed his son's arm, "Tell them to get out".

Barry turned slowly, his body strained, taut, even still his movement was fluid. "Wait, Dad. You don't get rid of people so easily. I want to find out what's going on. If they're really Devil possessed,then I want to know what that is."

"You'll get taken by them, Son, They'll pull you in. The thing is to stay away and don't listen to a thing they say." The older man's voice had become almost shrill, he edged backward, trying to pull his huge son after him. But he only succeeded in losing his grip. "Son, I tell you,come on, back into the house." When his son did not move, he turned, caught the door, and half concealed by it, yelled, "See for yourself, Son, but don't expect me to Heal you. You'll go to the purifiers. They're the only ones to help when that kind's done with you." When his son still didn't move, he shrilled angrily, "Son, don't do it. Leave them alone."

He backed into the house, closed the door and they could see him staring out the window with such a look of horror that Paul felt pity. He said,"My God,Tom, he's just terrified of us and of himself for knowing it. He's one who could learn, He has Talent of his own and doesn't know it. But who taught him to fear like that?" His eyes came back to Barry, "I'm Paul and I'm from Altos but my Family lives just out of Adwin. You must know, Tom, mayor of Adwin?" At Barry's reluctant nod, he went on."We've no intention of doing you harm, Barry, We simply want to talk. Would you come out into the yard with us?"

Barry settled,his whole body relaxed, he heard Paul's voice as though it were a balm. Paul's inexperienced use of that Voice, the modulating of sound to produce reflection of true intention, was weak but useful. He was learning to do what Tom did naturally. It put people at ease if his own intentions were good. He knew the limits of that use of Voice. But since it was built on genuine good will, it could not be subverted for selfish aims. They would have been revealed as easily. Now he watched with relief as Barry moved toward them. He had never seen a man so huge, so well proportioned, and so beautiful at the same time.

"All right, what's the problem." Barry stood towering over both Tom and Paul. His eyebrows shaggy and dark over the deepset brown eyes, but these eyes were not hostile nor afraid. Before they could answer, a woman came running up the street. She shouted,and Barry looked toward her."Janice! What's the trouble, Honey. Something wrong?"

She caught his arm,"Barry, I wanted to get here sooner because I want you to know that these men are friends. They aren't what your Dad thinks. They aren't Devil possessed." She was stumbling over her words and Tom wasn't sure she was helping,but she held to Barry's arm possessively and obviously she was a friend of long standing.

435

THE PEOPLE OF THE VALLEY

Barry nodded slowly, "I think I know that, Sweetheart. I think I know. Dad's been trying to get me to join the Builder's but there's something I don't like about them. Mostly I don't like the way they are afraid. They made my Dad afraid. When has the Valley been a place where people need be afraid of people? These men aren't afraid!" His big arm encircled her waist and he cuddled her against his hip. "Let's hear it, then. I guess you know me, but I don't know either of you, though I've sure heard of Tom."

Tom introduced them all again, telling them something of their own family. Then said,"We've just been at the other end of the Valley, probably made a record run from there to here.There are people there ripping up the sod, the old rooted mulch that's nearly three feet deep. It's at Tellings Field, Barry. They're ruining it! They're killing Telling's Field."   Barry waved one huge hand," I know what Tellings Field is like. No one would harm that Field. What d'you mean?"

"The Builders are doing it now."

"But why? Why would they do that?"

"We don't know yet. We couldn't talk to anyone. They wouldn't talk to us.They said," he stopped, how could he tell them it was William who encouraged them, and Dean who had told them to go on with their plans, "they said their leaders told them they must rip up the field and plant it. They said they had a right and they wouldn't discuss it. We wanted you to help. The big earth movers are cutting her up right now while we talk. We thought if you could stop the motors of the machines for a couple of days until we can figure out what to do, or get them to come to Council." He looked hopefully up at the giant. He wanted to reach, to Touch Barry's mind,offer an image, let him see for himself, but feared it might offend him. Janice would know, surely.

Barry held Tom's eyes. His face grim. "What d'you mean, stop the motors. Where d'you get that idea?" He sounded suspicious and uneasy and Paul felt his fear surfacing. That wouldn't do. They did not need to deal with more fear. He spoke again, using the Voice tones, projecting his intention of harmlessness.

"Don't imagine we've been studying you Barry. There's a lot of folk that could testify to your Talent." The boldness of his words were risky, but they didn't have much time. He saw Barry's eyes flicker, back and forth at them "You must know that some people have talents, Barry, You go to the Learning Center. You've been taught."

Barry held himself taut for moments more, his mind racing,faintly Tom reached and felt Janice there first. She Touched Barry's mind and let him see, let him observe in one vital, vivid picture what was happening at Tellings field and the need for his help. Swiftly she reminded him of the years they had struggled to understand his Talent and his old fear. Now,Janice said, "These people could help, help us know how to use it right.

"Thank God,for the Reach and the Touch," Tom thought.Simple as they are,they do the job with a picture. It would take so long to tell, and one picture told it all. Barry suddenly let his body loosen and smiled. "Well, all right, there's more of it than I thought then. But how can I help? I can't do anything here, I have to be within a thousand yards at least. He spoke so definitely and with such assurance that Tom realized he had studied this talent of his after all.

"We can be there in half an hour-- we'll be flying with the wind now. " Paul was breathing easier, taut with the desire to get back. To stop the brutality. For a moment there was silence, Barry looked backward at the house, finally shrugged, "Come on, let's go!" He turned to Janice, leaned to kiss her forehead, "I'll come to your house soon's we get back, Sweetheart. You wait there?" his voice was amazingly gentle. She nodded and stepped away.

They got in the car. Paul lifted off abruptly nearly unseating them. They laughed, lightening the tension further. Tom felt a great weight gone. Barry he had known as a strong man, he had not suspected such fascinating Talent. No wonder the Master Teachers had been so hard set on training in ethics and had let the training of Talents go so long. Tom realized that Barry also could Reach, though he obviously had not trained that Talent.

"How do you do it, Barry?"

Barry was busy watching the world below. He did not travel by air much, so the flight south-east was interesting to him. He had preferred long walks with the Vagabonds, found there his Mentors. With a visible effort he drew his attention back to Tom. "I don't know, I've just recently been willing to admit that I can do this. Hadn't been for Janice, I don't know as I'd have done it yet. She's remarkable. She's the one taught me not to be afraid." He shrugged, a half smile turning up his mouth lopsidedly, "Even got me to see it's not the only Talent, and that I'm not the only one. Taught me that it's ONLY a Talent, and not a Devil possession."

"You've spent time with the Vagabonds, didn't any of them help?"

He turned to look over the Earth again, "You know them. They'll never push. I was afraid and they let me be. They did little things, sooner or later, I'd have learned from them, but Janice -"he shook his head, laughed with affection, "She taught me pretty quick."

Tom persisted, "But don't you do anything at all? What does it feel like? We've been studying talents lately, trying to get a record of those Talents people have developed. And we come on few with yours. We need concentrated attention and we need people to talk about their special ones. Guess that'll have to wait 'til this crisis is past though.

Barry looked over at him again, "The fear people have's natural at first. But the Builders keep feeding it. Shouldn't be. Pa's got a bad case of it. He won't allow any of it at all now."

"How've you dealt with him?"

"Oh, Pa? He's got a Talent of his own. He doesn't know it, or won't let himself. Terrify's him. Like it did me at first. He won't let Janice in the house". He was chuckling now, a sweetness of expression in his face that made Tom think of the name 'Gentle Giant'.

"How about Janice? How'd she find you could make the Touch." Tom was surprised at himself, questioning like this, but a strange curiosity prodded him.

Barry looked searchingly at him a moment, nodded to himself and as if decided, said simply, "She loves me. And she'll be my Mate soon. You realize a lot about a person you love so" His eyes softened, had a far away look. Then he went on, " She showed me there's something greater than I ever dreamed. That Reach, and the Touch after it - it's different from talents. To Reach you have to go into yourself. Pay attention! You can see there's -- something different, something greater - maybe even holy inside us. It's then that I Touched on something grand in other people. I could tell. Some people are - really great. These talents, they're not something for just a few of us, they're for all of us. All of us together,." He spoke with a passion that surprised Tom, and Paul, listening as he concentrated on racing toward Telling, felt a great joy.

Tom knew that Janice had taught him these things, and that he had realized them for himself later. Barry went on, "When I began to look around, really see the Valley, really know about people, then I understood. At first, I thought Janice was nuts." He grinned.

Tom nodded, started to ask again, but Paul interrupted. Should we Reach to check with the Monitors, if they'd Touch with us that is?" He stopped, looked at the other two, "I suppose it might be interfering with their work. They must be busy right now."

"Well, it ought not to disturb just to send out a Touch, an inquiry. I'll make it, then they won't waste any time on us.But maybe I can find out." He closed his eyes, did not hear Barry ask, "Who are the Monitors."

His attention was drawn from the air car for only seconds but when he opened his eyes, returned to them,he felt shaken. his face was pale. Barry instantly frowned,"Not good for you was it? Whatever they are, you shouldn't have contacted them." His evident concern touched Tom sharply. A giant with a giant heart indeed.

Tom said, his face still pale,"It wasn't the Monitors, Barry, it was the Sensitives. I wonder what it must be like for them. The ones close by especially. Even I caught some of it. Their pain is like a long bleeding wound. It's not just the torn Earth and the dying creatures and plants, its the people who are willing to let that happen. Who don't know their own fears, greed and anger. All of it the sensitives feel. People like Jane for instance. He took his head in his hands, rubbed against his temples. What'll we do?"

Paul twisted in his control chair,his face worried,"Why? Tom, I saw the Monitor there. I saw her leading the little ones out."

"Yes, but it was too late for some, and she couldn't help the trees at the same time. They've started ripping out the great old trees in that grove near where we landed. Old,ancient trees they are. But it wouldn't matter, Young ones would suffer at that kind of ripping without warning too." He was silent,"The Earth is so close to us now. All of us must have some of that awareness. I felt it. But I wouldn't have if I hadn't focussed, Touched on the others. So there's pain as well as Joy in the Joining, remember."

Paul nodded slowly, turned back to his task,"How do they, the Sensitives,I

THE JOURNEY

mean, ever bear the Hunter's killing? Ever thought of that?"

Barry looked from one to the other, "What're you talking about."

Paul said, "Some people are so sensitive that they literally feel with the Earth. They feel the pain of people, of the Earth things as well as the plant world. They suffer from that pain too unless someone shows them how to shield. Because there is always some pain in living, always. Death and killing are a part of the natural order. But natural killing is different. It's the way the Hunters do it,I think. They have a ritual, before and after, and that ritual brings their prey ready, brings them prepared, so the pain is swift and done." He nodded to himself. He had wondered about the rituals many times. Now he knew he was right.

Tom stirred, "Yeah, they do. I've known that. This, though, it must be something like a rape, a tearing and ignoring of life." He reached out his hands to catch hold of Paul's chair back,"Paul, we've got to get there and stop them. The Monitors are busy, and anyway, it's really our job, not theirs now. Sensitives all over the Valley've been flocking into the Healing Centers. Even after the last time, when they found out they had to shield, they've not practiced enough. Then, some of our Healers didn't know how to teach them to build Shields." He was silent for minutes, then "Wow, never again will we -- any of us, be able to deny that the Talents and their training are real, or that we need to teach openly about them,."

"There'll be talents no one's ever known of revealed before this is through. But we've got to get there. Can we go any faster?" Barry was alerted now, worried with a knowledge that he had not had.

"I've got her at maximum, already, Barry.I don't see how --" Paul looked quickly back at the big man sitting behind him."Barry, could you do anything?"

"Do what? You don't want me to stop the motor. What could I do?"

"If you can stop one, maybe you could make one go a little faster, run more smoothly, more efficiently, so we'd get more speed. Would you try? After all, how can we know?"

Barry shrugged, "Never tried before up in the air like this. What if I -- "

Tom leaned to him,"Try Man, Just try. You can be careful."

Barry looked perplexed, started to speak, then with a another shrug, closed his eyes, let his mind move, roam into the gears, shafts, the oiled and efficient parts of the nearly silent motors running so well. He felt them, felt as he had never done, the nature of them, the fluid quality of the metals, molecular movement. It was as though he entered into them in some way,his mind 'joined' to them, merged with their faint consciousness and their patterns. He felt a fascination, a joy and slowly he began to see how the machine could increase her speed. Not much, but a little. There was a sudden smoothing of the sound, Paul and Tom looked at one another in wonder. The car did not seem to change, no lurch, no hesitance, just that smoothing and the speedometer moved up. It wouldn't help a lot, but it would make Tellings a little closer.

Barry seemed absorbed, a faint smile playing on his lips, his face relaxed,soft and they knew he enjoyed what he did. To stop a motor did not please him, but to make one work better did. Tom filed that away as one more bit of information he needed in this new world of Talents. They had passed Santiago, the emerald colors of the great flat Leaves, the brilliant globe homes and businesses, the vast trunks in which transportation whirled and industry produced the city's goods. The City blazed in the sunlight. Barry stared at it in delight. He'd seldom seen it so well. The Valley seemed to him to be so full of such beauty, such brilliance of creation. And yet there had been that rotten spot, that thing in them all that had not been noticed, that had been allowed to fester and finally to break out in pain. How had they been so careless?

Tom thought similar thoughts, watching the forests and fields, the small towns and lakes race past beneath. Fields planted with varieties of plants in patterns that seemed like great twenty acre paintings below, came to view, one after another. How had they let things go, had not taught the things that would have prevented this?"

Paul interrupted his thoughts, Touching,"Tom, you were one of the blind. How can you blame yourself?"

Barry was startled,he realized they had known his own thought. He also saw that he knew theirs. Suddenly he closed himself. It was as if he would not admit that he had seen - had known. Hearing Paul echo Tom's thought in answer, was a shock to him. They did it so naturally, so easily. As if it were all right! He realized, with a touch of envy, the depths of their friendship. They were so tuned to each other. He wondered whether he might be a part of such a Family group, if he might be a part of all this. There seemed so much to learn.

The land streamed away below and they were a few miles from Tellings Field. Barry could see the field stretching on between the rolling forested foothills. They could see no destruction yet, the vast acres rolled with tall pairie grasses, grains, flowers, it was a sea itself, rising and falling in the winds. Among these healthy, luxuriant acres were thousands of creatures. Something surely was happening there, had these men not told him, he still would have known. His heart beat faster, sorrow pressed down,and he looked at his companions. Were they friends? Would they be? He would like that. They knew the deep inner sorrow just as he did. He knew that dull resonating pain among the trees, knew and wondered. If he, who was not a Sensitive, could feel this much, then Sensitives were to be pitied.

Paul brought the little car down, circled the field, watching the people working, laughing and singing at their picnic tables. The three men watching knew those there were utterly unaware., Unaware! That, then, was the difference. How can you cast blame on those who do not know what they are doing? Barry's face was grim. He slid down into his seat, closed his eyes and fastened attention on the scene below. He searched mentally across the deep heavy grasses until he found the great machines. Then suddenly, as Paul and Tom watched, one coughed and died. The operator leaned forwad , puzzled, tried to start it again. When nothing happened, he got out and began to look into the engine cover. He had barely begun when the other machine just entering a grove a couple of acres away, quietly, with no sound, died and stood still. It's great teeth had sunk into the roots of two smaller trees and they were tipped, leaning toward the rest of the trees. People began to look at the two machines, began to gather around them, talking, gesturing.

Above them, the little air car circled once more then sped off toward Clandor. Paul looked with astonishment at Barry, still slumped, eyes closed, a faint smile on his face."You did it! And so quickly!"

Barry nodded, sat up, looking strangely tired. He was struggling with a sense of guilt. He said,"We could go home now."

Tom nodded, frowning, "But, you'll have to stay near to repeat the process when they get them started, won't you?"

Barry turned fine dark eyes to meet Tom's and said,"No, they'll not find the problem. And when they take out the engine, they'll still not find it, until they put it into a shaping unit and by then they'll know it can't be fixed. They'll need new engines. I only reshaped the main shafts slightly, but they can't be made round again." He seemed worried, "Maybe it was too much?"

Paul shook his head, "No, it will give us the time we need. It was NOT wrong to do that, Barry. You didn't hurt anyone at all and you stopped the whole operation." He looked anxiously at the younger man, wanting him to accept.

"Well, maybe I can show them, reshape the shafts after they wait for Council decision." he gave a curt nod, deciding.

Tom nodded, "Well, it's only a short way into Clandor so let's go there. I don't get down here that often, it'd be fun and interesting to see what people there are thinking ." They could see already the broad southern curve of the Green River on which Clandor was built. Nothing could be seen of the City because she was built into the trees themselves, and into the huge boulders that lay strewn across these fields like pebbles on a beach. Some were as large as small hills, scattered as though fallen from the high mountains. Tom had forgotten the geologic event that had spread them here, but people of Clandor simply cut into them and carved from the living rock their business offices, industrial plants, restaurants, and homes. Many more homes were built like airy tree houses between and through the vast forest trees, built into the branches, high in the air. Otherwise, they left the Earth untouched. To the casual passerby, only the paths and gatherings of people among the boulder buildings, suggested a city was there.

Paul was talking to the tower operator, dropped to the tree tops, to land on the grid projecting up out of the tallest trees. He sat for a moment, unable to move, feeling as though he had grown into his seat. Tom said,"Let's get something to eat. I'm starved."

They began to leave the car, Paul turned to Barry,"You're sure, Barry? How do you know?"

Barry smiled down at him, pleased with himself,"I've never really tried much before. I've not been so careful. But the little visit I had with your small motor, earlier, taught me that it's possible to go in --- go in and touch with wondrous delicacy. I don't have to stop or break anything. I can just cause the reshaping on one chamber, and the engine cannot run until it's replaced. They won't have any clues at all, so they won't think to check for such a thing. If they were willing to admit to the Talents they could find it in hours. "

Paul nodded, a look of profound grief filled his eyes, but his mouth smiled at Barry. "It's a sorrowful day, you know. A day I wish had never had to happen. We're divided. A people divided and I don't know how we can save ourselves."

But Tom grinned at Barry. "You're one of those who doesn't fight the Knowledge. When you see it, do it, feel it, you accept it. Not like some I know." He glanced at Paul and remembered Rose. Paul smiled too, nodding slowly. "That's a real talent, I think, to be able to accept what is obvious."

They stood silently for several moments, then Tom said, "Let's forget it for a few hours. We've been under a lot of pressure. Let's enjoy lunch." They walked to the lift disc that would drop them to the floor of the Tree City. He remembered a restaurant where fish was a specialty. The best River fish. They followed him, glad to do as he said.

CHAPTER NINETEEN

The Battle at Telling's field

    The breakdown of the machines at Tellings Field brought everything to a stop. But the Builders were becoming suspicious that some kind of sabatage had occurred. How it could have been done was unknown, but the brightest among them began to search that out, while others began to take the machines apart to find the flaw. Among certain extremists, the possibility of witch craft was rumoured. The implications of that created tensions between the different groups. Practical Builders who genuinely did not believe either in Talents or witchcraft, shrugged their shoulders and assumed the machines were just old. To believe either would have meant they must also admit that such evils were real. The Valley People found themselves facing what they had feared for so long. Clearly the Valley was divided. They were "them and us'.

    The Valley Council was deeply disappointed when the Builders refused to accept the World Market survey and insisted on doing one of their own. Thus this demand for more land. They firmly believed that they were right and that the market would be there for them. In the day following the stopping of the machines, the Emergency Council was deep in debate.

    Monitors, acknowledging the awakening of the people, began joyously opening their Stations, and also coming down into the Valley without any concealment. They took their places as Vagabonds, or town citizens, taking up life there in greater numbers, they wore their colors, deep blue or golden brown with scarlet edging, as freely as the Vagabonds wore theirs. All people must know of them and what they were. They saw first the danger of separation, of cleavage between the people and began to Teach and mediate even while their work at the Stations continued.

    Jessie left the Monitor Gather, enriched in spirit and mind. She was full of that new sense of possibility and Joy. Now they could truly begin,she thought. Above the steady ground of calm that grew from the roots of new realization she felt flickers of worry. Old habits sought to weigh her heart with fear that this transition would not be easy.

    At Tellings Field, after considerable argument and outburts of anger, mechanics reluctantly came to the conclusion that they could not find the problem with the machines. They decided to take them back to the museum and rent the only remaining one there. It took the two days Paul had counted on. Finally the machine was in place and they were ready again. The mood had changed however from one of holiday and picnic to one of grim determination. The stoppage had left them with confusion, anger. The trouble convinced some that evil forces were at work among them. But there were many who saw it only as hard luck. After all the machines were almost never used in these days. Those

THE PEOPLE OF THE VALLEY

who saw it as a contrived plan against them were convinced that they must best those forces by completing their work.

Every where in the Valley families held serious Gathers. The network of power the Monitors drew from that White City on the cliffs, was very real. It sang with energies such that few had known was available. Those who could See, who had begun to KNOW of the nature of Life and Spirit, whose minds were extended to merge with Mind itself,(those who had already made their Journey) no longer denied and so the speaking out, the acknowledgement cleared the air, made Gathers seem immediately necessary.

On the second day, when the Video News told of new machines already on their way to the Field, Rose and Annette came by air car from Santiago. They met with another Gathered Family whose members were friends, talked of the problem of the Sensitives and found there, Alicia, a young Monitor, already finished with her basic study. She heard their concerns and reminded them that the Sensitives must have a little time. The Healers and Station trained Sensitives would teach all of them how to Shield, but in the meantime, the western edges of Telling's Field needed to be cleared. All life must have time to leave the fields before they were ripped and plowed, the plants must have time to recede. Rose understood and agreed to ask for that time from the Builders.

They headed their little car south east, landed at the edge of the vast sun filled field. Already workers were bringing in the plants in great cases ready to be planted. Bags of seed waited on a table. The floats were loaded and young farmers waited for the signal to begin. This time, they would work immediately with planter cones following behind the Earth breakers.

Rose went toward a young man instructing an older woman ready to begin the work. The huge machines were already being brought into position. She didn't know either of them, caught at their minds faintly, testing, and that Reach caused them to turn to her. She caught her breath, keeping her balance, remembering to keep steady calm. She said,"I see you are ready to work. Could you give us just an hour? It would give us time to get the Sensitives able to work with the little ones living here. The Monitors have sent their own Sensitives to help. But we need an hour or so to prepare. So please give us a little more time."

" What do you mean? Monitors? I've heard of such people and never believed they even exist. I don't believe there are such things as Sensitives, either. They're both part of that fantasy the Valley must shed. Anyway there isn't time for more delay. What would such people do anyway? There is no need for paying attention to the animals out there. They can take care of themselves. You simply want to delay us." The young man's eyes held no sympathy, nor even understanding.

Annette had joined them and she looked with searching attention at the woman in the Mover. "You must remember. We always have prepared our fields. You must have seen it. The Plant Wizards began it, and then there were others who work with animals. Don't you remember? They can reach the animals, the plants, can prepare plants for death, or animals for moving. Give us time to bring them here. This is a very large Field."

THE JOURNEY

The woman nodded,"I've heard of that, Tommy, though I've never really believed it was real. How can the rodents in a field be talked to, let alone trees? But we've always allowed for it, you know." She frowned, looking from one to the other, "I thought it was just a ritual. Yet you say something really happens?"

Tommy scowled, his eyes hard,"No, we've been delayed enough. It's late in the season. Unless these crops are in soon, they'll not have time to settle before the cold begins. We've had enough trouble without a bunch of fools traipsing about singing rituals.

Rose held her feelings in check, reminded herself of the injunction that she must 'act with Love'. What did that mean here? She knew that if she could not stand in that energy of Love she'd never know. She said,"It only takes a little time. The Earth Sensitives will be here. The Singers are coming. and by that time,the Healers will have the new ones shielded."

"What do you mean, 'new ones'? The woman sounded suspicious, but curious as well.

Annette took advantage of that curiousity."When the work started three days ago, the people who are Earth Sensitives but who had never known or admitted to that, found themselves so full of pain, so full of anguish, that I can't describe it to you. They really had to be taken by the dozens to healing Centers because some didn't know what was wrong. Then since then, we've located others, young and old, who've not known their Talents." She felt an unexpected relief to be talking so directly about what had been taboo so recently, but the old fears still nagged behind that relief.

A woman standing near, gasped, they looked at her, her eyes streamed tears, "It's true. My own daughter, was taken like that. I had to call the Healers, She's still there, I didn't know what was wrong. It's a terrible thing to be taken like that."

Annette nodded, her eyes grateful but full of a sympathy the woman could feel,"You see, there are people who feel the pain of others more deeply than most of us. She spoke with relief that she finally could talk of these Talents that had never been mentioned aloud. Secrecy or misunderstanding from secrecy had caused more pain for humanity than talk, even harsh and selfish talk.

The woman's eyes shifted to the young man, in her own was worry, a softening."We don't want to be causing people pain though I don't see how we do. Whether I believe in it or not, they must be suffering from something to go to a Healer. Maybe we'd best let them have the hour, Tommy."

Tommy turned, looked around. The edges of the Field were lined with people coming from all directions. Their people were gathering. But carts bright with flags and the brilliant clothes of Vagabonds rolled through the hills toward the field. Many of the People riding belts like great butterflys flitted above the carts. He frowned, suddenly fearful,"Where'd they all come from? How'd they get word? How'd they know? Like that? All of them?" He looked at the woman, "We never told anyone we were going to start up again. There was no News Cast."

She shook her head. "I don't know Tommy. Maybe there's something to all this the lady is trying to tell us after all. Maybe we'd better let them do it. She says the ones that can do it are here already. We don't want any more trouble than we've had."

Tommy turned back to them, he seemed a little nervous now,"Well, then, tell them, one hour only. Just an hour."

Rose nodded, "Yes, yes! We'll need only that." She turned, caught Annette's hand and they ran to the edge of the field where she saw her old Vagabond friend Joseph standing beside Marian. They hurried toward her. With abandon, she broadcast the decision. Every person who could Send in a half mile radious would hear that Sending. The decision to give them an hour. She stopped herself, stared at Joseph. For the first time aware of the power of her Sending. He was grinning.

"You've finally admitted your power, Lady. And it's a grand one."

She looked around, the Sending had been heard. Healers, in their white and gold tunic and trousers, stood in clusters, they had come in on the floats from near by towns and cities. Monitors mingled, lost among the others. Earth Sensitives were being brought to the edges of the field. Some looked nervous,many had just learned how to shield and were not yet fully trusting of their ability. The news that there would be no destruction for an hour reassured them. No destruction, no pain. Most of them were children,though Rose saw several adults in brown and green colors. And there were Hunters among them. The Talent was wide spread cropping up in all kinds of people. Was this another manifestation of new awareness? Of expanded consciousness? She would ask Jessie, surely Jessie would know. And where was Jessie? She must be somewhere in the crowd.

She looked around, watched. There were Callers, ones who could make contact in a simple way with larger animals only. She felt a great relief. How had everyone known so clearly? How had they known to come right now? But she knew the answer even as she thought of the question. It pained her that they must do this at all. The Field must not be ruined. It must not be and they seemed now to be accepting the Builders right to do just that! What was wrong?

The Builder's permission, hard won, was a precious reprieve. They stood back, leaning against their machines, or clustered together at the edges of the field. Rose felt the huge hand of her friend, Joseph, engulf her own and she was drawn to the group of Vagabonds. "Rose, we want to make the song, we have dancers ready,look they're taking places at the four corners of the broken area here. They came in such a hurry some do not have their dancing clothes. But you'll see, they know how to lift. Now we need help to create the calm within which the dance occurs."

Rose shook her head, tears trembling in her eyes,"Joe,I'm not calm enough myself. Let me take a few minutes and I'll be ready. I can't bear the thought that we are preparing for what we cannot allow. How can we allow the destruction of THIS field. She watched the Sensitives waiting patiently in a long row the small white figures standing at intervals down the acres of freshly turned Earth. She

THE JOURNEY

met Joseph's eyes. He shook his head. She relaxed. They would need to clear no more than twenty acres on this side of the field.

He said,"This is only for protecting this edge of Tellings. There's no chance they'll harm more of it. The Council will have brought its decision. They Gathered yesterday, as soon as the news cast gave word of this. But they had to delay because they insisted that William of Altos be present and that the Monitors send someone to serve also."

"Monitor? " Rose was agast, "That's never been done. Never. They won't interfere in Valley business."

Joseph grinned, "Look!" He gestured across the field. Men and women in workers clothes were moving about among the Healers and the Sensitives. They walked with the Sensitives along the field, stood here and there among them. Their quiet seemed pervasive. And as Rose watched, her eyes cleared, she focussed, and saw without doubt the pure radiance that glowed through their bodies. The Monitors were already among them.

She turned to him,"That's unprecedented. It's -- it's -- wonderful. I'm so very, very glad." Her heart leaped and she felt a surge of real hope. A quiet,thin, small man moved toward them and with her Sight focussed, she knew he was one of those wise beings. He said,"Be at Peace, Sister. We will no longer be a divided people. We are one People together from this day on. You see that the People of the way need your help now with the Singing."

She nodded, thunderstruck,his nearness bringing her something of his stillness."Yes, Father, of course, I'll help." Then, in a plaintive voice she asked,"How is it that any good can come of all this?"

He stood watching the instructions being given to the Healers, knowing what they were being told as though it were spoken in his ear. He answered, glancing across at her, to meet her eyes,"There is always some good released when trouble is met! Disruption is not evil. It is often the clearing out of old forms for new. Much good will come if it is met well and fairly. Already we have found minds capable of what they have hidden from themselves and from you. Look yonder! The coming forth of the Earth Sensitives. We have pondered their emergence, their realization of their gifts. And the fact that they denied them. Now -- there are so many. Look too among the Healers, those with the deep and emerging capacity for compassion. We've known of them, but we had to wait for their self discovery. He nodded,smiling. "Oh, there will be good come of it, Child, because we WILL meet this well." He met her eyes,"Remember, you've been fearful of the division between you all, Citizen and Builder as separate groups? Well, now is the time for Healing, we are together!"

She nodded, trying to absorb the realization. "But you, you who are our Monitors. You are here, among us. Working among us. Isn't that interfering? You have the rule, the absolute rule that you must not interfere."

His smile was brilliant and reassuring to her,"Yes, we do indeed. That is another good coming from this. We see the People of the Valley able to take on the task. We see you choosing to lift and to refuse violence. You did not come in fury, but you stopped them gently. But best of all, you have asked for our presence among you, you called us. And therefore, we can now help. Now we do not interfere, but we join with our fellow men and women to create a greater Valley life. We need no longer be separate either, and that is a very great GOOD."

"Because we have made the choice, have chosen the higher Way, because we act from that highest nature in us, you can join us and help?"

"Exactly. You choose the highest Good and so we can stand with you. Therefore you are as we are. And we need no longer wait . We can Join our fellow men." He breathed a long joyful breath,"We too are full of Joy at these events, even as we know grief." He moved a litle away, then turned,"Excuse me!" He went down the field to the farthest edge. Rose turned to Joseph.

"O.K. Joseph. I want to be ready. I'll focus and try to sustain calm for all of you in this section." She closed her eyes, held her mind steady, higher and higher she Reached, out and beyond her self, knowing as she did that she was simply stabilized within her Soul. Higher she stabilized. And she felt the power of stillness, a breath of goodwill, of well being. Reaching, she felt the growing Touch of Love and she longed to be a part of it. To open her Heart to it. Where did it come from? She opened her eyes and walked to the great Oak under which the Vagabonds gathered. Joseph walked with her, his hand still touching her. He said,"You stand there, we need you."

She leaned against the tree, met his eyes, "Oh, thank God, Joe. Can you feel it? Someone has already begun it. Someone stronger than I."

He was turning restlessly his eyes racing up and down the ranks of people now lining the field. "We've got to keep the hot heads in check. We have few among our own people but those are angry. You have such too. They're mostly old ones. Funny isn't it. Used to be hot heads referred to angry youth. And we have those too. But look there - so many of our young ones are so still." Look!." He pointed and she followed his finger. a sigh of relief escaping her. Her eyes searched for children she knew. She trusted that her own were in Adwin watching these events with their friends on Video. Or were her own children here? If not, where were they? But the obvious readyness of those waiting, filled her attention. Maybe they could contain their anger, maybe they could act with Love after all. Then she heard the soft hum, the deep hum of a chant.She pressed her back against the tree and said,"Go ahead Joseph, We'll be here and I'll sustain the calm for you."

He nodded and went. She could hear the hum grow,then there was gently weaving into that hum the sound of instruments, violins, horns, banjos, guitars, whatever instruments anyone had, a drum kept a steady beat, others joined it. The sounds grew, and old field melodys threaded their way into the chant until it was lost in the swelling sound. They were playing the music of the Valley. so that the sound seemed to fill all the air. Like a benediction, music softly shaped and breathed through the air.

Then came the dancers out from among the People of the Way. Earth dances!

THE JOURNEY

They danced, across the fields, back and forth, weaving over the land, beneath the trees, lost in their utter absorption. Swiftly, identifying, out of years of practice, they became the dance of Earth Herself and moved it into visibility.

Finally, the Earth Sensitives began to move. Jane among them. Rose held her breath, watching the tall slim body, among the others, and there were so many small boys and girls. Their movement was also a dance, graceful, steady, they moved across the field. They raised their arms making intricate designs in the air, they lifted their heads, seemed not to need to attend to where they stepped. Then, startlingly, a Joining began, rising from the hearts of Monitors and the People of the Way, spreading out to wake and include citizens everywhere, people began to Join. Then, as that Joining strengthened, it became focussed and the completed moment of their Joining was an instant of lightning. The Light stirred around them, then subsided, so that only a faint glow continued as though from within their bodies. Visible only to those who could See. It was a wonderful reassurance.

How would those called Builders manage this? They seemed utterly entranced. Watching as though they attended a performance at Festival. They were being given visible evidence of all they had said was hidden and evil. Here, in Joy and Love, those very appearances of trance, the absortion of the artists, seemed appropriate. Here in the midst of dance and music, the sense of being uplifted, of being transported beyond oneself, seemed no longer to be feared. Rose saw puzzled looks cross the faces of those machine operators, but their eyes did not leave the fields.

Then, in the center of the area being 'cleared,' a man in brown, broad, short, with hair and beard shaggy, blond and blown by the cool wind, stood with raised arms. He seemed to leap a little, to laugh, and the merry gladness of his face was infectious for those near enough to see, and they smiled spontaniously. He rose slowly, lifted up, and no belt served him. He did this with his own power. The Builders stared, the dancers seemed not to notice, the musicians increased their speed and the music grew louder, until it seemed to reverberate throughout the land.

He lifted his arms again, and his voice rang out. The music softened and was slow, and his call, brought a change in the dance. The Sensitives and the dancers wove a pattern intricate, smooth, as though they had practiced for weeks. They followed his Voice. The music wove through the land, knitting the dancers together in one fragile fabric that grew stronger by the second. The Earth itself poured fragrance into the air around them.

Then they were suddenly still, everything so hushed it seemed uncanny. How? Why? But the answer was swift. The Callers came from here and there within the crowd. Moving also to the edges of the field, where the forests blazed with autumn colors behind them. They stood with outstretched arms, their heads up, concentrating. They began the soft intense, unceasing chant that was the Calling. The Sensitives still also, focussed their attention downward, Reaching those lives beneath the surface of Earth, reaching the trees, plants, everything that lived as well as every animal creature. Even earth worms felt that Touch though they did not respond. And the Dancers continued, moving on, around and among the Sensitives, now spread in a pattern all over the field. The people were doing this, the people. This was not a miracle of the Monitors, the Wise Ones but of the people themselves. Rose's heart sang. Already the movement in the grasses of the field were visible. The little creatures came following the sensitives, following and scattering beyond the field into the trees.

Air cars rose and fell beyond the edges of the fields, among the hills, in open stretches, they came and went. The edges of the field were dense with humanity. The Builders stood in amazement, wondering how so many knew, so soon, and why so many were here.The guards stationed at the edges of the fields, around the machines, seemed now redundant. The guns those guards held and that others had tucked away in their pockets, seemed incongruous. This was a 'DANCE'. Rose could see movement among them here and there, a whispering and questions. Then she saw William, talking to the guards. She Sent swiftly, suddenly free and rejoicing in that freedom to Send. Those near him told her that he did not trust this event, trusted nothing that was happening. She sighed in sorrow.

They must be very patient. She felt her body tense. They must restrain any possible touch of anger, violence. They must do more, they must FEEL no urge to violence. What was in them must, however, be admitted and met. Their choice was clear and it was a choice! They must be so filled with that finer, brighter power that all fear and its resentments were lost within Love. Almost with awe she acknowledged that they DID have that choice! She sighed, steadied and focussed consciousness. Beyond every part of her nature, the shifting, changing self, its many parts and reflections, she eased away, lifted attention into focus. And found further complexity of identity, but only one point of perception. Mind was a cosmic Kaliedescope, identity shifting and recreating itself endlessly. Only beyond Mind at the edge and entrance of Spirit itself, was there a point of singleness, acutely fine attention.

The word must be Sent, must be KNOWN.

Only by acting with Love could they prevent harm. And how could they act with Love unless they were within that state of Love? Aware? Rose fought to keep her point of highest perception and felt it slide, into personal identity. Again she refocussed, allowed, relinquished all struggle, and sustained attention. The point of Soul awareness was a Light that illuminated every part of her, mind and heart, body and thought. She knew what Love was, felt Its radiant Presence and stood still listening, awake to Its influence. If she could not herself stand in Love, she could at least act as Love directed.

Were all who watched capable of such sustained focus? Would the People be able to keep their own balance through out this hour? She focussed her attention, moved that attention here and there, felt the Touch of Healers.They were alert for emotional imbalances. And as she did so, she realized how many had known the same intense recognitions she had. Others too knew the

THE JOURNEY

necessity, the opening to allow Love to perform its miracle within themselves. People were Joining already in a literal bath of attention that lifted, Reached upward to that highest point of consciousness and intention.

She felt the powerful help of Monitors, finally taking their place as Valley citizens again, that right they had surrendered when they entered the Stations generations ago.

The brown man in the center of the field sang a verse, the Dancers and the people repeated and then built on it. They continued, the Sensitives were silent as before. Rose watched them, wondering. What would they do? She had never seen so many gathered, so many singing Earth Songs, and she had never heard this Song.

     Mother,Mother, life that surges through us,
We are your children, we are your voice,
     Give our voice strength, make it true.
Open the minds of our little brothers and sisters,
     Children of Earth! Open their minds to us,
That we may speak, may help them in this time.

     Listen, little friends, little brothers,
Listen Sisters, children of our Mother,
     There is danger, there is change!
There is danger, there is Change!
     We must move, must run to new places,
Take your young, your families,
     Move to new places,abandon these snug burrows.

Move! Move! Time to move to safety.
     All, everyone, Move, gently move, come with us
We will protect you, will make your Journey safe.
     Move out of home burrows, not in terror as in fire,

Not in panic,as when floods come.
     But in safety. Move through the grasses into the forests,
     Out of the burrows and across the land.
We will protect you, we will guide you.
     Follow our Light. See it, follow the good Light.

Follow the Light, See it! Follow the Light.
     Hunters will forebear from hunting,
None will persue,None will persue.
     We hold you safe,safe in the running,
Into the forest, into strange meadows.
     Safe into new burrows, new nests.

Let there be peace among us this day.

And as they sang the words, a virtual ribbon of images poured from their minds, focussed to any attentive mind, animal or human. Each phrase was an image, creating for those subconscious ones, meaning.

The singing grew quieter, creatures stirred slightly among the grasses, moving just faintly at first, through tall, wild plants. Then more and more, foxes, squirrels, chipmonks, rabbits, snakes, skunks, voles, mice, moles, and more, they came. The numbers seemed astonishing to the watchers. Earth seemed to literally move itself as they came from their burrows and began to run along just in front of the Sensitives, like a living stream growing in strength as they proceeded. Rose thought she saw the look of awe, of wonder in some of those intelligent eyes.

They lifted their heads, looked on those human guides, and scurried on toward the forests beyond the great Meadow. Only these few acres need be cleared, but as Paul watched, he thought how prolific was the life of this Earth. How could there be so many? They moved as creatures do before a fire, paying no attention to one another, simply racing for safety. How could they know why? They only knew the inexorable call, the powerful drawing forth from the Sensitives who walked above their Earth. They moved with fast beating hearts, excited but not afraid. And yes, there were a few whose eyes lifted, saw the shining presence of these who led and were wakened to an uneasy awareness. These were the Singers, and creatures knew already, through generations, the Singers would not harm.

The plants began too to change, a listlessness, a drop of leaf, a sagging of the grasses, life fled from them. The trees tipped half over by the Mover yesterday, began to loosen leaves, their color fading. The plants prepared themselves to die.

The soft singing, the steady movement of the dancers, beating their light rhythm upon the Earth, the absolute quiet of the healers and the rest of the watchers, created a quality of calm so deep that even the guards relaxed their hold on their weapons, the most militant among them found themselves wondering what they were doing there. William, returned from his appearance before the Council last evening, stood fighting against his own desire to acknowledge the sense of calm, of rightness. His attraction to this ritual. What ritual? And then he remembered. The Ritual of the Living Field. He had seen it performed once before, seen and thought it impossible. Now, he felt a deep troubling, a surfacing of his persistent doubts. Doubts he had been able to quell for several weeks now. He resented their arousal.

The sea of movement around the feet of the Guides grew like waves with a rustling audible within the singing. A family of rabbits, from one edge of the field, ran swiftly together, ignoring another group that came from the other side. Running! Their shining backs catching the sun, all the little creatures ran and as they reached the edge of the forest, they moved off, scattering in every direction, finding shelter, finding new entrances and beginning with a rapidity that astonished the watchers, to dig new entrances. The music grew, lifted over the trees, penetrated the land, seemed to tremble among the billions of leaves, turning already in the autumn sun.

The afternoon air was filled with light, a light that was more than the sun gave. Rose felt the flow of energy through the air, the tenderness of concern of those who sensed the Earth so deeply. The Builders had all turned to watch this exodus of creatures from the land. It could not be denied, it could not be called evil. Guards let their guns drop, no longer able to take their eyes from the remarkable scene. William stood finally silent, accepting and surprised. How could there be so much life in this Earth. What then happened to them when the great blades of the earth movers tore it apart? He had not thought of that, never imagined such life was there. Finally the animals were moved, disappeared into the forest with a quaking and rustling and digging of Earth where they deepened their new warrens.

The wide river of land, edged by the dark exposed soil ripped open two days before, was as though struck by terrible cold. Death lay across this ribbon of land between the ripe, rich flourish of life on every side. And the contrast was an informing.

There were hundreds of people now, gathered along the Field's edges, to the consternation of the Builders. The Council had not sent their decision, the Builders wanted some accomplishment now, before any decision was made. And so, they watched the strange exodus of the children and adults who had led the creatures to safety, watched until the dancers left the field, the Vagabonds moved their carts and themselves farther into the forests, as if seeking escape from this blighted land. Then impatiently Builders began moving their machines into position. The People turned away in sadness and utter quiet while this edge of Telling's Field was raped. Paul turned worried eyes to Tom, but what was done was done. Hopefully, they would hear soon the Council's order to stop. He was sure there could be no other decision. They too went, following the Sensitives and the Vagabonds, seeking new council among them.

-------- --------- ---------

Tom had no knowledge of a gathering in the north Valley early on the morning when he and Paul raced to try to stop the Builders. On that morning when the two huge machines began ripping out the land, young men gathered before the Video, watching, seeing what was happening, what the big machines did to this sacred land. While the boys watched the Healers had begun to come. They saw people coming to ask the Builders to wait, saw their refusal, and their anger grew. So they turned away from watching, they felt a profound necessity to act. They saw nothing of the stopping of the machines.

Young Steel, his face a mask of grim determination, watched and felt his heart beat fast with excitement. He interpreted it as indignation. He did not recognize the flood of righteous justification for his plans. He accepted this justification with simple gratitude. Now, there was ample reason, now there was excuse to attack, to demonstrate that the young men of the Valley were at least able to fight their attackers. To protect their people. Now the people would see who could protect the Valley!

"It's time, men," he cried out to those watching with him. "There's no one doing anything at all." Did you see how they ignored the requests to wait? They're not intending to stop. They'll have the whole field ruined in a couple of days."

Another boy frowned, "But what can we do, Steel? They're already at it?"

We've all been in the new Teaching. We know some of you can do something called 'Reaching!" He looked around furiously. "Well, now's the time! Reach! Do it,whatever it is! Get word to every man who's willing. We'll go down and stop them. We will stop them even if no one else will!" Steel felt the heady excitement, the rush of pure exultation. He said, "Just call and let whoever hears you meet us in the south east of Clandor."

They had experimented with new found budding ability to Send. Most of these young men could not make a true Reach. They all did their best, and each also called by video phone, reaching boys they knew would want to go. They got the word out. Four among them not only Sent loud and clear, but could make a tentative Touch. One was already an adept and knew Joining, but not with these friends. That one was Andrew. Within half an hour they all began the journey south to Telling's Field. They went as rescuers. Most clearly their excitement carried a feeling of urgency, emotion was easier to Send even than imagery, though humankind has been doing both for centuries without realizing it. Their friends responded to this pull, this fire of conviction, this tide of ancient fury and self righteousness. So they traveled toward Clandor, picking up others as they went.

The excitement caught at the minds of the five young men with Talent, attracted in spite of themselves, convincing themselves that they would go as rescuers. They arrived at Clandor and met their South Valley friends. They went to a cafe where good food was available to talk, eat, and plan. Steel was an astute general. He had read that an army moved on its food and pure excitement. He must keep the pitch of that excitement high. The Builders had played well into his hands. None of these boys knew of the stopping of the machines. They acted as conspirators, in secrecy.

Steel looked around the table drawn to a corner where they could have a little privacy. He was aware of the lift that hot food gave. Clandor was surprisingly quiet, he looked around, few people were walking in the pathways outside. He was puzzled, but shook his head, it wasn't his business. He talked easily,"We're the strong ones of the Valley now. The old ones aren't trained, they're afraid,it's been too long since the Valley has needed such help. But now, the Builders have shown their colors,they must be defeated. Absolutely brought to know their place among the People." He felt the resistance to that bigotry, felt and lifted his head to glare resolutely at one or two faces until they dropped their eyes. Surely they could see!

"The old ones are frightened, they've remembered too much of the past. Even the Master Teachers have gone off lately, you all know they left the Center two weeks ago. Some've not come back yet.I think they're as scared as the old folks." He stopped, let his eyes touch every young pair of eyes, gather that will behind those eyes to himself and then on to the next. "It's obvious that we're the only ones in the Valley with courage to meet this danger." He looked around, the eyes were responding more properly. He felt satisfied.

He looked at two young men, their eyes hooded, watchful, one from Clandor, one from Santiago. These were his rivals. He knew their power and their strength. He must convince them but also keep his leadership before them. He said,"I've got a plan." Everyone hushed, willing to listen. Their eyes shining, eager. He went on,"We 've got to get to the bald mountain from here. We can see what they're doing at that high point above the trees but we've got to get there without attracting attention. So we'll split up. Then go in from all directions one or two at a time, drifting in. We've done that before in games, so do it now for real! We'll make final plans there. How does that sound, Taggart? Ronald? You both are good at strategy." He must give power to them both,, so that they would not take it. The truth was that in that time he hoped to have his own plans in place.

Ronald, Santiago's fierce eyed young leader, champion of the Young Hunters, winner of the Valley trophy for decathelon for two years, turned to face Steel. Even sitting he towered over the younger boy, his voice deep, commanding. Andrew, listening, caught the undercurrent of humor, the easy confidence he radiated. Steel assessed this opponent rapidly, knowing that he could not defeat him, he must make him an ally. Ronald said, "You've been leading the north Valley for some time Steel. We've heard of you. So we'll go along with that, so far."

Steel heard his message, and they measured each other, their eyes steady. The others watched, seeing the judgement. Steel nodded with a jerk of his head, made his decision." Then you'll command the Mid Valley troop, Ronald." He knew he must be the one to speak that decision,even though it was an obvious one. For him to say it placed him still in command. He turned to a shorter, heavier, young man from Clandor, a young Forester and Archer, whose name was Taggart. He seemed to radiate strength, a quality that gave him height greater than his physical height. Steel knew here again was a leader, he must mark his own place swiftly. He said,"Taggart, you command the Clandor men!"

Taggart nodded, his eyes narrow, seeing Steel's strategy, but willing to let it be. He said,"Our men are ready. We'll come in from the south though. You take the west approach, Ron, and you, Steel,the north. "He knew that to make even such a command placed him in the minds of the others. "We can arrive without making a fuss." His quick direction surprised the other two. They met his eyes, no one giving way, and finally each boy nodded. Taggart's satisfaction did not show, he used his knowledge of the local countryside to advantage, "Right, we'll meet out at the Rock. It's an overlook and from there we can see the Field and what's going on."

Then, recognizing the need for himself to place at least one command among them, Ronald raised a large hand and said,"What weapons you use best, get ready, bring with you." There were startled looks. Though several had hidden weapons, no one had spoken of them. These boys were Learning Center trained, they would not think of weapons to settle a dispute. But the romance of the game had overpowered their better judgement. Most of them were mind-blind, knew of no Touch, had seen no glimpse of Light, of a higher way. But all of these young men knew of the IDEA of Spirit. All had been taught to practice the Convictions. Now, in the heat of excitement, feeling his own pack of arrows nestled against his shoulder, seeing a bulge of what must be a gun on Taggart's hip, he thought the rest should also have weapons. He forgot that his own training as a Hunter gave him discipline about when and when not to use weapons that the other boys lacked.

They thought themselves speaking in utter secrecy, yet if they had taken thought at all, they would have known that any strong mind could have over heard their careless unshielded attitudes and emotion. The law of privacy was so strong in the Valley,that it lulled their caution. Their skills were not honed enough to automatically shield.

When they left the cafe, the late sun blazed through the forest trees of Clandor. Great spreading oaks, half a dozen varieties, some red, some as yellow as the beech, ash,walnut. The world around them deep with the quiet, fragrant peace of autumn stillness.They did not think to wonder at the incongruity of this fury they would unleash in that lovelyness around them. Andrew and those who were Mind Aware with him, felt the strangeness, as though they walked in a dream. The still land around them, the slight breeze, the lovely autumn day,light gleaming through the colored leaves, surrounded them with magical beauty. It was almost a holy hush, thought Andrew, as he waited for his turn to climb the blue air and sail outward to the pinnacle.

Those who watched beyond,in the mountain Stations, who stood at the ends of every threading of that network of energy and awareness that blanketed the Valley knew the festering of thought, of youthful excitement rising like a knot, a dense,turgid knot, tied together by a passion understood but questioned by those who saw. One young woman, just recently completing her internship, allowed finally to stand among the net workers, was assigned the task of following that knot that blazed so fiercely with passion. It was not her task to listen to ideas, but to know of attitudes, images, and to pay attention to where the clustering energy went.

Alicia had come to the room at the top of the central tower where other Monitors were gathered, had been for days. They kept their numbers rotating so that some one constantly stood to keep the network whole. The young ones took a turn, saving the strength of the old for events that seemed crucial. The energy that flowed literally through their body-minds was enormous. She had practiced so long to learn how to release obstruction in herself and so to allow free unobstructed flow. For it was powerful energy, the energy of Love Itself that the Valley needed now. She too must know how to offer herself as a vehicle for that

THE JOURNEY

down flow of energy from that greater Source beyond them all. There must be no personal needs or confusions, no self righteous outrage, deflecting its flow at this time. Alicia knew the symptoms of her own self righteousness and had learned how to let it drain away. She had on the one hand to clear herself of attachments, stand Soul Conscious and empty of personal intention, except that of standing aware and steady. In this crucial time, they must yet wait. The human race had to choose as one mind, they, the Elders of that race, could not force that choice or it was no choice. But in her heart lay quiet the plea to her fellows to look to their highest Heart's knowing.

At this time, the two great machines were beginning their ripping of Earth. Tom and Paul had arrived to plead with them to stop, others came, to do the same. Alicia knew she must dampen her own desires, wishes. The choice was not hers.

There were rapidly fluctuating signals in Telling's Field. Alicia had listened as Father Charles explained. "Our task is to maintain the inflow and to stand firm against that dark energy that seeks to feed the lowest desires of humankind. We feed the highest, we serve the Soul Itself among humanity. Humankind is ready to make the choice toward the direction that we, their brothers have taken for so many centuries. We wait for them, and we cannot make the choice for the rest of our kind. But now, it's obvious, they begin to make it themselves. That energy of Love that we step down and extend to them, wakes the very Soul within them. Rouses the spark of Spirit that has lived in them forever. That flow of Love must grow stronger and nourish and care for the new born consciousness that is Humanity. You know, Alicia, that we believe that Humanity, the new 'humanity,' is being born." He smiled at her surprise.

"I suppose, Alicia, that none of us expected that there would be so many awake, ready to realize the Light. We've kept watch, done our work here, longing for this day, yet we didn't expect it. Now it is here, there are millions through the world AWARE. In these past months it rapidly grows to billions. Even still, some of us didn't dare to hope that it was truly time, that all this recent trouble was the disruption before the Awakening. Our Elders told us that when the old patterns break, begin to fall apart, the Light will come through and human minds will See. Now we know they were right."

In his voice was the radiance of a Joy still not fully released. Could it happen? Was humankind ready to choose to enter into its heritage of SPIRIT? He was silent, letting his thoughts run backward in memory. He watched her. "There! You have it. Your power is pure, is clean and open and you support the mind web. The strands of the web are strong. We will be able to count on your skills, Child. But right now, we want you to watch the movement of these young men. They are full of a primitive excitement, both conscious and unconscious minds caught up in it. We cannot know what it means. We cannot interfere but we know that in each of them is the Knowledge." He frowned darkly for a moment, "Though most of them are unconscious, there are five who are conscious. They all are devoted to the Convictions and we trust that they will remember them before they do harm."

"Then I must make no attempt to influence the action of these people?"

"No. You know that is not our task. We want you to keep watch that we may know their actions. If they reach for help, though it may be a blind Reach, alert us." He brushed the thick, grey hair back from his forehead, his hand slim and strong. The deep blue robe he wore whipped softly in the gusts that broke against the high tower. They stood on a balcony that circled it. The sun warm, bright on the green forests and fields below seemed utterly peaceful. She looked across the wide land, stretching for miles below, listening, her mind tuned in to the fine vibrations thrumming throughout the air. She reached out one slim dark hand to touch his arm for a moment. It was the gesture of a child. He smiled gently. She was little more than that after all. He watched her a moment. Her dark calm face framed in a halo of tightly curling hair. The snowy student tunic and trousers blowing softly against her body, emphasized her vital young figure. She said,"They're young boys. Surely they won't cause harm."

"Young boys, nearly men, who are filled with messianic zeal can upset the balance easily , my dear. The old habits and desires still live in most human hearts. We are a people breaking free from our past, from our darkness and that struggle to break free is not yet done. We must know if there is danger of regression here."He sighed, then smiled a joyous smile that comforted her," Oh, Alicia, don't fear. In these weeks, so many have made that choice. So many more open their minds. Already we are free to help more then we have ever been. Free to make ourselves known to these younger brothers and sisters."

She nodded, turned to the east, where in the distance she could see the pale green of the Telling's Field running like a broad sea and lapping at the edges of thick forests. She nodded thoughtfully,"I will settle down here then, Father. I will focus and hold steady."

He nodded, "Don't hesitate to Reach to us if need arises. There are two other students focussing on small turbulences. We will hear you if you call. I must go to change to tunic and trousers, there is work below to do." He watched her go, conscious that her skill was greater than she knew. She was rapidly becoming fully mistress of that power within herself. And when she did, the Stations would become another kind of place. For there were many now coming to them with such great sensitivity and strength.

Alicia settled into her seat at the edge of the Tower. She observed the arrival of the young men at Bald Mountain. They settled in like great crows, chattering in the soft night air. Their excitement growing, their sense of mission, of rescue, saviours of their homeland, strong. They watched the Builders under the great Trees, making fires, cooking dinners and it seemed to them a grand picnic. They could hear the laughter, sense the feeling of a party, celebration. They saw the huge machines stopped in their small rivers of dark open Earth and did not know why. They thought they had simply ended their work for the day. They saw mechanics working, the entrails of the machines brought out, parts being worked on, but they did not know why. The boys were sure that the Builders did not

THE JOURNEY

imagine that Valley people had courage enough to stop them. They thought they would have their way. Steel smiled grimly. They would teach these people a lesson.

"What happened to the machines. Why'd they stop? A young boy, thin and barely begun to stretch to his future height, came to stand before the two leaders.

Steel looked to Taggart before he thought, then hastily answered, wanting to be the one who could."It's evening, stupid, why shouldn't they stop for dinner?" He knew his irritation worked against him and was honest enough not to blame the boy. He started to speak a gentler caution but Taggart was searching the Field, watching, and shook his head, "There's something else. Something's gone wrong for them I think."

Steel got up, stretched his body to see better and finally said, "The machines are all fired old, no wonder to me they stopped. Maybe it'll slow them down. Make our work easier." The other boys nodded,

It had begun to grow dark and even the frantic work around the machines had ended. They saw people lift off, on belts and air cars, toward the north.Other people came back to the tents and cook houses for their evening food. The Valley people who had gathered to watch and to grieve, had begun to leave. They waited for word from the Council, perhaps during the night, or at least by morning it would come. They had word already that the debate was a difficult one, that the Council had sent again for William, and for Adam of the Vagabonds, others from Bend and Clandor. Did this mean they must make new laws, new Convictions, for their Valley Constitution? That could -- was - taking time.

The young men on their pinnacle, spread their sleeping gear, built small fires, but heated food in their power back pots. It felt more like a holiday, a celebration and old remembered childhood journeys into the wild. It was difficult to think of troubles.

Steel and Taggart sat together assessing the situation. The trees below rustled,the air was soft. How could there be danger here? But Andrew, watching them, felt something wrong. Something tugged at his mind. He cast his eye about. Let his mind Reach very softly, for he did not want to trouble anyone aware enough to Send but unaware of further Mind Reach. Instantly he felt the response. With him were four others whose Touch was true. Those also, he knew now, were tentative and uneasy.

Before Andy could identify any of them, Ronald strode over to the two other leaders, and standing before them, he turned to the gathered boys, most of them already sitting in their sleeping sacks. He said, "We've got to arrive early, before they've time to do more damage, arrive and surprise them. We've got to put a stop to this destruction . So we pray to Earth Mother this night. We must dedicate ourselves to this task." His eyes were full of a devotion, a conviction that Andrew felt almost like a constricting band through his mind. Yet Ronald was absolutely sure. The other boys felt that sureness. It steadied their thoughts, gave them greater courage. Andrew felt the power of it himself but resisted succumbing. He wanted to succumb, to give himself to that devotion and loyalty of Earth. He did not want to question just now. These three stood, establishing their leadership in these ways. He would accept their choices.

The plans were made. Each group would approach from a different direction. They would surround the machinery, prevent it from starting in the morning. At the same time, another group made up of boys assigned by each leader would circle the camp. They would stand with arrows ready. Guns raised.

It was then that Andrew found himself shaking his head as if to shake away a blur. What was that? This talk of weapons? The Hunters among them were deadly marksmen. Others had served apprentice with the Hunters as one or more of their Journeyings. The thought made the hair on his neck lift. He cried out,"Wait, wait, Surely you are not talking of killing, or harming anyone! We cannot harm them, we cannot --". he was silenced by Ronald who looked at him with a smile that condescended.

"Andrew, that's your name isn't it? You're one of those who Touch. Maybe you even Join, though I don't quite beieve what I've been told of that. But it makes you a danger to us,you know. That's one of the things they hate in us. The people who JOIN. You'd better let the rest of us do the planning. You see, you can't think rightly for this." He smiled, a strangely sweet smile. But Andrew looked at him in shock. He wasn't even listening to me, he thought. He drew himself in, not wanting to have to leave this band, not wanting to listen to his own caution.

Steel looked at Andrew and gestured, a sign of dismissal, "It's not a problem,Men. We don't have to hurt anyone. But we stand firm. We show our strength, make them understand we won't accept what they're doing. They'll back off! It's true we have Hunters among us, but we're not Hunters of people. If we're sure of ourselves, together, we can't be divided. If we're not divided we won't fail." He looked around at them, standing now,his thin, dark body seemed almost delicate beside Ronald's huge one and the short but powerful frame of Taggart."We just have to show them we mean business! All right? Everybody ready?"

There was a weak cheer, then it strengthened and rang out over the hills. They grinned, pleased suddenly with themselves. Most thought no one could have heard them, their cry would be like the wind at any distance. But Andrew knew better. Others frowned. They settled to get some sleep.

Andrew curled up in his blanket. His mind was troubled, his heart divided. He thought to Reach, to call to the Family, to ask someone to help him decide. But then, with a frown he shook his head. He had to decide for himself. After all, he wanted to be part of this and although most of these boys did not know of Touching, those who did, would learn of his doubts. His troubled mind wrestled with doubt. Then he closed off those thoughts, thrust them aside and was suddenly asleep.

He thought he'd had only a brief nap when someone was kicking him gently. Steel was going around waking everyone. He was again taking the lead, small things like this put him at an advantage over the other two. Andrew watched as the leaders woke and their instant consternation that it was Steel up first and taking charge. He had waited until last to wake them. Andrew yawned and pulled on his jacket. It was like a children's game, he thought. they were being so careful about noise. He felt his mind snap to attention, felt a faint Touch through his guard. He automatically had closed, he could not betray their where abouts. But a new question probed and would not be silenced. 'Am I playing a game here too?'

They all gathered where the food was being heated. He sensed without actually opening his guard that others wondered too. Well, he thought,if the Builders listened to them, they could stop this whole thing. And it would be them, the young men, who did it. A pride suffused him. The Builders must be taught that the Valley would not accept their invasion of its land. It was a right thing to do. He reassured himself and imagined them all standing there, clear eyed and strong, stopping the depredation, firmly setting things to rights. He imagined the Builders and other Valley people seeing their mistakes and honoring these young men who saved them. They would stand firm and the Builders would be convinced. He let the image linger a moment, then went to eat. Taggart had supplied Hunter's Pack food. They talked quietly, their voices hushed, but excited. Their faces shining in the early morning light, black faces, brown, ruddy round or slant eyed faces, Andrew, watching, was struck with their beauty, their youth and the fire of their convictions.

Then they saw the movement of machines, and watched,, astonished and puzzled as two machines were ferried out of the field and another, coming in the distance like a great clumsy dark cloud, approached, came closer and was finally landed down at the edge of the dark strip that had been opened. People cheered there and the boys looked at one another."Whatever's happened doesn't change our job." Taggart spoke quickly, wanting to have his voice heard before this new event."We've got to get ourselves ready. Close down the camp, but leave our stuff here, we'll pick it up later. It's time for us to go down there. And remember exactly how we planned."

Ronald shook his hed,,"Wait, we've got to eat. No one'll do well on an empty stomach. It'll take only a half hour more. they'll not do much in that time." The faces of the other boys registered such approval of that idea that the other two leaders nodded and food was taken from their packs. It did take nearly an hour, after all, but their spirits were high. In that time the new machine had begun its work.

They drank water from a clear spring twisting down from the rocks, strapped on their belts then, through the rising mists of the Valley floor, they lifted. The mists gathered and loosened, were thick as buttermilk and then faded away to nothing.They chose to travel inside the thick clots weaving where they could. Each group took off, they would approach the field from north, east and west. They landed without mishap on high limbs of trees,a little distance from the field .Their fingers and faces were cold,their breath coming fast and their expression set with conviction. In the distance through the trees they could see the movement, the great machine at its rumbling destruction.

And then, everything was stopped, people were talking, gesturing. Adults and children in loose brown and green clothes, barefoot silent had begun spreading over the immediate field. Each of the leaders of the young men, held up a hand, waiting. Something was happening. They heard the music, the sweet sound of pipes and strings, the voices. It transformed their world. They stood in astonished silence. Had their elders after all planned something? Would their own glory be taken away? They watched tensely. Then they saw the dance begin and recognized it as a dance of the Healers. They guessed that someone planned to clear the field. That, at least, they knew about though few had seen it happen. Well, they could wait for that. Fascinated they watched, their young faces tense, alert, glancing now and then at one another, frowning at their leaders, waiting for directions.

Now, the movement through the fields began and they watched in amazement, for they had never believed the possibity of such a quantity of small creatures that ran behind the feet of those who 'cleared'. Envious, a little angry that the impetus of their small army had been stopped, the three young leaders, waited, each nervous, trying to see beyond the activity through the trees, to be sure neither of the other leaders moved his troops into action prematurely. They must wait on the agreed upon signal. At least they had that. Andrew sensed their impatience with the obvious necessity of the wait. He wanted to Send an image, a picture to each leader, but knew he must not. These young men could not receive such a Sending adequately.

Then, finally the dance, the singing and the strange soft light faded, the Sensitives were entering the woods, walking among the trees near where the men waited. They flinched, some of their own excitement was being aborted, lost to this gentle work. They waited, impatient, angry, and filled with new turbulence of doubt, until most of the Vagabonds and the field clearers had gone.

Andrew looked around. In his group, behind Steel he saw that strange tight look on these young faces and was startled into awareness of that righteousness. He felt another stab of doubt. But pushed it aside in the need for action. The Builders had gone to the Machine, were readying it to begin the work. Now, the signal! Relief, heavy and exhilerating. They found their posts, lifted above the trees, drifted over the field and then, dropped from the air into position and to the utter amazement of the busy Builders. The young men stood surrounding the camp and each piece of equipment, their weapons held and aimed. Never had anyone of this Valley, seen weapons held and turned toward any group of human beings. They stood stunned, unable to fit the experience into meaning for long moments.

Andrew stood beside a huge floater with many fine sharp wheels beneath it that would pulverize the soil after the Rippers had broken up the sod. He felt satisfaction. They had succeeded. All would go well. Everyone was surprised. It would work. There would be no argument. Surely the Builders would see their determination and give up resistance, now that the issue was forced. It seemed so clear to him. He had no gun, nor bow and arrow. He had refused to turn any weapon toward any human being. He remembered the scene back on the

THE JOURNEY

pinnacle, a moment when he almost deserted.

His refusal had resulted in anger from Ronald. But Steel aleady knew Andrew would not. He had nodded,"We've got two others like that. They can do that thing called Reach though and maybe we can use that. They've got the most to risk because Reaching's what the Builders hate,you know. We can use them to warn us. They can listen in on the Builder's plans." He had grinned at Ronald, but turned an angry eye on Andrew.

At that comment, Andrew had felt a tentative Touch near and then Ralph stepped up beside him. He was grateful. Ralph said,"No! I'll never eavesdrop. Never!" Ronald had tried to argue, but Steel spoke with such absolute confidence, that they listened.

"You warn us, nevertheless, those of you who can do that. I don't know what it's like, but I'm told you can sense other people's attitudes. So, let us know if there's danger". He hesitated, frowning at them."We've got to show them we've got power, can't you see that?"

The others had accepted. Ronald had thumped his hand against a stone and said,"We've got a couple like you too. We'll use them as scouts. So be alert! We want to be warned!" And so establishing their control in these ways,the two leaders had accepted these five boy's refusal to bear arms. A number of others shifted position avoiding the distribution until their were not weapons left. Steel said,"There aren't enough for everybody, but the rest of you carry clubs. He indicated a bundle of stout clubs. The boys hesitantly took one and felt it's weight gingerly, then used it as a walking stick. Andy had managed even to avoid those. But he remembered the moment with a frown.

Now, beside the floater, with the Builders beginning to stir after the initial surprise, Andy waited, alert, watching, his heart full of conflict again. He could feel some powerful pressure against his mind like a persistent Touch. He shook his head. What? Who?

Alicia watching, saw his receptiveness,he WAS aware of the powerful energy flow, the streaming of pure Love through the net of Mind. She focussed, wanting to Reach, to Touch those of the young men who COULD Reach. Why were they so closed? She hesitated. Would that be interference, to press against that closure? The boys who had asked Andrew to warn them had not imagined what that could mean.

Alicia watching, saw the Builders surprise. Should she call for help? The weapons startled her too, but she felt no intention to use them. The Builders were looking around. She saw them frown as they realized these young men surrounded their camp. What were they doing here? She saw astonishment, then disbelief, then growing anger among the Builders.

"Hey,who the devil d'you think you are? What're you doing here? We've waited for that fool ceremony, now we'll not wait longer!" a red haired man cried out, running toward two boys standing braced, their legs wide, bodies leaning forward, their gun aimed toward the frowning crowd. He stopped suddenly, nearly tripping as he fully realized that those guns were there.

THE PEOPLE OF THE VALLEY

"We're asking you to hold off until the Council decision is made."

A woman came to them. Andrew saw similar confrontations across the field where other boys stood holding their weapons toward the crowd."I can't believe it," she said, "I can't believe any Valley citizen would threaten another!"

"Don't you realize you're threatening the whole Valley with this destruction here?" Andrew's hurt and anger was out. Said! He felt relief as if she would immediately see the point and call the action off. She simply looked at him in disbelief.

"Look, it's just a field of grass. Sure, it's a park, but it'll prove that the land can produce more than it's ever done." Her face was softer, her eyes moved from one boy to the other, then rested on the blue glint of the gun.She shook her head, frowning, Then with a sigh her face cleared, "How can you do this, bringing weapons against your fellows? Is that the way you want the Valley to go? Think, young man. Think!"

Alicia felt the rising tension and called out her report. Three were released from the Joining that was the Network. Three powerful Senders came to settle themselves near her and turned swiftly to her vision. She had a great Talent for visual image and they simply opened their minds to encompass it. They saw what she had seen. They said,"Yes, you must try to Reach to these minds among the young men who saw themselves as Saviors. Go ahead, do it. It isn't interference now. The people have decided. You are aware of the Gathers all over the land and what they have accomplished. People have begun to come together."

But as Alicia focussed her attention, she realized they were not surprised at what these young ones had done. It could be expected that such eager young men might imagine themselves able to save the Valley. It simply must be corrected. They would listen,wait and watch. The five mind-aware boys among the self appointed Saviors might become keys to resolution, if they could be Reached.

But the news of this happening spread through the now open Network. Through the growing power of mind to mind Touch, the sense of danger, of confrontation, woke people all over the Valley, brought them to their Video screens, worried again. Most importantly they saw how strong they could be as they Reached unhesitatingly to one another. Listening, the people opened their minds. Together they became aware of that great outpouring of Energy. Even as the Touch began, the news people reached Clandor and began broadcasting what was happening.

All over the Valley people gathered, recognizing their Joined power, and seeing through their Videos the need for attention. They sought to receive that energy that was available. They began to know that its Source was beyond consciousness and that IT was everywhere. A stream of that energy flowed from the City, carefully stepped down to make it bearable for humankind. It poured into the Stations and then, stepped down again,it flowed on into every listening, receptive mind. From there it could flood the Valley. The steady trickle broke through those few who resisted, who had not yet acknowledged their own capacity to be aware. With the gentle persistence of water entering into sand, it was pervasive, that power of Love.

As people focussed and became more aware, they were able to acknowledge that flow of impersonal Love, Love like none other they knew, yet holding in itself all love they ever knew or imagined. So great was it, so tranforming of the heart's vision that new understanding shaped in their minds as they were receptive. The trickle increased through joining minds, broke through old patterns of fear and of self created notions of what Love is, absorbed angers, lusts, desires, and illusions so that vision cleared. The illusions of what the world is, what humanity is, broke into the clouds and mists that they were and new perception of what was real was like Light entering darkness. Even the smallest corner of human life had new meaning, was revealed. The trouble at Telling's Field had waked the Valley after all.

Old thought structures that could not stand before this Light of Knowledge trembled and came apart as naturally as sand falls from a loosened hillside. Each recognition, created greater space into which further recognition could occur.

Monitors from the four stations held attention without wavering, distributed all they received as a River breaks into a delta before it enters the sea. They knew that none among them could have born alone the power of it. This which revealed Itself to them, had its seed in every person, in every living thing. And that seed broke its long closed shell, waked and began to sprout as that greater Light, like a water of Earth, softened the shell and drew that hidden Life forth. And these Valley people now had eyes to See. It was a revelation of Spirit. Only together could they receive, carry the power. And only together could the people of the Valley bear what they became aware of. The fourth level of life waked in people of the Valley, from eons of being conscious through body, emotion, mind, they were becoming conscious in Spirit. Humankind unfolded further into what it was becoming.

The awakening of mind to Spirit had leaped across eons of dispair and once begun, it swept all in its path. Human consciousness could not resist its own new birth. Monitors, realising this flowering of Consciousness, knew with Joy that the pressure created by the 'troubles' in this Valley had triggered an inevitable effect. The balancing of negative and positive could begin.

Now at Telling's Field there must be played out this part of the drama. The boys stood resolute. Taggart nodded to Steel, for it had been agreed that Steel would speak. Steel walked from his place, went to stand beside the Builders who stood in amazement that was turning to anger. They had just begun to sit down to eat, and their hunger increased their irritation. He said, loud, clear, in that voice that had brought him followers,"We have come to end this destruction. You do not have permission to destroy this field. This is a field sacred to every Valley citizen. Life has been here untouched for more than a hundred years. You desecrate a Valley shrine." He spoke proudly and was unaware, as Andrew and those who could Reach were aware, of the desecration he was doing to the egos of those leaders who listened. This upstart of a boy, telling them, older men and women who had helped build this Valley, what they should do.

Andy wanted to warn him, then knew he had no way. Steel could not 'hear.' Andrew saw the anger sweep like a fire among them. Here was something, someone they could aim it toward. Andrew tried to focus, opened his mind to Reach Steel even a little, but his effort was vain. He did however, feel another energy flowing into him, like a tent of power it came around them. He felt the Touch against his own mind of that watching one. Alicia saw the rent in his guard and Touched against it. But Andrew was so absorbed, so fearful of what Steel did, that he shrugged off that outside Touch.

"Well, now, at least there's a little life in the Valley after all. Took the young ones to see that we meant what we said!" A tall blond man walked out from the cooking area where most of the people stood. He frowned, startled when he saw how many young men there were, half hidden among the tree trunks, standing behind boulders. It seemed to him like an old movie set. He felt unexpected grief to see those weapons, then an all emcompassing anger began to build. He wanted to fight , to meet them one to one, but a stronger training calmed him. He took a deep breath. He resolved to talk those guns and arrows down."I'm glad to see that the Valley people have a little nerve after all." Then he made a fatal mistake. His idea of controlling was to humiliate. "But you boys can't meet serious matters with old movie programs. This is real." He wasn't astute enough to notice the tension, the fury those words engendered.But there was one there who did.

When Andrew saw his Uncle Will step from behind a table to come toward them, he shrank from the pain of that fact. But his feelings bore into his attention. He thought,' He isn't more than any of these others,nor less, but my personal attachment still makes him seem so. If I'm still drawn so much to my own, my heart is not free to know all people as my family.' He nodded to himself,and a trembling spiritual pride bled a little.

He saw Will walk to stand before Steel, his face a mask to Andy, except for the thin amused smile. When he spoke there was a silence all around. Will knew how to take advantage of a dramatic entrance, his voice had the timbre that had moved and held thousands during his life.

"You've come like brigands of the last century? You chidren of the Valley? Taught to know of higher things? You dare to stand in our midst and attempt to control what is not your affair? " His power, his pure personal magnetism shook Steel. For one instant he recoiled and his followers saw that faint shrinking. But he regained courage and held firm. Will was surprised. He saw Andrew from the corner of his eye, saw the other young men from Adwin and Altos. He felt a fury build in him and sought to suppress it lest it destroy his power. These were not just fools after all, they were young men of superior minds, excellent training. Why then were they here? For seconds he was rocked from his confidence, the amusement faded from his lips.

He was suddenly stern and cold as only he could be. He said,"Gather your boys together and go home to your parents so that they can teach you manners." The moment the words left his lips he knew the error. Intimidation would not work with these. But he was sure that the display of weapons was sheer bravado. these young men, raised in Valley teaching, could not use a weapon against other people. Anymore than his own people could. He was aware of a flicker of surprise at that thought these,'his own people'? Then what of his Family? Then he remembered that many of 'his people' had weapons with them, had brought them to this field. How then could he prevent their use if things got out of control.

He raised one hand,called out,"We will begin as we have planned with the day's work. Let's act in a civilized manner".

Steel was taken off guard. He'd never expected this. To be nearly ignored was impossible. He brought his gun higher, bent to aim and held himself steady. They must see their intention was real. They would not be ignored. These Builders must realize they meant to stop all action here. At least until the Council brought its verdict. And why had they not done so? He held firm, lifting his gun in a menacing manner toward the people, knowing the boys behind him had followed his example. "Stay! We must defend this field, whether it means harm or not."

What happened next was so unexpected that neither Will nor any mentally aware person, other than a Monitor could have stopped it. Alicia saw,before it occurred,and so did those watching Senders beside her, but they were too far away. The people, bonded in Joinings through the Valley, felt disruption like a jolt. They were absorbed in lifting of the Energy to all parts of the Valley, in guiding the flood of awareness, the lifted consciousness of humankind. At Telling's Field the Builders knew nothing of that flood,but they felt greater energy and intended to do what they saw as right. Builders began to move forward toward their machines.

Suddenly from behind Steel, who held himself in rigid control, came an arrow, then the report of a gun. Will grabbed his shoulder and spun around, then fell, a young man beyond where Will had stood cried out and sank to the ground. A second of horror and stunned disbelief caught them all as if in a tableau . Then Steel's boys, horrified at what two of their number had done, recoiled from their stance of readiness, were caught in the swift sudden charge of the Builders who ran over them in fury, over flowing straight at the lax guns, the dropped bows. They caught the boys off balance. But in sudden dispair at the loss of their command, they fought in rage, shrieked and howled in release of tension, a sound that Andrew thought, standing at the side, was like that of wild creatures.

Without thinking he Reached, drew into conscious awareness every mind Seeing person among them. Then they focussed. But they did not think to move out of the midst of the fighting. They Reached with all their combined energy and called for help.

Far off Alicia had seen the sudden break into fighting with equal horror, she felt the impact of those two wounded and brought it to those who stood with her. But they had already moved. Already turned the call back on itself and met the combined Joining on that dismal field. They could act. They had been called.

Andy knew that help would come. Those who had left the field earlier were aware, already attentive. If he could call again! But he dropped his attention and moved to try to stop what harm he could. Just as he turned he felt a terrible blow to his head and shoulder. Someone had hit him so hard that it knocked him to the ground. He shook his head to try to see. Dizzy with pain, he rolled over to see what was happening. All around the field was whirling with men and women shouting, wrestling, hitting each other in violence he had never witnessed nor ever had wanted to. But there were, astonishingly enough, many more just standing, unbelieving, holding out their hands in suppication as if to stop the carnage. A young boy ran past him, his face screwed in rage and a strange gleam in his eye that Andy, whose Touch sense was fully alert now, knew with a sinking grief was a killing glee.

Surely that could not exist among modern men and women. He tried to get up, but his body seemed paralyzed for a moment, the pain amazing. With deliberate persistence he got to his knees and looked around. Fury, fear and a strange excitement pulsed all around him and Andrew was aware clearly of a dark reddish haze through the air. Only those with the clear sight would see that haze, it was the overflow of rage and fear. He was also aware of how many did not enter into the fighting, who stood, some with faces filled with grief and tears, some trying to pull apart those who fought, picking up guns and flinging them far off into the woods. So unused to weapons they didn't think to empty them first.

There were the few non-Builders who had come this early morning responding to their own prescience and, with a calm that seemed unreal to Andrew in this situation, drew together, in a silent focus, Joining. Around them was a light that began to penetrate the dark haze. He looked, shook his head and tried to reach through the pain. Yes, there were those who, even though mind blind, knew this fighting must be stopped. It seemed to him a long time that he stood, but it was only a few moments before he could stand and begin to move.

His mind cleared, sight intensified. He Reached, Joined with the four other young men of his group and they were aware that the red haze was around them all. It pulled at them too, threatened to draw them under its weight. Guilty, they realized they had been caught in a trap of violence, of unbalanced emotions. That they had courted that violence even without intention. But now, belatedly, precisely attentive, they withdrew, helping each other, giving steady balancing rituals.

The youngest of the five, Benny, spoke slowly, as if just coming to awareness,"We did it. We brought all this about." Then anguished, his voice thin, he cried out,, "We didn't intend this. We didn't want people hurt!"

Jeremy sighed, sitting with his forehead on his knees. His left hand and arm was badly scraped and bleeding, but he seemed indifferent to it. He raised his head, his face wet with tears he made no effort to hide. "Those bastards, those sniveling, unconscious, selfish bastards! They drove us to it. It's their fault, the whole thing is their fault!" Anger relieved his shame and he sat straighter.

Meridith slowly shook his head, standing behind Jeremy, he leaned against the tree whose shade they'd both sought,"No, jerry, you know it won't work. They didn't drive us to it."

THE JOURNEY

"Well, who then? It's against everything we've lived by! How'd this happen!" It was as though he couldn't find the answer unless someone else spoke it.

"Benny spoke again, looking at Andrew still trying to stand and focus, "Look, Andy's been hurt but he's focussing, calling now, and we're stupid enough to waste time laying blame. People are getting hurt, we stop this thing."

Randolph stood looking at them, frowning, his left arm hanging crooked, the pain in his face real, but he would not succumb. "We did it, men, let's don't find blame on any other. We made our own choices." Then turning to walk away, he added,"We've got to live with that."

Meridith sobbed then, trying to wipe the blood from his arm with leaves, NO! No, I won't accept that. We didn't fire the shot that started it. We couldn't have."

Benny stood like a stiff mannikin, in a leaden voice he said,"One of our gang did. And a boy from Denlock shot the arrow. We started it, Merri, and we have to live with it!"

Randolph modded slowly, as if just taking in the enormity of their action. "We knew, more than the other boys, we knew and we came along, for the excitement of it, to make people do as we wanted, to prove ourselves heros. We are more responsible because we are more aware, we knew better! We KNEW better!"

Perry came toward them, his shoulder in a sling,"He's right! He's right. If we deny it we make everything worse. We are able to distinguish the lower nature, but able or not, we let it control us. The other boys don't SEE that difference. They've been taught, but they don't SEE."

With a terrible recognition, Meridith finally wrapped both arms around his head and sobbed. He couldn't deny. He couldn't bear to admit. Taking a deep breath, Perry said, "Let's at least try now, Reach out, call for better help, for the others who can See. We've got to do what we can and when they know our part, we've got to admit it."

Andrew, sitting in pain and grief, cried out a silent plea again for help. Where were the those who could See? Where were the conscious people of the Valley? Why weren't they here?

These few boys, acutely aware now,responding to that energy coming to them from Alicia and the Stations, lifted above their resistances and realized. Finally with hearts broken in self dismay, they accepted,were responsible for what they did. 'We knew better'they grieved.

Then like a light pulsing down out of every direction, came a power given them by Valley people . It reached, stimulated their young minds, their Hearts to listen and sustain calm. They WERE coming, but in the meantime the four of them could be the focus for the power that might turn the tide of human behavior. Might give hope in this furious battlefield. But they must sustain, hold steady, for even now, energy could be misused. Nothing less than the energy of Love could quell this uproar. An energy that drained the power out of fear and rage. Drew them both to itself and absorbed them as water absorbs fire. They knew it could be done.

A young boy,(Andrew knew him as Dennis's son, Joseph), had grabbed a fallen rifle, aimed it almost in childish glee, swung it around to sight first one then another, as a child playing a game. Andrew focussed, Reached, sent the flow of energy so that it surrounded him, Touched into him, the thought shaping,' one person must not hurt another'. The familiar Teaching already trembled in Jack's memory, and now he felt the power of it, but resisting its influence was all that was happening around him, his own pain and anger at the loss of his lover, knowledge of his inadequacy. At that instant, a pair of wrestling boys fell against his back and the trigger of the gun was pulled. Jack saw and heard as in a trance, watched in horror as Andrew fell. Pain coursed through Andrew's body, his chest was hot with the soaking of blood. He thought he could not breath. He caught his hands to his chest to perform the healing ritual but felt the hot blood seeping down his back. He knew the bullet had gone completely through his body. At least there wouldn't be a bullet needing to be cut out. The thought was strange, like something coming from far distance. He felt distant from that body in pain. Observing. What was this body suffering here in the midst of the mele.Jack stood a second,the gun hanging loose, then without a flicker of hesitation he dropped it and ran to Andrew.

    The other boys still linked with Andrew, were rocked by Andrew's new pain. They nearly broke their link, then re- established it. Andrew assured them he was not in danger. They spun loose, his pain racking their minds. They must separate from him, try with all their strength to dissipate that red haze through which they saw the Field. They were aware that they were focusing agents for the Monitors now. They gave them selves willingly, hoping for some correcting of their wrong choice.The Light grew around them, the air cleared little by little. Andrew lifted higher, aware beyond pain, his body, the torn hole that bled life from him. He Joined with them, sustained their effort and knew his People were coming. Then he withdrew from their effort, to attend to his body. He was aware of Jackson crying and touching his side, trying to stop the bleeding.

    He focussed all his energy now on the torn flesh, the splintered right shoulder blade and rib. He could at least slow the bleeding. He fought to keep himself conscious through the pain. He entered into his body, finding the torn blood vessels, gently, carefully drawing together the edges,the tissue, the scattered cells , and began the slow knitting, the blood flowed less from him, but he could not stop it, could not do a right job. He was not a Healer. The effort was exhausting, more than he could continue. Self Healing was very difficult even with a trained Healer. He almost fainted with the effort, so he shook tears from his eyes. What he had done would have to do. He turned again to the field, the people around him. It seemed to him that more people refused to fight, who pulled apart those who fought. The fury seemed concentrated in two small knots of people, the air around them dark with that strange reddish haze. Again he thought a long time had passed and glancing at his watch he saw it had only been eight minutes since the first shot was fired.

    He stretched his attention to his friends, Reached, and in a new humiliation,accepted his shame. Resolute now, able to distance himself from the pain a little, he focussed and joined the boys who still held their own focus steady. They must help to end this terrible thing they had started. Surely such fury, such actual lust to hurt could not exist in modern people! His heart ached, surely they could not desire --. Then he realized, these were NOT modern people regardless of how much they had been taught. These were the ones who were mind blind, whose minds were still those of their ancestors. Who could not KNOW. In these the spark of Soul had not flamed into enough life. They were not conscious of that bright, energy that healed and calmed and absorbed into itself all fear. They were not aware of LOVE itself, nor of the part of IT that came to them through the loving hearts of their fellows. Neither were they aware of that pulse of dark energy that strove to pull them down to the lowest they could be. So they didn't notice when it did.

He watched, unable to move as another boy, picked up the rifle Jack had dropped, and aimed it at someone. Jack, sitting now beside Andrew, his face dirty with streaks of tears, fashioning a bandage out of his shirt tail, cried out. He leaped to stop the child and Andrew focussed his mind at the same time, together they deflected the shot, and it entered only into the arm flesh of a man beyond. The man clutched himself, screamed and fell against a tree just as he had drawn back to aim a violent blow at Steel. Jack felt sudden elation. He saw Steel's glance toward him. Steel knew! Jack had saved his leader. But the sobering thought came swiftly, 'But I almost killed my friend too.' He felt obscure pride, rage, fear and finally a profound relief. Maybe now, it would be over, the pain that had eaten at his heart for so long was draining away. Andrew felt the boy's relief like a wash over his own attention, but he fell back to the ground, his exertion had re-opened his half healed vessels. He was shaking and crying now, tears blurring his vision, but his mind steadied, held, focussed with the others, who carried his pain with him. He was barely aware that the uproar had subsided a little, the men and women, exhausted, frightened, had abandoned their machines, had turned to try to stop the fighting. The incongrous fact of the wonderful smell of food, a great pot of stew, cooking on in the background seemed to mock Andrew's grief.

Jack knelt beside Andrew. He cried out, touching with great tenderness his friend-enemy's bleeding chest. "Oh, my God, what've I done. I never meant --, I didn't know - Oh, my God!" He tried to wipe the blood away, hurting Andy more. Tenderly he began to wrap the makeship bandage around Andrew, trying to stop the bleeding. Andy shook his head, but said nothing. All his energy going to focus with those who worked through him. They must bring that Healing energy down, the energy being sent to them like a river from thousands of people all over the Valley. They must lodge it in the hearts of every person it could Touch.

Then with great amazement, Andrew's vision cleared, sharpened. A tremendous power grew around them, coming from - where? How had it been released? The sense of great energy gathered, focussed and coming toward them, charged his mind and cleared his attention. He was awake in a new way. He saw that those people he had thought to be unable to realize at all also had in themselves that tiny flame of spirit, of Love Itself, to which Monitors could Reach, once permission was given. It was there, if only it could be brought into flame and life. Even the mind blind could be reached through that spark of inner fire if the power were strong enough all around. If enough people - and then Anderew knew what was bringing the inflowing power. His heart lightened, his hope returned.

Andrew said,"Jack! Jack, leave me. Thank you for the bandage. I won't bleed to death, I've got it stopped enough until the Healers come. Go out there, make them stop, Joe, make them stop." The increasing Presence of the penetrating Light was so evident to Andy that he marveled that the boy could not see it. But Andrew saw, with his heightened sight, the spark of light in Jackson's churning self, was nourished by its touch. The spark flamed up, intermittent, but alive. It caught and made conscious that faintest of recognitions. Jcckson nodded, staring at Andrew with unbelief, then turned to look around as if he saw this turmoil with new perception. In him, as in others, rising from the basic goodness of his nature, the living Soul attended and lit it's own reflection. It surged as if a wind of Light blew upon it. It held, undefeated by those dark urges,the raging fears that had engulfed him.

Jack met Andrew's eyes, his own wide, not focussed and then with a snap, He caught himself, reached out a hand in a gesture of farewell and stood. He began to shout, "Stop,Stop! We've lost our way! Stop. Stop! We don't want this." But the noise and confusion were drowning his voice. He turned and ran toward people around Will where he lay bleeding from the great wound in his shoulder. He began to talk to them, plead with them and he saw, in William's eyes, agreement. Andrew watched for several moments then, seeing that there was hope there, he turned again to his friends who still held their mental focus steady. They must hold steady, constant intention brought to bear on the mind and heart of the most militant of the Builders. Yes, they must focus now,on specific minds, whether they could receive or not, they could not ignore this mounting energy flow. Their minds were trained and strong. They did not know that this moment had brought its own intense training.

They began to be aware of that cry for help from the builders, from those whose hearts were not too filled with hatred or fury. The cry they made was a simple prayer,"Oh, God help us. Help us all!" But it rose from their hearts, true and strong and it was a call the sweeping energy of Love could respond to.

Alicia had been sent to carry messages, to relieve those who must keep the steady flow downward to the Valley, or to prepare the drink they must have to nourish their bodies as they worked. She watched the great ones, their faces serene, calm, full of a peace she longed to know. A peace that came with fine acceptance of humanity, of life and of death. They Reached out to the small group of young men who could receive in that mele.These boys, who had provoked the trouble, would be the ending of it. they seemed utterly open to that inpouring of Light as though fially repenting, waking fully. The power of the monitor's calm, their Love, filled the boys, two of whom were momentarily knocked off balance by violent blows from furious Builders trying to complete the removal of their attackers. The Builders had taken the guns from the boys, but were brandishing them themselves. Some had bows but were not archers so they did little harm. Shots were being fired, people screamed, and fell, bodies lay here and their, people in pain, some crying, blood made an awful stench in the air and the creatures of the Earth trembled and fled. The skies were full of a whirling of birds rising and sweeping and then gone. The land was in battle with itself through this humankind that is the highest consciousness of that land.

Another one of Andrew's group fell to a wound, but they held steady through the pain which now was spread among them. Slowly they were piercing the red haze, the product of rage and fear. It thinned out, clotted around one or two individuals, moved. The Light that radiated from the five boys increased. They were like receiving stations, learning how to send that Light as they received. Not fully aware of all that flowed through them.

Slowly the Light entered into the red haze, the dark cloud, and gently, softly, entering it, drew it into itself. Where there had been dark there was now Light. Those joining into a fight, would find themselves forgetting what they were fighting about, would look with amazement at one another, suddenly aware, suddenly conscious again of their actions. Their attention was lifted from their forgetting. The field around the boys became quiet, fighting was sporadic, and slowly the effects of the calming increased. The eternal spark of Light that is in every person was waked to life in some of the Builders by that power of inflowing Love and in those, profound grief broke the web of desires. They did not yet SEE, but they glimpsed and knew a turning of intention.

Finally the Builders drew back, still holding the guns, still wary. Only Taggart still fought and two men pinned his arms behind him and dragged him to that place where the other boys already had been gathered. Will, in a strange cold fury he could not understand, had sent men out to round up every still standing boy. But now, Will felt only an equally strange sense of shame, of dispair. What was happening?

Among Steel's gang, many held against a table were unashamedly crying. Many of the Builders were crying. Many looked on that field with horror, some with shock, some with a kind of satisfaction. But these were Valley people born and taught. Most bodies bent in an anguish they had never known. The deed was impossible for their mind's to absorb. Now that quiet had been restored, they could not believe that they had so utterly lost control.

Slowly the sound and fury calmed, people were brought to the tents for medical attention. Healers, arriving in flocks, worked silently everywhere. Some had seen them arrive, like great white birds on belts from Clandor, and other towns and cities. Ignoring the tumult, they had entered into the fiercest of the fighting and picked up the injured and begun to Heal. Now they were in tents, finishing. Andrew and the four boys who still held their Joining, still focussed calm over the field, stood at the edge of the group. But the Builders saw them as no different. As the calm grew. Builders found themselves responding, waking, clearing their minds and recognizing knowledge they did not know they had. Every human heart held its own flame of Spirit, no matter how small, and that flame responded clearly to this pure wind of Love that blew now through them all.

Finally Andrew was carried by the Healers to their tent, but he held his attention, Joining with the others. They must sustain and the Healers did not need his attention. He saw that his own power to receive had been greater than he had known. Alicia saw and felt that power and was pleased. He alone had focussed enough to spring loose resistances in the other four boys and introduce them to a Joining. He must be trained, she thought. He focussed that Light energy, he did not know that his body glowed during this effort, that the very Light he focussed helped the Healers to heal his body. The other boys felt it like a bright warm fire, drawing them closer. Monitors stood unnoticed here and there, taking over the task of focus, they charged the air with their Light. And the gathering energy of Good Will played on the anguished boys, the still furious or appalled Builders. They gradually became calm, felt all the compassion they had in themselves, not only for the Builders but for themselves. Builders could see the genuine anguish of their attackers. A strange quiet grew.

A Healer who stood over Andrew touched his face, brought his attention to herself. She realized his efforts to heal himself, knew it had saved his body much. She was busily reaching into that mangled flesh to draw together the blood vessels, knit them and bring the start of healing to the bone. She said, "You can sustain yourself completely if you will break the link with them and concentrate. You must save this body. The others will be all right now." As she felt him relax his attention and turn it to her, she smiled," Do you realize the amount of power you are focussing? Such talent, such capacity to participate in the Love that courses through our Valley just now, must not be lost. We will need it in the years ahead. So attend now to yourself."

Andrew roused himself, looked at her, "But they need me! " He felt drawn - his attention split.

"No, not now. It's over essentially. Monitors have focussed here. Attend! Look! And the wakened people from all the Valley have found their power!"

Andrew did, let his mind see and was astonished."My God in Heaven. How? The flow is like a River -- it's magnificent. It's everywhere!" His eyes filled with tears. "They don't need me at all. There are so many great ones coming now. So many who know, who -- like Jessie, I think." He closed his eyes, let his attention relax, "I'll be all right now. You can go help the others." She nodded, left, signaling a float to transport him to the healing Center.

Now, outside, still standing in a silence they could not break, the others waited. There were so many with minor injuries, a few broken bones, lots of scrapes and cuts, a number of bashed heads. Sadly a few more shot as Andrew had been. Were there any who had been killed? Every one shrank from the thought, the possibility, but they had to know. To have killed another human being would be unforgivable, to have done it in wild passion, uncontrolled, would not bear living with. If any died, then the mind Healers would have work to do.

Finally there was a soft cry, like an animal hurt, a weeping within and then suddenly cut off. The waiting men and women, their own children caught up in

THE JOURNEY

their arms now, heard the cry, knew it's cause and turned in a numb emotionless staring at the boys sitting close together in a huddle between the breakfast tables. Their heads were down. They did not see the numb staring eyes, the flicker of sudden refired rage, that was quenched as quickly, and again that grief that could not find expression. Floats were carrying out the wounded. The silence held. Finally, one, wrapped in a white sheet, still, was carried out. Tenderly, a woman who had been killed in the battle over Telling's Field, was laid on a floater and in the company of a Healer and her sister, lifted off to be carried away to the Ceremony of Death with her family.

No one spoke, the sense of grief was heavy upon them. And then a second float, carrying the body of a man, also wrapped in white, accompanied by a weeping son and sister, lifted and began the journey north. As they left, others came. Air cars were settling at the edges of the field. People coming. The Messenger from the Council was among them, but no one knew that now. They waited. Speech seemed meaningless.

The Healers left. The people gathered around the silent workers and the boys who had planned to save their land. William had been carried off, to his protest, for healing. The flowing energy from the network was steady now. Master teachers flying in from Clandor had taken the task of channeling energy so that the boys could rest. Could sink into themselves and feel their shame, their dispair. But already the mind Healers had arrived, and were moving silently through the crowd. They had air cars in which to carry their patients away. Steel, Taggart and Ronald allowed themselves to be settled on the floats. Unable yet to speak, they simply complied. The other boys leaned against one another, and the Healers came to them, spoke softly, and soon took them away. The Builders relinquished the guns and bows the boys had brought. They allowed their own weapons to be taken away, their faces bewildered. Those among themselves who had fired weapons, who had caused injury, and two deaths, were recognized by the mind Healers too and lifted off the field. The Builders seemed suddenly unsure, glad that the boys were gone, that the weapons were gone. They did not seem to know what to do.

After several minutes, they began to react. At first there was a tender touching of one another as if glad that they were there. They began to speak of their hope that their wounded would be all right. The deep palpable grief of the families of the two dead, came in a wave, of pain and dispair, of self recrimination. No one held it off, let it throb against their ears, their hearts, knowing that they deserved that pain also. Finally, they could begin to speak of the dead, promising that they would have the finest ceremony and be honored always. Then slowly the fact of those deaths, the brutal killings, the attack by the young men, the violent reaction of their own people, penetrated. They made no effort now to ask themselves who had actually fired the guns that had killed, they began to react. The dark energy, swift to find any crack began to seep into the heart's defenses. It was hidden from the Light by angers sprouted from their pain, angers that grew and were used to hide the fear and hurt, the confusion and guilt they knew was their own. But the

Mind Healers had taken most of those obsessed with violence, with hatred and fear.

So most of the people held that stream of acceptance, of Love sweeping its healing down into those hearts that threatened to harden with their anger.

Builders wondered about, unable to focus, to decide what to do. William was gone, the driving force for the Builders, but they began to gather around a younger man, Jeffry. He sat disconsolate on a bench, a very fair man, with blue eyes and a thick cap of curly copper yellow hair. His wrestlers body was hunched against the edge of a table, His elbows pressed against it . He glanced up, noticing that people were standing near.

Eyes met, and he stood, half a head taller than most, he exuded physical power. He said,"You want to know, What now?" It was a statement. He stretched his arms out then up, his face slowly losing its entranced look, his eyes flashed about, here and there, seeing the camp, the people, the dispair they expressed."It's a terrible thing that's happened here. More than you know. It's proof that we've not learned much after all. That with all our Valley Convictions, our new way of life, we've not learned." He shrugged and his shoulders seemed to fold into themselves in defeat."Those were children. Those boys. They meant no harm. But they were trying to protect their land in the old fashioned way. In the way we insist is right! Yes, they were defiant, but what can we expect of boys. Their only crime was that they wanted to force us to their ways." He took a deep breath, visibly swallowed as if reluctant to speak more. Then as if admitting to a crime, he said softly, "Just as we want to force people to ours."

The people around him shuffled, looked away, some stared at him in surprise."It wasn't the fault of our people, Jeffry. If they hadn't come here --"

Jeffry turned, shook his head,"Don't talk nonsense. You know that we attacked this field. A field that is sacred to all of us. It is OUR field, not 'theirs'. And then, we attacked them when they came to stop us. They were playing a children's game. A foolish one, granted, but still a children's game. Even William couldn't hold us. Let's not deny our guilt. I accept my share and I don't know how I can live with that." His face twisted in a mixture of grief and dispair. "If we hadn't had guns here, one of our number would not have been able to make that mistake, the first shot - " he swallowed, his eyes wet with tears, but persisted, " the first shot came from us, the Builders! We have to live with that!" Around him absolute silence grew to a palpable substance.

He looked across at the machines, then sighed. He said, in a voice loud enough for most to hear."Never in our Valley history, until today, has any human being killed another human being. And now, it's been done, twice. It was a scared Builder who killed Demelda. It was a scared boy who shot Abraham with an arrow. Had to be a Hunter. No one else could have done it. But it doesn't matter any more who. It was all of us! We will not put our guilt off on one or two scapegoats!" His voice had in it the terrible rasp of a man controlling an anguish that was a wound in his heart, but the roar of it sounded all over the land.. He shrugged again, "How can we go on with our work here."

THE JOURNEY

People stood unmoving. These were Valley people, raised in the tradition and Teaching of the Valley. They could not absorb fully the results of their actions. They could not start the big machine, could not continue yet. There needed a little time to absorb what had happened. With very little talk, some went to save what they could of the food, to call people to the tables, serve them silently . Others lifted bags of seed from an air car. But the eagerness, the confidence was gone. Jeffry, walked with heavy steps to the supply of lift belts."I'm going to find William. If he's well enough, I want to find out whether we'll have any change of plans."

The people began gathering at the tables, sitting waiting, their heads down, sometimes talking quietly, sometimes simply silent, few could eat. The fields were quiet, few calls, no laughter, and no singing rang out in this morning. Finally some talk began to rise and then fall again, as if there was little energy for it. People moved to sit with people they knew best. There were gusts of sound,of anger, blame, denial of guilt, then periods of quiet. The desire to blame the boys totally, to allow fury to build against those who had brought the violence to them,fought with the honesty of mind that told them differently, with the basic caring and love of the people for one another. The Monitors kept their steady network of energy flowing, the Soul Conscious of the Valley held their focus. They felt the counter flow of dark descending energy push against the lift of Love. The pull and push of these continued but those who Saw persisted patiently and the years of learning, of the intellectual understanding of their convictions gave these people of the Valley foundation and the lifting energy absorbed the darkness into itself. Slowly as the morning wore on, the Monitors felt the resistance weaken, the effort to deny finally recede. Acceptance of their share of guilt began. The people could settle their problems.

A turning occurred in the Earth. A shift and a recognition. Monitors at each Station still kept up the watching and the network of energy flow, though many moved among people and took their place there. Old passionate lusts for revenge were known, but they lacked energy, faltered and did not take root in the hearts of most of these people who had so long learned to listen, to care. Those few whose fury caught hold in dissatified hearts, found fewer and fewer to hear them. The mind focus coming from the Black Lodge seemed a trickle, a simple stain now in the fabric of this glowing Light.

It was Light that poured, flooded, filled every corner of the Valley and so it gleamed through even the last of that dark stain. The hearts and minds of people felt that power. Throbbed with pain, Joy, possibility, whether they were AWARE or not. Whether they knew why their hearts were so full, they could feel that fullness. Something in humanity had turned, chosen a new recognition of LIFE. And so, the Monitors were able to thrust forth upon that fine tension of consciousness an acknowledgement of that recognition. They no longer held themselves behind secrecy. They no longer had need to conceal anything of their Vision or of their Knowledge. They were Coming Forth! The anguish of the morning seemed to have broken some knot, some denial, and released a new quality of Life for humankind. Spirit woke within humanity.

THE PEOPLE OF THE VALLEY

Gatherings all over the Valley felt the increased energy, the stepped up level of LIFE itself. Receptive, jolted by it, unsure how to adjust to it, but trembling with a new Vision of what the Valley was becoming, they listened, watched, waited. Bathed in that Light, that flow of Love, vision cleared, minds extended into realization.

The trained and disciplined minds of those whose consciousness had expanded into the greatness of Soul found intellect shaping itself to begin to understand perception of these new dimensions. That shaping brought a fine mental pain, as at a birth, a stretching of the very self. A brilliance of Cosmic realizations, of possibilities beyond present intellectual capacities, was there at the edge of awareness , tantalizing those minds able to glimpse them. A hunger for explanation tortured those fine minds, so that they searched for words, created language,felt the terrible demand to put into their store of explanations, this immense realization. Explanation for what there were as yet no words to speak. No words, no mathmatics, too often not even a concept. But the Reach held, promising a future.

For those whose awareness was not already stretched by years of awakening, there was a new color to Earth, a new brightness and darkness to everything, a terrifying and exultant edge to thought. William's heart swelled, touched with a shadow of something he could not quite think about. He wept, found himself unable to talk for the first time in his life. What he began to know he could not name, yet the perception of IT would not disappear. It both frightened and elated him. For the first time in his life he clung to Annette and she rejoiced to see his tenderness.

The strength of Family groups was drawn to its highest possibility,the wisdom and understanding purified, focussed and shared,until they came into a Touch with one another in ways never before known. They had to lift themselves, sustain that focus, out of the dark morass of their agony brought about by their own actions or inaction. They could not deny their responsibility. There was no where to hide; their lives were open to one another.They HAD to find their way up - into that higher Spirit, higher consciousness wherein they could build the lives they could begin to See.

In the field where people waited still, eating desultorily, people were silent. Among them walked many of the awakened who had come to help. And among them another thought was shaping. 'Just as we must accept our shame, our guilt, we must also accept our greatness. We the people of the Valley, in the end, did not submit to our worst nature, but caught fast to the knowledge of Love and sustained ourselves in Light'! Slowly that thought did its own healing. This society would not imprison one or two as the blamed, and deam itself guiltless.

SOUL CONSCIOUSNESS! What was it? How could human minds bear that power, the energy of such knowledge? Life took on meaning that made the familiar, ordinary world seem limited, the way a room is limited in comparison to the sky. Exploration of space, the grandest dream of humankind, seemed child's play, an anachronism, for now, new dimensions including space and time and reality beyond them, beckoned. The world of Spirit was real and they felt it waking in their hearts. Now after the human mind had refined itself to be receptive, it saw that the human Heart woke, pulsed with new kind of awareness. A knowledge beyond present thought. Because all humankind began to KNOW, the power was inescapable, the recognition, unavoidable.

But they were essentially human after all, and relationships to one another dominated the thought that relieved the ache of mind stretched beyond endurance. Gathering together and talking, thinking, explaining to each other was a relief, like falling down to a simpler era of life. Spirit drew them beyond thought into Knowing, It was a relief to slide back down into thinking, shrink consciousness from that vast Soul Consciousness and explore those ideas born of this new realization. How could they accept this still terrible capacity for harm demonstrated in this morning's events? But more, how could they accept that seemingly infinite capacity for Joy, for Good itself, they equally began to glimpse. Knowing as they did, perceiving beyond their personal selves, they knew finally the nature of harmlessness, of selflessness. The idea of living so was no longer so preposterous. What had been unattainable ideals, were now possibility for living today.

Those called Monitors saw that their brothers and sisters were finally accepting of them. The people of the Valley could make themselves consciously receptive to a quality of Love that was Divine, was more than human. And in doing so, they could choose to be transformed in that Love. As they gave themselves to IT, gave their conscious attention to the reach of that flowing energy, they knew their own transformation taking place. They were themselves unfolding into that which they sought to be, that which they were becoming. The universe sustained itself in an attractive Field of energies rising from a,so far, unknown Source, but with this realization, came possibiity of some day knowing even that Source.

So the Builders worked mostly unaware, yet feeling a greater sense of life. Wondering, they plunged themselves into the tasks they had chosen. For they must stand together even in their wrong. Questions had begun to insist, to press against all the convictions of their days. That same rising energy that lifted the aware from their imprisoned lives, roused in the unaware the beginnings of sight, the shaping of ideals to lure their minds beyond habit. It stimulated all things, the hidden fears as well as the hopes and ideals. Some partook, as humanity has for eons, of immediate desire, but every person knew constantly a disturbing yearning beyond such desire.

As the People sought their own council, gathered and listened to one another, felt the flaming forth of that Love within themselves, they began to know what they must do to protect their Valley, to protect the life that lived there. And they set about to do that.

In the midst of this re-evaluation of themselves, the Council decision was broadcast. Coming now, after the life shaking event it seemed anticlimax, and yet, it nourished the recovery It was broadcast all afternoon.

THE PEOPLE OF THE VALLEY

"Telling's Field being a national landmark, a place revered and protected for nearly a century, will remain a Valley treasure and will not be broken! The practice of using land without license will be ended. No citizen can use land without full permission of Council and based on a voting of the people."

Some of the Builders heard, but many were still working at completing their old plans. They wrestled, felt anger, relief, grief. Builders at Telling's Field had brought no Video, still did not know their plan could not be fulfilled, were preparing to continue. The messenger who came in the midst of the mele, told them repeatedly the decision,but some insisted on arguing, though most knew it was a futile act, but they persisted stubbornly, refusing to give up.

It was then,in a silence so deep that it was a wonder the Builder's, mind blind, or not, would not sense it,the people called out to the Monitors andasked them for a True Joining.

The Stations, half deserted, for Monitors were everywhere among the people, still held their focussed attention to the network of mental energy. The Families were able to see and know of that network present.

The response to the request for Joining began. First, realizing the process needed, each Gathered Family sustained one another, each entered into a deep, focused Joining. As that occurred, the Monitors watched, and then when the peak of tension grew great, they stepped in. Could they do this? Could the People of the Valley, all of them, Join together in Love and Good Will?

From the Stations and wherever they found themselves, Monitors Joined as part of the people themselves, no longer separate. They lifted Mind and Heart, sought that Spirit in themselves to lift consciousness toward Spirit Infinite. They Reached beyond themselves as a people. Their combined strength Reached out over the Valley, like an atmosphere, a wind that spread into and through every mind. Joy was the evocation of the Gathered groups, and humankind in the Valley responded with a releasing of Joy pent up for just this occasion during generations. On this day humankind on Earth began to know Itself.

For the first time in the history, JOINING was complete. What Humanity was becoming, was glimpsed through that sea of consciousness. Knowledge in Spirit was a reality experienceable enough that they could later find a few words to begin the new language that would one day speak of it clearly. The poets of the world would have a task for generations.

The Joining waked minds and hearts into the life of single consciousness. It was as though Earth Herself sang upward into the sky, surged forth on wings of Mind that tore away the limits of a physical world and made the universe visible in all its glory. The three dimensions opened to reveal the fourth, finding themselves within and already part of that vast and wondrous plane. The Gathering of Humanity, already spreading through all the Valley, already drawing into its surge of Light the rest of the world, where such similar Reaches also had begun, grew, held, was alive. Every life was informed of itself, and of its whole Soul nature in the interchange and exultant cry of Earth. Spirit sang through Her, its voice Her humanity. For timeless moments that Joining held, lifted and finally sank into its components. Then, as that song soared outward, through dimensions of Being, the call went forth, the call to that Source of Spirit, the song that was prayer,chant, mantra, all the forms through which humanity had called out to that which WAS through millinia. The call of Humankind spoke the prayer of Earth. And in that instant, every heart radiated with response. Every Heart glimpsed its Source. The Joy of that Knowing was indescribable, but endless.

As they released that Joining,, as they turned to their lives and their Valley work, they knew they must yield themselves to unfoldment of Mind and Heart in order to remember what they knew. Individuals returned to ordinary living -- remembering what they could of their experience. Knowing of the vitality of it, they made their choice.

They came from hamlets, towns, farms and great cities. Streaming like gnats on their shining little belts. Like a cloud they rose from the north Valley and swept downward toward Tellings Field. And as they went, that cloud grew by the hundreds,then thousands that rose up from city and town through out the length and breadth of the Valley.

The Monitors who still lived in ordinary flesh bodies, joined them. They were joyous in their final oneness with all People. Some stayed at the Stations, keeping the vigil. Sustaining the ceaseless flow from the Silent City. The people riding swiftly through the autumn air, carried no weapons,wore, in honor of the City, white clothes. And then they were suddenly there, landing everywhere, filling the fields,the groves, completely covering the machines, a great rustling crowd moving through the forests, hundreds of thousands of people, and their feet crushed the grasses and Earth where she had been wounded.

The Builders looked up at the sound of their arrival, the ceaseless fall of the descent among them. They were afraid. They drew back, their breath caught in fear. Jeffry had returned from talking with William, but William was a silent, broken man. Nothing in him could have prepared him for what had happened. To Kill was to him anathema. He could not endure the fact of its having happened. He had sent Jeffry away, saying they would talk later when he had had time to rest and think.

Jeffry stood watching the arrival of the people over the Field. The silence unnerved him much more than their numbers even. He steeled himself and stood forth. Then a white robed woman came out toward him. It was Marian, the Vagabond Mother. They could be seen and heard by the Builders and by these thousands of the People.

Marian spoke,"We will not leave. We will not allow the work to continue."

"You have no right. " Jeffry spoke with a clear tone of doubt which he did not himself recognize."

"Enough Damage! You can see clearly the vote is No!" Marian would not debate. "The Council has voted, there can be no breaking of Tilling's Field. Now, you see the People agree."

Jeffry hesitated and in that hesitation his people knew their loss."No, we have the right."

"Not if the vote is against you!"

Jeffry turned to his people, they were milling about, talking to one another, a murmur growing. He said to them, spreading his hands, "They've got us. The numbers are against us. We'll have to quit." To his surprise he felt a gentle relief, as if something waited, something infinitely better beckoned. The awareness flickered and was gone, but he remembered. He stood, gazing for a long moment into distance, through bright autumn leaves.

A shouting of angry disappointment broke out but was brief. They had not really believed that their numbers were so small. To see themselves here, - to see the hundreds of thousands of people so concerned that they came now IN PERSON, gave them serious pause. The World Market survey, informing them that no markets could be built, had lost them many members, those whose only interest had been in making huge profits. But, with the little bars open, the new fabric being woven, those left had still thought they could win.

Jeffry could hear some comments around him, he nodded, turned again to Marian, "You say we must live in this Valley with people who openly practice witchcraft, who listen in to private conversations, who try to deal in the powers of evil? You mean we have no choice?" His voice carried no longer the harsh conviction he had always spoken with.

"No, your choice is to stay, using the land you now have. We will not take back what we have given, even though its use grieves us. Or you can leave the Valley. We will not impose what you call our witch craft on you, we will in no way intrude on your private lives. Nothing you call talent will demonstrate itself when we are within your cities without your permission. But in return, you must agree to study this phenomonon, learn what these talents are. Teach the knowledge to your children.

You know now that your children will be as we are." the last carried a tender apology, healing, reassuring, not divisive. "Many already are!"

But Jeffry shook his head, his voice livid with an anger he couldn't define. "How can we trust you?"

"You can because you always have. No one has ever imposed him or herself on anyone who does not share our awareness in all the years of our living here." She studied him as if unsure to add anything, then said, "And neither have your own children." The impact of that utterly deflated Jeffry, stunned other Builders who suspected their own homes harbored what they couldn't accept.

He stood, looking at her, letting his eyes finally move out and into the ranks of waiting silent people. The significance of their white clothes was not lost on him. He nodded to himself, assessing, knowing what she had said was true. He swallowed hard, knowing defeat! He shook his head, wanting to clear it of the surge of emotion. "You've got the decision from the Council?" His voice had lost its belligerance, The crowd knew he would not hold against them.

"We have. But it is not simply our own Council who has made the decision we bring. It is the World Council!" She turned, touching the arm of a very old man who stood behind her. She turned again to Jeffry, "Jeffry, this is Everett. Will you hear him?"

Jeffry blanched, startled and uneasy. The people behind him murmured, but he held up a hand. "Let him speak."

The thin old man stepped forward, his clothes were of plasilk, embroidered obviously by Vagabond craft. He was not as tall as Marian, but he stood smiling slightly, his deep grey eyes so calm Jeffrey felt their stillness like a personal touch of calm. Everett spoke then, his voice had a reedy quality, light and clear, but then, suddenly he broke into the use of the Voice. There would be none who would not hear, and yet, he spoke no louder. "Builders request the right to produce quantities of wines,beer, fabrics from their new short life fiber, and for the introduction of pornography studios where holographic simulated life dramas can be enjoyed. You want to make a 'Dream Park, where people can lose themselves in simulated realities, creating a reality of their inner life, endulging their fantasies, whether fine or impoverished. You asked also that cafes where these could be combined with sale of liquors, refined drugs, mind changing fragrances, etc. and such products could give customers an evenings entertainment. " He looked for a moment so sad, Jeffry wanted to stop him. Then he glanced around at the Builders and back to Jeffry, "In short, using these and a number of other businesses, you want to be wealthy, and to be world financiers Is this a correct statement?"

Jeffry frowned, moved nervously. To hear him say these things did not sound the way he wanted the business to sound. He answered, "I think they are correct, Sir." He felt unable to speak further. No one had expected to have a World Council member coming with a Voice report. It was unprecedented, as far as he knew. He felt uneasy, what did it mean?

"We've studied and given your request careful testing . There have been test cafes set up in a hundred cities, word of their offerings aired on the daily newscast. We've watched and aired everywhere your own advertizements that show scenes of your products in action, the persuasive little plays you created." He smiled,"Quite good they were, you know. You have dramatic talents, and great talent for design among your folk. We gave world wide airing of these videos of yours and in these months we have found so little interest that we had finally ceased to show them". He saw the frown, the look of disappointment, but also the belief that what he said was true."But don't dispair. There seems a small steady market, you will be able to market probably what you have begun to produce now. But there simply is not enough interest in the products to warrant any further development. People seem to have other things on their minds." His faint smile broadened a little, but his eyes never lost their gentleness, their interest in Jeffry the man.

Jeffry felt that interest and it soothed his feelings. He was irrationally relieved to hear the report. He didn't stop to think why he should be relieved, he was angry at himself. He turned back to the Builders behind him, whose silence now was total. Suddenly they began to break into talk. Someone shouted,"If that's so, then where can we live in peace? Who will help us build our city."

THE PEOPLE OF THE VALLEY

Everett turned to Marian. And she nodded,"We are one people.. We will always be one people. We know you as part of our family and we will help, of course, as we always have helped in this Valley and through the world. "You will have the same help every town or city has. We will send labor if you need it, skills, and credit until you are established." Everett seemed suddenly looking on them with a deep and tender sadness.

The same voice shouted,"You will honor our right to live without contamination by your kind?"

Everett nodded, his smile faded, "He nodded, the World Council has offered contract." He held out a sheaf of papers. An official world Seal could be seen on it's cover. With a gesture of defeat,Jeffry reached for it. Then Everett smiling said, "In return we ask agreement that all chidren will be educated in a Learning Center staffed by Master Teachers as we always have done". Jeffry stood numb with realization then finally nodded. He turned to the workers behind him. Their faces drained, miserable. They seemed to Marian, like lost children.

Jeffry held the papers up showing them to the people, and saw nods, reluctant nods, tears and frowns. He turned back, " Go then, all of you, Leave us!". His voice held the edge of tears.

"You will remove the machine?"

With a sudden burst of anger and dispair, Jeffry turned to Marian, looked defiantly out at the gathered people, and cried out, "Move it yourself". The old man's face did not change, he nodded sadly. And Marian nodded with him. Then the Builders behind him began to move back, gather their things, pick up their food baskets, their belongings and to turn to their own supply of belts. They began in silence, heavy with their defeat, to take to the air.

Marian turned to the People. No one spoke, there was no attempt, the entire group began a JOINING led by that old Teacher, Everett, World Council member and Monitor. And as the Builders lifted off, their sound like a buzzing of bees for some minutes the people felt sorrowful relief. They would clean up the Field themselves, and they would return the huge terrible machines back to the museum they came from. A few among them knew that Barry would have to come to the museum to correct what he had done to the first two.

After several minutes, in which people talked quietly, a young man entered the machine, activated it, and lifting its digging arms, drove it onto a huge Lift Car. It hummed softly and then wobbling slightly at first, it lifted off, and in a great whirring, rattling and noise, it started on the Journey to Santiago. The machines that would have smoothed and leveled the land were next, and within half an hour, all sign of Builder work was gone,, except for the great scar, the wide river of dark brown-red earth, exposed and barren. But the seeds, and even broken roots still lived beneath that dark surface, and those seeds and roots would bear green shoots come spring. Like a flight of white birds the rest followed, so that the machine was surrounded by that cloud for some distance and then suddenly, as at a silent signal, the people scattered to go to their various towns and farms.

Telling's Field was left, a few local people still wandered here and there,

THE JOURNEY

feeling the changes, wondering about them. But the Field would heal itself after the winter had given it rest.

CHAPTER TWENTY

Preparation

    The following days passed in bringing some order back to the Valley farms and towns. The tragedy at Telling's Field was burned into the hearts of every citizen. Among those who did not go to the field, there were none who had not seen it via newscasts or through the visualizations of mind-conscious friends. The injured were given healing and sent home to let the body complete the job. The most dedicated Builders turned their backs on the field as if it had never occurred, but there were many again who turned away, horrified at the results of their actions. Some sought someone to blame, but many more knew that blame was, as they had been taught, an avoidance. They knew 'people' were responsible.and did not exclude themselves.
    The report by the World Council member and the revelation at Tellings Field of the indisputable fact that Sensitives and people of great Talent were in the majority in the Valley, had such an impact on Builders that hundreds of them sought out Valley Teachers to help them understand. Instead of thousands, as there had once been, the hundreds who withdrew further, angry and bewildered, clustered together for mutual comfort. Charges of evil seemed ridiculous but these Builders who still could not tolerate the differences, gathered together in a tight community to plan their own town. A petition had already been accepted by the Council.
    The third day following the disaster, when most of the wounded were somewhat recovered, everything in the Valley was suspended while a ceremony was held in every town or village for the two killed at Telling's Field. Those ceremonies revealed a grief so deep it seemed to penetrate the very Earth. For Jessie it revealed a great advancement of humankind. No one placed blame except for the most fanatic of the Builders. Most people simply took responsibiity for their own capacity for harm and vowed to practice more intensely the kind of harmlessness, based on selflessness that they had been taught. The people had been tested.
    Following the ceremony the Council suggested that Builders choose land beside or within the fields they had been previously granted, and submit a city plan that the Council could help finance. The plan gave the remaining Builders new hope and something to work toward. They vowed it would be a place without the talents they distrusted but as Jessie listened to their eager talk, she saw they planned without understanding their own youngest children. When she asked them what they would do for these children, they fell silent, refusing to discuss them, and said finally they would make their own plans for them. They did not deny the presence of true Talent among them,but they could deny that any higher Knowledge or expanded consciousness existed. They could deny the presence of

Spirit as a reality in life, saying they would wait until after death to deal with whatever Spirit was.

But those who had sought out the Teachers for understanding began to accept the idea of that greater reality. They could understand possibility even though they experienced nothing of it themselves. Such people were a levening influence within the Builders organization, and Jessie knew that they would protect the growing conscious children.

William lay silent on a couch for two days, refusing to talk, gazing out the window at the vast wonder of the Valley below and the mountains that framed it. He made no effort to turn the thoughts away. He would meet them, try to understand though his heart felt numb. Early on that third day Jennifer arrived to see him, Annette brought her to him where he sat watching the sun slant across the Valley below and reach narrow streamers into the deck that overhung the cascading roofs below. The late September sun was warm, but a cool breeze rustled among the vines and leaves of a young acacia. She brought her guest to the couch and Jennifer bent suddenly, unexpectedly to kiss William's forehead."My dear friend, I am more than sorry this happened to you." Her entire bearing testified to the fact of her grief. He looked at her speculatively for a moment then laughed, a short sound of irony.

"Serves me right, don't you think?

To go against Valley decisions and even Convictions the way we did? Who better to be wounded?" His smile was thin. "We've got a bitter pill to swallow. It's been sticking in our throats too long. We've got to swallow it." He turned his head away but she saw pain in his eyes.

Jennifer glanced at Annette and saw there the sadness of her own knowledge."Will, everyone of us is at fault. None of us saw, or was willing to see in time."

He was silent, turning his head so he met her eyes and she was startled at the sheer grief she saw there beneath a sharp bitterness that pushed the grief away. Then, suddenly he smiled at her, loosening the tension in his face. "Oh, Jennifer, it's true. I don't intend to go on with this defeated martyr attitude." Then, to her relief, he grinned and his face lost some of the bitterness, leaving only the grief. "I suppose we've got to admit that we're anachronisms. That we're left over from the past?" He was deliberatly hurting himself and she frowned.

Annette shook her head, "It seems wrong to me when you put it like that, Dear. I can't believe that anyone could ever call you an anachronism."

William shook his head, his eyes bleak,"My Darling, don't try to protect me now, I can see my fault. I can't deny what I saw at that field. Talents are real. They do exist and the people who have them are a new breed of humankind. Whether I like it or not! If the ones demonstrated there are real, then all the others probably are. Those amazing things Jessie's done, that I called slieght of hand," he laughed harshly, " marvel at how clever I was in explaining those creations of gold coins and that marvelous emerald. I still have it you know and it is still marvelous. I've had it tested and it's genuinely very valuable." He sighed, raised a hand in a gesture of finality,"I dought if Jessie ever tricked anyone in her life." He shook his head again, glanced briefly at each of the women then pressing a knob at the side of the couch, he lifted his body to a sitting position. "I never would have believed that one bullet could bring such pain." He grimaced as he adjusted himself and asked,"How's Andrew?"

Jennifer nodded, "Benjamin called this morning. It's what I wanted to ask you. The Family is meeting all together, they want to - to just be together to re-establish ties , to affirm our love."

"And you want me? The blind one? What do you want me for. I'm of no use!" The bitterness of his voice was a pain to the women, and seeing this, he patiently tightened his lips again, then shrugging heavily, he seemed to throw it off."I can't help this terrible bout of anger. I'm really furious, you know, that I'm left out of it. All of us, who call themselves Builders. And a good number of others, I understand who don't hold with our attitudes. It's hard accepting that we're not - not -", he drew a long breath and said it,"we're not developed enough to perceive what the rest of you do. And to admit that we can't even build ourselves a city and have it to ourselves because we can't do without our mates, or our children, who are --" his smile was tight,"enlightened. We'd be cut off from our friends, our Families, everyone we've loved." This time he nearly sobbed and Annette started forward but checked herself before he raised a hand. He had let his anger drain and that anger was his only defense from pain.

He went doggedly on, as if wanting to hurt himself as completely as possible. get it said. "We'd be cut off. Like a city of lepers. The Builders who plan that separate city don't know what they're doing at all. I can't seem to make them understand. They've quit coming to talk to me!" He grinned feebly, glancing at them. "That means though they'll have to find this out through the pain of it, but it'll be slower, and maybe less painful that way." He sat silent for a time, then, "I suppose I won't be able to avoid it for a while. I am bitter. It infuriates me to know that I cannot -- CANNOT - no matter how hard I try, learn what you all are born with." He looked at Jennifer as if she were the cause of his hurt."I don't deny that there IS something."

She felt tears pushing past her restraint. She must not cry now. He must bark it all out. Jennifer was helping, he had not talked like this before. With a deep breath, she said, "Oh Dear Willy, we've talked about this before and you know and I know it can't be helped. I've never known you to feel sorry for yourself." She spoke with calculated brutality, deciding it was the only way.

He turned to her, met her eyes and she bore the pain she saw there, the anger, the flicker of hate at her truth. Then he looked down at his hands, finally shrugged, "It's true! You're exactly right. I'm behaving like a child. Andrew would do better, I'm sure. But I can't help it. My life is thrown down the drain. I've denied so many years, even when I saw what was before me. Oh, yes, I did see, sometimes. But I couldn't bear to admit it. Underneath I knew that to admit the facts that I can no longer deny, would leave me exactly where it has left me. Good God! How would you feel if you'd suddenly discovered you were retarded and had never admitted it?" Neither woman spoke. He was right. they had to allow him anger. Allow him to put the facts as brutally as he had to in order to get the thing there before him to live with. He slid his legs over on the floor, the argument was making him feel better and he didn't understand that but accepted it. He thought he might even get up, walk around a bit. He had told the Healers that his body could finish their job and went home earlier than they would have liked. Annette watched him, her face streaked with silent tears, but her heart lighter. He was getting out a lot of what had stopped his throat, ached in his heart, for so long. With Jennifer he could do that. He sat, but didn't attempt to stand yet. The one attempt had told him how dizzy he was. He looked at Jennifer and said, "That Joining you speak of, it's like a world wide computer system isn't it? All anyone has to do is plug himself in? D'you see how that'll put the rest of us out of business?"

"Oh, no, Willy, Joining is not at all like a computer. Its another process entirely. We'll need skilled Comtechs more than ever." Annette sounded finally worried. It was a relief to feel only that.

Jennifer nodded, wanting to stop such thought, "No, wait, William, you've got the wrong idea. The joining comes from so deep in us, it extends into such a higher state of consciousness it can't be used for such practical things that a computer does." She knew she bent the truth, but basically it was true."You see, we can't just talk to each other, it isn't telepathy in the old idea of that. We've still got much to learn, we don't use it well yet probably, but we do know that Joining is only a beginning." She looked at Annette, seeking help, but Annette only smiled. Maybe someday we'll have power to Join on a world wide basis. Maybe Monitors can do it now. I don't know. We've got a lot to learn! But right now we need communication grids, computer systems more than ever. Most of us link only with friends and families, when we do we share feelings, attitudes, and imagery primarily. We don't exchange information about such things as business, politics, etc. Some people can't even do clear imagery yet. Yes, we need even better computer systems, a world system in fact." She realized she was holding out a straw to a drowning man, and if he grasped it, he might be saved.

William's need was naked in his face for an instant, then hidden, but he said, "Is it possible one of you could hook into a computer suystem as part of the system?" She looked startled, frowned but he went on."You ought to find out, you know. Might be some interesting results." With a loosening of his whole body, he sighed,"Well, it might mean I'll have a place. I've been wroking to build that world system for years. It's not long before it'll be in place.But what else, how else could such a system help?" He seemed to be pleading, though his voice was harsh.

"You've got the kind of mind that could help us speed up training. You realize that children almost all have some new Talent and they're reaching out to dimensions of Spirit - into enlightened states more and more. We need computer help to design training, and to probe the possibiities. To help people all over the world understand before we have any more things like Telling's Field. You can do that. You have that kind of mind! You have friends who think that way too, they'd need to help." She nearly held her breath, as he looked down, out the window again.

Finally he said, softly,"You mean like the one who can market the works of an artist even when he doesn't know how the artist creates the works. Well, maybe I'm good for something after all." Then, drawing himself up, he stood a moment, his height above them, seemed to comfort him."We'd best be getting at it then. And that Gather, you came to tell us of. We ought to go, I think. We ought to keep together." He turned to Annette, "Would you Send to them, either of you could, I think and tell them we'll all come?" There was still resentment in his tone, but suddenly his face changed and when he spoke again they heard the forlorn note in his voice,"I want to be part of our Family again!"

Annette shook her head,"I can't Send that far, Will. We'll call Paul and have him make an ordinary call. She hesitated, not wanting to bear more anger, not wanting to tell him how sorry she was. She said instead, "You must realize William, that we aren't just being kind at all when we ask for your help. We've got an awful lot to learn.

His face softened and he reached to take her hand, "Oh, my darling, I know I'm being fearfully unfair, and acting like a bitter, disappointed child. But I'll get over it, just give me a little time. I'll try not to be so hard on you, my dearest." He was silent as he took several steps toward the couch and sat down again, then with his old grin he said, "But it does help to rage and rant a bit now and then." He looked almost sheepish, his eyes loving and Annette found again the man she married. He had not been so tender toward her in years.

He settled himself with cushions and said, "You know, when the Healer was mending my shoulder bones actually getting the bone growth started, shutting off bleeding, and so on, I watched her. her eyes were so full of " he gulped, then said resolutely,"yes, so full of Love. I can't deny that. She seemed unable to work without that attitude. Once a woman was being healed but she was so dispairing, so hurt by all the violence, that a younger Healer began to grieve at the awfulness of what happened. She had to leave and let another take her place. She said the healing was a way of using the energy of Love itself. And at that time I thought that statement so foolish I laughed at her. Told her she was a fool. She didn't seem to mind, just smiled, but later I was ashamed. I had a chance to tell her so. She was an inspired woman, no doubt. And there was a young boy with her, not over twelve, already learning. I couldn't believe that." He shook his head again, needing to talk, to tell all he had realized. Annette looked over his head to meet Jennifer's eyes grateful that her visit had brought this outpouring. He had been almost constantly silent since he came home.

Annette said, "Children seem to have the Vision even when they're very young now-a-days. If we can help them, they could develop to their fullest abilities much sooner and without suffering as our older children have. They will be seeing beyond ordinary vision to what none of us know." Suddenly she burst out,"Oh, Will, we're ALL mind blind, it's just that some are more so than others." She turned away, regained her calm and turned to them again." We must find a way to train them, Will. I see that Jennifer is right. You could do that, you know!" Her eyes were sad, "Too often we've denied our chidren even acceptance and some of that sensitivity has been lost. Maybe forever!"

"Then its' true! There's more, isn't there? It's not just the Joining, and the psychic Talents, the children show. There's what we've always called mystic Vision, and these kids have that?" He stared at them one after the other, then shrugged, his good humor reasserting itself, "Yes, it's pretty obvious. Early this morning, while you were working in your studio, Annette, the Valley Video broadcast a talk between two Monitors. Believe it! Monitors on Television. We hardly thought they were real a week ago. They were explaining. And yet, they hadn't language either, so it wasn't making much sense to me." He stopped remembering all he'd felt this morning. They waited, Annette taking a chair opposite and Jennifer sliding to the floor. Softly she asked,"What else Will?"

In moments William went on, " But they did speak of a Vision. The literal seeing of a Vision. It didn't sound that much different from the kind of thing mystics have reported for centuries except it wasn't tied up with religion. They said they had training too. That they could teach the awakening ones, but they didn't have enough people to do it now. too many coming up for training. A bent old man, with a blue robe on, said with training, children could take steps beyond ordinary consciousness into what none of us know of. He said they first need discipline, attention, focus! I always thought I was already doing those things. That's standard training in the learning Centers, isn't it?" He stopped, shrugged finally and then went on, "He said something else that puzzled me, but from what the Healers said, I suppose it must be true." He heaved a sigh, as though a burden was loosened, "He said that opening the Heart to Love was necessary if the Vision was to be developed. That kind of training is crucial." He reflected on his own words before he turned to the women,"Does that - do you both know what he meant? I was dumfounded. It sounded like the vague talk of ancient philosophers?"

His voice had dropped to almost a whisper as though he feared either a yes or a no. He watched their faces and knew before they spoke. Jennifer said,"I do know what they speak of but remember, Will, that ability to perceive, to stand at that state of consciousness beyond the familiar is also a thing that must be trained. We have the ability and up to now it's come on us from within, kind of awakening of perception, a bursting forth, but it's incomplete, only a glimpse. Most of us are scared by what we experience. We explain it away, or deny it even." She looked to Annette for help, but Annette only smiled and nodded.

Jennifer frowned, then went on. All these years the Master Teachers have been teaching us to pay attention, to meditate and to reach out beyond our ordinary thinking mind. They insist on training children to see, to be aware, to be conscious of being conscious, if you will. And to go on from that first glimpse, takes many further steps, much further training and the ability to stand in silence of awareness is one of the special ones. But there are many more we don't use yet. But because we'd been trained to be aware, most of us recognized our own

Vision when it came. So when we began to step across that great gap between the physical and astral worlds, and were able to recognize dimensions of Spirit itself, we were more prepared than we knew. But no one can really be prepared. Such experience tips over the whole perception of reality. Nothing is as it was, yet, as every mystic has reported, everything is the same, except more! So much more!" Her voice was soft, she gazed far off into memories. Those of us who had help were able to avoid total denial or worse, explaining the power of that as some private religious scheme. But it's still a shock, that awakening, and the Vision that follows.

She was a little embarrassed, taking so long to explain, but he had listened patiently and now he nodded slowly,"The Silent City! It had something to do with all this, didn't it?"

Annette sighed with a great relief. Jennifer seemed to have this effect on people, they opened up to her. She was relieved that he had ended the silence that had held him since his return home. She could bear anything better than silence. Jennifer was nodding, "It truly has. there seems to be some power running through it, from it, out to all the Stations of the Valley, and so down to us all. Some people say it's a kind of stepping station for an infinite power that we could not bear at all. It might even come from - from the Source of Life Itself, from what people have called Eternal Spirit but I don't know. I don't think anyone of us knows. That's why we need help, William, good minds that know how to analyze even these things." She looked at him hopefully, wanting to emphasize that need.

"He nodded slowly,"I see your point, my dear." Then, hesitantly, he asked,"What - what's it like, Jennifer. What to See beyond our world. What's it like?"

Jennifer's heart quailed. How could she tell him? "Well, at first, it seemed to me like getting high above a Valley for which you have no map and being able to see, actually see all the roads, the rivers and streams, the towns and how things go together. Only it's seeing a map of the inside of yourself too, seeing what you are and what you've been. It's seeing into human life, into the way of living things. Oh, dear, that's not right at all.

" She sighed, grimaced," At first it's pretty uncomfortable. After seeing everything in bits and pieces, suddenly you see it all as a pattern, and sets of petterns, and it - well it enlightens. Because you SEE!" She frowned, wondering if she made sense to him at all. She knew that she was making sense to herself, teaching herself in fact.

Then Annette spoke,"There's more to us than we've ever known. Remember our Teachers telling us that?" At his nod, she said, Well, at first it's like 'seeing a Light, as if there's someplace beyond where we are, beyond this very universe, Will. And we have to learn to allow that Light to illuminate everything for us so we can begin to realize some truths." She talked rapidly as if finding thoughts she had not known were there. She glanced at Jennifer again, and knew their linking supported and strengthened her perception.

William was slowly nodding, his eyes fixed on her face." That's what the teacher on the video said. Almost the exact same words, in fact. I suppose it must be true."

Annette breathed a long sigh of relief, then said brightly,"Well, shall we go then? Paul has his car at our section grid. We'll fit a belt on you Will, You shouldn't walk that far yet." At his look of skeptical amusement, she frowned but he didn't hide his pleasure at her concern. She said, as she brought him the belt,"If everyone's begun to Gather, they'll be expecting us."

The Family had indeed begun to Gather. Andrew stretched his long thin body on the floor, his healing complete enough that he had little pain, but the healer insisted he rest. Give time for his body to complete its knitting. The others came, one by one. Ned had swept in alone very early in the morning, wanting to know their stories of exactly what had happened. He had not been to Telling's Field and had only seen part of the News reports. Tom, Angy and Mary with both children rode in on the morning air like a covey of huge dark quail. It had been years since they'd all been to a Gather. The Family waited in a strange unexpected quiet, little talk, mostly a brooding tenderness to one another, as though each sought and gave with great care. Silvia and Jerry were preparing a special brunch in the kitchen, compliments of their new restaurant. Delicious fragrances drifted out to meet people coming over from the Temple. Jessie sat in a comfortable soft chair near the window watching everything, a pleased smile on her face, for she already knew that William would come with those from Altos.

Cassie came running in from her cottage, greeting, in high excited tones, Nathan and Justin as they landed with their parents. They came in chattering with one another, then suddenly were quiet. "Did you all see the video last evening? Did everyone see?"

Jerry nodded, wondering whether he should tell them to calm down."We saw Cassie, sweetheart. Any one who didn't would still know most of it, it was Sent by thousands of people all over this Valley." He watched Justin's face as he stood there, between Cassandra and Nathan. The two children focussed clearly to surround Justin's mind, knowing he could not Send or receive imagery. Nathan frowned, protecting his brother,"We already told Justin and he saw the Video news. Justin nodded, mildly interested, but he looked with worry toward Andrew, seeing his hurt, the paleness of his face. He went to him, bent and touched his shoulder with one hand lightly, his face intent. Andrew took the hand, and drew the young boy down beside him. Jerry sighed, how could the chidren manage to protect and even communicate somehow with Justin? How could they know to do that so gently?

Jerry went to the door, then across the deck, waching the sky toward Altos. Sure enough, the air car was already past the river and would begin to circle ready to land. He felt excitement and a new deep joy. The other Gathers had been exciting but also frightening. He did not feel that now. So much was being realized by them all. But this! This was something special and William was here! The Monitors had talked to the whole Valley last night on Video, told them to talk, to tell everything they knew, to sort out their own feelings and share them with Mind conscious and mind blind alike. Secrecy, they said, had done too much damage. There was nothing to keep secret.

Jane was talking in the Hall, Jerry could hear her fine, light voice, "They said we must practice, must practice the Joining, because then we can share our perceptions through imagery. They said we must talk too." She laughed, amused at the thought. "We have to make language whenever there isn't any. How can I tell of knowing of so much fear and pain. Or the rest of it either? But what we know now has to be common knowledge." She was reciting the admonitions of the Monitors as if reminding herself of a new lesson. Her eyes were dark this morning, the pain of the past week still a shadow in them.

Steve stood beside her, his arm about her waist and his eyes often on her. He had suffered knowing of her pain, feeling something of it through her. He wanted to keep her from ever knowing such pain again and he knew he could not. "It was just the keeping of secrets that got us into trouble. The Builders refusing to search out their feelings and tell us; ourselves refusing to tell ourselves even, let alone each other. No more secrets among us. We will not have secrets again, Love. Never!" His voice had a trace of anger but was also a plea. He frowned at Jane, then at the others, and hugged Jane close. "You know, had we talked, you would have learned to shield and to manage all that came to you." She nodded, curled into his arm.

Silvia called out, "Any body hungry? It's ready." The tables had been drawn into a circle so everyone could sit together this day. The Altos family came in, talking, exuberant, a joy sang around them that startled Silvia when she went to them. Everyone was there to touch, hug them, make them welcome. William need not feel singled out as they all reached for him, wanted to touch him, meet his eyes. They could ask about his hurt, make him comfortable in a special chair, express their delight and relief that he was here. He looked around, almost suspicious of this warmth, but he shrugged; he was surely welcome. He had not stopped them from lifting him from the grid to the Hall and settling him in a chair, and his eyes were moist as he laughed at them.

They began to gather around the table and finally everyone was seated. Silvia said, "We'll have brunch in a few minutes but we've some talking to do first, I think."

There was silence then, for moments when every mind was focussed and a blessing to their health and harmony was designed and formed in the air above the table. It was mental imagery, created by their Touching minds. It was beautiful. Jerry looked at Justin, Cassandra was whispering to him and he nodded, looking all around. Then he said, his voice bright and clear above the murmur in the room. "So, our blessing needs to be heard too, you know, so Uncle Will and I can be part of it." So simply and so bluntly he began the ending of secrets.

They all looked at each other, surprise, chagrin, wry humor on their faces, and then suddenly they began to laugh. After a minute, William joined in, his face a study in relief. It was a clearing out of whatever tension was left. It was a great heaving collective sigh.

Paul grinned, so full of happiness he wondered at it himself. "It's so good to be together, all of us. Angy and Mary even managed to be at home the same month. How's that?"

Mary laughed," During the last few weeks, we knew we must begin to be here more". Justin piped up again, "Daddy told us we had to come. He told us to come."

Tom nodded, "I did actually. I thought in light of what's been happening that we needed to be all together. " He said it mainly for Justine's sake and remembered it was also for William. He felt a gentle gladness that that good man would be here to be a companion to that little boy who must live his life without the beauty the rest of them knew. But he wondered whether the gain would not be William's more than Justin's. Then they were all silent, just being together.

After a while, Paul said, Jessie, we've heard so little from you lately, especially since we came home from Telling's Field. I wish you could help us shape into words what our hearts are trying to communicate right now. Justin's right, it must be heard as well as seen." He frowned at his own words, wondering if they were fair.

But she smiled, nodding slowly, her eyes clear and bright as though they held in their depths something of that beauty Paul sought. She was silent for several minutes and then slowly she began to speak.

"There is a sorrow, a deepness beyond all pleasure, all senses and all thinking, where words fail. There is emptyness lying beyond the doorway of the heart. It seeks to be filled and it is our choice whether it fills with darkness or Light. We've spent years denying our Heart's need, and our Hearts Vision. Now we are aware enough not to do that anymore." She was silent. They all reflected on her words.

Then she went on, her voice soft. "Where can resolution come when there is no named problem? Where can relief occur when there is no recognizable strain? Yet from the depths of ourselves we've cried out for what we now begin to know, for what we See and realize. It is so far nameless but it holds in itself all possibility. Every breath we breath in this atmosphere expands the self, makes visible what has been invisible and unknown. In this new atmosphere we will find knowledge that will erase pain."

"Oh, yes, there are yet fears, there are struggles and the way is not easy. But what Light hovers just at the edge of that terrible chasm of perception inviting the leap? What Light stains through the interface beyond which Life measures Itself within us, speaks bouyantly through consciousness beyond our own and speaks of That for which there is no name? Yet we know it more clearly than we do our own."

Every eye was on her, and she held their attention utterly while they began to realize this was the beginning of the final phase of the Journey. Her voice lifted, stronger, sure. "There it has been lying at the bottom of the Heart, at the edges of the awakening mind. It reflects itself daily in that pool of mind that is our communion with one another. Yet still we have recognized nothing! We hear the heart singing, singing its own celebratiuon of THAT which streams into it like a wind, or a rising of oceans. The Heart knows the nameless as clearly as its self, yet we suffer, unable to know our own Heart's knowledge." For some minutes she was silent and they sat benumbed, absorbing all she taught them.

Suddenly her voice was strong, penetrating their attention and waking them further. "Take thought! Aware! Stand at once in the company of seeding grasses, of fruiting trees, of sunlight slanting down the dim faces of stone and reminding us of the rising up of Life from its numb depths, the catapulting of Life, like a great song pressing itself out of miles of Earth. We look into ourselves , together, reminding each other of that same Life wakened in us of which we become conscious."

A voice cried out, "Jessie, is Life that which we call God?"

"No, What we have called God is that which is nameless. Life is an attribute of That."

Another, anxious now, "Then, is it Love, or Consciousness?"

She laughed, " It is neither of these, they too are attributes. And look to see from where you insist on naming. But remember, the first requirement of a student is to listen. That which is nameless cannot be defined." She hesitated and then added doubtfully, "At least not by our brains."

For moments again they were still and then she said,"Pay attention! From THAT utter joy is born and infinite possibilty. It is the same fire that plunges through Earth into Sky and then streams with light to sing from a birds throat. It's the fire that races through our hearts and calls out like a lost child incessantly. It is that which shapes in us the shadow of our incompleteness, our pain, because we stand blocking the Light and will not wake to See."

"And then, we understand that the Nameless is That which we seek but before we celebrate, the smallness in us longs to give it name, to hold it in our small hands and reduce it to our size. Then finally, we see that the demand within us, bringing vast griefs, is the longing to stretch ourselves large enough to live conscious of That always Nameless! To be ourselves large enough to contain some awareness to Life! To have strength to bear that knowledge."

And they knew she had finished her Teaching, she had spoken the visualization into words. For long they sat in silence, letting all she had taught settle in memory. Then with a deep long breath, Paul looked around. The shape of their world was shifting. Surely nothing would ever be the same again. But he did not grieve. He said, "Jessie, I wish you had written that because I need to speak it to myself often to realize it all."

She said,"It has been done."

Jerry said,"You don't think I'd start a Gather like this without a recorder do you." He lifted his hand, and they saw the small silver case he held. He was grinning as if he had caught them out. Then slowly, soberly he said, "There's a light that literally stings against my brain, illumines perception and wakens life in

THE JOURNEY

me such as I nearly cannot bear. I see that what Jessie says is true. And I remember how we fought ourselves and would not see what we were discovering. Now, we see our dual nature. We are of Spirit, Christ Conscious, Buddha nature. But we also see that we are animal nature. We demonstrated that at Telling's field. We must never forget all that we are."

"Why is it, Uncle Jerry,? If we are a new people, how can we also be the old?" Jason spoke seriously, his dark green eyes like shining gems behind long lashes. Paul looked at him, knowing he must see more of this boy.

Paul answered, "Jason, you saw the videos of Telling's field. You saw us behaving in many diverse ways. We are like creatures stepping from ancient seas on to dry land. They had to learn. For generations they returned to the sea for important periods. Some even reverted and did not learn to live on the land at all."

Tom nodded, "Yes, Son, you go with your mother to the city beneath the sea and learn to live there, to live where life seems alien to us who must feel the dry wind blow around us and see the sky.. You have begun to adapt more fully than your mother who took you there. So you know there are other states through which to live. Look at your developing gill receptors. By the time you are grown, you will be able to swim the waters free as your friends the dolphins, for at least a few hours at a time. There are times I envy you. And yet, I know that all of us are entering into another realm of existence even more dramatic if we think ahead as if we look back from a couple of hundred years. We can imagine the direction." He was smiling, but then he sobered again, "Jason, we know we are not immune to selfishness, to various lusts. Unless we remember our ability to fall into the least that we are, we cannot climb outward to be all that we are."

Jason did not take his eyes from his father, he said,"Then harmlessness rises out of the knowledge that we are capable of harm."

"If we're to live Mind conscious and therefore expressing of Spirit, we must remember. But so much is offered us now, if we can let our Heart's lead the way, not our intellect. Look at your possibiity. You may be one who will open up the universe of the intelligent under sea creatures, the Dolphins and the Whales. I understand that already you share much with them." He saw Jason flinch, look around, he almost never shared that very secret part of his life.

"Dad, I'm afriad, when you speak of my private life here in our Family. And yet, I've seen what secrets can do. I want to tell you all. I want to let you know. And I will. It is in fact what I hope to do, to learn to communicate with those vast lives." He was silent, then, "I can see how it resembles this other, this entrance into that realm of Spirit."

William spoke then, rasping so he had to clear his throat, he said," I've known something of that undersea life. But he's so young. How can he -?" Will shook his head, set his mouth and then went on, "Just a child. Maybe there's more going on in this world than I've dreamed of." He frowned, looked angry then blurted out,"But how do such people do business? How do we manage the governing of this land?"

Tom and Paul locked glances, then turned to the others, but no one spoke. Finally Jessie reached out a hand, then dropped it to her knee and said, "William, you've begun to speak of yourself as separate but you're our teacher as much as we are yours. We are none of us more than standing in the doorway to that brighter realm. We can try to tell you what we see, and you can help us shape our world to function from that vision. Only the great avatars, such as Christ, Buddha, Krishna, others approaching their states of consciousness, have actually left us to live beyond everything physical and astral. For most of us, the physical world IS our world. We have to learn how to live again with new vision, to know the worlds of finer substance."

He nodded, slowly watching her face and she felt as though he sought to trust. "I don't understand most of what you've been talking about. I'm glad Jerry copied what you said, maybe I can listen and begin to realize at least the idea of it." After a minute, he added, "Then there's the Silent City. I suppose I must accept that too." The resentment and anger was barely noticeable in his voice, "Why couldn't you have told us long ago what you knew?"

To his surprise, Anna spoke, "Oh Uncle Will, I always wanted to, all those years, tell you and everyone. But we didn't understand all we knew and you seemed so unwilling to listen."

William frowned, looked down then nodded slowly, "I suppose there's something to that."

Silvia got up and Jerry followed her. "It's time now. The food is ready and piping hot. So we must serve." She spoke with a gayety that was like her old self. She was proud to demonstrate the talent that was making their restaurant a success. As she got the trays ready for Jerry to carry in, she looked out at the blazing leaves, the silent slow fall of one after another. She felt the gentleness of this year ending, the sweetness of the dry autumn, but the sadness that lingered beneath it.

In the Hall, Andrew had taken his tray, picked a bit at the steaming food, and looked up." Uncle William, look at me. I'm an example of what we've been talking about. It's true we see more, we know of what Jessie calls 'That for which there is no Name'. Yes, we begin, just barely begin to KNOW of That." His voice was intense, strained as if he had to make this Uncle understand. "Don't you see, that if we should lose balance we can do more harm, more harm, just as I did." The pain in his voice was sharp, ripping down the edges of his words like a rasp.

Rose made as if to go to him, but he was across the table, and she sat back down. She said, "Andrew, pay attention, feed your body too, just as you are explaining, it all has to be done at once, all the levels of living."

He smiled at her sadly, "I hate to hear the reminder, but you're right." He ducked his head to hide his tears, then lifted it again to meet his mother's eyes without flinching, the tears glistened but did not spill. Swallowing to steady his voice, he cried out, "Look at me! I was attacked because I provoked attack, Uncle Will. I went there thinking to gain glory, to save the Valley, to be a hero! I was full of excitement and the lust for adventure, and what I did I knew better than to do."

THE JOURNEY

His voice rose suddenly, breaking to that of a child, then dropped again, to deeper tones. I had seen the larger vision. I knew! I knew! Yet I was drawn back down by old desires, unfinished business of desire. My heart kept warning me,, but I had too much pride of thinking. I believed I was smarter than other people. I wanted glory and what I got was a teaching so profound that I will never again step out of my cottage until I have made certain that I am balanced in that Light I know. Have lifted myself to stand in Soul Consciousness. My cottage has become my Temple because I don't trust myself to walk even as far as the temple before I balance, before I stand clear of myself." His voice had a btter tinge, yet as he talked it softened and finally looked around as if some dark shadow had been dispelled from his heart. Finally with a great sigh, he said, "I know, Mother, I know! First I must forgive myself!"

She nodded, tears spilling from her wide brown eyes. Benjamin watching, thought he had never been so proud. Yet there his daughter sat, she who had not succumbed to old urges, old desires. Didn't she deserve approval for that strength? And then he knew he thought in the old patterns. No, she was a new person, she would see beyond those childhood needs. But she was so far, so far beyond, he felt alien to her almost. His son's very struggle made him precious to his father at that moment. Had she also struggled and her father did not know? No one knew and so no one felt pride in her accomplishment? Had she won through in loneliness to step beyond that need? Can we be proud of those who have fought the struggle so far beyond our own we don't know its nature? Alone, utterly alone?

Jessie touched him, her hand across the corner of the table and he felt the power of her touch. She too would not longer close herself from them. She said, "We're looking with fresh eyes upon ourselves and that's good. But we must lift our eyes to what we perceive beyond our smallness. Look! Know yourselves there. Waste no more time on guilt and grief. In recriminations. Be aware and set aside those sources of dispair. We are a people renewed. Lift up your hearts and recognize Joy!" She looked around, smiling and radiating that very Joy she spoke of."There is still much to learn. We have far yet to go."

Andrew frowned, then suddenly, he too smiled,"It's true, I've grieved enough. I've made my confession and I am forgiven. I will not forget but I will learn to forgive myself." He let his tears fall, then gave a curt nod and turned to his plate of food. He started to lift a bite to his mouth, then stopped,"But if any of you see me falter again, promise that you will tell me and I promise I will listen."

"We have to ask that of each other, all of us. You aren't more prone to forgetting than any of us, Son." Ned picked up his cup and drank, and then said softly, setting his fork down into a nearly empty plate,, "How do we plan how to go from here?"

Silvia looked up nodding, "Yes, where to go from here, because we cannot go back! None of us, not even the Builders. Whatever they choose, it'll be something new, not somethng that once was."

Jerry stared at her, "My darling, you've said it right. We've all been taught in

THE PEOPLE OF THE VALLEY

the ways of awareness, and that's made all of us a different people, even those who don't See beyond this immediate life."

Rose was pensive, looking at the children all eating with good appetite now. "It must have been hard on you children. With adults all around to whom you couldn't talk. I don't easily forgive myself that."

Young Steve laughed,he was helping himself to a large piece of berry pie and the aroma of the juices seemed irresistable to Rose as she watched. He said,"Aunt Rose, you're right. All of us've talked of it. It was why we didn't always come to Gathers, you know.It was almost as if we weren't of the same family sometimes." He met her eyes, saw there bleakness, glanced at his own parents, saw Paul;s sad glance at Jennifer. "Oh, now, it wasn't so bad, you know. It made us work things out for ourselves a little. We did trust that you'd come round one day." He looked a little embarrassed. "There was Grandpa too. He couldn't sense much of anything at all. We had to learn how to talk to him. But we did".

Andrew nodded, curious,"How did you Steve, you and Rachel, manage to keep out of the - the sort of thing I got into with Steel? Weren't there young people wanting to change things there in Altos?"

Steve nodded,"There were, and I know the attraction, Andy. I know! But you see, I'm a little older and I was working so hard in the Domes, and learning plant culture, that I just haven't had much time to think of politics. Or much of anything else. You know, getting a talent like this in control takes a lot of time and energy."

Andrew shook his head, a wry smile softening his face,"Thanks for the try Steve but I've been as busy with music and with science study, and sometimes with girls, I can't use that excuse. You're just made of pretty fine stuff, Cousin."

There was silence while everyone finished the desert, a silence finally broken with everyone telling Silvia and Jerry how great the lunch was. Then taking cups of hot drink, they went to sit in the big soft chairs at the windows. The sunlight outside came and went behind gathering clouds.

Jessie began a slow gentle Touch. Tom nodded, then said, "William, Justin, we want to begin a meditation together. Are you willing to join us?" It seemed so simple, and so thoughtful for him to ask them. Rose marveled at Tom's unfailing good sense. The man and boy both nodded, finding better positions. The others settled themselves, their cups on tables near by.

Will raised a hand,"Before we do that, I need to finish this. We - the Builders - have failed you know. Our plans aren't going to work because this world is not the same at all . We had a hard time seeing that. I don't know that everyone has yet. We HAVE admitted that we're far outnumbered. It's still astonishing to me that that's true. But there'll be some who'll build that separate city." He sighed, looking away, then he went on, his voice sad."It'll not last. Their own chidren'll break the walls down. Already are to some degree, though too many won't admit that. Many of us envy you, and I hope that doesn't create too much hate."

"How can we prevent that, William?" Benjamin's eyes held Will's, his own full of the love he felt for this brother.

William nodded slowly, "I suppose just what you're doing. Talking about it, openly, making no pretense. I think we've got to be sure no one feels left out, feels his own finances are less because of it, that's a crucial point, you know. Money. Access to power. They've flamed fires of hate before. We'll have to do a lot of work with my --" he sighed, turned thoughtful eyes on them, "among our people to help them accept. Maybe find a Teacher - the right kind." He was silent, letting his eyes move from face to face. "Actually I don't envy you. I think it's that I don't quite know what I'd envy you for. People'll resent most any attitude of superiority, you know that. It's natural, and you'll have to watch that." Again he was silent, "But I suppose that very thing you call the awakening, realization, prevents you from feeling superior?" So far I don't feel any different from any of you, so no envy strains our friendship. I want that to continue to be true."

Paul nodded, "It is true. We aren't superior, and we sure won't have more credit, maybe not as much."

William simply nodded slowly," Lots of people can do things I can't and I don't envy them. But I had important work to do too. We've all got to have a place! That's crucial!" he stopped, frowning, his head turning from side to side, watching their responses. "But if that's done, then I think it'll work out. But I insist you talk to me as much as you can about it. Let me try to understand. That's important for all of us. I think it was the feeling that something was being kept from us that made us angry and afraid."

Jessie nodded, "I do know a Teacher. One who has a special Talent for offering understanding. He has great compassion of heart, and great knowledge of humankind. He could come to you, teach any who would listen."

"It's what we need. He was silent, sad. "It's come to that, hasn't it? I still think of the Builders as my people and I won't do that. We are one peple. We are and we must remind ourselves." Then suddenly he grinned, the recent pain and worry seemed magically to leave his face and he looked his old self. "We've been taught that every person has the right to live according to his deepest nature as long as we do no harm to others. And I see that it applies to you too, to all of you with the Vision and the Talents."

The courage necessary for William to say these things was enormous. They all recognized that and turned the combined force of their compassion and appreciation to him. He did not know it's presence but he felt relief as though he had recovered something and set out upon a surer path. Jessie nodded briskly and Paul said,"The Valley will survive."

They sat in silence, turned into themselves, a meditation that could include them all and for those who were able a deep Joining. The entrance into that mental closeness was easier and held steady. They projected no images; they held a unity of Stillness that renewed them.

After a time passed, they began to open their eyes, feeling a peace and calm that balanced every heart. Jennifer was the first to break the silence,"There is that strange sense of having known somethng larger when we Join. It's like being more aware, like seeing and experiencing more, like being a little in love".

"Can someone be a 'little in love'? Silvia laughed.

Everybody else laughed but Jessie nodded her head vigorously "Someone once described this as feeling as though he had fallen in love with the human race. He said he thought everyone he met was truly a sister or a brother. It's a wonderful feeling when it's known."

It's just a matter of learning how to see, you know." Cassandra spoke so matter of factly in her little girl voice that no one could suppress a smile.

Finally Rose asked, "It IS Love, isn't it? The energy of Love we work with when we Join?"

Jessie nodded, "It is! The energy that attracts and holds things together in the universe."

After a while Tom asked," I've heard talk of a Valley Gathering this winter. People are asking about hooking up for a World Game. You know, everybody able to hook into computer networks to see things from a world view. We ought to learn the possibiity for World Communion."

Cassandra asked,"How could a World game work?"

It's built on the principal used for simulated reality games but far more inclusive and sophistocated. Instead of just entering into the lives of people of any country or all countries,we can move out into space, to the space colonies, the moon city. We can watch from vast distance, then move in slowly, until we are part of the action. We can travel, join people in small forest villages, or huge cities." Tom's eyes were shining, "When I was in New York two years ago I tried the beginning version and that only was introduction. the world would be surely one world. And to add to all that the ability to Join , might be something no one could imagine."

"We'd better try something limited to the Valley itself first. It would probably take a lot of credit to link into a world game. Besides we could include everyone, mind blind or not." She'd used the phrase before she thought and saw William frown. Justin, only looked excited and interested. It would include him. He was already a whiz at computer networking, in his own opinion.

Jessie said, "You could do a lot with it, create a combined technology and mind process even. You might find language that will help express what you realize. I think it's worth developing."

Mary spoke softly, her quiet smile catching Jessie's heart at its tenderness,"You use the word 'you'. Aren't you going to play at all?"

Jessie held her eyes a moment,"No Mary, I must not. I must allow all the people of the Valley to play this game or to begin long distance Joining as they become able. The channels are open. It's your game. It's not for me, for us, those who have been Teachers, Monitors or Travelers. " She looked around. Perhaps some day, when you've settled the matter among you as to how you want to begin your new way of life, we will be part of it. "She was laughing now, her delight so infectious that the others began to smile. "There's so much to learn, you've just begun, you know."

And what about that Journey you've always told us of? Isn't it about time for that?" Paul watched Jessie as her face sobered.

THE JOURNEY

She nodded, "That's so, Yes, its so. We must be ready to go immediately. Before the weather changes. Besides we must be back home for the birth of our new son, Christopher." She looked at Silvia and smiled,"We'll make final plans after supper tonight."

The after noon was moving into early evening. One by one they left to do chores, to go to their cottages, or just to walk around the gardens. The need to be alone was distinct and even Steve and Jane went separate ways for a time this evening. Clouds had gathered, rumbled about the sky but little rain would come of it, too much turbulance, and high winds that were already blowing the clouds apart. The breeze was fresh and cool however and felt good against the faces of those who walked down to the River's edge.

CHAPTER TWENTY ONE

The Journey begins

It was the first week of October. The late autumn sun fell through the barren trees and the high mountains had already had their first fall of snow, on which that sun shone in dazzling intensity. Winter was still more than a month away, but her stillness already made itself felt in the Valley. Harvests were in, the food processors and graneries were full. The mills ground what flours were needed daily and then closed their doors. In the cavernous storage barns to the east of the Industrial Rings a busy crew loaded fiber plants into the stripper. The leaves were sent to the paper mill and the medicinal processor, the stalks overflowed onto a moving carpet that slid them into the vats for softening. In a couple of days they were rolled free from their husks and the fibers loosened and cleaned to bundles of soft,tough, four foot long threads that were loaded on the running carpet again and sent to another section of the mill to be separated, sorted and twisted into long yarns. Some were fine as a cotten yarn, some coarse as hemp, but they all found their place into the dying and weaving barns. Thus, one of Adwin's most lucrative industries was underway. Not until summer would the work slow down. Harvesters brought in dye plants, and a neighboring barn housed the strong odors of husks, hulls, flowers,roots, etc. that created the endless variety of colors for those yarns.

Adwin was engaged again in the familiar autumn cleanup that preceeded the pruning and replanting time. Farmers took choppers into the fields to break the old vines and stalks of harvested plants so they would rot more quickly and ready the Earth for new plantings.But every where the meadows and self seeding fields were bright with their new green of winter. Within a few weeks much more time would be spent indoors, time for learning, practicing numerous arts, entertaining one another with stories, holoroom adventures and historical replays, for all the less active labor and play of winter time. No town or village would be in need this winter. The People of the Way were steadily moving to the south land, and only a few hardy families would still travel the northern Ways.

Creatures of Earth were settled into their winter burrows, their stash of food as carefully stored as those of the humans.It was still bright autumn, with warm afternoons and cold nights, but people had begun to draw inward as is their wont when the cold begins to close the world into itself. In these respects what difference there was between animal and human was a matter of degree. For humankind could create more luxurious dens and nests, could create a simulated summer in their great halls. But it was in that vast new world of mind and Spirit that humankind left their little companions of Earth so far behind.

But now, in this new time, this new dimension into that world of SPIRIT, as strange to imagine as the world of deep thought and science had initially been to ancesters of these new people, there was both inexpressable joy and at times, great fear. For what is truly unknown has always brought with it fear. What is an opening of another dimension of consciousness will bring with it great joy.

Jessie mused aloud as she stood just before dawn watching the light grow grey-white through the darkness. The full warmth of Indian Summer was on the Valley, and it brought a pleasant drowsy urge to contemplation and reflection. "That transcendence of our old world brings great change. This is the time of conscious evolution and we participate in our own awakening."

"Now, we must find out whether we can bear that awakening. But it is said, nothing is given that is too much to bear. That doesn't mean it might not be ALMOST unbearable, however." She smiled at her own mild humour.

She stood silently watching the sky brighten, the mountain edges redden with the approaching sun,"Will we bear it? Have our bodies been born with strength enough, our minds flexible and strong enough? Can our hearts stretch to this kind of Love, the demands of that Love?" In all the years of her service, she had felt that change occurring, had known it in herself, had endured as had all Monitors the times of recognition, of awakenings one upon another. She said with strong conviction,"Well, surely a good number of the Valley people have already born much of that stretch and have not receded into fear."

"We must adapt to all this." Her heart swelled with Joy and the trembling fear that had so often darkened it, faded and was gone. "How can we, human, unfold into beings of Spirit, alive and conscious in flesh. That is the task, is it not?"

She fell silent, thinking of those Monitors who already lived at those levels of consciousness, lived and worked among their kind."There are babies born among them whose greater physical, mental and emotional capacity from birth houses the unfolding Spirit. They grow up and live as a people and we see what we will all become. These few, give the promise." She started with a smile, remembering, "There is Christopher, he is one of these. He'll be born with Heart and Mind equal to the Elders of our Stations."

She looked out into the land, felt the powerful impact of the sweet curve of mountains, the lift and fall of hills like breathing and then the smooth rounding of the plains that sloped so slowly to the Great River, shining now in the autumn dawn. "Is it that humanity enters into a stage when the physical world fades into the background, and the mental world carries our consciousness through into that world of SPIRIT. Or is our relationship with that physical world simply changing to something we have never known. What then is the Spirit in us? What is its nature? How can we endure to know ourselves SPIRIT? This is our task now. And we approach that new dimension of ourselves with minds honed through millenia to fine skills in thought that will make us able to penetrate the outer limits of Spirit and bridge these worlds we live in. Have we finally broken the barrier between mind and Mind, between mind and Spirit? Or have we only seen the possibility? Is the life of Spirit so far beyond us, as far as primitive physical life was from the mental life of Einstien, Aurobindo, Hegel, Dante, Shakespeare, and such as they? It is that which I know now. That which I long to understand." For all growth there is something lost. Must we die to that which has been. Is this the way humankind as previously known will become extinct. What will we take with us. What did the Cro Magnin inherit from the Neanderthal and what did they sacrifice? We don't know the nature of Spirit. The unknown is our universe.Perhaps as the body cannot understand MIND's greatest leaps, neither can ordinary mind understand those of SPIRIT. But perhaps each can be AWARE! Each is an extension of the other."

    She fell again into silence. The sun had broken across the mountain tops and spread light down over the lower hills and fields. A clustering of bright white cotton ball clouds, their undersides painted softly with rose colors, spread upward into the heights of blue. The shadows in the Valley were like dark pits waiting for the rising light to penetrate their depths. The scattering of leaves in the oak below her house,hung utterly still, like coins suspended in the black branches, themselves sheaned with the silver of dawn. The stillness of this entrance of light through the land, transforming as it came, brought tears to Jessie's eyes. How could such beauty be spoken? This wonder, repeated so endlessly every single morning of life, filled her with an awe for the simple wonder of life itself, that she thought she could not bear that either. She laughed again, this time a low chuckle of amusement at herself,"There! See! In that simple fact lies a clue. For there, in that absolute beauty that is Earth's nature, is the first demonstration of SPIRIT to humanity. We have had it before us since time began." She was silent and then softly she added,"And it has done its work on us without our knowing." She watched, pleased to have found that thought. She turned to go out of her cottage and walk the winding pathway up to the Main Hall. The whisper of the morning wind in the pine above her as she walked across her needle covered court,seemed beautiful beyond description. She felt the needles thick under foot, and walked with hushed care, not wanting to disturb the quiet. She walked up the hill, wondering where eveyone was. It was early, but usually someone would be out and busy by now. Perhaps their impending Journey kept them longer in Temple. Surely that must be it. She walked on, listening, aware, absorbed in being alive. Perhaps she would spend this day in communion with that Mother through whom she lived.

    Early, the next day, the air quiet and cold, there were no voices anywhere on the Farm. The Hall was quiet, a breeze blew through the empty rooms, the morning warmed slowly from the cold autumn night. A curtain lifted lightly,swelled high, lost it's fill of wind and fell silently. Nothing stirred. The people were gone. Rob lay on his side, at the head of the steps where they had left him. He lay, eyes open in a nameless grief. For they had gone,and he felt for the first time in his life, truly separate from them. Vague thoughts of a changed world stirred and faded. Feelings of loss rose and he shook himself, lifting his head to growl softly. Some unseen danger, unsmelled and unknown threatened. He barked, listened for his mate's answer, and was comforted when she appeared. The cats had come, sitting near by, they were as silent as statues for some time, seeming to ignore him,but he knew they felt and needed his company. Finally, they left, one by one,

THE JOURNEY

to go and open their food bin for their breakfast. They were practical, life must go on, but for Rob, there was no hunger that food would satisfy this day.

The Family could still have been seen, Jessie at their head, walking lightly single file down the trail toward Adwin. They carried packs on their backs, and walked in silence. They crossed the Great Highway, seeing no one along it's visible length, and started up the slope toward Adwin, but half way up, they turned to another trail, that led out and down again to the Green River shore. Curving around the headland there, below the Industrial Center, the knoll broke into graduated benches, each smaller than the one below. Very steep steps had been cut into the rock ciff but mostly it was a long easy walkway. They arrived at the River's edge as silently as they had left home. A few boats still lodged in the slips along the front, but most were already out fishing, or pulled in out of winter storms.

Now there were intermittent comments, or cautions about the path. They felt both an uneasy question, and an unspoken excitement and eagerness. A driving force pressed against their hearts, this Journey, was not to be questioned. Neither was the question, had it been voiced, to be answered. It just was. Cassandra stood aside and waited until Jane passed near and she took her hand and held it tightly. The broad plasteel waterfront plaza, extending from the rocks of the shoreline out over the water for some forty feet, curved around the edge of the bank and across some fifty feet of the cliff face beyond. Cut into the rock cliffs were temporary lodges for fishermen, stalls for gear, and two larger meeting places where a good beer, or tea or coffee could be had along with some thing to eat. Wide easy steps wound into the rooms and up through walls on either side as they climbed to the town above.

There was a small crowd of people there, waiting on the quay, sitting on the rough carved benches of heavy planks solid and shining with their frequent oiling. Who were these? And then, as though the answer was born of itself in their brains, they knew. These were those who had themselves traveled this Journey and would see off their fellows out of respect and love. There were others who knew of this Farm Family climbing to that place of discovery. Many who remained at home, aware of what happened around them by casting their attention far, like a net that caught impressions and intentions.

William was not with the Family. Though he sat at this moment there in Altos, knowing of their going, wondering what it meant. Feeling so little he wondered at himself. No envy, no fear, no anger, little except his old familiar curiousity. He felt a wearyness with the struggle of the past months. He felt relieved that the old pull from that far Black Lodge, that pull that had fed something subtly insidious in him, was fading. He turned away from what he felt of it, with distaste. .

He sat silently, alone and lonely. Annette was not with him for she had fled to spend some weeks in Australia with her sister and he had been glad for he felt himself guilty. Yes, she would have known the hour they left. He only knew the day. Why can't I know too. Why is this so? He shook his head. He had not yet accepted all that he now admitted to. He said aloud,"And Rose probably Reaches to me. I suspect that, because she does that, and Paul certainly will. Yet I can't know. I am like a child to them, a child who cannot yet read or decipher what they see with ease. Vaguely I can grasp something of their ideas of what is happening to us. I can even believe that they must be right. But it means little to me, I cannot really imagine what it is like at all. They seem unable to tell me what it is like." He was silent, watching through the windows the cold light rain falling across the roofs and gardens below. "Perhaps it is a kind of blindness. And I will have to accept that fact, bitter as it is". He sat, wishing Annette were here, suddenly wishing and then as suddenly glad she was not.

The Family stopped at the River's edge, then turned on a pathway to the north that ran long the banks. The beaches here were narrow, but they broadened as they walked until after a few minutes they were several yards wide and sandy with heavy grasses making a thick carpet before the forest shadowed Earth too much. They must cross the River, but that would come later. The sky was blue, and the sun warmed the air a little; it was a beautiful morning. They could enjoy that. There were streaks of high clouds here and there. There might be rain before they -- returned? The idea that they would return seemed distant. This morning seemed to be the ending of life for them, as though there would be no life beyond this Journey. The thought brought a strange, sad relief.

Then they saw a flat, broad raft-like boat waiting ahead against a sharp edge of bank where the River turned. Tony, Jerry's friend, whose farm land ran along the River for a quarter of a mile, waited there, watching them arrive. They climbed onto the barge, and he activated the power pack that would silently propel this huge hand made River tool, which Tony used to carry his farm products to town and from which his whole Family fished. They moved out into the stream, the trees overhanging here made the River a green tunnel into which the sun gleamed.

Jerry asked,"Tony, how was the skenna crop in your wet lands this year?"

Tony nodded, smiling at him, his eyes flashing response that it had been good. But he didn't want to talk of that,He said,"Been several families going up this summer. You know." His glance swept over Jessie sitting at the other end of the craft, gazing over the water, "Her! She goes with people a lot. Or sometimes Adam does, or Margo. I'm always surprised, you know. "He grinned, tossed back his long hair, his eyes assessing this new group of 'travelers'. Jerry nodded slowly, his mind busy with these new thoughts. He hadn't really known, until the response to Telling's Field that millions of Valley people were already aware. That majority was what tipped the scales for humanity finally.

Tony got the barge, a bit clumsy to steer, pointed upstream and settled into its slow steady pace. They could see ahead up river where the morning shadows lay dark over the trees. The Valley narrowed slowly, until the hills finally came near the River. Then on up, where the water was running faster through narrower banks, they would see the mountains to either side with steep banks that made walking along the shoreline nearly impossible. Now, however, they watched the farmland of their neighbors pass slowly by. The tiny fishing villages receeded back into the trees in this late autumn. Only the water fronts, still floating, were busy. Fishing boats steadily worked the waters, the people ashore ran packing rooms, refrigerating and shipping out the crop. Many had returned here from their shoreland farm fields, not needed there with harvest done.

Tony glanced at the cluster of quiet faces where they were all seated together at the stern, their backs to home. He smiled at them, wanting them to relax. "You're all on your way then. This is a great day for a Journey. Looks as though it'll hold too with the weather turned warm for Indian summer." He gestured to indicate the far, blue sky above the trees.

Jerry stood beside Tony. He realized that the rest of the Family was already deep in the thoughtful attention that this Journey demanded. They seemed absorbed in a strange stillness of body , so relaxed, yet alert. The world around them seemed hardly to move , so silently the barge rode the shining green water. Tony steered carefully into mid stream,away from a tumble of massive boulders spilled out into the River from the shore line. They were familiar to Jerry, he had often come among them to fish. But now, they seemed different, as though he saw them for the first time. He met Tony's eyes and then asked,"How many years,Tony, have they been dong this?

Tony was thoughtful, ten or fifteen years people've been making the Journey. Not many at first. My Dad took them across then, but lately, there've been lots more. I thought all the Family groups of the north Valley must have gone. "

"What about your own folks?"

"It's near time, I think. Adam's been telling us to prepare. He wants us to go in a few days, because the mountain'll close down for winter soon. Strange, Jerry, for the first time since I've been ferrying people up, I feel like I'd like to be on my way too." His smile seemed pensive now, his eyes serious."You know, my Marya sings of the City. She's from the Vagabonds and has a deep bond anyway, but lately, she's been eager. She watches out to see the first light strike against the cliffs." His voice had a note of wistfulness and his eyes were fastened on the farthest point ahead.

Tony turned to attend to the maneuvering of the barge. The river current was increasing and he shifted the lever controlling the power unit beneath it's thick plank deck. He let his eyes follow the shore line, the familiar beloved land, the yellow, red and orange fall of leaves like gay curtains to both sides of them. No grass strip here, nor any fern covered bogs. Along the banks was a sweep of stiff stemmed Skenna plants that reached back into narrow finger like fields among the trees until they joined together in broad acres of flood plain. Here the River banks were forested but broken by steep rocky outcrops. Just north of the fording point the hills closed in, but the hardy Skenna persisted wherever a flat bit of land held water during long spring months. The rough thick stubble, green with a late leafing, still gave protection to the river birds and otters.

Silvia sat feeling the slight motion, wanting the silence, holding herself contained. Her eyes turned downward at the clear roll of green water and seeing it she allowed her thoughts and feelings to sink into those depths until she lost them beneath the green fields of microscopic life that fed the world of creatures living there. She vaguely felt Jane's hand holding hers, and knew that Jane's other hand was as comfortingly in Steve's . This was the beginning of something they knew was crucial to their lives, and which they longed for,yet they felt fear. After all, who enters into the unknown blithely, except children.

They knew that there were many forces combining to bring them to this day. And they could feel their own inner nature responding, waking further somehow,with each mile traveled.There was something ahead that was already drawing them, already had caught at their hearts, their Souls ,and intended to bring them to Itself.

They arrived at the edge of the forest path up which they would travel.Here the banks were higher and grass covered. Tony drew the barge in with barely a jolt as it bumped gently against the bank. They climbed off, one by one, gathering along the bank and saying their goodbyes. He stood, watching them turn, then begin to move across the small apron of grasses before entering the rocky trail that began to climb upwards through the thick trees,a look of envy on his face.

This was the country they did not know very well. Few traveled here. The forest was a mixture of conifer and disciduous trees, and the sun broke through thinning leaves in a spangled pattern of shade and light.The ground was deep in rustling dry color. Here and there small meadows claimed the land and they walked silently for moments across the deep green grasses.Then they were climbing in earnest through steep hillsides. At that it took only a short time for them to reach a considerable height. They walked steadily, slower now, keeping to the narrow trail. The ancient trees murmurred,evergreens whispered,as they passed. It could have been a party of friends out for a hike, except for the utter quiet.

Shadows lay down across their bodies and that cold woke the darkness within them. The cool shade brought a pall of chill, a reflection of inner doubt. Now faintly they felt a relentless backward pull which they , at first, consciously attributed to the steepness of the grade. These hills seemed twice as hard to climb as they ought.

Jane stopped suddenly, leaned against a pine and the thick foliage surrounded her, she could see the others still steadily moving there on the narrow path, heads down, lost to one another,. Jessie came finally at the end of the line, her old body moving with an ease that surprised Jane and made her wonder. It was not right, when even the youngest seemed to toil just to set one foot ahead of the other. Jessie stopped, lifting her face through the dappling light and shade, smiling with a joy that caught at Jane's heart and troubled her.Jessie seemed to be absorbed in the trees above her and Jane imagined she did not see her. She thought that she ought to just wait here, in this quiet place . She felt sleepy and tired. They could find her on their way back. She let her body slip down to sit on the thick needles. It felt so good. Earth life around her, seemed to her so welcoming.

Then, she felt a strange tugging within her own body, a flash of something loosened in her mind, and from it grew a desire that resisted the urge to rest. She felt herself standing again. The others were gone, she couldn't see them ahead at all. She must go on. In conflict, she felt her weariness, a longing to return home, to leave this confusing forest and find again her old identity. The trees around her were so vast, so old, Their spreading quiet became a contemplation, a conscious awareness that spoke to her, nudging like a soft cascade of rain in her mind. So physically real did it seem that she glanced upward, expecting clouds but there was only the sunlight, pouring through and on the needles and the ruddy leaves of oak, gleaming silver. The yellow heat of it covered her face, her hands.

Then there rose again that deep inner tugging, a desire to reach, to know those lives around her, the vast power of the forest life. The longing rose and grew until it was a song and she could hear at some inner point of listening. She did not think anymore, but responded with that deep urgency toward that great, vivid Life. The dark and light, the Sun and Earth, Life and Death, receiving and letting go, here juxtapozed, and at their edges flickered a new meaning for her. She felt some tough knot snap within herself. Snap and release her. The world she had left, the dream of accomplishment, seemed a drifting cloud, non essential. As she watched within the stillness of this place, immersed in the dark Earth force, old memories began to take on a new look,they seemed transparant, incomplete.

Gradually old memories fell and softened then dissolved as mist does in sunlight. She looked through them, saw there a new Earth. Every living thing seemed to her to be pulsing with a golden life. She felt awe. It was as though all life presented itself as this tender gentle smile, and she was included. All bitterness all hardness and suffering, cruelty of living, dispair, all that was created of pain, stood within that smile. Suffering was the resistance to life then, the refusal? But she herself was more-- she was herself a way - a passage, through which this new Earth could be found. Herself-- and all other human beings, they -- we -- are the Way. She found the thought pulsing there in her mind, and wondered fleetingly where it had come from. And exactly what it meant!

Jane opened her heart to receive, to accept and doing so, she saw that the old familiar was encompassed within this new Light. There -- that which had been, was rearranging itself within what was becoming,. She herself was no longer what she had been. And all she had been was -- lost? -- gone? No,only absorbed into this larger nature.

She straightened, her eyes wet with the tears of realization, of struggle and of loss. A great sob broke from her, she held her head in both hands and the grief broke through her like a tearing, leaving her emptied. She felt as though an unspoken knowledge grew through that emptyness.She stood straight, lifting her head with conviction, the trees seemed to her to support her direction. She began to walk again on the path, climbing with a renewed energy, a sureness she had never felt before. She did not notice Jessie there behind.

They climbed on, the day was nearing noon. Andrew was in the lead, his young body finding these trails more demanding than any he remembered. He glanced back now and then, seeing the older folks bent and quiet. He stopped at last. "This looks like a good place to rest and eat our lunch." They stopped and looked around. They had reached a small meadow, nearly flat among the rocky up thrusts. Familiar trees seemed smaller, older, struggling in the thinner soil. Evergreens were in their element, tall, piercing the blue above them. He waited, watching, while the others moved out into the meadow, to sit down, to lie flat on their backs, weary and glad to rest. He shrugged and joined them. He saw Jessie coming round the last boulder that twisted the path and knew they were all here. Something was happening -- something he didn't understand.

Steve voiced it for them all. he felt it like a dark, weight in his body. His voice was a whisper, "We're not going back! Not ever! We're leaving our home forever!" The edge of panic made his voice high.

Silvia sat up to study his face, then swiftly those of the others. She turned finally to Benjamin who sat leaning with his eyes closed against a huge grey boulder. "What does he mean, Ben? Is it true? I feel something like that too" . She shook her head, grimaced, "Can it be!" Her questions were staccato slaps in the air. Then suddenly frowning, she drew a huge sigh of relief. "Oh, you don't mean that, Steve. Of course, we'll go back. Where else would we go?" She seemed satisfied with her own answer and leaned back against a small tree.

Benjamin turned to meet her gaze, his eyes full of such deep sorrow that she gasped to see it. She leaned forward, "Wait, you do mean it! Tell me, what's going on."

Steve looked around. The others seemed lost in some kind of communion, some quiet of-- he studied them -- of grief? It was what he felt. "The whole Valley, all our lives, friends down there, all we've done. All the work, our Farm, that we built , that we love. We couldn't leave it all. How can it be true that we're not going back!" His voice was angry. He looked at Ben but Ben had closed his eyes, his face composed. He seemed to Steve to have died. He turned worried eyes to the others and found Rose's eyes on his. Fear shook his anger into life.

There was a presence of sadness among them and Rose acknowledged it with a shake of her head, acknowledged as though the right thing was to deal with it firmly. "There is that, Silvia. The world there, below us, that we can barely see now, through the trees, spread out like a landscape painting. We can spot so many loved spots, and we must know that that world is gone for us. Forever gone. Even if you went back now, it wouldn't be there."

Silvia was horrified, she jumped to her feet, anger renewing her energy. She looked from one to the other, "Come on, quit playing games. This is no joking matter. It's impossible but with all the things that've happened I'm not going to risk anything more. The Valley isn't going to disappear just because we've left it. You're not making sense."

Paul touched her, he among them all had not sat down. He took her hand and held it close to his side as children do. "They mean that it's gone the way your childhood is gone. But you won't be allowed years to realize it this time. The world is changed when a young person does something significant, like getting married, or completing his first youth school, or having a first child. The world is never the same. In that sense, hasn't it gone?" He dropped her hand, his eyes holding hers for a moment, his serious but smiling, her's still defiant, but softening. Then her gaze passed beyond him and into the distance below.

He turned to find a seat on a flat stone, bending forward. "It's true, we'll never go back. What we will be when we have completed this Journey, I don't know. But it has to be found out." A sorrow, like Benjamin's, caught at his voice now, and his own eyes sought comfort in that distant scene.

Again there was silence. Again the bodies stretched themselves into comfort, rest and renewal. Water was passed around, someone opened a bag of apples and big golden complums. Then a package of sandwiches, and everyone was busy eating. The droning of the autumn day around them seemed to comfort them. So natural it was, so familiar. There were tears in some eyes, a grief that rose from depths below thought. And yet no sounds were made. Steve's cry spoke for them all. "Why? Why must it all be gone? I had so much left to do? I had plans, and -- there was so much."

Tom turned to look at him, his eyes hard. "Just don't think about it now. It doesn't make sense except after the fact. Just the way it does with any important event." He couldn't understand Steve's worry.

Then, slowly there came a quality of Presence, of power focussed. Someone had Reached gently, and a Joining began. Paul bent his head, bringing all his energy to Reach. He knew Rose and Ben already had created a triangle with Tom, he entered and felt Jennifer with them. Then vaguely but without doubt, he knew that another triangle had formed between Jessie, Andrew and Anna. He knew instantly that it was right. The triangles first, then the melding of two triangles. Paul recognized with an inner sight, that Tom and Ben had become the base of theirs and Rose the apex and that, Jessie as apex of the other, swung in that heightening consciousness toward them. The others entered, one or the other triangle, and then bringing themselves into balance, the second triangle came against the first, base to base and a diamond was formed. They were a great diamond of energy that pulsed and drew from the universe itself, then gave to all the life around it. A great wonder grew in their faces, as they realized this fact.

The form was shaped and held intact by their combined minds. Cassandra reached out her hands, as if to touch them all, and then with a soft cry of relief and gladness, she let go of her past, her child world, her longings for what had been, or might have been. She gave her own power, so strong and stable, rich beyond the few years of her life, her mind melded, fused, and she was conscious of them all there, a powerful single Mind. Then she turned herself, moved into another position and there was a three dimensional diamond and Silvia and Jane were another base, Paul, steady at that apex. Clustered there, firming the multidimensional center were the others. At that moment, Andrew shifted mental focus, to make that diamond four sided. As he did, Anna loosed her position to

Jennifer at the base and she, moving, through, out of sight, between states of visibility, drew their attention through and beyond the mental space they were shaping. Instantly the diamond was known to have existence in that fourth dimension that extended through the veils of the worlds. Could they hold? Could they keep that shape firm? It needed something more, for shapes were not the same thing in that fourth condition. Mind was a tangible substance. Jessie left her place to Paul and moved herself there, between worlds, invisible to familiar thought, but visible to the focussed minds of that multidimensional Diamond of Consciousness. Her strength, her knowledge, stabilized their perception.

Steve had felt his daughter leave them, move out, and sorrow engulfed him. Then a knowledge filled him, and he felt that great Love that filled this creation they were building. The energy of its very shaping was Love. He turned himself to realize, knowing that he would give up his life to this family in the process. And as he did, it seemed so very natural. All that was lost seemed little in comparison. Yet he knew well that he entered into what was unknown to his old, small brain-mind. On wings of his faith, knowledge flooded through all sorrow and left him free.

Silvia felt those events, felt them soundly and with astonishment. She knew also that Jane was already moving, already stepping into that pulsating jewel of human relationship. She saw and knew and felt herself turn toward the Valley below. Her mind flooded by what she knew there. She felt her own desires rise and pull at her, felt old hungers gnaw, and then subside. The old dreams had seemed so important. The loosing of these ideas, longings, was like the sloughing off of old skin, natural and beneficial. She felt herself watching them fade as from a distance. And yet, she knew they would be there again, diminished, but present to be lived. They were simply not so central to things anymore.

At that moment she thought of the child within her, all she had dreamed for him, for his greatness among people. She began to turn away from that mind pattern they built, the quiet steady shining of energy. She blinked and saw nothing except people gathered in an odd arrangment among the meadow grasses. Even as she did, she felt the stir of life in herself, a powerful choice made , and she recognized that she could make no plans for this one who lived already there. He was already moving into that center creating itself among her people. And so she followed, awed by the amazing power of that unborn mind. There again in the meadow the great pulsing diamond of Light stood visible in the winter air. To her surprise, she and her child entering so, created another three dimensional point, another triangle that opened a full facet of brilliant Light. To bear that Light-- now, she had become part of that many dimensional form, to perceive something of that farther dimension, whose very existence stunned and stretched her consciousness to pain, and within which this familiar world was held like a dream. Slowly the fact of it was clear and understandable. But to bear that LIGHT, now that she chose to enter fully, took all her strength. Then, giving way to simple awareness, allowing her mind to empty, to be aware, she saw it was very simple and took no strength at all!

THE JOURNEY

The energy they drew into focus and form here, multiplied so many more times than the simple addition of their numbers. Informing, cleansing, reaching from somewhere beyond them all, it was also rising from within them. She realized with a great dawning knowledge,"We have been the focal point of such Light energy all our lives and we did not know. It has always been in us, like a light lit waiting for the wind of recognition to blow it to flame." The thought shaped itself, fastened itself into her consciousness and she knew it was true.

She knew without doubt that the source of this Diamond of Light was good, that though it seemed to disappear into further dimensions, it was nevertheless shaped by great forces of Good. That quality of selflessness, of harmlessness, was radiant within it, was inherent. Silvia sighed, Reached out to those around her and accepted without doubt.

They sat for a while, their bodies resting, their consciousness building. Then slowly they shrank to familiar limits and sat watching the Valley, the day's business creating movement here and there, the flitting of air cars, the gleam of the River and the river boats, like tiny chips floating in it. And they wondered! They knew with acceptance and a gentle sorrow, that they would never enter into that world of their childhood. They had passed through a doorway toward adulthood, they must begin living from a new knowledge.

Rose said, "It's so quiet here. But the stillness is actually in me. Perhaps in all of us?" She looked around, then went on,"Together, we realize something that's beyond our minds to fully remember. Yet, I carry the memory, the shape of it, the possibility, like a promise. Even when thinking stops, imagery continues."

Benjamin looked at her, took a long breath, as if coming up from deep water. He nodded absently, "Reducing ourselves down to what we've always been is to lose -- so much. And yet, we barely sustain consciousness of what we are becoming."

Then slowly they realized that the goodbye had to be made by each one alone. Paul said,"As close as we've been, the Valley meant something different to each of us, our lives have been actually very separate. To let go of what was, isn't to lose it, but to extend outward-inward to what IS. The multiple diamond expresses an inclusive reality. We did see that!

Rose's heart leaped - a glimpse of that old chasm on whose edge she had felt herself standing so many times in longing and fear, unable to cross, yet knowing that she must. There it had been, unattainable, and yet, -- now, together, supporting one another, they might -- . She breathed the thought into shape,"Together we might meet that terrible emptyness, that point at which I have always balked, and go on. For is that point that appeared to be emptyness, not actually the other dimension of the diamond of perception we've created here? A shape that extends out into Mind substance? So unfamiliar it seems nothing at all?"

Silence grew around them, they each withdrew into themselves. Rose realized she deliberately could make the choice, to step into emptyness and risk the unknown beyond. To set aside the limits of thought and stand beyond. Now, with the others she had seen so much farther, as though from a satalite looking down on Earth, she had seen that the mountains were not impassable. There was in her that which could exist, live there, beyond this limited dimension, and still retain connection. Oh, it was clearly a Reach of Mind alone. But then, Mind was clearly more than she had ever thought it to be. Was a lucid abstract MIND state that other dimension? But how could a 'I' exist there? How did the physical world relate to that state? She shook her head as if to free it from an unsettling burr. Thinking was like a hedge, protecting and limiting, but to think of THAT troubled and frightened her. She said to herself very slowly,"Take heart, I've just shrunk down into this limited world view again." She let the fact of that settle into perspective.

Yet she herself had stretched, not just from the strength of the others. She herself also, now was --'more' -- surely, each of them was. With a sudden swift abandon she let herself flow from the safe mooring place of her physical body, moved on through surrounding sheiths that were subtle bodies, with their own extension and their own limits. Then growing vastly more aware, her body felt tension grow. She thrust against that limit, and the act brought pain, fear, astonishment and unbelief. But it was also a great swelling of JOY that threatened to catapult her into that unlimited surrounding awareness, not emptyness at all--but rather - - a place of no limits. And she clutched at the limits as though clinging to her mother's hand.

Thus released, consciousness Reached out, encompassed the Valley beyond and felt the color, shape, smell, taste and size of everything from the smallest sand grain to the greatest solid cliff, the microbe and the shaggy wild horses, the dying of a calf in the fierce jaws of wolves, the sleepy safety of a bear finding her place of hibernation and birth. The power of it, the pain, rush of urgency, eager acceptance; the birth of young. There was everywhere a sudden intent charge and then, hot blood and pain and sharp odor of death. The strange, melancholy giving up to death, withdrawing of life from that torn body before it knew complete pain. She had seen a rabbit once being swallowed by a snake and having released its own resistance entered a comotose state. And this was life itself. And yet, knowing, aware, she felt the others realizing with her. There was a lack, something missing, a terrible jagged draining sorrow of something lacking. Something that was not there! Within everything of Earth there was something missing -- something she could not name,, touch, sense, speak of. Something nameless, like a fire burning far beneath showing no smoke yet, but never ceasing to warm. That nameless thing that offered itself as an ultimate threat and ultimate possibility if one were to enter into it. Annihilation in fact! And yet, without it, there would be no Life at all.

How to define, name? She thought she had to find a NAME!

She wanted the others, their help, wanting to fall back on them. But she knew she had to find this herself. What was it? It was there, just beyond -- beyond what? It was precisely clear, yet unfocussed as though any second she would SEE. There was something preventing -- she drew back, down into herself, her body, her senses, and started again, seeing now the tree before her, the leaf, a purple scale on it, the mite gnawing away on it, and always there was that thing beyond vision, just barely beyond. How could she know it was there at all?

But the knowledge rose up out of her deepest consciousness, swept inward through her from beyond consciousness. She did not doubt.

Where to search? She focussed down into her own body, the flesh, the skin, the inner organs and their tissues. The blood, hot and steady, flowing as if it knew its own business, nerves carrying instant messages everywhere, as if they ran the body with care. And then she turned her attention to her own brain, watched it's function, sending minute dicharges of chemicals out, sending electrical impulses on to organs that performed their function as if intelligent. She tightened her focus, entered into cells and found there, another kind of intelligence, producing, dividing, shifting --- and then, suddenly, going no further, she realized, "Who enters into this tiny life and knows it? It is I. Then I am Mind itself? I am that which knows?

There she sped from those internal functionings, realizing -- "I am myself knowing as I am becoming and there is no separation between mind and body." The thought shaped, distracted her from knowing. "Mind shapes physical substance from mental templates?"

Then the idea was drowned in thinking. But moving from that cage of thinking as though pulling herself free from molasses, she could simply see it as fact. Physical Earth did not come first, but was a blossoming forth of Matter infused with Spirit, shaping, creating. She was AWARE, not thinking, BEING. And all things were as was she!

No time was. Yet inherent within the physical forms through which she passed, time marked itself through events. Thought isolated itself, shaped itself like a mist, and firmed until she knew a passing knowledge. All else was Being shaped in Mind extended from Spirit, and there was nothing that was not of Mind. Yet each was also separate and there were many dimensions of Being. But there, beyond THAT, beyond everything knowable was -- what was beyond -- unknowable? Unnamable? Yet clearly THERE! Her mind quailed at the edge of something else.

She drew back as swiftly as an amoeba might touch then contract. Recognition yawned and threatened to drown her.. Experience, phenomonon, were of the nature of Mind itself. They were not separate and there fore -- neither was Mind itself separate. A single reality. But drawing back, thinking again, shrinking, identifying into experience, she lost the far OTHER. She shuddered as at a painful loss, the sense of it so acute it bled through every cell of her being, energy seemed to pour through her and drain on, like the impelling waters of a sea washing through its creations. How could she follow? But now she knew!

Shaken loose, submerged again in thinking.in shaping thought, she knew that the impression from that endless mind substance, was felt in every living thing. She could never cease to know of it, even paying no attention, it was there beneath everything she was. She lay in a profound stillness, realizing, awareness was a pulsing of electrical energy, a flow shaping and forming. She thought that she, herself, had performed the way a sense organ might, receptive, reactive, responsive, and she wondered if perhaps human beings were not subtle sense organs of Earth Herself. Was her job to extend consciousness out into the physical world, further, more subtly, then through the mental world even further into subtlety? Was it to know and sustain that knowing?

Or was she only another ubiquitous human ego functioning again? Her body wept softly, her mind sustained its touch with power like an arching rainbow. Grieving at ignorance, lacking, she also knew fullness, completion. Could human life extend beyond each personal self? For her there was no possible doubt. Thoughts whirled, but beneath them, surrounding them, she was quietly waiting, still. Since all this was part of being aware then it was also part of being human. And so being human was vastly more than any one could think of. Beneath the whirling cacaphony of thought, was a wonderful stillness an amusement, a watchful knowing. And surprisingly, the thinking did not interfere. That stillness was like an ocean into which she plunged and from which she brought all she could absorb to - to think about! Why couldn't she simply accept without having to explain everything -- everything. Explaining had been her nemesis forever, would it be again? Or did it have purpose also?

She sank into herself, drew down, realized herself in her physical body, her face wet with tears, her heart sore, and aching, her body exhausted and her mind flaccid. Slowly she began to sense all this, then the grass,Earth beneath her, the trees, the sky, the Family around. She dug her hands into the grass, thrilling to the feel of it. Simple and familiar.She pressed the ache of her mind down through that Earth, the pain of her fingers in the dark sandy soil drew her mind out of itself, left her to sensation. She let her self cry softly, sought to comfort herself.

She opened her eyes wide, looked around.Everything shone as from an inner light, a radiance of Life that spoke to her mind as clearly as words could have. She could SEE Earth anew. And then, as if finally she relaxed enough to recognize, she Knew. What is beyond is also this, This, our familiar world, is also THAT!

She did not doubt or argue.it was fact now. She could let it be, healing her mind, her body with the knowledge. She found herself thinking, trying to explain again and she smiled. Well, let that be too. her mind would always explain,or try to do so. But there was that known. She could not bear to realize , to Reach so far again soon. I am so tender, memory holds my life hostage. I remember!

She moved around, feeling movement, touching things, looking, smelling, entering into herself without restraint. Enjoying being this one limited human person utterly.She laughed suddenly released, it was her choice. She stroked her skin, her hair, clasped her hands together, feeling the wonder of them. She thought of Benjamin and her love for him. And she felt it surge through her body like a wave. She thought of the Family, looked at them,sitting there, and their very presence swept through all doubt.

But continuing,as though discovered and permanent,that quality of

THE JOURNEY

amusement filled her mind, her heart. It released her from the bonds of thinking. Nothing could ever bind her to the smallness of herself, her old self again. She reached through herself and felt the Joy of it.

She felt the others knowing their own discoveries and turned all her attention to them. She felt the steady flow of strength from Jessie pooling about them. Rose felt comfort in that flow. Yes, the Journey meant a loss, acceptance of that loss, but it was most of all a finding.

A rising flood of grief poured through them all. A grief at first not understood. Finally Silvia nodded, realizing. "It's so sad, you know. So sad that we must end, let that life die away. It's true. It's true, that we will not be, are already not the same." She was silent, then with a sad, small smile, she said, "I remember when I was fourteen, and I knew with absolute certainty that I could not be the way I had always been, the child I had been. I wanted to grow up, to be a young woman, and yet -- yet, I found myself grieving to lose those old simple joys, the comforting pleasures of being a child." She nodded abruptly, "There is something of that now, the sense that we will not be, cannot be as we were because now we consciously choose to stand beyond what we have been." The fact that she herself had made the group statement surprised her, as did the fact that she noticed that.

They mourned in a quiet acceptance. No one had imagined such a sorrow as part of growth. They all knew well that they would enter that Valley again, would return to the Farm, but they would not enter into that old life. The old days were gone. Done! What the new would be could not be imagined.

They began to stand, look upward toward the trail. Only a short hour had passed, though it had seemed so much longer and they were refreshed. Then, just as they were ready, single file in the narrow trail, they began spontaniously singing the old Valley song of Farewell.

> Go with the day, our brother , our sister,
> Go to the new world you seek and enjoy it.
> Know all of its treasures, its greatness and grief,
> And bring them back someday to us.
> Fare thee well, Fare thee well,
> Our Love will go with you,
> Hold you and keep you safe.
> Know our Love around you friend,
> Until you return.

The familiar song took on new meaning now, the words softened their grief and gave them a sense of finalizing the fact. When the song was done, they commenced again to climb. The trail led them past a small pond from which deer were drinking. Now they stood and watched the passing human beings without moving, curious, unafraid and silent. Their great dark eyes unblinking and at peace. The calm acceptance by the deer was healing to the Family, though they couldn't say why.

THE PEOPLE OF THE VALLEY

Thus the first day of the Journey passed. From the meadow they wound up a crooked rocky trail, treacherous hard climbing, through deep forest lands, so dense that the light was for some time only a scattering of gold on the ground around them. It was not until the light began to fade at evening that they found themselves suddenly rising out of the forest. They climbed through a sheer rock fall, sharp edged boulders, clumped so that they must work their way round them, over them, until they came out on a broad flat tableland. The peaks rose above, but here, all around, there were clean cliff sides, benches breaking over one another, like a series of high narrow steps up into the slopes covered with stunted trees and shrubs. Before them were huge slabs of gleaming grey stone, shot through with a blue vein that formed tables, clustered leaning giants that created small caves and tunnels between themselves. They stood on the broad flat surface and after being so long in the high trees, it seemed in the evening sun, very bright and clean. Small trees pushed their way through crevases between rock, clung to the steep cliff faces and were clustered here and there where sand and earth fall had made a place to sprout.

They dropped their packs, let them lay while they sank down to look around. Here would be a good spot for night camp. The air was cold now, a steady wind blew across the side of the mountain. Unshielded by forest, they felt it's full force, so they drew back behind a tall clump of boulders. Without much talk, the children began gathering dry fuel for a small, clean burning night fire. They drew out long thermal cloaks, light and warm enough to sleep in, yet easy enough to wear if need be. They were water proof yet soft to touch. A threaded power pack ran heat through the cloth when activated.

Grief seemed suddenly far away. Already old patterns, old habits seemed to have split away. There was left a wounded feeling, a hollow ghost of sadness that they folded into themselves and accepted. But there was also the clear sharp excitement and interest of that Journey and what it would mean. Their minds fled from analysis, sought quiet contemplation. they felt moved toward stillness more than toward thought. It was as though thinking had exhausted itself. A large pot made of cylinders that crushed together to form a single ring and which had been hung on Ben's pack, was opened out and filled with water from a spring that threaded down through rock crevases. Paul looking at the site, reckoned it to be a familiar camp site. He glanced at Jessie, moving so familiarly about and knew that she had brought others through this land.

Even Cassandra seemed absorbed in her own quiet Between them, there flowed a mutual awareness, a gentle desire to attend to each other's small physical needs and to forget the rest of the Valley for the moment. Fragrant odors of dinner rose from the heat units within half an hour, and everyone gathered around, hungry, eager to be doing something so simple and familiar. They talked lightly of the day, the surroundings, as they ate. But as they did, there grew a sense of themselves there, on the high mountain, and their place in that Earth universe, in the scheme of things alive. A subtle knowledge began to shape itself. They realized themselves more sharply as extensions of Earth, conscious spawn

THE JOURNEY

of Earth along with the trees and the clean smooth grey stone. They settled into the mountain side, subdued, feeling that deep relationship.

They cleaned and stored their utensils. The sense of physical and mental weariness gone. Good food and rest had restored them. Rose smiled, noticing how different she felt. Food was always a miraculous restorer. And here there had been food of many kinds. For some time they sat enjoying the novelty of this new place, the high mountain world, the high forbidding peaks above them, behind which the sun had set.

Tom spoke,"Strange, here we are reduced to very simple needs, surrounded with little of our civilization and yet we're able to fit. Wouldn't you agree?" He looked around, still judging himself in this environment. Could he survive here, physically survive?

Ned followed his thoughts and questions, nodded and was himself wondering. "I always think of that when I come to the forests, Tom. I haven't ever really answered it to my satisfaction. I've spent weeks living alone in the Valley forests, with only a few tools to help me, but never in the winter. That I doubt I could do. What would happen to me here?"

Silvia spoke impatiently,"Seems foolish to speculate. The natural creature has a life pattern which guides his survival. People who live in the forests remain when the season is best for them and leave when it's not. If you lived with forest people long you'd have a regular path to food supplies learned through generations. You'd know the skills for keeping warm in winter, but it's still pretty primitive. And there are few such people today."

They all knew they were avoiding the talk that must come. There was silence. Tom studied Silvia, absently, appreciating her beauty, his mate Mary leaned against his shoulder, his arm around her. He thought of his sons, they had been sad but proud of Nathan who chose to wait to make the Journey with Angy, because Justin, mind-blind, would not go at all. Nathan said, with the caring of a parent, "Dad, he'd feel better if we leave him with you and the rest of the family later." He squeezed Mary's waist as he remembered. He thought of his own fears, familiar, tough, resistant. They would not be displaced easily. But somehow, he was comforted by their familiarity. They were resistant barriers within them all, they would bear attention soon. There, he thought, that's something to get settled. But when?

Jessie spoke aloud,"Are any of you aware of where the Silent City is from here?"

They were unprepared for the question. Rose, Benjamin, Tom and Anna, then Paul and Andrew immediately nodded, surprising themselves. They realized the direction had been clear to them during the day, that the City had acted as a beacon, drawing them, guiding. Jerry, Jennifer and Cassandra shook their heads, frowned, focussed their attention and then, with a look of surprise, nodded too. They had not been aware of Her, but now, they knew without question. Ned, Mary, Steve, Jane and Silvia looked at Jessie, puzzled, wondering at the other's confidence.

THE PEOPLE OF THE VALLEY

Jessie did not speak. After a few minutes,, Silvia said," Why, maybe - it's --. I have a strong feeling that I must continue to the south east. If I were alone, that's the way I would go from here, but I didn't think of the City at all. Does that mean anything?"

"It's a way to test yourself. Try it, those of you who do not know. Which way would you go?" They were silent again, and she saw the look of surprise come also to their faces. "Why, yes,it's true." Jane stood up and walked a little way in the direction she would take. She looked over the trail ahead, through the rock, the jumble of great weathered boulders. Beyond them, a faint trail wound for a short distance and then seemed to disappear. They could not take that trail , surely.

True to her nature she began to talk of what she knew,"It's the Earth that tests us, isnt' it? It's through Her barriers, her cliffs, her narrow ways, that we'll either find our way or not." She turned back to them, her eyes wide, her slim body looked fragile in the fading light, its very real strength concealed by the soft loose shirt and trousers, tucked into light,calf high boots. It's the Earth who is our teacher on this part of the way, isn't it?"

Jessie nodded," And yourselves. Each of you is a teacher here,remember. But you must know the Earth, know Her as Jane does, and as Benjamin does even though he has not acknowledged so." She sighed and added softly, "Tomorrow will require a lot from us all. It's dark and though it isn't late, let's let our bodies rest and restore the energy we'll need to use. Earth is not niggardly, though She can be ruthless. Her energies will pour through us to restore us while we sleep, if we so request."

It was only a short time that they were settled, each one a little separate from the others. Each one feeling a desire to contain his own thought, to make communion with himself in these last moments before the final stage of the Journey. The night was clear, they had no storm to deal with at least. They were grateful for that as they drifted off to sleep.

In the twilight time of consciousness, between sleep and waking, there is sometimes a rent in the fabric of things, a place where waking consciousness is releasing its hold and the deeper consciousness, alert during sleep is already a little visible. What has been known in those deeper realms of the psyche but hidden from view of the outer attention, is visible. A clarity of vision, wherein recognition can occur and be remembered.

The doors of perception are open, what is seen through those doors however, may be glimpses of beauty, of those gone before us to that separate realm called death, it may be a wisdom about our lives or hidden intentions that cannot surface through the watch dog of the conscious mind,it may be glimpses of what is immenent in our future, or it may be a descent into our deepest miseries, and our basest longings. The hidden is both wonderful and awful.For those who are timid of spirit, these glimpses may be forgotten in the ensuing sleep, but for the strong souls, seeking to know themselves regardless of pain or joy, recognition is held and known. Consciousness had expanded for people of the Valley and it had long invaded that realm called subconscious, illuminating and bringing more and more into full consciousness. In the study of dreams they had learned to be alert to their wisdom or their warnings.

The Journey lifted every sense to a height that held it focussed and taut. It was a time of excitement and of the surfacing of hidden feelings and attitudes. It was a time when the gates between worlds traditionally are loose, when the Soul takes its opportunity to speak and to show the person through which it expresses Itself, something of the nature of things. And of Its own nature.

Tom let himself relax in the quiet enjoyment of this lovely night, a great yellow moon rising in the east spread light everywhere and he roused himself to look around, before sleep. The moonlight itself seemed to him to be mysterious, full of a promise that he could not name. He thought,'The moonlight has saved us for eons from that expected darkness of night, and it's presence after the day's sun is gone is still a light of wonder'. Now, its magic worked again on the world around. He lay watching it rise into the sky. He was excited and pleased to think of the day's Journey, and of all that must be coming ahead. There would be rough mountain country to cross, to climb through. There was adventure ahead. He closed his eyes, feeling himself drift away, enjoying the sense of giving himself up to the sleep that pulled at him.

As he drifted, he was aware of a strange sense of unease; his attention turned to it, though his eyes remained closed, he felt the ebb and flow of sleep and attention. Resentment, crowded up from beneath attention, pushed away sleep. He could not deny it, that resentment was strong! What? Why? he drew himself into a watching attitude, the familiar practice of balancing. Why am I so angry? The fact surprised him, but he didn't doubt. Many times Tom, had found himself feeling what he didn't know he felt.

" I might as well find out. I won't sleep until I do." Thoughts swept into view, overpowering any resistance, thoughts that rose from that anger as bubbles rise from disturbed water. He felt sinking sorrow even as he felt anger. Thoughts formed," Alone, I could climb through that mountain within a few hours. With this crowd I'll be surprised if someone isn't killed before we get there. Besides,there's Jessie. She's too old to be climbing such country. Why's she doing it anyway? We could go on alone. She could come by Belt. Why the devil didn't we bring Belts anyway? We're going to get into real trouble. Why can't I just get up and go on alone. Or Jessie could Send, Reach back to Adwin,. I know she's got people there who can receive, they could bring Belts. Why all this struggle?"

Unable to believe his own anger,or these questions, he searched himself. What made him so restless, so resistant? The thought of Silvia, pregnant and the burden she would present, flashed into mind like one more thorn to rouse resentment. Then he soberly shook his head, bringing the inner eye into focus, for the outer eye, critical and sharp, had questioned.'Is there something in me afraid?' The ability to read himself, see within without flinching had made Tom known for insights others seldom had.

He saw his fear, it astonished him. He shifted focus and saw that the others were struggling with their own questions. That knowledge released him from fear for a moment, a reminder of his love. Then piercingly, the thought, "If you love them, you'll see that they don't go into that danger ahead." Resentment was using that very love to further its aims." I'm the only really qualified person except for Jane, to do such climbing." The thought lay in his mind like a seeping acid, disturbing the quiet, eroding the sense of companionship, of unity. He shrank to himself, suddenly seeing that he was resentful of his love for them. Did loving them mean he had to be responsible for them?

The recognition stung, stung and rose like a bitter acid in his mouth. He said in a whisper as though talking to another, "You think you're superior to the others, that you are better able to enter the City. You're afraid they will hold you back. Cause you to forfeit the whole Journey."

There, the statements, standing before his attention, seemed evil. He cringed from them, refusing the accusations. He countered, "How could that be true? I'm concerned that someone'll get killed. After all, I do know what climbing can be like!" I am concerned!"

"You aren't!" At the recoil of rage at this self accusation, he almost exploded in fury of self defense. But something broke free before his vision, something released in this interchange. He could see his own fear raw there before him. "It's true. I AM afraid." The admission rocked him. He felt betrayed. He wept to see his own duplicity, and his own cowardice.

Then the voice, speaking from those depths, urged on now by that clear voice of reason, before which no cloud of denial could conceal the truth, spoke gently, "I am afraid for myself. Myself!" The fact jolted him anew, spoken aloud, it brought pain.

He felt himself become still, accepting. Finally he moved through the self disgust, and stood free. He said clearly to himself, "I don't want my fear to endanger anyone on this Journey. I will not! I will draw what courage I have. I will look to them, because it is together, only together that we can make this Journey at all. After all, that is a fact."

He lay then, absorbing, reflecting, allowing the knowledge to settle into his whole being. Sobering and humbling, it enabled him to recognize himself anew. He left off thinking, and simply watched, realized. Out of inner silence a thought took shape. He spoke it. "ONLY as a people can we -- humanity, take the next step. I do know that! I cannot forget -- or deny it." the fact of that knowledge sobered him again. "Now, in this simple way, we practice for that greater unity!" He was aware of the resentments, the fears, the excitement, many feelings, and he sighed, swallowed them all and said, as he turned to sleep, "They've all got to be taken as they are. But before them all, I intend to take my part and keep strength. I may be afraid even, but fear won't control me. I will keep balance." Then, reflecting on that decision, he spoke, "Standing at the point of Light at the apex of my being, in Soul consciousness, I will balance myself." These were the final words of the ritual of balancing, and he spoke them with relief.

Jessie sat unmoving on a flat stone by the little fire that still burned faintly. She felt the night, the Earth surge, and the moon pull. She enjoyed each. She held herself apart from the Family she watched over. They must be on their own now. Their growth was sufficient, they could meet what came. She saw Tom throw his body sideways, roll over on the thick grass, the air sponge of his bag cushioning his bones against the ground. The air had grown colder, he drew the bag higher, settled and was instantly asleep.

Jessie observed the nature of her own desires. Deeply she wanted them all to come through, to complete the Journey. If she had taught well, if she had judged well, they were able. But she knew this was her own desire. It was not to be given attention. The rise and fall of feelings was familiar to her. The pull of them quickened her attention and her wary mind was attentive. This was the power that could pull her off center. The power of personal desire. She watched it ebb and flow and smiled at herself. The still center did not yield.

What could she do, for this lingering thorn of pride, of selfness must be met. It could, catching her off balance, lead her down to its blinding caverns where she might -- she laughed then, aloud."Oh, No! too many times I have watched myself, known myself and guided myself through these labyrinths." But the task now was to meet head on, once again, the hidden, so that it could not work unseen and gnaw at the foundations of her knowledge.

She sank toward those old memories, the old voices, the dreams of her youth, the fears of her age. She worked her way back to clear recognition, so familiar that path, seeing and refusing to deny. Yet how many times must it be done? When the recognitions came, then she must hold herself steady against them. Hold that still center where balance existed. She watched them, familar, dear, hated, decried, hungered for, repulsive, beautiful. All the desires of her personal self, still looking for recognition before the absolute purity and stillness of the SELF, watching and compassionate. The most seductive of desires for her, was that desire to succeed, to save, to control those lives that were in her guidance, to give them that vision she must not, could not, give them. They must find that for themselves.

Ages of time poured through her, she knew herself living, a hundred years ago, a thousand, and all the voices of human nature whispered through her so that she felt invaded, cast from herself, spread thin as air in an atmosphere of humanity that sought to negate her into itself. Jessie, this personality in which she lived, feared to lose herself so utterly, she wanted to stand out, to be there before the others. To BE a person before others! Long had she met this melting of herself, this loss of her nature within this ocean of memory, of lives clamoring for existence through herself. She thought and the thoughts held paradox, a multitude of understandings each one as valid as the other. There was only one way to deal with this longing and this fear. How many times must she re-establish balance?   She focussed, stood at the point of highest awareness, stood in Self

Consciousness, what she knew as Christ Consciousness. Stood and observed in deep compassion her own struggling self.

Gradually the voices wore themselves out so that she heard only the strongest left. She felt the longing of old loves, old hates, injustices, joys, all that being human had meant."What are we?" she asked out of that subsiding invasion, "What are we that we have this endless connection with all other lives? That we are as though an extension of Earth Herself, not separate actually from any other life?" These were old questions that had racked her from her birth. Then with a breaking free of questions she said,"All forms are separate, Life is single. There is no loss."

And then, as she had so many times, the living person, Jessie, sought herself. She held herself intact. refusing submergence, retaining herself as a point within an ocean. She felt the waters close over her and claim everything she was. Reaching beyond that submerged identity, the stillness held, did not waver, the point of attention watching, was firm. She knew, and there at the point of that true Self she found Jessie also clarified. What she was, was nameless, and in no place, no time. Drawing up and out, she was also that point from which vision occurred, vision that extended beyond Jessie into what she knew as 'Soul consciousness'. With humour, she focussed,spoke the name of her active form, "Jessie!" She lived after all, just now at least, as Jessie, this life form. What she was must sustain Jessie. Bring into full consciousness, this person.

Beneath everything was the consciousness of existence, and in that was the surge of all lives. She knew herself again as an issuing of consciousness literally reaching out to those voices, because clamorous, seductive as they were, they were humankind, animal kind, plant kind. What was this crawling, infestation of life in Earth but the awakening surge of Spirit in Matter. All those living forms were Life in expression of ITSELF. The great core of her Heart expanded and swelled to include, to reach on, and to receive knowledge, She felt a vast willingness resolve her questions.

And then, more personal, she heard the voices of those many lives lived in every state, lives of greatness, wealth, poverty, great scientific or philosophic knowledge, lives of academic ignorance but astute awareness of Earth. This Soul living through a woman called Jessie, had also lived through those many varied lives, owned great industries, managed vast lands, struggled up through poverty, dealt with the temptations of wealth, governed nations. This consciousness knew of that, remembered and could work from those worldly knowledges. Now, those lives clamored in her, cried out to the Soul Consciousness looking through these weary grey eyes. The wisdom there,deep in those eyes seemed fathomless, and the compassion without limit. LIFE realized ITSELF again and again through these endless series of festering lives that filled Earth and made Her conscious. There within everything, unfolding within world knowledge, was that fathomless KNOWLEDGE that had no name.The spark that lit the ever present fuse. Life realizing its own nature. Jessie realized and then thought shaped.

" Let them inform me , listen to them, my own old selves. Realize that I

THE JOURNEY

have known through ages what my task would be. Always when I have wanted to make this world what I thought it should be, I've said to myself, "There is a world here ripe for the glory for which it is destined. Let me point the way! Let me, in this life time, use these new minds, hearts, Souls that I as Jessie, have taught, have brought through these narrow passes into the Great City of Light. Am I not the Soul that has consciousness of the Eternal, that lives now through this woman, Jessie. I, can lead those Souls that I have taught and save this world. Use their minds and hearts to create that magnificent world that could be. Isn't that what this has all been for?"

The voices of all the lives she had lived, clamorous, stung her heart with promises and dreams. I, Soul could command the legions I have led to their awakening .Could command and build before the universe that possibility I know the world might be. Save it, rebuild it! The possibilities are endless. Why not? Surely that would be the greatest service, the greatest gift to the infinite ONE who IS. Surely I would stand then within that circle of absolute LIGHT."

Jessie felt herself drawn and persuaded, felt the rising temptations swarm around her inner consciousness, felt power touch against her heart, draw her the vivid images that would result. She knew that she could persuade those who had followed her through these mountains, those who had followed her through other lands, other places of holy intent. Perhaps it could be done! She had brought thousands to their point of Journey.

Jessie looked into that maelstrom of herself, all that she had ever been, could be, was part of this struggle. And there against that Lighted point was the conscious knowledge of evil.And evil was: to take this sacred trust she carried like a pearl in her hands and betray it to this temptation , this hungering need for power, presented as a cause for the good of humankind.

And she knew the lie, even as she saw the dream of glory rise before her eyes. To respond would be suicide, a dying of Soul Self into world fascination. Then all those eons of lives lived in order to reach this point of consciousness, this knowledge that there did exist THAT WHICH IS, would be wasted. She would have to return again to the beginning and start as one unconscious. And because she was conscious, she knew her danger.

Her mind shaped thought, which itself should have warned her, "Yet every thing that IS is of that ONE. There is no other, Nothing else. How can I BE other than THAT, how can I act other than in harmony with WHAT IS? Yet, I long to turn from that Knowledge. I long to try, to make! I have a choice, I can choose to save this world myself, I, SOUL, conscious, can choose to go my way and insist that I know the way. For I have seen so much of that vast and cosmic Light.

She felt herself lost and regained. Then torn away again to agree to the plan. Then swinging back to see the emptyness of such a plan. The paradox, in fact. This struggle, of SOUL still bemused by personality, of personality still wanting to use for itself the infinite powers of Soul,wore indentations in the fabric of the very universe. This struggle of mind within Mind, relentlessly making its choice, was a cosmic and inevitable struggle.

Gradually from the great core of her life came a quiet power that rose out of Spirit within, rose gently from the center of her being. With still focus, the cry reverberated,"Let be!"

And in a quiet tone, she heard the voice of her Heart. "I know of THAT WHICH IS but the DIRECTION of the Infinite I cannot know. My way could be little more than a dream again, another dream that would itself fall in on itself as have all other human dreams. I make the choice! I choose to let go of desire. To live according to what I know is greater than Life itself!

From that moment she knew release as abruptly as though all doubt had fallen like a stone dropped. Desire to control, to be the savior of a world once lost, dissolved into the wisdom that lived deep in her heart. The wisdom to know that humankind must come to its own salvation through itself and as one whole. No 'one' person could 'save' the world. For no one knew or could know what 'saving' meant. Only an infinite Mind might discover that.

Energy fountained outward, an energy she knew as Love, coming from the calm depths of her being, it streamed, unobstructed, absorbing old desires. All voices fell silent and one harmonious sound drew steadily into a clear tone. The Soul sound, that lived through this lifetime. She focussed then, on the small physical body that waited on the mountain side. She knew suddenly again taking comfort in this cluster of tiny cell lives that were this body. She crooned to herself, knowing the ancient trail of herself from single cell to multiple, each working and living as one aspect of a whole beyond its own consciousness. But harmonious, always. She heard, through Earth the sweet strong notes of other conscious lives singing through personhood, and she joined them in harmony. After a while, her attention shrank and Jessie rested within herself., She quietly remained, in a vast and unceasing existence, softly breathing through itSelf.

She chose and choosing, listened to her Heart. Her Mind watched the ululations of possibility moving into strands of reality and stabilizing there. Often only an act or a word drew the final direction firmly to its focus. Choice was infinite. To watch and offer no interference was as difficult as it had ever been. To need no recognitions for herself, Jessie, was like a child denied its toy. But there was Vision that smiled at her, steady.

So many possibilities.There were so many ways that those who knew themselves even faintly were beginning to coalesce into what would be. She tightened her resolve,firmed her direction and focussed again on that distant blazing fire of LIGHT. She smiled,then, in her small waiting body, smiled also in that vast patient Soul. Smiled with an infinite relief to rest and BE as Being occurred. She, the woman, turned her attention to enjoy the sounds, odors, beauty and lives of the night.

Ben stirred, then turned to lie on his back. Sleep was far away from him. He knew he would wait. He watched the high dome of the clear sky peppered with stars already invisible near where the moon rose. He felt the quiet awe of that distance, that infinity of space. He reminded himself that there were human beings our there, at least in the nearest points of light. People carried on their own power to planets and their moons, settling them, avidly, eagerly trying themselves in that limited but vast and wondrous universe beyond their home world. He thought,"I would like to go out! I'd like to go with Rose, the two of us to take a journey there some day, for the pleasure of it.We've never done that together and we must. To see those strange and changing other earths."

Then his eye fell into the Valley, and saw there the lights scattered like the stars among the darknesses of Earth. He wondered at them also. Sharply he realized he was avoiding something. He sighed, and the thought spun swiftly into focus. "Why must we climb this mouuntain, this steep impossible mountain when an air car could have put us down at the top in minutes? It's foolish. Jessie's a wonderful woman, I don't doubt that, but this -- she IS old, after all."

Resentment at the inefficiency nagged at him,"Waste time! Wasted days." Why was it that any thing that seemed inefficient angered him so? There had been so much to do, too much to do, in building this Valley. The years of work, hard unceasing work, for all of them, meant that inefficiency could not be tolerated. Most people seemed to Benjamin to waste energy, to waste motion itself. He struggled with the idea. After all, they were finished mostly with the intensive labor, the endless pressure to complete the original plans. Couldn't they relax a little now? Was there something here he wasn't seeing? Was it just habit to resent inefficiency. Couldn't they allow a little relaxation now? No! Inefficiency took away from relaxation as well as from work.

He sighed, "Jessie is no fool, call her an old woman or not, she is no fool. There must be something else!" His own necessity,a gnawing need for doing things right prodded at him, brought a tightness to his throat - chest- - an old familiar feeling.Yes,it was. Where did it come from? Why was he feeling it so much now? He was at the edge of danger ahead, could that be it? But why? He remembered the struggle he had had to prod people into thinking, approaching a job with efficienct care. They never could have done it had he not kept after them. He and others who bore the burden of the Valley plans.

Without that focus, that clearing of waste time, motion, supplies, they would not have escaped from the horrors of the past, the devastations,the losses. Now, it was done and he felt drained, weary. Even their own wonderful, beloved town was generally finished. And here he was, again with another impossible task. The Journey itself! He shook himself. Had he taken it on as his own task? Had he assumed he must be responsible? The way he had been for so much of the Valley? He thought of the distance ahead, he knew the rock and cliff faces he would have to travel through, around, past. he shuddered and felt a rage rise in him,,snuffing out the calm of a few moments ago,"Those cliffs are dangerous and they're too steep for ordinary people to climb. There's no sense to that. There are obviously better ways to get people up this mountain. Otherwise what've we accomplished , as a people?" The thought, spoken like that, relieved him a little. He wanted to yell it out to the others, to make them aware.

He remained where he was. Silent. The thought of telling the others gave him a brief glimpse into their response. He quieted his emotions, settling them with a movement of attention outward the way that allowing water to spread relieves its racing power. And in that separation from attachment to those emotions, he saw behind his anger a curling fear that clung to the darkness within him. With a surge of courage and brutal strength he turned to it and the anger died, sucked out of existence by the permeation of this darkness. He was suddenly alone naked before his fear and he shrank with a whimpering cry. He saw there the shadow of his own self, the shadow of a small and unfamiliar Ben, sitting within that darkness huddled and helpless against the walls of his mind, surrounded by fear so dark he could see nothing except that fear.

Then, slowly, sustaining attention apart, he watched himself, observing without judgement. He looked with a quiet compassion and reached out one hand tentatively. Surely this terror need not include such lonliness. Yet he was alone with himself, he had only himself now. His mind trembled in meeting this rage of emotion. He saw there before him the small dark self, there, hiding in the red darkness of fear and rage. Then the dark figure looked up and that watching Self met those frightened eyes. A forlorn hope flickered there. The small figure crawled toward the extended hand, caught at it, pulled against it. Fear felt the pull of knowledge. Knowledge felt the weight of fear. But Benjamin held firm. Finally he saw himself standing, drawing that fearing part of himself out of its darkness. The scene was so real, as visualizations always were for him.

But the small dark form swelled when it was exposed, He felt himself being inundated, the tiny hand clutching like a hot needle at his heart. He screamed in his head, heard himself and was startled. All identity focussed now in that tiny frightened form. He knew existence now only in this deep place, the caverns of his being. Then, suddenly he saw light. Someone was coming, other tiny lights appearing from no where, and the light reached beyond the one who carried it and touched upon the edges of his darkness. He had been drawn into that small place of his terror. Now, even this terrified self knew that there was an outside, a place where terror did not exist.

He felt hope, and took strength from it. He loosened from the terrible limitation and was again conscious of being both fear and observer of fear. He stood firmly then, he in the dark, and he the one who watched. Finally he cried out to the light -- reached for it.

He was surprised at the power in that dark hand that clung now to the edge of his heart. But there was power in his heart that refused to yield or be drawn into that helplessness. He shook himself and stood conscious in his refusal. He couldn't understand how, but at that refusal, the clutching hand released its hold, pain faded. That which sought to engulf him, faded, light surged in, leaving only a pale and grey less frightened self. He felt the strength borrowed from that distant Light, so steady, so unmoved by the dark. It broke free the upthrust of his own inner Light, rising to surround, to begin a slow seeping into, that dark. Nourished by the incoming Light, his own was radiant now, streaming through the dark, dissolving it. Fear melted away, revealing what he was afraid of. He stood now, looking into the obvious answer. Even now, he hesitated to shape that revelation into words. He knew that the Light came from those who had traveled this way before. Those who were his brothers in some deep,human sense.But now, he must meet it alone.

He stood attentive, drawing that small self into his own Self, into that Light of his own courage, he shaped the thought that defined both."I'm afraid of what that Silent City means." As he absorbed that thought, he sighed,"All my life I've sought for that knowledge, and all my life I think I avoided finding what I sought."

"I was afraid the Valley couldn't be built. That we would fail. And so I had to keep every possible pressure in place.I had to constantly demand absolute care, efficiency. Now, I'm afraid I wont be able to meet what the City is. I fear my inadequacy. How can I be part of what I imagine that to be? What am I that I could -- could enter into it?"

Was it true? What a monumental ego! Had he really felt responsible for creating the Valley? For building, for designing Adwin, for planning the Convictions,the governing bodies, all that they had done? With a long sigh of dispair, he remembered he had surely worked hard, given all his time, and yet, had it been that much more than most other people? He sighed, tired, troubled by this revelation. What complicated creatures we are. Unreasonabile assumptions that he must do it all? That he couldn't trust others to do as well? He reached back into those days, remembering, with pitiless persistance to see himself. When failure occurred, he felt it his own, when a building was not complete on time, or the Learning Center had no equipment for some special skill, he saw himself to blame. Yes, he had felt that. He had been so angry at the Teachers at times.Yet it had not been their fault either. He had never seen himself so sharply. Never questioned his anger until it revealed the fear behind it, nor questioned the fear until it revealed its source. And now, this! That fear that others would not do their jobs right, was only a cover for his own.

The truth was his own deep fear of personal failure spread out into the community. What harm had he done? How had he hurt his people, his family? His attention turned back to that dark shadow that he now held before himself, held, but not harshly, rather with a kind of sad tenderness. There was a soft pervasive light filtering through him, through consciousness within himself so that he saw himself clearly now. This much at least. The Light seemed very real, and gradually he knew it was Light that flamed higher from within himself. Revealing,not accusing. The doors were opened and that Light was not shadowed. With a sense of discovery,of awe, he murmured,"What the teachers call Soul Consciousness. I see the Light and I am that Light. It shines through everything I am, and I can SEE.

To assume that he was to blame for community failures was unreasonable. It was too grand, too exaggerated. It had smothered reason. Balance was lost, yet people often praised him, for his attention to the Valley plan, his persistent demands that it be perfected. And so that had been his pain? To be out of balance causes pain, he had known that. To be responsible means that I'm important, that I have power, that I can-- CAN take care of things. It was an ego hunger after all, hidden behind need. My own need for being important, for seeing that everything was taken care of and for not trusting others to be as able as I. But at the base of it, I didn't trust myself at all. Had I trusted myself, I might have trusted others. So there I have been, and now?

His mind was centering, his body felt easy. This nature that feared, that couldn't trust itself, could be given balance. He could learn to do that. Now that he knew. Cascading down like a cool water, through his sorrow, his disappointment with himself, came a pure joy of relief. He thought of the others, their presence around him. They would go on. They must meet these things together and he must allow them their power, their ability to meet as much as he. He must trust that he could do what was needed to make this Journey. It was, in a sense, an offering of one's life to take this Journey. He knew that now, and that was all one could hope to do. To offer and to trust.

He thought of the City, the power of HER. Unknown power! Fear throbbed faintly, and he knew he would always be capable of fear. But it was not all up to him, he could rely on, must rely on, all the others. He felt fear subside, the quiet stillness of this new awareness absorbed it like a sponge. He must trust others, must know their strength was as great as his own. "I think that I've actually felt that I was in danger of dying in these mountains." Now, he shook his head, he had to repeat the realization. "I have to remember it's fear of my own inadequacy, that I can't do what's expected of me. That's what had me tight as a cork. I will die! Yes. We all will die to what we were. But we must risk whatever that is. Dying the little deaths, is worse than the final one." He spoke aloud, softly, his mind was clear, his senses alert, he thought he would never sleep. But when he turned, flattened himself against the soft pad of his bag and closed his eyes, he was asleep instantly.

Rose felt excitement, there was danger ahead, that she knew. She was cold. The Valley was far behind. At first she had felt such delight that they were finally on the Journey. But now, fears etched erosive patterns through her mind. Discomfort enabled fear and convinced part of her mind it was true. They were lost to the Valley, to the old life. Surely that was true. Did it matter? The alien thrust of this question startled the complacency of her self pity. That pity had drained her will to flaccidity and she had not noticed. Where did this strength to question come from? She saw the numbness of that self pity had quenched her delight, and now, the question was a brutal reminder of that indulgence and it's damage. What she had realized earlier today at the lunch stop, pushed its way to attention.

She turned to her other side, restless as if something else prodded. Finally, curling up, to wrap her arms around herself, she shook off the clutch of an insipient dispair. She had to think. What did she expect of this Journey? Was she still seeking what had happened to her so early in life, that initial awakening, that fleeting moment of brillaint prescience? Was she longing for a repeat of that first wonder? The fire of revelation, the mystic experience that had opened her eyes initially to that greater universe of Being? Did she expect that? Demand it? And also dispair of such? The teachers had told them that nothing repeated itself in the realm of Spirit. That it was ever new. She had never known what they meant.

Suddenly like a gift the sharp, memories flooded her mind. It had been a touch out of the infinite, surely, nothing else could have such power. Who would not long for a repeat of that shattering awakening, even though it had so frightened her, had resulted in her hiding from it, never speaking of it, being afraid that it was a mark of her strangeness. Or had she coveted that sense of strangeness? Resolutely she catachized herself, endured the probing of her frightened mind by that same mind. Was that thinking mind frightened that it might lose its seat of absolute power over her life? But what else was there? There could not be two minds! From whence came this relentless questioning, was it another depth of mind? Intuitive and higher reason?

With a sinking dispair, she stopped the debate. There again, that never ending debate within, that gave her no rest, that had driven her nearly to crazy hopelessness, or immodest assumptions.

In the quiet that unsued, she simply realized, as though out of a smiling stillness. "You know that that awakening had to be strong to shake you from your sleep. It had to jolt your complacency, You are no longer asleep. You don't NEED another awakening. You need to pay attention!. You need wisdom."

She was silent. Her mind, as if subdued, moved into reflection. During the past years, since that moment of revelation, she had had to learn to live, to practice all that was revealed in that split moment of SIGHT. She wondered,"Have I done that?" Ruefully she let the question probe. Then," Well, I believe I've tried. But I still don't know how to form into thought all that I know. And without making it thought, how can I believe it?"

And now, we're about to face the reality of something as powerful. What can I find here in this City? Will I perceive that blinding Light again? Or that other time of Touch, that moment, timeless and unexplainable, when the very universe seemed to wake in me and there was a sense of vast tenderness that filled me until I could bear no more and my heart broke with Its beauty? I could not have imagined or taught myself that. It had to come from beyond myself. I have nothing so pure in me. Is that what I seek again? These gifts, these visits, or perhaps the waking, of what has to be Spirit?

Will I know again of That which is beyond thinking? Is that what I want, long for, and yet, am so afraid of? Is that what I covet? As she reflected, she said aloud, "Experiencing that waiting and silent Self, realizing Life, is overwhelming and yet, I long to know again, that Light. That perception of what is beyond this life." She longed to know and at the same time, she was afraid. "Nevertheless, I would seek that doorway again".

Thinking stopped, she entered into silence. Aware of every touch of air, drift of sound, the shadows of tree limbs under moonlight, her body pressed against uneven Earth, and instantly, perception swelled, included the arching sky of stars of space the ranging hills, the valley below, the extending universe, until she knew herself one with that universe and time had no existence.

And suddenly, as if something snapped in her mind, she was aware she was thinking again. There, I was at the edge of that realization and I would not sustain attention. Is that what I realized this morning, that I deny the very thing I seek. I remember that the Teachers have told me that pride in perception, hunger for experience of that which is absolutely NEW, can be in itself a barrier to development. A barrier, not a way. Is that what I've gotten to?" She sighed, turned her body into a more comfortable position, reached out to touch the edge of Ben's hand lying on the ground beyond his bag, wanting suddenly his comfort. " In such moments there's so much -- such a power of LIFE itself. I want to know that LIFE again. And yet, I see how the desire, the endless thinking about it, is holding me from what ever might be." Her heart ached at the confession.

"Wait," an inner voice murmured, "take heart. What will be will be." Then suddenly she laughed out loud. "Life of Spirit doesn't repeat Itself. When we desire that awakening so much we imagine it, or try to make it happen, we block every revelation of the real." Slowly she sighed,"It's a matter of being aware long enough to SEE. To sustain awareness, just what I didn't do!"

Now she looked up through the trees at the peaks above them, They seemed almost to tower over them, so close, so white in the moon light. There was danger there, between here and there. She had done the usual small climbs that all children did in this Valley, but she had not learned to climb the way Tom or Jane did. Could any of the others make this climb alone? No! Only as a group, as people in a deep union of trust could they make that Journey. Could they trust that much? She lay, finally mentally still, finally released from thought, aware.

She lay still, letting the question remain unanswered. Tomorrow would give them that. She felt a drawing near by, and intuitively reached, and Touched Tom's mind. He struggled himself, just as she did. She held steady, and knew that unaware, he had partaken of her stillness. She felt a deep hope. Perhaps they might accept and trust enough. She wriggled against uneven turf, finding a better place. Then, thought slammed against her stillness breaking the calm.She could not distance herself,she was caught in a swift fear. With a small cry, a whimper, she turned her head to look across the meadow. She saw mounds of other people all around. "How can I be so stupid. After all, no matter how I feel, we won't physically die." The thought was hardly formed when it was attacked,"Oh, yes you could!"

She refused,"This Journey is a spiritual Journey, not --" She sat up, stopped by the realization. "But that can destroy me as surely as a fall from these cliffs. There is the fire of it in me already." She stopped her thought racing."My God, it is truly a fire,burning, and already it threatens my very life. Everything I've become aware of."

"There is something in me, a knowledge, that burns against my consciousness and ignores my simple human fear. There is something I KNOW, that I have not acknowledged." The realization silenced thought. She held her body,wrapped her arms around herself,protective. Softly she said,"Now this, the burning fire that reveals that there is the unknown,will not be denied. I cannot hide, nor refuse longer. It is before me and whether it means some kind of death, physical or astral, then that I must enter into." She felt the hot tears coursing across her face sideways running into her ears. Doggedly she said the words that she knew were true. "It's why I've preferred to imagine, to recreate a vision out of own mind, because I fear the genuine Vision that will take me from myself."

Gradually she felt her tension subside. The inner voice was clear and strong. "It's the Heart's way. It's the longing that's not in error." She was still, knowing this. Willing. Accepting. Finally softly she said as if reaching acceptance, "It may take away my familiar world, as it did before, or open my eyes to what I've refused to see." Dispairing, she turned her head from side to side, her throat aching. " What ever it does, I willingly accept. Because I know that it is REAL. She was aware of all the explanations coming like a tide to screen her from possibility but shook her head out of great weariness. How many times had she grasped at the questions, threw them up like a dike before the unexplainable. She would simply let be.

For a long time she lay, nearly asleep, but knowing suddenly that she could not sleep. A thought formed itself as if magically before her. It dawned like a rising sun on a dark morning, illuminating. "I sought experience, a sacrifice of all my world that I might live above that world. That I might be -- be-- 'HOLY'. And what is that? With sinking dispair she admitted it. "Yes, that's what my life's been, denying the longing for the Real by trying to create my idea of an 'EXPERIENCE OF HOLINESS'. I've refused to utterly open my heart before the absolutely unknown. I wanted that which I could understand. Again her thought ceased, she lived in a breathing stillness of her self waiting. "Isn't that what life is - what we're here for?

She shook her head, knowing of some flaw here, needing to find it. She glimpsed her life, seeking what was imagined. The idea had mesmerized her, had held her through the years, had given her a kind of power, but it was a blinding barrier to what might have been. She had spent years clutching the longing for an 'idea' and had not LOOKED. She had thought it offered power, love, admiration, but all she got was fear, comfusion. These had resulted in a desparate refusal to share, both out of pride and out of fear. She thought she was partaking of something greater than anyone else knew.

She writhed with confusion now, with pain of recognition. A knowledge that persisted just behind thoughts so painfully breaking down. Suddenly like a strong light soaking through all her consciousness, she KNEW. Slowly she spoke the knowledge.

"I wanted my revelation, the purifying of my Soul that I might be pure and holy in THIS life. I would have willingly given up the world around me. I offered sacrifice in pain that I might be purified and illumined with truth, but I limited that truth with my self." The very thought ached against her mind.

She heard her own cry, the words flung soundless out with the passion of her aspiration, seemed to rise, fall over her and carry her away in their flood. Then in a strange mockery, they fell backward, crumbling in impotence upon her. She saw the shift, that flung her from beneath that wave of emotion. Gradually she felt the loss of passion, the stillness of acceptance, indiffernce, the emptying of herself as though all passion was spent. She stood appalled, spent! From some still point beyond turbulence there was strength that held. From that still point identity waited, patient and serene. and a steady vision held through the recurring flood. She did not sink again.

"I wanted so much to be beyond ordinary life! I denied daily the Self that is not ordinary. What is REAL is immeasureably beyond my self!" Old desire drained itself out, as though an ocean drained itself into sand. Slowly she was aware of a new silence, a stillness of heart and mind. Thoughts spun like angry bees around that silence, then drifted off. Slowly recognition settled into her, she looked at her hands before her, felt her flesh, warm and alive, touched Earth, let her eyes roam almost hungrily through the trees, and the sky full of light. It was as though she saw them for the first time. Knew her own body as if afresh. She lay realizing unaware of time.

Later, she knew she must explain all of this to herself. For her mind was an explaining mind. But right now, she would simply be at ease. And everything could be as it is. She felt her self sink, felt her body weary, her eyes heavy and without another thought, she slept.

CHAPTER TWENTY TWO

Jane sighed as she snuggled down against Earth, adjusting her body to the curves and unevenness of the bed of grasses she lay on. She felt good, excited and full of eagerness for what she thought to be an adventure that was worth entering into. She rolled over onto her back slowly, watching the trees above her and the sky above them moving into view as she did so. The tall white oaks looked slim here between the whispering green of the broad pines and firs. She smiled, they were comforting friends. She enjoyed the pattern of the limbs against the star lit sky, and she responded to the conscious presence of these great lives. "They know of us here, these lives that reach their limbs to trace the sky. They are aware !" the thought was clear, sure. A faint grief nudged aside her contentment. She turned mentally to meet it. This wild land, this Earth where human kind was not. Could she join in this primeval Life? Did she want to? That strange new experience of Joining, was so different from the Touch with Earth that she had always known.

She thought of the Valley below, remembering the details of pathway, trees and fields as if she stood beside them now. Always the land called to her, never ceasing, so beautiful, so utterly beautiful. Sometimes she felt the Earth beauty so great it hurt as though her heart was caught and measured by that beauty. She could not quite FIND what it was that was there, just beyond the edge of all her senses. So often this autumn, in the ripening fields, she had sensed it. Once while watching the still, slim stalks of ripe, wild barley that began to gently move in the air, catching and releasing light from the sun. It caught her as well, drew her out of herself into itself. Drew her to some wonder that hid just behind its shadow. Or on another day, under the soundless scrape of leaf shadows over still water, or sometimes sitting in quiet grass, hidden in the deep folds of hills rumpled with living trees and the dry thick stalks of old autumn weeds, there was a breath of possibility, and in it she had wholly forgotten herself. She wound herself into the memories, then murmured, "No, this night, I think it was remembering my Self." In a thousand other events; a hen's merry singing on a hot afternoon; a bird's sudden sweet call out of silence just at sun-up; the white shimmer of moonlight down the tracery of barren branches; any of these brought her to an urgency of attention that threatened to break the very air apart and reveal --what?

And the pain of it was that she never could quite sustain her attention deeply enough to enter into that hidden possibiity. It was ever there, ever enticing, beckoning, as though these visible forms, this utter beauty, was only a surface, a colored skin over the REAL. Somewhere she must find what was beyond that surface. Yet, she both longed and feared to find, to See.

Now, sensing again the throat tightening wonder of moonlight spreading like a living light over the low hills below, she found herself fleeing again, unable to bear the near revelation. She remembered her dream, her plan that she had once told to Jessie. How she would like to see the Earth made into garden, a wonderful place where humankind nourished all living things, but carefully removed the scars, the ugly, the tangles and cluttered places. A garden of Eden, she thought. She smiled at the thought, the vague images that tried to shape themselves in her mind. "It's asking a lot, but then all human endeavors have asked a lot." She frowned, thoughtful, wanting now, in this silence, to shape the plan more precisely. Maybe this Journey, this entrance into these high places would clarify, would give her new vision.

She abandoned herself to imagery, to shaping the vision of such a world. The land around her, how would it need pruning, shaping to make it so. But the vision faltered, would not form. A powerful forest presence had grown around her, was reaching to her, pushing away the thought process and attempting to enter into awareness. She trembled, momentarily at the edge of panic. Frowning, she began rapidly to think of old plans. Thinking was a safeguard from the nearness of that Vision.

The air was clear, the moon's light, brilliant. Usually she could hide in rapid, invasive thinking, from the overwhelming of beauty, but now, her defenses crumbled, realization shook her. An ancient knowledge stirred in the depths of her mind, a knowing that shoved through intellectual perception and broke all barriers. With deliberate decision, trembling, she Reached through fear and found to her surprise an immediate strength. Hesitant at first, she clung to it, wondering at its source.

Again taking courage, she accepted the Presence of strength around her, was aware of how utterly still everything was. As she allowed herself to respond, a delicate joy grew and it drew her to a new edge. She knew without reason that this depth she approached was of Earth's vast heart. She was sinking, entering into a conscious Earth and felt it envelop her. A question flickered,'Could that consciousness, of Earth, know of her?' In that instant she was aware that she was known, and wept at the Touch that told her that.

With a small shuddering sigh, she willingly entered and was entered. Strange that there were no words to fit the thing that happened. Quick flickerings of thought swept briefly through her mind as the experience proceeded. They were as secondary as they would be to vision. Could a human being know of anything without accompanying thought? She realized what was there behind the Earth form, the living envelope of LIFE that had taken her into itself. Knowing was an ocean in which her life moved, like a flowing of intelligent waters. Thought faded, could not hold all this. A flicker of memory reminded her this ocean would not fit into a familiar bucket. And then the flicker was gone.

She stood alone, slowly becoming aware that aloneness was illusion. The stillness, rootedness, interconectedness, with networks of consciousness was alien, yet subtly reassuring even as it threatened her autonomy. Consciousness was inclusive. To be within this - to be so aware, was astonishing. On the other hand,it seemed so natural, as if -- identity was multiple.

She was awed by that quality of life that Touched against her, was herself, even. She realized that to be conscious meant to include lives of which she had no previous awareness. The idea needled across attention and was gone, leaving a sadness, a slight fear. Then, slowly, swelling like a great wave rising out of its own energy, Earth-Joy grew . Holding in itself all anguish, fear, pain and gladness of living, it brightened through itself, cascading darkness like drops of rain. It rose and broke against Nothing. She was stretched into its vast dimensions, realizing, past thinking, past ordinary senses. She spun through herself, through IT, and was aware. She knew that something was immenent,something she must realize, be given.She feared and longed for that gift. Then she was aware, "It's not that Earth knows of me but that I am the knowing". The fleeting realization was a shift in perception, rather than thought.

Then without warning,her will balked. Fear pulled at her, created a whirlpool, a blindness,a refusal to see. It stirred, grew,was a cloud before the Light, sought to close her away into itself. Like a membrane of doubt, it cut her off from the brilliance of Earth-Joy she had known. All things that she saw had grown sordid, dulled, -- the leaf, once silvery in the moonlight, was thick, dark and it sucked sight itself into its darkness to end it. The leaf was a 'thing', a leathery shape that would shrivel and crumble into dust. It was no longer a window through which she could see. The trees, the hills below, the sky, dulled to shapes, to objects without true life. This was the end of all hope, all vision and all JOY. An opaque membrane of doubt, opposed --? Opposed to what?

She shrank with her doubt,but the question flung itself free, ripping loose some threads of that dark hold. And the vast Earth LIFE shimmered through the torn edges, glowed with its own laughter. Potent!

Then it was that some fierce energy of will shaped itself, a shaft that tore through attention. The probing edge of that Will cut against the hardness, the dim, senseless, one-dimensional dark. The edge of that dark she had torn loose needed to heal and the Light laughed through, a seeping joy that curled around it and reshaped its form with Light. That which refused, that thickened itself to conceal, became a revelation to her. She could see that dull dispair was designing a name for what it hid. To know a name for darkness would give her mind a key with which to open it.

She focussed vision, penetrated that dull exterior,probed a crack in the calloused surface that was her denial. Light seeped like a water to give her Sight. Darkness that hid her vision came out of her own name and her own memories. The darkness was herself. She spun back from the realization and shuddered even as she felt release and a surge of joy.

Now, the dark shaped into thought. She could see the desire the intention to shape and make things according to her own intention, to redesign Earth in her own image. It was the flaw that blinded her. That thickened against her vision. This came from her self, not from without. In HERSELF was denial of Joy,of the living swell of LIFE. In herself still clustered the needs that must make all things fit her own dimensions, adjust to her own size. A thought shaped,"Evil then, is the refusal of LIFE? Is it the denial of the flow of living energy. Is it the limiting of life to myself?"

The thought sped like an arrow puncturing the membrane of doubt. That which had drawn the curtain across her vision snapped. In its place was light, Joy enfolded and infused her with Itself. She was beyond herself and aware as Soul.

She never knew how long she remained thus deeply tuned to that Vision. She descended into an acute Earth awareness. Long she was aware of its great lives, its brief and tiny lives, its still slow lives, and its quick flashes of life that faded into others. But there was no separation - in Soul consciousness, all lives are One Life. Time ceased, she realized the nature of Earth intention, as though she herself was its writing. Intention was written by her life.

Then, slowly, from knowing, she fell, felt herself limited, then more limited, until she was simply the woman Jane. Thoughts began to pile one on another, like an avalanch of reaction. Gradually she allowed herself to hold the thought steady, to know without doubt what she was. What Earth was. There was too much to think of. But here was one underlying knowledge. The Earth is permeated with Life, is itself a vast life. Life breathes through Earth as through a membrane of its own body. And humankind is an organ of Earth life. "Then, have we no special task?"

Softly she formed the words of her understanding. "The role of humankind is not to remake Earth in its own image, But to listen, discover the true nature of Earth and our part in that whole. It is a purpose of the plant world to serve the animal world, but it is only one part of its purpose. It's only a part of the purpose of humankind to serve the simpler orders of life in Earth, but it is surely one important part."

"I see creatures fight death, but accept it utterly when it comes, give themselves to it, as they give themselves to the animal that eats their form. I compare that with the endless thinking people do about death and the fear of it, the refusal. I see how life moves constantly through all living things of Earth. Earth is life shaping and reshaping itself through a kaliedescope of forms, rising and dying away and rising again anew. For Life shapes ceaselessly as an ocean shapes waves. And every new wave lifts consciousness a little higher."

"There is something else, something that eludes me. I must listen, the way Earth artists listen. I must watch, the fields and hills and creatures, the way we listen to children when we help them learn. I must learn to listen and discover the nature of Earth Herself. So now, my life work, that I thought was to transform Earth into a great garden, I see, is not that at all. It is to discover. To see how I fit into the garden that Earth is becoming. But even more, to be conscious that Earth knows of us, humanity, and we are the knowing."

Jane sat still. The dying of her own dream like a scatter of leaves beneath her feet. She felt a sorrow, and an elation. The burden of it had been great. It had seemed like such a grand idea. And now -! "Well, there it is." She said softly."I have a life time to learn and to listen." She sighed deeply, sadly and felt the night

THE JOURNEY

around her, felt a cradling response from the Earth and the trees and the small lives beneath her. "Life' would teach her. She had only to pay attention! She curled herself into her warm bag and went to sleep.

Silvia huddled in her sleeping bag. Comfortable as it was, she could not relax. The night was utterly still,so still that cry of an owl, or brief scurry of a mouse,sounded sharp and clear. The moon's light poured clean and soft over everything. She felt a power in that light, a beauty that lay against her mind like an invitation. A sculpturer, she was highly sensitive to the shapes of things,and now, these shapes in the moonlight, the nameless, indefinable beauty of the night, drew at her heart and mind with a power that amazed her .

Slowly she released herself to the night, to the beauty, the sounds silence full of soft rhythmic cricket and tree toad thrumming.. A feeling of life permeated the air, Life that promised, that was full of something she could not name. It was a presence, as though Life itself had entered into their circle. She frowned, thinking that -- it seemed an unlikely thought.

The power of it was great, however and she could not avoid that power. She felt an uneasy sense of something greater than she knew. Suddenly she grabbed the top of her bag and stretched her legs, to roll herself, bag and all, over the ground until she stopped near Steve and Jerry who were settled head to head beneath a pine. She rolled so that her own head was near theirs. She wanted company. Silvia had never lived alone in the wild land, as had the others of her Family. She had gone with another young woman, neither of them willing to do it alone. And so her capacity to bear this solitude was not complete.

The three bodies were three spokes of a wheel on the ground. She did not speak, nor explain. She felt comforted. Something in this whole mountain seemed to her to be filled with 'intention'. That was the word, 'intention'! She felt a slow surge of fear, there was something here she didn't understand. She felt a tautness in the two men near her. And then, with surprise, a stir in her belly, as though THAT one wanted to be included. He was here, one of them. Somehow, she shrank from that knowledge.

She waited, quieting herself, accepting that they were four together. Jerry spoke then softly,wonderingly,"Silvia,he knows of us, knows of our Journey."

She shook her head, tears of anger filling her eyes. She did not want this. She said, "I don't want to know that."

Steve moved slightly,"What is it? What's happening to us? I feel naked here, naked of mind, and of heart and body too, altogether vulnerable." His voice trailed away."I don't know!"

Jerry realized with a sudden flash of knowledge that he must take responsibity here. That he must offer strength. He at least had some idea what they would meet in this Journey, but he had to quell a surging resentment, always it had been others who had been there to support him. Rose, Ben, Paul, even Tom, and now ? Well, was he not a man grown?. Lying flat, he felt his shoulders straighten as he accepted. He slid his hands out and up until his fingertips reached toward Steve on one side and he slid Silvia's hand into his own on the other. He said,"What does it feel like to you?"

Silvia broke from her swirl of confused thought with gratitude. His question gave a focus to her thought. "It's mostly fear! And yet, I feel such a longing, an unreasonable longing. On the other hand, I am afraid to meet, whatever it is that might fulfil that longing. It's only because we are together that I can dare be here at all. I've thought more than once today of running all the way back home ."

Steve sighed. He wanted to reach to her, to Jerry, but could not yet move his hands. With a sudden jerk he slid his arms out of his warm bag, reached his hands outward toward them as Jerry had done. But he did not touch their hands. They were unaware that their six arms reaching out, formed the points of a star.

Jerry spoke then, knowing that they were joined in a web of energy, an energy that could free them if they would acknowledge it."There IS something here among us. A presence perhaps, just as you sensed it, Sil." She wondered how he knew of her thought. " It's strong energy, and I am sure that it's good. It is not to be feared." He felt the stillness that grew about them, a sense of awe, familiar to him, yet always surprising, lifted them from their ordinary awareness into a larger, stronger point of knowing. Jerry recognized there was another Touching among them, wondered, but did not search. He thought that this sharing of deep knowing, the Light within, was itself something he had never thought could be. To share that power, that overwhelming beauty, the threat of the unknown, the terrible longing for That Unknown, was for him impossible and yet, -- why not?

With a dawning excitement he thought perhaps it was possible. Perhaps he could teach Silvia and Steve, as he taught himself. He felt eager to try. Hadn't they noticed they could focus more, realize more, when they Joined? Well, the same could be true for that Reach across into the still ness of Spirit. Couldn't it? Neither of these had consciously made that choice. He felt proud, strong, full of a new responsibility. The sense of the stranger's Touch faded as he realized. Was it then up to him? Perhaps he could make them notice, He said softly, "To share all this, the four of us, this way. Isn't it what we want?"

Silvia slid her hand to touch his, clutched it, feeling the literal flow of their combined strengths, but she thought the strength was Jerry's alone. She said,"Well, tell us. Explain!"

Steve frowned, feeling invitation, something nearly touching him. Something lurked at the edge of his mind, so beautiful, he felt suspicion. How could that be, and yet, he shrank back. His mind veered away and unconsciously he stretched his fingers and his mind at once to Reach. He found Jerry's mind and hand at the same time. Clutching both, he said softly,"It's true, Jerry. You've got to help us. This is so strange. And yet, I'm so grateful to be here."

Jerry nodded, a part of him searched for that lost power he had felt, the light, the energy, like a stream of joy. It had been so 'full'. Why couldn't he show them? Rose and Paul were always doing such things, helping, guiding. And why couldn't he? I've got to help these two. They need me. They can't See well enough yet. He felt restless, impoverished, groped for the cause, and thought that the energy,

THE JOURNEY

the power he had felt was lost, was faded. Something was wrong, he felt off balance. He knew their Touch, and their confident waiting. He reached out further, searching - what was it? Already he felt the power lost!

What had happened ?

A sense of panic swept him as at a danger. He reassured himself, holding steady,Reaching with the strong focus that he had practiced, striving for control,thinking rapidly, hunting in his mind for answers. And then, astonishingly, he felt- heard a tinkling, merry laugh.It was so clear, almost as if it came from himself. Well, what was the joke? Who laughed? Why? He said,"Yes? What is it?"

"Pop? You are my Pop. But you seem to have slipped from your senses,Pop?"

Jerry was thrown utterly off guard. His thoughts whirled, he felt the Touch against his mind, responding to his Reach. His tiny son, lying floating there within Silvia, laughing softly. He had spoken!

Jerry flushed, as if caught at something he felt shame for. Why? What was wrong? He frowned and remembered himself, went swiftly back over his thoughts.. How he had wanted to save them, Steve and Silvia, these two he loved. To save them, be their protector, the wise one who could lead them. He had wanted that? But how could the baby know?

Settling back, accepting the thoughts that wove themselves through his mind, he realized that Christopher had broken the weave of his intentions. He felt exposed, revealed. And so then, the intention was not right? This child - not yet born, able to flush him out and expose his weakness. Monstrous!

Then he felt shame. The exposure had happened just in time. He refused to respond, not wanting to admit, yet knowing.

The baby shrank back, disappointed but Jerry avoided him. He turned to Steve and Silvia, said aloud,"Steve, Silvia, our baby, our son, he's here with us. He knows -- as much as we do. He's taking this Journey before he's even born." The three of them lay trying to absorb the knowledge.

But there was not strength in that very young life to reach beyond the fear and revulsion that shaped itself in his elders. Jerry held off the fact made obvious. Silvia tried to be accepting of her son's consciousness with them. Steve did not, but rather felt a shuddering fear as if presented with something unnatural, a monster. On the other hand, he understood there was something, something full of -- of simple love, that he might acknowledge if he would.

Jerry steeled himself, drew his emotions into focus, settled them gently into place and turned his attention to what was happening. He recognized his own anger, his squelched pride and struggled for moments. Then, his natural good nature, impulsive good humor, surfaced like a great bubble of pure air, freeing him from the weight of guilt. He grinned,"You're right Son, I hate to admit it, but you're right! But now, we've got a new trouble. We've got to deal with the way they react to you." He could feel the baby shrink from Steve's refusal. Even his own mother resisted him.

Jerry felt the child's eager Reach aborted. His joy weakened with

THE PEOPLE OF THE VALLEY

disappointment, he too held himself separate. Jerry feared that they would lose that growing mind, lose it's trust. Would their rejection of wonder, of that love that poured around them, sentence them to loss?

They all knew, vaguely that they needed help. That they had not courage to get past their separateness at this moment. There was a gulf of fear and of disappointment, of rejection and of very real distress. The tenuous threads of their Reach began to shrink. The sorrow of their hearts increased as the loss was glimpsed. Jerry cried out for help! Then -- without warning, came a flood of energy, a fire that held and burned through them all, that Reached past their fear, melted it into such an awareness of themselves together that they caught their breaths in awe. It swept and released their resistance and was gone.

They were there together and in Touch. Fear dissolved in the expanding Light so that love swept through and extended beyond them, reached and included the child's arena of life. It reassured. As it swept through, their Reach amplified into Joining. They were together, each participating in Love.

Jessie had let her strength live with them for a critical moment, then withdrew. She did not need to make herself known. Once the initial Touch was done, fear broken enough that Love could fill the void, they woke to what they were. Their own desire for Joining asserted itself anew. That moment, returning to one another, still seeing the darkness of the near rift between them, they would never forget the power of fear. But now, they knew the limitlessness of Love. Their size was stretched, they could See through themselves a little more clearly now.

Jerry asked, "What was that?" There was silence, and though they thought of Jessie, they did not know. She knew they did not need to know. Jerry asked, "Why were we so afraid, all of us?"

The answer came this time from the unborn child. Both Steve and Silvia were lost in the wonder of what had happened. Christopher said, "We were afraid, and of each other! I too. I won't forget that. And not being included hurts." None of the others could have Reached thought out so clearly.

Jerry nodded, wanting to help Silvia find that understanding. But he checked himself. She would find it for herself. She too had felt that jolt of power, of realization. Finally, after chasing fragments of idea through her mind, after bringing to focus shreds of feeling scattered and faint, she said, "It's what we've always talked of. Unity! An including. There it was, so amazing yet so simple we almost refused." She hesitated, then gaining courage she went on, "Yet this isn't all of it. It isn't just ourselves. There's something here, among us, in our gathering tonight. There's something -- OTHER, beyond ourselves."

Then, they were silent again until Steve said, "Couldn't it be just that -- what you said? That 'unity" that's all of us together, more conscious? Isn't that something a whole lot more than any of us?"

Jerry laughed, "You've hit it Steve, in my opinion. It's exactly that. Together we become something far beyond ourselves."

Silvia persisted, 'Yes, I'll agree, but there's something -- something triggering it all. Helping us. Something like -- I want to say a Holy Spirit? A Touch from God?" It was a question, the idea more than they could grasp.

Christopher stirred again, pleased with his Mother's thought.But Jerry shook his head,"I still think it's Spirit.Maybe it from what's Holy in Life. I suppose that's what people mean by - God. Whether or not, it seems irrelevant, the name." They were silent, feeling the power around them, the generative energy that seemed just then to be great and sure. Silvia was still, realizing, and she thought that it was true, a fire did seem to burn in her Heart.

They lay realizing all that had happened. Knowing that they must learn from within themselves, that they must be responsive to other human calls. But it was responsiveness itself that made the difference.

Finally after a long time, they each said good night, rolled into more comfortable positions and fell asleep.

Where were Andrew and Anna in all this night's events? Listening they had heard much. Waiting they had recognized the changing. They felt the others around them. They knew the rising and falling, the turbulence and the quieting. They knew of the sudden interjecting of Jessie's watchful mind. They had held their own council separate. Wondering.

Now, they let their minds roam in curiosity up and down the peaks and the narrow clefts that they must climb tomorrow . They could accept that. They could extend their consciousness on toward that waiting City above. Without hope, or expectation, they could observe Her relation to themselves. They settled into themselves, Touching.

They began to wake to the relationship between the two of them. Found it harmonious, but saw the inner conflicts like sharp breaks in that harmony. each personality, conscious of itself, strained for and resisted inclusion. Each feared a loss of itself, already knowing how that refusal left it limited.

Anna recognized these facts. She saw that Andrew did, but she felt him withdraw, to attend to his own attitude. She felt the isolation of his leaving, and the specific freedom of it. She waited patient, wanting nothing, empty of herself. At this time she felt essentially alone. More so than ever before in her life. She watched her thought reflecting all that was happening.She had become a mirror, aware of reflection.

As she watched, silent, balanced with the precision of a dancer, time stopped in the second of that balance but she knew change. A sense of amusement, then awareness of that outpour of love through every life here, then slowly a lessening, a drawing into her self,and a sense of unease. Suddenly,she knew the Touch of a strong consciousness, that swept through into herself and Andrew and brought their attention together in one.

It brought color, a fire of life to the communion that occurred between the three of them. She recognized the third and focused. She must remain in balance, must sustain and give herself wholly into the elastic consciousness beyond themselves. Jessie showed them how to enter into that higher relationship. A realization. "Our entire family - no one is alone, not one can ever

THE PEOPLE OF THE VALLEY

be alone. Together, we are a source of energy. All of Humankind - what would we be all together?" The thought spun away, carrying them into possibiity.

Jessie's Touch dissolved. She was alone. Andrew turned to her slowly, acceptance rising with his laughter so that they felt intensely the foolishness of their old hesitations. He smiled. Then he too was gone.

Anna felt the silence like a palpable presence. Strong, around and through her, it heightened her awareness of the others. She must hold herself separate, each of those around her was at a point of decision.She could know that. Each must find his or her own way. She held that right in absolute trust. She withdrew into herself. Waiting.

Andrew enjoyed his separateness, listening to the sounds of the mountain forest. His thoughts were on the City above them. He sensed an expectancy there. He thought that a city does not 'expect'. Then realized that a city could, since a city is its people, not its buildings. There fore who ever -- or whatever -- lived in the City, must be expecting them. The thought excited him, but gave him pause. Surely, it is not the physical city that effects the People of the Highways when they make their daily reverence,nor can it be even what she stands for. It has to be the life of that City. The thought surprised him.

He was silent, listening. There is power here, a stabilized energy. What is it? He focussed his attention, listened, intently aware. Gradually he knew a stirring as of many voices, faint, hushed, distant. An urgency woke his mind to attention more precisely focussed. It was as if his very consciousness lifted, tuned to finer senses; a broad, vivid alertness of mind that Reached into that Mountain itself. From the depths of it then, from the layers of stone, soil, metals, waters pouring and seeping through in veins and great pools, rose the consciousness that had thrust up peaks and ranged them one against another. It had extended the massive cliffs that were the walls of the City He knew it and was awed.

Life! The living mountain.It was alive even as his own body was. Not living flesh,but living rock and soil. The knowledge of it stunned him, yet he held on, listening with his whole mind. Wanting to know, to be part of that Life,. He was filled with a deep permeating sense of power, fused and radiant with profound Love. It staggered him until he hastily withdrew, over come. For that Love seemed to him without mercy. That seemed a paradox. How could Love be without mercy? Surely. He must have mistaken something, missed something.

Shrinking within himself to that tiny selfness that was Andrew, he intuitively sought Anna. She the other half of him, the twin that lived so close. She was shaking her head, busy with an effort to dispell some of that radiant power that she knew even as he did. He realized that he had not been alone in his realization of that EARTH LIFE. Surely no person could bear to know Life like that alone. He hadn't been able to. He was glad that she - and Jessie - were with him. Then he turned to her.

Anna Reached to him. A reverence seemed to hush everything around her. "Andrew, is it possible? Possible that we can know? All that? Could WE receive that Touch of Earth Herself? Could we bear it? The brush of IT against us just now was like a burning, a tenderness that stood against my heart, immoveable and -- tough. Not to be touched by pity! Is Earth Life a reflection of Spirit itself? I felt such wonder. Such strange beauty, and pain too. It's like a fire burning through my mind. And I know that it only barely brushed against us. How could human beings Join at all, how could we even Touch, with THAT?"

Andrew nodded, trembling, Reaching to link himself wholly with her, their minds supporting one another, their awareness enlarged in multiples, not just doubled. He knew that even together they had barely been able to know a flicker of what had Touched them. He sighed, "Anna, what was it? What did we Touch against? What drew us -- like moths into a flame, so great, so full of life?" Then he knew, they both knew the answer and they could not have explained at all." I think maybe THAT was a tiny glimpse of Love itself!"

He nodded to her as she met his eyes in the moon light. They were still, as two children might be who have met an unknown they cannot grasp at all. Slowly, they regained their balance.

Anna murmured, 'Whatever, it was too much, too much for us alone." They felt a longing to Reach out again, to Touch again that ocean of power. But they shrank in terror at the idea. They remembered their childhood, their learning together, alone, to receive one another, how frightening it had been at first. Then when they had felt that first Touch of trust, of love and Joining, how vast it had seemed, how grand and beautiful. They saw that their courage to meet this, this unexplainable vast power, would depend on their mutual trust. Could it truy be Earth Herself? the thought echoed through their minds, penetrating, shifting perception. "Perhaps with many people together we could realize more. It would take more than all humanity together to sustain that Earth Touch. We'd have to have lived our lives - lived through Love for generations, I think."

"We couldn't even stand a glimpse of that, just the two of us, you know," Anna said to him. "We never will! We have to Join with others who are willing to make that contact. It's too much, the power would roar through us like a hurricane in a hollow tube and break the very walls of our consciousness."

He nodded, her hand clutched in his, and both of them held to thick tufts of grass, as if wanting to keep their contact with this physical earth. Andrew quieted himself. his trembling faded. He let his mind extend, Reach to the others, flow like a water among the familar family.

Their first Touch was to Ned. He lay in a chaos of thought and feeling. He was calling out, with feeble energy as if he thought no one would hear. How long has he been so? Anna felt contrition. Anna and Andrew tightened the balance of their Joining, made it stable and were surprised at how easy it was. Ned knew someone was close, but he did not trust his knowledge. He was like someone lost in the dark who calls out hopefully but when someone comes, cannot turn to them, or believe that they are there.

Then, drawing himself up, focussing his own mental energy, he figuratively stood, stood and recognized help. Already his composure was regained. He had caught himself intact not knowing whose presence had provided the crutch. From

THE PEOPLE OF THE VALLEY

the deep great center of his generous heart, Ned looked out at the inner world of his mind. He would hold! But what he had come up against, he could not accept, could not and yet did! He cried out again, this time in astonishment and terror. Andrew and Anna entered near, their very real love surrounding him as though it were light. They did not know how to do more. They waited.

He began slowly to respond, his fear ebbing, so the barrier weakened between them. Andrew called, " Uncle Ned, it's Anna and Andrew, Uncle Ned!" Ned was not aware of the words, the names, he knew only of help. With a wrench, he jerked himself away from the fascination of his terror. Anna felt the waves of resistance the terrible pull of his fear. Then, in a moment,from somewhere outside all of them, there came a quiet firmness, a silent strength, nameless but present. Ned felt it. He righted himself. Focussed and stood quiet but free. Anna and Andrew were grateful for Jessie's Touch. It enabled them. Now Ned could hear. Could see again.

It was as though he pushed his way through a darkness, shadows that held threat and doom. His vision seemed dim, he could make out forms there, his mind felt something Touch against it, something that Healed and comforted. Like a rope to which he could cling, it wound into his grasp. He held on. Knowing there were others now, others who cared. He realized that wash of Light was their Love, finding and guiding him. He felt gratitude. He turned to them, but they seemed so far away, he felt disappointment. He had opened his eyes, and was looking at them, across a small stretch of the meadow. How could everyone be so far away. Then he closed his eyes, entered down into himself again and found them with him. He sighed, deeply comforted and yet,peculiarly ashamed. After a moment, with his usual good humour, he smiled and they smiled with him. He nodded, his head moving as his thoughts reflected his mood.

He spoke to them now, mind to mind, accepting and knowing that he did just that. He visualized his experience and they shared it."Everything is so much more than it ever was. Life reaches through things, I feel it." He was amazed even remembering. Anna and Andrew knew as he knew. He was amazed to feel them so near him. He could 'see' the soft extending glow of energy that was their presence with him. He knew he saw now with mind, not physical eyes, and he was awed. So that was what had brought so much trouble into the Family?

In a world so changed, multidimensional, he felt off balance. He heard the soft murmur as of a multiplication of thousands of separate tones, each emanating from different life forms. It was as natural as fragrance. He thought he had lived as a blind man. Now he glimpsed something of the complexity of the universe, and he glimpsed also something of the Love that wove it together. There were lives in every dimension, not only in this physical one. Love filled his heart, found there the great natural pool already well developed and enlarged it. But for Ned, the realizations were overwhelming. He said,"My God, do you see all that? Do you realize -- what it means?" He was silent regarding them,"Of course you do. Have been, for years, haven't you? That's what it's all been about,isn't it. The Joining, the Reach, the learning how to SEE. We're beginning to know

THE JOURNEY

physical life is only a small part of Life. He nodded, acknowledging.

Andrew grinned, "We do know something about what you were experiencing, yes, You remember when we were all taught that there are modes of consciousness that extend beyond our senses? Well, now it's making sense, Huh?"

Ned was silent, focussing intently with Anthony. as if absorbing meaning beyond his words. "I think we're not built to cope with it all. It's too much. It'd drive me crazy to live in a world that was so -- so -- multidimensional."

Anna said, "You did, cope. And you will learn how to screen, how to build a shield to adjust to what you can bear. Gradually you can bear so much more. It's natural after all, you know." She felt relief, glad that he was balancing, adjusting now, more than he knew. "You aren't asked to do it all at once, but change is endemic, things are really fluid, you know."

Ned swallowed a grief that kept building . Unwilling to acknowledge it, he struggled. He knew then, gently that grief was natural. Thought was a rippling through awareness. 'The changes are strange, they make most people feel a great sadness, as if they've lost their old familiar world, somehow. We grieve at a loss of -- of that limited cradle we've all lived in. We're out into reality a little farther now. We can't go back.' The knowledge was instantly his own, and he accepted.

He sighed and allowed his grief to rise, his eyes to flow with tears. He bent his head, the mixed, violent, emotions of the past hour had taken their toll. He bent his head into his arms and cried for several minutes, allowing. Then he said softly to himself, "It's like -- like suddenly knowing when you get to be fifteen that you'll never be a child again,that you've lost that, can't have it back. And yet, there's the same wonderful elation that now, now I will know, experience, as an adult .A new life, in fact."

He looked over at them, lying in their two bags, watching him there, Anna sitting up now, and though he could not meet their eyes, he heard their words. He said,"You knew, have known, haven't you? Even though you are so young. You had to meet all this as children, little babies,in fact. My God! You're children and you're teaching me!" He sighed, felt again lost, realizing that.

Finally he said, "It's really all right. It's really something pretty wonderful. You can't help being kids." He hesitated, looked around at the other sleeping forms in the meadow. "All of us. We've begun to realize so much. We've begun, we are making that Journey Jessie brought us to." He grinned, his good humor coming back. "I think now I know what it means to be together."

"But to be like this, it means so much. I don't know whether I can -- I feel as though I've lost myself, and yet, --" He grinned again, "Obviously I've not. I'm as separate and myself as ever, but I have that choice. I could reach in there, -- could again reach the depths and look into that." He was silent for minutes, then turning, stretching, he said, "You're a pair of wonders, that's for sure. I love you both."He slid down into his bag, "I'll think about all this tomorrow."

Anna and Andrew slid down too, settling into their bags to sleep. The grass seemed lumpy here, Anna rolled about to find a place where it was soft. Andrew felt Anna drift away into sleep."It's all so much. We're learning to give support, the way Jessie told us. We might one day,study to be a Teacher the way she is, or even a Monitor. It's not just study though, one has to be -- to have the Talent, I suppose. " He remembered his doubts and fears, his attractions to the excitement his gang had brought him, the near entering into that pull toward violence, love of control. He sighed, "No, I have choice, I have choice.I know that now. And I choose Life, the LIFE that pours the Love through our Valley and brings us to these new dimensions of living." He too drew his sleeping blankets over his shoulders, and slept.

Off to one side, two bundles lay, one bent to the side from theo ther. Mary had been sitting with Cassandra when they decided to sleep and had just settled where they were. Now, Mary stirred, sat up, looked around, needing to pee. She slid the opening free on her warm bag and stepped out, dressed in loose sleeping clothes. She got up and walked to the bushes beyond the rock fall. The moonlight made the night golden. The distance was misted, soft as in a dream. She stood a moment, just being aware of it, then squatted to relieve herself. When she returned to her sleeping place, she slid only partly into the bag, sitting, she looked all around, filled with the wonder of the high mountain night, the moonlight, the hush and the intermittent call of creatures.

This air, this fresh, blowing air, delighted her. So different it was from the re-used air of the undersea city. They had not yet found a better way, but the city itself had taken all their strength, their time and imagination, just to make it liveable. Some day, they would know how to live in the sea.She turned on her back, staring straight up into the sky. Shadows played about on the rocks, the pale cliffs. A light wind blue the thin limbs of trees, creating movement even in this stillness. And then, paying attention, she was amazed at the stillness. Seldom did she have time to come to the mountain country when she was home. And the quality of that stillness was utterly different from that of the depths. She let herself attend, realizing it with all her senses.

And in that stillness, Mary found the Touch of another mind. She knew at once it was Cassandra, gentle, far more caring than any child had a right to be. She turned her face slightly, toward the small lump that was Cassandra's sleeping pallet. She was hidden beneath her covers, but her mind ranged, sought others. And Mary smiled, pleased at this companionship, the ability of this child to let another be with her without any expectations.

Then, frowning, she thought of what Jessie had said when they were eating. That business about the City. In her own childhood she had taken her times with the Vagabonds, she knew of their reverence but she also knew the City as symbol, not worshipped. She focussed her own attention toward that point above and slightly to the south east. She found it easily, the power of it drew her, its real presence could not be denied. Cassandra was still there, a faint presence. Together they sought out that point from which the energy seemed to flow, an energy that Mary would not deny, scientist as she was. She had seen too many remarkable things occur in that ocean city, the intense high level of focus, of Reaching out toward creatures of the sea, the Touch of alien consciousness barred from ordinary communication by an utterly alien perception of reality,but still making tentative Touch, to doubt the profound presence of mystery beyond her own rational mind. She listened, with her heart's acute focus.

Remembering, now, she listened and gradually felt the delicate, rhythm of response. A rhythm not unlike that of the unceasing currents of ocean. There it was, streaming through everything, the air, the land, herself. And she held herself utterly silent, receptive. In this Journey, might she find a key for opening that vast universe that was beneath the powerful waters of the Earth's seas. The greater part of Earth in fact. The unknown, a frontier that fascinated her far more than space exploration even could. A thought gradually shaped out of some knowledge heretofore unknown. This journey was a way toward finding the key into herself. If there, another key existed that might open her awareness to new thought, that might be, but it might not. She smiled, nodding and was still for a long time.

Finally, chilled, she slid down into her bag, snuggled in, shivering slightly, and slowly, she felt the drift down into that small mind that functioned in this body. Without any words at all, she Reached out, Touched with gratitude that great Soul that was Casssandra and then, with a long sigh, she turned away, to sleep.

CHAPTER TWENTY THREE

The Testing

It was only a few minutes later that Anna stirred, lifted her head and listened. She felt strong energy course through her body, sleep eluded her. She Reached to Andrew, wanting his company, and he woke, his sleep light before the restlessness of his mind. They focussed attention and knew the touch of Jessie's mind like a smiling -- a sweet laughter -- then it was gone. They were still.

A cry like a child in pain stabbed at their attention. Without thought, both children Reached. Here in this inner realm where astral substance shaped itself into whatever forms thought took, such forms could be seen in that physical world as reflections. They watched the movement and found the source of the cry. They could see Jennifer as the awakening Soul she was, full of the beauty of color and wisdom, but half submerged in a cloud, a clinging of pain.

Jennifer had put her sleeping bag under a pine tree where needles were piled thick and soft. The scent pleased her and she had fallen asleep swiftly. Now in a dream, she was again above the City. Suspended there in an air like shimmering diamonds, air that was sweet and full of energy. She trembled. Her dream had been of Joy initially but shadows formed and the events troubled her until she descended into fear. She felt power here, power such that she shrank away. Such power could destroy her. How could SHE stand against such power?

In the instant of her cry, she knew with an illogical certainty that she truly WAS above the City -- just as she had been on that fateful day months ago. At the same time, dreaming, she knew that she dreamed. Neither less real than the other. At that moment, she felt the surge of support from the twins. A bright flame of warmth around her that lifted then subsided. They were there, like two strong currents of energy on which she was free to draw. She leaned toward them, surprised in a bemused way that Anna and Andrew were the heart of that current. Her own children had not come to this Journey. Knowing of it, Stephen chose to wait, to make this Journey later. But to her amazement, Rachel confessed that she had already made that Journey, had even accompanied another group to help them make it. Jennifer had stared at her daughter in disbelief, then slowly a dawning understanding had settled, troubling her at first. Why did she know so little of her child?

Now, setting those thoughts aside she focussed into her dreaming, felt a surge against herself, and knew it came from the City itself. A surge that drew her, and of which she was afraid, even as she longed to respond. Could she tolerate that pulse of -- of Love? Yes, nothing else could name it. It was Love that rose from that City and its purpose? What was that? For surely even Love must have purpose! Instantly she knew it was to nourish her, to inform her. With this help, she could tolerate it. Her fear fell away like a heavy stone falling and gone.

She felt strength in herself unlike any she had ever known, as though that nourishment wakened a strength already there.

Her mind raced, this then was that Love the others spoke of. This! So powerful, so vast, so -- so literally omnipresent. Literally! She sustained her attention, aware, full of wonder. Love without question, made one free. The fact of that startled and amazed her. It had so long been a cliche. But here, wanting nothing, needing nothing, she was free to participate in loving without limit. The nature of that Love, utterly real, filled her mind, swelled her heart. In moments, she absorbed, realized and could not conceive of life without it.

Strange. Had she always known this presence but never acknowledged? She thought that all the love she had known had been nothing in comparison. In spite of all she found in the creation of music, now it was clear that that creating was an expression of all she knew of life, but it was equally a deep and unfilled yearning for a something beyond it. At its best, it was a drawing forth from the depths of her being that power that was Love. Now, it seemed nakedly present, the foundation of living itself. She wanted to flee, run away from the power of it and at the same time, she longed to move deeper into it. To accept.

She was aware that there was help near, help from lives old and constant. But instantly she remembered that those who had come to her were Anna and Andrew, she frowned, disbelieving. Not possible. They are too young. At first her impulse was to refuse them, to keep her separation, but the Presence of Love sweeping through her, lifting her consciousness, included them. She turned.

The two young people Touched, gently, hesitant, extending the Love they felt for this Aunt Jennifer, a love very personal and real. And around them all swept the powerful flow of Love that tossed their own personal feelings like a shell in a powerful river. Here in this dream state, she could literally see that River, feel its cool movement. She was so quiet, so still in her attention, until finally she drew away, separate and able to think. She said, "So that was another dimension of Joining! I've not practiced much, even though we all promised we would. I've avoided, I think, and it was a loss, surely. This Touch with you was different, alive, like a pulse almost but that was only the initial breath of it. The sweep of it was beyond any intimacy I've ever known, -- " she was silent, and then," and yet, that intimacy is included. Yes, included."

The sense of floating, of hanging light as a dry leaf above the Silent City was reinforced by the company of the twins. It could not be dismissed now as dream. She frowned, uneasy but turned her attention to the City below. "Look the air here is so clear, the City so pure and bright, as though Light glows from every stone of the walls. As though it's Holy after all." The thought was a sigh, and she knew it. An old longing. She wished Paul were near; so acute was her desire it translated into a Reach.

To her utter astonishment Paul was instantly there with her, bodyless, and conscious of their Joining, he took her hand and floated with her in the bright sun that he knew was the City. He was with her. The children waited a moment, and then withdrew.

Paul felt a vast joy to find his love here, poised in awareness above this bright revelation of what the City was. He met her, wholly surrounded her with his love, felt the steady pulse of that greater Love that surrounded them both. He saw his own drowned in that grandeur. He knew the sweet wonder of Jennifer's willingness to give and receive. She who had held herself so distant these past months, was truly present. They circled one another, making contact, withdrawing, Coming closer and each time, a deeper Joining grew. They were knowing one another as they never had. As she had never allowed. They merged in an intercourse of mind and Spirit that woke their half sleeping bodies to its ectasy of Joy and fulfillment.

Paul finally drew thought into a sentence,"Oh, my dear, dear Love, how long I have waited for your company here."

"Oh, Paul, I feel afraid. I feel as though I could be lost. Please don't leave me alone, not yet,not until I know how to be here without --- without fearing that I will lose myself. You understand Love?" She was anxious, even in the midst of his reassurance and he poured out to her his recognition. He reminded her that such fear of being lost from oneself was natural and everyone knew of it. He quoted a Teaching that both had heard but had always half understood,"The little self feels overwhelmed by the vastness of the true Self, and fearful that this great identity will swallow into oblivion this small one."As he repeated the words, she nodded, soberly. Finally it made sense.

They watched the play of Light, color, sound, fragrance below and soon he said,"You, know, Love,that the others know of our being here ?"

Her Sending had almost a physical jolt to it."In this? Our own intimate time?"

He smiled, "No, Dear,No. They don't enter in. They wait, but we've been Sending pretty strong and loud, you know. Several could hear our Joy. It's roused the same in them, in fact, for their mates. So it's done good, No?" She felt his grin. "After all, they're family, you know."

She moved a little, felt the sudden pull back to her body, then with renewed confidence, she strengthened the separation. She wanted to be here, above this City. Wanted to know its truth. Now, Reaching out, she included the others faintly. She accepted. "Yes, I think I see. The children were here, you know. They showed me, helped me. I was so surprised at them, Paul. I think they worried about me. But I want everyone to know that I'm no longer afraid. Not at all,afraid.

He nodded, feeling a great happiness. "It's a miracle, all this. It doesn't seem possible that we're here together and that -- that you accept it all." His arms were around her, he drew her close, his relief and joy wrapping them both.

But before they could know more, they felt the unorganized Reach of the little girl Cassandra as she came tumbling into their presence. It was as a child comes tumbling into bed with her parents. She laughed, full of lightness and exuberance. They both laughed and received her. She said, "Aunt Jennifer, Uncle Paul -- you can be with me here now. It's wonderful. How did you do it?" They were astonished at the power of her Touch - so young to have depths of mind stirred so, so able. Awakened thus so early, she would surely grow into a great and noble woman. Paul felt her potential only half expressed. He felt a little envy, but mostly a great fatherly pride. What wonderful things would her life bring. So much waited for the young ones of this Valley.

Cassandra laughed at them, while she descended a little, to stand firmly on the tip of a glowing tower of the City. She looked up at them, and said,"It was Jessie, talking about the City. I dreamed of it then, I -- I just came here to see." For a time they were silent, and Cassandra nodded at them suddenly, then left.

Paul too, felt the pull to return, took his leave of Jennifer, felt the familiar locating in his body. He wanted to allow these events to shape themselves into thought. "How do I manage all of this? Make sense of all the power here? All the feelings, the grief, the Joy, the knowledge?" Thoughts faded and slid away into tendrils of sleep that claimed him. A last thought lingered as he dropped into dreamless sleep. 'It can all be thought about tomorrow'. And Jennifer waited until her dream returned her again into her body.

There was Mary, sleeping now near Tom, wanting to feel his nearness in this strange place. And she woke, as though some one had called her name. She looked around. The night was bright with moonlight, the air seemed to her charged. And then, slowly, she felt the questions with which she had wrestled for months, rising, like a swarm of bees, shoving the quiet away, demanding. She sighed, wondering if that meant she would not sleep. Surely she would need rest before tomorrow. Her doubts of this Journey, the very fact of it, was a cloud through which she looked and was troubled. The old questions seemed suddenly unimportant, details, and she shrugged them away. She no longer needed to answer for herself the nature of life, to find ideas that held that answer. The nature of life seemed to her eternally discoverable, never findable. The thought comforted her. She could rest from that. Then what was the sharp call that had waked her?

She sat up, looked all around, saw the rounded lumps of human bodies here and there. Like a stage setting, it seemed, a grand and dramatic scene. She smiled,the moonlight laid down shadows of great limbs over them, the night seemed so still. Too still, as if a breath was being held. She thought fleetingly of her son Justin, his unknowing, and his loving, his wonderful talent for loving. Then, as swiftly she turned from thoughts of him. He was all right. Surely, more than that. Angy and Jason were with him and they would make their Journey, or perhaps they already had in another way. As the thought left her, she felt her mind empty, cleared, swept dry as though long hours of deep contemplation had passed.

This stillness, was within herself, or it projected from some depth that was in more than herself, it came -- was there in everything, in them all together , but more, the mountain, the trees, the air, everything. The stillness was a 'way', a path through herself into some nameless brilliance that was Life itself. And then, what was Life was no longer as it had been, but like a fluid, an orderly changing, a growing or an unfolding, it was becoming, unceasingly becoming Itself. Just as her beloved Ocean was never still, ever rolling with the currents of its changing, even though it never ceased being Ocean. It was not a 'THING', it was a condition, one of the qualities of reality. That was it. Yes, she had it. Life WAS. Without cessation.

And she was part of the changing! She was entranced, utterly focussed, attentive to that giving of things to the ceaseless changing. Of herself, of her own heart, and finally, self aware, of her entire mind substance. And here she drifted, knowing its realizations and unable to pin down a single one into crystalized thought. For moments she was frantic to find solid shaping of thought, and then, shrugged off the need as if it were an old coat. Astonishment flickered, because, as if in play, a thought formed. "Absolutely! Mind is fluid, but it creates as it relates to Life. Creates out of its own substance. Mind too is an ocean." The realization seemed to her an enlightenment, so intensely did she know it. And as she did, she felt her body loosen, slide down into her sleeping bag. As from a great distance, she saw the questions that plagued her, that had nagged at her for years, and each dropped, like pieces of a jig saw puzzle, into a vast pattern whose dimensions stretched on beyond comprehension. Obviously, in this part was an understanding, a knowledge of the fluidity of mind. The light of awareness was stretched on to illuminate a bit more of that which was hidden. She turned over, feeling the quiet of sleep claiming her again.

Jessie, watching from that light and fragile place slightly beyond the perceptions of the others, relaxed, felt her eyes grow heavy. It was done. They were awakened and now their bodies rested. She was like a light that had drawn in upon itself and now began to pour outward, to invade shadows, and dissolve them. To clarify and reveal a world of mystery. In the air, the moonlight seemed to intensify, to grow deeper, and all the life around seemed to hold magic of delight.

The morning dawned cool and with a light wind blowing down from the cold peaks. They woke with some sense of apprehension. each one looked around, at the clean fall of barren cliff and forested crevasses, at one another, wondering, feeling the surge of joy, the weight of fear, the hope of promise. For several moments no one stirred from their bags, Then the sun swept down into the tops of trees, painted naked branches with its light and shone in the needles of pines. The wind sloughing through those conifers was soothing, but the air was cool. Before the sun had reached the ground around them, Tom leaped from his bag, rolled it up and pulled on his clothes. Jessie watched him, smiling, enjoying the energy he so casually used. She slid from her bed, nearly as swiftly if not as effortlessly, and began to make ready for travel.

As they drew from sleep, pulling on clothes, packing things, she noticed shy smiles, a meeting of eye, a gentle touch here and there. It was as if they saw one another for the first time and needed to get re-acquainted. She sent a clear thought of anticipation and went walking down the path that they must take after breakfast. The sky was a cave of bright blue above them. Ben carried his pack into better light, poured a quantity of grains and mixed dried fruit and nuts into a transparant bowl and touched a power pack at its base. Hot breakfast would be ready soon.

THE JOURNEY

Everyone could smell the heating porrage, and it gathered them near. Ned opened his pack to hand out small, orange Com fruits, sharply sweet and nourishing. They sat, not talking, each absorbed with memories of the night, and ate their hot breakfast and drank hot tea. The heat of the food was comforting and the quiet time together reassuring.

Jane stood up, waited a moment, her hands wrapped close upon the roughbark of a tree. She glanced down at the heads of hair shining in the spreading sunlight,and then she looked up into the gleaming needles of the pine above her,. As if taking courage from it, she heaved a great sigh and REACHED. She felt the strength of this first consciously chosen effort. Then she came against another, a Touch in response. Her face broke into smiles, delighted with her new perception, she chuckled. And at that, there was swift response from everyone, acknowledgement, their delight in her willingness. Jessie smiled at the mental clamour ahead of her as she returned to them. They had a lot to learn. Yes! But they had learned so much!

They repacked and began to move into the trail. Paul said,holding his head and grimacing through his smiles, "Wow! That was something !" He turned to look back at the others, beginning to find a place in the line up on the trail."Were going to have to learn how to shut up and take our turns, how to distinguish,how to stay out of each other's way." He shook his head, "Out of each other's MENTAL way!" But he laughed."There's a lot to learn!"

Ned straightened up,slinging his pack to his back and settling it into place. "I hope it doesn't take as long for humankind to learn mental manners as it did to learn physical manners. We've only begun to learn to be considerate of each other as we were."

The joke relieved the little tension that was shaping. They had begun to read each other's needs, guided by those strong experienced minds among them. They relaxed consciously so that order could establish itself. Some did not know how to select and choose, how to shield adroitly and yet not miss what was wanted. Ned said,"It's as if the night has dissolved barriers, dissolved some kind of blindness and torn down all our hiding places." He was silent, he knew he spoke for himself . He reflected on what he'd said and added, "No! There it is. I can see that I am also hiding again, can avoid or conceal just as I always have, but-- it's different. I think that now I have choice! I've got on to myself." He turned to meet Jessie's eyes and found agreement there.

Ben clamped down the cooking utensils, stored them away and hoisted his pack to his back. "It'll take time, you know. No use being impatient" He let his own thoughts subside, but Reached out, Touched here and there, flickering Touches and then drew himself away. He accepted whatever responses he got, whether refusal or acceptance. He had not known that he could recognize the feelings, the way another person 'was' so clearly. He turned to the Earth around, and nodded, satisfied.Yes, it was so there too. Everything seemed so much more responsive, steadily so. Unlike the intermittent surges, the flickering recognitions of his past life. The lives around him seemed so present to him. He could Touch and know response or refusal clearly. He sent out a deliberate call to Jessie, wild, impulsive, full of delight and joy. He felt the Touch of her response, brief but tender and pleased. He felt like a child who has just learned to talk seeing the approving smile on his mother's face.

In that time, more conscious than they had ever been, they knew of emotions, fragments of thought, shafts of anger, fear, envy, eagerness, that came and went. It was as though they stood at a little distance from themselves and watched the process of their living. The familiar practice of self observation. This time it was sobering, but fascinating. Each sought to bring his or her own mental-emotional climate into balance. Each saw resentments of a life time, angers of childhood, old unfulfilled hungers, staining and shaping present reality. They could see that without new fears, but with a little sorrow. There was an all pervading delight at the astonishing 'thereness' of the other. A 'withness' that seemed to have erased walls of distance, of blindness. It was constant reassurance. Loneliness had become a thing of choice. The very movement of their bodies, legs hung perfectly in the sockets of hips, the sweep of shoulder and the lift of heads, seemed this morning so precise, so powerful.

Without further comment, they began the Journey again. Tom in the lead walked across the flat surface of the ledge where the path seemed to end. A sharp turn of the cliff face hid what was ahead. He turned to them, seeing their trusting faces. Jennifer moved ahead, exploring beyond the great boulders that created open caves as they leaned against one another. Tom said, "I think we guessed we'd have to travel some narrow trails . So we weren't without warning, but this cliff face is something special. To cross it isn't easy. It's a climbers job. It's sheer falling on one side, straight up on the other. It varies from a foot wide to four inches, I hope nothing less. It has little to balance us. Fortunately, the cliff slopes backward just a little, from the ledge, thank God, or we'd not have a chance, but there are places where it doesn't. We've got to hug the cliff flat and tight."

He stopped and studied their faces, the eagerness, fear, simple interest, that he saw. He continued, "For an experienced climber it's no problem at all. But for beginners, or those who've not climbed at all, it could be very difficult."

Benjamin shrugged, "There's no one in the Valley that I know of who's completely inexperienced in climbing. We've all been taught as kids."

Rose said, "That's true, but experience is very different among us. Some have only a minimum. But we've got other help. We've just demonstrated it, our greatest strength. We must rely on each other. It's our only chance."

Tom was nodding, " But that's exactly it. The weakest link can bring us all down." He spoke brutally to convince them they must be serious. Until they were on the cliff face, they couldn't know. Unless they'd had experience and there were several who had little. He saw a few faces blanch, one or two grin, others look quietly serious. Those too eager could be as dangerous as those afraid. He Reached, made brief mental touches down the line, bringing firm demand to shaky confidence. "We can do it if we Join. If we support one another completely."

Jennifer had returned, was standing near him watching, she nodded,"We take each other's lives into our hands. We are responsible! All our physical courage and mental power is needed now. This is no time to pretend, nor to deny. If you are afraid, admit it and we can support you. If you feel as though this is nothing at all, just a big jaunt, then you're dangerous to us. We need to know exactly where everyone is." She looked serious, but her eyes were smiling, an eagerness visible in her eyes. She was going to enjoy the climb, but she worried about the others. Nevertheless, they felt her delight in the challenge and it lifted their spirits.

Tom watching them, knew they were as ready as they would be. He turned to Jennifer,"Tell them what it looks like out there. You've just seen it."

She nodded,"There's a tunnel between those house sized boulders there, when we come out, the ledge begins. It isn't too narrow at first, and it climbs a little. It narrows as it goes though, so we must rope ourselves together." She drew out the lines, the harnesses that each must wear. They passed them down the line and began fastening them on. She went on," We'll need to hold together physically as well as mentally. We've got to use every skill of balancing we know." She watched as they attached the lines, and adjusted some, she and Tom checking every connection.

They began to choose their positions. Jennifer would lead, Tom bring up the rear. Those who feared, who knew the least of climbing, were distributed among the others. Silvia was at the center, Jane whose heart ached with her fear of heights,talked to herself. Steve walked behind her, she turned to meet his eyes,then gritting her teeth, prepared herself with a long slow breath. She didn't want to let her fear grow -- or be known. Jennifer stopped. Turned, met Jane's eyes, tenderly. " Jane, it's no use. Unless you let us realize with you, we can't help. It's too dangerous for us to conceal anything now."

Jane looked around, shame fighting wisdom, her face was tight with anger at herself. She knew Jennifer was right. She studied the others, who else knew? They revealed their identities, without guile, looking at her with love and firm resolve. She felt naked there, furious and then, with a swift emptying of anger, she sobbed with relief, then, taking a deep breath, she said, "All right.I've got to admit that I'm phobic about heights. I don't see how I can manage, but I have learned to use belts, to fly with them. So -- I thought -- I'm determined to do it!" With a fierce frown to hold back tears, she added,"Don't worry about me. I'll not cause trouble."

Steve met her eyes again, touched her lightly on the arm,"Dearest, don't you see what Tom said? Nobody's feelings pay attention to reason. If they overwhelm you, reason won't help you. You know that yourself. Neither will determination help much. Just let us stay with you all the time, every minute, close watch. " He poured all his love into his request, and found himself deeply Touching, knowing her longing to receive him, then with a sudden release of her tension, she did.

Jane's tears fell then, her eyes dropped to the ground. "All right! All right!" her voice was brusk with anger and relief mixed. "I'll stay open. I'll keep contact. I WILL do that. I see that I must. I can't gaurantee that I won't panic, but this way,you'll know as soon as there's any chance of it." She grimaced, trying to smile, her tears disregarded. She was holding on to Steve's hand as they turned to move on, her hand reaching back to him, clung for several minutes before it withdrew.

They moved off, the world below was visible, a light morning haze softened the low valleys, the River gleaming bright through long distances. They felt the Valley's pull, felt their love for that home land and yet,in this night's passing they had released their clinging to it. The mild sadness of that fact,was gone with the gladness of release. A release that surprised them. So it must be, one's personal loyalties, a virtue ordinarily, were also limiting. Their loyalty was to Life itself.

Jessie carefully chose her footsteps where she walked just in front of Tom. She smiled at their brief backward glances, and then was pleased to see no more. No heart seemed torn with indecision. The choice was clear. It must be so, the path ahead was irrevocable. She could feel the Reach of their minds toward the City now. Their thoughts were centered on It.

The trail wound through the shadows under the great rocks, a wide sandy surface, easy to travel. As they came out, the long stretch of forests covering the rocky slopes below, seemed finally familiar and the path more safe. As the path rose higher, the tree line fell and they were out above the tall trees. There were small wind twisted trees and hardy shrubs clinging to the cliffs. The Alpine pear, planted so long ago in the mountains grew in sturdy little clumps, fruit still clinging stubbornly to the thorny little branches. They would cling so, until some creature came along to pick them off. The deer, and birds, even the wild cats, and coyotes were known to eat them when other food was scarce. Mice and rabbits fed on them regularly.

Tom breathed a sigh of gratitude that it was not stormy weather. Had Jessie known and so chosen this time? They arrived at the sharp turning of the ledge and it's narrowing point. They crowded on the last wide shelf looking at the trail they must traverse.

Jennifer studied it, then turned, her face serious." Well, we've come to it, the narrow part. I can't be sure how far it goes, but surely around that next turn at least. That means it's going to be long enough that several of us will be some time on the narrow part together. We'd better adjust the ropes, so there's room for spreading out." Just in front of her the trail narrowed to about eight inches wide, it widened again to twelve, then narrowed again. What it would do beyond the turn, no one could see, though several knew. It would narrow to no less than three inches. But those three inches were firm and smooth. It should do. Jennifer nodded, confident.

"Well, we'll have to take a final tally. We've not actually heard from each one of you. Let's see how we stand."

They looked at one another. Ned said,"I've done enough climbing that I'm

THE JOURNEY

fairly confident for myself. But I don't know how much help I'd be to anyone else."

Silvia spoke out of a burst of fear,"My God, with my belly, how d'you expect me to cling close enough? It'll be impossible! She turned to Jerry, to put her face into his shoulder more afraid than she had thought she would be. And she knew that some of that fear was not simply because of her child. She was uncomfortable, though not actually afraid, of heights. Jerry drew her to him, kissed her hair and whispered softly,"It'll be all right, Love. We have plenty of rope and everyone will be watching you."

Jessie stood watching them, her face a blank, her eyes attentive, measuring, non judging. She waited. Suddenly Jane cried out,"Jessie, how could you have done this? You knew that this situation existed. Why did you allow her to come, or me even? Don't you realize it's dangerous?" Her eyes were angry.

Jessie nodded, but Tom said,"Jane, we have to do what has to be done. We can't have special privileges, even if we have what we see as special problems. No one else has ever been given special choice." He stopped, how did he know that? But no one noticed, they were busy considering the words spoken.

Benjamin said,"Will we go on or not?" It seemed to establish the choice. "This is only one task among many that will follow. If we're defeated by the first real difficulty, what are we? We aren't worthy to -- to enter the City. We're finding what strengths we have or don't have. We have to know -- we can't risk not knowing anything about each other that is relevant." He searched their faces, several eyes dropped, Then one by one they looked at him, at Tom and at Jennifer. Anna and Andrew had climbed since early childhood, taken to it well and enjoyed it. They were eager and confident, Ben thought a little too confident. He said,"Fear is natural to anyone who hasn't done much of this. But over confidence is also natural and just as dangerous. Look to yourselves, discover any over confidence and give it to us. We have to know what we're dealing with." Tom was nodding, grateful for Ben's brusk decisiveness.

Anna frowned, drew her attention into herself, searched out her attitudes and met Andrew's eyes. Each grinned sheepishly. He said, "O.K. Dad, we're eager, looking forward to it. Maybe wanting to show off, huh? You call that over confidence? I'd not thought of that". He reached back to Anna, their hands clasped. They watched their father's face, waiting. Ben nodded, no change in his expression but they all heard the relief in his mind. "We can work with it, Son, if we know it. But especially if we know you know it! Thank you, both."

"Well, I'll admit I'm scared spitless. But you all know that." Silvia said, "I don't even mind saying it. Climbing's never been a hobby of mine, though I've done the basics in School."

Paul glanced at his wife's happy easy face,"Here's where Jennifer has it all over me. She's always been a natural at this. I don't think I feel afraid, at least not yet." He grinned ruefully at Tom. Both remembering several climbs they'd made together, as boys testing each other, as men, enjoying the solitude of the peaks. Tom nodded, and turned to Rose, she said,"I don't think I'm afraid, but who knows until I get out there on that trail. I think I'll be able to handle myself.

"You've climbed, Rose. You're good at it." Benjamin looked with impatience at his mate.

"I know. I have. But only easy climbs to get where I wanted to go. I've never really made any hard climbs."

He grinned, "Honey, what you term a hard climb is what I'd term impossible. I don't think you need to worry much." She smiled then, and their open love cheered those watching, for it was inclusive.

Ned stepped from his place at the back of the group. "Jerry's got more skill than I, we've tested each other lots of times, so I know." He glanced around wtih a downcast look, "But I'm big, bigger than any of you. It's not going to be fair for you to have to keep tabs on someone weighing as much as I do." His eyes were worried. Silvia reached over to take his big hand in hers, he reached down to lift her face, pale and small, in his great black hand.

Silvia said, "We depend on you too, Ned. You may be big but you have strength. And your body has always had the grace of a dancer, balance is second nature to you. I know I couldn't help you if there was trouble, but I'm damned if I'd bring you hurt".

Tom nodded, He studied Ned, wondering whether this friend had told all he felt, then said, shrugging , "I suppose I must tell you that I have a few fears. I'm afraid for all of you. Not for myself, But for you. " He grinned sadly, "So who have we here with no fear at all?" He was looking at Jennifers happy face, where she waited leaning against the huge boulder.

She laughed, "Well, no one in her right mind would be without fear, and I know that there's always an edge of fear beneath the excitement. But I'm confident we can do this cliff," She looked at Silvia, "I climbed when I was pregnant, Honey. I don't advise it actually, but I did. As for your phobia Jane, well, they're painful, but we can manage. We can protect you." She grinned again. "I'm so confident that I've offered to lead if I have Tom at the rear." He nodded, realizing something of what she was doing, "First we have to realize that we actually, absolutely CAN cross that cliff face. We can! We have strength, a lot of able climbers and no one is without rather good knowledge of climbing. There is no one who has not had some practice. We've got good equipment, and we'll do it!" Her grin flashed again. "I know that we will."

Paul watched her with pride. His mate was not one to brag. She had spoken so calmly, so matter of factly, that a listener believed that she spoke fact, not opinion. He felt relief. This was what they needed.

Then Paul said, glancing at Jessie and seeing her nod, "We've not mentioned our greatest asset. We have a mind link. We can know how each person is doing as soon as that person knows it her or himself. That is if everyone keeps an open mind. Keeps within the link. We can know when another is suddenly afraid, panics, or whatever, even if someone loses footing, we can know and respond instantly. Because we are linked and because we are trained climbers. So now is the one time we must form a true Mind Link. The thing called a group mind, a single mind intent on itself, multiple mind, we could call it. This must be the tightest

Joining we've ever known."

Andrew nodded, realization surprising him, "Why of course! Alone we might not do this, each of us alone. But together, we surely can."

So Tom nodded to Jennifer, she turned, checking the ropes one last time, Tom took his place in the rear and they began to move on. No one spoke, their attention was on their path, on their balance and on the recognition that their mind's had begun a clear, strong Joining. The trail narrowed immediately, until they shuffled into it. Moving slowly, they wound their way around the sharp bend and found the narrow edge even less, almost halved. It was enough to keep toe holds. It was enough to grip the wall above, fingers pressed into crevasses, while Jennifer ahead, stopped to pound in a piton at certain points. Those were bright points to keep ones eyes on, something to cling to. Here and there vast slivers had broken, through the years, from the cliff face. And in some cases took the path with it entirely. They must step across that empty air. In some cases these slivers falling out had left deep indentations that made walking easier, Ned, trying to balance his big body and Silvia searching for space, were grateful for those extra inches. There were cravases cutting down through the stone, like veins empty of the water that might have made them, and in these their fingers clung. Jennifer reflected that for her alone, it would have been a piece of cake.

Jane wanted to stop, to hold to the solid pathway, to cling to the first piton and not let go, but she knew that she must keep the proper tautness to the rope, she must not let that edge of panic rise. She did not look down, but pressed her face against the smooth cliff. Steve worried, watching one then another, and knew that he must not do that. Anna was in front of him and he was astonished at her skills, felt she could reach to Jane ahead of her with help, were it needed. He wanted to know how Cassandra was doing but would not look back. He could see Silvia ahead of Jerry with Rose on her other side. He watched, willing that young woman to steady confidence. He finally laughed at himself, feeling all their combined mental energy, their Mind link, and seeing it was far beyond what he had imagined.

They kept on, their eyes on the pathway, and on the cliff where they felt for hand holds. Their minds attuned, they focussed. They did not look down at the hundreds of feet of clear blue air, and the forests rolling like a dark green rumpled rug below. To fall into that would be to die painfully. Ned, glanced down, and knew that if one fell, all could fall. At the same time, if one lost footing, the others could hold him or her. He did not have any idea that Jessie could have lifted any one of them back onto the cliff face. No one knew her powers, or thought of them and she held herself constantly ready, but confident that such help would not be needed. She would not have brought them on their Journey were it not so. And yet -- there was the possibility, there was this testing of what was unknown but must be known, in themselves. And always again, in her.

Ned, turned his face into the cliff face, watching the thin threads of veins that gave the cliff it's characteristic rose color. Then, with a start, he realized that this was the cliff just beneath the City. The cliff face they saw lit by the sun on summer evenings, glowing as with its own inner light. No wonder people were not accustomed to climbing to that City.

The fact awed him a little and he forgot momentarily the dangers. He Reached outward, felt Silvia's fear, her tension, her faint trembling. Then he knew her gratitude for his Touch. He was close, he could help. Then, like a sharp loosening in his mind, he was aware of the steel strength of the mutual Touching. The fact of it shook him. He drew back his hand. The reality of that mental Touch was still hard for him to trust. Jerry, just ahead of Silvia, kept the ropes at right tension,,and yet, he was aware every second of her welfare. Ned, knew that, knew it and marveled that he did. He too was part of this weaving of mind.

The heightened awareness resulting from the link,was a revelation to Steve. Like a clean streaming of water, he felt the clear presence around him of the others, their minds present to his own. Their senses alert. He renewed his focus, attention at a precise point, he knew the new sensation of Touch. The setting of will to be aware and then, like a balloon of energy, the sudden spreading out of Touch. It was instant, swift enough that his attention did not fail as his hands searched for a place to cling, as his feet felt for a firm place. His mind seemed reaching out in a dozen different activities, sharply focussed,able, confident. To be able to do so much at once surprised him . He caught his breath, wanting to laugh.

Ned, held his mind steady, also learning how to use this amazing energy of himself and of his Family. He felt awed by how much he knew of everyone, and even more astonished at how sure he was of himself. He watched as Jane, there ahead, struggled with herself as well as with the task. She fought her fear and she was learning these new recognitions even as the others did. Her years of Reaching to the minds of creatures, had taught her much. She saw that this new focus, this human Joining was not that different. But it was amazingly more exciting. So much more to realize here. The delight of it relieved much of her fear. Caught at her attention and lifted it from old fears. Steve knew he must not touch her, but Steve was Reaching as he had never done before. He poured his Love to her, sent her the Joy and Pride he felt in her. He was undisturbed that the others knew and gave as he did.

The ropes were at a correct Tension, Tom sensed their spread, the balance of the climbers. He felt alert to what ever might happen, but he was relaxed. Tom caught an idea that the ropes were only for their comfort, that they were not really needed.He frowned. Could that be? He was not going to find out. He could feel Silvia especially among them, could find her familiar mental tone merged among their Joined minds. Jane too. She seemed to sparkle among them. Gradually he became aware of another quality of mind, a deep,pulse, as though some great heart beat bringing power amomng them. He could feel that power threading through everything, steady, powerful. He literally felt that they leaned against that weaving mental cord of strength. He realized gradually that it was not only one who offered that mental strength, but a braided cord of four combined powerfully focussed minds. And they wove their strengths through the unsure Joining of the others, creating a single strength. He did not search to see from whence that original centering came. He was grateful. He wanted to be part of that steel strong thread.

Jennifer felt the presence of them all. Felt their trust and marveled. She and Tom were doing what neither had done before and she felt the tug and movement of the ropes with wonder. Yet, there was something far beyond that. The Linking, the force of that power running through their bodies, their minds. It was like a lash that held them to this cliff face. She reached back, felt her own consciousness threaded within that braiding of energy. Felt it's unbelievable power. They didn't need the ropes! She knew it absolutely.

A thought came, needling into her attention. She probably was not needed. Then instantly, she knew that was false. She was surely needed for her knowledge, as was each one. Jennifer sought to understand, and as she reached, questioning, she felt the power run through her, open her like a steady stream of realization until she knew how to use this power. How to take part in its work. The molecules of air, stone, flesh , all together, formed a net through which energy wove itself. She was utterly astonished at the flexibility of Earth, of flesh. Mind strength ran through all of it, like a water permeating a sponge. She had never before thought of mind so. She'd thought of it as mistlike, as insubstantial, having only vague existence through and around the human brain. Now she could see that it was powerful, tough, resiliant, usable!

The rest of the Family responded to that stream of energy running through them now. They welcomed and allowed it. Such energy could be directed.

Jane noticed Cassandra, touching her out of that woven mental chain. Her heart lurched with another kind of relief, for Cassandra wound around her a great loving concern, like that of a child for its mother. Finally she could accept that Cassandra held no resentment at her entering Steve's life . She could accept Jane into her father's love. Jane felt tears start at that clear knowledge and realized how fearful she had been at the danger of Cassie's resentments. She could see now the open generosity of Cassandra's nature. Cassandra's small face swam into mental view, her eyes so bright, so often laughing, or so sober she seemed old. Simple human relief broke through old defenses, dissolved old imagined fears.

They were inching along, facing into the dense, hard stone. The spider web of rosy viens, left also a web of narrow crevasses in to which they could fit fingers. Jane composed herself, listened and felt a good sense of accomplishemnt. Balance was crucial, She refused to look down, she could see wiry twisted little shrubs growing out of the crevasses here and there along the cliff. They seemed somehow to reassure her. Again she was aware of the singing thread through her mind, like a flexible fine steel that wrapped around her and held her safe. It helped her to forget that she was walking along over nothing at all.

With chagrin she thought that she gave little to that strong guiding thread of mind. She stood there, among them all, helplessly, barely able to sustain her control,. She was not of any use but rather a burden to the others and the knowledge broke the will that had held so firm.

In an instant the waiting panic flooded through her, rose like a wave,inundated her will She fought back, surfacing from under it, riding aginst it, pushing it down and then with a great sigh of pain and dispair, she allowed it -- there before her, that terrible reasonless fear of falling. It seemed to her that the distance below them pulled at her, caught her at the nape of the neck and at the groin , creating fine sharp spasms of fiery pain and excitement. Almost as if she wanted, -- sought -- the leap outward, down. Was that it? She fought against a terrible desire to jump? The recognition rivetted her attention.The panic subsided,she looked at the possibility and was aware of the thrumming mental band that focussed now on her, held firm,, even as her hand slid and she felt her balance topple. It held, held as if she were merely a leaf. The force of it stabilized her. She felt light, loose and sustained as if in slow moving dream and slid her hand slowly back across the rock and found her hold. She realigned her body, felt the good pull tighten. Then she deliberately reached into that strong mental band and found again her place. She would sustain, she would affirm her desire NOT to fall.

It was at that moment she felt a tremulous whisper ahead of her where Silvia clung with bleeding fingers to the rock. She felt all of her attention leave herself and swing with powerful concern to her little friend. To that baby who was at their mercy. In that movement from herself all panic drained away.Jane was conscious then of Jennifer and Tom at either end of the line. Conscious of Silvia's degrading connection to them. Tom knew they must not hesitate, must continue on, steadily, steadily. Silvia was crossing a very narrow stretch, the upper rock seemed to lean out toward her, she was afraid that she was losing balance.

Then came a command, no longer soothing comfort, but stern lash of command. A mental Voice that cut like a knife through all thought and routed fear. This fierce slim thrust of attention came from Rose, Anna, Andrew and Paul then Tom and Jennifer. They were vaguely aware of Jessie's absence with a thread of resentment that revealed their desire for dependance on her. Then seeing that, they knew another Voice thrust through. "We can do it! We don't need any other help. We have the power" From whence did THAT come. Then altogether they realized that it had come from those six who found power they did not know they had. It was their own Family who had spoken.

The path wound steadily upward, but at least now it kept it's width. The climbers shuffled carefully along, a quiet, firm linking running like a steel band between them. Another break! a little wider this time, but the climbers at the head of the line found it no great problem. When Silvia reached it, however,she was lulled a little by the firm width of the trail. But she heard the warning and stopped, to test her reach. She stretched her foot, finding safe footage, inch by inch, wondering when she would reach the broken edge. And then, it was there. She reached out, could not find another edge, did not know it was longer this time. She cried out, dug fingers into the cravases between the rock, clung, but slipped, her bleeding fingers could not find another crack. She was tiring, and the sudden loss of footing unbalanced her confidence. She wanted to scream, to quit this never ending struggle, to let it all go.

She couldn't give up! The others were roped with her, she would pull them all off balance. She had to reach the other edge. Her foot reached out again, keeping precarious balance with one foot, she was not aware that she pulled against the rope behind and alerted every climber behind her. But before they even felt the pull they had known that surge of fear and dispair, the wish to quit, the fear that she couldn't go on. Never in her life had she felt so much depending on her. She caught hold again with her fingers, their tips sticky with blood. Then, they slipped and the loss over powered her will. She cried out and slipped loose, felt herself falling. Terror engulfed her.

Instantly she felt her falling cease, felt herself hanging, without support, the ropes loose, not yet taut. The toes of one foot wre still dug into an edge, but she was off balance. She felt herself sway, then knew she was not falling. It had taken endless seconds for her to realize she was not falling. Now only the edge of her foot still touched the path,she was not falling. There was a moment's wobble as if she might, but suddenly, like a hand come up beneath her, she was held. There was a low hum all around her, she heard it like a singing and it engaged her mind away from terror. Within her belly it lifted, closer and closer from everywhere around. It was as though she was in a net, and that net grew tighter,, more firm. Minds around her reeled themselves into her, drew together into strength that she would not have believed had she not experienced it. Neither would any of them have believed it, had they not found themselves sustaining that strength. And they knew that the instant's trigger for that strength, that steady power, that had forged through them the knowledge, was now gone. Had been there only for the moment it took for them to acknowledge they must. They held this strength alone together. Jessie was no longer with them at all. Silvia only knew one vast thought,"It's impossible!"

Then, lifting her feet, sliding her toes upward and forward,she was on firm footing, bore her own weight. Silvia had found the other side of the broken path. Now it felt so wide, so firm, she thought it was all she needed. Her face soaked with tears, she clung, her fingers gripping through ignored pain. Now she could lean, press her face against the cold white stone. Feel it's firm solidity. But more! She could feel that net still there. Still around her, tightly, supporting. She was safe!

Somehow the Family had supported her, had sustained her there in the air hundreds of feet above death. She realized they were not only emotionally, mentally Joined, but that their power could support physically as well. She felt numb with relief and astonishment. Every person had kept balance, emotions calmed, so that none followed her into panic. They had held as one consciousness, firm.

As she relaxed a little, she knew that they had to have known as soon as she did that she was slipping, no, before she did. That their attention had been complete. Every person -- each one, even the children, had been focussed, alert.

Had she been? She shuddered. She had let herself slide into the assumption that the danger was over and that the path would remain solid. She would not have been ready if one of them had slipped. They had been able to brace their bodies BEFORE she actually slid, had actually fallen. They had known before she fell. The knowledge rearranged her thought of the whole possibility of Joining.

She knew now, felt it, and was slowly feeling the invasion of a Joy unlike any she had known, replacing all her fear. They all knew clearly that this kind of awareness of one another, had been a safety they could rely on. They had trusted utterly, themselves and each other. She turned her face slightly to see other faces, and found them full of that same joy, that love that she could not fathom. Yet, it seemed natural. They too had final proof of their power together. They too felt elation at their success. All Jessie had had to do was point the way and they had done it.

Tears wet her face, blurring her eyes, But she wanted to move on, she shook her head, sliding her fingers along, feeling for new holds. Alert now, focussed, sensing the entire line of moving bodies, Joined Minds. Faintly they heard a song, a melody, touching their minds, uniting them further. It was a power, a song of power.

Anna was aware that the Mind Song had initiated with Jessie,and,like a slim cord it had wrapped around their attention. Then, as they caught hold, as it was reverberated through all of them , she knew that Jessie had withdrawn. Said, in effect,"You do it!"

They all moved slowly on, the knowledge of that power a wonder and a Joy, but also, a threading of fear. Slowly it settled into proportion, settled into a benediction that eased out the knots of doubt and pain. They could -- they did -- have that power.

For an hour more they climbed. For a while the path opened out onto a broad shelf on which they rested a little and climbed with ease, then it narrowed again, and wound on. Their strength was now an act of will. The sky was filling with clouds, but they were barely aware of that. The sun broke through intermittently, the air grew colder, and wind penetrated their clothes. Their faces and exposed hands felt freezing cold. Rain would come soon,or worse, snow. Tom worried, glancing at the sky, measuring the distance of the storm. But they must have time, they must!

Jane was near dispair. The few moments of elation when she had known that she herself had joined with the others in supporting Silvia, had helped so much. But the cold wrapped around her. She had not drawn her jacket tight before she started. Steeling herself, she looked at her own panic, her strange wish to let go,to fall. Literally fling herself out into that clear, blue, empty air. There like a curtain fallen, she saw it as the source of her panic. I'm afraid of myself, she thought. I'm afraid I will give into that crazy desire. The simplicity of it gave it question. Could it be so? Well, she still had choice. She said aloud,"Well, I don't need to do that. I won't honor that dispair, from where ever it comes. I simply won't. I choose to walk this wall and live!" She said it so decisively that Jessie hearing the thought forming before the words, smiled. But the others listened, watching, wondering if they must again focus strength to her.

But Jane deliberately firmed her mind. She pressed the roused emotions into a kind of cushion, into which she leaned, smoothing them, bringing them into a rough balance. Then, a new thought struck her forceably. She turned her attention, Reached into Earth, Reached into that mountain on whose edge she clung. The Earth sense was all around her, through her. She took it into her hands, felt it flow through herself. Could she make it work for her, for them all? She could, the Earth sense released in her something familiar, something she knew and could trust utterly. She would not be a burden to her family, even if the storm broke, greased these cliffs with rain, she would not slip.

Then as suddenly as she had found that strength, had pierced her own terror to find the energy that was behind it, she knew that the end had come. The narrow trail had ended. Tom had stepped off onto the wide apron, yards wide, many yards long. Just ahead. Her heart leaped with relief, as she made her way to it. Could see with physical eyes the great shelf that her mind had shown her. They all moved back, away from that edge, feeling that this space was vast, so wonderful, to sit down, to lie stretched full length again, to release themselves from the ropes. There were tears, hugs, laughter, and quiet satisfaction.

There was little talk at first. A communion like a steel spring ran between them. Jessie moved to the back, along the cliff wall, setting up lunch and a kettle of hot tea, a mixture of herbs that she had brought and that tasted so fine, unfamiliar, but immediately strengthening. They gathered together then, ate and drank, touched one another, a shy, new touching, as if they had just come together after years apart. Steve with out any restraint, caught Jane and then his daughter to him. One on each arm, he settled against the cliff wall, looking out over a lowering sky. Wind chilled their faces, but the clouds raced by so fast that only splashes of rain dashed against them. Steve murmured, "More of a squall than anything else."

That broke the silence. They began to talk. No one could look on another face without wanting to reassure -- to make clear how precious each person was. Paul watched them, watched himself, going about, suddenly taking hold of another's hands, meeting another's eyes, hugging one another again. He thought they were all acting like foolish children. And yet, he laughed, enjoying it. Finally he laughed, and cried out, "Hey, we made it. Let's celebrate!"

Every one began to talk, then stopped, then started again. Then they were laughing, and Jessie watched to note any note of hysteria, but it was not there. The laughter was free and full of fun. They talked a few minutes, wondering at their accomplishment. They looked over the land below, no one thought of the return trip. Finally their talk faded into silence. They sat quietly, reflecting on all that happened . Paul stood, an arm around Jennifer's shoulder. He had been telling her how proud he was of her wonderful skill. She had laughed, relief like a wine running through her. He said, "I thought -- out there -- when we were struggling, what my life would be without you, my darling. Like something cut away from myself." She reached a hand to touch his face, her face serious now."And I thought that we might think how we have forged a Joining among us all, one that would bring unbearable pain one day." He couldn't tell why he had to speak of this nagging worry, this thing that stuck in his mind. He frowned, even as he heard his words.

She turned to him,"Why Paul! Why pain.?"

The others were listening, watching them and he answered her slowly,"When we must be separated, when the Joining is broken, by - - death or-- loss." He felt old fears surface, old childhood pain, old memories, like a cluster of thorns they stood out against his relief at their safety. He said,"Do you think we've made a mistake to give ourselves to one another so deeply?"

Steve stood against the back wall, his head leaned back, feeling the firm,solid hardness of it. He was watching Paul, then his eyes moved, glancing to others, his voice was quiet, almost resigned,"There isn't any Love anywhere without risk. There's no way to avoid pain -- and still live!" His own heart had finally fought out this problem. Had risen from its protectiveness. He had allowed the possibility of love again. He would not deny life any longer, and life included suffering. As long as one clung to it. He reflected silently on that last knowledge.

The children, laughing and joking at the far end of the shelf, had turned to listen, puzzled at their elder's solemnity. Ben nodded at Steve, "There's no doubt there's a risk. But, we've met each other so much more deeply, we've passed beyond friendship. We're truly 'FAMILY'. " He drew a sigh, pictures began forming and with a startled confidence he was aware they were Sending. That they were sharing memories, ideas.He drew away,"It's natural there will be pain. We can't limit ourselves for that!" Then he found his own mind flooded with memories , the struggle to accept committment, the loss of parents, friends. He realized the memories of the others, until there was a hush, they knew of each other's pain in a way never before imagined. The experience silenced even thought for some minutes. So much each one had born in lonliness, unable to share until -- until now!

Suddenly Silvia cried out,"That's not the way it is!" They were jolted out of their quiet. She stood, both feet planted far apart, balanced beside Jane. "For heavens sake, you've forgotten what we've been taught since we were born, in fact. What we know, even from experience. The Teaching has finally made sense to me too." They knew sharply of her lost parents, her brother, and a friend as close as these. They saw her sorrow flash like a lightning of fire upward through her body, and subside as suddenly. She dropped that sorrow deliberately. "Death is not a permanent loss. You all know that! Or we've been fooling ourselves for a long time. Nobody is really 'gone'.We don't need to hold on. We can let each other go." There was a caught breath from the whole group. To have such come from Silvia!

Rose nodded. Benjamin drew near her as though a breath of that cold separation touched his heart. "It's true, dear one, It's true. But then -- you know too that the exact person, this physical person, that I can see, that I've lived with, loved for so long, is precious to me. When you die, Silvia, I will lose YOU and for that I will grieve deeply." She sighed too then, and smiled,"That other is true too, when a person can recognize it. When I can let go of the one who has -- been lost to me. At least lost for the time and the condition."

Ben kissed her lightly on the neck,"This talk seems pretty strange for people who've just been given a new lease on life. I think you're original thought was real Paul. We will feel terrible loss, at times. But then, we can bear it together better than we could alone." He walked to the edge, looked over, whistled, and turning said,"Well, We're willing to accept what we've been taught, to realize it. Because now, we can See more. It is as if my brain has fired up and every one of my senses is sharpened. My thinking is clear, as though a fog has burned off." He was looking at them with surprise. He hadn't intended to say that.

Ned shook his head, moved out from his stance behind Silvia, and went to gaze at the distance, beside Ben. His gleaming cap of curls shining with drops of rain. "Well, sure as Hell though, we don't have to learn it all in one day. Took me -- most of twenty years to get here. To learn -- anything at all. And now, I feel as though -- just what you said, Ben. Just that!" He spread out his long arms, creating a cross of his body, against the stormy sky beyond. The rain spattered against him there, exposed at the edge of the cliff. He shouted,"Thank God, we're all all right! Thank God!" And relief changed to Joy in his cry. He whirled then,"Where do we go from here?"

Tom got up, he'd been lying flat on his back, listening and looking as if he slept. He said,"We've got a ways to go. So we'd better get on with it. Nothing else could be any worse than what we've already done, I think. But look out there! We'll be soaked in a few minutes if we don't get our rain gear on." He turned to Jessie. She was waiting at the far end of the platform, "That's true isn't it? That's there's nothing worse?"

Jessie met his eyes,"That's to be seen. Let's look ahead now and see."

They turned to look toward the east, across the platform and he went to peer on beyond the far edge. He turned, his face drained of color. "NO!, No! It can't be. There's no way to go on. The trail ends here. This cliff is it!" He turned to her again, his face a mask of puzzled hurt. He couldn't believe such betrayal.

Rose glanced at Jessie, "Looks as if we're going to have to fly!" The joke wasn't funny. But suddenly, as if ignoring, refusing to think of this new problem, Silvia turned to Jane,"I wanted to tell you Jane that I don't think I could have done what you did. I could not have faced the kind of fear you did. As afraid as you were, you didn't let out a peep."

Jane sighed, touched Silvia's cheek lightly with one finger, "I was too busy, you know. I had to trust you all. I had to learn that! But to do it, I had to trust myself!" It was as if she confided a secret that she had found."It was like all the other refusing I've done. Refusing to accept your Joining, when I've been doing that -- in other ways, all my life. Denying my very senses. Denying and pretending. No, I'll not do that again. Ever!" She dropped her eyes, her tall figure towering over Silvia, yet she seemed almost a child at that moment. They let her go on. Seeing she needed to speak. "It was when I stopped thinking, when I focussed, entered into Earth, because I can always trust Earth, that I could turn to you all, trust you too, accept what we are together. It was then, that I lost that panic, but not the fear. It was like something draining out of me. I had become as still as the stone around me and in that stillness, I found -- courage, maybe. Because I never lost that fear."

Rose reached up to kiss her, "You never knew how strong you were, Hon. Neither did we.!" Then she turned to them all,"But we've got to find a way to go on."

Jane ran a knowledgeable eye over the cliff ahead, her gaze moving swiftly from the obvious end of the apron on which they stood, backward to the scree, the piles of debris fallen out behind them. She said,"Silvia, let's redeem ourselves this time and find a way. There has to be a way!" She walked rapidly across the ledge, around the slippery mounds , where dust and chips and sand had gathered through centuries. The others watched, a new confidence taking hold at her decisiveness.

Then they heard her cry out, a glad cry, a reassuring cry. She reappeared from behind the boulders , grinning she said,"There's a way. Yes, just the kind of a way we need with this weather." She laughed then, as at something that pleased her. "We'll be traveling through Earth herself and there's no safer place."

Paul glanced back at Jessie, trailing, silently behind. He thought in a sudden irritation of the thin barrier that seemed to have risen between himself and her. He wondered if the others felt it. They seemed almost to have forgotten her. With a quick remembering,he Sent, and Touching,knew! She entered his mind like a dart of fire, a sensation of burning, and then was gone. Instantly he saw. the barrier had been there all along, all these months, this year. They were only now aware enough to notice. That barrier was not to conceal her, but to protect them. The fact sobered him. That tremendous power of her. How could they meet it wholly? He dropped his eyes and turned to meet Jane. She was coming to them like a child with a surprise. She said, "There are tunnels, caverns, there, winding through the mountain, and then, finally we will be beyond and outside."

"How can you tell? We could get lost in there." Paul was sharp, angry at her confidence.

She frowned, it had not occurred to her that everyone would not be delighted. "Why, it's in the Earth! I can read Earth signs. I can --" Her eyes swept their watching faces,"I guess there's only Benjamin who knows about that?" The knowledge saddened her obscurely, she said,"Well, let me show you."

Ned shook his head,"Oh, my God, I might have known the only way out of here would be THROUGH. Jane it's not your fault, after all. But, Honey, I'm claustrophobic. Have been since I was a kid. It's all right in large caverns, I've learned to deal with them, but narrow tunnels, really get to me. I don't know whether I can do this."

Jane felt some of her delight leak away. Was there always to be some pain for one, no matter what the joy would be for another? She looked around, knew

THE JOURNEY

she was already in charge. How could they trust her? Then her joy and confidence in what she had sensed beyond the entrance swept away all doubt. They can trust me because I know the way. It is clear to me. And she said, "Well, we'll have to regroup. Those who find tunnels uncomfortable, will move to the middle of the line. Let's alternate ourselves so everyone has support. Old cave hounds, to the rear and front." Her eyes were shining again.

Ned shrugged, tightening his muscles and then he met Jane's eyes. "If you could do what you did, Baby, then I've got to manage this. What makes you so confident. Maybe if you tell me it would help?"

She smiled, her eyes distant and soft. "When I enter into the Earth, I sense all the lives there. I sense especially Earth Herself in a new way, I am surrounded by a consciousness that cradles. Yes, strange as it may seem, cradles me. It's what finally saved me back there, I realized I walked against the edges of Earth and focussed into the mountain itself. It lent me strength. There are other lives, other kinds of lives -- other -- conditions. I think one would say, other conditions of consciousness. The deep, deep stone itself, solid, depths of Earth body. The streams of metals, the bright slow, slow crystals, the waters, where they run like veins. There are the living creatures,, mostly at the surface. The very thin surface layers, are where the creatures live. The little ones, in the dark places. So quiet there. I sense them there, I know them. There is a communication that is like a reverberation that runs through my body, my mind. My Mind extends and knows. Focussed that way, it is as if I am also Earth. But there it is, Mother Earth, is real to me." She met their eyes and her own held no apology as they would have done a few weeks ago. They held a joyous pride.

She stood, uncertain, a faint frown creasing her forehead, then she said slowly, "D'you think --would it be possible for us to Join right now? Maybe I could visualize and you would see! I -- don't know, but maybe I could --" She was silent, looking at them uncertainly.

Rose nodded vigorously, "Yes, yes, Jane, absolutely! It's possible. You can do it too. You know that now. You can visualize, can take us to where you experience, you can open a way for our minds into what you know. After all, Sweetheart, that's what it IS." Her voice had a faint ring of impatience. It seemed to her to take Jane so long to accept her strengths.

Jane nodded. "I'll do it then, Rose. I'll focus when we begin."

But Silvia was staring at Jane. She had listened with astonishment to the talk of inner Earth. She frowned then breathed out her words, "Well, all that may be, anything seems possible at this point. I've got no fear of caverns. I've crawled through a lot of deep holes, for fun. But I wasn't as fat as I am now, I was littler! I don't know about narrow tunnels."

"Come now, Sil. You're no wider than Ned's shoulders, or even Ben's for that matter. We'll make out all right." Andrew was impatient. To him this was adventure, exciting and promising. He could feel the nearness of the City, feel it in a way that he shared with Anna and Jessie. The simple adventure of the Journey delighted him.

Silvia glanced at Andrew frowning. then she grinned with a sigh."I suppose you're right, but that doesn't help if Ned and Ben and I all get stuck someplace together.

They all smiled, except Ned, though the humor was grim.He said,"Oh, No, Silvia. Don't think such things at all." And covered his face in mock horror.

Jane shook her head, suddenly angry,"Wait, I wouldn't take any of you into such a place.I'm not going to enter a tunnel that isn't wide enough for us anywhere along it's length. If I can see in Earth, then I CAN see." She met Silvia's eyes, her own angry, "Sil, focus, try, Join with me. Maybe you can see with me. You'd feel better if you knew. We've shared imagery before."

Silvia began to laugh,"Good God,I couldn't --", then her mind was caught in the Touch and focus of Jane's mind. It was a fine tuned Reach, led subtly by Jane's intent survey of the tunnel ahead. The images were sharp, clear. This new skill, this mind Reach, was still amazing to her, but it pleased her. She felt the lift and flow of Mental attention. She cried out."Why of course, of course. Why haven't I done this before. We're together, I see through your vision! It's as though I'm living on two levels at once, as though, -- why,I couldn't have imagined, and yet, there it is." She was silent, watching the unfolding of vision, like a map she saw the inside of the mountain, and the tunnels running through them. They led on and on and there somewhere far ahead, was light, a plateau and -- beyond it, --. She had to break contact, the intensity hurt her head. But she had seen. A light seemed strangely to glow through the walls of stone beyond that opening from the tunnels. She was very excited,"Jane, Jane! I think I do see. I could see it. It's unbelievable. And you see all that all the time!" She turned to gaze in astonishment at Jane, then added,"There IS an Earth vision. I think I see a little of what you do." Her face was radiant with revelation.

Jennifer had stood in silence watching, listening. All her confidence of the past hours fading. "Silvia, is that real? Can you really See with her? I can't, and I need to know for sure that there's a way out. All I can do is hold on to myself because I'm afraid too. I won't panic, it's not a phobia, but I've always felt afraid since -- since childhood. Something happened then __" With a wrench she blasted them with that memory, she could not deny it. Like a demand it rose to flood her inner vision. Those tuned to her at that moment, saw too. She had been caught, locked accidently in a storage tunnel for two days and no one could hear her cry. Today every city in the Valley had alarm systems built inside every storage shelf no matter how small. They were designed to be used by children and children were taught how to use them ever since that day when Jennifer was found. But she said,"I need your help if I'm to travel through that dark ahead." She was smiling a wry self deprecating smile, 'The strong have fallen, the weak have gained their strength.' She laughed shortly at the quote.

Silvia put an arm around Jennifer's shoulders,"It's true Honey. I do see, and I'm sure that Jane does see even more. There is an ending and a way out."

Jennifer started to speak, looked embarrassed, then realized they were attentive and could pick up much of her thought. "I'll ask it then. Why did Silvia find your support even when she didn't know how to ask. But I had to ask, to expose my fear? Why didn't you know?"

Rose looked back, assessing the question,"Well, Jen. Silvia's body asked. She was emotionally incapable of asking. So we could interfere. We've agreed to support each other, but we can't interfere in another person's choices.

Jennifer stood a moment, then she curtly nodded."I think I knew that. I think I'm delaying, just delaying!" She drew a long tremulous sigh. "Well,Ned, how can I complain when you don't? She grinned thinly and he reached to squeeze her hand. They found places in the line,, moving forward behind Jane now. Ben took the rear behind Jessie. Ahead of Jessie were the twins, then Ned,and Mary, Silvia and Jerry. Jennifer walked in front of Jerry with Paul and Tom ahead behind Jane. They could manage.

Jerry remembered exploring caverns with Ben and Tom. He'd gone a few times with Jane. But never had he known Ben's broad shoulders to be a problem. He thought his only worry now would be his mate, Silvia. But those trips into Earth had taught him and given him knowledge. He was enjoying this. They moved into the Earth! The rain had begun to fall, only misting at first, it had become heavier with large drops like tiny pellets cold against their skin. The wind whipped hard lashing their backs until the stone ceiling covered them. In moments the sound receded, the quiet was comforting, as though they had entered into a protection.

Rose moved along deep in thought. They had learned, surely in the climb around the cliffs, that they must focus. They must not wait now, but must link, practicing, seeing just a little differently, sharing all they saw. She had an image of a crystal, polished and cut to bring out the brilliance of its beauty, many facets, like many eyes, reflecting all beyond it. We are as separate and complete as each facet, brilliant with its own light, and yet, together we are immeasurably greater. She felt finally satisfied, finally at peace.

She Reached, wanting that Joining to sustain them, give them that strength they had used before. After a moment, she felt the others joining in. Then, the link established itself. Anna and Andrew fixed themselves like solid pillars of attention. She could feel the firm solidity of Ben's and Paul's attention. Her own, ran steadily into their growing consciousness. It was like an unfolding, an awakening of perception, another greater 'SENSE'. The flexible power of their bonding grew. And for those with eyes to see, a Light emanated from their bodies and it was a radiance of blue 'light of the mind'. But beneath it, sustaining and pre- existing, was that soft golden light of Love. They were annealed in that Love.

Jane moved carefully, but at first there was only a winding cavern, plenty high enough that neither Ned nor Tom had to bend. Wide enough that they could have played a game of Three Basket had nets been hung. They breathed with relief, and Jane walked with the light attentive tread of one wholly listening,,sensing the Earth around her. She began to know of the structure of the rock, to see its defects and its solid strength. There was no danger here.

They walked silently, enjoying the closeness, the silence. They could see little, their small hand lights giving them vision for their footsteps. After some time of darkness, a time hard to measure, perhaps an hour of walking, they saw ahead a shaft of light. It was a crack that slanted downward a number of feet into the solid dome of the roof. Through that crack light poured like a stream. In the darkness it seemed literally to flow over the rock below. The tunnel widened into a small cavern beneath the crack and it was lit well. Lizards scattered at their approach, Silvia cringed, not wanting them to touch her. A snake wound itself along a ledge, but Jane was the only one who saw. She Reached to its tiny brain, soothed and left it quiet, while the others passed. Their noise and their energy created a wave of disquiet inside this mountain, as though a great creature passed there. Jane watched to comfort tiny ones who felt their passing with fear. She wondered once how she could do that, then forgot the question in the doing. She knew herself to include them.

She exulted in this new found wonder, thoughtlessly expending her energy in abandon with the delight of any child who has discovered a new skill. The others were aware of her control,her delight. They too felt awe at her discovery and watched mentally as she recognized these creatures they had seldom seen. . Gradually the cavern narrowed, and she must take her attention toward it's ending. Abruptly they were at the point where it divided. For those who could tune into Jane's attention, it was like looking through a window, seeing beyond themselves.

Jane stopped, let her mind Reach far ahead, sliding through stone and Touching another consciousness whose subtle presence seemed to the others,experiencing it only through their Joined minds, to be barely there at all. How could she know anything from that? But Jane did know, things communicated their shapes to her, she felt their dimensions,their merging into one another. The shift from solid stone, the taste of metal ore, of water,of other kinds of rock form. It was for her like passing through a known landscape. Reverberating through this landscape she tasted a vein of copper, unknown by miners in the Valley, she was sure. Then another of iron, fascinating to her, she had never risked such searches before, but now she had to pull her attention away. It was a temptation to reach further, to Taste again the presence of metals.But she drew back to the business at hand. Tom, following her visual projections, reminded himself that he would question her about those metals one day.

She settled her attention to the immediate way ahead. The tunnel to the right would go where they wanted, some distance ahead it linked to another cavern where travel would be easy. She knew that there were narrow places in this tunnel, but they were traversable. However,the left hand tunnel,at first wide and promising, was a dead end. Half a mile in ward, it was blocked.

So they turned right, having to slide past narrow walls sideways,feeling cold wet stone burn against their skin, the scurry of tiny creatures in the darkness, a rustling of sounds unseen and Jane informed them that a cluster of snakes had wrestled themselves away from their path. Silvia covered her mouth with her hand but everyone heard the scream in her mind. Jane shot back the same soothing Touch that she was constantly sending ahead. It seemed as though she had blossomed, had become grand in her own strength. Silvia saw as Jane saw for a moment, felt her tender concern, her response to the little creatures, their nature as animals, not as unknown scurrying 'things'. She was seeing them finally, no longer wrapping them with her own fears. Their tiny but bright alert eyes, their fast beating frightened hearts. Her way of seeing shifted.

They had passed the place where light came in. Darkness deepened, they walked by Jane's vision alone. She walked with feet that listened themselves for any sound of lives moving across her path. Then, with an abruptness that surprised them all, they came to a halt at a narrowing of the tunnel. The roof was lower, slanting downward, so they must bend. Jane stopped, turned to them.

Softly, she said, looking at their anxious faces all in a line behind her. "There is a narrow tunnel here, it will flatten a bit before it opens out again. But there is room, don't fear. It is not long." With quick intent glances at each face, she assessed their willingness. Then, smiling cheerfully, she turned to go on. She heard the great heaving sigh behind her.

She went on, bending only her head at first, then her waist until finally, she was on her knees. The sandy floor made footing firm, softened the pressure on their knees. Then, the walls closed further. Ned, gasped, it had been already too much and not this! The others kept unceasing Touch, spread their own strength around him. He took conscious grip on himself. But clung unashamedly to Jerry's hand. He fixed his mind on Jane's, seeing as much through her vision as he could. His vision blurred, he felt faint, but righted himself, Jane focussed to him. The others increased the clarity of the visualization. He could see something of what was ahead.

Then, like a twist of torment, the way ahead became even more narrow he bent his shoulders, felt the ceiling press against his back. He could no longer crawl, he must lie down. Must slide on his belly. He heard the grunts and groans of the others, complaining of the discomfort but for him, it was a matter of being able to sustain sanity. To keep control. The air seemed red before him, his chest burning with a liquid fire. He thought he might explode, might -- be crushed. And terror numbed him, made him for moments, sure he would scream, batter against the walls until his arms bled. With pure unceasing balancing, he endured. Jane kept steady, projecting images as she saw them ahead, the widening out, the opening of the tunnel. And had she not, Ned was sure he would have screamed. She kept telling them there were only a few yards more. Then with grim humor, Silvia informed them it wouldn't even take one yard for her to stick. Ned vomited. Gabbling apology,shamed and angry, he broke the grip of his terror. The stink of it was so strong the others had to keep themselves balanced carefully to pass by the splashed walls. The release comforted Ned a little. Ned could hear those behind him scattering sand against the walls to soak up the vomit before they passed.

Jane felt the fear rising among those behind her. She whispered reassurance, sending the consciousness of the Rock, the deep Earth, the presence that surrounded them. Then, the narrow neck ended for her, she stood beyond it, standing in a pale light like green mist. Looking around, she tried to Send back to them, but the fear had grown so for Ned and Silvia that the others were attending to their support. Few knew her Sending. She steadily Sent the image of a lovely cave, faintly lit, echoes sounding hollow in the distance. They couldn't see to the other side. Rapidly she got those behind her out and turned to help the rest.

Jerry felt behind him, caught Silvia's ankle. She had simply stretched out on her back, letting her arms scoop her along through the sand. He drew her forward, whispered above this mind link, reassuring, encouraging. And slowly he helped her slide through into this strange wonderful light. Any light would have seemed heavenly at that moment for her. She sat up, then immediately reached back to find Ned's hands. Jerry caught on and together they drew him, with a few curses, more sounds of vomitting, visible trembling and he was out. He sat up, his head between his knees, trying to stop shaking. The two, so exhausted, relieved, did not notice they plugged the outlet for the others until some one pushed from behind. Then guiltily they both slid away and sat holding to each other, surrounded by laughing, comforting Family. Even Ned's trembling thin voice saying, "Honey, don't touch me. I stink!" They let their eyes accustom themselves to this huge, space.

Hundreds of yards wide, it descended at least twenty feet below where they stood, It was a vast Hall, narrow stalactites formed ribs down one entire wall, like a curtain of changing color. The floor below was covered with sand, clean, broken here and there by gigantic stalagmites, rearing themselves into the air, leaning sometimes against one another, some slim like needles of colored stone, some great, hulking, fat pillars that looked as though fold after fold of molten rock had laid themselves down one layer upon another until they reached the ceiling . A column of pale tall towers marched down through the center toward the far end. There, to the left of that column, was a gleaming pool of water. Absolutely still, it seemed more a mirror. At one end, a faint ripple at a narrow end revealed the source of its supply. Their eyes moved to find the source of the pale light that made the cavern a cathedral to them. A long, wide crevase through the side wall was broken edged, and rough, with plants growing into and through it. The light that came though it was made green by the filtering leaves.

Tom eyed the cavern with the eye of a city planner. Winter and spring there's probably a lot of water coming through. Wonder how it gets out. Some subterranean stream, or another lower cavern? People could live here, you know, and widen that crack, for an entrance. That opening must be pretty high in the mountains but I bet it doesn't freeze in here."

Ned snorted. " Thank the Lord you don't plan to have them enter the way we did." Everyone breathed easier. His sense of humor was intact. He went on, "Surely, we don't need caves yet, to house our people?"

Tom nodded, still studying the walls, the size , the possibilities. "Some people

THE JOURNEY

like cave towns. You know that. We've got several in the Valley that were chosen over outside towns. They have their advantages." He shrugged, "It's just something to keep in mind and make a report for the library. We've learned a lot about how to live in a cave and not harm it. Someday, it might be needed, you know." He laughed, but we've other things to think of now."

Paul felt Andrew's arm slide across his shoulders. His first response was one of irritation, thinking the boy was offering reassurance, and then, he asked himself if it might be a silent request for comfort. He was puzzled at his own suspicions, resistances. He reached up to grip Andrew's arm then slid his hand out to find Jennifer's shoulder, he said, "Well, Dear, we've made it through." He smelled the fragrance of her body and with it the sweat smell of her stuggle. "Maybe this is the worst of it."

Jennifer breathed a long, tremulous sigh, "If I hadn't been able to lock my attention into Jane's visualization, I couldn't have done it. I don't have the courage you have, Ned." They were all silent, looking around, listening to that great, silence. In it tiny sounds stood out, a fall of a pebble, a scurry of some tiny creature. They sounded sharp and clear. Then Jennifer said, "Look, there is a stream, a narrow, stream."

Ben moved nearer, "If the water's clean, we could all use some. It's time to stretch out and maybe have a little snack, anyway."

Ned reached out his long arms, "Oh, to scrub off this smell of me, and the stink of fear."

They began walking down the winding trail into the floor of the cavern. Only Tom and Jane noticed that the trail was odd. Why a trail here? Narrow crooked ledges rimmed this end of the cavern and they walked down from one to the other, until they reached the bottom and what seemed to be the bed of an ancient water way. A thin stream of very clear water ran at its middle. It continued out into the broad flat foor. They passed through the tall columns, turned to the right and were beside a pool whose edges were uneven but smooth as glass, worn here through ages as water poured over the upper lip with enough force to push most sand through and off to the outer end. There was a clean, pond more than two feet deep that leveled rapidly off to the sandy stream bed that wound on through the cavern. Their voices were hushed, as they marveled at the shapes all around. Many seemed to have been consciously carved. There were many colors twisted into the columns, striping the walls, and Anna said, softly, "Why, it's really beautiful here."

Jane went to the spring, touched its water, leaned to taste it, and Jessie brought her a little flask in which there were a few colorless crystals. She said. "Do you need the help of these?"

Jane turned to her, her expression bemused, then her eyes focused on the bottle and she smiled, "I do not! I know that it is good water. But, let's test it this way too so there'll be no doubt in any mind." She was smiling, and dipped the bottle in to fill it. The crystals dissolved and the water remained clear. She handed it to Jessie and Jessie turned, holding it high. "Now, you can trust Jane for another talent. She can distinguish pure water from harmful water. Here is the testing of that!"

Jane looked at her thoughtfully, then curtly nodded. "Yes, it needed to be done." They all came forward to fill their flasks and to drink. They sat on stalagmites ,some low and rounded like stools, some high but not too sharp for comfort. A thick pale moss grew over some of them, some seemed very old as if they had ceased their growing long ago. Where enough light fell, moss had spread over the floor, around the spring and among the clusters of stone stools. Silvia cried out, covering her mouth in sudden self conscious shame. Jane looked where her finger pointed, her eyes narrowed as she watched the creature there.

A lizard, the size of a grown spaniel, moving slowly across the bench above a little dripping spring. Another shrugged itself through a hole in the wall and watched with dark expressionless eyes. Suddenly they were aware that there were many of these watching creatures. They moved slowly, curious, not attacking. Jane sensed immediately they had no fear. She Reached, and they turned toward her, but not even surprise registered in the bony faces, the sharp, small eyes. Her eyes swept upward, to the jagged narrow steps in the rock where a couple of them moved along a narrow bench, worn into the high dome, toward the crevase and the growing plants of the outside. She nodded, satisfied. They went out there to feed on the leaves and grasses, but it would be the rare predator who could come upon that entrance bench. They came in here for protection and safety. She nodded to herself,then turned to the group."Well, we might as well get on, hadn't we?"

They gathered together their flasks, bits of fruit not eaten, and turned to look for the way out. Jane searched, her eyes sweeping the lower walls. Paul moved out among them, he was feeling calm enough,but he had been pleased to get out into this space. He wasn't looking forward to entering another tunnel. Tom walked the length of the flat 'field' before them searching for some natural 'path'. Others began to climb around, seeking out some direction to another opening. They climbed here and there, searched across to the far side. Jane told them they must go to the left if they were to keep on the trail toward the City. Others nodded their heads, Jessie noticed and smiled. So there just to the left of the spot where a small swarm of lizards moved slowly about, they finally focussed their search.

Steve followed Jane, watching her as she stood, She was lost in her intent deep Reaching. He touched her hand and felt his fingers folded into hers. Immediately, he was drawn into her intensity, her Reach. He responded, curious, eager.He became aware of something of what she realized. His mind holding attention in amazement. Ben came to them, his own mental focus reaching out, into the Earth, then he Joined with Jane, adding his vision to hers, and they were both stronger. Steve, to his surprise, felt that his own steady calm was helping. It was as though they leaned on him.

He felt their Reach extend, become more precise, feeling through the walls,knowing the surfaces of these great pocked and punctured walls. Lizards

THE JOURNEY

moved restlessly, some moved out, others simply stood and then sank into their sleep. Then among all the openings and small tunnels, Jane and Ben found one that continued. Though it was narrow, it was not low as the one they had just come from. It opened into a small cave thirty feet high and broad, with a floor of smooth polished stone. Animals used it often. Jane wondered why. Then, they saw. It led into another cavern, only fifty yards beyond, smaller and less colorful than the one they were now in, it had no natural light. But it would take them on their way.

Jane called the Family together. She showed them, images flashed like sharp clear pictures through her mind and they saw, as they focussed attention. Finally with a brisk nod, she led them to the tunnel. No one spoke. They left the great cavern behind them, its light persisting like a watching eye. Jane thought that it was benevolent. She felt that sense of calm, acceptance. She knew that dangers lurked among those cold hard pillars, but no evil lived in that natural world. Only among humankind was there malevolence and the thought was a sadness. She showed them the way, the narrowness and the openings ahead. They sighed, steeling themselves for more.

Ned resisted, looking for anything to delay the entrance into that new tunnel. He was disciplining himself, holding his fear in check with all his strength. "What'll we do with our packs. We can't keep them on through that little tunnel. The last one was short enough to slide them ahead. We've got to do that again"?

Jerry was tying a rope to his pack, and then linking that to the others, "We'll have to drag them after us, close enough to keep loosening them if they get stuck, but behind. Jane felt the fear among them, crowding down, invading those who had known little before. She sensed that difference so clearly, it surprised her. Was she growing more aware? She knew that that fear could weigh down their hearts, grow, if they did not watch. She turned to the tunnel entrance, walked in and then bent to the sloping roof. It wouldn't be bad for a while yet. She said, "Stop, we've got to do better this time. We can't have Ned suffer so much. We can give him more support."

They turned to her, Paul nodded shortly, his attention focussed. He had forgotten his own fears in concern for Ned. "You go on guiding, showing us the way, Jane. We can keep helping Ned to see and to handle this." Jane nodded curtly, in appreciation, heaved a sigh and turned to go on.

After an hour of fairly comfortable walking, their spirits had lifted, they even joked a bit. Then the tunnel closed down, was small around them, and Jane crouched, bent to her knees. It was easier to crawl. The other followed suit. Silvia was not comfortable, but she was laughing, back there with Jerry, at her dragging belly, trying to make a joke. Ned worried her the most. Paul could manage, she was sure. Ned was down again, the bones of his legs were too long to crawl normally. He was literally stretching himself out, using his elbows and knees and toes to shuffle himself along. He couldn't crawl. The position was painful as it was prolonged. Finally, as they kept up the steady slow journey, Ned simply flattened himself, worming his way, the elbows of his jacket were already badly worn.

THE PEOPLE OF THE VALLEY

Sweat greased his face and hair, his face twisted in an agony of self control. He sobbed intermittently, swore fiercely, unashamed, unable to stop himself. It was a relief. But steadily, Paul,Rose and the twins focussed the images Jane saw, made clear the way out. They had begun to learn the technique, creating a sense of space around them by that vision of the far ahead space. If Ned could focus, free himself from panic enough, he felt the difference, and slowly, he was learning to do that. It took tremendous discipline.

They kept slowly on, Jerry talking to Ned and Silvia. Silvia pushed on but pulled at Ned's long hands now and then, wanting to help. He was too bound up in his control even to tell her to stop. When he broke out in a paroxysm of cursing, it was a relief to them all. Finally Jerry helped Silvia turn over on her back, rolling her gently so that the baby was on top now. She felt better. He pulled a little on her extended wrists, she grumbled and he let her. Jerry swore suddenly, releasing some of his own frustration. Rose felt the tension increase, she imagined what they must look like, all of them, stuffed into this tunnel, all of them, suffering. It made her smile grimly. Jessie and Ben in the rear dragged packs behind them, pulling them with their feet sometimes, sometimes with their hands. But mostly, they were simply paying out rope, so they could pull them through when they all got through.

Finally, Silvia stopped, "Oh, God in Heaven, what a way to travel. I should never have come to subject myself to this. And right at the time when I should take better care of myself." She hitched herself up on one elbow and a foot, bending a knee to get leverage. Jerry looked through her knees at her face and shook his head. He Sent, strong and forcefully to the child they both worried about. He got a sleepy response. Christopher wasn't worried. That made Silvia smile in spite of herself and the pressure seemed to relent.

Jerry said,"Ah Love, we'll be through soon."

She said, anger rising again, "How do I know that? We might go on this way for an hour and I can't do it. Or maybe we're hitting a dead end, and will have to all back out again. How can Jane know? How can she be sure?" She dug her elbow in so hard in emphasis that she cried out with the pain of it. "Damn it," and her voice was a loud yell,"It's not fair to Ned." The thrum of sound she created seemed to shatter her own anger. It scared her that she could fill space, this narrow world, so utterly with such anger. For moments there was absolute silence.

Ned rumbled behind her, "Sil, Sweetheart, if there were no cave coming up very soon,, I'd have refused this trip for sure. But I can see it myself through Jane's vision. I know it's there. And you can too. Focus now, Sil. It's what keeps me sane. That and all this sweat from my terror. The very sweat of fear lubricates me enough to slide me through. Without fear, I'd stick. Some benefit to pure terror." Jerry grinned. Ned's humor had brought them through more than one scrape.

Silvia grunted,whining,"Damn it, the walls are so rough, the chips and debris that's fallen cut at my back like a bed of knives. How could we have chosen a worse route.

Ned, lay a moment, his breath coming in gasps, but he fought to bring quiet to his rising panic. Breathing steadily, slowly, deeply, he felt the immediate surrounding lift of several minds. He felt them at the same time he felt himself able to breathe more easily. It was as though vision cleared, an image of wide space around him was so strong he was convinced for seconds. His eyes were closed accepting that help. His panic subsided. Jerry reached back to find and grasp one of Ned's hands. Ned clutched at the offered hand and clung in a spasm of sudden crying. Everyone was still, the supporting minds, surrounding him, the clear Vision of Jane's sight ahead, her powerful reflection of the benevolence she knew through this Earth, was shining like a light in their minds. They were surprised to be able to see that light. Surprised at Jane. Never before had she Sent so clearly, filled their minds with such assurance and calm. Tall strong Jane who had never seemed to have time for an inner life at all.

Ned said aloud then," If we didn't have Jane's sight,we could have chosen that other tunnel, Silvia, like you said. And we'd be back tracking by now. That I couldn't imagine. I prefer even this." Ned never lost his capacity to respond, even through his sobs. Silvia caught back angry complaints, swallowed them, seeing the effort this cost Ned. She took a long breath, focussed her attention, Reached and was aware of the ending of the tunnel, as Jane visioned it. She clung to that promise and began again her slow motion.

Silvia reached ahead, realized that those ahead had gone on. She began to struggle again, wrestling and scraping to slide forward. Jerry pushed, helped. She let the cuts and bruises have their way, determined to ignore them. If she didn't hurry, Ned might not make it. She could hear the trembling of his voice, even when he spoke.

Then the message poured back to them, Jane was through, in the new cavern, free!. She sent the message, more clearly than she had ever dreamed she could. She could recognize their reception. She could give them the visual image of that open end and beyond it, the clear wide cavern ahead. She stood now at the outside, standing, stretching her cramped muscles, the dirt and sweat smearing her face and body. All her attention focussed on Sending that wide space before her. She marveled at the cavern she could see there.

Ned locked his inner eyes on that mental picture, and held it as though clutching it to him. The twins and Paul expanded the perception, made it more real. He released Jerry's hand and they began again to follow Silvia as she dragged herself ahead. Silvia felt someone take her reaching hands and literally draw her the last few feet ,then out and up. She held on to those warm arms. Paul and Jennifer held her, and they stood out along the ledge from which they could see the cavern beyond.

They had moved so Jerry could turn to reach in to take Ned's hands. The long black body squirmed and wrestled as if desparate, as indeed it was, to get out, and Ned lay, stretching his hands, then rolled over and began to get up. Ned stood, leaning on Jerry,"Man, Oh, Man. I ain't ever gonna forget. That's the worst thing that could happen to any man. Nothing can ever be worse. I ought to be satisfied now to face anything life has to offer."

Jerry grinned, steadying his friend as the others drew themselves out, one after another. Breathing sighs of relief, smeared with dirt, tired and gasping a little with the fresh wonderful air. Jerry walked Ned across the ledge, down a few steps into the main floor and everyone felt relief that this big man was finally cleared of that suffocating control. Ned was shuddering, helplessly, still crying, and yet he grinned,so great was his relief. He had no shame. Tears were, to Ned, simply normal healthy expression of what had been the worst hour of his life. He loosened his grip, stood back, wiped his face with his hands, straightened his long dark body and cried out in Joy."Look at this. Look at it! Jane, Honey, you didn't do it justice, when you visualized, but you did it well enough to save our lives ! For that you deserve a hundred hugs and kisses."

Jane , who had walked a little way on, stood beside a clear stream of water, gleaming, running rapidly; it's soft chuckle was the only sound when they themselves were quiet. She turned to look at Ned."I'll collect them all too, Ned. I'm so sorry you had to do that. It wasn't an easy route, but it was the only one that would have worked. But look, everyone; can you imagine a cavern more lovely? Literally lovely? Her eyes were shining, her face sweating and dirty, radiant with the delight in the accomplishment and the beauty she had found.

The last of the group was helped out of the tunnel, out of the dark into this strange lavender light and the packs pulled free. The room was half as large as the previous cavern,but surely large enough to house a few Family groups were there need or desire. The bottom of the cave was nearly flat, rounded up into a sharply vaulted ceiling through which dropped tendrils of vines, their leaves pale where they grew inside in this dim light. The domed ceiling was split at the top left side, running downward a yard or two before it closed again as though a slice of mountain had been cut out. Light poured in through green limbs and vines. There were no signs of heavy rain fall through that opening,and yet it was surely open to the sky. Tom studied it, looked directly beneath it to the sandy floor and decided either that a cliff over hang protected it, or that the rain that did come in sank beneath the sand so that only a narrow pool was left. He looked around the dome.

A smaller narrow crevase off to the left side, admitted air and light and the glimpse of trees and sky.To their delight they could hear bird calls. The opening was three fourths of the way up the side wall curving slightly toward the domed ceiling Tom wondered whether it could be reached from outside. Probably not, he thought, it must be high into the peaks there. But there might be trees and birds ? He decided he would investigate later when he returned home.

Jessie watched him, guessing much of his thought, and was amused that he among all those she had taken through here would actually follow through in that investigation. Tears stood on many faces, for the glimpse of that outer world seemed then so precious. There were no standing columns or hanging ones, the floor was broad, extending around a deep bend in the side walls, so that further

THE JOURNEY

extensions of it couldn't be seen. Only the thick dust of the centuries and fine drifting sands covered the floor or concealed here and there the brilliant colors running in wide stripes and curling ridges through the hard white walls. A precipitation of minerals had built up along those sides into a webbing of intricate stone vines thick as a man's arm and colored with red, green and grey shades. The echos of every movement emphasized the emptyness around them, The stillness was intensified by the faint intermittent call of the distant bird They walked slowly down and into the lovely hall, luxuriating in being able to stand straight, to stretch. They brushed the dirt from each other. Ned took a handful of sand to wipe once more at the stains from his vomit. "Oh, will I ever smell sweet again?"

Paul sighed, moved by the silent beauty. "Well, Jessie,this is surely a lovely place. As though it were created especially to welcome us. But look, there,!" He walked rapidly across the hard path to the edge of the winding stream of sands that had drifted to this lowest part. He pointed down, then knelt. "Look, footprints, a lot of people have passed this way,I think." Then a thought struck him,"It must be the only way after all."

Jessie stood then, looking down, a strange smile on her face,"No, this is not the only way. But it is surely true that many have passed this way."

"And they never spoke a word of these great living spaces, never told us of the land beneath the City, the country of caverns where people could find homes. He was puzzled.It seemed to him a great discovery. People of the Valley were beginning to know that their kind could not multiply endlessly, for the Valley would be destroyed if that were done. Here, were future spaces, room for them. But now he shook his head and was silent. There were other things to think of now.

Paul was more directly worried for their Journey. "How do we go on? We can't scale those walls, they swell out like a globe. He looked up, watching the cascading vines sway lightly in the movements of air."Somehow it reminds me of Altos and her cascading gardens."

Jennifer laughed, meeting Jane's eyes. Ben had walked off, searching along the caverns walls, his own concern seemed greater than the others. He turned away and returned to them after a while. "There's just nothing along that side but the smoothest walls I've ever seen in a cave. We might have to break up and everybody start a search the way we did before.But it's surely time for lunch, isn't it? I'm hungry."

They settled down at the other side of the sand 'stream' where a pool surfaced. The footprints seemed to them to speak of friends, perhaps neighbors. Ned went farther down the stream bed to wash himself. The water accepted his stench, dust and sweat and cleared itself miraculously. Then scooping a small pool in the sandy bottom, and taking off his clothes, he soused them in the water exuberantly. He sat down in the pool and soaked his head, cleaning all the dirt from the thick curled cap of black hair. Then he put his clothes on. It was warm enough, he thought and his body heat would dry them as he walked. Somewhat recovered he sat quietly watching everyone. Finally he said,"Well, unless there're piles of bones lying over there beyond the curve, these folk had to get out of here." They were silent, eating their sandwiches and fruit. They drank from the small pool, whose waters were clear as glass. "This pool has to have an outlet too, or it'd have filled the floor." Then, pointing, he cried out,"Look at that!"

They followed his finger and saw, sitting on the round smooth boulders at the side wall,a half dozen of the great lizards they had seen before. "I suppose a number of people might survive here if they could bring themselves to eat lizard meat".

Rose was nodding, her thoughts running over the possibilities much as Tom's had,"Well, lizard is more acceptable food to most of the Valley people than most other animals. They're barely conscious, I think. But they are aware, see how they watch us?" They sat some time, eating slowly, stretching. Some dozed a little, some lay watching the strange slow beasts.

Jane finished eating, cleared her lap, repacked her bag and stood up. She looked down at the others, sitting or lying on the floor of the cave. "I'm going to search. I think I know where the way out might be. "She met Ben's eyes, and he looked puzzled for a moment then with surprise lighting his eyes,he smiled too. "You'll come with me Benjamin?"

He nodded, and got up, gathered his supplies and settled them on his back again. "Jane, you've learned to send images so fast. I've never had a clearer picture."

She laughed,"Well, everybody who was paying attention should have got it. Learning to send pictures wasn't hard for me,that's the way I've always contacted the little ones of Earth." Her smile was rueful,"It's just that I never thought to direct them at any person."

He nodded and they were off walking straight on from where they had entered. The others began to pick up their gear, scramble to their feet and prepare to follow. Jane was walking ahead, moving with an easy rolling stride that ate up the distance. Ben,shorter, had to lengthen his own stride to keep up. Her hair hung lank and heavy at her shoulders, the dirt that had fallen fairly well from their clothes, clung to hair and sweat made it like glue. Ben scratched his own brown thatch and wished for a bath. He rubbed his hands, cleaning off still damp sticky bits of mud. Jane turned, seeing his movement and laughed."Ben, we might as well wait until we find water enough for a swim. I never mind the field dust, but this stuff, it irritates my skin and I don't like the smell.

They kept walking, surprised that the distance was greater than they had either of them thought. She turned once to see that the others were following near behind. When they reached a scatter of very smooth,semi-transparant columns, looking as though they might be some kind of quartz, Jane turned a moment, her eye sweeping over the lot of them. They seemed to her to be tired, but game. She smiled. When they were near, she said,"Help me concentrate. There're some holes in the walls beyond these columns." She gestured to the small forest. Some were clean to their tops, gleaming in the light, others were rounded, moss covered, They had been there for centuries and seemed to her to be sleeping in their absolute stillness. "We'll have to do that Earth Search again, I think. To find the path that's best for us."

Jessie was again in the rear, at attention focussed. Paul and Rose next to her. They exchanged glances and Jessie smiled,"Wait, just a minute,Jane." She spoke softly but her voice carried in this closed space. They all turned to her, wondering. She had been so silent up until now. Suddenly the room filled with brilliant golden light, shining in the fine dust they had kicked up, so that the air seemed to shimmer. The sun had come to the point in the sky so that it was just over the crevase. It's light fell into the fracture on the west side. The great cavern was transformed, colors gleamed in the walls, a streaks of mica caught the light and sparkled and the boulders glistened as though covered with fine diamonds. The water in the stream behind them was silver. "It is a benediction and a farewell." Jessie said bemusedly, enjoying their delight and surprise."It does this also earlier in the day,just when the sun reaches that larger opening above and to the east. Only there it lasts longer. Here it is only a half hour or so. But sometimes, at the right time of year, it lasts until the sun sets. It's always a delight to see."

With that she let them know that she had been here many times, had passed through this way at all times of day, and perhaps night. They stood a few moments, realizing that, wondering at it. Then with a curt nod, Jane turned, walking as she did so, standing before the wall, eyes on the openings. She let her mind travel, her senses Reach. Paul standing behind her, gave her strength, Benjamin beside her, seemed so sure she thought he might have been in these depths before.

She focussed then, using her vision as she had never done before. Focussing her attention down the tunnel she had chosen to follow as it wound its way through rock and over debris, fallen long years ago, already dusted thick. They saw it narrow, widen, open into small caves, shrink to a chimney, then expand and then -- suddenly -- it ended, a dark, small cave with no way out. Jane sighed, and withdrew her attention."We should have known, at the first. There were no footprints anywhere, it was obviously never traveled." She shook her head. The walls had been only a few feet thick in some places, beyond those few feet was another space, where there might have been a way. Someone could come through here with a stone laser and cut out openings. With an engineer, a sensitive engineer, to guide the doing of it, to keep strength at maximum, they could easily make a route through these mountains that anyone could travel. Why hadn't it been done? She resolved to ask later.

The second tunnel lasted only a hundred yards, ending in a small rapidly descending cavern at the bottom of which some water falls roared and fell. An underground River? A lake at its bottom? It was a temptation to follow her mind sight, to go on, seeing mentally the many fascinations of this underground world , but she knew she could not. The third one they entered, watching now for whether it had been used. It was the last. Now, they knew they must find a way out. This one ran deeper for some distance, wide smooth walls and floor, very little debris, it was used by animals and snakes, by the lizards surely. But now, they knew that foxes, mountain cat, many other den making creatures including bear, used these entrances and the many branches. Jane knew of a den where a bear had come last winter to sleep through with her cubs. Her spirits lifted. No creature could come in unless there was a way to the surface.

Finally there was a narrowing, then a widening and they could see daylight, they smelled fresh air. They returned in mind to the others, who stood silent, waiting, not even trying to join and know in advance. They were elated, telling of the pathway out. They had hoped this would have no tight place. Jane said, It's a good route, but it gets narrow for about fifty feet, though its not a low ceiling." She took a deep breath, "You must have seen my image of that one spot, about a yard and a half, where a bulge downward will make us crawl. But only that short distance. Can you do that? All the rest you can stand up straight!" Her face held the worry and concern that had grown in this journey. She tried to sound cheerful. And now they knew the ending was near,they felt their spirits lift,they had seen her image of that ending. Not very far, and altogether open. They breathed long sighs of relief, of renewed effort.

Ned shuddered dramatically and then shrugged. "Well, down to the dungeons again,it is. Through your eyes, Jane, I saw that narrow flute,but it's only a yard or so long. I saw that myself, so I can endure." He wiped his face with his hands, and went to take his place. Silvia nodded too, somehow cheered by his joking she went to her place in the line up. He bent to her, "We're going to get through this,Hon. I never thought I could see a picture through someone else's mind. But then, that's what a poem is, isn't it." His sudden seriousness, surprised her and Jerry, coming to them, slid an arm around each of them, to draw them toward the tunnel mouth. He said,"It is, my friends. And we will make a wonderful song of our Journey, and sing it through the whole Valley next Festival. I've heard some Journey songs, Ones others have made, and though I didn't know why, I never quite realized all they were singing about. Now I know."

Silvia nodded, the realization striking her forcefully."That's true, Love. I heard them last Festival, and though there was a haunting beauty to them, I didn't really notice the words, more the melody. Almost as if I didn't want to notice." She turned then fully to the task ahead. She clutched Jerry's hand, "It'll be easier if we start the way we were in that last tunnel. When we get to the horizontal chimney, I'll just flatten and you can pull me through. I don't mind the scrapes, since this one is so short.So you go first this time." He met her eyes and she saw that he worried about Ned. She shook her head."I'll attend to him, Love. I think I can do that. Besides when he's worrying about me his mind's off himself."

Ned laughed,"She's right there,Jerry. And there's Benjamin right behind me. He's got the strength of two of us. So let's get on with it."

Jerry leaned down to kiss Silvia's dirty face, wishing he could pick her up and carry her through safely so that she might avoid any more pain. They entered, following the others who had gone ahead.

True to Jane's visual picture, they traveled along a comfortable channel for some time, it's walls wide enough for two together. Then there it was, the sudden narrowing and the low, tunnel. He bent to peer inside it, saw a pair of boots disappearing beyond it, and then stand and he sighed in relief. It was true. Hardly more than a yard. He lay down, pulled himself into the narrow space and began shuffling on elbows and knees, pulling himself on, and almost immediately, his head was through, he looked up, saw the others standing there, waiting to help. Some already moving on, making room. He grinned with relief and tried to call back to Silvia, but his voice was a blur to her. He reached out to catch at a leg he saw in front of him and drew himself rapidly out and up.

Silvia had begun, lying down, she pushed herself with her feet . Jerry called out, "Nothing to it Honey, just stretch out and reach your arms through and I'll have you through in a minute." She followed his directions and in minutes, she was standing in his arms and he drew her close to still her trembling. They broke away at once, however, Ned was next and they both knew that the darkness here was worse even than the narrowness for him. They must be ready. Paul watched, waiting to help. Jennifer had gone on, following Jane. Jerry said,"Paul, we've got to get some light. I don't think Ned can take another place like this without at least light." Paul nodded,his face worried,"There's light in my pack of course, Damn, why didn't I think. And Jane's gone on with hers."

They felt someone moving through, and Anna was beside them, her lithe body slipping through the tunnel with ease. Behind her came Andrew, and they stood close, touching Paul and Jerry.

Andrew said, breathless, anxious,"Uncle Paul, We heard you. We do need light for Ned. Listen! You can hear his growing panic. I don't see how he contains it. It's like some kind of pressure in him. We thought we could help."

Jerry caught Andrew's hand, said,"I don't know how you're going to do it, but whatever you can do, do it now."

Anna and Andrew moved in the dark, closer to one another, Jerry could feel their touching, Paul moved in,"Let me help". Jerry felt the twins move closer to him, and then, he and Silvia felt an energy, a surge, a brightening of the air, and gradually a soft glow. It was as if a tingling occurred on their skin, and a faint breeze moved. Then suddenly, the tunnel, was lit. A soft glow, filling the air, exposing the grey walls of the tunnel. Jerry laughed,"Wonderful,Wonderful. Now let him come!"

As he said the words, They could hear the scrabbing and sliding of a big body through the tunnel, and Jerry reached in, to find a large hand stretched out almost immediately. The narrow chimney was not as long as Ned himself, so by the time his belly was in the center of it, his head was out. Jerry pulled, Ned, wriggled, swore, cried, and then his head was out,but his eyes were closed, and he gave a great heave. His shoulders moved out and he leaned on his elbows, resting a moment. His body trembled, and Jerry reached, touched his tightly controlled mind, and then helped him crawl out into the shelf. Ned holding his head, until they Touched to inform him that he must open his eyes. That he could stand here. That there was room and light. He rolled over to his knees and then opened his eyes and looked all about. The trembling ceased, his face streaked with dirt and tears, glistened in the soft light. He stared at them all."How - how did you make it light?"

Jerry drew him up then, gripping his hands tightly, sliding one arm over his shoulder, pouring his own strength into this friend- brother. Silvia leaned into Ned and his arms wrapped around her, feeling comfort from her soft warmth. He buried his face down into her hair, and was enclosed between the two of them. Jerry said,"It was the kids and Paul, Ned. They made it. Anna says she can keep it here if we don't talk to her." Ned looked at Anna, swept out one huge hand to catch one of her small ones for a moment. Then, lifting his head, he grinned feebly,"Let's go before the others accuse us of jamming the roadway."

They moved on, the others came rapidly through. They followed the cone of light that Anna held about Ned. And slowly the whole group walked through the larger tunnels, looked with amazement into small 'rooms' that opened out from it, Listened to the subdued roar of the distant water fall rumbling beneath them,wondering at its power. It took less than half an hour of walking and the air became sharp and cold, freshened by a breeze that grew stronger as they approached the light beyond them. And then, suddenly there it was, the opening out into that mountain side where fresh air and the evening light seemed like paradise to each of them.

Ned stretched himself down again, wrapping his head in his arms and letting himself cry silently in relief. He was so full of profound relief he could not believe that he could ever forget. Open air, the open Valley would forever be wonderful to him just because it was open. Jerry picked Silvia up, lifted her up to nestle close, her face pressed into his neck. Weary and relieved, she lay finally accepting his strength. The others stood for moments silent, looking at distance and light. Rose came to put both arms around Jerry and Silvia, kissing them, crying a little. And then, to Ned, and she sat with him,her body so small beside his and finally he turned to draw her toward him, accepting her gift of comfort. Finally he lifted his head, the familiar wry grin on his face, "Well, either I spend the rest of my life here in the Silent City, its only known citizen, or I fly home. I won't go back that way." He eyed them all, speculatively,suddenly somber, "Although, I would never have thought -- if it hadn't been for you all, for the steady support, the absolutely unceasing presence I felt from you - from all of you. I'd not be here now. After that, I think, together, we could do anything."

Rose nodded, "You must not go through that again!" Though she didn't know how to get him home otherwise. She turned to the gathered Family, "Well, where do we go from here, we're obviously not there."

This time, Jessie walked ahead, her smile full and sweet. They could not feel worry looking at that radiant face, that Joy she poured out to them. They cheered up, following her, Ned moved slowly, stretching his body up, swinging his arms, dancing a light jig and then suddenly, to their astonishment, he howled a long wolf call, in sheer exuberance that the trial was over.

In moments they had walked across the stony land at the exit from the tunnel. They entered into a narrow valley that lay between two peaks, small, bright with green growth, it seemed almost an entrance way to something. The walls of the high peaks ascending sharply on either side. They rounded a corner, and stepped out on a broad shelf that hung high over that Valley that they could see again below. Beside them were the clean shining white cliffs that they had looked up to all their lives. The evening sun fell over those cliffs, and woke that golden radiance they had all seen from afar,. Here it was like some fire that burned within the stone. They stood, dirty, tired and full of a piercing sweet joy.

They walked the length of the broad apron of stone and green growth. How did it keep so fresh and lush? Then Jessie called and they came to her where she stood beside a wide clear pool that filled a broad depression in the stone. Water ran from a spring pouring silently from the walls of the City. They looked at it with pleasure and instantly fell to pulling off their clothes. Drinking from the spring, leaping into the water, washing the dirt and fatigue from their bodies, they relaxed. They didn't stay long in the water, it was too cold. But they washed their clothes and hung them, brought out the camp power unit to dry them rapidly. And then put them back on. Some one began taking out food packs, and everyone settled, silent, feeling the wonder of their accomplishment, eating, drinking and resting. Finally, feeling utterly refreshed, they lay, wondering, looking down at their Valley, feeling the energy that seemed to pulse from the walls of the City. Talking a little softly, they waited. Then, slowly they became silent.

Evening drew shadows down, surrounding them, making the air colder. But the cliffs poured a very real radiance into that air, the polished stone of the walls, gleamed with its own light. They gazed in wonder at it. Saw with astonishment that though the Valley below grew darker, the shadows lengthened across the fields and River,here, the light persisted. "It's a real light, not just reflection from the evening sun." Paul said in awe. He touched the walls, felt the delicate vibration of the energies that pulsed through them.

Jessie went to the wall, stood leaning back against it, as if seeking there the brightness and energy it gave. But the Family was startled at the radiance from her own body. She concealed nothing of herself, the brilliance of her eyes, the love, like a physical emanation pouring to them, the Joy, that unceasing centering of Joy. The power pulsed beyond her body, Jessie herself was far more than that little, dumpy body. Then, they saw too how very old her body was. Old and tired with life itself. They had not really noticed until this moment. How weary her body must be for it had undergone so many Journeys. She was stroking the stone, smooth against her palm. They watched her, wondering, hesitant before this City with no visible doors. She turned slightly to them. intending them to watch closely. Her eyes were shining, full of her joy.

Then they felt her Touch, drawing their minds, Reaching in one powerful fan of energy. Was it augmented? For she had never seemed so strong. How much had she restrained her power before. Now she seemed ruthless , unconcerned that they know of her . Her Touch was so strong, they felt themselves Joining with her even though an aching pain accompanied that Joining. It did not stop as they entered into it, it seemed to arch , ascend, spread out. They Reached further,the strongest minds supporting the lesser. unashamedly leaning against one another. Like rods vibrating they felt the pulse of energy, adjusting, shifting the fiber of their substance to a new pattern that could endure that kind of energy. Jessie nodded, Yes, they must depend on one another, together they could do what they must do.

Like the conductor of a small orchestra, she drew them on, focussed, brought them together in a new intensity of attention. She brought to the surface every shred of their power, she persuaded, comforted, persisted, and slowly their minds responded. They found themselves Joined in a single consciousness, a single Seeing. And their recognition was astounding. All fear was wiped away. The basis of this Joining was an unremitting flow of Love. They found themselves knowing of one another, of themselves in depth and in wholeness. They were each offering everything of themselves and finding their offer valuable. They found their own names within that unity.

Clearly, each sought the point of inner Light, the transcendant purity of mind-heart focus. Finding it, focussed there, each was aware that they stood now in that highest level of SOUL Consciousness.

As they knew, the reality seemed as natural as life itself. Jessie held firm, bringing harmony and focus. Her hands still lightly touched the shining wall. Anna and Andrew moved to stand beside her, their hands reaching out hesitantly, then confidently, to touch that wall with her. Rose felt Paul's hand in hers and together they moved to join the three. Slowly each one broke free from him or herself and allowed that streaming of energy-- of Mind- Heart itself, to pour through their individual minds. They allowed the unity that opened vision. Vision that no individual mind could endure. They saw and knew then beyond all life as they had known it. They did not see in glimpses as they had done before, instead, perception persisted, widened far, and they stood beyond the darkness of human sight. They stood in the brightness of clear vision. In this way, and at this time, Jessie could teach them this final knowledge that they must use in order to proceed into that City.

CHAPTER TWENTY FOUR

The City

They stood at the gateway between two worlds. A point between two perceptions of Reality. At first glance, they saw this point as a dead end. Gradually they were aware that they stood at an invisible doorway through which was Life, infinitely greater, deeper and more vivid than they had ever known. But none here were wholly unfamiliar with this doorway. They had seen that Light that shone through those doors, had seen it briefly, but clearly. It was a Light that blinded the mind and the senses at first, but beyond which a few of them had caught swift recognitions, although of such transcendant nature that it either eluded the conscious mind or, inexpressable, it too often slipped from memory and left little more than an enduring longing that could not be fulfilled. There was a strong conviction that there WAS SOMETHING there, beyond that invisible barrier. Something that drew attention,so that in moments of utter stillness, it was there, causing all other thought, memory, to recede into meaninglessness. Beyond that initial Light was a key to the nature of reality.

And the Light itself? Was it a true blinding or an illusion of blindness that struck the human consciousness at its discovery? More than one had already found it was simply an exposure of their own original blindness. When we open our eyes in the morning at the sun's first light, we realize we've been asleep. So it was. They knew now, surely that their ordinary life was a kind of sleep and that now they could, if they chose,keep their eyes open to that new immensity of Vision. They could begin to LIVE wakened from the ancient dream of living.

Now, they could see that Jessie stood there, on the first of three broad steps. They realized that here they could participate in a promise that was greater than any dream. Now, a fire woke in them, woke memory of knowledge that roused consciousness as a breeze rouses flames from coals. They were waked from an ancient sleep and that waking had shaken them alive.

Jessie spoke, her voice like a current that blazed through their minds,"Through these years you have refined the very substance of your bodies, hearts and minds so that now you can endure something of the Vision that you have seen. You've learned to See,to Listen, to focus attention, to know with all parts of your triple nature. You are finally aware! Otherwise you would not be here. Much of this you have done from within as you learned discipline and absorbed the Teaching, without consciously realizing it, but much you worked consciously to learn, to train yourself to realize. You have found identity with Soul and stand Soul conscious together. You have done this! Body, mind and heart awake to all memory,as to a liquid in which you bathe."

She showed them the nature of the Wall, the nature of the City itself. As she did, they knew their own bodies as they never had. Perhaps a talented Healer might know of the nature of the living universe that was a human body, but few else. Here they entered into those bodies, saw that every complex functional organ was made up of cells joined in a mutual task, organs whose every function was intelligently arranged so that each harmonized with and supported or complimented every other organ. Not until now had they realized the miraculous nature of that fact. Each cell, an intelligence, knowing its task, fulfilling its responsibity,and even sometimes, failing to do so.

And they looked closer and found themselves to be an essence, a fluid substance sustaining this universe of molecules and atoms that made up these cells. Each person lived through these vast spaces of the body. Like galaxies, clusters of such cells together formed the organs and between each was vast emptyness. And consciousness that was themselves inhabited that space and permeated every cell. These were the recognitions.

And then they looked at the Walls themselves and saw that structure as very similar. They could see then that as these physical bodies could pass through these walls, these walls could allow passage through themselves for there was space enough between all matter. It required only a subtly refined attunement, a synchronicity of molecular vibrations .Focus of mind made the passage possible, and they had been trained to focus mind since childhood. How obvious it seemed, seen from this deeper view,that it was not magic at all, but simply a focus of attention and harmony.

Their eyes were opened,they knew the nature of mind substance, flexible, strong, resistant to harm, infinitely malleable. What could be imagined, could be. They saw that things were not what they had seemed. Mind-emotion permeated body and extended far beyond it. And they saw the color of emotion playing through their lives, the power by which they could sail beyond their universe and the still currents of Mind that swept beyond human ken and offered unlimited discovery as the ocean once offered what seemed unlimited discovery to sailors who learned to sail the seas. As they knew these things, they turned to the doorway, watching alertly as they had watched the immediate life of Earth as children. They watched the wall fade, solidify and fade again. Their own bodies seemed to them to have a consistency of smoke and then to become heavy, dense. They could see together without blindness. There, where the walls had been, seemed to be now giants of radiant armour, standing with raised swords, repulsing the approach of any who were not ready to enter this City. Their swords, upraised, flamed with a bright fire of pure energy and that itself made the City unapproachable. They were not there to protect the City however, but to protect those who came from entering what they were not ready for. This City was a fountaining focus point of Life. Its fluid energy broke through the structure of this physical universe, as a spring of water breaks through a mountain of rock.

For this Farm Family, however, that terrible fire seemed now to be a nourishment. They stood full in the flow of it, and it fed their hearts and Minds and each grew in stature and strength. The flames of the guardians played over them, making visible the three bodies in which they lived. The heavy physical body, radiant with its new inner life. The subtle colorful astral body, a little larger, purified and visible now. The mental bodies, less visible, encompassed the other two in their soft pearl light. Thus, they absorbed that fire and knew a little more of their nature at last.

Their minds were fully conscious of that unity they had achieved. As atoms gather, drawn by that strange attraction of their kind, to form into molecules which become then miraculously a new substance, so these human beings began realizing a new consciousness, there at this doorway, catalyst to awakened spiritual existence. This new nature partook of its parts the same way water partakes of oxygen and hydrogen. Now they were conscious of themselves together so that a great wonder rose up in them and a Joy that burned as a light. Below, in the Valley, there were those who could See, and who saw that flash, then the stabilizing of the trembling until it was a steady glow and those who could see turned to their night's rest, with pleased smiles.

Jessie knew they must enter the City if they were to complete the Journey. They were drawn by irresistable aspiration. The fear, doubt, amazement rose and then drained away as if irrelevant. Eagerness grew. Longing -- that age old longing, reached its peak. Here now, surely,. Here now, finally! They moved forward, not thinking, but responding. They knew the radiance of Joy, they partook of it as people thirsty might drink. What were they that they could pass through walls? The question was not asked. Whether they were still human was not asked. The answer preceeded the question: they were Conscious. They knew themselves so alive they felt joy as though it were air they breathed. The human intellect, still persisting in trying to explain everything to itself, was stilled. Thinking would come later. Thoughts formed, and they slid past attention and were lost. The wonder of this new dimension had stretched mind beyond itself. They were taking a step forward, they KNEW,(though they did not intellectually understand), the mechanisms of what they experienced. But they were wise enough not to call it magic. Someday they would unravel the details of this dimension as humanity had unraveled so much of its old universe. But now, it was essential to live in it, to step forth, and claim that birthright.

It was not true that they entered the City without pain. There was a tearing of old patterns, a tearing that was actually the final dying away of patterns, old and worn and no longer functional. They had spent years wearing down some of those patterns, assumptions, habits of thinking, and so the pain was brief and sharp . It was a calm recognition, as when one sees that he has grown too large to wear an old garment and must put it off. They stood quietly together, clinging a little to one another, letting the old concepts, patterns, fall away, naked to such newness that they felt raw with tenderness. They knew these deaths with a faintly lingering sorrow and then a breaking away of relief. They looked up then and saw that they were in the City.

They walked into the gardens, each taking his or her own way, moving with ease and freedom, absorbing and feeding on that astonishing beauty. They could see a great shimmering of Life glowing through every thing, stone, leaf and water.

THE PEOPLE OF THE VALLEY

The air tingled with the presence of Life. How had they imagined themselves alive before? The air was a nourishment. There was a beauty of form here not fully visible to them. They still had much to realize, their minds were still expanding and the stretch of it ached and tingled as though electrical currents were loosed through their brain cells. They saw that the buildings were of stone, but that they extended beyond the stone, and were more than stone. This Being that was the City, taking form during the cosmic act of Love, had taken one of the innumerable forms of Love. So it was ever evolving, ever renewing itself. It was gradually visible to those who had chosen to arrive here.

Their brains were filled with awe, wonder, Joy but their Souls rejoiced in this coming home. This union of the self with the Self was a necessity for being here. They stood in paradox, for they were aware of themselves being more than they had ever known they were. Such an awakening was a kaliedescope of experience and of knowing. Running through cells of the body, the oceans of the emotions, the vast spaces of the mind, was that new flickering fire of recognition that was an expansion of consciousness. Transformations were steady, gradual and persistent. They knew and entered in, consciously they participated in their own illumination. All those names they had revered rose from memory, Buddha, Krishna, the Christ, Mohammad, Mary, Kali, Shiva, the Mother, the Father - other names, all shaped and faded. Surely such great ones had come this way? They had no language to hold this vision and they knew there was no name.

Finally, they began to hear the sounds of the towers, the subtle music of great architectural wind harps. The sound included and went far beyond the sensation of hearing. It grew slowly to fill their consciousness creating in them a deep resonance that pulsed through their flesh, their minds, and shaped into thought patterns. "Here is the truth of our lives, the possibility of humanity." The thought stood as a fact. Indeed this was what they were becoming. The strong reverberations of Soul resonated through them and continued the refinements of their transformation. The pulse of transcendant consciousness beat through their very beings, waking them. A sudden cry, a deep sigh, a whimper, escaped here and there, but none retreated. They felt gradually that their bodies were vibrating as delicately as the strings of the wind harp. As though this sound, subtle, yet so full of power, tuned them so that their own notes could sound true.

They moved back, retreating slightly from the insistence, the invitation, then they swung forward again, eager, filled with desire to respond. As in a dance they hesitated and then leaped ahead, fearful and fearless, willing, then shy and the gradual ebb and flow drew them forward toward the harmony that they could faintly hear, a harmony that grew slowly near. The dance was intricate, and they were wholly involved. They felt their minds engaged, wholly immersed and knowing all that they entered into.

They entered and began to recognize their own sounds, the tone that characterized themselves. They could extricate it from the intricate symphony. They could hear the harmony, then the loss of it, the regaining of attention, shifting of emotion like a scattering of fireflies, flashed into play. Both trifling and

THE JOURNEY

overwhelming they stirred for moments conscious of their part in this group consciousness, coloring and deepening, for they were part of this symphony also. Then gradually they began to find balance in the serene steady focus of this Mind-Joining.

How could this be? What -- who-- Joined with them? Yet, a new consciousness of Life beat through every thread of existence, Love blown like a constant wind within every breath, allowed them to see what they had once called life. Looking back they realized it was so small, so one dimensional, their world seemed a toy in their hands. A toy humankind had spent millions of years striving, dying and reliving to create in imitation of what prodded against their hearts. How poorly we strove, they cried in their Souls, yet what massive courage! They could feel the tranforming power of this growing sound, of the harmony of those Minds that were surely present somewhere near. Without knowing more, they responded and accepted as reeds weave in the movements of wind among them, filled and complete.

They were pleased,filled with a delight in themselves and each other. They stood at the edge of a vast sea of consciousness and knew of it. The lapping waves of that sea washed against them, shimmering, splashing over them and drawing them into its depths. Its sparkling light rippled against their minds, their hearts. Fear was held in abeyance, like a marble, taken from a game, is held in the pocket.

They clung to one another. Thoughts exploded like showers of fireflies, registering then fading. "How could the children endure" And the children laughed! " Who were children here?" They felt pleased with the shapes and fragrances of the garden, they knew language that could speak of much they realized, but they lacked language for most of it. Then thought began to shape, thought that did not have to settle itself into a rigid clutch of words, but would sing in flight, moving with realization keeping pace. Now they communicated,and knew at those edges, perception that woke meaning all around them. Other minds somewhere near informed them. They drew back against one another, wondering, shy suddenly, like children again, at a new place. They wondered where their hosts were.

Jessie stood a little beyond them, they had clung to her at first, but they saw she had abandoned them. The quality of her nature was beauty too great for them to look at long. Yet! Many feelings came and went, sudden shafts of pain that gradually settled into a vast unease. Had she always been so and they simply had not seen? That which was becoming known to them was unsettling, brilliant with wonder. Could humanity be what Jessie obviously was? Capable of such Love, such depths of courage and expressing a Will- to-Good that dwarfed anything anyone of them had imagined. Such Will had to know something of that which is Good that is unknown to most. Such a one must be a transparent expression of Spirit Itself.And yet,she was - or had seemed - still human. They looked at her in wonder.

Then the landscape began to change -- or seem to. It dimmed,then grew clearer, began to sparkle with an inner light that was like an essence of diamonds. Everywhere this light grew stronger, making leaves and flowers stand out in such precise detail that they fascinated attention even as the vision passed on to every new form.. Surely it must be night in the Valley below, yet here was a brilliance of light. They could see that every living thing in this amazing garden was 'aware' of the Life around it. The relationship between plant, animal and human was a complexity that began to reveal itself as if unfolding from a fold of invisibility.

There was a subtle, brilliant movement in the very structure of things, the air, in human bodies, in the branches of the trees,the leaves moving so lightly above. They were conscious of a pervading upsurge of Joy as if it had been there within things all the time. It was there -- the dance of Life itself, echoing, reflecting through everything non-living, waking there a slow, response.

Sound increased, cascading all round them, their own individual tones, so clear now, lifted and entered into the vast universal sound, the music that reverberated through them now, a streaming music, of a symphony too large, too complex and vast to be heard in its entirety. They too, entered in with one note each. They each knew that music growing clearer, lifting and enfolding them, rearranging the very cells of their bodies and minds. It was the Heart's wisdom informing them, reaching out as if on wings. Then, Mind itself, something beyond simple mind, woke them to Itself. They learned, though they would not remember it until much later, how to use sound, notes of the voice, the complexity of great music, to create change. The power pulsing through them now came from that source that was Life itself. For Jennifer and Andrew it was an ecstacy of realization, creation of music such as neither had dreamed, but had felt whispering far in their hearts. The knowledge humbled and quieted their hearts.For this wonder was given, offered, as though they each deserved all that it was.

The resonance of music pounded through them, softly lifting and soaring with them higher and higher, tenderly infusing them, rousing to acute awareness their finite personal minds. The shapes of things, of relationships between things, was itself a flowering of sculptural art, woven in that warp of sound. This must be the source of all art, all human creation! Through everything a simple fear reached out, like a sharp pang, echoing its minor key in the harmony. It was as if the sudden shadow of a hawk, might darken a sunlit meadow, where young creatures played. Then, slowly, settling into that light itself, it clarified, revealed it's part in the pattern. Where was that lost humanity? That which they had known as human? What was this new dimension that Humanity entered into? The sense of 'otherness' as of something alien, was softened, faded in this insight.

With simple astonishment, and at the same time, with absolute naturalness, they realized the ensouling of all form; the fact that Spirit, that new dimension of aliveness, was the heart of everything that existed. It was not an idea, but a clear knowledge, seen, known, and realized in totality. Mind was the body of that which they knew so far as Spirit. Spirit embodied and made functional in the material world, but there it was, and THAT brought them to utter stillness, in contemplation.

How beautiful it was, how simply obvious. For looking about, they could see with ease, that inner flame of Spirit, that inner fire of LIFE itself. And seeing it in one another, they saw that they could not desire other than that harmony they now knew. There was nothing other, Life itself meant harmony that included all conflict, all pain. It was an intensity of growth rising out of that deeply sprouting awakened Spirit. And this was only a doorway! What might come beyond this? What might LIFE include then, if this was a beginning?

New meaning formed, as if some mental flowering was occurring. That new meaning formed and informed their taut receptive minds. but meaning extended beyond the language of thought, in its unerring flight, it stretched mind stuff. It stretched consciousness into a stillness where meaning out distanced comprehension. That was the center of deep knowing, knowing that could not be shaped into thought at all. Paul wondered, and words shaped a fleeting thought, "The greater part of the whole mind knows beyond thought? And thought is only a firefly in that wind?"

Rose spun down into identity of herself, Rose. Found herself aware as though she was one tiny, firm point of a vast and limitless cone, and that cone spiraled into infinity. To perceive was to flow through impossibiities into a melding that sprang immediately into new possibility. That process was like a new condition of being alive. Her attention wondered in and out of that complexity that her own previous life kept shaping from this absolute simplicity. It was, she was, they were, the medium through which the energy of Life kept forming endlessly. Could there be any understanding of this? There was no shaping it into an idea for understanding. Could it only be realized, wordlessly? And yet, there it was, at least the shadow of this immensity reflected by her stretched and suffering mind.

She Reached out, then knew that Joining was already complete, that without it, they would not KNOW as they now did. There was a surge of Spirit moving through Mind. She knew that what she had grasped had been what was left behind as it moved. Like a bit of melody haunting the memory, they knew of new life from that moving, ever recreating symphony that was already far beyond. She sank, giving herself over again, allowing thought to swim again through the endless realizations. Thought was like small cups immersed in that vivid streaming consciousness, like cups trying to fill themselves with an ocean. It filled them, spilled over and they emptied and refilled, so that holding and defining seemed futile. She knew that without their mutual strengths, their deep Joining, they could not have born the power of this filling and refilling.

Briefly small shafts of thinking occurred like little dark knots in the fabric of consciousness: a desire to run away, to bury herself in some busy intersection inside the markets of Santiago, some distraction with things to catch and hold her attention in littleness and end this fluidity. But the idea faded as easily as mist before the sun. Some steel strong center of herself ignored these desires that burst into rigid little shapes now and then, as one might ignore the disturbance of gnats behind one's ear. She could feel herself grow in strength, that strength twined through the strength of the others.

Silvia drew strength from her, Jane and Steve were steadied by her balance. And they gave back their own. She found calm from Paul and Anna and Andrew, and Tom thrust himself into their need like a pivot. They held firmly, their hearts singing, all the others also offering their strengths, greater than any had thought. Joy rang through them so great it threatened to shake them from their senses. The idea amused her. Amused them all.

The idea of explaining all this, slid through her mind like an anchor to which she could cling.. And she felt an upwelling of laughter, merriment that seemed to have no end. How could one even begin? Perhaps explaining would not make its endless demands on her in future. She might simply accept. She could hear her own note within this, the notes of the others and their place was real. The realization was something her mind could hold to. She felt herself sway, recede, expand, become what she had not been, recede again and give herself altogether into that vast and uncontainable fluid knowing. She was merged into that wholeness and yet, she was herself.

The rhythm grew, merged, was carried on a flow of sound so pure as to nearly release them from themselves. What was this? Where? What were they thus all together? Astonished, she gave herself, willing, She was conscious of Life Itself peering through this Universe at her, through her, as if, Life contemplated Itself through its forms. The recognition emptied everything of idea out and left stillness.

THAT! Even the faint touch of That, once more realigned the very cells of their Joined Minds. That which was Nameless Present? Had That been the source of the idea called by the various names of 'God'? Power beyond power, Life beyond life, Being beyond all being. A reflection shaped again, thought sought to mold itself to that shape, but the substance of Mind itself was inadequate. The reflection itself shone like a gift.

Delighted laughter sounded through her bones. As swiftly, she felt a terrible grief inundate all thought. She swayed, unable to sustain so much, they swayed, even their Joined awareness was overwhelmed. They were unable to BE so much. And yet they were.!

Music descended to a minor throb, left them quiet, separate, feeling the relief and loss like a scalding pain. Slowly, the world around became visible to their physical eyes. They were here, just here, a Family.

They knew a soft, tender fear, feeling as if their mutual nature was swollen with pregnancy, with Life that had been unknown. They had been transcending all they had been, they had broken open, giving birth to something greater than themselves. And greater than this Joined Self. It seemed terrifying and infinitely desireable. Rose, drew a focus through them. They must rest and wait. There could be no more birth. They released one another from this sustained attention. They knew one another again but with an intimacy that was both physical and mental, emotional and of Spirit. Then Jessie came to them.

THE JOURNEY

She took from herself, from the mental substance of her nature and created a star, a symbol that she held up and projected out to them. It's many points extended into dimensions beyond senses, invisible except to eyes open to Spirit. It had many facets, many reflections. It drew from each of them and was drawn into each so that a point of mutual attention occurred. The star was the symbol of a possibility of unity.

They knew of one another now. But they knew also of those who lived in this City, who surrounded them now, but who were not yet visible. They knew beyond the conscious thought that flitted within this limitless knowing.

Together in a helpless sorrow, they saw how limited those flickers of thought were, they were, after all, human. They were alive to the breath of Life in themselves, But the shadow lingered there too. Their humanity both offered them possibility and limited that possibility. They were matter stretched to its utmost in this weave of infinite Spirit. Now would it fall back into its familiar mode? No, the stretch would not fall back. It had become too strong. The wakened, expanded consciousness, was permanent.

Rose said, "Together we can return to that place of LIGHT. And each time we do, we will realize more, and sustain that realization longer." They were full of such a sweet calm that Rose marveled "Together we can also remember. That memory is embedded in every cell of our three fold nature. For once in my life I finally know what that means."

Anna came to her mother, stood close, to slip an arm around her waist, her face held a pensive stillness,"Mama, it's all true, isn't it? What our Teachers have taught us and what we began ourselves to realize a little? Life is so endless we can't ever discover it all. That seems so very good. There's no end to it all."

" Look, Look," Andrew cried out happily,"Listen! we can hear even our own sound!" And they could hear the full notes of their own natures, the harmony of their Joining. It was small, in that vast and grand music surrounding them, but it was pure and sweet. "We have that to take home. We can remember. Perhaps I can make a music from it." His smile was wide.

Jessie was smiling at them as they moved about now, walking through the lush gardens, touching bright ripe fruits, bemused by the beauty of the buildings. She said,"Life may have dimensions no single human mind can bear. Not as it is at least. To learn to bear more of Reality, one must enlarge constantly. But to know that there is no end, gives freedom and possibility. No one can grow weary of life knowing that." She laughed,"Although life may not always be in a physical body"

Finally with a long sigh, Ben moved his body, walked briefly here and there, as if testing himself out, feeling his body alive again. The exhaustion of the journey was gone, he was physically present to himself, he felt closed off a little from that extended vast universe in which he had so recently lived."We've got to remember. Surely we will when we are together and when we Join. I don't want to forget -- anything!"

Tom nodded, sitting and then standing, restless now in his long body. "It's only together that we can fully know or remember. And yet, how can I believe -- even now it's already lost a little." He looked so sad, Jennifer, who stood beside him took his hand.He looked around at them, "At least,I know that I can find something of it. I can remember with you all. I don't want to forget."

In this garden their bodies seemed light, so that their feet barely touched Earth. They saw Jessie beckon them and followed her into the Temple. She drew their attention and then, as though a veil dropped, they saw it was half full of people. A stillness hung through the room. As if their ears had not yet learned to hear. Then a hollow cone of Light spun like a fierce point of energy through the air of the Temple. They knew invitation , greeting and joy sweeping from that cone to permeate every atom of the space. They were able to Join with all that company and respond. They stood, absorbed in that nourishment. All that had blinded them, fogged their perceptions, or dimmed their senses was washed away, as dust before a spring rain. The power, the transforming light and Knowledge, completed the birth. After long, long moments, while time turned and swept in on itself, they moved again. Conscious as they had never been, or imagined being,their minds fragile with renewal, they left the Temple.

The Temple breathed the winds softly through the harps of its towers. Sound blended with the rising fragrances of Earth, grass, trees and fruits. Fountains rose and fell, leaping out in fans that sprayed into one another and filled pools that ran over and fed a small stream that wound among the ferns and moss. The people of the City came with them from the Temple, and began to show them all the wonders of their home land. They wandered here and there, attending to the vivid life around them. They entered other buildings, and finally found small nooks and crannies where groups of benches invited sitting. They climbed narrow stairs to the tops of slim towers, and walked among rooms laid ready for whoever came . They did not ask. They saw chairs and tables, wrought by artists more than human, cabinets, beds, ordinary things to live with, dishes, utensils, and yet each a work of art, enduring, and beautiful. This was a place for human living surely! And with that thought, they began to search the faces of those who guided them, and saw the depth of their humanity.

Finally, they all came together to lie in the grasses in a small meadow beside the narrow stream. There under a towering tree they could see beyond the mountains and even to the Valley floor. Their eyes comforted them with memories. The silver glint of the Great River flowing past their old home was familiar and made all this more real.Jane stood looking down at Ned's lean, black body stretched on the grass beside Ben's shorter stocky, very fair body. So different they looked. Ned brushed away an insect that crawled down on him from the end of a long blade. She looked up and met Jessie's watchful eye and saw her nod. With a smooth gentle focus, she touched that infinitismal insect life, that consciousness, so limited and so delicate. She informed it, informed all those similar lives now roaming and busy among the moss and grass. She glanced at Ned and Ben who were watching her, aware of what she did. She grinned. Then Jessie said,"Sleep now,if you like."

But no one wanted to sleep. They watched the scene below for a little, and felt such love for that land they had cared for. Paul sat on a low stone, cut and polished into smoothness. He looked out at the sky above them, it's blue so deep it seemed he could swim through it. His thoughts focussed and he said,"All these millinia we have been intently fighting evil, fighting to conquer those who threatened us, absorbed in searching for evil all around us,,and all along it was there in ourselves. All we needed to do was refuse to provide the energy for it to flourish in ourselves. We did not EVER trust Love and it the only truth greater than Evil. And yet, our Teachers have told us since time began. The ancient Mother Gods showed us in their time, but they feared and were unable to find the balance with the Father Gods who pushed them aside." He shook his head. "Humankind is stubborn, hard headed, slow to shift perception and suspicious of Balances. It's the Balance between Earth and Sky, between Matter and Spirit, between Life and Illusion that we must seek forever." He nodded slowly, accepting this thought.

They wondered again, unable to get enough of the wonder of this City. Looking at the people of the City, quietly going about their daily lives here. They were puzzled that the people took them so matter-of-factly until Jessie reminded them that this was not an uncommon event in this City.

They could hear conversation, light and musical when it was audible, but mostly mind sent and therefore soundless. Here was not the simple Touch, the heightened awareness of attitude and idea that their own Joining brought, but an ability to discourse in sentences if they chose. A true telepathy. Even still, they caught only fragments of such conversation. They did not talk among one another for a long time. Finally, Ben rolled to one side, looking out over this lovelyness and said,"How can we ever leave this? It's everything any human could desire."

Ned turned to look at his friend,"It is, Benjamin, that's why we can leave." He grinned impishly at his joke. "We can come again you know. It'll be here forever, I think."

Silvia was gazing, half seeing them, half hearing, and she said slowly, as if finishing a thought,"Reality is a new word for me now. I don't know whether I can even think what it once meant anymore."

Jane laughed at them, standing above them, her body half hidden by low hanging branches. She began to dance lightly, her body bending, leaping lightly, somersaulting, then catching herself and spinning and then bending again. She laughed aloud, the dance delighting her. She finally stopped, caught at the branch above her and said,"It's so beautiful, so delightful to be here. I want to remember everything.!" There was an ache in her heart that persisted and she accepted it. Such beauty hurt.

Rose looked around at the others, and saw that neither Anna or Andrew were with them, and wondering, she began to look around, then, as if a voice spoke, she knew. They were still in the Temple. Their places among these 'People of the Light' as she thought of them, was different from her own. A stab of jealousy cut and faded into fear, then pride, then a sense of loss. She shook her head. The garden around her spun and faded, she was caught in old emotions, damping vision. She reached in wild impulse outward to Benjamin and encountered all the others, ready, willing and with swift precision she regained herself. Silently, she went to the Temple entrance, peered in and was momentarily blinded by the Light there. She could see nothing, hear nothing and yet, she knew that a profoundly important ceremony was taking place there.

Anna and Andrew had waited when their Family left the Temple, knowing they must respond to that point of radiant light that revealed Itself to them at the Center of the Temple. They did not know at first whether the others were aware, but saw soon that they were not. It held the attention of these two children, captivating their minds. They waited, and when the Family left, some of the people remained with them. The Light grew, surrounding them like a liquid and they waited. They made their choice in that instant, they were fully prepared, their minds responding to a familiar pull. Choice made, they sank to their knees, willing, knowing the choice was permanent, that they had passed from one point of being to another. And yet, they were as they had always been.

As the Light burned into their minds,, strengthening and affirming all that they had become in these last years, they felt the attachments of their past lives fade and fall away, the last clinging remnants of desire and need turn to nothing and dissolve. They were finally aware of a great cleansing brightness that flamed through them. Steady recognition blossomed in Minds here-to-fore choked with old hopes and dreams. Silently they took this pledge that grew from depths of themselves wakened and set afire by this living Light.

They felt the finger of that Light everywhere through themselves. It's power in every hiding place of their natures, it permeated every flicker of what they had been and merged into what they were becoming. It was a fire that burned away, leaving them hollow. Silently, they were completing years of growth, of expanded and deepened perceptions won through a steady effort to reach that Light since birth. The ripping away of old assumptions, of ancient patterns built into the race they were part of, was full of pain and grief. But they stood without faltering.

Finally they spoke knowing the words."I will serve all life, all humanity and all lesser lives, of Earth. I will to offer my life, my consciousness, to stand steadily in this Holy Light that glows now clearly within my Heart and Mind." Then Anna said softly, "This entrance, this journey we take here fills us with what we need to give to others when we return."

Andrew murmured ,"That service we will become, it is what our lives are for - a meaning that never fades."

When it was done,they stirred, felt the Light recede into its point at the Center of the Temple, felt the over whelming power of Love that had engulfed them so that they might know something of that possibiity. Tears flowed over their faces. They knew an energy, a power of the Will to Good, that would keep them moving toward that possibility of Love forever. That Will, penetrating as a sword might, woke, and set into new functioning their own strong wills, their perceptions of Good Itself. Old doubts and fears would not erode away their committment again. Whatever new doubts might arise, those old ones were gone, lost in this vision, great and broad as the possibility of truth.

They sat, silent, wanting to rest here a little. Among the other people Jessie stood. Coming to take their hands and kiss them with such Joy as they could not explain. She wept with the power of that Joy, laughed and turned away to allow the others to come to receive them.

To a person viewing this City from the air at this moment, there would have been visible twelve people lying quietly on the grass or moving with amazing grace about the pathways. There would have been no others seen. But to a careful observer there would have been knowledge that much was happening. A stir of power lit the City and poured outward down into the Stations, where it was received with understanding and then, it was channelled outward through the world beyond.

Ben said aloud, "The universe is different, everything is absolutely different." He stood contemplating that fact. Alert and focussed as he had never before been. Then, he said slowly,"No, we are different, the universe has always been so, and we have not known." Over all familiar things was a polished newness, a shining in every living thing he saw. It puzzled him, but seemed so right.

Ben looked around, all his senses alert, tasting, seeing, smelling, as if for the first time,fascinated by every experience, however slight. There was a quality of that aliveness in everything, the Earth, the stone Temple, everything! He said, to Tom who stood beside him," Look, the buildings have a light in their stone work. Somehow they are alive too, in a way I don't understand, but I don't doubt". Other senses for which he had no name woke in his shaken self. "Tom, I think my brain feels sore from so much -- so much more that it has to make room for." He laughed.

Tom nodded,"It's stretched, Benjamin, no doubt of it. It's what I feel, and it IS a feeling of being sore."

Ben caught sight of a group of people gathered before the Temple and nudged Tom,"It really floors me. Who are they? Where have they come from? How long've they been here?" He sighed.

Tom eyed the group thoughtfully, "What's a surprise to me is why we never saw them when we first came in. Surely they were here. They obviously live here."

As they watched, the outlines of the gathering people became clearer, they seemed to firm up, round out into living physical bodies, yet how could those bodies be physical? They could see Jessie among them now. Some event had just concluded inside the Temple and they were emerging. The two men were surprised at how many had been inside. Jessie moved nearer them, talking to a short bodied, dark skinned man whose brows beetled into a frown. His powerful arms lifted as he talked,waving at the air in a gesture graceful and arresting. A woman was with them, slim and fragile, yet with a quality of body strength expressed even in her manner of standing. Jessie seemed to Tom and Benjamin to be her usual self except she totally lacked that self effacing quality they had known in her. She seemed straighter, taller, and all three of them radiated power, sureness."She seems different too."Ben muttered.

Rose joined Tom and Ben then. She said,"She does seem so. So balanced, so self accepting. Now, when I think of it, she always has been, but the way she sat back, kept in the background among us --! " She shook her head. Jessie was and she wasn't the same. She looked around at the others, "They are all like that! It's a miracle that they can be like that." She watched, wondering exactly what it was about them that gave that knowledge. Then she sighed,"Oh, I wish I could be so!" The desire filled her and she saw Jessie turn and nod. Her eyes met Rose's. The process that had begun years ago, that process toward self realization, self knowledge, was given strength. She felt the gift, like a centering and a clarity . She too would one day know that same freedom.

Then they saw Anna and Andrew leaving the Temple. Rose caught her breath. Tom and Benjamin stared. Had these kids been in there all that time? The children seemed to glow, their bodies radiating light literally, just as the citizens of this place did. Rose cried out,"Oh, my dear God, Ben! Our children, Ben, Look at them!" She caught at his hand.

Ben squeezed her hand, staring,"They're wonderful. Oh, how can it be sweetheart?

Jane moved sideways through the gathering crowd to stand beside Steve. Her hand seeking his and he turned to smile into her eyes,"Honey, they're amazing, I can't quite believe what I'm experiencing. People like this! How can there be people like this? So many of them?"

Jane simply nodded,she could not trust herself to speak. She felt unusual shyness. They heard Ned say, "As strange as it is, and everything is strange, I feel good. I'm not afraid. I KNOW this is all right. That surprises me." He was grinning like a child at a fair. Enjoying every minute. Jane looked at him curiously. Yes, he seemed full of joy, a bursting joy and she acknowledged it. She knew because she felt it herself. As though it would lift through her self, wanting expression through her face, and her distrust kept her face serious. How could one feel such Joy? How could it be real? It actually hurt in her throat.

Steve squeezed her hand, sensing her dilemma,"It's real, sweetheart, I've never felt like this and I can't keep my face straight. I'm worse than Ned for grinning." She looked over at him, barely needing to look up. He nodded,"This kind of Joy can't be harmful, nor false, nor anything but wonderful. Enjoy it, just enjoy it! There is such trust here. No wonder your throat hurts if you're denying all that!"

Jane watched his face, saw it wreathed in a delight she had seldom seen there. She was pleased, comforted and relaxing, felt her own face responding so that her smile was irrepressable. Surely this was not simply some euphoria rising out of the height and the strangeness. It was genuine, and very permanent.

Silvia had taken her hand and Jane turned to her, the question in her eyes, the puzzle communicated,Silvia nodded,"Yes, I wonder too. Look at Jessie, look at Rose and Ben and Tom there. They're so full of -- of Joy, it's like we've suddenly realized how wonderful life is."

They looked at each other, touched each other then, began to know the Presence of the garden. Like an air, breathable, and yet, they could only describe it as Love Itself. They would not have said that they felt loved, nor that they loved, but rather that Love was simply a quality of the atmosphere in which all things here lived. It was unity, inclusiveness, absolute acceptance. It was of the nature of Life itself, as though perhaps Life had risen from Love in some remote beginning. Yes, that was it! The knowledge sobered and awed the most sceptical. They could, together, give themselves over to that wonder and feel release from doubt. Here Love was a stable condition of living. It absorbed and made impotent all fear.

Cassandra went to her father, clung to his hand and without taking her eyes off the radiant people said,"Daddy, do you see? Do you see now?" Her eyes met his and received his affirmation. She nodded and went on, "They are so beautiful, they are Teachers you know! They don't have to say anything to Teach.It's just their living, and that's what I want Daddy, that's what I've always wanted." Her voice was wistful, her meaning not quite clear to him.

You mean -- you want them to teach you too?"

She shook her head, bemusedly, "No, I want to be like that. To be so alive!" He was surprised, she did not usually talk so.

He searched her face, watchful, soft, the longing clear in her expression."I can't think of anything greater to want, Sweetheart. But I doubt if you have to worry about their disappearing from us. Perhaps they will help us learn that.If only they would live among us, if we could see, have an example of what such living is."

Silvia was saying, "How the devil would I ever tell my friends? I want to bring them all here. To show them!"

Paul nodded,"I don't know whether I could tell anyone at all. I think you have to see it, experience this, to believe it, or even imagine it. Surely though --" He looked around at the others,"Surely, though, some of our friends have already been here, or will be and you notice they didn't try to tell us." He met Silvia's eyes, they nodded.

Then Paul shrugged,"Wow! It's no wonder William was afraid. He's probably able to feel some of the energy rising, increasing in the Valley and can't explain it. This same energy effects him with fear. But he didn't have the clues we did to See more." He frowned."It's a grief that I won't be able to talk to him of this." His voice was sad, his eyes locked on the pavement of the court.

Ned frowned, "No, Paul, you must talk to him, must do just that. Just what Steve just said. The people here teach by being, and we want such people to live among us. Could my life teach anything at all to anyone?"

Rose was nodding,"At least, we'll no longer live with fear. There're other people in the Valley now, who know, who have opened the door into Light. We can talk to them. We can learn from them. Because, you can see we've only just begun the Journey."

Andrew was watching Paul. The two children Touched lightly, wanting to reconnect with their Family. Now Andrew's gaze moved from one to the other and finally settled on Paul. He was aware of the stream of sensation, of general thought trend, of emotions rising and falling. He realized their efforts to digest, to understand in ordinary terms all that was happening. He caught Paul's memory of William's discomfort in his birthday journey, and Andrew realized Paul's worry. Their eyes met and he took of that grief. He said softly,"Uncle Paul, I see so much more today. I feel so glad to be free of all those old questions" He laughed,"But probably now I'll have new ones."

Jennifer sat huddled into herself, but her attention was open, listening. She reached to realize the thought patterns, the stream of feelings. She felt gratefully the Presence the others had accepted and though she had not named it, accepted it too. Jane leaned against a tree, her eyes looking far off into the Valley.

Benjamin went over to touch Paul's shoulder, "It's not an easy thing to leave our friend, our brother, behind. It's like deserting him." He was silent, a nagging concern."But he's only one you know, there are others.There must be communion for them too." Paul nodded, slowly, his heart comforted. Rose frowned and said "Life hasn't changed, we'll still go on with it, somehow. Though right now it doesn't seem as though it'll ever be the same. But we'll include other people just as we always have, and we'll be included in their lives."

Rose was sitting with her arms across her knees and her chin resting on them. Now, she looked up, swept them all with a serious thoughtful look,"You all know they'll know there's a difference. I just hope they don't resent that. A sadness was sweeping among them. Sadness of separateness.

"Depends on us, you know. How we live our lives!" Jennifer was smiling, unaffected by that sadness

Tom looked at her, "Exactly! We never did resent Jessie. We saw her difference and we loved her for it. Just liked being around her, Even William said that once, he liked being around her and didn't know why. Surely, if we practice living from this point of perception, just living ordinary lives lifted to their highest, others won't have anything to resent."

"We're gonna have to search our hearts for any trace of superiority, of being better." Jerry sighed, "Take Jessie for a model, we never felt that about her."

Rose nodded, "Nor Grace, nor Edsil!"

Anna said,"Mother, there's plenty of practice. Everybody has had it. Look at Andrew, we don't think he's special because he can make music out of a dream, out of anything. We don't resent Jennifer and her music, or Annette's sculpture. We don't resent Daddy when he comes up with an invention. There's so reason to assume anyone'll know any difference,if we don't."

Cassandra spoke up,"Uncle Will did like being with Jessie, he said so. Even though he also said he didn't trust her?" She laughed. "He didn't trust what he didn't know, I think. But then, neither did we."

Anna looked down at the little girl, nodding, "Yes, Cassie, I think you're right.

THE JOURNEY

He might enjoy being with us, feeling loved, the way we do with Jessie." She glanced around the garden, "With all these people here. He might!" She was silent, then she said, "It's a matter of keeping balance. Like we always had to do. 'Til we find out how to live well? Did Jessie ever make mistakes?"

Rose frowned. "I don't know. I always thought she didn't. If Jessie made mistakes, she surely did correct them. And we'll make them too. More, probably, because we've had no experience living -- living from this perspective." He hesitated, "Besides, we've got ourselves to live with still."

Paul finally breathed a long, slow sigh and laughed, "Mistakes aren't the end of the world. We can tolerate a few if we notice them. In fact, we've got so far to go yet, we'll have plenty.

Ned, lying at ease eating a bright yellow fruit, looked up at them, then stretched to pick a twig from an over hanging branch. "You know, what some one was saying earlier, I too've thought it'd be such a great thing to be a truly holy person. I imagined I would know everything, that I would walk above the grasses, and that people would just know my holiness by sitting and listening to me." He laughed, shaking his head, "That was when I was first taught the Training and the Convictions. When the Master Teachers taught us what a holy person might be. But we never knew of one, we never saw one. Or rather, we didn't recognize them when we did. Holy people don't act like holy people. There were neighbors, or Master Teachers who always seemed -- seemed good to be with. They never had special privileges, on the contrary, they were always giving to other people, time, themselves. They had nothing for themselves. They didn't seem to need anything." He was puckering up his face, remembering. "Yes, that's the way those people were. They never withdrew from us, or lived in isolation with only a few favorites. They always mingled with us all, talked to us all. And so, my idea of a Holy person was a true fantasy." He was silent, remembering, then went on, "I listened to Teachers and to the Elders like Grace. What they said fascinated me, though I didn't understand it all, but the way they lived, moved, LOOKED at us, was their teaching. And so, I didn't think they were Holy at all, they didn't ACT Holy. But then, what did I know what that kind of acting would be? They acted as if they loved us. And I think now they do."

"And now, you know more about that, eh?" Tom grinned at his supine friend.

Ned rolled his head to look at Tom, nodding, "I think I do. I think now, I know the Master Teachers were so simple, so pure in their way. They were so deeply utterly AWARE and that awareness literally seemed contagious. We got it by infection." He laughed again. But his voice was more serious than any of them had ever heard in Ned." You said we need models, to live with us. Well we've already had them. Actually, they made us independant, refused to allow us to devote our time to them, refused to be set apart. They were so ORDINARY. So now, I think that's - greatness of Spirit because I would not use that term 'Holy,' it's been to long misused." He had seldom been so serious so long.

Listening, Jerry nodded slowly, " Remember how they always insisted that we learn to 'Pay Attention!' Pay attention to everything, to the tiniest flying creature to identify it as it flew, to the stars; to know how they related to other stars; to the voices of people; to the sound of birds so we'd know who sang; to the colors and the shapes of leaves that we know the tree they fell from, and so much more. We learned it all in our infancy, but we were able to do more than name, we were AWARE of all those things, we saw when we looked at things, we heard when we listened. All our lives. To be so aware - we learned how to pay attention to the inner shape, the inner sound of things too. The inner life!" He sighed and shook his head slowly," It came with the rest, and we didn't notice. We all see within things now. No way we can deny that. I think life'll be different, you know." He stopped with a grimace that ended in a wry grin, "I suppose I'll be living just as I did. Can't imagine another way.

Ned nodded, murmured, "But with new understanding, Brother, new understanding!"

Tom settled himself against a bench, leaning back against it, looking up through the trees, watching the people of the City come and go, wondering about them. He wanted Ned to go on, but he wanted just to be silent too.

Andrew squatted down beside Ned, his eyes shining with a light Ned had never seen, "I believe my old idea of Holiness was full of wanting power and worship. Wanting people to admire me. Full of mystery, that I'd be mysterious and no one would really underhand me. Wanting to be important and admired. Yes, that's it! I thought I would be better than others, higher. And everyone would love me and want me for a friend. I made a fantasy of being given a wonderful home where worshipers would spend their time taking care of me just so I'd make a speech to them, preach, maybe, once a day." He shook his head, I'd gotten that from old novels and tales. Not one of our Teachers would tolerate "disciples" running around 'taking care of them'." He looked at Rose,"Mom, d'you suppose the people here are Holy people?"

Rose laughed,,"The way you describe that, I doubt if they'd want me to say, yes. But I think they are people whose minds are vast and full and whose Hearts are actually fountains of Love. They can't glance at us that I don't realize that. They don't have to say much at all. They aren't aliens, they aren't a strange race, they're simply our elder brothers and sisters. I know that clearly. And to live with them, among them, would be all the teaching I would need."

Andrew said, "I think of my friends, the gang I ran around with there at home. I wonder whether any of them have made this Journey. Surely there must be some." He bit his lip, drawing his attention into focus,his face cleared,"Of course, it's so obvious when I pay attention. There are two who have already come here. I can see why I didn't notice. They never tried to tell us anything, it was just the way they WERE. --" He was silent then added,"So that's how it is then!"

They were all silent, remembering their friends, seeing them in their mind's eyes anew, and knowing more than they had thought they did. They watched the people who passed here and there through the gardens, and buildings. What business could they possibly be attending to? Paul asked aloud,"Who are they all, Jessie?"

THE JOURNEY

As he spoke the words, a man turned from his conversation and looked at them with gentle interest. Rose gasped, aware of how utterly he had moved his attention, an absolute attention, from his conversation to theirs. Such attention was like a light, directed where he chose. "As you pay attention to what you know, do you notice how much you still deny of what you know?" They looked at him and knew his name like a whisper in their minds, he was called, Phillip.

Ben was surprised, resentment surged then subsided. he shook his head as if to clear it, then said,"Wait! Yes! You're right. We still are-- doing just that!"

Paul touched his arm."It's not a surprise, We've only just begun to acknowledge. Just Realized so much of what, what we actually do know!" He nodded emphatically, recognizing that in himself. He looked at Phillip, who had turned to step toward them,"Are you saying we have to live it NOW ? We are Soul consciousness. Let's sustain our focus of attention from that point. We DO know who you folk of the City are!" His voice dropped into near inaudible softness,but everyone knew the realization flooding his mind. Barriers fell and were allowed to fall. They accepted another depth of themselves.

Rose said to Phillip, speaking for them all,"You are God Conscious people. Just ordinary people who are God Conscious. Isn't that true?"

Phillip nodded," That's one way to describe us. We are becoming, just as you are. All of us here spend our lives in different places, not all of us on Earth, in fact. But many of us do live lives just like yours, even among you. Some are Valley Citizens. A few are Valley Vagabonds, the People of the Way have lived in Knowledge for long. A few are also working among the Monitors, our siblings. " He grinned so disarmingly that their slight unease faded and they felt willing to question him.

"Your lives are gifts - isn't that so? Gifts to guide people toward their own waking? You live as mirrors for the rest of us to see ourselves, what we are becoming?" Tom spoke as if just finding these thoughts shaping in his mind.

Benjamin nodded, summing up what they knew so far,"You don't preach, and don't persuade, or found ego-centered ashrams, you just live your lives as Spirit Conscious people. That in itself teaches!"

Their new Teacher nodded,"Just as Jessie has always done." He laughed at their looks of surprise, that shifted to recognition."Of course, you See now. To See is to be joined in Love and Consciousness - God Consciousness -. Then we live from there."

Steve spoke aloud. "But we aren't able. We don't have such wisdom. My life hasn't been one of living for others -- not even for good. How can my life be of value to others?"

Phillip laughed again, merrily, his face full of delight that swept away any sense of strangeness. " Do you think wisdom comes instantly? It gathers as you live consciously. 'A questioning mind has more value to your world than a devoted closed one'. Isn't that one of your precepts? Therefore your deep questioning, refusing to accept anything until it proved itself to you, that has been a teaching you gave others. Each person does his work through living and through the complexity of relationship with all other lives. We have not had the luxury of isolating - or perhaps the need to isolate - our Seekers and our enlightened ones, for several generations. Our teaching is strong in the minds of the people, we are a waking generation of humanity, Joining in full consciousness. We are becoming a people of Spirit as well as of Mind. And you don't yet know even what that means."

" But, look at all we've done. Our Valley people. We haven't learned much, or we don't See much as a people." Jerry was sure he could not live to these standards, that he had not the vision to do so. "We destroy when things don't go our way. We ignore the welfare of others sometimes, look what we almost did just a few weeks ago, almost had civil war. We are a selfish people --" But Phillip was laughing and waved a hand to stop him.

"Oh, of course. You are human! Accept that. We have!" Jerry subsided after starting to speak and then falling silent."You must notice that human beings are not evil. There is evil around us, among us, we are attracted to evil and we can perform evil actions, but within, we Know. We have choice! And those few weeks ago, your people made a choice. They did NOT end in war." He was silent, letting them recognize the difference,then went on,"We have that flame of Life, of Love that cannot be completely extinguished no matter what happens to us. We are HUMAN!. We aren't simply animal. We have a responsibility. Don't ever forget that. We are the carriers of that task of rousing and nourishing consciousness in all lesser lives. You feel it in you! The Spirit that is waking like an ancient breath from within Matter. It reaches out to embrace and welcome the original, the infinite SPIRIT from which it once separated itself. We are the children of -- call it God, if you will!" He laughed then,"I've just been doing what I've said we don't do. I've been preaching. But that's what I once was, a preacher in a small church in western Ohio."

." How did you discover that there was - more. That there was Soul Consciousness, for instance?

"I did what many others did in those days. I found an itinerant Teacher who told us. She truly knew the Light, the Spirit was alive in her, there was no doubt, but she-- she lost her way a little."

He seemed so sad, they hesitated to insist on the story. But he went on. "She had read all the great books on the esoteric knowledges, studied Zen, Buddhism, Christianity, Sufism, Muslim ideas, everything until she was a walking encyclopedia of all knowledges. And then, she began to formulate her own blend of these, something many other Teachers have done and perhaps still do. And she made it easy to understand, her life was one full of love and honor, but she had not stilled her appetites, nor had she brought Balance into her being. That is why the Balancing is taught you all before any spiritual instructions are given. Because it is so vital. But she had not that teaching and -- she did what many Holy ones have done, she thought that in order to perfect herself, she must isolate herself and speak only in little discourses, hidden away from us. We never saw her interaction at daily levels, never saw how she met anger, frustrations,

THE JOURNEY

resentments, lusts, greeds, and all the other powerful forces influencing her. We couldn't learn how to balance because she did not practice that. She had become a "HOLY ONE". And so, we either worshiped and offered blind devotion, or we left." He was silent for several minutes, then, "I left." Sadly he gazed at the rough curve of a great boulder grey in the sunlight.

With a sudden smile, he looked up and said,"So there, you have it. Most people don't CHOOSE wrong, usually they just fall into it because it fits a need or hunger of their unbalanced nature. It gets them something. And that something might even be as intangible as revenge. People don't CHOOSE to be foolish either. But we sometimes are."

They looked at each other, fearful, hopeful with a deep joy underlying all their thought. Jessie nodded, "It's together,as a group that you will teach most accurately. Joined, you are able to extend consciousness far, and you will notice when you've shifted from the flow of Love to your self."

After some time, Steve asked,"Are you then mortal, you who live here?"

Immortality is a characteristic of life, not necessarily of any specific form." Then, "Look about you. Open your minds to see fully. Notice that the Earth repeats that trust over and over, again and again, there in front of your noses,. You see it if you are paying attention. This body is not immortal, neither is personality, though all each personality learns, in each lifetime, is remembered in the Soul. And the Soul is conscious of THAT which does not cease, just as you are now, in this state of Soul consciousness. Life and death are processes of LIfE."

Then another of the shining people came nearer, a woman, dark haired,and full bodied."Look - you can see that Spirit illuminates Matter. You KNOW. It is before you every day. A flower bursts from the living plant, utterly filled with beauty, fragrance rises, unseen, lifting the heart, birds sound out, for their own purpose, but for joy of life also. Children dance spontaniously, so full they cannot contain all their delight. Spirit is very practical, for Spirit is Matter at its highest point. Joy, beauty, consciousness are all ways it perpetuates its Presence."

Jane nodded, looking suddenly awakened,"Yes, why yes, there is always a power of Love that pours out from the trees. It is never absent. And beauty is the very nature of Earth."

Paul nodded,"Remember how we've always said that a quality of love seems always to rain around Annette? Everyone senses it? If some people can be so , then maybe we can learn too."

Jennifer sighed, "It is so! Yes, I see. it is what is meant by the phrase, 'Here through life,the Eternal creates Itself endlessly.'"

There was silence. They absorbed all they had received, and realized that they themselves had taken over their own teaching. All the longing through the years had brought them to this place of rebirth. Now they knew what they had sought.

"Once, humankind used mind for little more than survival, but one day, some began to dream, imagine, create thought that struggled to express meaning to life. Yet, none could have imagined what thought would bring us to. Now, we see spirit as a spark, a light to wake us, we cannot know where that power will lead us either. That's enough for me!" Tom was slowly running his hands up and down a slim young tree, feeling the rough bark, enjoying the sense of life in it.

Jessie nodded,"Look, do you see how that very matter of your bodies now shines with that inner light of SPIRIT? That should tell you something of the nature of what you enter into."

They looked at one another and they could see nothing at first, then, focussing attention, looking through the broad spectrum of non-focussed vision, they could see a radiance shining through their physical bodies. There! Like a pearl white glow, it surrounded them. They opened their minds, seeing with that sharpened inner vision. They were aware of the electric touch of these people of this Silent City. In stillness they listened, were receptive, knowledge growing like sprouted seeds in their brains, as though that seed grew downward out of that high bright Consciousness into this lower mind. Rousing and upsetting familiar assumptions, they saw the nature of selflessness and it was no longer a mystery.

The air seemed to be full of a mist, but it was the result of that non-focused vision, through which attention could focus so precisely beyond ordinary sight. Their brains were enflamed with the powerful impressions of knowledge, as if consciousness roused itself within them and nourished every cell. They knew quietly that they were on an edge of discovery and there would be no end to realization. But the power of it was overwhelming finally and they withdrew attention. Wonderingly,Paul asked,"How can we learn how to live constantly aware of such glory, such ceaselessly unfolding realization? Where do we get the strength?"

Then, like a thought echoing in their minds came the answer,"You will learn how, because you have begun and know the Journey is possible. You will continue until you join us and then you will realize where to go from here."

Paul nodded, feeling his heart overflowing so that he wept without noticing, "It is so wonderful, that glimpse. We can't hesitate. We must continue. How can we think ourselves accomplished at all. We are not any farther in knowledge than our friends at home, our only accomplishment is that we know that there is so very much more to Being Alive than we once did,and perhaps than William does." He felt a dawning humility, a recognition of how barely within the doorway they had come. There was a great stillness in the gardens, the air seemed to hang moveless, time to have stopped. It seemed as though curtains had lifted, a universe beyond revealed in new Light.

Gradually the beauty around them was effecting a kind of healing of these stretched and raw edges of mind, of heart. There was so much to Being! So much More! They wanted to be willing, to be able to respond, and to sustain that brightening consciousness. That steady pulse of energy they knew as Love, reassured and healed so their astonishment did not turn to fear. Then their attention fell to the level of ordinary senses, they smelled the fragrance of the garden,saw colors they could not name, and uncountable living beings. Such

THE JOURNEY

heightened perception in ordinary vision, delighted them. They felt shaken with this birth and cried out as ones new born.

Ned shook his head, his voice rough with feeling, "Well! There it is! They've made me see, understand even! It's really something! I know there's no point in telling anyone about the Journey. I wouldn't've believed it if someone had told me. The power of it still shakes my heart. My mind feels peeled down and so sensitive it literally hurts." He laughed at his own images."I never would have believed that either."

Tom turned to look around at them, meeting their different faces, pensive, radiant, wistful, wondering, and he nodded, then looked farther to the few people still with them, there with Jessie outside their group. "It's like something's gone," he said "I've lost something. Yes, but I've found something so great - so big - I feel lost in it. " He snorted, looked all around, aware, conscious of himself within the whole as he had never been before. "I remember hearing an old wondering Teacher tell us we must let go of ourselves. That to See we had to stop standing in front of our own eyes. He was a man who lived that way, he always was amused, always seemed to be smiling with us. But not at us. It was like warmth.

Mary spoke then, from her silent observing of everything."Yet, it's not exactly what our teachers called surrender. I think surrender is when a person no longer needs to have power over anyone at all, or anything, either. Power belongs to Spirit. For Spirit harms nothing." Her voice was pensive, shaping words around new ideas. "Here surrender is a revelation, an inclusion. That Light, that knowledge, is so vast, so immense. I am filled so full that there's no room for myself, except inside everything." She nodded, her eyes far,"And it's also as if I'd given myself away to Light." she frowned, remembering and began to quote." 'In giving myself away, I find mySelf.'" She shook her head and laughed, "The old words come back and are accurate after all. Not mysterious, but real".

Ben nodded, in his turn, understanding more as each spoke. He wondered at that, his need to hear words, to set into language these ideas and understandings. "We've lost our littleness, that's it, Tom. We've lost the old limits. and yet, they're right here in what we've found. What are we ? What are we becoming after all?" He shook his head, his eyes reaching out into the farthest distance of the sky.

Rose took his hand, conscious of her need to link physically with her mate to connect on that old familiar way. "We are weaving in and out. Identifying with old small familiar ways of being, then feeling constricted and inadequate there. I feel almost unable to contain myself,because there is so much more to me than I knew. Shifting mind - shifting attention, I stand fully able to extend and Be what I am. What we all are. Have always been, in fact. And didn't know. Didn't know!" She spoke with subdued wonder.

   Paul came then to stand closer. "We just have to learn how to keep our attention at Soul level, and then go on living as conscious human beings. If the ebb and flow of living is a conversation between Soul and self, then we might go on with the discovery. I think that might be one way." He drew Jennifer into the circle of his arm and reached to draw Steve with the other. All of them drew closer, the children in the center.

Rose said,"Jessie, don't leave us yet. I need to know what happened to my children this day. What happened to them there in that temple? "

Jessie looked at Anna and Andrew,"They can tell you."

Andrew turned to his mother, took her hand, "Mama, there was -- there was -- so much Light, and Anna and I, we felt it like a vibration at first, we both knew how it was for each other, and we stood strong together in that Light. Then it became like something loosening going on inside us, my brain felt like it was on fire, my heart ready to burst. I could feel that energy coming into my flesh, the bones and muscles, the nerves, every part of me, the littlest cell even. It was infusing my whole self, not just my physical body but astral body, mental body and every part of each. I hadn't known they had parts. It was all we could do, together, to hold steady. Oceans seemed to me to heave up through me, and they were all the emotions of my life, all roused and stirred at once. And I knew I must bring them to stillness, must calm them as if they were actually water. And we did that, Mother, we did it because, you see, the Light was filling us and was like an oil that stilled all these waters. It was the Light, Mother and we knew that that Light was Love itself." He looked away,"It changed everything I am, I think. In me that tide bore everything on its ebb and flow."

He stopped, his voice breaking, his eyes moist. He looked around, a faint fear flickered in his eyes and was gone, when a radiant smile blazed through his face." Love, Mother, is what makes Life beautiful, makes it happen in fact. That and the Will to Be. The will to take form. When that Will is strong, then the form is full of Love and then it cannot be other than beautiful. Just as no natural thing is other than beautiful. We knew that, Mother, as I've never known anything before. We knew and Anna and I wanted to offer ourselves, to be of these People who are the True Teachers. We offered our lives, both of us, together, in service and that was the ceremony of acceptance." He looked at her anxiously, as if she might not understand.

Anna nodded, leaning in against her father, one hand sliding down between her parent's clasped fingers. "The changes in us are going on, unfolding, and I haven't the words to tell you!" She was silent in her turn. Then finally, "It's just that, Mama, just what Andy says. We will be helping to make it happen, make the Light blaze up in every living thing of Earth. Just as Jessie helped it to blaze in us. But then, Mother, all of us will be doing that, you know"

Rose leaned up to kiss her tall daughter, pressed her son's hand and nodded. "What you know and are already, is more fine than I think I can ever be." Tears were in her eyes, no jealousy darkened her heart, though a fierce pride shadowed it. There was acceptance and understanding. You've gone beyond your old parents but then, you always were, weren't you?" She touched her daughter's cheek lightly, then stroked the shining hair that fell over Anna's shoulders. Her eyes were moist. She felt gratitude for the strength of Benjamin's fingers around her own. Together they tightened their hold on Anna's.

THE JOURNEY

Then they began to feel the vibration of a Joining, it came welcome, drawing them all together. They knew the golden power streaming through them, waking them further to Itself. Their minds formed the understanding for which words would no longer carry concepts. Even the two words, 'Love and Soul' were words of a narrower world, smaller, a world of Learning Centers, here they faded, meaningless. Valuable as they were, such words held only a faint shadow of the real.

Thus was the birth completed. Thus did awakenings occur in each of them. In this great cradle, this Silent City, this place of familiarity and utter strangeness, those who had traveled so long were gently brought into full companionship with those who knew and Served that Spirit they Glimpsed. And that Spirit, vast beyond comprehension, poured its benediction down into all those come to awaken Life in their fellows.

For a long time they sat together thus. Thoughts came into the silence of their minds, then drifted away. What they knew here was beyond thought, but from it's influence, thought would be created all the rest of their lives. Minds, reflecting that vast Light, loosened and woke whole sections of brain tissue never before functioning. Mind claiming and extending through its vehicle, wove itself a way. These changes were experienced by the thinking brain as Light and as mysterious Knowledge. Slowly, through the Joining which required no language, they realized the nature of Humanity. Then with that came drifting memories.

Tom wrestled with resistance, doubts, a refusal of everything that was happening -- an urge to sum it up as hysteria, to leap the walls and run screaming that hysteria out in shrieks down the mountain. But he held firm, looked with steady honesty at the recognitions and soothed himself. He saw that he could not still that ocean of emotion as wholly as the children had done. But he could bring much quiet. He saw old fears and identified them, contained them. He accepted the pain of a stretching, transforming brain, of this breathing of new birth. The others steadied and supported him, finding their own doubts reflected in his. As the heaving of his old nature subsided, as he grew steady with knowledge and acceptance, they rejoiced. He thought it was like a birthing. What he realized they did also. For they were Joined in One Mind.

Silvia stretched herself, rejoicing in this release of old limits that had seemed to her too tight . Now the full deepness of breath filled her. She thought she could extend to her full nature at last. She could consider this new life she carried with new understanding. Christopher must meet this new Earth they all had entered into, must experience this birth even before his tiny physical body was born into this world. They all felt his Reach, his confusion, the conflict in body and mind, the frustration at this so tiny vehicle in which he must live. Then they felt his wrenching free of that body-mind. It was a fine, deeply conscious Self who righted itself to stand among them. Again the Reach, the calling, and they sustained, offered him themselves, until he could reach out free from his limits.

And so he joined them here, in this garden, consciously able to know of this vibrant place of Life offering. He was there and he spoke to the Old Ones, swift mental sending that sped from mind to mind as a flash of warm light might. He turned in sudden eagerness to Touch Anna and Andrew as if they were his own. Then he turned to the others, Touching, naming, and greeting as if he had known them long. Then finally he Reached out with a strange sweet Joy to his father, Jerry.

Jerry ached with the recognition, it hurt in his throat to realize this new Touch that was his son, his unborn son. The radiant Love of this new life finally swept away all resistance. Jerry focussed and firmly Reached out to Touch and know this one who would soon be among them. The child turned at last to his mother and Joined with her like a breath of cool air, his character visible to her, knowledge of him real and she longed for that little body to be born that she might gather it into her arms.Then he retreated into his warm close physical world of the womb and slept.

Paul thought of the power that had grown among them, his recognition an affirmation. He thought,"Was this garden -- this City - another expression of that very Spirit they sought - of God Itself? Was that urgent demand rising through all of them, through so many in the Valley, coming from the necessity of life to reach to LIFE? Surely the smaller, sought the greater! That urgency to Join, was it related? Was it part of that quality called Love, the urge - the intention that responds so deeply, that brings together all things that are separated? He found his mind filled with these questions, perceiving as he had never done. And then he knew clearly that a new, finer will, a fervent steady intention, was wakened in them all.Through the action of Love and Will,Life projected itself, created through space, forming all the myriad expressions of Itself. He sat, overwhelmed with this knowledge.

But he finally realized that they had all realized with him, they were all gifted with the same knowledge. The power of knowledge reverberated through them, wresting them from old patterns, old karma, old thought and freed them to know. Clearly recognized was the thought -- the FACT that the nature of Life was Love, and consciousness is a probe of Spirit into matter to waken and purify. Thus they took their places participating in that unceasing Creation.

Ned shook himself and looked around,"How can we ever live so? Only a few days ago I was wondering and learning about the Monitors. Those who live like this - who participate in Love itself. They respond to us with a Love that I couldn't imagine. How could we be a part of that? Are we able? Is that what this Journey asks of us?"

Tom nudged him, his sense of humor still as sharp as usual. "You Ned! You can ask that? You've already found the world we knew of little interest to you, I remember you were wondering how you would keep interested in it for a life time. Well, now, look at us. We -- the rest of us -- will just have to live as Jessie lives." He was grinning and Ned gave him an indignant glance but he refused to be riled, he simply looked at Tom blankly and then finally, smiled.

"All right, old friend, I'll quit my questions . But this Garden! It fills my heart.I want to stay here!"

THE JOURNEY

Rose laughed, Silvia smiled and said,"So do we all!"

The People of the City were fading away. The Family never knew whether they went into buildings, far back into the gardens, or just faded like mist before sunlight. They simply noticed that there were fewer and fewer present. They were themselves feeling more and more 'normal'. They began to think of going home.

Rose stood up, looking around, her heart was full. She felt a tenderness, a sensitivity to everything around, to light, color fragrance that poured around them like a breeze. The soft music of the towers rose and fell. They knew that they were citizens of this City now. The thought was exciting.

Paul came to her, taking her hands, reaching to Silvia, Jennifer. Then others came and they embraced one another, feeling as if they had arrived out of a long Journey far from home. Rose felt her eyes filling, she thought the love she felt from them all would burst her heart. Silvia kissed her and Rose looked into her friend's eyes. It had been some time since they had felt this closeness of their youth. They all felt a need suddenly to cling to one another, as if all they knew would overwhelm them otherwise.

Tom was holding Cassandra's hand. She clung to him seeking reassurance, turning this way and that, to look at this wonderful City. She said, "Uncle Tom, look how the people fade. They were so bright before"

He laughed, "We saw them with Mind Sight, with that inner seeing that is able to see beyond ordinary things. Isn't that something? You and me, Cassandra, with Mind Sight!" He was grinning happily, and she laughed with him. He said,"We can still do it, sweetheart, we just have to focus you know."

The others laughed, and then they heard the People of the City laugh too. They could hear them like chimes in their minds. Then they realized a thought ,"You've waked up. Welcome to our City. Welcome! You are one with us now. This is your City too.!"

Rose said, "We can't thank you. We can only go and carry your message out to our people below."

The response came sweetly, like a gentle memory almost. "Yes, now you will go and live as you have realized here. You'll carry knowledge through your very lives through out the Valley."

Jerry walked rapidly up and down the walkways, testing himself out, releasing his taut body,"I feel as if I've gone through some madness --- found its center and rebuilt myself out of stronger stuff. I'm tired. But I'm so glad to be here, to know of your presence here." He turned to look around at the fading people who watched them.

Then Anna cried out, pointing toward the Temple. They all turned. A growing light came from the tall doors , figures seemingly made of that Light took shape and came toward them. They were more than twice as tall as themselves, radiant Beings, and the Family had to blink their eyes to adjust to seeing them. Anna said, "Who are they?" She felt fed by that Light.

The Citizen who had talked to them said,"Speak to them. You will know! Ask and it will be clear!" Anna had stepped ahead, as if this were her own task. She reached out one hand, She said, as if to herself,"Surely, these must be the HOLY ones."

Then they heard the sweetest laughter they had ever heard, coming like fragrance into their minds,"Ah! No, not yet. We are the guardians. We have come to welcome you." There was the clear sense of pride, as though parents rejoiced at a birth. A great Joy pulsed from them and the Family shivered with a shy swift denial, as if they could not possibly be worthy of this wonder.

But they said again,"Every life rising out, every life breaking from the bonds of the old limits, every life beginning the life of harmlessness and selflessness, consciously chosen, is a great and wonderful joy to us. And we welcome you into this company of those who stand in the Light."

The Family stood speechless,over whelmed by their outpouring Love, by the stern strength and Will that held them each inviolate in their path. Rose, conscious of that, quailed a little at the demand of that strength and will, of that beauty. She knew that each of them must find this will within themselves. The Lighted ones shimmered and were gone.

Jerry breathed a long sigh,"Wow, they're out there in some other dimension, even beyond this. And I thought we'd arrived, just getting here."

Jessie was there, She seemed her old self, but had a new lightness of movement, of voice and a gladness in her eyes revealed that she too knew change. "It's time. We've got a journey of return to make, Loves." Her eyes carried her smile to each face and they nodded. Her words turned them swiftly to that ordinary world below where their lives waited . They felt the pull and attraction of old familiar thoughts. They stood together to say farewell to the gardens, but there was nothing to say. They went out, moved with ease through the walls and stood on the smooth bench at the cavern entrance. Below them lay the Valley, open now to possibility. They stood there looking down. A few of the City people floated or walked among them. They felt glad for the companionship. Their path held no impediment now, they moved with mastery over their Earth through which they had struggled such a short time ago. Or was it an eternity?

They drifted across the narrow ledges with sure feet, confident balance, and began the trail down through forest and meadow. As they neared the Valley floor their hosts of the City left them. Jessie was still with them but they watched with unease, thinking she too might disappear. As the last of the others left, she settled herself firmly on the ground, and said,"I'll remain with you for a while. but among you I won't wear my old habits. Sometimes I'll be visible and sometimes not, according to your vision and my work. Soon I must leave, because I have work in many places in the short time of my life left."

What is that work Jessie? We thought you were -- were " Tom stumbled at the sudden realization of the great assumption they had all held. "We thought you were OUR Teacher". Then hastily he added. "And now I grieve that we have one another and you must always be alone."

She laughed, "Don't be chagrined. You know something of my work and it is among many. As for being alone, You have thought I was alone. But after seeing

THE JOURNEY

all those you have just seen how can you imagine anyone is alone?" She smiled at him,"There's no space nor time between us. We're always together. When we desire to be. But now, we may all work more openly among one another. Among the Valley people, maybe soon among the people of the world. You've seen that your elder brothers and sisters have already begun to join you. Those you have called Monitors. Well, these of the City also rejoice that their younger brothers and sisters are ready, more and more ready, to join them. Remember that! It's important." She looked at them with such Love that it set fire again to the love in their own hearts. "Today, I must leave you, but I'll be back soon because important events are near. I'll be as near as you are to one another, all you need to do is call."

With a gesture of embracing them all, she looked on each face briefly, with her wonderful smile. Then she turned to walk away. They watched her go, feeling a great sorrow to see her disappear down another path. At the same time, joy and resolution filled them and they went on to cross the River into Adwin. And so on the third day the Journey was done.

CHAPTER TWENTY FIVE

The Birth

  The days that followed the return to the Farm were days of adjustment at first a tendency to separate, to sit alone in Temple or private rooms, alternating with a clinging to one another. No one wanted to leave the farm. On the first day, there was little talk ,then the dam broke and for two days they could not get enough of talking, of telling each other over and over the way it had been for them. There would be intense talk, between two or three, then suddenly, a leaving, each seeking a quiet place to meditate or to think alone. They tried to assimilate all that had occurred;the new powerful thought,the swift access to Joining, the unbelievable fact of the fine network of mental connection that they knew now was spread over the Valley. But above all else, the recognitions of themselves, their true nature, exposed now and visible, the nature of all things living,Earth, Sky, and Humankind, revealed to them each day more deeply. They saw the futility of much humankind had striven for, and the utter wonder and preciousness of much else that had sometimes been given less value.

  A majority of People of the Valley saw with new vision. Together millions began to look backward to the patterns of history and see the endless repetition in human behavior, the awe-ful senselessness of political, industrial, military convictions and how each had drawn humankind willynilly into destructive patterns of suffering. They saw how people had designed and been attracted to such patterns, maintained them, fought and died for them, and they knew the needs and desires that had kept them attached to those false values. They saw the remarkable freedom from such attraction that people had begun to live by and they knew clearly that new direction must be nourished. They saw themselves,their own needs and desires, and their gradual loss of these, and that perception, both painful and full of a great promise, was the mirror through which they began to solidify a new freedom. There began a plan, not yet formed, to enter one day into a Valley wide Joining. The thought was electric.

  But at the Farm north of Adwin, those returned from the Journey went down now and then to open the door of Jessie's cottage, realizing finally her absence, sitting sometimes in the little living room, aware of her presence.

  The third evening the entire family was gathered again in the Hall. Altos folk would be leaving the next morning, Tom, Angy and Ned in the afternoon, but now, there was a quiet time together. Paul came in from a long walk in the fields, He felt refreshed, ready to go home and to begin work - the work of his life. He said," You remember the way we knew the network? The Monitors network? Probably none of us were ever truly aware of it until that trouble at Tellings field." They nodded, interested."Just now, down below, in the fields, I was focussing, really Reaching out and I think that I felt it, felt the tension and power of it there. I

THE JOURNEY

thought, if we Joined, if we reached all together, we might make contact. Conscious contact!" His eyes were flashing in excitement, he looked from one to the other."We might be part of a Valley wide communion."

There was general agreement, willingness, but he found himself searching out Anna's eyes. She seemed so - attentive, smiling with that strange, sweetly distracted smile she had had these past days. He turned to Andrew, and saw him meeting Anna's eyes. Then Andrew said,"Uncle Paul, let's do it right now. Why wait?. Let's reach to them,find out whether we can Touch, maybe even enter into the Net." Paul felt disconcerted, they seemed so matter of fact.

Paul frowned, his eyes moving from one face to another, everyone in the room watched him. Why me? he wondered. Then, shrugging, he nodded. "I can't see any reason why we shouldn't try. Maybe we'll understand all that's happened better if we can make that kind of Joining." With a wry grin he added,"Maybe we'll prove once and for all that that Journey wasn't a dream."

They focussed, Reached to one another, then when they began to know the singing balance of Joining, they gathered strength and turning from their own center, as a Joined consciousness, they Reached to the Valley network. For the first time they Reached as a family without Jessie. Then, miraculously, through the fine silvery distance, there it was, as though it was visible, a ringing net of communication, a powerful force usable and vital. It was true, it spun out from the four major Monitor Stations,built into a dense webbing reinforced by numerous Family groups all over the Valley. The number and extent of the Joined groups astonished them as they felt their own merging into the network. The power of it was astonishing. And they knew it grew each day. There was much to be learned, and they felt others discovering how to be part of that energy flow. How to be AWARE. How to Join into that communication line and support it. The experience reassured, awed, and delighted them. They were fully part of that Valley strength. This was not a telepathic sharing of ideas, but rather it was a knowing of attitude and heart knowledge,of feeling and health of the Valley. It was a sharing of relationship awareness. They would practice that Valley Joining each week, but in between times, families must practice with one another so that they would be ready for the growing power of the webbing. They returned and were separate but they felt excited by this discovery. They were ready!

They went back to their jobs, their Teaching and their Learning. Paul's air car lifted from the roof grid like a humming leaf spun upward on a gentle wind. Then later, Jerry stood watching the little figures move through the air to Adwin. He drew Silvia close against his side, put one hand on the mound within which slept their son. He said,"Honey, when will it be?"

She drew her thoughts back, slid her fingers into his hands and wriggled her body against his warmth. The wind blew a cold sharp reminder that winter was close. She turned her face slightly to rub it against his shoulder. "Soon Love, Soon!" Her voice was soft, distant and he thought she was still far away in that City." I think the Journey brought him to birth sooner than I thought. It will be soon". Suddenly she moved with a little cry, pressed closer into him and turning, wrapped her arms around his tall, dark body, burying the small, pale, shell of her face into his chest. He wrapped his long arms around her and poured to her the comforting of his love. After a bit she looked up, her face serious and tear stained."It's a new time, Jerry! I feel somehow sad and alone -- the way I did before __ then I realize all over again the wonder of knowing what -- what we all know. I will never be alone again!" She shook her head,"What a blessing." She clutched him and he felt a sigh of relief.

They stood in the bright winter sun, feeling its warmth when the wind died. Leafless trees reached smooth limbs into the blue air above them. Small shrubs rattled against the wall below them. A clump of soggy yellow Chrysanthemums bent against each other. There would be snow to cover it all soon.

Jerry nodded and spoke as if to himself,"Yes, everything is new, all the old assumptions seem - not false - but just inadequate. There is some kind of freshness to things, to people too. As if I'm seeing them for the first time, seeing so much I never noticed before. I think it'll take years to absorb, to understand it all." She watched him, smiling, and nodded.

The world seemed strange and dear. Familiar and different. They found themselves watching with fascination what they had previously stopped seeing. Rob, one of the cats, a familiar bird, or the way the hillside fell away dark with the winter growth of grasses beneath the dry rattling seed cases. Everything seemed abruptly new, sharply beautiful, astonishing, and yet -- so achingly familiar. They looked down the graceful fold of the hillside, into the stretching length of the Highway, empty of travelers in this cold season, Silvia said,"I keep noticing things, like that leaf there, the last one still hanging, so orange, so full of color and so very dry. And that grass blade, moving in the morning breeze and yet that dew drop, absolutely clear on its tip, doesn't fall. Look Jerry, " She waved one arm across the fields, beyond Adwin, misty in the morning light, where woodland and field joined and separated again along the Highway. "Looking down from here, you can see that the shadows the clouds make are only passing things. We must remember!" He smiled down at the top of her head, He thought he could smell, see, feel for the first time fully.

Jerry nodded, "I walked in the fields today, with Tom. I felt the Earth energy rising, the green energy, like an electric current. Even through my shoes I felt it and I took off my shoes and Tom thought I was nuts, but then he did too. We both knew it, that current, alive, showing us the way, revealing the life knowledge all the time. It's always been there, we just never noticed. There"s so much we just never noticed." He bent his head to meet her eyes again, "And now we know Jane's always known that Earth Touch, and didn't know what she knew."

Silvia said,"I want to know these things, I want Jane to teach me too." She turned away,"Paul says we are alive at last, that we've remembered what we are, what the Earth is. I think that's right."

Jerry drew her toward the Hall door. "Honey, you'll get chilled if you stay here long. Rose turned away from her own absorbed attention of the world beyond them. She wrapped a woolen shawl around Silvia's thin shoulders and smiled at them. "D'you notice? We seem to need to touch each other a lot lately. As though we need reassurance, to remind ourselves. I feel as if I've come back from a far place. There doesn't seem to be any time when someone isn't in the Temple!" She laughed, "But then, it's no surprise. So much has happened."

Together they stood, comforted. Then like a thin whisp of calling, a whistle in the mind, there was a shy Touch. Together they turned to Send, finding that Reach from Jane trying out her skill, affirming her new presence among them. Jerry nodded and sighed,"It's true Sis, we're here for each other." He drew her into his embrace with Silvia, and said,"We've got lots to do. And Silvia,my Love,we're going to have that little fellow out here among us soon and we want to be ready." Silvia laughed, little else was on his mind lately.

Rose nodded,"It's true, little Pearl. We all have to be here for his birth. We have to know exactly when so we can let everyone know. Do we need to call a Healer to tell us exactly?"

Silvia grimaced, shaking her head,"I don't think so. Finally I've accepted that a lot of you are aware of more than I am. Cassie's been communicating with him. Of all things! The impertinence!" Then she smiled, "But then, she can! And the twins too. They know each other already.I'm jealous. I think the rest of you know him too."

Rose looked apologetic,"We don't want to interfere, or be impertinent, Love." Her dark face radiated concern, worry, and Silvia pressed the hand she held clasped in her own.

"Don't worry, Rosy! Don't worry! I got over it. Poor Cassie. I think I scared her at first. But afterward I told her I was glad he had such a family. That he was not coming into a strange world. I don't resent it. Especially now that I've found I can reach him too. My own little son. Here in my body. We are --." She shook her head, a shy happiness filled her eyes and softened her face."When I finally Reached to him - I could see we aren't at all apart. I feel him with my mind,know something of his thought and feelings. He is so THERE for me now." She laughed this time, You'll see! It's new to me, this Joining, but I am doing it a little. On my own. And it's wonderful. It's not like mind reading, the way I thought, at all. It's just being WITH, being with others in a very deep and total way."

Jerry grinnned,"Honey, I know you're with him, I've felt you too,you know. So we both know that he's about ready to come out of there,.."

Silvia nodded, absently her thoughts searching,listening. Rose said,"Cassandra wants to do her birth room training with you and Christopher. She's only attended once before and she needs more experience. She'll be with us anyway so its a perfect time. Anna and Andrew are old pro's already, so they'll help prepare. We won't lack for help." She nodded, deciding. "It's partly because they can all communicate with him already that they can be so much help, you know." She saw Cassandra running across the garden with Rob,playing again, back to her old self. She called out and when the little girl came they told her she was to help. Cassandra put her hands on the mound in which her little brother lay, her face radiant, looking up at Silvia,"He's ready ,Sil. He does know."

THE PEOPLE OF THE VALLEY

Silvia nodded, "I know that Sweetheart.I do know. And you're right, he's ready. Just now he gave me a jab, like he wants us to hurry." They all went into the Hall, where the warmth stopped Silvia's shivers'.She said, "We might as well plan for this week then. It's time."

Jerry said," We'll notify the Healers and the rest of the Family." It was with a sense of celebration that they went in to breakfast.

For the next three days everyone was involved in the preparations. The birthing room had to be made ready, the birthing bed-chair, and the hot teas that would help Silvia relax. Already she was practicing the birthing skills every young girl learned. The children sang the birthing songs in the garden to have them letter perfect. For the first time on this Farm a child would be born consciously participating in his own birth.

It was the evening before the time of birth that Jessie arrived. She came up the path quietly, slowly enjoying the experience of coming home again. She entered among the trees and gardens, stood looking around at the changes that winter had brought . Gardens were beautiful in their naked emptyness too, she thought. Possibility stored in them like a restrained power. The sky was mottled with great fast moving clouds, the sun shone intermmittently. She glanced back at the Valley, beyond Adwin, then slowly let her eyes sweep the eastern cliffs until they rested on the white stone of the City. She felt the connection as acutely as she would have a click of a computer key. She frowned, sustaining the power of it and then, turning, felt it break. She watched the sun glisten in the pine needles above her own little cottage. It would be empty now, she thought, but then, it would be ready for Christopher when he was old enough.

The gentle sadness of leaving things, of being so soon gone away from this life, stirred in her heart. She shrugged, "Nevertheless, it is time. But first I want to enjoy that new life coming to us. This little one, born of Earth and heaven." She smiled at her image. She turned to go into the Hall but before she reached it Rob and his mate came bounding from the garden to wriggle and lift one paw and then the other toward her. They did not touch,their manners were far to good. But they loved this old lady and were excited to see her. Rob barked once in excitement and she knelt to rub his head. The cat called to her, standing balanced on a slim branch of the walnut tree. She balanced,then leaped into Jessie's arms. Jessie laughed, delighted at their joy.

She felt Rose's Touch, then surprisingly, Silvia, tentative, a little awkward, but Jessie reached through, clearing the blur, surrounding her with delight. Rose was at the door, opening it. "Jessie, Jessie! We're so glad you're here." She drew Jessie into her arms and Silvia was there, hugging and crying. Why,she didn't know, but she had wanted so much for Jessie to come.She cried out,"How did you sneak upon us this way. I was listening, I had planned to meet you part way. I didn't know you were here!"

Jessie laughed,"Surely you don't imagine I always let my presence be known. Perhaps that's one more skill I must teach you. How to shrink into your own Silence. Knowing how to Reach, includes knowing how NOT to Reach." She

THE JOURNEY

smiled at Rose's consternation."It's not so hard, Dear. You already know how,it's just in noticing that you do."

They went in together to the dining room and gradually everyone of the Family came and they ate together, drank hot drinks, warmed each other with reassurance. After a while, they went out to the deck where the winter sun was high, lay like a thin warmth in the air. The light clothed the world in a glow of rose and gold. It had never seemed so beautiful to Silvia watching, looking out at the fields and forests. For some time they stood, intimately aware of one another, their trust. However, there was a difference. Jessie was not the small quiet woman she had seemed. She no longer restrained her power, her presence before them. She seemed so familiar, but also she seemed a stranger. Would they ever know her? Her Touch was a fiery tenderness, brief and infrequent. They must learn how to be in such company. She was there,-- sure, warm, loving, but at the same time,she was other.

Cassandra sat at Jessie's feet, her head leaning on her knees, while Anna sat on a low stool beside her. The fragrance of the day was deep and held the bitter sadness that comes in early winter.

Jessie looked from one to the other and then said,"Perhaps you already know that I'll be leaving soon. Leaving this body. Letting it die. There is a balance there, you know. That this old body dies just as Christopher's new one is born. I'll wait for that birth,and a little time to be with all of you. I've taken leave of all the others with whom I work. So now, there is nothing else left to do." She was silent, listening to their responses, unspoken, but clear. She knew there must be sadness and she wanted to demonstrate her gladness too.

"You know, this is a great joy for me, the leaving, that is. Not that I don't feel sorrow, always there is a sorrow at parting, but it is a breath that blows off and away. Mostly, I am eager, filled with Joy. This body has become a burden to me, it cannot function well anymore. It has served well, but what I must do now, is too much for it. It has narrowed itself for dying for some time and I have held it on. My leaving is a simple natural thing as the leaves falling from a tree is natural and neither do they damage the tree, but make it ready for the new growth and life of spring."

There was silence that encompassed the wave of grief, mild shock, for they had not expected this. These feelings faded swiftly for those who were most aware of how temporary was their loss. But for others, the loss of this person, who had become so important to them, was very real. It knotted the stomach, felt like a thorn in the heart, that loss. The fact of her dying came harshly and Jane looked around, offended at the silence. She said,"Jessie, I wish -- , it's been such a short time. We know you and love you as one of us and we need your help." Tears filled her eyes, stung behind the lids as she held them from freely falling. "I'll miss you terribly."

Jessie shook her head, "Stop and realize! You know you don't need to miss me!" Jane looked startled. "You know, anyone of you can Reach through, can call me with an act of will, a shift of mental state. You Reach through into that subtle

astral world where I'll be -- at least for a little while."
Jane's eyes were wide with questions, puzzlement."Oh, No! Jessie, I can't. I don't know how to do that!"
Jessie was patient,"Jane you've just seen your resistance to growth proven a mistake. Don't make the same one again."
Jane looked at the others, then shook her head, frowning. Then precisely focussing, she Reached, and with grateful relief, JOINED. She felt the edges of this familiar physical dimension , then was aware that it pressed against another subtler realm, a larger inclusive universe, was in fact within it. She shrank back, then, because she felt the children insisting, drawing her on, she sustained awareness.

She felt their excited thought,"Look Jane. Look, we can move through together, it just a matter of pushing on out, farther into the Astral universe. Beyond it are others, even more subtle, but they are so far, this Astrral is so close. Watch!" Then it was as though a veil fell in the room, a shimmering of light filled the air, a stillness hung. Jane let her vision adjust, knowing her mind saw through the old limits of vision. She could not see through with her eyes, but the vision was no less clear. And then, as though an adjustment occurred in her brain, her eyes worked for her. She looked around, awed, silent and within a silence that she could not penetrate. There were people there in this same space with them that she had never seen. They were talking to one another as if they felt right at home, but were disinterested in this Family Gather. Then they turned, as if their attention had been drawn to her. They caught her eye and smiled at her, pleased and amused. She caught her breath.

Then Jane saw an amazing thing. People stood beside Jessie,people they had not seen until now. They had obviously accompanied her. Friends of long standing but ones who lived no longer in bodies. It startled her so she erected her barrier instantly. Perception clouded. Then, paying attention, she shied at the obvious existence of a barrier, but vision had to clear so that she could see again. She knew she could not speak to, nor touch, anyone there. She didn't know why. It was as if a window had appeared, shades up, but the glass in it still intact. With a long sigh, she nodded and instantly let those shades fall. The scene ceased to be for her. Only the familiar family members were in the room. She said aloud,"O.K. Jessie. I see and I accept that. I don't know whether I will do it, but I see that with help I COULD do it. That is at least comforting. It's a matter of shifting vision - inner vision, isn't it?" She was silent, thinking,"It's a shift of attention,in fact."

Jessie nodded, Jane looked around again, met Steve's sympathetic eyes, She felt a sharp longing to be back in the old familiar days, when things like this were not known about. Jessie felt the longing and smiled. But Jane was aware of its nature and saw that same longing ebb away like a wave that rose then broke against Jessie's steady strength. Steve said, "Well, that's all well and good, but it's your physical self that I'll miss, the sight of you, the going and coming, the talking and the company in our daily lives." He frowned, going to take her hand

and holding it in his own, looked down at the small,brown,wrinkled flesh. "It's this, the human physical touch that I'll miss too."

She nodded,"It's true,Steve, that's still true for us all." And they were silent, honoring that loss. After some minutes, Jessie shrugged and spoke softly.

"Well now, we've settled that. So now, perhaps it's right to prepare for the birth. It's obvious to you that birth and death aren't really much different. Depends on which side you're on." She gestured outward,"Those others waiting my arrival there, are much like us here, waiting this child's arrival". She laughed, "Except that I've got the advantage. I can go there without having to live in a baby's body and take time growing up."

The silence that followed that statement was broken by a collective sigh. Amused by their varied feelings and this sudden united sigh, Ben laughed outright. Cassandra said with a gentle seriousness no one had heard in her before, "When will you leave, Jessie? I want to prepare some things and I need to know."

Anna shook her head, then nodded,"You're right, Jessie. It couldn't have been kept secret, could it? I know how to answer you Cassandra. She'll leave us just a week after our brother is born."

Cassandra nodded and smiled softly,"Oh, yes, our baby! He'll be here tomorrow, and for Jessie we have seven days."

Silvia frowned at the thought of her baby being 'our' baby, and then relaxed with a wry smile. Surely he was, they all knew him already. He was so important to them all. For a moment a strange resentment circled around her, fear that her child would not be hers alone, hers and Jerry's. But that fear, that resentment, drifted away like a mist confronted by sunlight. She wanted him to have this full and whole family.

Rose said,"Remember, Christopher DOES have to live in a baby's body. The only way he can endure that is to be not completely in that body much of the time these early days. He will not be there for your Reach. Sometimes there will not be anything more than a helpless and needful baby. For that body must be allowed to grow and begin developing some skills for living enough to make life bearable for Christopher." The others nodded.

Silvia was paying attention to the mixture of feelings she had to all this. And she felt Jessie's demand, for steady holding of attention, a gathering of strength. Sure it was sometimes a painful stretch.It was relentless too, and would continue to be. Then she withdrew, felt herself leave them all. Hold separate! She began to realize the nature of solitude, the nature of that utter presence of herself in Silence. She had drawn away, separate, defined only as herself. She knew that self as clearly as if a four dimensional mirror had brought it into focus. She saw the inner worlds of herself and knew they far surpassed her small outer self. As yet her mind was a country little traveled. There were depths she had no name for yet. There was power available, vision that enabled, and she realized all over again that she could CHOOSE.

She could SEE the rightness of their mutual connectedness. The miracle of it.

THE PEOPLE OF THE VALLEY

It enlarged each of them, loosed limits and gave Vision. She knew clearly that she wanted to be a part of that Vision.

Jessie glanced around at them, they seemed to her wonderfully responsive." There's one thing I'd like to ask. Can you tell me what's to be done? Where do we go from here?"

Benjamin nodded,"It's been in my mind. I think we all know - It's what our lives have been about. There's only one thing to do - to give everything we are to the Valley!"

"To the whole world, to every living thing." Jerry spoke slowly.

Anna was nodding, and she leaned into her mother as she said, with an authority new to her,"To every living thing, Uncle Jerry. Yes, to every living thing. It's the Knowing -- we see a new way of being human, of running our world, of being with Earth. It seems obvious to me now. I can't imagine how we missed it before."

Steve murmured aloud the old Learning Center Maxim,"To Serve and to Learn in harmony with all Life" Yes, that's what it is isn't it? And that was just a phrase to me before."

Jessie nodded,"I feel grateful to you. You've put an old lady's heart at rest. I needed to hear it said, spoken in the old way, though I sense it constantly now in you. I know that you'll not let the power of that knowledge fade. It's born in your flesh, your hearts and your minds. Every part of you speaks of it.

Cassandra turned to her father, leaned on his chair, she said,"Daddy, since we got home I feel different. Things aren't the same. I don't know exactly where I am now with some of my old friends, and yet, other friends, look at me and I feel welcomed."

Steve sat up, alarmed, shedding his objectivity. Even as he started to speak, he saw the loss and grinned, he closed his eyes. Cassandra watched him puzzled. Steve drew from himself a new balance and turned to her,"Honey, you're playing with your friends just as you used to, aren't you? Yesterday when I saw you out there in the field, you all seemed the same."

"I know, Daddy, I know. It's O.K. It's just different" Then she bent her head. " Maybe I do know what's different. Some of them have taken that Journey too. Some of them, and we link up, sometimes, even when we didn't intend to. But some can't do that. We can't find them with us." She sighed, as if there were more to understand. Then she leaned back into his lap, and snuggled down in his arms. He nuzzled her head with his chin and realized that it wasn't as easy to do as it had been a year ago. He laughed, thinking of how fast she grew.

Jessie nodded, It's true! that's the task for everyone. To learn how to meet the difference, how to relate to those whose bodies and minds are not able to realize, to hold that power. You know that every person has the flame of Life in them. But they might not always be awake to it."

Silvia snorted,"Oh, dear. What I've learned in these past months is enough for me for my lifetime,I think! And yet, I want to go ahead too. There has to be understanding. Things have changed. One hour I feel no different, as if it's all as it was, and then suddenly,I look around and I know I have never seen the world, the Earth, anything as I do now. Either I've changed drastically, or the universe itself has changed. It's easier to believe the change is in me."

Jane spoke slowly with a new confidence, her reticence faded. "It's as though there is an energy in me that informs my mind, informs me as though thought is a medium that can be shaped, inpressed with a new possibility. I know what I didn't even imagine. Things have changed, surely, none of us can doubt that. And yet, it's as though I always knew but didn't admit." She was silent, taking in her own thoughts.

Ned, nodded, reaching for her hand, his great black hand totally enclosed her slim long one. "Me too, I guess it's all of us - shaken up, you know. Me, I feel shattered. Broken a litle inside. the pain of it is a surprise, but I can't resist the pull, the pull to See, to Know again. Actually, I don't want to resist, I really WANT to know. It's the same as you all say, the whole universe seems different and I know its me whose different. But old habits die hard." He absently slid his hand up Jane's arm as if testing the skin.

Silvia moved a little closer to Jerry, his brown arm twined with her pale one. She sat curled into his side,their hands clasped as if she did not want to let him get far away. "It's scary, the whole thing. It hurts to Reach, to respond to the Touch. To feel you all there - so - so - present.But then, it's the most exciting thing too, full,of wonder, full of being part of something very fine. I know what you mean Jane when you speak of something that 'informs, a second Self. It's as if a greater part of me is available finally. A part with talents, knowledges and consciousness that I've never known. I experience this and it's REAL. I feel fragile against this strange great strength that is actually mySelf. I can finally admit what I am."

They were silent, letting their thoughts settle. The day grew a little later and the time together was precious. The time seemed to stop. They were aware of those moments as if they had no end. But finally Andrew stood, and said,"Well, let's finish getting ready for our baby."

Silvia said, "Wait a minute. Whose baby?" Then her frown cleared and she laughed, a sharp pain breaking in her heart, a shard of possessiveness that cut and then fell away, leaving a small scar. Finally she nodded, " All right, it is 'our' child. He is being born among people who will know what it is to be so alive! He will never suffer what we have. He'll grow up without denial of his inner life. He will be Soul Conscious from birth. He'll grow up accepting whatever Talents he may have and feeling no fear of them." She looked around,"That, in itself, is miraculous. Wonderful!"

Jessie said, "It is! The life of greater consciousness includes those deeper and new senses. They accompany growth and the presence of the energy of Love. But they are focussed through that energy called Will. Together they tranform our human natures. You can see that?" She looked at them. "We become more fully human."

Jessie was serious, "There is danger, always has been, that people don't distinguish a crucial difference. They confuse themselves. Imagine as egos that they are 'holy' perhaps, and don't listen for that deep informing wisdom. Exactly what Silvia and Jane spoke of. Soul INFORMS if you listen. But if we don't, we have justification for selfish actions, harmful thoughts. Soul is selfless, harmless. Personal self is not. You must always remember the difference. Until -- until you identify so utterly in Soul Consciousness that selflessness is normal." She looked apologetic, "I didn't mean to give a Teaching but there's so much, and I'm going soon ."

Cassandra took her father's great hand in her two small ones and drew it to her chest, cradling it there. "Jessie, it's just the thing we kids have called the 'knowing'. We've known about it, but we didn't call it 'Soul". A name does help, doesn't it?"

"It does help us. Our personal minds seems to need that."

Anna glanced at Andrew and he nodded,"Jessie, it's true. We did know that if we were still enough, the 'knowledge' would come. If we waited, listened, we would begn to See. So then personal benefit wasn't in it." She looked around, wanting to make herself understood. "We knew that! And we were only kids."

Rose smiled, wondering what she thought she was now. "You did have a protection. I always thought so. You knew how personal selfishness could twist what you realized."

With an quick grimace, Andrew nodded, "Look how obviously it happened to me. I'll never forget."

Rose nodded at him and then sighed,"And Christopher will be as aware as any of you. He'll know right from birth and we won't handicap him as we did you three."

Jerry sighed, pulling himself from his thought,"Jessie, it's still a danger. How DO we know how to distinguish between inner knowing, true perception and some personal idea we want to convince ourselves of. Humankind has spent centuries destroying itself because of notions called Holy!"

Andrew coughed,"I don't think that danger will ever end, until, maybe we're much farther along. As long as we're human, have egos at all, we'll make the mistakes. We are aware now though. We can See." He hesitated, looked down and then firmly went on, "When I followed Steel I knew, I did distinguish! But I refused, denied my Self as though I had never recognized It." He hadn't spoken of those events before Telling's field. His voice faltered,"I convinced myself that what I wanted was true. What can we do?"

No one spoke. Finally Benjamin said, "Maybe it's just that, Son. You were so sure you refused to question. But you wanted Steel to be right. You didn't know your own needs, wants. Being willing to question, to doubt always, to listen to all of us together when we Join and then listen to that deep Self.Really listen in Silence. I think we can distinguish."

"But Dad, it didn't help that I could! It was as though something in me wanted something so much that it could overpower everything else I am!" His voice was anguished, he had to put into words that thing that had happened. Had

THE JOURNEY

possessed him." He stared at them, wanting help.

Anna shook her head, "Wait, Andy, remember, it is yourself, not some devil who haunts you, or some evil power that can bend you to its will. It is yourself! And the little self is devious."

He was angry, his face full of dispair,"Oh course, Annie, I know, I know. I didn't sustain vision, sustain Self consciousness. I fell down into the miasma of animal blindness.I let that happen even when I knew better!" He was quiet, the dispair dissolving from his features and from his heart, he looked at them from clear eyes, nodding slowly,"It's something I'll never forget, that I am able to destroy everything I love. That I carry my own hell within me. And that I also have choice." Nodding slowly again, he was looking far into distance,"I have to practice making that choice anew every day, -- " he sighed, a small smile beginning, "Maybe every hour. So, now I know the danger, I can keep watch on myself." He glanced around,his eyes dropped then met theirs firmly,"And I can ask for help."

Anna was beside him, her hand lightly resting on his arm, "She says it's a surrender that gives Soul a way to function in our lives. All we have to do is make a choice and wait." She sighed, knowing it was not easy," Then surely we'll gradually be Soul conscious more than self conscious and we won't even have to make a choice. It'll be a given. We won't fool ourselves if we listen, pay attention, like Daddy says." She looked off across the distance, "What we have now to do is to check. Is it harmless? Is it selfless? Is it an act of Love?" Her voice faded.

Andrew looked at her sadly,"I managed to ask those questions and answered them every time with a rational that sounded like a 'yes' to me. I've heard Mama say that we can reason a way to justify anything we want. We have to simply lift our awareness and then, See. If Love is functioning through us, we don't have any question. For me it wasn't but I pretended it was. How do we distinguish? I say it's through mutual Joining, sharing perception with one another. It's the one thing I didn't do. Together we could have lifted into Soul perception,out of my self perception and I would have KNOWN. It's the only way that'll work.

Jerry broke the quiet,"Yes, to always check ourselves out, in Silence. To ask those questions everytime we think we know. Finally we know we can trust one another to help.IF we have courage to ask."

The evening was coming, the air was growing cold. The Hall was warm, but outside the cold seemed to shrivel the few dried leaves still clinging to branches. They stood comforted by the good warmth. The Solar batteries had absorbed enough energy through the day to maintain themselves for an indefinite time. If the gathering clouds kept the sun away tomorrow,the rooms would still be as warm. That thought was a comfort when the wind blew so fiercely. Silvia looked out to the deck, stood suddenly and ran to the window. Along the trail coming from the northern hills, came a brown and white goat. She walked slowly, her big belly swinging from side to side. She was full, laden with kids. She had come in to bear them in the protection of the home barn. Behind her trailed several other goats. Silvia cried out in joy. "Look, Anath is coming in. She's really returning. I was afraid she might not." She turned to them, her joy delighted them.

In the morning Silvia was up and down at the barn, finding that Anath had given birth already and had three shiny curly coated kids. She gave them all good hay, fresh grain and saw that the water trough was full. She played with them, letting the tiny kids leap into her lap. laughing at them. And finally, feeling so deeply conscious that this day her son would be born, she went back to the Hall. She had spent half an hour in the Temple just after dressing, and now, she felt ready. She sat, sipping hot tea and grinning, as if she held a great wonderful secret.

Rose came to her,"Silvia, the room is ready, Jessie is there now. Jerry is finishing the morning cleanup in the kitchen and the children are all cleaned, sterilized and waiting. It looks as though everyone is eager - and here you are, sipping tea as calmly as though you'd done this everyday."

Silvia laughed, and slid one hand across her belly, "I can feel the pull beginning, he's pushing against me. It's true, already therre's been some pretty hard waves. I'll just about finish this tea. You know, I've helped at a lot of births, Rosy, your babys included, and so I know." But Rose saw the tension in her face. Suddenly she tensed and a great heave of painful pressure flooded through her lower body. She stood up, took Rose's hand and said,"Yes, let's get in there. I'm going to have a baby."

As they walked to the room, she slid an arm around Rose's waist, leaned her head against her shoulder, "I'm so glad to be here, in this Family. It's -- the best world I can think of to be born into." Jerry came hurrying to them, and slid an arm around her shoulders. He laid one hand on her belly,and felt the upheaval there.

"It's sure time, Love". They all laughed, tears coming to their eyes, "Look, he's insistent. We'd better get you into the chair. The mats and birth bath were set out. The chair leaned in position, ready to be adjusted as Silvia needed. The Health Center Air car landed on the Hall roof. Two middle aged women followed by two young boys, new ones, getting their first midwife training, walked down the stairs.

Jessie had begun the music, special music designed to greet the newcomer. the lights were so dim Silvia could make out only the large objects and she could see Jessie's figure as she readied some padding beside the birth basins. With no hesitation Silvia stripped off her clothes, and Jessie handed her a soft specially decorated gown. Silvia saw her own name embroidered in tiny stitches around the collar. On the front was printed the large blue design that was Silvia's personal symbol, given her shortly after her own birth. the light warm garment was like vestment for ceremony. The children came and Jerry appeared, wearing his own gown, with his own symbol.

The contractions increased, she grunted and then relaxed, began the rhythmic push and release that she had been taught and had taught others. The music kept tempo, Then gradually increased as the contractions increased. Silvia felt sweat run down her face and neck. She gripped Jerry's hand on one side, Rose's on the other. She looked up at them, found their faces intent, their effort

THE JOURNEY

almost as steady as her own. She felt the music echo her breathing, supporting her effort. She bent to her task, causing the chair to shift and pull into a straighter position so she could have full access to her own body muscles. Her body pressed within itself to expell this foriegn object. The movement of the baby in its tiny sea, was a rising and falling, a disturbing that could have been frightening had not he been aware of the cradling of their minds reassuring him, comforting him in this utter destruction of his familiar safe place. There was a short time when everything seemed to halt, to wait.

Suddenly the sea waters spilled out and he was sunk there against hot cushioning flesh, no longer against that utterly responsive water. The rhythm of the waves to move him toward that unknown became stronger and he felt the tightening, the closing of space around him, the caress of infinitely soft flesh. The waves for Silvia increased to a crescendo , pain and pressure,release, alternating. The time between each wave decreased gradually. She thought hours had passed. The baby was accepting,,unresistant and Silvia focussed her body's effort to smoothly, steadily push this object out. She worked at it, keeping a rhythm to her breathing. Jerry's hand was at her back,he was breathing with her. She gasped, in great grunts, she cried out,then, giving attention to her whole body, she loosened tight places, let herself focus, slid her attention around the babies slick little body and finally, the head was out, visible, fine dark hair, knowing the air of the Earth for the first time.

Silvia gasped and cried out, pushing hard, eager now, feeling the success. Knowing of the Minds supporting her and her child. She felt cradled,even as the baby was ,in that mind strength. With a smooth sliding motion, pressed on by the strong muscles behind him, the little body slid out,softly down into the hands of his mother and Jessie. They swept the clinging mucous away, lifted him, cleared his mouth and throat and he caught breath with a loud cry. He opened his eyes, clearly he looked at the faces, those strange moving objects around him. They brought him up to lie against his mother's belly, and the beat of her heart, familiar, comforting, reassured him. He felt the strange roughness of human fingers sliding against his skin, caressing and gentle. The fluids of his birth made an oil to insulate his mothers touch and she made tender little cries that he heard and remembered because they were not different from her voice during those long months in that dark safety.

He was bathed, and he cried a little, Jerry leaned close, touched him, and their eyes met. Jessie, lifted him, brought him to be laid on Silvia's warm stomach. He felt the touch of her, his mother, and he knew her. He opened his eyes again. The strange light, revealed things. Faces, and he heard voices, and they were familiar. He began to notice, but mostly he wanted to sleep, to cling and sleep. The birth chair was smoothly drawn back and brought to a resting position. Silvia was tired but full of Joy. She was exhilarated and wanted to sing out but she was too tired and so she just smiled. Slowly, softly she began to sing the birth song. Familiar to every person over twelve in the Valley. She chanted the old familiar words that she had sung to so many mothers in her young life.

The Healers stood at the side, watching, ready but not interfering. Silvia heaved out the after birth and relaxed, finally done.

Soon the Healers cut the umbilical cord, finished the final washing and dressed the baby. They had examined the baby rapidly, mentally focussed into his flesh, his bones and nerves so that they knew his condition well. He was healthy. They began bathing Silvia and they moved her to the small bed at the side of the room. The birthing chair was folded and set aside. The room was clean and fresh. The two boys and Cassandra moved back and forth, handing towels, removing the soaked clothes that would be taken and completely cleaned for the next baby of this family. Then they brought the fresh sleeping robe.They were doing what they had been taught. And they too, smiled and were delighted at this beautiful small child.

Then, everyone in the room began to sing the birthing song. Silvia realized that all the Family had come. William too. She saw him at the back, trying to catch her eye and she smiled, blowing him a kiss, so deeply glad that he was there. He was in the usual white birth room robe, looking strangely soft, gentler. She thought that Jessie had been right. The Builders had taught them so much. They had seen their various urges to possess, demand to keep, the fury to control, to run the world their own way, disregarding the rhythmway of Life. And these had been met and transcended. Could their combined love for William heal the gap between them? There were so many families with one or two members who were mind blind. There were those who had formed no Family. The thought came to her, lying there weary with the task she had just finished, stroking her new baby softly with her finger tips, that Adwin itself must learn how to Join, to include every single person in a deep Joining. Conscious or not.

She was surprised that she was thinking these things at this moment. But she looked down at her baby, given back to her, after others had passed him around, had touched and looked and wrapped him in warm, very soft blankets. She knew that he was truly there with her, his eyes met hers, he smiled. She was aware that the whole family was in Touch, these ideas were shared. They too were aware of William and of Joy at his presence. The children too, Rachel and Steve, and Tom's children and both his mates, all there today. Annette, looking pensive and sad, but smiling. All were here. Life suddenly seemed wonderful to her. She listened now as the others sang the song a second time, their harmony like a caress around her.

  Welcome - Welcome, little one, little One!
 We greet you with our hearts full.
  You have come to join us,,to join us
 On our Earth and under Sky.
  Christopher, our newest brother,
 Christopher, our blessed son,
  Christopher, will be among us,
 We rejoice that you have come!

THE JOURNEY

They had swaddled him in soft clothes and handed him to Silvia to cuddle down between her arms. Cassandra and Anna brought the tiny robe on which was the emblem that was a combination of his mothers and fathers emblems, and he would wear it until he had an emblem of his own. Then the song rose louder and stronger. Silvia snuggled down into the soft pillows, ready to rest, to sleep. She wanted to look at him, to touch and feel his tiny wonderful presence. The baby turned his head, opened his eyes wide and looked around, met his mother's gaze, then that of the others. He was clearly aware of them. His eyes were blue, deep, clear blue. The kind of blue that would hold. So large and bright and luminous they seemed themselves to speak. William reached to touch one finger to the tiny hand and it wrapped around that finger and held him there.

Then the baby smiled and everyone laughed. They stood silent, unable to leave, and then when they saw both Christopher's and Silvia's eyelids closing, they began to leave.

It was a grey day, the storm that had blown in the evening before, had pounded on the roofs all night, the air was wet and cold still, though the rain was intermittent now and the sun broke through in brilliant light. Rose went into the main Hall. A sense of holiday, of celebration filled the house. Andrew and Jennifer had gone upstairs to the music room and were there playing together new music Andrew was writing. He wanted Jennifer's help. Anna joined them with her flute. They wove a new melody together, creating a song for Christopher. Tom and Ned and Rose and Angy were in the Communication room of the Hall. They began sending bright, messages, designed with flowers entwined around a baby, and other foolishness, to every friend and relative. Benjamin sat with Steve before the little fire and silently drew on his pipe, at peace, thinking of all that had happened. None of the three spoke. Mary and Cassandra and Steve could be heard in the kitchen planning a special celebration dinner. It was time to think, to meditate on all that was, had been and would be. The Valley had weathered the storm, both that of humanity and of the elements. She was giving birth to a new humanity and the evidence for that was fast growing.

Jessie sat in the Hall, near a small window, seeing the movement around her, hearing the low talk, that broke now and then from those at the fire, hearing the music upstairs, and so very aware of the peace that had settled on this land. She felt a shiver of excitement and a thin thread of fear. Would they be able to walk into that new world they were creating? Would those new people, being born even now here and there throughout the Valley, even as Christopher was, be able to meet all that this new life would bring? She smiled, this intermediate generation had met what it had had to, and she thought they had not done too badly.

CHAPTER TWENTY SIX

Jessie--an end and a beginning

In the morning of the fifth day after Christopher's birth Silvia was back in her own cottage with Jerry. Christopher was settled in the trundle bed beside their own. She woke several times in the night to draw him to her to nurse. On this morning she still slept, catching up for those interruptions, her shining black hair a web beneath her head and across the white pillow. Jerry stood, half dressed, watching her, his face full of the tenderness he felt when he thought about the fact that she had chosen him as Mate. "I can't believe how it's worked out, we're together and we've got our son." He let his eyes slide to the sleeping baby. "There's no doubt that your mama's my Mate, and you little son, are our first achievement together."

The baby stirred, opened those incredible blue eyes and stared steadily at his father. Jerry did not Reach, he waited to find out what his son would do. Then with a start, he knew clearly the demand for cleaning, an image of uncomfortable wetness so sharp Jerry felt it himself. He laughed, "Hey., wait, I hear you, Son!" But his astonishment held him motionless.

Such a clear image, demand, recognition of him as father, from that tiny body? Christopher opened his mouth and uttered a loud cry. His eyes still on his father's face. Jerry leaped forward to pick him up, he must not wake Silvia. "I hear you little Son, I hear you! I'll have you fixed in a jiffy. I just was too startled to move." He began busily changing the wet diapers and clucking, he murmured comments, endearments, but he did not Reach. Then, realizing that, he did.

He had tried to Reach several times since the birth, and had found only a vague sense of a life present there. But there was no doubt there was someone there now. Now, the Touch that met his was not that of a speechless child. He felt the strange quality of 'idea'then laughter,this was a joke. His son was laughing at him. The baby reached out his arms and Jerry picked him up. He smiled happily into the little face, tuning his mind to this one. Christopher's eyes moved around the room, and Jerry saw an expression of amazement at all the objects. Saw his pleasure at the color and shapes. The blue eyes flickered up to his own face a moment and then, some of the light in them dimmed, and he was only a very small baby, needing again to sleep.

Silvia woke, her eyes on the two of them, a smile on her lips, she watched. He turned to her. "Oh, my Dearest, it's such a joy, our Son. I feel so happy, so proud." She nodded faintly and he went on, "When Rose had the twins, they were so wonderful, I loved them right away and it was a miracle to me even then. But this --- this moment with our child seems the most complete I've ever known". Then with a frown, "But, d'you know what he just did? He ASKED me to change him, showed me VERY graphically that he was wet! Silvia, I didn't expect that!"

THE JOURNEY

Silvia nodded, sat up and reached out her arms for the baby, and he brought Christopher to place him in her arms to nurse again. "My Darling, he's done that with me too. But some times he doesn't. He just cries until I find out he's wet. But Jessie says that it'll be like that for a while. That the total committment and entrance into this body will not happen for some months. That he'll be intermittently present. After all,she said the great Soul that has chosen us as parents might find it a little cramped to fit in this tiny, helpless body all the time." She laughed,but he heard the note of unease that the knowledge had given her. They were silent for minutes, watching the nursing child, so safe,so very simply a child. Then she looked up at Jerry and said, "But whatever else is happening, he's our child Jerry. And I know he's no diffrent from anyone else's child but I feel as though we've got a miracle here. A real miracle."

They heard a cry from the gardens outside. Jerry went to find the cause and Silvia finished nursing Christopher. She could look at this, her first child, for hours and not grow weary. A heavy sky darkened the morning. There was little wind but the clouds hung, dark grey and heavy. It was colder than it had been and the sky had the look of snow, already a few flakes were falling. There was a feeling of anticipation,something important was imminent. Jerry felt it, but couldn't decide what it was. He stood watching Rose walking up the lower pathway from Jessie's cottage. She saw him and waved, her breath making small puffs of mist before her. He went toward her, stepping down across the low evergreen hedge that bordered the path. They met at the Hall.

"What's the hurry, Sis? What's happening?" He saw her brown face full of sorrow, and knew instantly."It's Jessie, isn't it?"

She nodded,"She's ready Jerry. She wants us to Gather. She'd like to have the ceremony today. I thought it would not be so soon." Then with a sob she caught him and pressed her head into his chest, but only a moment was needed. Almost at once, she lifted it again and she was smiling. "It's as it should be. She's so excited, so -- just so glad, Jerry. I can't help but feel some of her anticipation."

It's going home for her, you know." They stood looking back toward the little house where Jessie had lived for this year of her work. Then Rose shook herself. "Well, we've got to get things done. Will you call everyone? Tell them? I'll prepare the Hall. She wants only a very simple ceremony."

Jerry nodded as she turned."I think she'd as soon not have any at all except for us. We need one. She knows that. "As they crossed the deck to enter the Hall,he added, "I'll call a Gather. They're all expecting it."

It was an hour before they'd got the message to everyone. Paul and Annette first, the farthest away, then realizing that Angy had gone back to the sea city, Rose spent twenty minutes making contact. The others were in Adwin and she got them with a first try. They were already on their way. It took only half an hour to prepare the Hall. When Paul and Jennifer, Annette and William arrived with the children,coming in Paul's car through freezing air from Altos, everyone had gathered. The Adwin folk had taken off their thick coveralls for belt riding in winter, and were seated, warming themselves with hot toast and tea, coffee or

639

chocolate. There was a hush in the room, a mixture of sadness, and of anticipation. Jessie sat in a wide, deep chair, her excitement obvious. She had greeted them all with great affection and warmth, then smiling all the time, had taken her place among them.

They settled themselves around the little raised platform where Jessie would sit. She came in, her face a wreath of smiles, but a gentle grief in her eyes. She said softly, "Death may be only a passing through, but there is a body that must fall away, go to Earth again. And the body is so intertwined in mind and heart, so enmeshed in the whole of the nature, that withdrawal isn't slow, though it appears to be. I've been at it for days already, you know. I cluster around myself already. Look and you can see." She cast a piercing glance among them, urging them to focus. "The pain that has throbbed in this body for some years now, the pain of disintegrating parts, makes leaving it even less difficult. The sorrow is a leaving of the familiar, the loved and known." Her eyes were distant, soft, and yet, as she looked at each one, they seemed to speak directly to their hearts. She went to the platform, settled herself into the cushions there. She sat straight, winced as she crossed her legs beneath her, that pain would not occur again. Her hands were folded in her lap, her hair, nearly all white now, hung loose around her face, and her blue gown, also loose and embroidered with her symbol, seemed too softly light for the winter day. She wasted no time with explanation.

"You've all known the time was near. We have talked and we have bid our Goodbyes. It is near the end of the year and the beginning of the new one. Now it's time to gather your strength the way Earth does in sleep of winter. There is commonly a habit among people to draw into themselves in winter, to simply endure, to suffer the cold, the stillness and lifelessness of this time. Don't do that. USE this time! Listen, penetrate the depths of your hearts in this time, live there, at your deepest level and know yourselves as you never have. Remember exactly! Until your habits, attitudes, behaviors and the process of your humanness, both the mean and the finest in you, is utterly familiar . Now it's time to meditate, listen to the silence within yourselves that will tell you where next to work. You all know now that from silence comes true understanding. Thinking only shapes that understanding into words after it is known so it can be shared. And if you don't listen to the silence, you will know nothing at all except a repetition of words." She grinned impishly, shaking her head. "How I do go on. I seem unable to stop teaching even at my last breath."

She bent her head, composed herself again, let her hands loosen in her lap and finally with a slow, deep breath, she said,"For you,it's the time to gather strength." She frowned slightly, "For me, it's the time for great change." Her face became serious, so quiet, it seemed to them fragile and they were abruptly aware of how very old she was.

Then her face opened out in a great, wide, sweet smile. It transformed her with youthfulness. She laughed at her own seriousness,"Even now, as I accept this time to take what for me is a gift, I feel the old pattern shape itself. I feel apologetic that I am acting for myself and not for others. Strange how the

THE JOURNEY

besetting habits of one's life cling through every learned skill of balancing. Even now, I notice that old assumption that I should not leave those who need me. But you don't need me at all. I must remind myself of that. I turn from old patterns that this life has lived out, and outgrown finally. And so, I won't allow them power. I have no apology for leaving. It is my time!" The last words were said with a strong friendly vigor. She was silent then, shrugged and with a wry smile, asked, "Well, is there still anything left to say?"

Paul moved restlessly in his chair, feeling the intensity of this moment and unable to imagine anything beyond it. Something of life itself was leaving them with Jessie's departure. "Jessie, you're leaving us, can you tell us how - to go on. There seems so much to do, so much in the Valley -- the harmony we long for, the Teaching we must continue. Can you tell us something to help?"

Rose was nodding, her throat so constricted with the pain of loss that she couldn't have spoken. Jessie looked at them all, meeting their eyes. She remembered so well that first time a loved Teacher had left her in this same way. How devastated she had been, how wanting to hold on just a bit longer. She smiled, "I have told you, listen within. Take time to listen and to remember. You have the task before you. You know what is to be done. It's up to you to find the way. And you have plenty of skill and knowledge. You don't need me, my dear ones. You don't need me at all!" She sighed, was serious, "There is that place where each of you can go at will. At will,mind you! For inspiration, for realization. That place within your selves, where knowledge is. And you can help one another to find that place when there is need. You can find it together as a group and then there is even greater realization. Don't forget that! Your own heart is truly a place of inspiration! It is familiar to each of you and you must make it a daily contact. Deliberately retire to that place. Stand firmly conscious. Soul Conscious! Because you are Soul Conscious human beings. You will see what is true." She stopped, watching their faces, listening.

"You see me leaving you. You know that I leave this body, and that I leave that astral body that clings for a little longer. I lay aside much of what I've seemed to be. I do not know yet all that I am. We are what we know as human. The Soul infused flesh. So does life struggle upward. The lesser lives of Earth, you bring with you as you become conscious.

Listen to your Hearts and act from that knowledge. It is as simple as that."

Rose bent to adjust the small box before her, and Jessie smiled at her, nodding abruptly. She saw that they were stereotaping in three dimension, this event.That they could remember and hear it all over again in later years. She didn't mind. She knew they would gradually forget it. Her face had the soft amused look they were so familiar with, of that Mother who knew their weaknesses and was willing to allow them for another final time.

Then suddenly her face became stern, the tenderness drawn inward into a powerful intensity of precision and Love. "Stand Forth"! It was the speaking in the VOICE! The note was so powerful it startled them. Brought a flush of shame to their faces, broke them from sentiment. "You know your tasks. Learn to draw down from that place of Light such conviction as you know there and learn to sustain that through daily work. Keep forever in your heart, keep minute by minute in your hearts and minds that conviction and that knowledge of Love Itself. Your mind focusses at that conscious recognition of Love. You act with Love, think with Love and become an expression of Love, nothing less. Nothing can best THAT. There ! That's it!" She met every eye with that piercing look that woke into flame the knowledge within them. They stirred from themselves and woke Soul alive. Their faces lit, aware. Jessie saw, and let her eyes drop. They watched the soft movements of her hands slowly gently moving against one another. She smiled again.

Rose said, "You told us that we do not need to miss you even. You have reminded us that you are as close to us as ourselves. And we know that's true. And now you remind us that we are as close to Love itself as our hearts will allow. We live from that Christ Consciousness, which is Love. We live from our Heart's Center. That, I keep forgetting. It's what you mean by cautioning us to remember! We thank you Jessie." She drew a deep sigh, then smiled. "Well, there it is. It's time. Yes, it's time!" She did not wipe away the slow tears. She watched Jessie without blinking.

Jessie nodded, smiled again,"To say forewell to this small body that has served me so well for so many years. These hands that must return to their source, just as I will. These feet that have carried me so far. It is farewell to all this." She put her hand across her chest and another on her head. As if caressing this body gently, she closed her eyes. Then with a curt nod, a quiet relaxing, she let both hands fall again to her lap. A deep long breath slowly exhaled, three short in drawn breaths and then silence, her breath so quiet now it seemed gone. They watched , saw the slight droop to her shoulders, the sudden tightening of her hands and then release. There was a faint tremor that ran through her whole body from feet to head and then -- ceased.

And they knew she was no longer there. No longer in that small tired body that waited there in the cushions. The change in it was so immediately apparent that they were startled. 'Anybody could have seen she is gone,' Silvia thought. 'Even I could have seen it a year ago. You don't have to be very aware to see that. Her body is so empty, so still in itself. It is so small, and though a pale glow is still present, the Light has gone out'.

Rose sat stunned, her mind seemed to stop working. With a sharp pain, she felt a waking, a pressure and knew Anna present, Touching her, she heard her daughter's mental call,"Mother, notice! Mother, pay attention!" And Rose was grateful, realizing she had something she must do. She did not think that her daughter could have done it as well. Attention came back to her eyes, and she looked around. She shattered the silence with a cry, and her words came with the force of the VOICE! "Pay Attention!"

Swiftly they felt the Joining, each entering into it, each adding their focussed attention. They lifted that attention, drew their Joined minds into a stream and then loosening from their own bodies, just as Jessie had, they released

THE JOURNEY

themselves from that stream, knew each other there in that place where physical laws no longer held. Where astral laws did hold. And there was Jessie, laughing, greeting people they had never seen, people radiant as globes of revolving pearl colored light. For moments they held this state, oblivious of their physical surroundings, attending only to that clear fact, that Jessie was as near as themselves. Even knowing that soon she must die away also from this state, leave this astral body too, they were comforted. Rose laughed at the surprise and unease among those who had never looked into this dimension of being before this day. "You'll get used to it. It's so near the familiar physical one, it's easy to come here. The veil between these dimensions fades away in these times. It's so thin now,. Humankind has drawn away all its energy and it fades away everywhere." The words were like tiny bells in their minds. They had not heard words in their Joining before.

They drew aside, letting Jessie greet all those come to welcome her. She would rest here for a little while and then she must make another death. These friends, who gathered with her would send her on the next step of her way. The Family withdrew,broke the Joining,and sat again in their living room at the Hall. All of them had known Jessie's presence in that lit place except William. He sat watching the small, silent body drop in on itself and wiped a slow tear from his cheek. He said, "Regardless of everything, I did like that old lady." He turned to them, wholly unaware of their momentary departure. " He sighed, shaking his head,"And she did it. What she said she'd do. Seems so impossible to me that she could. I am slowly recognizing the fact that there are things in this world that I cannot explain. I have decided that I must listen to you, listen and accept that what you say you know, is real, not just real to you, but real, to life, whether I understand how or not." The past year had taken its toll and given its learning. Annette reached out to him to take his hand.

"Yes, Dear,she's gone. She was truly a good woman, a great Teacher. And now we must continue with the ceremony of death. This is for us alone now."

"Not until a Healer pronounces her officially dead" He turned to her, his eyes showing some of that old anger. "Has anyone provided for that?"

Benjamin stood, actually relieved at the abrasive tone, the very human dissension broke for him the purity of their Touch. Now they could just get on with the rest. Yet, what had she said? To keep the highest realization of consciousness even as we do this? He nodded to himself,allowing his thoughts to reach out, Touching and knowing the others were ready, "Let's go on. Who has the Robe?"

Rose had not forgotten the laws of this world. She had called a Healer and she watched as the man came into the hall. He went to Jessie and without any surprise at all on his face, examined the sitting body. He pronounced her officially dead. His eyes met William's, then swept to the others, a hint of amusement in them.

William nodded curtly, stood and as the others began to gather together their belts, he said, "But we haven't prepared the pyre. No one will know. She hasn't even been sick, nor has she shown any signs of dying soon. It will take some time to get things ready."

Paul shook his head,"No Will, when you say that you will believe us when we tell you what we know, please do so. She told us, remember? She said she would die this week. We've been preparing. The pyre is ready at the Temple grounds in Adwin. We needed to have it there because many others will be there,you know."

It surprised Paul that William just nodded,after heaving a long breath, accepting all that. He frowned, "It's not something I can accept easily, you know. But I suppose you'll -- Send,is that what you call it?" At their nods he went on, "You'll Send to them so they'll know and be there when we get there?" They glanced at one another, knowing that Jessie had already sent the word as she died. Those Jessie had taught, already knew, but how to explain THAT? They just nodded again."Oh, well, it isn't something I can keep denying. It's obvious it happens. And it's become obvious to me too that none of you are evil. You're not monsters, nor conspiring against Nature." For seconds they watched, wondering and then to everybody's relief, he laughed and there was in that laugh something of the old confidence, the old power that William had always brought to their lives. He was thoughtful again,"I believe you when you tell me that it isn't actually mind reading, you do, but another deeper connection that comes from intuitive knowledge. Without language even. At least I'm aware of the nature of intuition. I think that is easier to bear. It's taken a long time. It's taken us near to battle between us. It's almost taken --- my sanity! But finally I am willing to accept that there is something you all -- that's the amazing fact for me -- that all of you, ALL, have this gift. This talent, you call it, and I don't. It's that simple, isn't it?"

"It doesn't make you any less, Uncle Will," Cassandra said, slipping to him and huggng him about the waist.

He nodded, putting his arms around her. He bent his head, he did not see the moisture in the eyes of the others, but he did see their smiles. He said, bruskly, "Well, we'd best get on with this. The others will expect the ceremony."

Rose turned hastily, Touching the others, setting the plans into action. William was surprised as each one began doing a part of what had to be done, to get Jessie's body to the town. He explained to himself that someone had obviously organized things well after all.

A white robe was brought to wrap Jessie's body which was moved, still sitting,to the padded floater. A pale grey cover was fitted over it so that the wind of the travel would not pull at her robe. She was carried out onto the deck, everyone had their belts on. They settled Jessie's body there and circled around it, and then they began to sing the song of Farewell here for their own house.

    Farewell to Thee, Farewell to Thee,
Loved one who leaves us now.
    Let Thy Journey be true, Thy joy be near,
And Thy return among us be soon.

THE JOURNEY

Farewell to Thee, Our hearts are full
Our Love goes with Thee all the way.

We place this body in which you lived,
This home of your life on this Earth
Into the pure flames, the bright light
That it too may return to its Source.

    They lifted off, everyone touching the floater, each one Joined, except Will who flew at the front,,and took charge of the direction, which they were pleased to have him do. When they arrived above the Temple, above the open space around it and looked down they could see the crowd. There had been so many Jessie knew, taught, loved. They could see there were people from every small town and many Vagabonds. The Vagabonds seldom used belts but this time they had. Outside town, carts and Gathering camps brightened the Roadside. Rose realized the Vagabonds had known, even though no one had called them. They had known as surely as they knew the time for the leaves to fall.
    They lowered the disc slowly.They sang the Song of Farewell softly as they descended, and the crowd of people below sang with them, and the sound carried far beyond the Rings of Adwin. They slid off the cover of the Float, and, still hovering in the air beside the top of the pyre, they moved the small body out to sit on the platform. She looked as though she had just come to offer a Teaching, except her eyes were closed. Then William drew the disc away, took it to the landing grid. The others dropped to the court yard, settled among their neighbors, greeted with their eyes without sound. Adam touched Rose's arm, his mind Reaching and she met him gratefully. He turned to include Deborah and then swiftly together they lifted, focussed and were half outside their bodies, able to see beyond them. There above the small white form at the top of the pyre , quiet in the air,, stood the glowing form of the woman they honored. So many in that crowd could see her. Some could not. Some did not know there was anything to see. She met their minds lightly and then she was gone.
    Rose caught at Adam's hand and squeezed it in gratitude that he had thought to notice. Now, William,, settled down at the edge of the Pyre, took his place with three others. They went forward with lighted candles and as the Song of Farewell once more was sung, they set the dry wood ablaze. The flames rose orange and yellow through the cold winter air.
    Such a simple thing. So cleanly of Earth. So ancient, so tied to the condition of being human. It was a reminder to them that there was this life to live and to complete. This world to recreate and to transform according to their highest understandings. They must live so that those transformations would occur through that very expression of Life itself.
    Finally as the day moved into late afternoon,they left the ashes still smoking faintly, to begin that task.